THE
Newton
HANDBOOK

THE
Newton
HANDBOOK

Derek Gjertsen

ROUTLEDGE & KEGAN PAUL
London and New York

First published in 1986
by Routledge & Kegan Paul plc

11 New Fetter Lane, London EC4P 4EE

Published in the USA by
Routledge & Kegan Paul Inc.
in association with Methuen Inc.
29 West 35th Street, New York, NY 10001

Set in Bembo
by Input Typesetting Ltd
and printed in Great Britain
by T. J. Press (Padstow) Ltd
Padstow, Cornwall

Library of Congress Cataloging in Publication Data

Gjertsen, Derek.
The Newton handbook.
Bibliography: p.
Includes index.
1. Newton, Isaac, Sir, 1642–1727. 2. Science—
History. 3. Physicists—Great Britain—Biography.
I. Title.
QC16.N7G54   1986   509'.24[B]   85–28160

ISBN 0-7102-0279-2
British Library CIP Data also available

Contents

Preface and acknowledgments

Some time in 1691 Richard Bentley, later to become the foremost classicist of his day and a notorious Master of Trinity College, Cambridge, approached Newton for advice on how he should tackle the recently published *Principia* (1687). Many, since Bentley, have felt in need of similar help. It is unlikely, however, that many, as with Bentley, could have benefited much from Newton's advice. After having mastered, Newton emphasised, 'Euclid's Elements' and 'the Elements of ye Conic sections', the prospective reader should then consult van Schooten's *Commentaries*, 'Gassendus's Astronomy', and 'Hugenius's *Horologium oscillatorium*', before being 'ready' to understand *Principia*.

Newton was of course correct. There are no short cuts, visual aids or pedagogical tricks which can ever dispense with the mathematical skills required for a full understanding of *Principia*. Equally, it can be argued, only those with a good command of Ionic Greek could be expected ever to gain a full understanding of the *Iliad*. Some knowledge is also required of the Arcado-Cypriot dialect, the Attic variety of Ionic, comparative religion, anthropology, mythology and, perhaps, several other disciplines as well. The truth, of course, is that while few of us possess such skills, many of us enjoy the *Iliad* and, in our own way, attain an acceptable level of Homeric understanding. A comparable adjustment is attainable, hopefully, with such works as *Principia*. Just as Homer is not the private property of a few Greek scholars, Newton is not the exclusive preserve of specialised historians of mathematics. A full and deep understanding may always be denied most of us; our interest, however, remains and can, perhaps, be satisfied by shallower levels of comprehension.

Many of the great Newtonian experts have, in fact, appreciated the point and have sought themselves to provide such assistance. The process began in 1687 with Edmond Halley preparing an account of Newton's work for James II, and has continued ever since. An attempt by I. B. Cohen and A. Koyré to compose a history of the commentaries on *Principia* alone was abandoned when it was realised that it would require some '1,500–2,400 pages of small type' (Cohen, 1971, p. xi).

PREFACE AND ACKNOWLEDGMENTS

There is, clearly, little need for yet one more commentary on *Principia*.

Other areas exist, however, for which there is a clear and genuine need. While there have been hordes of willing translators of Newton's ideas and texts, the humbler post of guide to the Newtonian corpus has long remained vacant. When approached by Bentley in 1691, Newton had published no more than a handful of papers on light and *Principia* itself. There are now literally dozens of Newton's works available, ranging over such fields as mathematics, physics, chemistry, alchemy, church history, chronology, metrology, theology, biblical studies, physiology, economics, and much more besides. Some of these appeared piecemeal, during Newton's long life, and throughout the eighteenth and nineteenth centuries. Many more remained, unpublished, unread, and unknown to even specialist scholars. So much was confirmed in the 1880s when the Portsmouth family passed over to the University Library, Cambridge, their rich holdings of Newton's scientific manuscripts. A catalogue was issued. Half a century later the remainder of the Portsmouth family's holdings were auctioned by Sotheby's of London in 1936. A further catalogue was issued. The welcome results of such dispersions was at last to make aware to scholars both the magnitude and quality of Newton's unprocessed manuscripts.

Newton, it appeared, was a compulsive writer. He could not, apparently, read or think without a pen in his hand. More importantly, he seemed incapable of changing his mind, or developing a position without first writing a number of drafts. Some quite lengthy items from the collection are available in a dozen or more drafts. One consequence has been to enable the modern scholar to reconstruct in some detail the development of a number of Newton's more important works. A further consequence has been to release such a mass of material as to occupy fully an army of scholars for an entire lifetime. Estimates of the size of the surviving collection vary; it is clear, however, that Newton left some tens of thousands of written pages running to several million words.

Serious research on the collection began after the Second World War. By now much of this early work has been completed. The eight volumes of the *Mathematical Papers* (1967–81), and the seven volumes of the *Correspondence* (1959–77), have been available for some time, while the first volume of a planned three-volume edition of Newton's *Optical Papers* (1984) has already appeared. Other texts and manuscripts have appeared in monographs, journals, collections and appendices. Some works are available only in summary, much more remains unpublished.

Readers of today are thus presented with a problem unknown to Bentley in 1691. How do they find their way around, or locate an item from, the mass of material? It can be a confusing quest. Some works are simply difficult to locate. Neither *A Dissertation upon the Sacred Cubit of the Jews* nor the 'Form of the Most Ancient Year' have appeared in print since the mid-eighteenth century. Other works may be more readily available yet still remain difficult to locate. The simple title *De motu*, for example, can refer to any one of eight distinct works, variously located, not all published, nor always carefully distinguished by commentators and biographers. The works are, of course, listed in a number of excellent catalogues and bibliographies; the ways of the bibliographer, however, are not those of the guide. While the former is more concerned with correct identification and description, the guide is keener to deal with the contents of the work, to trace its history and pursue its significance and reception.

One basic theme of the present book is accordingly to survey the Newtonian canon, scientific and otherwise, and to find out of individual works how they came to be composed, what they say, how and when they were published, their significance, and where they can be found today. An attempt is made to bring out the extraordinarily wide range of Newton's interests, his competence and learning in these fields, and what they could have meant to Newton and his contemporaries. A further theme pursued is the birth, growth and persistence of the Newtonian legend. Why did the feeling of Newton's uniqueness arise? What vicissitudes has the belief undergone? How does it stand today? Answers are sought in literature, art, language and biography.

Equally in evidence are the basic data of Newton's life and career. Covered in this way are his character, mode of work, domestic arrangements, social life and finances. Given the material Newton himself left, and the interest of his contemporaries, it is usually possible to find well documented and detailed accounts of such matters.

In works of this kind it is often customary to scatter around the text asterisks, italics, underlinings, bold type or some other acceptable convention with which to cross-reference the various entries. Such a policy has not been adopted in this work. One reason is that the number of such signs needed to make the convention work proved to be excessively large. A simple sentence, 'Halley★, as secretary of the RS★ reviewed★ *Principia*★ in the *PT*★', requires five asterisks; others were found to demand as many as twelve. A number of less obtrusive aids have none the less been included. Amongst them are the following.

1 An alphabetical list of entries is printed at the end of the book.
2 Some items in the text serve, in part, as surveys of entire fields. The item Priority dispute, for example, should lead most readers to almost any further heading they feel inclined to pursue. Examples of other such surveys are: Calendrical writings; Mathematical works; Mechanics, Writings; Mint, Writings and documents; Optics, writings; Priority dispute; Life, career and works; Works.
3 If it is felt that the reader may be in some doubt where precisely further information on a topic may be found, related headings are listed at the bottom of the entry.
4 It is sometimes unclear whether an item will occur under its full

title (*Tractatus de quadratura curvarum*), or under a more commonly recognised form (*De quadratura, De quadratura curvarum*). In general, entries are listed under their full heading, with shorter titles entered as cross references only. An exception to this rule is *Principia*, known so widely in this form that it would be unduly perverse to list it as *Philosophiae naturalis principia mathematica*.

The entries themselves break down into the following broad categories.

1 Works of Newton. Well over a hundred named works are listed under the heading 'Works', along with basic bibliographical data. Most of these works are also listed separately where a fuller account of their nature can be found. A few works are not listed separately; they are, however, cross-referenced to other headings in their entry in Works where further data is listed.

2 Personal/biographical entries. An attempt has been made to identify and describe all those individuals, whether as kin, friends, enemies, editors, artists, colleagues, disciples, or servants, whose life had some notable impact on Newton. It should be appreciated, however, that the emphasis is on the impact on Newton, rather than the subject. It is thus not intended to provide detailed surveys of the lives and works of such subjects as Leibniz, Bernoulli and Descartes. Sufficient data is provided, it is hoped, to enable their influence on and relations with Newton to become intelligible. Some 250 such entries are provided.

3 Scientific entries. The aim has been to take the main concepts of Newtonian science – such terms for example as gravity, inertia, centrifugal force, fluxions – and to indicate what they meant to Newton, where they derive from, how Newton deployed them, and how they were received by his contemporaries, and by later scientists.

4 Other intellectual interests. Entries are also provided on such items as Newton's work in alchemy, history, chronology, theology, metrology, prophecy, and politics. The relevant works are identified and described, while particularly important concepts are given entries of their own.

5 Institutions. The main institutions of Newton's life – Trinity College, the Mint, the Royal Society, etc. – are all listed and described.

6 Life and personality. The main events of Newton's life – school-days, student days, career, offices held, parliamentary career, residences, health, death, funeral – are separately described, as are a number of supposed features of his character and personality.

7 Legend. Such well-known items as the apple, the dog Diamond, and Newton's supposed inability to add up, are examined for their plausibility. An attempt is also made to trace the source of the particular story and to follow its later history.

PREFACE AND ACKNOWLEDGMENTS

No one could ever hope to complete a work of this kind without incurring numerous debts to the scholars who, during the last thirty years or more, have struggled to make so much of Newton's work available. Pride of place in any such list must go to the two great collections issued by Cambridge University Press: *The Correspondence of Isaac Newton (1959–77)* and its three editors, H. W. Turnbull (vols I–III), J. F. Scott (vol. IV) and A. R. Hall (vols V–VII); and the eight volumes of *The Mathematical Papers of Isaac Newton* (1967–81), edited throughout by D. T. Whiteside. Together they have formed the basis for this and virtually every other book written on Newton during the last two decades. Two other invaluable collections are A. R. and M. B. Hall's *Unpublished Scientific Papers of Isaac Newton* (1962) and I. B. Cohen's *Isaac Newton's Papers and Letters on Natural Philosophy* (1978). Two other works frequently referred to are the *variorum* edition of *Principia* (2 vols, 1972) edited by A. Koyré and I. B. Cohen, and Cohen's own companion volume, *Introduction to Newton's Principia* (1971). Equally valuable, and as frequently consulted, have been R. S. Westfall's definitive biography of Newton, *Never at Rest* (1980), and the superb bibliography compiled by P. and R. Wallis, *Newton and Newtoniana, 1672–1975* (1977).

No less valuable, although more specialised, have been Betty Jo Dobbs's *The Foundations of Newton's Alchemy* (1975), J. W. Herivel's *The Background to Newton's Principia* (1965), John Harrison's *The Library of Isaac Newton* (1978), A. Koyré's *Newtonian Studies* (1965), A. R. Hall's *Philosophers at War* (1980), Henry Guerlac's *Newton on the Continent* (1981), A. I. Sabra's *Theories of Light* (1967), E. J. Aiton's *The Vortex Theory of Planetary Motion* (1972), and the Frank Manuel trilogy – *Isaac Newton, Historian* (1963), *A Portrait of Isaac Newton* (1980) and *The Religion of Isaac Newton* (1974).

In addition, I am indebted immensely to a large number of papers, essays, and monographs, on a wide variety of Newtonian topics published by E. J. Aiton, I. B. Cohen, A. R. Hall, R. S. Westfall, J. A. Lohne, J. E. McGuire, A. Koyré, D. T. Whiteside, John Herivel, Henry Guerlac and M. C. Jacob, and to whom reference has been made in the text of the book.

There are also a number of more personal debts. The encouragement and help of Ted Honderich did much to make the book possible, while the patience and consideration of Wendy Morris enabled it to be completed. Two friends, Roger Thomas and Terry Walz, have been kind enough to trace for me two particularly elusive items from the Newtonian canon in the libraries of Cambridge and New York respectively. I have also benefited from the help of my daughter Veronica in the final preparation of the manuscript. The work itself I would like to dedicate to the memory of my parents, Rasmus Gjertsen (1900–51) and Anne Elizabeth Gjertsen (1903–83).

Abbreviations

The following abbreviations and short titles are widely used throughout the text.

Account
An *Account of the Book Entituled Commercium Epistolicum Collini & Aliorum*; available in facsimile in Hall, A. Rupert (1980) *Philosophers At War*, Cambridge, Cambridge University Press, pp. 263–314.

AE
Acta eruditorum (Lipsica).

Brewster
Brewster, Sir David (1855) *Memoirs of the Life, Writings and Discoveries of Sir Isaac Newton*, 2 vols, Edinburgh, Thomas Constable & Co.; (1965) New York, Johnson Reprint Corp.

C, I–VII
Newton, Sir Isaac (1959–77) *The Correspondence of Isaac Newton*, 7 vols, edited by Turnbull, H. W., Scott, J. F. and Hall, A. R., Cambridge, Cambridge University Press.

Cajori
Newton, Sir Isaac (1962a) *Sir Isaac Newton's Principles of Natural Philosophy and his System of the World*, 2 vols, edited by Cajori, Florian, Berkeley, University of California Press.

Cambridge Catalogue
Luard, H. R., Stokes, G. G., Adams, J. C., and Liveing, G. D. (1888) *A Catalogue of the Portsmouth Collection of Books and Papers written by or belonging to Sir Isaac Newton, the Scientific Portion of which has been presented by the Earl of Portsmouth to the University of Cambridge.* Cambridge, Cambridge University Press.

CE
(1713) *Commercium epistolicum D. Johannis Collins, et aliorum de analysi promota*, London, Royal Society.

ABBREVIATIONS

DNB	*Dictionary of National Biography.*
DSB	*Dictionary of Scientific Biography.*
Halls	Newton, Sir Isaac (1962b) *The Unpublished Scientific Papers of Isaac Newton. A Selection from the Portsmouth Collection in the University Library, Cambridge*, edited by Hall, A. R. and Hall, M. B., Cambridge, Cambridge University Press.
Horsley	Newton, Sir Isaac (1779–85) *Isaaci Newtoni opera quae existant omnia*, 5 vols, edited by Horsley, Samuel; (1964) Stuttgart–Bad Cannstatt.
JL	*Journal Littéraire de la Haye.*
KCC	King's College, Cambridge.
MP, I–VIII	Newton, Sir Isaac (1967–81) *The Mathematical Papers of Isaac Newton*, 8 vols, edited by Whiteside, D. T., Cambridge, Cambridge University Press.
Opticks	Newton, Sir Isaac (1952) *Opticks or a Treatise of Reflections, Refractions, Inflections and Colours of Light*, with a preface by Cohen, I. B. and an introduction by Whittaker, E. T., New York, Dover.
PC	Portsmouth Collection.
PLNP	Newton, Sir Isaac (1978) *Isaac Newton's Papers and Letters on Natural Philosophy*, 2nd revised edition, edited by Cohen, I. B., Cambridge, Mass., Harvard University Press.
PT	*Philosophical Transactions.*
QQP	Newton, Sir Isaac (1983) *Quaestiones quaedam philosophicae – Certain Philosophical Questions: Newton's Trinity Notebook, Cambridge*, edited by McGuire, J. E. and Tamny, M., Cambridge, Cambridge University Press.
RS	Royal Society.
RSW	Westfall, R. S. (1980) *Never At Rest*, Cambridge, Cambridge University Press.

ABBREVIATIONS

Sotheby *Catalogue* prepared for the 1936 sale of the papers in the
Catalogue Portsmouth Collection; Taylor, John (1936) *Catalogue of the Newton Papers sold by Order of Viscount Lymington*, London, Sotheby & Co.

TCC   Trinity College, Cambridge.

ULC   University Library, Cambridge.

A

Aberration

Makers of optical instruments in the seventeenth century soon became aware of two common defects revealed in the blurred and distorted images formed by their lenses.

1 Spherical aberration, in which light passing through the centre of a spherical lens focuses further away from the lens than light passing through more peripheral areas, as in Fig. 1.

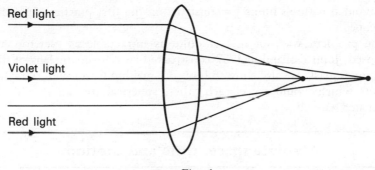

Red light

Violet light

Red light

Fig. 1

Spherical aberration decreases as the square of the focal length, so one solution was simply to increase the length of telescopes. Johannes Hevelius responded accordingly and designed a 150-ft telescope; others began to contemplate a 1,000-ft-long instrument. An alternative solution considered by Newton in his *Of Refractions* at the beginning of 1666 involved the grinding of non-spherical lenses. His growing awareness, however, that such lenses would still suffer from chromatic aberration led Newton to turn to other problems.

2 Chromatic aberration, in which a distant white object is seen as a number of distinctly coloured images. It is caused by the fact that

long light waves, such as red light, have a longer focal length than the shorter violet waves, as in Fig. 2, where A is the focus for violet rays and B is the focus for red rays. Other colours fit somewhere in between.

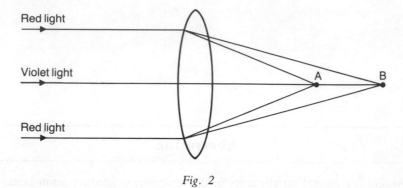

Fig. 2

As soon as Newton became aware that chromatic aberration was caused not by a defect in a lens but arose from the fact that light itself is 'a heterogeneous mixture of differently refrangible rays', he realised that a limit had been set by nature to the 'perfection of telescopes', or, at least, to the perfection of refractors. Within a few years, however, Newton had avoided nature's limits by constructing the first practical reflecting telescope.

The problem was not in fact quite as intractable as Newton had supposed. John Dolland in 1757 constructed an achromatic lens of flint and crown glass. He also showed how, by making lenses with refractive powers which would cancel each other, spherical aberration could be eliminated as well.

Absolute space, time and motion

Principia begins with eight definitions and continues with an important *Scholium* in which four further definitions are offered of absolute time, space, place and motion. Thus, 'Absolute, true, and mathematical time . . . flows equably without relation to anything external', while 'Absolute space', in its turn, was also presented as being 'without relation to anything external'. The remaining concepts were subsequently defined in terms of the previous two: absolute place becomes a part of absolute space taken up by a body; and absolute motion is merely 'a translation of a body from one absolute place into another' (Cajori, pp. 6–7).

An alternative view had been expressed by Leibniz in a letter to Huygens.

> For if there are 1,000 bodies, I still hold that phenomena cannot give us any infallible way of determining which are moving and in what degree; and that each separately could be considered as being at rest.
> (ALEXANDER, 1956, xxvi)

Newton, however, thought he could distinguish absolute from relative motion, and once having demonstrated the existence of absolute motion, the existence of absolute space and time would follow as a matter of course.

There was, he insisted, a real distinction between motion generated 'by forces impressed upon bodies', and relative motion which could be 'generated or altered without any force impressed upon the moving body'. In this latter case it was only necessary 'to impress some force on other bodies'. The example Newton selected concerned circular motion. Water in a spinning bucket, he noted, 'shows its endeavour to recede from the axis of its motion' without depending upon 'any translation of the water in respect to ambient bodies'.

Not only the Leibnizians found Newton's views hard to accept. Berkeley in his *Principles* (1710), for example, could find little sense in the idea of an absolute space which was unperceivable. It received its most devastating critique, however, in Ernst Mach's *The Science of Mechanics* (1883). Shortly afterwards in 1905 Einstein proposed alternative foundations for physics which began by dropping Newton's assumptions of absolute space and time.

Académie royale des sciences

While informal meetings of scientists were being held in London and Oxford in the 1650s, similar groups, discussing similar problems, met in Paris at the house of Habert de Montmor. In 1662 the English scholars were duly recognised by Charles II and received from him the Royal Society's first charter. Stuart monarchs seldom had the funds to back their schemes and consequently the fellows of the Royal Society were expected to pay for their membership a fee of 6d a week.

A few years later, in 1666, a similar *Académie royale* was formed in Paris with Louis XIV, on the advice of Colbert, providing two rooms in the Royal Library for the Academy's use. In contrast to London, however, membership was much more restricted, with no more than about 20 members appointed initially in 1666. Further, members were servants of the crown and were accordingly paid by Louis and granted funds for equipment and research. In return they were expected to work on government projects like the design of the Versailles water works, as and when it was thought they could be of use.

In 1699 the *Académie* underwent a thorough reorganisation. It was decided to appoint eight foreign associates, three on the nomination of Louis and five elected by the *Académie*. Louis chose Leibniz, Tschirnhaus and Domenico Gugliemini; the *Académie* selected Hartsoeker, Johann and Jakob Bernoulli, Romer and Newton. Newton's election was noted by James Gregory in May 1699 together with the false claim that '1500 livres of pension' went with the post (*C*, IV, p. 311). Foreign associates received no such payment. Others, like David Gregory, complained that Newton had been slighted in being ignored by Louis and in being elected into the very last position by the *Académie* (Hiscock, 1937, p. 9). Newton's relatively lowly position was, in fact, the result of two factors. To begin with, his reputation in France in the 1690s was not especially high. Unlike Gregory, the scientists of Paris were unaware of the riches contained in Newton's unpublished writings. To them he was the author of a rather doubtful hypothesis on the nature of light and a mathematician of some power who had been misled in *Principia* into a physics based on attraction. Secondly, according to Conduitt, Newton had been approached in 1698 by Jacques Cassini with the offer of a lucrative post with the *Académie*. Newton had declined the offer. It was most unlikely, therefore, that Louis XIV would have been inclined to nominate Newton personally to the *Académie*.

Newton's membership, though not of any great importance, was not without its significance. Most importantly it brought with it the obligation on the part of the *Académie* to note the death of any member with a suitably composed *éloge*. No such obligation was assumed by the RS. Consequently, at the hands of Fontenelle, Newton's *éloge* was released shortly after his death and played no small role in stimulating interest in Newton and in helping to create the still burgeoning Newton legend.

See also *Éloge*; Newton in France; Royal Society

A Demonstration that the Planets, by their Gravity towards the Sun, may move in ellipses

---

A Demonstration was found by Lord King amongst the papers of John Locke. It was first published in his *Life of Locke* (1830, vol. I, pp. 389–400), and has since appeared in Rouse Ball (1893, pp. 116–20, incomplete), the Halls (pp. 293–301), Herivel (1965, pp. 246–56), and *C*, III, pp. 71–7. Locke's copy, in the hand of his amanuensis, is endorsed in his own hand: 'Mr. Newton March 1689' (1690 new style). The original manuscript, in Newton's own hand, is to be found in the PC in the ULC (Add. MS 3965). A Latin translation was published by William Whiston in his *Praelectiones physico-mathematical* (1710).

How Locke came to have a copy is not known. He met Newton not long after his return to England in February 1689. It is consequently assumed that Newton provided his new friend with a more elementary derivation of the inverse square law. The work itself consists of three hypotheses and two propositions. The first two hypotheses are variants of the first two laws of motion formulated in *Principia*; the third hypothesis does not, however, present the third law of motion but is rather a statement of the parallelogram of forces. The propositions assert: a body 'continually attracted toward an immovable center' will describe 'equal areas in equal times'; and that 'a body attracted towards either focus of an Ellipsis . . . ye attraction shall be reciprocally as ye square of ye distance of ye body from that focus of ye Ellipsis'. In Newton's own manuscript a third proposition had been added which considered only 'the attraction at the two ends of the Ellipsis'.

It has been widely assumed that *A Demonstration* was composed especially for Locke sometime after February 1689. Herivel has, however, argued that the date on the manuscript of March 1689 is the date of receipt and not composition. This latter date he assigns either to the winter of 1679–80, or to 1684 (Herivel, 1965, pp. 108–17). Why, he asked, if it had been written after *Principia* (1687), did he not simply refer to the published laws instead of formulating them at length? In any case the description of laws as hypotheses was a usage abandoned by Newton before 1690. There is also something odd about the inclusion of hypothesis III. Long before the appearance of *Principia*, Newton had ceased to consider the parallelogram of forces as a hypothesis or law, but instead had succeeded in deriving it from more basic assumptions. For these, and other reasons, Herivel feels that *A Demonstration* is in truth an earlier document than *De motu*. The matter, however, remains controversial. Although supported by Cohen (1971, pp. 147) and Westfall (1971a, pp. 429–31), it has been dismissed by Whiteside (*MP*, VI, pp. 553–4) and the Halls (pp. 238–9).

A Description of an instrument for Observing the Moon's distance from the fixt Stars at Sea

---

Newton's paper was sent to Halley in 1700. It somehow became mixed up with Halley's papers and was found unexpectedly amongst them after his death in 1742. Publication was quickly arranged, with it appearing first in *PT* (1742, pp. 155–6). Thereafter it was republished by Brewster (1831, pp. 308–10) and is today most readily available in *PLNP* (1958, pp. 236–8).

The instrument described is a reflecting octant fitted with telescope, two parallel mirrors and a moveable index. When the index was set to 0° 0' 0" the same star would be seen both directly and reflected by the mirrors. If, however, the moon and an adjacent star were observed, the angular distance separating them could be read off the scale by moving the index until the star touched the circumference of the moon. The advantage of the instrument, Newton pointed out, was that even though it could not be held level at sea, 'as the Moon and Star will move together . . . an Observation may be made as exactly at Sea as at Land'.

Newton's work was genuinely innovative. Its appearance in 1742 was, none the less, of little more than historical interest for by this time a similar device had already been described to the RS in 1731 by John Hadley.

A Dissertation upon the Sacred Cubit of the Jews and the Cubits of the Several Nations; in which from the Dimensions of the Greatest Pyramid, as taken by Mr John Greaves, the Antient Cubit of Memphis is Determined

---

The most elusive of all Newton's published works, it is known in just two editions, neither of which is easy to obtain.

1 London, 1737. Translated from Latin into English and published by Thomas Birch in his *Miscellaneous Works of John Greaves* (Greaves, 1737, vol. II, pp. 405–33).

2 Lausanne and Geneva, 1744. Translated back into Latin it appeared in *Tome III* of Castillioneus.

Horsley ignored the work.

In origin the cubit is simple enough to describe. It is the length of the forearm. When, however, questions are raised about how many English inches are contained in the cubits of Egypt, Rome, Persia, Israel and other ancient kingdoms, matters are less clear. Equally mysterious is why Newton should pursue the matter. No indication is given in the text of the paper. Throughout, Newton's argument is clear, detailed and precise; it is also without direction, a study in pure metrology. As with many such works, both before and after, however tight the reasoning, the reliability of the conclusions will still depend upon the accuracy of the initial assumptions. As many of these were, in fact, no more than guesses, Newton's conclusions lose much of their initial plausibility.

He began by accepting the claim of Greaves that the Great Pyramid was 693 English feet long. As it was also supposed to be 400 cubits long, Newton had little difficulty in calculating the length of the Memphis cubit as 1.7325 English feet. Confirmation of Greaves's assumption came when it was found that the King's Chamber, a site inside the pyramid, measured 34.38 and 17.19 English feet, figures very nearly 20 and 10 cubits respectively. Other dimensions also fitted as neatly into the same scheme. 'Who will therefore imagine,' Newton asked, 'that so many dimensions not all depending upon each other should correspond by mere chance with the length of the Cubit assigned by us?' (Greaves, 1737, p. 410).

Newton thus accepted the Memphis cubit as 20.79 inches. Various other cubits were examined, including the Babylonian (24 inches), the Arabian and the Persian. Eventually, Newton turned to the Jewish cubit, the main point of the paper. Two main sources were considered: the *Talmud*, with its claim that the human body was three cubits from head to foot; and the dimensions given to the Temple by Josephus in his *Antiquities*.

With such a wealth of data, Newton had little difficulty in identifying two quite distinct lengths. One of 24 inches he claimed to have been adopted by the Jews in the days of the Babylonian captivity. This was the Jewish sacred cubit and had been used in the construction of Noah's Ark. There was also a vulgar cubit used by the Jews, which Newton casually identified with the Memphis cubit.

It remained to link the Jewish cubits with Roman values. If the Roman cubit and the sacred cubit were expressed in the same basic Roman units we have: 1 Roman cubit = 18 *unciae*; 1 sacred cubit = 25 1/5 *unciae*. These Newton somewhat dubiously claimed 'are to each other in round numbers as 2 to 3 very near'. In this way, Newton concluded, whenever Josephus had written 3 cubits he had really meant 2 sacred cubits. Applying this key to the measurements of the temple quoted by Josephus, Newton was able to reduce them all by one-third and to bring them into harmony with the figures quoted in the *Talmud*. The agreement between the *Talmud* and Josephus has not so much emerged or been derived, as to have been engineered by the adoption of the appropriate key. Other keys, no less arbitrary, were available which, if adopted, would have led to quite different results.

See also Solomon's temple and the cubit.

Age of the earth

Newton lived at a time when the earth's creation could be seen as a relatively recent historical event. In this context the name of James Usher, Archbishop of Armagh, has gained a certain notoricty for proposing in his *Annales veteri testamenti* (1654, Annals of the Old Testament), that the earth was created in 4004 BC. John Lightfoot, a Vice-chancellor of Cambridge in Newton's day, went further and offered the more precise date of 9 a.m. on the 23rd October 4004 BC (Gjertsen, 1984, pp. 297–8).

Doubts on such a naive chronology began to appear in the eighteenth century. One such doubt originated with an experiment described by

Newton in prop.XLI of Book III of *Principia*. Speaking of the heat obtained by a comet from the sun, Newton noted:

> A globe of iron of an inch in diameter, exposed red-hot to the open air, will scarcely lose all its heat in an hour's time; but a greater globe would retain its heat longer in the ratio of its diameter . . . and therefore a globe of red-hot iron equal to our earth that is, about 40000000 feet in diameter, would scarcely cool in . . . above 50,000 years. (CAJORI, p. 522)

Obviously unhappy with his findings, Newton could do no more than speculate about 'latent causes' which might speed the process up, and to recommend that the subject be further investigated 'by experiments'.

It was, in fact, taken up by the great naturalist, the Comte de Buffon. In his *Les époques de la nature* (1778, The Epochs of Nature), he reported the results of similar cooling experiments which gave the earth a history of '74,047 years approximately'.

Akenside, Mark (1721–70)

The son of a butcher from Newcastle-upon-Tyne, Akenside qualified at Leyden as a physician in 1744. As a poet he is best known for his *The Pleasures of Imagination* (1744), a work which happily incorporated the science of Newton and the philosophy of Locke. It is interesting to see Akenside dismissing the later Romantic claim that knowledge of the structure and genesis of such natural phenomena as rainbows was incompatible with their appreciation. Akenside made the quite opposite claim, that the 'rainbow's vernal-tinctur'd hues' had never appeared so pleasing until:

> The hand of science pointed out the path
> In which the sun-beams gleaming from the west
> Fall on the watry cloud   (NICOLSON, 1966, p. 33)

See also Poetic tradition

Alchemical Notebook

The Alchemical Notebook can be found in the Jewish National and University Library, Jerusalem (Yahuda MS, var.260). It consists of no more than a number of headings and subheadings. Amongst the headings are such items as '*De sale*', '*Solutio*', '*Conjunctio et liquefactio*'. Why Newton chose not to pursue the headings is not known.

See also Alchemical papers

Alchemical papers

Few things shocked Victorian scholars and modern scientists more than the realisation that Newton was a serious alchemist. The evidence appeared to be indisputable and lay primarily in the wealth of material discovered in the PC.

HISTORIOGRAPHY

Newton's chemical interests were no secret to his contemporaries. With Robert Boyle and John Locke, for example, he would discuss and correspond on technical chemical issues. He even permitted the publication during his life of a chemical text, *De natura acidorum* (1710). There are, also, vivid descriptions from Humphrey Newton of how in the 1680s the fire in Newton's laboratory scarcely went out night or day while Newton himself would rarely retire before '2 or 3 o'clock, sometimes not until 5 or 6'.

None of his unpublished papers, however, attracted the interest of such early editors as Thomas Pellet and Samuel Horsley. It was left to Sir David Brewster to reveal to the general public just what was contained in Newton's surviving chemical papers. The shock is still discernible. How, he asked, could 'a mind of such power . . . stoop to be even the copyist of the most contemptible alchemical poetry, and the annotator of a work, the obvious production of a fool and a knave'. In defence of Newton, Brewster noted, the work was not undertaken to enrich himself, but out of 'a love of truth alone, a desire to make new discoveries in chemistry, and a wish to test the extraordinary pretensions of their predecessors' (Brewster, vol. II, pp. 374–5). Having drawn attention to the existence of such material, Brewster moved on to more congenial matters.

He had not, however, given any indication of the scale of the material. Nor did L. T. More, the next major biographer of Newton, have anything to add in 1934 to Brewster's comments. It was left to the Sotheby sale in 1936 of the PC to reveal just how vast and prolonged Newton's alchemical researches had been. Some 650,000 words, 'almost all in Newton's hand', were offered in 121 lots. They are fully listed in Dobbs (1975, pp. 235–48). Keynes acquired fifty-seven lots which are now deposited in KCC Library; a few others are to be found in the Babson, Yahuda, and Bodleian collections; the location of twenty-eight lots is unknown, and three further lots are unavailable in private hands.

Serious work began on the manuscripts after the Second World War. Some of the texts were published, first by F. S. Taylor (1956) followed shortly after by Geoghegan (1957). Scholars also began to survey and to analyse the details and the nature of Newton's alchemy. Some, like

Boas and Hall (1958, pp. 151–2), sought to play down the alchemical content of the Keynes collection. 'Newton was not', they declared, 'in any admissible sense of the word an alchemist.' His reports 'read like those of a rational, experimental scientist at a time when alchemy could not be discounted'. He had never, they insisted, ever written an alchemical treatise.

A more detailed analysis of the Keynes manuscripts showed Boas and Hall's initial confidence to be misplaced. It was only too clear that Newton had written a good many alchemical works. What was not, however, immediately apparent was the purpose of many of these manuscripts. Were they simply chemical reports written in a strange and antiquated language? Or were they really genuine alchemical texts? It was to such questions that detailed investigations by Dobbs (1975), Figala (1977) and Westfall (RSW) began to address themselves.

DATE

The papers come from the period 1669 to 1696 with, according to Westfall (RSW, pp. 530–1), only four fragmentary notes being dated with assurance to the post-1696 period. Westfall (*ibid.*, pp. 290–1) went on to estimate their distribution in time. He found 20 per cent to have been written by the mid-1670s, a further 30 per cent before 1687, and the final 50 per cent to date from the 1690s. The interest was thus an abiding one. Conduitt reported Newton talking with pleasure in later life about what he termed his 'furnace days'. It seems, also, that not even the demands of writing *Principia* were powerful enough to keep Newton out of the laboratory. Dated experiments were recorded for both April and May 1686, a period when he was still working on *Principia*.

COMPOSITION

Keynes proposed a fourfold classification of the various works.
  1 Transcripts of other works, by far the largest group. Examples include transcripts of works by Edwardus Generosus, Nicholas Flammel, Artephius, Thomas Norton, Michael Maier, George Ripley, John de Monte Snyder, Basilius Valentinus, and numerous others.
  2 Translations.
  3 Indices, glossaries, bibliographies, summaries, etc. Examples are *Alchemical writers* (a list of 113 writers on alchemy), *Index chemicus* and *De Scriptoribus* (a bibliography of over eighty books).
  4 Works by Newton himself. *Alchemical propositions, Clavis, Praxis, Vegetation of Metals* and *Essay on the preparation of star reguluses* are

examples of such works which have been either published or described.

SOURCE

One feature of a number of the texts listed in the Sotheby *Catalogue* (1936) is the lack for them of any published source. In some cases Newton copied texts which differed from the published work; in other cases he took notes from works some years before they appeared in print. Some, indeed, of the treatises copied in Newton's collection are still unpublished. Where, then, did Newton obtain them?

Some he probably borrowed from Cambridge colleagues such as Henry More, Isaac Barrow and Ezekiel Foxcroft, also known to be interested in alchemy. There are also a few references and hints in Newton's papers and correspondence to a wider set of contacts, amongst whom views, recipes and manuscripts were exchanged. Thus, in March 1696 Newton noted the visit of 'A Londoner' with whom he engaged in a technical discussion sufficiently important to be recorded in a *Memorandum* (C, IV, pp. 196–9). Newton may well, also, have entered into a continuing alchemical correspondence with a certain Francis Meheux (C, II, p. 386). There were, no doubt, others. Such vague hints present the intriguing picture of a Newton repeatedly discouraging the mathematicians and physicists of Europe from seeking his views while, at the same time, eagerly receiving the letters and visits of a number of shadowy alchemists.

Of the source of the bulk of the manuscripts copied and noted by Newton, there is no mystery. Harrison (1978, p. 59) has identified 138 (8 per cent) alchemy titles in Newton's library, including such major compilations as Zetzner's six-volume *Theatrum chemicum* and Ashmole's *Theatrum chemicum Britannicum*.

See also Alchemical principles and aims

Alchemical principles and aims

Newton's library contained 138 books on alchemy, while his papers on his death ran to some 650,000 words, mainly in his own hand, on alchemical topics. Such was Newton's concentration on the subject during the period 1669 to 1696 that Dobbs (1975, p. 88) could judge that Newton had probed 'the whole vast literature of the older alchemy as it has never been probed before or since'. Why did it attract Newton so? To what end were his enormous labours directed?

Traditionally alchemy had been concerned with the search for a substance, commonly known as the philosopher's stone, capable of transmuting base metals into gold and silver. Given also the traditional understanding of the nature of metals, the programme was not implausible. Metals were thought to be compounds of sulphur and mercury but not, it must be noted, the ordinary chemical elements S and Hg as we know them today. Alchemists well knew that if they combined sulphur and mercury all they ever got was cinnabar (HgS). The sulphur and mercury they had in mind would be described as the 'spirit' of sulphur, or a 'philosophic mercury'. Alchemists felt that it was their failure to extract from crude, impure samples of sulphur and mercury the pure spirit of the elements that had prevented them from achieving their aim. If they could produce pure samples in the laboratory then it would only be a matter of time before they discovered how they should be mixed, and what needed to be added to them, to attain their aim of transmutation. The first aim, however, remained the production of 'philosophic mercury'.

Alchemists, for a number of reasons, had been most reluctant to express such a straightforward programme in a coherent language. They were, of course, hampered by the absence of any agreed, common, public chemical language. This would only begin to appear in the nineteenth century. The lack of such a language was compounded by the unwillingness of alchemists to reveal their secrets to their rivals or to their potential customers. The result was the development of not one, but a variety of esoteric languages. The difficulty could range from the simple abbreviation A for Aqua, to an unambiguous cypher in which the reader was told to mix xknk with qbsf tbmkt (Crosland, 1978, p. 41).

The subject seemed an ideal one for Newton, combining his love of bookish pedantry with his delight in experimental work. Newton's first instinct was to survey the literature, a task he could never undertake casually. The result can be seen in the 650,000 words on alchemy in the PC. Much of this is concerned with Newton's attempt to master an extensive and obscure literature. It was, admittedly, no more extensive or obscure than the literature on the interpretation of the *Apocalypse*, or on the chronology of the ancient world. In all cases Newton seems to have shown the same single-mindedness and the same capacity to master a complex and novel field. Perhaps the best indication of the magnitude of his approach, outside the Sotheby *Catalogue* (1936), is his *Index chemicus*. Started in the 1680s, it included, when finally abandoned in the 1690s, 879 entries with references to about 150 alchemical texts from which some 5,000 page references were listed.

In addition, from the late 1660s onwards, Newton had begun to tackle the discipline in the laboratory. Early experiments were concerned with the extraction of the 'mercury' from the other common metals. Two ways were pursued: by dissolving mercury and a metal in aquafortis; and by mixing common sublimate (mercuric chloride) and sal ammoniac (ammonium chloride). Although the only thing to emerge at the end would be ordinary mercury, alchemists argued that it was in fact a rather special 'philosophic mercury'. In later work, as with the *Clavis* for example of the mid-1670s, Newton's interest turned to antimony and the preparation of the various star reguli.

By the time Newton performed his last experiment in February 1696, shortly before taking up his appointment at the Mint, he seems to have discovered, to his own satisfaction, the secret of multiplication. The claim was made in the conclusion of *Praxis* that 'each stone' could be multiplied '4 times and no more'. Such works and claims have strongly suggested to readers like Westfall (1975) that Newton was undoubtedly an alchemist. He may well not have been a vulgar alchemist concerned with enriching himself or baffling the credulous, but he remained an alchemist none the less.

Both Westfall (1975) and Dobbs (1975), however, have claimed to identify insights gained from his alchemical researches operating in more orthodox areas of Newtonian science. Thus, for Westfall (1975, p. 224): 'The forces of attraction and repulsion between particles of matter, including gravitational attraction . . . were primarily the offspring of alchemical active principles.'

For Dobbs (1975, pp. 210–13), the crucial step in Newton's scientific development came in the late 1670s with his realisation that a mechanical ether had little to offer the theoretician and, in any case, lacked the appropriate experimental support. From this time Newton, consequently, began to accept 'the notion that active forces were operating generally'. The results can be seen in *Principia*, with its willing acceptance of forces of attraction and repulsion. The source of such ideas, Dobbs has argued, can be traced to the *Clavis*, in which reference had been made to a distinctive 'mercury' operating as a 'magnet' with clearly displayed attractive powers. This crucial step, Dobbs argues, was taken in the period 1679–80 (Dobbs, 1975, p. 212).

The issue remains unresolved. The claims of Dobbs and Westfall are entirely speculative and, though suggestive and not implausible, are no more soundly based than the proposal of Frank Manuel (1980) that Newton's concern with attractive forces derived ultimately from his early separation from his mother. Further, it has been argued by M. B. Hall (1975), the language of chemistry has always been unduly vivid and figurative. Newton's adoption of this familiar linguistic convention should, therefore, be taken no more seriously than the modern physicist's attribution to the quark of such properties as charm, beauty and colour.

See also Alchemical papers

Algarotti, Francesco (1712–64)

The son of a wealthy merchant, Algarotti was educated in Rome and Bologna. After travelling widely throughout Europe in the 1730s he settled in 1740 in Berlin at the court of Frederick the Great. He soon quarrelled with Frederick and in 1742 transferred his allegiance to a new patron, Augustus, the Elector of Saxony. Amongst other duties Algarotti served as artistic adviser to Augustus and was instrumental in buying for him several Tiepolos.

He had earlier in 1737 published his *Il Newtonianismo per le dame*. Translated into six languages and published in thirty editions, it served as one of the main channels through which Newtonian ideas reached the general European public. It was not, however, to everyone's taste. Nancy Mitford (1959, p. 56) has noted that Voltaire and Madame du Chastellet, in private, considered the work to be 'too frivolous, with too many jokes and not enough stuffing'. Nor does it read well today. Translated into English by Elizabeth Carter as *Sir Isaac Newton's Philosophy Explained for the Use of Ladies, Six Dialogues on Light and Colours*, first in 1739, later editions being known from 1742, 1752, 1765 and 1772, it is written in the form of a discussion, rather than dialogue, with the 'Marchioness of E____' and 'composed of certain Discourses which I had with that polite Lady on the Subject of Light and Colours'. The first five dialogues are concerned with light, and include 'a confutation of the Cartesian system' (dialogue 3), two dialogues (4 and 5) on 'the Newtonian system of Optics' and the final dialogue on 'the Newtoniam universal Principle of Attraction, and Application of this Principle to Optics'. The discussion throughout is interspersed with numerous digressions on such subjects as the nature of English verse.

Algarotti's tomb in Pisa, paid for by Frederick the Great, carries the inscription 'Algarotti . . . Newtoni Discipulo' (Algarotti . . . disciple of Newton). It can be seen in Levey (1980, p. 25).

An Account of the Book Entituled Commercium epistolicum Collini & Aliorum

The *Account* first appeared anonymously in the *PT* (February 1715, pp. 173–225). Newton, its author, was keen to see it more widely circulated and, under the title *Extrait du livre intitule Commercium epistolicum*, had it published in a French translation in the *Journal Littéraire* (1715, pp. 114–58, 344–65). He also, in a Latin translation, included it as *Rescensio libri qui inscriptis est Commercium epistolicum* in the second edition of the *CE* (1722). The original English *Account* is conveniently available in facsimile in Hall (1980, pp. 263–314).

While the *CE* sought to make its point by presenting all the relevant data with the minimum of interpretation, Newton, in the *Account*, chose to state his case against Leibniz at some length. Hall (1980), in his analysis of the work, has identified five main themes. He began with the claim that he had gained the crucial aspects of his mathematical method by 1669 and described them in *De analysi* (1669). He secondly claimed that Leibniz only began to develop his ideas on the calculus in 1677. The June 1677 letter from Leibniz to Oldenburg was, thus, a report of new work. Thirdly, he argued for the superiority of the method of fluxions over the differentials of Leibniz, while, fourthly, he went on to insist on the practical benefits of the new system of analysis. With it, he declared, most of the conclusions of *Principia* had been derived.

For the final point Newton moved from the calculus to the principles of natural philosophy and offered a seemingly independent evaluation of the work of the two rivals. While he found the work of Newton based on 'Evidence arising from Experiments and Phaenomena', he found the work of Leibniz dogmatically insisting that nature was a 'perpetual Miracle if it be not Mechanical'.

Newton also chose to answer the charge that in the *CE* 'the Royal-Society gave judgement against Mr Leibniz without hearing both Parties'. But, Newton replied, judgment had never been given. The Society had simply appointed a Committee 'to search out and examin such old Letters and Papers as were still extant about these Matters'. Ever ready to take the offensive, Newton concluded the point by warning Leibniz that 'by taxing the Royal-Society with Injustice in giving Sentence against him without hearing both Parties, he has transgressed one of their Statutes which makes it Expulsion to defame them' (Hall, 1980, p. 311).

There is a curious air of unreality about the *Account*. It is, after all, supposed to be an account of the *CE*, a work mainly written and assembled anonymously by Newton. The *Account*, equally anonymous, and equally by Newton, is a review of the first anonymous work. Despite such a deliberately misleading situation, Newton still felt free at one point to break off for a moment from judging the strength of Leibniz's case to appeal to the principle: 'But Mr. Leibnitz cannot be a Witness in his own Cause.'

Newton's authorship of the *Account* was only revealed in 1761 when James Wilson discussed the calculus dispute in an appendix to B. Robins *Mathematical Tracts*.

See also Anonymity; *Commercium epistolicum*

Anagrams

It was not uncommon for seventeenth-century scientists to record their more valued results in the form of anagrams. Thus, Galileo published his discovery in 1610 of the phases of Venus in a thirty-five letter anagram, Huygens announced his 1656 observation that Saturn was surrounded by a ring in a sixty-three letter anagram, while, in England, Robert Hooke and Christopher Wren resorted to similar stratagems. The advantages of the ploy are obvious. Priority was established yet nothing was given away to potential rivals. If, by chance, the work failed to stand up to further analysis it could be quietly forgotten without the embarrassment public failures tended to incur. Such anagrams were nothing like the single, clued words found in today's crosswords. Invariably in Latin, clueless, and of immense length, they were virtually insoluble. One of the simpler examples is Hooke's announcement in 1676 of his law of elasticity, proclaimed in the form: *ceiinossstuu*. Its solution, *ut tensio sic vis*, translates neatly and briefly as: as the strain, so the force.

The technique seemed ideally suited to someone like Newton, who combined an extreme reluctance to engage in public controversy with a fierce regard for his priority. Consequently when, in 1676, he came to discuss his work in a letter to Oldenburg intended for Leibniz he broke off from discussing his theory of tangents to comment: 'but because I cannot proceed with the explanation of it now, I have preferred to conceal it thus: 6accdae13eff7i319n4o4qrr4s8t12ux' (*C*, II, p. 134).

The convention was to present anagrams as frequency counts: six As, two Cs, one D, one AE, thirteen Es, etc. Mistakes were inevitable in such a system and Newton, in the example above, had failed to record the correct number of Ts (the solution requires nine).

The letter, known to scholars as the *Epistola posterior* (*C*, II, pp. 110–61), contains an even more formidable anagram. With over 270 letters, in a foreign tongue, and with little indication of what it might contain, it was as secure as if it had never been published. Discussing two solutions he had developed to the problem of tangents, Newton perversely concluded that:

> It seems best to write down both, at present, in transcribed letters, lest if others should discover the same, I should be compelled to change the method into another:
> 5accdaeI0effhIIi413m9n6oqqr8sIIt9v3x,
> IIab3cddI0eaegI0ill4m7n603p3q6r5sIIt8vx,
> 3acae4egh5i414m5n8oq4r3s6t4v
> aaddaeeeeeeiijmmnnnooprrrsssssttuu. (*C*, II, p. 148)

As if the anagram was not absurdly difficult enough on its own, it was inevitably transcribed incorrectly with one I too many and two Ss too few. Newton prudently noted in his own Waste Book the solutions of the two anagrams.

The first and shorter anagram reads:

Data aequatione quotcumque, fluentes quantitates involvente, fluxiones invenire, et vice versa.

Which, translated, becomes:

Given any equation involving fluents, the fluxions can be found and conversely.

The longer 273-letter anagram translates as:

Una methodus consistit in extractione fluentis quantitatis ex aequatione simul involvente fluxionum ejus: altera tantum in assumptione seriei pro quantitate qualibet incognita ex qua caetera commoda derivari possunt, et in collatione terminorum homologorum aequationis resultantis, ad eruendos terminos assumptae seriei.

Or, in its English translation:

One method consists in extracting a fluent quantity from an equation at the same time involving its fluxion; but another by assuming a series for any unknown quantity whatever, from which the rest could conveniently be derived, and in collecting homologous terms of the resulting equation in order to elicit the terms of the assumed series.

The solution of the first anagram was disclosed to Leibniz in a letter from Newton dated 16 October 1693 (*C*, III, p. 286). The solutions to both anagrams were first published by John Wallis in the third volume of his *Opera* (1699). They were published once more in the *Commercium epistolicum* (1713) and are to be found today, amongst other sources, in *MP*, II, pp. 190 1 and *C*, II, pp. 153 and 159.

The patent security of the anagrams did not prevent Newtonians like Raphson, in his *History of Fluxions* (1715), from suggesting that Leibniz had in fact deciphered them and derived from them Newton's general method of quadratures. The absurd claim was apparently omitted from the Latin edition of 1715 (More, 1962, p. 192).

One further anagram is to be found in Newton's papers. Like most compulsive writers he was tempted to see if the letters of his name could be so arranged as to yield any significant results. When spelt Isaacus Neuutonus it yielded the no doubt pleasing Ieova Sanctus Unus.

See also Epistola prior and Epistola posterior

Analysis per quantitatum series, fluxiones, ac differentias

In 1708 William Jones acquired the papers of John Collins. Amongst them were some unpublished mathematical works of Newton. It was clearly about time, and, with the priority dispute with Leibniz quickening, very much in Newton's interest to have some of his own earlier work in the public domain. Consequently Newton, for once, had no second thoughts about his decision to cooperate with Jones on his plans to publish some of these texts. The work itself, presented to the Royal Society on 31 January 1711, contained the following:

1 *De analysi* (first publication);
2 *De quadratura*;
3 *Enumeratio linearum*;
4 *Methodis differentialis* (first publication);
5 *Epistolarum fragments*:
     letter to Collins dated 8 November 1676 (*C*, II, pp. 179–80);
     Epistola prior;
     Epistola posterior;
     letter to Wallis dated 27 August 1692 (*C*, III, pp. 220–1).

The work also contained a Preface drafted, no doubt, with Newton's assistance. It contained no mention of Leibniz. It did, however, contain the claim that Newton had:

> Deduced the Quadrature of the Circle, Hyperbola, and certain other
> Curves by means of Infinite Series . . . and that he did so in 1665;
> then he devised a method of finding the same Series by Division
> and Extraction of Roots, which he made general the following Year.

The Preface also contained a critical reference to the 'harsh Hypothesis of Infinitely small quantities or indivisibles'.

There proved to be little demand for the work. Since its appearance in 1711 it has been re-issued only once, appearing in Amsterdam in 1723 both separately and as part of the reissue of the second edition of *Principia*. The trouble with the book was basically that it was out of date. The works published were too advanced to be of interest to the student while, to the mathematician they were no longer new. Half the works printed had already been publlished and contents of the rest had been spread by word of mouth and in manuscript many years before. Its publication was thus, for many, a statement of history, not mathematics. It also proved more convenient for editors to extract and publish the individual tracts one by one rather than to re-issue the whole of Jones's collection.

Ancestry

Shortly after being knighted in 1705 Newton went to some considerable trouble to establish his ancestry. On 22 November 1705 he filed what he took to be his family tree with the College of Arms. Autograph drafts are to be found in the Babson, Keynes, and Yahuda collections. It was first published by Turnor (1806) and thereafter can be found, variously modified, in Stukeley (1936), More (1962), RSW and *C*, VII. The essential details, tracing his ancestry back to a John Newton of Westby in the sixteenth century, can be seen in the diagram in a much simplified form.

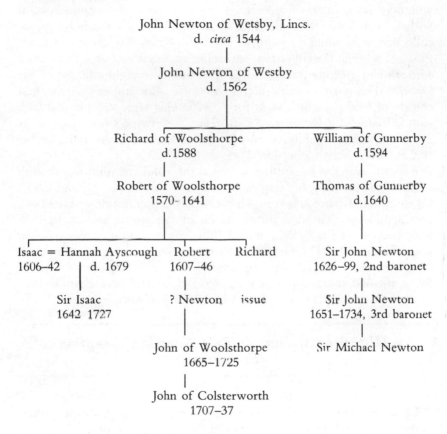

The document carried the note: 'This pedigree above written, I do aver to be true to the best of my knowledge. Witness my hand. Isaac Newton.'

In later life Newton seems to have changed his views somewhat, telling James Gregory in 1725 that his grandfather had come down to London from his East Lothian home with James I (Brewster, 1831,

Appendix I). There were also reports that the Newtons of Westby were descended from the Newtons of Lancashire.

See also Family; Heirs; Scottish kin

Andrade, Edward Neville da Costa (1887–1971)

A physicist who worked with Rutherford at Manchester and who held chairs at University College, London and the Royal Institution, Andrade was also a Newton scholar and the owner of an extremely fine collection of early scientific works. It is unlikely that anyone of average means will ever be capable of assembling such a collection again. Sold at Sotheby's in 1965, the collection fetched £69,581. At the heart of the collection were some forty-six works of Newton. No less than sixteen *Principia* were in the collection, including two first editions, three third editions and a Motte translation. There were also eight editions of the *Opticks*. The most valuable piece was a two-line imprint of the first edition of *Principia* which went for £2,400. This same volume was later seen in *Blackwell's Centenary Antiquarian Catalogue* of 1979 on offer for £14,000. Andrade published an account of his collection in *Endeavour* (1953), 'A Newton Collection'.

Andrade was also the author of two slender and unambitious, though accurate and readable, biographies of Newton (Andrade, 1950 and 1954). Of more significance was Andrade's role in the publication of Newton's correspondence. The committee set up by the Royal Society in 1938 had, because of the Second World War, made little progress when it was reformed in 1947 under the chairmanship of Andrade. A competent editor, H. W. Turnbull, was appointed and finally, after many years of delay, the first volume appeared in 1959. Before Andrade's death in 1971 four of the seven planned volumes had been published.

An Historical Account of Two Notable Corruptions of Scripture

---

The two supposedly corrupt texts are:
I John 5:7 'For there are three that bear record in heaven, the Father, the Word, and the Holy Ghost: and these three are one.'
8 'And there are three that bear witness on earth, the Spirit, and the water, and the blood: and these three agree in one.'
I Timothy 3:16 'And without controversy, great is the mystery of godliness: God was manifest in the flesh, justified in the spirit.'
With its clear statement that the 'Father, the Word, and the Holy Ghost' were one, the Bible would seem, in I John, to have provided an unam-

biguous declaration of the doctrine of the Trinity. As a direct challenge to Newton's Unitarianism, the texts forced him into a major investigation involving all his formidable biblical scholarship and calling upon his profound knowledge of the patristic literature.

Finding it impossible to reinterpret the texts in any natural way, he chose instead to deny their authenticity. John, he pointed out, was not to be found in any early Greek manuscripts. Nor could it be found in the writings of the early fathers. Surprisingly, it was not used by Athanasius and his supporters when the Arian heresy was debated at Nicaea in 325. Consequently, Newton concluded, the text was an interpolation added to the Vulgate of St Jerome in the late fourth century. Modern scholarship has tended to confirm Newton's insight and has identified the first appearance of the text as a gloss by the Spanish writer Priscillian in the late fourth century.

Of the Timothy text Newton noted that the word 'God' was absent from all early versions. The claim made was merely 'great is the mystery of godliness which was manifested in the flesh'. This time the interpolation is claimed to be a Greek one dating from the sixth century. The culprit was identified as Macedonius, the patriarch of Constantinople. And, for this, Newton added, he had been deposed and banished in 512.

The two corruptions described above formed the subject of a long letter to Locke dated 14 November 1690 (C, III, pp. 83–129). It was followed shortly afterwards by a further letter in which Newton announced his intention to identify some further corruptions (C, III, pp. 129–44). Not surprisingly he found that most corruptions originated in the fourth century during the period of the Arian controversy; further, 'Catholicks are here found much more guilty of these corruptions than the hereticks' (C, III, pp. 138).

At one point Newton considered publishing his discussion of the first two corruptions. It was decided first to have it translated into French and published on the Continent. 'I may perhaps after it has gone abroad long enough in French put it forth in English', Newton told Locke (C, III, p. 82). Locke cooperated enthusiastically. He had copies made and arranged for a friend, the theologian Jean Le Clerc of the Remonstrant's Seminary, Amsterdam, to undertake the translation. He was not informed of the identity of the author.

Newton, however, as had happened often before, began to have doubts about the wisdom of publishing such a work. On 16 February 1692 he finally instructed Locke 'to stop their translation and impression so soon as you can for I designe to suppress them' (C, III, p. 195). By this time Le Clerc had worked out the author's identity, and although he scrupulously followed out his new instructions, he also ensured that the manuscript was safely placed in the Seminary's Library in Amsterdam. There it remained until 1754 when it was finally published by an unknown and anonymous editor.

The work is known in the following editions.

1 London, 1754. It was published under the title *Two letters of Sir Isaac Newton to Mr Le Clerc* from the 'authentic' manuscript found in the Library of the Remonstrants. The text has, in fact, been described as 'imperfect and erroneous in many places'.

2 London, 1785. A more accurate version based on 'a MS in the possession of the Rev Dr Ekins, Dean of Carlisle' was published in Horsley, vol. V. The manuscript passed, via New College, Oxford, to the Bodleian Library.

3 Bath, 1803. Included in *The Recorder*, vol. II, edited by W. Mathews.

4 London, 1812. Included in *On the Object of Religious Worship*, edited by G. Clarke.

5 London, 1823. Included in *A Collection of Essays and Tracts in Theology*, vol. II, edited by Jared Sparks and reissued in 1830 and 1841.

6 London, 1959. The 'Two letters' are included in *C*, III, pp. 83–129 and are taken from the original texts in the Bodleian Library. The *Correspondence* also includes the third letter to Locke (*C*, III, pp. 129–44). It is taken from Newton's original manuscript in the Bodleian Library, and is concerned with a number of further corruptions of scripture.

See also Le Clerc, Jean; Unitarianism

An Hypothesis Explaining the Properties of Light Discoursed of in my Several Papers

---

Newton's so-called second paper on light and colour was communicated to the RS, in the form of a letter to Oldenburg, on 9 and 16 December 1675. In a covering note he observed that fearing 'vain disputes', he had resolved never to write again 'any hypothesis of light and colours'. A decision announced in advance 'to answer nothing' should free him from that fear. His aim in the paper was no more than to render his other work 'more intelligible', even though, he dismissively added, he had not concerned himself whether the new paper 'shall be thought probable or improbable' (*PLNP*, p. 178).

The paper is nonetheless noteworthy for containing Newton's first public speculations on the fundamental structure of the natural world. In the first part of the paper Newton presented the following five propositions.

1 'There is an aetherial medium much of the same constitution of air, but far rarer, subtler, and more strongly elastic.' As evidence Newton pointed to the way in which a pendulum slows down in

a vacuum almost as rapidly as it would in the open air (*PLNP*, pp. 179–81).

2 The aether is 'a vibrating medium like air, only the vibrations far more swift and minute' (*PLNP*, p. 181).

3 It is not, however, evenly distributed throughout space. 'though it pervades the pores of crystal, glass, water . . . yet it stands at a greater degree of rarity in those pores, than in the free aetherial spaces' (*PLNP*, pp. 182–4).

4 As for light, 'it is neither aether, nor its vibrating motion, but something of a different kind propagated from lucid bodies'. One possibility is that it consists of 'multitudes of unimaginable small and swift corpuscles of various sizes, springing from shining bodies at great distances one from another' (*PLNP*, pp. 184–5).

5 'Light and aether mutually act upon one another, aether in refracting light, and light in warming aether' (*PLNP*, pp. 185–6).

Much of the rest of the paper was spent in showing how the hypothesis of the ether could be used to explain such familiar optical phenomena as reflection, refraction, and the colours found in thin films. It also did much more. Above all it showed Newton as determined to tackle a wide range of problems – chemical, physiological and astronomical, as well as optical – and to attempt to understand them within a comprehensive framework. To do this he was prepared to speculate as readily as he had previously been willing to experiment and calculate. Static electricity, surface tension, muscular contraction, the dissolution of metals, fermentation and many other issues, all were raised and discussed without dogmatism or preconception. There was even a reference to the 'gravitating attraction of the earth', and the query as to whether it could be caused by 'the continual condensation of some other such like aetherial spirit' (*PLNP*, pp. 180–1). Newton may not have progressed far with any of the problems he raised; it was clear, none the less, that he was a thinker of imagination and range, willing to consider a wide variety of problems and solutions.

He did not, however, gain the freedom from 'vain disputes' he claimed to value so much. First there were requests for further details of his experimental work. This was followed by the comment of Hooke that the bulk of the paper 'was contained in his *Micrographia*, which Mr. Newton had only carried further in some particulars' (*PLNP*, p. 199). Newton replied on 21 December 1675 insisting that the only thing they had in common was a belief in the existence of the ether. In any case, he counter-charged, Hooke seems to have taken most of his points directly from Descartes (*PLNP*, pp. 208–9). The correspondence continued briefly between Newton and Hooke into 1676, but neither of the protagonists seemed to have much interest in pursuing the matter further and it was consequently allowed to drop, amidst much strident insincerity.

[23]

Newton rejected Oldenburg's request to publish the paper in the *PT*. Although some of the material was used in the *Opticks* (1704), the paper itself first appeared posthumously in Birch (1757, vol. III, pp. 247–305). It can today be readily consulted in Thayer (1953, pp. 82–99), *C*, I, pp. 361–86, and *PLNP*, pp. 177–99.

Annus mirabilis

Sometime in the summer of 1665 the plague appeared in Cambridge. Shortly afterwards the University closed down and Newton returned home to Woolsthorpe. He remained in Woolsthorpe from summer 1665 until April 1667, with the exception of the period March to June 1666 spent in Cambridge. Over fifty years later, at the height of the priority dispute, Newton wrote down for des Maizeaux his recollections of the period.

> In the beginning of the year 1665 I found the Method of approximating series and the Rule for Reducing any dignity of any Binomial into such a series. The same year in May I found the method of Tangents of Gregory and Slusius, and in November had the direct method of fluxions and the next year in January had the Theory of Colours and in May following I had entrance into ye inverse method of fluxions. And the same year I began to think of gravity extending to ye orb of the Moon and . . . I deduced that the forces wch keep the Planets in their Orbs must be reciprocally as the squares of their distances from the centers about which they revolve . . . All this was in the two plague years of 1665–6. For in those days I was in the prime of my age for invention and minded Mathematicks and Philosophy more than at any other time since. (RSW, p. 143)

The document was first published in the 1888 Cambridge *Catalogue* of the PC. Since that time it has been customary to refer to the year 1666 as Newton's *annus mirabilis*. The description is clearly misleading, for even the most cursory examination of the text reveals that Newton assigned his discoveries to a two-year period and that no special priority can be given to either 1665 or 1666. It would therefore be more accurate to recognise, with Westfall, 'the myth of the annus mirabilis' and that '1666 was no more mirabili than 1665 or 1664' (RSW, p. 144).

It remains true, none the less, and without too much exaggeration, that in a remarkably short period the twenty-four-year-old student created modern mathematics, mechanics and optics. There is nothing remotely like it in the history of thought. A comparable achievement is sometimes claimed for Einstein and the year 1905, when he published three papers in which he laid the foundations for the special theory of relativity, successfully analysed the photoelectric effect in terms of the new quantum theory, and revealed the atomic basis of Brownian motion. It would be pointless to attempt to belittle Einstein's achievement in order to preserve Newton's uniqueness; more is to be gained by noting the contrasts. Above all, the most impressive feature is the sheer isolation of Newton. Not only was he young and without any genuine training in science; he could have had few, if any, to talk to in a backward Restoration Cambridge, or a remote Lincolnshire farm. There can, consequently, be no doubt that whatever Newton did create in 1665 or 1666 came from no other source than his own creative will, and from his private reading. Einstein, by contrast, though no one's disciple, and as much his own man as Newton had been, was still much more aware of the science of his day, both through his education at the Zurich Polytechnic and through his reading of Maxwell, Mach, Helmholtz and others.

One further contrast is to be seen in the response of Newton and Einstein to their work. Whereas Einstein, very much the modern scientist, promptly and efficiently wrote up his results and published them, Newton for the most part, clung on to them obsessively for twenty years or more. Indeed, many of the mathematical results remained unpublished until they were finally revealed forty years later as appendices to the *Opticks* (1704). Others were only revealed many years after his death.

Anonymity

A persistent and surprising feature of Newton's attitude to his work was his willingness, and sometimes even his eagerness, to see his books and papers appear anonymously. Thus, to John Collins in 1670 he agreed to let his work on annuities go to press but, he added, 'without my name to it. For I see not what there is desirable in public esteem'. Shortly afterwards he was again insisting to Collins that he would only allow the title page of the proposed *Observations on Kinckhuysen* to carry the note, 'Revised by another author'. Later works to appear anonymously were the substantial *Arithmetica universalis* (1707), the slight *Scala graduum caloris* (1701), and the triumphant *De ratione temporis* (1697). Even the first edition of the *Opticks* (1704) failed to carry Newton's name on the title page. Evidence of the author's identity was reserved for the Advertisement which carried at the end the initials I.N.

It is difficult to grasp Newton's motive at this point. It certainly cannot have been to hide his identity. There can have been few, if any, scientists who were unaware of the name of the author of such works as *Opticks* and *Arithmetica universalis*. If they were, numerous statements could be found inside the book revealing the author's identity.

There was also a second class of works in which something more than anonymity was sought, and for reasons only too distressingly clear. Thus when Newton published the *Account* (1715) and Leibniz the *Charta volans* (1713), it was not obscurity they were seeking but camouflage. They sought not so much to hide behind an anonymous front, as to present openly a counterfeit appearance. Hence, the regular use of the third person to describe oneself. 'Mr Newton did this' and 'Mr Newton did not do this', Newton informed the readers of the *Account*. This, however, was merely the first level of duplicity. Having once issued an anonymous work, there was nothing to stop the author issuing a second anonymous work which quoted, as evidence, material from the first work. Or alternatively, the first work could be quoted by a second author, and subsequently re-used by the first author in a later signed work. Other variations were possible.

Confusions of identity, and slips of the pen, could and did arise. The best known such case befell the unfortunate Johann Bernoulli, who published in 1716 the unacknowledged exercise in self defence *Epistola pro eminente mathematico, Johane Bernoulli* (A Letter written in favour of the Eminent Mathematician, Johann Bernoulli). An inadvertent reference to a formula of Bernoulli's as *'meam formulam'* (my formula) revealed his identity and allowed the English mathematicians thereafter to ridicule him for his presumption. Despite their own willingness to issue anonymous material, they still felt free to lecture Bernoulli on the impropriety of his behaviour. Newton, for example, warned Bernoulli that any future unsigned letters 'wherein you are applauded . . . or your enemies abused' would be looked upon 'as written by your self' (*C*, VI, p. 387).

One final form of anonymity often adopted by Newton was the use of a front man. Unwilling to engage his critics directly, he would sometimes prefer to see his own views expressed under the name of another. The priority dispute with Leibniz was pursued under the cover of John Keill, John Raphson and Pierre des Maizeaux. A secondary dispute with Leibniz was directed through the figure of Samuel Clarke. Earlier, views of Newton on the nature of ancient science, the so-called *Classical Scholia*, had appeared in a work by David Gregory. It should be emphasised that disciples like Keill and Clarke were doing something more than merely defending their master; they were actually publishing Newton's material for him under their own name. The process, well documented in the surviving correspondence between Newton and Keill, was as self-conscious as it was deliberate. Not many readers, however, are likely to have been misled by the manoeuvre.

Antimony

Central to much of the alchemy, both theoretical and practical, of Newton's day, is the element antimony. Alchemists actually worked with the ore stibnite (Sb_2S_3) which was then reduced, using charcoal and a variety of metals, to the metallic element known as *regulus* of antimony. If charcoal alone was used in the reduction process, the metal was known as *regulus per se*. If, however, a metal had been used it would be variously known as *regulus* of Saturn (lead), *regulus* of Venus (copper), etc., depending upon which particular metal had been involved. To the modern chemist all such *reguli* are equally antimony. The traditional alchemist, however, would insist that they still contained within themselves the influence or the seeds of the metal from which they had been derived.

Antimony showed one further feature. When reduced with iron the crystals will occasionally form a star-like pattern. It was much sought after by alchemists and known to them as *regulus antimonii stellatus*. If iron had been the reducing agent it was known as martial *regulus*; if copper had been used the result was venereal *regulus*. One sign of Newton's interest in such processes can be seen in his detailed *Essay on the preparation of star reguluses*, published in full in Dobbs (1975, pp. 249–50).

One reason why antimony was of interest to alchemists was that it was widely used in the purification of gold. If molten gold ore was mixed with stibnite any impurites would combine with the sulphur and rise to the top leaving the pure gold and antimony to sink to the bottom. To the untutored it could well look as if antimony had been transformed into gold. To the more sophisticated it suggested that antimony could be an appropriate place to start in the quest for metals which could be transmuted into gold.

There was, however, a further reason for Newton's interest in star *regulus*. A star is normally seen as the source of lines radiating outwards. Dobbs, however, has pointed out that it can be seen just as naturally as a centre to which rays are attracted (1975, pp. 148–55). Antimony could in this way be seen as a potent agent attracting, like a magnet, the essence or spirit of metals such as gold. Dobbs claims to recognise such views hinted at in the alchemical literature Newton knew so well. As a result Newton spent much of the 1680s and 1690s working on the practical chemistry of antimony while pursuing, at the same time, references to it in the complex and confusing literature of alchemy.

See also Alchemical principles and aims

Apostille

The heading refers to a postscript added to a letter from Leibniz to Conti and dated 25 November 1715 (*C*, VI, pp. 250–5). It was clearly intended to be shown to Newton and Conti, in London at the time, accordingly obliged. The postscript was mainly a prolonged attack on the basic presuppositions of Newtonian science. Amongst other points, Leibniz insisted that:

1 gravity was either an occult quality or a miracle;
2 Newton had failed to prove the existence of a vacuum, or of atoms;
3 Newton was mistaken in requiring God to intervene to preserve the stability of the heavens;
4 nor is God a sensorium;
5 Newton seemed to have abandoned experimental philosophy in favour of speculation.

Newton replied, through Conti, on 26 February 1716 (*C*, VI, pp. 285–90). Although he took up a number of points made in the body of the letter on the priority dispute, of the postscript, he recorded in a draft: 'The more I consider the Postscript of Mr Leibniz the less I think it deserves an answer'. There was, thus, only the briefest of answers to the charges of Leibniz. Replies came instead from Samuel Clarke. Similar arguments had been presented in November 1715 to Princess Caroline. Her intervention at his point led to Clarke taking up Leibniz's points and thus beginning the important Leibniz–Clarke correspondence.

The postscript also contained a brief but important reference to the priority dispute. He could not accept, he insisted, that Newton had discovered the infinitesimal calculus before him. In support he cited Bernoulli, who had 'judged well' in his favour. Such a reference made it clear to all that Bernoulli must be the 'leading mathematician' referred to in the *Charta volans*.

See also J. Bernoulli

Appearance

In addition to the portraits, the prime source is John Conduitt.

> He was of middle stature, and plump in his latter years; he had a very lively and piercing eye, a comely and gracious aspect, and a fine head of hair, as white as silver, without any baldness . . . never wore spectacles, nor lost more than one tooth to the day of his death. (TURNOR, 1806, p. 165).

Two other reports are less flattering. Bishop Atterbury, for example, denied 'the piercing eye' of Conduitt's description, and spoke instead of a rather 'languid' look which 'did not raise any expectation in those who did not know him'. Another eyewitness, Thomas Hearne, agreed with the bishop that Newton, 'a short well-set man', was of 'no very promising aspect' (Brewster, 1831, p. 342).

Apples and apple trees

The subject of comedy sketches and cartoons as well as learned articles, the story of Newton and the falling apple is undoubtedly the best-known anecdote in the entire history of science. Inevitably the current £1 note displays, with the other familiar Newtonian icons – a prism, a reflecting telescope – a spray of apple blossom. Inevitable also has been the often-drawn comparison between the apples in the gardens of Eden and Woolsthorpe:

> And this is the sole mortal who could grapple,
> Since Adam, with a fall, or with an apple.

> BYRON, *Don Juan*, canto X

Was Newton's apple any less mythical than Eve's? David Brewster, Newton's first biographer, thought not. As the story 'is mentioned neither by Dr Stukely nor by Mr Conduitt, and, as I have not been able to find any authority for it whatever,' Brewster concluded in 1831, 'I did not feel myself at liberty to use it.' He could have added that Fontenelle and Whiston ignored the story completely, while Henry Pemberton (1728) spoke of a meditation in a garden without ever mentioning an apple tree.

None the less, Brewster's hesitation was misplaced. A more comprehensive search of the early literature has produced several accounts. The most detailed is that of Stukeley, not published in full until 1936. On the 15 April 1726 he had dined with Newton in Kensington. After dinner, he reported:

> The weather being warm, we went into the garden and drank tea, under shade of some apple-trees, only he and myself. Amidst other discourses, he told me, he was just in the same situation, as when formerly, the notion of gravitation came into his mind. It was occasion'd by the fall of an apple, as he sat in contemplative mood. Why should that apple always descend perpendicularly to the ground, thought he to himself. Why should it not go sideways or upwards, but constantly to the earth's centre. (pp. 19–20)

Conduitt's account confirmed Stukeley.

> & whilst he was musing in a garden it came into his thought that the power of gravity (wch brought an apple from the tree to the ground) was not limited to a certain distance from the earth but that this power must extend much further . . . Why not as high as the moon said he to himself.

But Conduitt does not actually declare that an apple fell in Newton's presence, although such an event is compatible with the passage; the falling apple could be an illustration of a thesis and not the observation leading to the thesis.

There were, however, two earlier published accounts. Voltaire, writing in English in his *Essay on the Civil War in France* (1727), spoke of 'Sir Isaac Newton walking in his Garden had the first thought of his System of Gravitation, upon seeing an Apple falling down from the Tree'. He repeated the story in his better known and more accessible 1733 *Letters Concerning the English Nation* (Voltaire, 1980), although in this work he spoke not of an apple but of 'fruit falling from a tree'. Voltaire's source was probably Catherine Barton. The final early source was Robert Greene, on the authority of Martin Folkes, in his *Philosophy of the Expansive and Contractive Forces* (1727).

It thus seems likely that Newton some time in the 1720s told a similar story, describing events of half a century before, to four close friends and relatives – Catherine Barton, Martin Folkes, John Conduitt and William Stukeley. There is no reason to believe that an eighty-year-old Newton could not remember with reasonable accuracy such distant events. If there is a problem, it is why he waited so long to tell the story. Why had not an earlier generation of friends – a Halley, a David Gregory or a Fatio – been told of the falling apple?

The story inevitably attracted later additions. Isaac D'Israeli, for example, noted that 'the apple struck him a smart blow on the head'. Accurate the story may be; if, however, it is taken as anything more than a pleasing anecdote and even thought to be capable of explaining the origin of Newton's ideas on universal attraction, then it is indeed, in Westfall's phrase, 'a vulgar myth'.

As to the actual apple tree at Woolsthorpe, its fate and nature are well documented. Edmund Turnor, the manor owner, reported in 1806 that the tree had survived and that he showed it to visitors. In the eighteenth century it grew pear-shaped apples with a very distinctive flavour.

Brewster saw the tree in 1814. It was badly decayed, he noted, and was taken down in 1820. An account of this incident was later published by C. W. Walker in 1912. His father, born in 1807, attended school near Woolsthorpe. One night, presumably in 1820, after a severe storm, the apple tree was found lying on its side. It had been propped up for several years before but the wind had finally been too strong for the decaying tree. The teacher, a Mr Pearson, 'sawed a good many logs from the branches. My father got one of these pieces . . . various friends and other people often tried to induce my father to part with this, but he always refused, as he prized it very much indeed.' Walker presented the fragment to the Royal Astronomical Society in 1912.

Scions had been taken from the tree and grafted on trees belonging to Lord Brownlow at Belton. Grafts were sent to the Fruit Research Station at East Malling, Kent. At a meeting of the Royal Society Club on 3 November 1943, with J. M. Keynes present, E. J. Salisbury of

Kew produced two apples from the Belton tree. He went on to identify the Woolsthorpe tree. A further graft was sent to the US in 1944 to the orchard of Pennsbury Manor, Morrisville, Pa., the home of William Penn. A scion taken from this thriving tree in 1954 was planted in the driveway leading to the Babson Institute Library. The apples produced by the tree have been identified as a variety of cooking apple known as Flower of Kent. Pear-shaped, the apples have been described as flavourless and coloured red with streaks of yellow and green.

Fuller details of the story are available in McKie and de Beer (1951; 1952).

A Problem in College Administration

Lot 310 bought by Keynes in the Sotheby sale of the PC in 1936 consists of a document prepared by Newton in 1708 for Richard Bentley. Keynes donated the manuscript in 1939 to TCC and it was published under the title *A Mathematical Analysis by Newton of a Problem in College Administration* in *Isis* (1958, vol. 49, pp. 174–6).

Bentley asked Newton to determine an equitable allocation of the college dividend on the basis of the rules which assigned livery expenses, stipends and commons to Fellows on the basis shown in the table. Using the formula:

$$s^2 = 81L - 342$$

he calculated that the Master should receive a stipend of 25 nobles and, consequently, a commons of 275 nobles. He recommended that dividends should be paid in proportion to their total incomes of 26, 31, 35 and 312 nobles. The noble had the value of £1/3.

Rules assigning livery expenses, stipends and commons to Fellows

	Livery	Stipends	Commons	Total
BA	5 nobles	8 nobles	13 nobles	26 nobles
MA	6 nobles	12 nobles	13 nobles	31 nobles
DD	7 nobles	15 nobles	13 nobles	35 nobles
Master	12 nobles	Joint award of 300 nobles		312 nobles

Arbuthnot, John (1667–1735)

The son of a Scottish clergyman and a graduate in medicine from St Andrews, Arbuthnot was a figure of some importance in the literary and political circles of his day. He settled in London and worked initially as a maths teacher before being appointed in 1705 physician to Queen Anne. A friend of Swoft and Pope, he formed with them The Brothers, a Tory club in competition with the better-known Whig Kit Kat club of Montague and his associates. From it there emerged eventually Pope's *Dunciad* and Arbuthnot's *Memoirs of Martimus Scriblerus*. This latter work, a satire against 'false tastes in learning', is comparable in many ways with the latter parts of *Gulliver's Travels* (1726). Arbuthnot also produced works of political satire, *The History of John Bull* (1712) for example, as well as a brief but original paper in probability theory, *An Argument for Divine Providence Taken from the Regularity Observed in the Births of Both Sexes* (*PT*, 1710). The argument would be much repeated throughout the century.

A figure of some influence at court and in fashionable literary and political circles, Arbuthnot was a valuable figure for Newton to have on his side in his disputes with J. Flamsteed and Leibniz. A fellow of the Royal Society since 1704, he was one of the members of the committee set up in 1712 to examine the papers and correspondence in the possession of the Society relating to the Newton–Leibniz priority dispute. Arbuthnot had earlier served as one of the referees ostensibly appointed by Prince George in 1704 to oversee the work of Flamsteed. On his role in this latter affair Flamsteed commented:

> Being one of the Prince's physicians, he was taken in to serve Sir Isaac Newton's purposes. He saw what was designed, and testified to me, by some expressions, that he approved not such proceedings; promised once to assist me in a particular affair; and, though he met with obstructions, performed it handsomely. (BAILY, 1835, p. 77)

It is not clear what Flamsteed was referring to. However, Arbuthnot's name was absent from the referee's letter of 13 July 1708 announcing their intention to print Flamsteed's papers with or without his help (*C*, IV, p. 524). A later correspondence between Arbuthnot and Flamsteed on the same subject and covering the period 14 March 1711 to 23 May 1711 has survived and been published in Baily (1835, pp. 280–90).

Argumenta and Twelve points on Arian Christology

More (1961, p. 642) quotes from a manuscript, presumably from the PC, listing 'fourteen *Argumenta* in Latin, with supporting passages from the Scriptures, to show that the Son is neither coeternal with, or equal to, the Father'. More summarised six of the *Argumenta*, the first three of which are:

2. Because the Son is called the Word. John I.1.
4. Because God begot the Son at some time, he had not existence from eternity. Prov.VIII. 23,25.
5. Because the Father is greater than the Son. John XIV.28.

A similar christology, although of twelve rather than fourteen points, and lacking Biblical references, has been published by Westfall (pp. 315–16). Taken from Yahuda MS 14, Westfall assigned it to the period 1672–5. Typical examples of the points made are:

5. The son in several places confesseth his dependence on the will of the father.
6. The son confesseth ye father greater than him calls him his God, &c.
7. The son acknowledgeth the original praescience of all future things to be in ye father onely.

Newton never seemed to tire of drawing up lists of this kind. Whether they were theological, historical, Biblical or linguistic, he would seem to have little difficulty in conjuring up a dozen or so objections to some particular aspect of orthodox christian theology.

Arithmetica universalis, sive de compositione et resolutione arithmetica liber

Newton gave David Gregory a somewhat obscure account of the work's origin.

He was forced seemingly to allow it, about 14 months agoe, when he stood for Parliament-man at that University. He has not seen a sheet of it, nor knows he what value it is in, nor how many sheets it will make, nor does he well remember the contents of it. He intends to goe down to Cambridge this summer and see it, and if it does not please him to buy up the copyes. It was read by way of lectures many years ago, and put in Public Library according to statute. (HISCOCK, 1937, p. 36)

Why Newton's candidacy should require him to publish a work on algebra is no clearer than why he should be forced into buying copies of his own work rather than simply forbidding its publication.

As Gregory indicated, the book began as lectures. In fulfilment of his obligation as Lucasian Professor, Newton first lectured on algebra in 1672 and seems to have continued until 1683. Although the manuscript of the ninety-seven lectures in the ULC (Dd 9.68) carries marginal dates from October 1673 to 1683, it should not be assumed that the lectures were ever delivered. There are no contemporary accounts of them and, apart from Cotes, who made a transcript of them in 1702, they seem to have been totally ignored. Whiteside (*MP*, V, p. 5) believes they were composed 'over a period of but a few months' during the winter of 1683–4.

For whatever reason, and however reluctantly, Newton did give William Whiston permission to prepare the lectures for publication. They appeared without Newton's name on the title page, although references inside the work made no attempt to hide the author's identity. Nor did he show much interest in the work. Instead, he complained that the titles and headings were not his and that it contained numerous mistakes. Yet when he did come to prepare a second edition in 1722 the changes he introduced were 'primarily reorderings of his own manuscript, not corrections of Whiston's editions' (RSW, p. 649).

The universal arithmetic of the title was meant to contrast with, what Newton termed, '*arithmetica particularis*', or an arithmetic which considered specific numbers. He did, of course, begin with operations on natural numbers, and did so at a remarkably elementary level. Here for example is Newton explaining to the undergraduates of seventeenth-century Cambridge how to add 1357 and 172: 'Write the one, 172, below the other, 1357, so that the units, 2, of the latter lie beneath the units, 7, of the other' (*MP*, V, p. 65).

The subjects actually covered were notation, addition, subtraction, multiplication, division, extraction of roots, reduction of fractions and radicals, the reduction of geometrical questions to equations, 61 problems, and the resolution of equations. Newton is thus seen posing such traditional mathematical problems as: 'If 12 cattle eat up a 3 acres meadow in 4 weeks and 21 cattle eat up 10 acres . . . in 9 weeks, how many cattle shall eat up 36 acres in 18 weeks?' Not all the problems are so perverse. Many, in fact, such as Problem 55 ('To describe a conic section through five given points'), would find clear echoes in the mathematical machinery developed in the *Principia*.

Newton also took the opportunity, once more, to dismiss the Cartesian approach to mathematics. Modern analysts, he complained, had confused arithmetic and geometry.

> The Ancients so assiduously distinguished them one from the other
> that they never introduced arithmetical terms into geometry; . . .
> recent people by confusing both, have lost the simplicity in which
> all elegance in geometry consists. (*MP*, V, p. 429)

The work was, however, more than an introduction to algebra. Leibniz, who reviewed it in the *AE* (1708), identified in it 'certain extraordinary features which you will seek in vain in vast volumes of Analysis' (RSW, p. 398). In particular, Newton extended Descartes's rule of signs to imaginary roots. The rule, in Newton's terminology, stated that there are as many true (positive) roots of an equation as there are changes of signs, and there are as many false (negative) roots as there are like signs following each other. Thus, the 4th degree equation:

$$x^4 - x^3 - 19x^2 + 49x - 30 = 0 \qquad (1)$$

with its three sign changes will have three positive and one negative roots. There are, however, equations in which the rule breaks down. For example:

$$x^3 - 4x^2 + 7x - 6 = 0 \qquad (2)$$

has only a single real root and not the three demanded by the rule. In actual fact, as Descartes's rule set an upper bound to the number of positive and negative roots, it has not been violated. Equation (2) still has three roots; two of them are, in Newton's words 'impossible', or, in a more modern terminology, imaginary. The roots are 2, $1 + \sqrt{-2}$, and $1 - \sqrt{-2}$.

Newton set about formulating a rule which would allow mathematicians to determine the number of imaginary roots of any equation (*MP*, V, pp. 347–53). The rule was complicated and offered without proof and without any indication of possible exceptions. Some idea of its originality, however, can be gained from the fact that it was not until 1865 that the rule was derived in a rigorous manner by James Sylvester.

Despite Newton's somewhat churlish attitude to his own work, and despite its incomplete nature, the *Arithmetica universalis* proved to be one of the more popular of Newton's books and is known in the following editions.

1 Cambridge, 1707. Edited by William Whiston, it contained 343 pages and sold initially for 4s. 6d. It also contained Halley's *Halleiana aequationum radices arithmeticae inveniendi methodus* (Halley's method of finding roots of equations arithmetically) published earlier in *PT* (1694, vol. XVIII, pp. 136–48). It was reviewed by Leibniz in the *AE* (1708, pp. 519–26). Newton's name does not appear on the title page or elsewhere in the edition, although references by Whiston made the identity of the author plain to all.

2 London, 1720. The first English translation, under the title *Universal Arithmetic*. It was prepared by Joseph Raphson and revised and corrected by Samuel Cunn. Halley's paper was retained.

3 London, 1722. A second Latin edition, seen through the press by John Machin. Although Newton had complained of Whiston's work, and although the new edition was advertised as having been revised and corrected by the author, there were in fact few changes. Halley's paper was dropped.

4 London, 1728. Based upon the second Latin edition of 1722, this second English edition carried Newton's name on the title page for the first time. It also restored Halley's essay.

[35]

5 Leyden, 1732. A Latin edition prepared by 'sGravesande and containing tracts by Halley, Colson, de Moivre, MacLaurin and Campbell.

6 Paris, 1732. A Latin edition published by C. A. Jombert.

7 Milan, 1752. A three-volume Latin edition, with a commentary, prepared by G. A. Lecchi.

8 Amsterdam, 1761. A two-volume Latin edition, edited by G. Castillioneus.

9 London, 1769. An inaccurate reprint of 4, edited by Theaker Wilder and to which was added a *Treatise upon the Measures of Ratios* by James Maguire.

10 London, 1779. Included in Horsley, vol. I, and the 1964 facsimile reprint.

11 Paris, 1802. A two-volume French translation by Noel Beaudeux.

12 Moscow, 1948. Russian translation by A. P. Yushkevich.

13 New York, 1967. 4 was included in vol. II of Whiteside (1967).

14 Cambridge, 1972. The text of the Cambridge *Lectures on algebra* 1673–83 was included in *MP*, V, pp. 54–491, together with an English translation and much other relevant data.

Arius (260–336) and the Arian heresy

A Libyan, and a pupil of Lucian of Antioch, Arius served for many years as a presbyter in Alexandria. He begins to appear on the world scene when, in about 319, he is first recorded as arguing heretically for a subordinate position for Christ. Although he gained the support of Eusebius, Bishop of Nicomedia, he was excommunicated in 320 by the Alexandrian Synod. His position was further weakened at the Council of Nicaea in 325 when he found himself condemned and banished to Illyria. Shortly before his death he was summoned to Constantinople where arrangements were made for him to receive the sacraments. But, according to Athanasius, and in Gibbon's phrase, 'his bowels burst out in a privy'. It was a point Newton would challenge.

The controversy persisted for much of the century. The Arians insisted that Christ was not God by nature, that he was created and not eternal, and was thus subordinate to God. Support for Arianism was variable, depending largely on the politics of the imperial court. It was embraced by Constantius (317–61), third son of Constantine and Eastern Emperor from 337, and led to his persecution of the orthodox. It was tolerated by Julian (361–3) and supported by Valens (364–78). The West felt no such attraction for Arianism.

Arians themselves became divided into fanatics like Aetius, who would not even concede that Christ was in any way 'like' God, and the so-called 'semi-Arians', who accepted that Christ was indeed 'like' (homoiousia) God. The end came, however, in 381 at the Council of Constantinople called by the Emperor Theodosius (379–95). The Nicene creed was endorsed and, for a variety of reasons, Arianism ceased to be a serious option available to ancient theologians. It would, however, be raised once more during the Reformation and would prove to be irresistibly attractive to Newton.

Artemidorus

A late-second-century AD Ephesian who wrote the extant treatise *Oneirokritika* on the interpretation of dreams. Newton had a copy, a Latin translation, *De somniorum interpretatione* (Leyden, 1546) which he used extensively as a source for the interpretation of symbols found in the prophetic writings.

Artistic interests

In a number of well-known stories Newton is presented as something of a philistine. The tradition began with Conduitt's report that Newton never diverted himself with music or art. It was continued with Stukeley's account of Newton's single visit to the opera: 'The first act, said he, I heard with pleasure, the 2^d stretched my patience, at the 3^d I ran away' (Stukeley, 1936, p. 14). There is also Newton's judgment on the Earl of Pembroke, a famous collector of statues, as 'a lover of stone Dolls', and his description of poetry as 'ingenious nonsense'. That this was indeed Newton's attitude to poetry is confirmed, it has been claimed, by the absence from his quite extensive library of Chaucer, Spenser, Shakespeare (with the exception of *Hamlet* and *The Tempest*) and, before 1720, Milton.

Against such fragmentary evidence a set of equally fragmentary data can be arraigned. As a youth Newton was clearly interested in drawing and painting. In later life there is the evidence on the contents of his London home from the Inventory; over 200 prints and sixteen pictures in a house shows some interest in the graphic arts. Further, while Newton's library did contain little of the literature of his own day, it was well-stocked with editions of Homer, Ovid, Vergil, Horace, Terence, Aristophanes, Euripides, Sophocles, Catullus, and other items of classical literature. Newton's interests in such works may well have been primarily historical and theological; his acquaintance with classical verse remained, none the less, closer than many who have sought a less workmanlike contact.

A Scheme for Reformed Spelling

The six pages of the Morgan Notebook concerned with phonetics have been reproduced by R. W. Elliott in his 'Isaac Newton as phonetician' (1954). He dates it to the period 1661–2.

The topic was very much one of contemporary interest. The Royal Society had set up a committee in 1664 to advise on a 'more certain orthography'. One of its members was Wallis, who had published in 1653 his *Grammaticae linguae anglicanae*, one of the earliest works of modern phonetics.

Something of Newton's proposed orthography can be seen from his transposition of the following brief letter:

Loving ffreind
    It is commonly reportd yt you are sick. Truely I am sorry for yt. Yor very loving freind I.N.

which becomes:

Luvin ffrend
    It iz ripωωrted ʊɑt yw ar sik. Triuli Oy am sori for ʊɑt Yor veri luviy ffrend I.N.

Linguist's have pointed out that Newton's phonetics show very markedly the influence of his Lincolnshire pronunciation.

Ashmole, Elias (1617–92)

The son of a saddler, Ashmole was educated at Lichfield Grammar School before training as a lawyer. He benefited from a rich marriage but, following a too public support of the Royalist cause, he spent the years of the Commonwealth out of government service. With the Restoration his loyalty was rewarded with the posts of Comptroller of the Excise and Windsor Herald.

A student of alchemical and hermetic literature, Ashmole published in 1652 the six-volume *Theatrum chemicum Britannicum*. Basically a collection of twenty-nine rare British alchemical texts, it contained such important works as Thomas Norton's *Ordinall of Alchemy*, published in its original English version for the first time, and George Ripley's *The Compound of Alchemy*. Newton owned a full set, which can now be seen in the Van Pelt Library of the University of Pennsylvania.

Ashmole is, however, remembered today not for his work in alchemy but for his collection of 'rarities and curiosities'. They were offered on his death to Oxford University on the condition that the collection would not be dispersed. They thus formed in 1693 the nucleus of the Ashmolean Museum, the first such institution to appear in England.

A Short Chronicle from the First Memory of Things in Europe to the Conquest of Persia by Alexander the Great

---

The history of the *Short Chronicle* is complex, even more so than most other of Newton's manuscripts. Newton used to hold regular discussions with Princess Caroline, wife to Prince George, the heir to the throne. At some point she heard from the Abbé Conti that Newton had developed a new system of chronology. This was sufficient to arouse Caroline's interest. The subsequent request to see some of his work was met by a reluctant Newton in 1716 with a summary of the main points of his chronology. It is in fact no more than an annotated list of dates revealing little of his methods, assumptions and aims. Starting from 1125 BC when 'Memphis reigned over upper Egypt', with such details as '1005 BC Andromeda carried away from Joppa by Perseus', it concludes in 331 BC with the entry, 'Darius Codomannus, the last King of Persia, slain.'

Unfortunately for Newton the Abbé Conti seems to have been shown the manuscript by Caroline. His inevitable request for his own copy was predictably refused. An appeal to Caroline led to Newton's agreement but with two conditions: Conti would publish no details of the work, nor would Newton be expected to answer any queries.

Conti could not contain himself for long. Back in Paris in the 1720s he soon showed the piece to the leading chronologists E. Souciet and N. Fréret; they were allowed to make copies. Another who saw the work was the printer Guillaume Cavelier. On 11 May 1724 he wrote to Newton that he had seen a copy and, because Newton's name was 'tres estimé', he wished to publish it and hoped Newton would let him have a corrected copy. Newton ignored the letter. But, on 9 March 1725 Cavelier wrote once more, announcing that he would take silence for consent. This time, on 27 May 1725, Newton did reply. Unless he saw the manuscript, he told Cavelier, he could not say whether it was his or not. But his position had not changed: 'I intend not to meddle with that which hath been given you under my name, nor to give any consent to the publishing it' (*C*, VII, p. 322).

Cavelier went ahead none the less. It was actually printed with critical comments added by Fréret in which he tended to dismiss all Newton's innovations. Newton received a copy in November. His response appeared almost immediately as a paper in the *PT* (1725): 'Remarks on the observations upon a Chronological Index of Sir Isaac Newton'. It was one of his most effective. Would any man, he asked, 'be so foolish as to consent to the publishing of an unseen Translation . . . made by an unknown Person, with a confutation annexed and unanswered at their first Appearance in Publick'? Conti, he accused of abusing his friendship and, an old charge for Newton, involving him in disputes. Ever the aristocrat, Conti met the charge with all the arrogance of a Venetian nobleman: 'At bottom I do not hold it in any greater esteem than the quadrill or hunting . . . I apply myself to learning neither to make a fortune nor to acquire a great name. I study as I travel . . . for my own pleasure.'

More detailed criticism came from the polite, but radical, analysis of Souciet. He warned that a full appraisal of Newton's work must await the publication of the *Chronology*. Nevertheless, he went on to deny Newton's law of regnal length, his dating of the Argonaut's expedition, the identification of Sesostris and Osiris, and to insist on the antiquity of Egyptian civilisation. Despite the politeness, little of Newton's work remained. Newton's response was to turn to the pages of his *Chronology* and to prepare them for publication, work he was still pursuing at the time of his death shortly afterwards.

After an initial spate of interest the work has been virtually ignored and was last published in 1785. The following editions are known.

1 Paris, 1725. It was translated into French by Fréret under the title *Abrégé de la chronologie de M.le chevalier Isaac Newton, fait par lui-meme, et traduit sur le manuscrit Anglois*. It also appeared as a supplement to the seven-volume French edition of Humphrey Prideaux's *History of the Jews*.

2 London, 1728. It was added to the first edition of the *Chronology*, edited by Conduitt, and entitled *A Short Chronicle from the First Memory of Things in Europe, to the Conquest of Persia by Alexander the Great*. It carries a dedication to Caroline and the note that 'it is entirely owing to the Commands with which you were pleased to honour him, out of your singular care for the education of the Royal Issue', and was also issued in Dublin.

3 London, 1728. A further English edition, translated from the French by an unknown 'Gentleman'.

4 Paris, 1728. A further French edition was added to Granet's translation of the *Chronology*.

5 Lausanne and Geneva, 1744. Included in Castillioneus, *Tome* III.

6 London, 1785. Included in Horsley, vol. V and the 1964 facsimile reprint.

A number of manuscript copies of the work are known. In addition to his own numerous drafts, two copies are preserved in the British Museum, and a further copy is in KCC Library. As none of these three surviving manuscripts is in Newton's hand they are unlikely to be the copy prepared for Caroline.

See also Chronological principles; *The Chronology of Ancient Kingdoms Amended*

A short scheme of the true religion

This short piece is to be found in KCC as Keynes MS 7. It has been published for the first and only time in McLachlan (1950, pp. 48–53).

A short scheme is very similar in content to the *Irenicum*. It contains the same insistence on the two basic laws to love God and to love one's neighbour. Newton also went on to insist that the nature and existence of God, and the duties imposed on us, are aspects of natural religion and therefore available to all mankind.

Aston, Francis (1645–1715)

Educated at TCC, Aston seems to have formed a friendship with his contemporary, Isaac Newton, which lasted from their student days until his death in 1715. Students together, they were elected fellows of Trinity together in 1667, and also together became fellows of the RS in the 1670s. Aston served as the Society's joint secretary with Robert Hooke from 1681–5.

An intriguing survival of their friendship is one of the earliest extant letters of Newton. It is dated 18 May 1669 (*C*, I, pp. 9–13). Aston had apparently told Newton that he would be travelling throughout Europe and for some unknown reason had asked his friend for advice. Newton, who had travelled no further from home than Cambridge and, for a couple of brief visits, to London, was evidently willing to play the role of man of the world. He began with a number of general rules in the manner of Polonius. Aston should, for example, 'seldom discommend anything' and, if affronted, 'pass it by in silence'. Such views, trite and pompous as they may be, turn out not to be Newton's own but taken directly from a work, Turnbull has noted (*C*, I, p. 13), amongst his papers in an unknown hand and with the title *An Abridgement of Sir Robert Southwell's Concerning Travelling*.

In the second half of the letter there is a change of tone and Newton's own distinct voice can be heard for the first time. Would Aston, he asked, make some observations for him? Some were concerned with the organisation of trade and industry. Towards the end, however, when Newton began to ask Aston to investigate how the Dutch ground and polished lens, and whether they were able to use the pendulum clock to discover longitude, the questions and the words were undoubtedly his own.

In later life the trustworthy Aston was one of the figures Newton assigned to the supposedly impartial committee of the RS set up in 1712 to investigate the priority dispute with Leibniz.

Athanasius (296–373)

Athanasius attended the Council of Nicaea in 325 as a deacon. Thereafter the rest of his life was spent in a vigorous defence, mainly against the Arians, of the Trinitarian position declared at the Council. Appointed Bishop of Alexandria in 328, he was, according to Gibbon, 'in a perpetual combat against the powers of Arianism'. Such was his commitment to orthodoxy that not even the demands of emperors could deflect him from its defence. Subsequently, on five occasions, under Constantine, Constantius, Julian and Valens, he found himself either an exile or a fugitive. It was, however, despite the uncertainties of the fourth century, the will of Athanasius which prevailed, and consequently it is the Nicene Creed which most clearly continues to express the conviction of Christians today.

Newton came to see the fourth century as the time in which the church allowed its original divine revelation to become corrupted by human additions. At the centre of this conspiracy he saw the Council of Nicaea and the figure of Athanasius. Newton soon became obsessed by the period and set out to master the largely polemical and frequently meretricious literature spawned by the period. He had no difficulty in finding suitably scandalous stories to confirm his initial suspicions. One particular charge, the murder of Bishop Arsenius, proved especially exciting to Newton.

The Meletians of Egypt were deemed by Athanasius to be schismatics, in the manner of the earlier Donatists. One such was Arsenius, Bishop of Hypsele, of whom Athanasius was accused of conspiring to murder or, at least, to mutilate. Severed hands were produced, witnesses were called who swore either that they had seen the crime committed or that they had spoken with a perfectly healthy Arsenius a few days before. The only reasonably clear detail in the whole story is that Athanasius was tried and acquitted.

It is of course impossible to judge the truth of the charges against Athanasius, not so much because the event is so distant, but rather because all witnesses and writers of the period seemed quite indifferent to the demands of truth.

Newton's own quite extraordinary views on Athanasius received their fullest expression in his *Paradoxical Questions*.

Atomism

The atomism of antiquity, associated with the names of Democritus, Epicurus and Lucretius, was little considered during the medieval period. Interest in atomism revived, under the influence of Pierre Gassendi, in the first half of the seventeenth century. It also spread to England where it could be seen in the 1650s in the writings of Walter Charleton and Thomas Hobbes. The appeal of atomism to the new breed of natural philosophers is clear. The demand of the new mechanical philosophy for mechanical explanations of all phenomena led to some seemingly unmanageable examples. What was mechanical about magnetic attraction or the expansion of metals when heated? Nothing at the visible level. It was therefore tempting to suppose that some non-visible mechanism was operating to produce the observed effects, and nothing was a more plausible candidate for such a role than the atoms of antiquity.

Consequently, Newton was exposed to traditional atomism as a student at Cambridge. As a sign of this his early Philosophical Notebook contains extensive transcriptions from the *Physiologia* of Charleton. The Notebook also contains, in the *QQP*, Newton's first recorded commitment to atomism: 'It remaines therefore that the first matter must be atomes.' The same commitment can be seen in *Principia*, where in rule III in Book III he had laid it down that:

> The extension, hardness, impenetrability, mobility and inertia of the
> whole, result from the extension, hardness, impenetrability,
> mobility, and inertia of the parts; and hence we conclude the least
> particles of all bodies to be also all extended, and hard, and
> impenetrable, and movable, and endowed with their proper inertia.
> And this is the foundation of all philosophy. (CAJORI, p. 399)

The message was repeated in Query 31 of the *Opticks*:

> God in the Beginning form's Matter in solid, massy, hard,
> impenetrable moveable Particles . . . incomparably harder than any
> porous Bodies compounded of them; even so very hard, as never to
> wear or break in pieces. (*Opticks*, p. 400)

There was much more to Newton's atomism than the mere assertion of the existence of hard particles. It was, for example, used to develop a theory of light. 'Are not the Rays of Light very small Bodies emitted from shining Substances?' Newton had asked in Query 29 before going on to argue that all the properties of light could be derived from this assumption. Also, in section V of Book II of *Principia*, Newton demonstrated how the density and compression of fluids could be dealt with on the assumption that 'a fluid be composed of particles fleeing from each other' (Cajori, p. 300).

There remains one further aspect of Newton's atomism. In the draft Preface of *Principia*, and in the suppressed *Conclusio*, he spoke briefly and obliquely of unsuspected harmony in the physical universe. 'Nature is . . . conformable to her self', he declared on a number of occasions (*Opticks*, p. 376; Halls, pp. 307, 333; Cajori, pp. 398–9). By this he meant: 'Whatever reasoning holds for greater motions should hold for lesser ones as well.' Consequently, corresponding to the 'greater attractive forces of larger bodies', there should be 'lesser forces, as yet unobserved, of insensible particles' (Halls, p. 333). Thus, just as the sun attracts the earth by gravity, there is an equally specific force operating when, for example, 'spirit of vitriol' is mixed with 'Sal Alkali'. The violence and heat produced by the reaction convinced Newton that there was a 'vehement rushing together' of the acid and alkali particles. Although Newton could not name or measure the reaction, he could still sense the presence of a force, operating at the atomic level and quite distinct from gravity.

See also Attractive and repulsive forces

Attitudes to Newton

In the whole history of science no one has ever been held in such high esteem as Newton. Other major figures – Einstein, Darwin, Gauss or Lavoisier – may be universally admired for their genius, their creativity, their sheer intellectual power; they have remained men none the less. With Newton, however, the idea quickly emerged that he was not as other men. Praise went beyond mere hyperbole, and it became customary to speak of the divinity of Newton; 'Does he eat and drink and sleep? Is he like other men?' de l'Hopital had naively asked John Arbuthnot in the 1690s.

While few would go so far as to assert the actual divinity of Newton, many would adopt alternative expressions of his apotheosis. Thus, Halley, in the Ode which prefaced *Principia*, took the note followed by many: if Newton was not in fact divine, he had come as close to that state as man could ever reach: 'Nearer the gods no mortal may approach'. Others, like Pope, chose to emphasise that, though human, Newton had been especially selected by God. Hence, the opening of Pope's famous couplet: 'God said, Let Newton be'. The theme was also pursued in the Stowe memorial, where Newton's bust bears the inscription: 'Sir Isaac Newton whom the God of nature made to comprehend his work'.

A third option conceded Newton's humanity but insisted, as with Andrew Reid in 1728, 'Had he lived in Greece and Rome . . . he would have been ranked among the gods'. Conduitt argued in the same manner:

'Had this great and good man lived in an age when those superior Genii inventors were deified . . . he would have had a better claim to these honours than those they have hitherto been ascribed to; his virtues proved him a saint and his discoveries might well pass for miracles.'

More rational minds were happy simply to stress the uniqueness of Newton. Thus, John Locke, in the Epistle to his *Essay* (1690), was content to speak of the 'incomparable Mr Newton' while David Hume in his *History* (chapter 71) spoke of Newton as 'the greatest and rarest genius that ever arose for the ornament and instruction of the species'. The theme of Newton's uniqueness was pursued by Lagrange later in the century. There was only one universe, he lamented, and it was Newton who had been fortunate enough to be born at a time when 'the system of the world still remained to be discovered'.

The emergence of romanticism brought with it a new rhetoric concerning Newton's divinity. The architect E. L. Boullée could thus speak quite simply of 'Etre Divin! Newton'. Others of the period, including such well-known figures as Henri Saint-Simon and Charles Fourier, began to fantasise over the idea of founding a new religion of Newton. The dottiest of this group was the otherwise unknown F. C. C. Pahin-Champlain de la Blancherie who, in 1796, chided the British for failing sufficiently to elevate Newton. He proposed we recognise Newton's divinity, make Woolsthorpe Manor into a sanctuary, and relocate the beginning of the calendar to 1642, the year of Newton's birth.

Not everyone looked uncritically on the notion of Newton's divinity, however rhetorically it may have been expressed. Some of Newton's contemporaries were even willing to describe some of his faults. Locke, who knew him well and admired him, still conceded that he was 'a little too apt to raise in himself suspicion when there is no ground'. Whiston, in his *Memoirs*, could be more forthright, and noted: 'He was of the most fearful, cautious and suspicious Temper, that I ever knew.' It was left to the Astronomer-Royal, John Flamsteed, a bitter enemy of Newton, to insist that Newton was really 'insidious, ambitious, and excessively covetous of praise, and impatient of contradiction'. When the ever-helpful Flamsteed pointed out to Newton 'some faults' in *Principia*, Flamsteed complained, instead of receiving Newton's grateful thanks, he was asked: 'Why I did not hold my tongue.'

Equally critical of Newton were several of the poets of the Romantic movement. Blake, in particular, built up an elaborate mythology in which Bacon, Locke and Newton were held to be responsible for the dehumanisation of man and nature he so raged against:

I turn my eyes to the Schools and Universities of Europe
And there behold the Loom of Locke, whose Woof rages dire,
Wash'd by the Water-Wheels of Newton

(HEATH-STUBBS and SALMAN, 1970, p. 165)

Keats too would complain in *Lamia* how philosophy could 'clip an angels wings' and, by Newtonian analysis, place a rainbow in the 'dull catalogue of common things'.

Romanticism, however, was an interval. Soon, writers would return to the challenge of finding superlatives adequate enough to describe the genius of Newton. The hagiography of Sir David Brewster, Newton's biographer, is well known. Compared with more popular works, Brewster's descriptions of Newton appear quite modest. Thus, *Chambers Miscellany* for 1871: 'The character of Newton cannot be delineated and discussed like that of ordinary men; it is so beautiful, that the biographer dwells on it with delight . . . a power of intellect almost beyond human . . . his modesty was such, that he thought nothing of his own acquirements.' Another, out of dozens, who could see no fault in Newton, was Robert Routledge in his *A Popular History of Science* (1894, p. 182). Newton's life was described as: 'One continued course of labour, patience, charity, generosity, temperance, piety, goodness, and all other virtues, without a mixture of any vice whatever.'

There were some nineteenth-century scholars who suspected that Newton's life and personality were more interesting than conventional panegyrics represented. The first to raise such doubts was J-B. Biot in his entry on Newton in the *Biographie universelle* (1821). Newton, he revealed, had suffered a breakdown in 1693 and such had been the impairment to his intellectual faculties that he was incapable thereafter of serious scientific research. Although Biot's facts and conclusions might be disputed, they drew attention none the less to the contrast between Newton as Cambridge scholar and Newton as London official. Some found the transition distasteful. De Morgan, for example, argued in 1846 that, 'it would have been better for Newton's fame if he had left all the coinage, clipped and unclipped, to those who were as well qualified as himself' (de Morgan, 1914, p. 43). He went on to refer to a 'gradual deterioration' in Newton's 'moral intellect' from the 'the time . . . he settled in London' (de Morgan, 1914, p. 153). Oliver Lodge, later in the century, also found it strange that 'a man sent by Heaven to do certain things which no man else could do', would be 'clapped into a routine office with a big salary' (Lodge, 1960, p. 198).

One who provided evidence of the 'deterioration' in Newton's 'moral intellect' was Francis Baily in his *Account of the Revd John Flamsteed* (1835). The published documents revealed Newton, at least from Flamsteed's point of view, as manipulative, insensitive, arrogant and authoritarian. There was little here, amply documented, of the 'patience, generosity, temperance, piety' spoken of by Routledge. Further evidence came from de Morgan in 1852 in his analysis of the priority dispute with Leibniz. Newton and his associates had been less than fair. They had, in fact, according to de Morgan, shown 'atrocious unfairness' and been guilty of the 'gross suppression of facts' (de Morgan, 1914, pp. 70–5).

The voices of de Morgan and Baily were largely ignored and for another century or more, as anniversaries of birth and death came around, the Newton of legend and phantasy remained preferable to the Newton of history and reality. The 1927 celebration of the bicentenary of Newton's death was the last occasion on which such simple views on his life, work and character could be honestly avowed, for, in 1936, the bulk of Newton's papers were auctioned at Sotheby's and subsequently became available to scholars for the first time. The sheer size of the collection, together with the interruption of the War years, delayed somewhat their impact on popular conceptions of Newton. The first clear signal that a new picture of Newton was being formed came in the belated 1946 celebrations of the tercentenary of Newton's birth. In a posthumous paper of Lord Keynes, the RS heard for the first time that Newton was not to be seen as 'the first of the age of reason' but 'the last of the magicians' (Keynes, 1947, p. 27).

Keynes's paper was just the beginning. Before long the detailed work of scholars, based mainly on previously unpublished material, began to construct an unfamiliar yet more realistic picture of Newton. It revealed a Newton as interested in theology and alchemy as in mathematics and physics; a Newton generous to friends and colleagues, but ruthless to any who opposed him or who sought to deny the purity of his work. Some scholars, like Manuel (1980), saw an intensely neurotic Newton, driven by his inner compulsions into his own private scholarship, and into battle against the enemies, secular, scientific and religious, he saw all around him.

One result of such revelations has been to enhance the appeal of Newton to a generation as indifferent to the purity of saints as they are attracted to the corruptions of sinners. At the same time, while Newton's personal reputation may have been somewhat eclipsed, his scientific reputation has, if anything, been enlarged. Intense scholarship by Cohen and Koyré on *Principia*, by Whiteside on the mathematical papers, by Hall on the correspondence, and by numerous other scholars on various other aspects of the Newtonian canon, has so far failed to challenge the intellectual eminence of Newton. Despite the identification of Newton's main intellectual roots, and despite the exposure of a number of inevitable errors and slips, the pivotal role of Newton's thought in the history of ideas has yet to be seriously questioned.

See also Biography; Poetic tradition

Attractive and repulsive forces

One of the most significant aspects of Newton's system of the world, made even more notable by its contrast with rival Cartesian theories, is the presence in it of a number of universal attractive forces. The presence of gravitational attraction operating throughout the heavens is, of course, one of Newton's more durable legacies. With it, he claimed in the Preface to *Principia* (1687), he had deduced 'the motions of the planets, the comets, the moon, and the sea'. He wished he could have explained the rest of nature in the same way, but in 1687 he could offer no more than the suspicion that all natural phenomena depends 'upon certain forces by which the particles of bodies, by some causes hitherto unknown, are either mutually impelled towards one another, and cohere in regular figures, or are repelled and recede from one another' (Cajori, p. xviii).

The existence of such forces was explored further by Newton in a number of unpublished works and occasionally surfaced in some of his published texts. Nature, he insisted on several occasions, 'is exceedingly simple and conformable to herself'. Consequently, he argued in the suppressed *Conclusio* to *Principia*: 'Whatever reasoning holds for greater motions, should hold for lesser ones as well' (the Halls, p. 333). It followed, therefore, that to the great attractive forces holding the heavens in sway, lesser motions should be governed by lesser forces. When, for example, acid is poured on to a metallic powder, 'there is a vehement rusing together of the acid particles and the other particles'. Another common example often offered by Newton was the existence of homogeneous bodies. What, he asked, held the particles of such bodies together?

Some, Newton noted in Query 31 of the *Opticks*, had proposed that particles 'stick together very strongly', or even that atoms were hooked. Such answers merely begged the question because hooks and glue, as homogeneous bodies themselves, were in as much need of explanation as the bodies they were supposed to hold together. The answer, to Newton, was clear and he was led to infer: 'Some Force, which in immediate Contact is exceeding strong, at small distances performs . . . chymical Operations . . . and reaches not far from the Particles with any sensible Effect' (*Opticks*, p. 389). A further use for such forces was demonstrated in *Principia*, Book II, prop. XXIII. If the particles of the atmosphere repelled each other with a force inversely proportional to the distances of their centres, the result would be 'an elastic fluid, whose density is as the compression' (Cajori, p. 300).

The use of forces of this kind made Newton appear to many a contemporary as a distinctly old-fashioned thinker. Thus, to Leibniz it seemed that: 'It pleases some to return to occult qualities or scholastic faculties,

but because these have become unrespectable they call them *forces*, changing the name. But the true force of bodies are of one sort only, namely those affected by an impressed impetus' (Hall, 1980, p. 154). Such charges were both widespread and persistent. They were heard as frequently in Moscow as amongst the Cartesians of Paris. Long after the death of Leibniz, the French *encyclopédiste*, Jean d'Alembert, could maintain that 'arguments concerning the measure of forces are entirely useless in mechanics'.

Physicists who were unwilling to use the Newtonian language of force could opt, in general, for one or other of two extreme positions. They could, like d'Alembert and many of the French school, mathematicise physics to such a degree that it became little more than geometry. An alternative view, developed mainly in nineteenth-century Britain, accepted forces, but only those forces which could be modelled in a quite literal manner within the domain of classical mechanics. In a celebrated passage Pierre Duhem spoke in 1903 of attempts made by a British physicist to expound modern theories of electricity. He found in the textbook examined (*Modern Views of Electricity* (1889) by Oliver Lodge):

Nothing but strings which move move around pulleys, which roll around drums, which go through pearl beads, which carry weights; and tubes which pump water while others swell and contract; toothed wheels which are geared to one another and engage hooks. We thought we were entering the tranquil and neatly ordered abode of reason, but we find ourselves in a factory. (DUHEM, 1954, pp. 70–1)

Against such extreme positions Newtonian physical theory could have its attractions.

See also Chemistry and the Newtonian tradition; Gravity; Iatrophysics; Occult causes and qualities

---

Auzout, Adrien (1622–91)

A Paris astronomer, member of the Royal Observatory, an observer and instrumentalist who, by 1667, and independently of William Gascoigne in Britain, had developed the cross-hair micrometer eyepiece known as the 'filar micrometer'. Auzout was committed to the traditional telescope and was even contemplating constructing such an instrument 1,000 ft long.

When he first heard of the much smaller reflecting telescope of Newton he raised a number of practical objections against its feasibility. What precisely these objections were can now only be inferred from

Newton's reply in the *PT* (No. 82, April, 1672). Auzout's own letter has been lost. He must have complained that the metal surfaces of Newton's reflector would tarnish too rapidly to be of much use, that it would be difficult to store when not in use, and would absorb more light than a glass lens. Newton replied in general terms admitting that there was much truth in Auzout's warnings but that, with the development of new materials and new polishes, they could be ignored.

Ayscough, William

Newton's maternal uncle, the brother of his mother Hannah. Unlike the illiterate Newtons, the Ayscoughs were generally well educated. William was a Cambridge MA and a cleric holding the living of Burton Coggles, two miles east of Colsterworth, Lincolnshire.

Newton was deeply indebted to his uncle for one intervention in his affairs. When his mother in 1659 seemed determined to end her son's education and turn him into a farmer, it was pressure from William, amongst others, which persuaded her that Cambridge would be more appropriate. Newton was able to discharge his debt many years later when William's daughter, Katherine Rastall, wrote to him in 1714. Apparently penniless and desperate, she asked Newton for 'sumthing' (*C*, VI, p. 183). Newton must have responded, for there is a later letter in which she offers Newton 'a thousand thanks for ye many civilities' (*C*, VII, pp. 166–7).

B

Babington, Humphrey (1615–91)

An early influence on Newton's career, Babington was rector of Boothby Pagnel, Lincolnshire, and a Fellow of Trinity College, Cambridge. He was related to apothecary Clarke in Grantham.

Stukeley reported that Babington's presence 'was the reason why he went to Trinity College' and that 'The Dr is said to have had a particular kindness for him'. He supported Newton in his stand against Judge Jeffreys in the Alban Francis affair. Clearly a man of principle, Babington temporarily lost his Trinity fellowship when he refused to swear the oath of allegiance to the Commonwealth. It was restored with the return of Charles II.

Newton presented Babington with a copy of *Principia* in 1687. It seemed lost on him for he declared with unusual frankness that he 'might study seven years' before understanding 'anything of it'.

Babson, Roger Ward (1875–1967)

Babson created for himself a sizeable personal fortune, first as a speculator on the stock market and later as a market consultant. With his wealth he built the finest collection of Newtoniana in private hands. Known after his wife as the Grace K. Babson Collection, it is housed in the specially-built Babson Institute Library, Wellesley, Massachusetts. As well as a superb collection of Newton's published works, the Library also contains a number of important Newtonian manuscripts and is rich in Newtoniana of all kinds.

One unusual feature of the Library is a 'faithful re-erection' of a room from Newton's house in St Martin's St, London. When the house was dismantled in 1913 all of the wainscoting and trim was carefully preserved by the owners of the house, the antiquarian firm of Phillips based in Hitchin, Herts. They initially intended to re-erect the house at another site. As much of the material was too decayed to make this scheme practical, the woodwork was subsequently acquired by Babson. This was used, together with period furniture, a copy of a Vanderbank portrait of Newton, and details described in the *Inventory*, to re-erect, as far as possible, an actual room from Newton's house. The results can be seen on page 32 of the 1950 *Descriptive Catalogue*.

Babson was something more than a rich collector indulging his passion for antiquarian works of science. It was, he claimed, his study of Newton that had created his wealth in the first place. Newton's third law, the principle of action and reaction, Babson argued, ruled not only the physical world but also the 'field of human relations'. Whether in practice this meant more than selling when the market was rising and buying when it was falling, Babson did not reveal.

Yet, with his success on the stock market, Babson's interest in Newton deepened. In 1948 he founded the Gravity Research Foundation in order to develop materials capable of absorbing, reflecting, or insulating against, gravity. Also sought were alloys capable of converting gravity into heat, and other means to harness the power of gravity. Babson offered prizes, organised conferences, and founded journals to promote his views. 'Gravity chairs' were built and houses specially designed to maximise 'gravity ventilation'.

When charged with his failure to develop gravity absorbers and reflectors, Babson, an MIT-trained engineer, responded with the example of Edison, who had tried more than 8,000 materials before he finally found one suitable to be a filament of an electric light bulb. Details of Babson's life can be found in his appropriately-titled autobiography *Actions and Reactions* (1935); a more critical view is presented in Gardner (1952, Chapter 8).

Baily, Francis (1774–1844)

The son of a banker, Baily worked first as a stockbroker before retiring in 1825, wealthy enough to devote the rest of his life to astronomy. He is still eponymously remembered for his description of Baily's beads, the bright dots or beads which appear around the edge of the moon during a total solar eclipse.

In 1835 he published, 'by order of the Lords Commissioners of the Admiralty', *An account of the Revd John Flamsteed*, together with Flamsteed's *British Catalogue of Stars, Corrected and Enlarged*; two years later in 1837 he added a lengthy *Supplement*. The *Account* consists of Flamsteed's own 'History of his own life', a catalogue of his manuscripts and, the bulk of the work, some 281 letters. Of these, 124 were written by Flamsteed himself. Of particular note are the thirty-six letters between Newton and Flamsteed extending between 1682 and 1716.

Baily took exception to the common view of Flamsteed as, 'a mere selfish and indolent observer . . . unwilling to communicate the result of his labors to others' (Baily, 1835/1966, p. xvi). Yet, to defend Flamsteed against such charges, Baily found it necessary to query the propriety, honesty and courtesy of much of Newton's behaviour. This was the first well-documented and clearly argued suggestion that Newton was not in fact quite the noble figure legend had made of him.

Inevitably, Baily's work was greeted with outrage by traditional Newtonians. Twenty years later Brewster could still refer to the *Account* as a 'system of calumny and misrepresentation unexampled in the history of science' (Brewster, p. xii). Baily had, however, patiently disposed of most objections to his work in the *Supplement* of 1837. It also contained an impressive study of Newton's lunar theory and its relation to the work of Flamsteed and Jeremiah Horrox.

The *Account*, excluding the stellar *Catalogue*, but with the *Supplement*, is available in a single-volume facsimile edition published in 1966 by Dawsons of Pall Mall.

See also Flamsteed, John and the Flamsteed affair

Ball, Walter William Rouse (1850–1925)

Rouse Ball, a lecturer in mathematics from 1878 and a fellow of TCC, is best known for his still read *Mathematical Recreations* (1892; 11th edition, 1939). A man with wide interests, considerable learning, and a prolific writer, Rouse Ball produced a number of valuable historical studies on such subjects as TCC, Cambridge mathematics, and mathematics in general. Amongst these studies was his important *An Essay on Newton's 'Principia'* (1893) in which, following the lead given by S. P. Rigaud in 1838, Rouse Ball sought to present a detailed and documented account of the development of *Principia*. He began with the 'Investigations in 1666' and in 1679. Further chapters were concerned with *De motu* and the period 1685–7, and the later additions and modifications made to the text between 1687 and 1726. The final chapter, 'Analysis of the *Principia*' presents a detailed analytical table of contents. In a series of appendices Rouse Ball published the fullest then available texts of the 1679–80 correspondence between Hooke and Newton, and the 1686–7 correspondence between Halley and Newton. The work thus remains, according to Cohen (1971, p. 13), 'an indispensable handbook for the student of *Principia*'.

Banville, John (1945–   )

Few modern novelists have sought inspiration from within the history of science. An exception is the Irish writer John Banville who, after two historical novels, *Doctor Copernicus* (1976) and *Kepler* (1981), attempted in his slim novel, *The Newton Letter* (1982), to introduce into a contemporary story echoes of Newton's 1693 breakdown.

Barrow, Isaac (1630–77)

Barrow entered TCC in 1645 and thereafter spent much of his life there as Fellow from 1649, Lucasian Professor of Mathematics from 1663 and finally, from 1673, as Master of the College. One of the most durable of all Newton legends has grown up around the name of Barrow and, like all such legends, it had more than a little help from Newton himself. The story began with the Abbé Conti who reported having been told by Newton that Barrow had once brought him a troublesome problem on the cycloid. Newton had solved it on the spot in six lines. In amazement at such mathematical power, Barrow immediately resigned his chair in favour of Newton, commenting that he was the 'more learned' (RSW, p. 206n). Barrow himself presented a different story of his resignation in 1669. He wished, he declared, 'to serve God and the Gospel of his Son' and realising that 'he could not make a bible out of his Euclid, or a pulpit of his mathematical chair – his only redress was to quit them both' (*DNB*). There seems, however, to be no doubt that, on his resignation in 1669, Barrow did see to it that he was succeeded by Newton.

Equally erroneous is the common assumption that Barrow was Newton's tutor. That post was held by Benjamin Pulleyn. According to Conduitt, the first official contact between the two scholars took place in 1664 when Newton, as a scholarship candidate, was examined by Barrow. As Newton knew 'little or nothing of Euclid' Barrow formed 'an indifferent opinion of him' (RSW, p. 102).

Whatever the truth of the Conduitt account, it is clear that by the period 1668–9 Barrow's view of Newton was more favourable. Thus when, in early 1669, John Collins sent him a copy of Nicholas Mercator's *Logarithmotechnia* (1668), Barrow could reply on 20 July 1669 that a friend of his in Cambridge, 'a very excellent genius to those things', possessed far more general methods than any displayed by Mercator in his work (*C*, I, p. 13). For the first time, thanks to Barrow, the name of Newton was heard outside the narrow confines of Cambridge.

Barrow may well have rendered Newton one further service. In 1675 it appeared that, unwilling to take orders, Newton would be forced to abandon his chair, fellowship and all hopes of an academic career. At this point someone intervened at Court and persuaded the authorities to exempt the holders of the Lucasian chair from the general obligation to become ordained. Barrow had connections at Court and had served from 1669 to 1673 as a Royal Chaplain. Although there is no hard evidence linking Barrow to the decision, he remains by far the most likely candidate.

Newton, in return, is known to have helped in preparing Barrow's *Lectiones XVIII* (1669) and *Lectiones geometricae* (1670) for publication, and even to have added one or two small improvements. As a mathematician Barrow is well-known as a pioneer in the development of the calculus. He proposed a new method to determine tangents, and introduced the so-called differential triangle into mathematics. Barrow also presented, although in geometrical form, the fundamental theorem of the calculus, in which integration and differentiation are shown to be inverse operations. His preference, in this respect, for geometrical proofs over algebraic manipulations, though somewhat limiting, could well have had some influence on the young Newton, who later expressed his own distaste for the new techniques introduced into mathematics by Descartes and his followers.

See also Landor, W. S.; Lucasian chair and the Lucasian lectures; Trinity College, Cambridge

---

Bartholinus, Erasmus (1625–98)

A Danish mathematician, the brother of the distinguished anatomists, Caspar and Thomas, who after studying at Leyden and Padua held chairs in mathematics and medicine at Copenhagen University from 1656 until his death. In 1669 he published his *Experimenta crystalli Islandici* (Experiments with Icelandic crystal) in which he described for the first time the strange phenomenon of double refraction in Iceland spar (calcite). Neither the undulatory theory of Huygens nor the particulate account of Newton could make much sense of the phenomena and it was not, in fact, until the early nineteenth century that science could offer anything like a plausible account of Iceland spar.

See also Double refraction

Barton, Catherine (1679–1740)

Undoubtedly, after his mother, the most important of Newton's relatives. She was the daughter of Hannah Smith, Newton's half-sister, and the Rev. Robert Barton. Her father died in 1693 and sometime after 1696 she moved into her uncle's London house in Jermyn St. When, precisely, is not known. The first documentary evidence linking them is Newton's only surviving letter to her, dated August 1700 (*C*, IV, p. 349), in which he was enquiring about the progress of the smallpox she was then suffering from. Were her scabs 'dropping off apace', he enquired. Never able to resist the chance to offer medical advice, he went on to suggest that her fever might well respond to 'warm milk from ye cow'.

By all accounts Catherine was a figure of considerable charm, beauty and intelligence. She was a friend of Swift and appeared frequently in his *Journal to Stella* as well as being celebrated in verse by the wits of the Kit-Kat Club:

> At Barton's feet the God of Love
> His Arrows and his Quiver lays,
> Forgets he has a Throne above,
> And with this lovely Creature stays.

Nor were her charms appreciated only by London society. Remond de Monmort met her in 1715 at Newton's house and thereafter could scarce contain himself. On his return to France he sent Newton fifty bottles of champagne; to be drunk, he added, by 'des bouches philosophiques, et la belle bouche de Mademoiselle Barton'.

Inevitably, the presence of such an attractive relative in Newton's house aroused comment. There were first obscure references in the *roman-à-clef* of Mrs Mary Manley, *Memoirs of Egypt* (1710), followed by typical bitter mutterings from Flamsteed. It was left to Voltaire in his *Dictionnaire philosophique* (1757) to make public what had obviously been a subject of gossip for some time. The charge was that Newton's career had been advanced by Charles Montague, Earl of Halifax, and supposed lover of Catherine: 'I thought . . . that Newton made his fortune by his merit . . . No such thing. Isaac Newton had a very charming niece . . . who made a conquest of the minister Halifax. Fluxions and gravitation would have been of no use without a pretty niece' (RSW, p. 596n).

On the point raised, Voltaire was simply wrong. While it is true that Newton was appointed to the Mint in 1696 by Montague there are no grounds whatsoever for the suggestion that Catherine influenced the appointment. In 1696, when the post was offered to Newton, he still lived on his own in Cambridge. It is doubtful if Montague had even heard of Catherine at this time.

There was, however, a second charge to answer. The accusation was made that for several years, and while resident in Newton's house, Catherine had conducted an affair with Montague. Further, it must have been an affair known to Newton and one he tolerated. The evidence for the affair is more substantial than the gossip of a Mrs Manley or the hints of an embittered Flamsteed. Montague's much older wife, the Dowager Duchess of Manchester, had died in 1698 leaving him a wealthy man. In 1706 he added a codicil to his will leaving to Catherine the sum of £3,000 and all his jewels 'as a small Token of his great Love and Affection'. Whether £3,000 was a small sum or not, it was increased in a further codicil in 1713 to £5,000 cash and property worth £20,000 'as a small recompence for the Pleasure and Happiness I have had in her Conversation'. These *are* substantial sums, even by the standards of today. Few who knew of them were willing to believe they could have been awarded except by a lover.

Nor is there any doubt of Newton's awareness of the bequest. He was, Hall has noted, 'deeply enmeshed' in the relationship and strove 'to give his best advice in order to ensure that she should enjoy the fruits of Halifax's intentions' (C, V, p. xlvi). Hall has, however, doubted whether Catherine actually received her inheritance. He has noted drafts in Newton's hand of agreements between the new Earl and Catherine. The Earl seems to have acquired the property left to Catherine while she gained an annuity of £200 (C, V, p. xlvi).

Yet, whether Catherine enriched herself or not, there was sufficient in the gossip to trouble Newton's later biographers. Montague's official biographer insisted that Catherine had been no more than 'Super-intendant of his domestick Affairs' and that, despite the 'censure' passed against her, she was 'a Woman of strict Honour and Virtue' (RSW, p. 598). It was a view proposed, at least in public, by Newton's leading biographer, Sir David Brewster (Brewster, vol. II, pp. 270–81). He too insisted that the relationship between Montague and Catherine could only have been one of friendship. In private correspondence with de Morgan, however, he confessed, he found it 'the most disagreeable portion of Newton's history'. The only way he could preserve Newton's reputation was to insist that 'Miss Barton *never lived* in Halifax's house' (de Morgan, 1968, p. 110).

On this last point the facts are far from clear. Montague's biographer had described Catherine as the 'Super-Intendant of his domestick Affairs' to explain her presence in his house. Against her presence are reports from Swift and Conduitt. Swift, who saw both Montague and Catherine frequently during the period 1710–11, never actually recorded their joint presence and seemed to be under the impression that Catherine was staying with Newton. There is also the claim by Conduitt that Catherine lived with Newton for twenty years. When, then, did she find time to oversee Montague's household? And when did the supposed affair actually take place?

If anything can be doubted it must surely be the claim that Catherine served as Montague's housekeeper. Newton as a knight, President of the Royal Society, Master of the Mint, and a bachelor, was clearly in need of a housekeeper. It would have been unthinkable for Catherine to have moved into another man's house except on grounds of marriage. She could still, however, have had a long affair with Montague while continuing to reside in Newton's house.

But even if she did so, Macaulay argued to de Morgan, it affected Newton's reputation not at all. For, Newton, with his child-like simplicity and given also 'the coldness of his own temperament, was a man incapable of seeing the passions in others' (de Morgan, 1968, p. 70). It is a view of Newton's personality no longer favoured by his biographers.

A third view, that Catherine and Halifax were married, was argued at length in de Morgan's comprehensive study of the affair. The crucial new piece of evidence produced in favour of his claim lay in a letter sent from Newton to Sir John Newton apologising for 'not waiting upon you before your journey into Lincolnshire'. The reason offered was the death of Halifax and, Newton continued, 'the circumstances in which I stand related to the family' (C, VI, p. 225); clear proof, de Morgan insisted, that Newton and Halifax were related. Why then, critics have pointedly asked, was the marriage kept secret for so long? De Morgan strove mightily and at some length to explain away the silence of all involved but, despite his efforts, no later biographer has followed him.

Some two years after Montague's death Catherine married John Conduitt. Significantly she described herself at the time as a spinster. Two years later their only child, Kitty, was born. It is through Kitty and her marriage to John Wallop, Viscount Lymington, that Newton's papers would eventually pass into the hands of the Portsmouth family, for it was to Catherine and Conduitt that Newton's papers found their way after his death in 1727. Conduitt showed some initial interest in them but soon seemed happy to leave them unpublished and unread. Catherine, in contrast, after her husband's death, seemed much more determined to see her uncle's work in print. Consequently she added a codicil to her will expressing her intention to print several of his theological works. Aware of her health, she instructed her executor 'to lay all the Tracts relating to Divinity before Dr. Sykes . . . in hopes he will prepare them for my grave'. Nothing came of her plans.

On her death Catherine was buried in Westminster Abbey by the West Wall of the nave, together with her husband, where she is overlooked by the more elaborate monuments to Newton and Montague.

See also Conduitt, John; Family; Manley, Mary de la Riviere; Montague, Charles; Portsmouth Collection

Barton, Hannah (b.1652)

As the daughter of Newton's stepfather, Barnabas Smith, and his mother, Hannah, Hannah Smith was Newton's half-sister. She married a clergyman, Robert Barton of Brigstock, who died about 1693. There were four children: Hannah (1678–82); Catherine (1679–1740); Robert (b.1684); and Margaret (b.1687).

When she was widowed some time in 1693 she wrote to Newton for help. It was a bad time as Newton had just undergone a severe breakdown of some kind and could barely cope with his own life. Consequently it was not until 1695 that Newton was able to help his half-sister. He sent her £100 and took out an annuity for £100 to be divided between the children on his death. Also, sometime after his move to London in 1696, Hannah's daughter, Catherine, came to live with him.

On his death the two surviving Barton children, Catherine and Margaret, were amongst Newton's heirs and must therefore have inherited over £3,000 each.

Barton, Robert (–1693)

The Rev. Robert Barton, a gentleman of Brigstock, Northants, married Newton's half-sister, Hannah Smith (Barton). They had three children: Robert (see below); Hannah (died at the age of 8); and Catherine (Conduitt). Hannah wrote to Newton in late 1693 informing him of her husband's final illness. The only surviving contact between Newton and his brother-in-law is an undated letter from Newton informing Robert and Hannah that he had sent them a barrel of oysters (C, III, p. 393).

See also Family

Barton, Robert (1677–1711)

The son of his half-sister, Hannah Smith, Robert Barton was Newton's nephew. He married Katherine Greenwood, with whom he had three children, Newton, Catherine and Robert. A soldier, he had reached the rank of colonel at his death in 1711 in the shipwreck that ended the Quebec expedition of Brigadier John Hill. On hearing the news, Newton sent a message to Hannah informing her that 'her friends here will take the best care they can of her concerns' (C, V, p. 199) and went on to ensure that she did obtain the appropriate pension. Shortly before his death Newton purchased a £4,000 estate at Boyden, Berkshire, for his nephew's children.

Barton was also the brother of Catherine Barton (Conduitt). According to Jonathan Swift, however, Barton was 'a sad dog' and a 'coxcomb'; Catherine grieved for her brother 'only for form' (*C*, V, p. 200).

See also Family

Bentley, Richard (1662–1742)

Bentley is remembered today as one of the foremost classical scholars of all times; to his contemporaries he was recognised as an opportunist, avaricious and, while fiercely defensive of his own rights and privileges, indifferent to the needs of others. Like Newton he began as a sizar, at St John's College, before advancing his career through the early patronage of Stillingfleet, Dean of St Paul's and later Bishop of Worcester, to whose son Bentley served as tutor. From 1694 he was Royal Librarian and in 1700 obtained the appointment of Master of TCC. There followed forty deeply divisive years for Trinity, with Bentley seeking to enrich himself, acquire personally or control all available offices, and to humiliate and expel anyone who opposed him. Typical of his compulsive behaviour was his determination to gain in 1717 the vacant Regius Chair of Divinity, despite the clear statute that Heads of Colleges were excluded from the post. Such was the tenacity and deviousness of Bentley that, despite the statute, he gained the chair. Much of his later life was spent in isolation in the Master's Lodge, ostracised by the bulk of the Fellows. To Bentley they were 'stupid, drunken sots', 'the Scab, the Ulcers, the Abhorrence of the whole University'.

Bentley's first contact with Newton was probably as a student when he attended his lectures. He is known to have approached him in 1691 asking for help in understanding *Principia*. Newton responded with a formidable course of study, starting with Euclid and 'the Elements of ye Conic sections', and advancing through a number of algebra and astronomical texts to Huygens's *Horologium oscillatorium* (*C*, III, p. 155–6). Contact continued throughout 1692 and 1693 when Bentley, as first Boyle lecturer in 1692, asked Newton to help him develop a number of arguments for the printed version of the lectures. His subject, *A Confutation of Atheism* (1693), called for arguments taken from 'the origin and frame of the universe' and it was clearly prudent to consult Newton on their validity and content. The result was the revealing correspondence first published in 1756 by Bentley's grandson, Richard Cumberland, as *Four Letters from Sir Isaac Newton to Dr. Bentley*.

The main impact of Bentley on Newton's career was directed towards the issue of the second edition of *Principia* (1713). Roger Cotes, in his preface to the work, reported that 'since copies of the previous edition were very scarce and held at high prices', it was Bentley who persuaded Newton 'by frequent entreaties and almost by chidings . . . to grant him permission for the appearance of this new edition . . . at his expense and under his supervision'. Newton had of course intended to issue a corrected and amended edition almost as soon as *Principia* first appeared in 1687, but with his capacity to delay and his propensity to retain rather than disclose material, it is an open question how long Newton would have prevaricated without the pressure of a Bentley behind him. Whatever his faults, Bentley stood in awe of no man and consequently felt in no way inhibited by Newton's name or reputation.

Bentley was an odd choice to entrust *Principia* with. To begin with, he was no mathematician. Secondly he had a reputation with texts that he 'spared neither the living nor the dead' and was as willing to rewrite Milton's verse in his edition of *Paradise Lost* (1732) as he was to correct Halley's *Ode*. He was also extremely greedy. When asked why he had allowed Bentley to handle the edition Newton replied: 'Why, he was covetous, and I let him do it to get money.'

When Bentley first received permission is not known. Certainly by 1708 he was at work on the project and had progressed far enough to have had one sheet, comprising the first eight pages, printed for Newton's inspection. He also invested in a hundred reams of paper imported from Genoa. Bentley informed Newton: 'In a few places I have taken ye liberty to change, some words, either for ye sake of ye Latin, or ye thought itself' (*C*, IV, p. 519). Bentley also had the sensible idea of adding running titles to each page.

Shortly afterwards Roger Cotes, a protégé of Bentley, took over the editorial duties. Whether Newton had objected to Bentley's assumed textual licence or whether Bentley realised only a mathematician could complete the task is not known. Bentley retained financial control. His accounts have survived and show that while still holding seventy-one copies he had already made a profit of £198.

Despite his numerous faults, Bentley did much to advance the cause of science in Trinity. It was due to his patronage that the young Cotes was appointed Plumian Professor of Astronomy in 1706. Bentley went on to erect for Cotes, above the main gate, a well-equipped observatory. He also provided for Vigani, appointed Professor of Chemistry in 1702, a laboratory within the college.

Full details of Bentley's remarkable career can be found in R. J. White, *Dr Bentley. A study in academic scarlet* (1965).

Berkeley, George (1685–1753)

Born in Kilkenny, Ireland, Berkeley was educated at Trinity College, Dublin. After several years travelling in Europe, and after spending three years in America, Berkeley was appointed Bishop of Cloyne in 1733. He is best known for his idealist philosophy with its commitment to the apparently ridiculous claim that *esse est percipi* (to be is to be perceived). Although his views might seem initially absurd, Berkeley possessed the ability to detect in his opponent's case absurdities and contradictions by the dozen. It is thus not surprising that a man who could find our commitment to the material incomprehensible would be hardly likely to accept the mathematicians' notion of the infinitesimal without comment.

Berkeley launched his attack against the mathematicians in his *Analyst* (1734), a discourse addressed to 'an Infidel Mathematician' (Halley ?). Were, Berkeley asked, 'the Object, Principles, and Inferences of the modern Analysis . . . more distinctly conceived . . . than Religious Mysteries'? The idea of the exceedingly small he found absurd. Mathematicians, he noted, customarily took $32 \times 16dt$ to be the same as 32. When pressed to justify their procedure they would dismiss the quantity $16dt$ as being so exceedingly small that it could be ignored. Berkeley insisted that either $16dt$ equalled 0 or it did not. If it did then there can have been no increment in distance; if it did not then $32 \times 16dt$ was obviously greater than 32.

Berkeley went on to note that if 'Objects extremely minute' were puzzling, how could we be expected 'to frame clear Ideas of the least Particles of Time'. As for higher order fluxions, 'the incipient Celerity of an incipient Clerity, the nascent Augment of a nascent Augment', Berkeley could make even less sense.

Yet, Berkeley conceded, mathematicians had attained true conclusions. How was this possible on such shaky foundations? Somewhat implausibly, he maintained that a twofold mistake had been made and, quite fortuitously, the mistakes cancelled each other out. In this way, 'you arrive, though not at Science, yet at Truth'.

Berkeley's arguments were taken seriously by the mathematicians of his day and led to a vigorous controversy. The first to attempt to meet Berkeley's objections was James Jurin in his *Geometry no Friend to Infidelity* (1734) and *The Minute Mathematician* (1735). Berkeley, however, in his reply, *A Defence of Freethinking in Mathematics* (1735), had little difficulty in exposing Jurin's incoherent attempts to define 'a nascent increment' which, 'though just beginning to be generated', had not yet attained 'any assignable magnitude how small soever' (Boyer, 1959, pp. 228–9)

The definitive Newtonian reply to Berkeley came a few years later from Colin Maclaurin in his *Treatise of Fluxions* (1742). While following Berkeley in his dismissal of the infinitely small, Maclaurin went on to provide rigorous geometrical proofs of Newton's mathematical procedures. Only towards the end of his lengthy text did Maclaurin allow himself to use the notation of fluxions.

Berkeley found Newton's natural philosophy as distasteful as his mathematics. In the *Principles of Human Knowledge* (1710, sections 110–17) and in *De motu* (1721), he directed his attention to a 'treatise on Mechanics . . . by a philosopher of a neighbouring nation, whom all the world admire'. He sought, in particular, to reject Newton's concept of absolute space, time and motion. For a body to move, he argued, 'it is requisite, first, that it change its distance or situation with regard to some other body' (section 115). Space, time and motion were thus, for Berkeley, all relative. Any other approach, he insisted, led us to the dangerous dilemma of 'thinking either that real Space is God, or else that there is something besides God which is eternal' (section 117). Newton was sensitive to such criticisms and sought to answer them in his General *Scholium* and throughout the *Leibniz–Clarke Correspondence*.

Bernoulli, Johann (1667–1748)

As the brother of Jakob (1654–1705) and the father of Daniel (1700–82), Johann was a member of the famous family of Swiss mathematicians. He held chairs of mathematics at Groningen from 1695 to 1705 when, on the death of his brother Jakob, he took over the Basel chair.

Bernoulli's contact with Newton arose from the dispute with Leibniz over the discovery of the calculus. The role he chose to play in the dispute has done little to enhance his reputation. Thus to Hall (*C*, VII, p. xxi) he was 'a lion by night, jackal by day', while Westfall (RSW, p. 762) dismissed his behaviour as arousing 'only disgust'. In 1713, for example, Bernoulli happily encouraged Leibniz to defend his priority claim against the Newtonians while carefully preserving his own position:

> I do indeed beg you to use what I now write properly and not to involve me with Newton and his people, for I am reluctant to be involved in these disputes or to appear ungrateful to Newton who has heaped many testimonies of his goodwill upon me. (*C*, VI, p. 5)

Bernoulli's involvement in the dispute was, nevertheless, the most prolonged of all. It was, however, a complex and varied involvement and covered the following issues.

1 Bernoulli established his mathematical reputation in 1691 with his solution of a long-standing problem, namely: the form adopted by a chain, the so-called catenary, freely suspended from two points. He was thereafter employed by de L'Hopital on an exclusive contract to teach him the methods of the newly discovered calculus. De l'Hopital went on to publish Bernoulli's work without any

acknowledgment in his *Analyse des infiniment petits* (1696), the first textbook on the differential calculus to appear.

2 In the June 1696 issue of *AE* Bernoulli raised the problem of the brachistochrone, the curve of quickest descent, and offered it as a challenge to the mathematicians of Europe. Newton, like Leibniz, had little difficulty in solving the problem.

3 The first real sign of hostility to Newton emerged in 1710 when Bernoulli spotted an error in *Principia*, Book II, prop.X. He informed Leibniz of the error and became convinced that Newton's mistake revealed a genuine inability to deal with higher-order differentials and was no momentary lapse. He had also become convinced that Newton had lacked a full understanding of the inverse problem of central forces and, accordingly, had failed to demonstrate that they, given the inverse square law, implied elliptical orbits. Papers on the two issues were prepared for the *AE* and the *Mémoires* and timed to appear after the publication in 1713 of the second edition of *Principia*. Things did not work out as Bernoulli had hoped. He had earlier conveyed details of Newton's error to his nephew Nikolaus Bernoulli (1687–1759) who, on a visit to London in late 1712, met Newton and informed him of the error. Newton moved quickly. He accepted the error, insisted that it was trivial, and informed Cotes on 14 October that the 'reprinting of about a sheet & an half' would be needed (*C*, V, p. 347). As an acknowledgment of his debt to Bernoulli he arranged for his election to the Royal Society on 1 December 1713. Bernoulli thought the acknowledgment inadequate, having expected an attribution to appear in the new edition of *Principia*. Newton made no such acknowledgment, nor, indeed, even bothered to indicate that the first edition had been modified in any way.

4 In 1713 Bernoulli drew the attention of Leibniz to the *Commercium epistolicum*, thus provoking him to write his *Charta volans*. The anonymous fly-sheet referred to the judgment of an unnamed 'leading mathematician' who considered that 'the true way of differentiating differentials was not known to Newton until long after it was familiar to others'. The 'leading mathematician' was of course Bernoulli.

5 Bernoulli's criticisms of *Principia* had appeared in *AE* (February–March, 1713, pp. 77–95, 115–32) and *Mémoires* (1714, pp. 59–72). Inevitably they had led to rejoinders from Keill. Bernoulli replied in turn in his unacknowledged exercise in self-defence, *Epistola pro eminente mathematico, Dr. Johanne Bernoullio . . .*, published in *AE* (July 1716, pp. 296–314). By this time Bernoulli was having some difficulty in keeping track of who was supposed to be in defence of the 'eminent mathematician, Johann Bernoulli' and inadvertently allowed a reference to appear to '*meam*

formulam'. The slip was lethal to Bernoulli's reputation and he quickly found himself ridiculed for his presumption in describing himself as an 'eminent mathematician' and then to do it so clumsily as to give away immediately his identity. The editor, Wolf, argued that the *'meam'* was a misprint for *'eam'*. The story was too good to be allowed to go away so easily and both Keill and Newton, with remarkable hypocrisy, began to fuel each other's rising indignation. Keill drew Newton's attention to the *Epistola* in 1717 and went on to comment that 'there was never such a piece for falsehood malice envie and ill nature published by a mathematician before' (*C*, VI, pp. 386–7). Keill submitted a draft reply for Newton's approval. Ignoring his own recently published anonymous *Recensio*, Newton warned Bernoulli that 'whenever I meet with such anonymous papers wherein you are applauded or cited as a witness or your enemies abused: I shall for the future look upon them as written by your self or at least by your procurement, unless the contrary appears to me' (*C*, VI, pp. 387). He chose, however, not to send the letter immediately and delayed its publication until a further outbreak of hostilities in 1720.

6   Leibniz died in 1716, and with his death most reasonable men could well have expected the dispute to die. Newton, for one, seemed anxious not to provoke Bernoulli and, as mentioned above, held back on a particularly abusive letter from Keill. Another who thought the quarrel should end was Pierre Varignon in Paris. When Newton sent him several copies of the second edition of his *Opticks*, Varignon sent one to Bernoulli as if it were a direct gift from Newton. Bernoulli consequently wrote to Newton – 'illustrissimo atque incomparabili' – in the most fulsome of terms. He also went so far as to declare 'in the name of everything sacred to humanity' that the variously published anonymous fly-sheets had been 'falsely imputed to him'. It was not his custom, he informed Newton with disdain, 'to issue anonymously what I neither wish nor dare to acknowledge as my own' (*C*, VII, pp. 45–6). Keill was all for having another go at the 'Lipsick Rogues'. Newton, however, seemed prepared to accept Bernoulli's lie and so informed him on 29 September 1719 that he wished to 'court your friendship and esteem'. Now that he was old, he declared, he took 'very little pleasure in mathematical studies' (*C*, VII, pp. 69–71). Bernoulli replied on 10 December and appeared willing to accept the truce offered by Newton.

7   The truce was soon broken. Des Maizeaux in his *Recueil* (1720) had revived once more the charge that Bernoulli was the 'leading mathematician' of the *Charta volans*. It was sufficient to stimulate Bernoulli to further complaints. For two years, despite the attempts of Varignon to re-establish harmony, the dispute drew on. With

the death of Varignon in 1722, and with no other intermediary willing to take his place, the correspondence at last came to an end. Newton's final defiant word was to issue in a more convenient form a second edition of *CE* (1722). Bernoulli's own final contribution came in a letter to Newton in 1723 in which, once more, he denied that he had ever attributed the title 'eminent mathematician' to himself (*C*, VII, pp. 218–23). The charge had been raised yet again by Nicolas Hartsoeker, and obviously continued to irritate Bernoulli. He was thus looking to Newton to defend him. At the age of eighty Newton had at last had enough. He ignored Bernoulli and with no reply the dispute finally ended.

If Bernoulli is revealed today as a liar and a hypocrite, it must also be conceded that few scholars, on either side, emerged with a faultless reputation. Newton and Keill were as willing as Bernoulli to dissemble and to condemn in others standards of behaviour they frequently adopted themselves.

See also Bernoulli's problems; Priority dispute

Bernoulli, Nicolas (1687–1759)

A nephew of Johann Bernoulli, Nicolas served as Professor of Mathematics at the universities of Padua (1716–22) and Basel (1722–59). In September 1712 he visited London where he was introduced by de Moivre to Newton. It was a timely meeting. Twice he invited Nicolas to dine with him and was rewarded for his hospitality by hearing how uncle Johann had discovered a serious error in prop.X of *Principia*'s Book II. Nicolas's warning thus enabled Newton to correct the completed text of the second edition of *Principia* (1713) and so saved him from serious embarrassment. On 1 October Newton wrote to Nicolas, with some satisfaction: 'I send you inclosed the solution of ye Probleme . . . I desire you to shew it to your Unkle – return my thanks to him for sending me notice of ye mistake' (*C*, V, p. 348).

See also Principia, Book II, proposition X

Bernoulli's problems

1

In the June 1696 issue of the *Acta eruditorum*, Bernoulli challenged 'the acutest mathematicians now living throughout the world' to solve the 'Mechano-geometrical problem about the line of quickest descent'. The problem, more fully defined was:

To determine the curved line joining two given points, situated at different distances from the horizontal and not in the same vertical line, along which a mobile body, running down by its own weight and starting to move from the upper point, will descend most quickly to the lower point.

Bernoulli later went on to illustrate the problem by supposing there are two points A and B, as in Figure 1. An infinite number of lines can join

• A

• B

Fig. 1

A to B. The problem was to select 'one line of such a nature that, if along it there be bent a metal plate shaped as a tube or groove, a small ball placed therein and released, will pass from one point to the other in the shortest time' (*C*, IV, p. 225).

Bernoulli originally allowed six months for the problem's solution. In January 1697 he announced with uncontrolled delight:

> But lo and behold, the final date is now past, and no solution has appeared apart from the fact that the celebrated Leibniz . . . informed me . . . that he had successfully unravelled the knot of what he termed 'this beautiful and hitherto unknown problem.'

Leibniz and Bernoulli were clearly enjoying themselves too much to allow the competition to end in January. Consequently they announced that the time limit would be extended to Easter lest anyone, they condescendingly declared, should complain about 'the shortness of the time'. They further decided to give greater publicity to the problem. Bernoulli also chose to add a second problem to the copies of the original problem he sent to the *PT*, *Journal des sçavans*, Newton and Wallis.

Newton's reaction to the problem was later recorded by Catherine Barton:

> When the problem in 1697 was sent by Bernoulli (Newton received it on 29 January) – Sr I.N. was in the midst of the hurry of the great recoinage did not come home till four from the Tower very much tired, but did not sleep till he had solved it wch was by 4 in the morning. (RSW, pp. 582–3)

Indifferent to Bernoulli's plans to reveal the solution at Easter, Newton pre-empted his revelation by announcing anonymously in the February issue of *PT*: 'Concerning the ratio of the time in which a weight will slide by a straight line joining two given points, and the shortest time in which, by the force of gravity, it will pass from one to another by a cycloidal arc.' He had sent earlier to Montague on 30 January 1697 fuller details of the problems and his proposed solutions (*C*, IV, pp. 220–9). His discussion of the first problem is short enough to quote in full:

Problem I   It is required to find the curve ADB in which a weight, by the force of its gravity, shall descend most swiftly from any given point A to any given point B.

Solution   From the given point A let there be drawn an unlimited straight line APCZ [see Figure 2] parallel to the

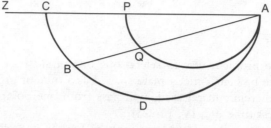

Fig. 2

horizontal, and on it let there be described an arbitrary cycloid AQP meeting the straight line AB . . . in the point Q, and further a second cycloid ADC whose base and height are to the base and height of the former as AB to AQ respectively. This last cycloid will pass through the point B, and it will be that curve along which a weight, by the force of its gravity, shall descend most swiftly from the point A to the point B. Q.E.F. (*C*, IV, p. 226)

Bernoulli had no difficulty in identifying the author of the solution; the lion, he declared, can be recognised from his footprint ('ex ungue leonem'). Newton's own attitude to the incident was revealed in a 1699 letter to Flamsteed in which he complained about being 'dunned and teezed by foreigners about Mathematical things' (*C*, IV, p. 296).

In addition to Newton, Johann Bernoulli and Leibniz, the problem was solved by Jakob Bernoulli and de L'Hopital. David Gregory, Pierre Varignon and John Wallis were known to have made unsuccessful attempts. Full details of Newton's solution can be found in *MP*, VIII, pp. 72–91.

Newton's ability to solve the problem in a single sitting has frequently been presented as a sign of his unrivalled intellectual powers. A less indulgent view is presented by Whiteside (*MP*, VIII, pp. 72–3) who finds in Newton's response signs of 'a mental rustiness' brought on by 'a year's total break with things mathematical'. A few months before,

Whiteside insists, Newton would have had the solution, not in hours, but in a matter of minutes!

2

In August 1697 Bernoulli posed to Leibniz the problem of 'constructing a general orthogonal to a given parent sequence of curves' (*MP*, VIII, p. 425), and sketched for him an outline solution. Some eighteen years later Leibniz revived the problem with the aim of testing the 'pulse' of the English analysts. The ever-willing Abbé Conti, conveniently in London, was thus chosen to deliver to the English mathematicians the challenge problem: 'To find a line which cuts at right angles all curves of a determined sequence of one and the same kind – for example, all hyperbolas having the same vertex and same centre – and that by a general way' (*MP*, VIII, p. 62).

The problem had reached London by January 1716. John Keill, John Machin, Brook Taylor and, no doubt, other mathematicians close to Newton, had little difficulty in solving the problem as it applied to hyperbolas. It proved less easy to tackle the general problem. Newton's initial reaction was to grumble to Conti: 'I have left off Mathematicks 20 years ago and look upon solving of Problemes as a very unfit argument to decide who was the best Mathematician or invented anything above 50 years ago' (*C*, VI, p. 285). Such a lofty attitude did not stop Newton seeking a general solution and, indeed, publishing his results anonymously in the March *PT* (1715) under the title 'Problematis mathematicis anglis nuper propositi Solutio Generalis' (General solution to a recently proposed mathematical problem about angles).

It was, Whiteside has commented, 'the last occasion on which Newton came creatively to grips with a mathematical topic of any real difficulty' (*MP*, VIII, pp. 61–2). He failed to analyse the problem adequately and was consequently reduced for the first time in his life 'to uttering loose generalities'. Unlike 1697, Bernoulli failed to identify behind the anonymous paper any lion's claw and rather supposed the piece to have come from Brook Taylor. When, a few months later, Conti circulated a further problem, Newton seems to have made no attempt to solve it.

See also Bernoulli, Johann; Conti, Abbé; Cycloid

Bible

Newton's knowledge of the Bible and its associated literature was impressive by even the highest standards of scholarship. According to Locke, who was himself extremely well read in this area, there were few his equal. There is also the evidence of the *Variantes*, with its collation of variant readings from the Apocalypse sufficient to impress a professional Bible scholar like John Mill.

More direct evidence can be seen in Newton's library. He owned thirty Bibles which break down into the categories shown in the table. There were also two editions of the *Cambridge Concordance* (1672 and 1698) and Walton's six-volume *Biblia Sacra polyglotta* (1655–7).

Newton's Bibles

Bible	Old Testament	New Testament
English – 6	Greek – 2	Greek – 7
Latin – 5		Latin – 3
Greek – 3		Syriac/Latin – 1
French – 1		Greek/Latin – 1
Hebrew – 1		

Two comments are needed. Some of these, and commentaries not mentioned, may well have come from his stepfather, Barnabas Smith, who left Newton some two to three hundred theological works. Secondly, impressive and unusual though such a collection looks today, it may well have not been all that extensive for a scholar of the seventeenth century. Locke, for example, with over fifty Bibles, certainly had more.

The background literature of the church fathers was also present and included ten volumes of St Augustine (Paris, 1531–2), five of St Ambrose (Basel, 1567) and various volumes of Justin, Clement of Alexandria, Origen, Tertullian, Irenaeus and many more besides.

Bibliographies

A number of bibliographies of different aspects of Newton's work have appeared over the years; only two of these are in any way comprehensive.

1 *Bibliography of the Work of Sir Isaac Newton*, with notes by G. J. Gray. Only 120 copies of the 1888 first edition were published. A second revised and enlarged edition was issued by Bowes & Bowes of Cambridge in 1907. Though obviously out of date and even incomplete in its time, it has remained a useful and easy-to-use guide to Newtonian literature.

2 *Newton and Newtoniana 1672–1975* (London, 1977) by Peter and Ruth Wallis. Published seventy years after Gray, this is a much more ambitious and comprehensive work. Not only are all

Newton's works listed, but an attempt has been made to list the critical and secondary work of the last three centuries. A measure of its success is the clear need for a comparable work to cover the years since it was published.

Although not complete bibliographies, there are three specialised catalogues which are, in many ways, just as essential.

3 *A Catalogue of the Portsmouth Collection* (Cambridge, 1888). A work of variable value by H. R. Luard, G. G. Stokes, J. C. Adams and G. D. Liveing.

4 *Catalogue of the Newton Papers* sold at Sotheby's in 1936. It was prepared by John Taylor.

5 *A Descriptive Catalogue of the Grace K. Babson Collection of the Works of Sir Isaac Newton . . . in the Babson Institute Library* (New York, 1950). For the most part only material found in the Collection is described. This is less of a restriction than it might at first sight appear; the Collection is so fine and the annotations so detailed that it is often of more use than more comprehensive bibliographies. A *Supplement* prepared by H. P. Macomber was issued in 1955. Limited to 750 and 450 copies respectively, they are handsome but expensive and hard-to-find volumes.

6 A Newtonian bibliography by H. Zeitlinger (1927) in Greenstreet. Although a bibliographical essay rather than a bibliography, this is still of use.

More specialised bibliographies can be found in a number of separate works.

7 *The Foundation of Newton's Alchemy* (Cambridge, 1975) by Betty Jo Dobbs contains a description of all 121 alchemical lots listed in the 1936 Sotheby catalogue; it also contains a comprehensive bibliography of related material on the chemical and alchemical background of the seventeenth century.

8 *Isaac Newton's Principia* (Cambridge, 1972, 2 vols), edited by I. B. Cohen and A. Koyré (Newton, 1972); an appendix to volume 2 contains a full *Principia* bibliography.

9 *The Library of Isaac Newton* (Cambridge, 1978) by John Harrison contains the fullest bibliography on the fate of Newton's library.

10 *Cinquant' anni di studi newtoniani (1908–59)* (Florence, 1960) by Clelia Pighetti. A chronological bibliography which allows the reader to see how interest in Newton has grown and changed year by year in the period 1908 to 1959.

Unfortunately there are no published bibliographies of the important manuscript holdings in the ULC, KCC and Yahuda collections.

Binomial theorem

The expansion of $(a + b)^n$, where n stood for a positive, integral exponent, had long been a familiar procedure to mathematicians by the time of Newton. The required coefficients could be read off from Pascal's triangle (see diagram) as and when they were needed. Thus, the expansion of $(a + b)^6$ can immediately be seen to be:

$$a^6 + 6a^5b + 15a^4b^2 + 20a^3b^3 + 15a^2b^4 + 6ab^5 + b^6$$

Although the triangle bears Pascal's name and was discussed by him in his *Traité de triangle arithmétique* (1665), it had in fact been recorded in print in textbooks since the *Rechnung* (1527, Calculation) of Apianus.

$$
\begin{array}{c}
1 \\
1 \quad 1 \\
1 \quad 2 \quad 1 \\
1 \quad 3 \quad 3 \quad 1 \\
1 \quad 4 \quad 6 \quad 4 \quad 1 \\
1 \quad 5 \quad 10 \quad 10 \quad 5 \quad 1 \\
1 \quad 6 \quad 15 \quad 20 \quad 15 \quad 6 \quad 1
\end{array}
$$

It soon, however, became apparent to seventeenth-century mathematicians that this was not enough. John Wallis, in his *Arithmetica infinitorum* (1655), for example, working on the quadrature of the circle, began with the equation of a circle

$$x^2 + y^2 = r^2$$

where r is the radius. Let $r = 1$, and the equation becomes $x^2 + y^2 = 1$, which can be rewritten as $y^2 = 1 - x^2$. Taking the roots of both sides yields:

$$y = \sqrt{1 - x^2} \text{ or } y = (1 - x^2)^{\frac{1}{2}}$$

Neither Wallis, however, nor any of his contemporaries knew how to expand equations with fractional indices. Instead he was reduced to using methods of interpolation. Newton began at this point, reporting later that:

> In the winter between the years 1664 and 1665 upon reading Dr Wallis's *Arithmetica infinitorum* and trying to interpole his progressions for squaring the circle I found out another infinite series

for squaring the circle and then another . . . for squaring the hyperbola.

This first approach to the problem was recorded in the manuscript *A Method whereby to Find ye Areas of those Lines which can be Squared* (C, II, pp. 168–70).

Details of his work was made public in the 1676 *Epistola prior* sent to Leibniz.

The Extraction of Roots are much shortened by the Theorem

$$(P + PQ)^{m/n} = P^{m/n} + \frac{m}{n}AQ + \frac{m-n}{2n}BQ + \frac{m-2n}{3n}CQ + \frac{m-3n}{4n}DQ + \ldots$$

where $P + PQ$ stands for a Quantity whose Root or Power or whose Root of a Power is to be found, P being the first term of that quantity, Q being the remaining terms divided by the first term and m/n the numerical Index of the powers of $P + PQ$ . . . A stands for the first term $P(m/n)$; B for the second term $(m/n)AQ$; and so on.

Newton's theorem is much more complicated than the form of the binomial theorem seen in modern textbooks; the details become clearer when seen in the context of Newton's own example, $(c^2 + x^2)^{1/2}$. In this case:

$P = c^2$

$Q = x^2/c^2$

$m = 1$

$n = 2$

$A = P^{m/n} = (c^2)^{1/2} = c$

$\frac{m}{n}AQ = \frac{1}{2}(cx^2/c^2) = x^2/2c$

$B = \frac{m}{n}AQ = x^2/2c$

$\frac{m-n}{2n}BQ = \frac{1-2}{4}\frac{x^2}{2c} \times \frac{x^2}{c^2} = -1/4(x^4/2c^3) = -x^4/8c^3$

and the expansion of $(c^2 + x^2)^{1/2}$ begins:

$c + x^2/2c - x^4/8c^3 + x^6/16c^5 - 5x^8/128c^7$ . . .

and continues indefinitely.

The theorem was presented without proof or explanation. Further details, however, were released in a second letter to Leibniz, the *Epistola posterior*, sent in October 1676. Wallis, he noted, had succeeded in working out the area of certain curves, and had had no success with others. His results can be presented by the equations in the table, where the curves have the common base x and the ordinates y. Newton began by noting:

Curves and areas calculated by Wallis

Curves	Areas
1 $y = (1 - x^2)^0$	x
2 $y = (1 - x^2)^{1/2}$	–
3 $y = (1 - x^2)^1$	$x - \dfrac{1}{3}x^3$
4 $y = (1 - x^2)^{3/2}$	–
5 $y = (1 - x^2)^2$	$x - \dfrac{2}{3}x^3 + \dfrac{1}{5}x^5$
6 $y = (1 - x^2)^{5/2}$	–
7 $y = (1 - x^2)^3$	$x - \dfrac{3}{3}x^3 + \dfrac{3}{5}x^5 - \dfrac{1}{7}x^7$

In all of them the first term was x and that the second terms $\dfrac{0}{3}x^3$, $\dfrac{1}{3}x^3$, $\dfrac{2}{3}x^3$, $\dfrac{3}{3}x^3$ etc, were in arithmetical progression, and hence that the first two terms of the series to be intercalated ought to be $x - \dfrac{1}{3}(\dfrac{1}{2}x^3)$, $x - \dfrac{1}{3}(\dfrac{3}{2}x^3)$, $x - \dfrac{1}{3}(\dfrac{5}{2}x^3)$ etc. (C, II, p. 130)

Newton proceeded to intercalate other terms of the series. The denominators 1,3,5,7, in arithmetic progression, presented no problem. The numerators, Newton noticed, for curves 1, 3, 5 and 7 above, were 1; 1,1; 1,2,1; and 1,3,3,1 respectively – precisely, Newton must have recognised with some excitement, the coefficients to be found in the first four lines of Pascal's triangle.

It remained for Newton to represent his insights in terms of the equation reported in the *Epistola prior*. The theorem was first used in print by Newton in his *De quadratura* (1704). Newton offered no rigorous proof of his work. Proof of the binomial theorem was, in fact, a lengthy process and came piecemeal, being completed only in 1825 with Abel's demonstration that the theorem applied to the general expansion of $(1 + x)^n$ where x and n were complex numbers.

Biography

The Newton biographical tradition is long, rich, and still continuing. It has already produced three major biographies and a number of memorable works which, though not strictly biographical, belong on the fringes of the tradition. This in itself is no slight achievement. Scientific biographies of merit are rare creations – none yet, for example, has appeared on Darwin – and for one man to inspire three such works is unheard of elsewhere. Surprisingly, the first biography did not appear until 1831. Before that, knowledge of Newton's life was derived from official eulogies or entries in encyclopedias. The tradition begins with John Conduitt and Bernard Fontenelle.

CONDUITT

As the husband of Newton's niece, Catherine Barton, and as his successor at the Mint, Conduitt was well placed to be Newton's first biographer. To this end he wrote to such friends and colleagues of Newton as John Machin, John Craig, A. de Moivre and others 'who had so great a share in his esteem' and asked them 'to put down anything that occurs to your thoughts, and you think fit to be inserted in such a work'. He guaranteed to 'acquaint the public in the Preface, to whom they are indebted for each particular part of it'.

He was remarkably successful. Amongst other items, he assembled a forty-two-page manuscript on Newton's life prior to Cambridge, sixteen pages on his life and work at Cambridge, seventeen pages of miscellaneous anecdotes, seventeen pages on Newton's character, one and a half on his final illness, two on his manual dexterity and a further two recording a conversation he held with Newton on the night of 7 March 1725. Virtually all of this material was acquired by J. M. Keynes at the Sotheby sale of the PC in 1936 and can now be found in KCC. Although extracts from this material have appeared in Turnor (1806), Brewster (1831), More (1962), Cohen (1971) and several other works, it has never been fully published. For some unknown reason Conduitt failed to complete, or even for that matter start, the contemplated biography. Despite this the material he collected so promptly has formed the basis for all other biographies published since. The first to use Conduitt's material was Fontenelle.

FONTENELLE

Ironically, the first attempt to sketch Newton's life was made by the leading Cartesian of the day, Fontenelle, *secrétaire-perpetuel* of the *Académie Royale des Sciences*. Called on in his official capacity to deliver the customary eulogy for one of the deceased *académiciens*, he sought the aid of Conduitt who prepared the *Memoirs Relating to Sir Isaac Newton sent by me to Monr Fontenelle in Octr 1727* (Keynes, MS 129 A). Demand for the *Éloge* was considerable. Two editions were published in Paris in 1728 and five in London, with a further thirteen editions appearing before the end of the century.

Fontenelle sketched the main details of Newton's life and even gave a first airing to many of the anecdotes that have ever since been associated with Newton's name and retold by all later biographers. The most famous of all the anecdotes, however, the apple tree and gravity, was not used by Fontenelle.

Having done his duty, Fontenelle could not allow the occasion to pass without measuring Newton against Descartes. He made it clear that he found Newton's concept of attraction a retrograde assumption. Surely, he protested, it reintroduced into science the occult qualities thrown out by Descartes. Newton's insistence that he was concerned only with manifest qualities failed to impress Fontenelle, and drew from him the response:

> But are they not properly causes which the Schoolmen called occult Qualities; since their effects are plainly seen – besides, could Sir Isaac think that others would find out these Occult causes which he could not discover? with what hopes of success can any other man search after them? (*PLNP*, p. 463)

The *Éloge* failed to impress its principal source. Conduitt complained 'I fear he had neither abilities nor inclination to do justice to that great man, who has eclipsed the glory of their hero, Descartes.'

EIGHTEENTH-CENTURY ENCYCLOPEDIAS

For the remainder of the century Newton's life was explored almost entirely within the context of the large multi-volume encyclopedias and dictionaries which had begun to appear for the first time. One of the first to appear in Britain was the *General Dictionary* (10 vols, 1734–41), an English translation and adaptation of Pierre Bayle's famous *Dictionnaire historique et critique* (1697–1702), 'interspersed with several thousand lives never before published'. The Newton entry appeared in 1738 (vol. VII, pp. 776–802), composed by Thomas Birch. In addition to the *Éloge*, Birch had access to material published by Henry Pemberton in his *A View of Sir Isaac Newton's Philosophy* (1728) and to material culled especially for him from the Macclesfield Collection by William Jones. Birch was thus able to publish for the first time, in addition to extracts from Newton's works, items from his correspondence with Oldenburg, Collins, Flamsteed and Halley. A French version was included in the *Nouveau dictionnaire historique et critique* (1750).

Birch published a fuller account in the *Biographia Britannica* (1760, vol. V, pp. 3210–44). Described by Westfall (1965b, p. xxxv) as 'a remarkable essay', it 'established the main features of Newton's life as they are known today'. It was the first work, for example, to attempt to trace the origin and development of *Principia* from the 'insights of the 1660s' via the 1679 correspondence with Hooke to the visit of Halley in 1684.

Thereafter, for the rest of the century, the details recorded in the *Biographica Britannica* were repeated regularly in such derivative works as Benjamin Martin's *Biographia Philosophica* (1764), the second edition of the *Encyclopedia Britannica* (1777–83), and the *New Cyclopedia* (1802–20, 45 vols) edited by Abraham Reed.

The first work to break away from this tradition and add something new was the *Collections for the History of the Town and Soke of Grantham* (1806) by Edmund Turnor. The Turnor family were the owners of the Manor of Woolsthorpe and, as an antiquarian, Turnor took the opportunity to publish any items of local history relevant to Newton's life. He was also allowed access to the PC and made the most of his opportunity by publishing long extracts from memoranda by Conduitt and Stukeley containing much of the basic material on Newton's life. While by no means the work of hagiographers, the memoranda published still tended to present a view of Newton held by his close friends, relatives and disciples. No one had yet suggested that there was more to Newton than the image presented of him by Conduitt as a man renowned for his generosity, charity, humility, courteousness, affability, piety, meekness, sweetness, modesty, simplicity, and much more besides. The one exception in Britain to this rule was William Whiston, who had, indeed, been critical of both the behaviour and character of Newton. Whiston, however, was a notorious heretic and eccentric whose judgment could be safely discounted.

It was thus left to the Frenchman J. B. Biot to be the first to suggest and document the claim that there was more to Newton than the published record had so far revealed.

BIOT

Biot contributed a long entry to Michaud's *Biographie universelle* (1821, vol. 30, pp. 367–404) on Newton. It contained two startling new claims. He reported an entry in a notebook of Huygens dated 29 May 1694 claiming that some eighteen months earlier Newton had gone mad. The incident proved to be too well documented to ignore. Biot went on to make the second point that as a consequence of his admittedly temporary insanity, Newton never undertook any further original scientific work. Everything published after 1693 had been written long before. Biot's work was not allowed long to remain in the obscurity of a French encyclopedia, for Lord Brougham's *Life of Sir Isaac Newton* (1829) was little more than a rehash in English of Biot's original article.

Biot thus became the first to suggest that Newton's life and genius were not without their problems. As often happens, once an initial blemish is noticed, other scars are soon detected. In 1835 Baily published his *Account* of Flamsteed in which a strange and far from flattering portrait of Newton was sketched.

Such disclosures could not be rejected out of hand; nor could they be allowed to stand. It was thus clear to one scholar and admirer of Newton, Sir David Brewster, that only a full-length and carefully documented biography could put the revelations of Biot, Baily and others into their proper context.

BREWSTER

Thus, in 1831, Brewster published his *Life of Newton*, declaring it to be 'the only life . . . on any considerable scale that has yet appeared'. It proved a popular work, appearing seven more times in Britain, sixteen times in the US between 1831 and 1874, as well as being translated into French (1833) and German (1836). At this stage he had little new to offer. His main source remained the *Biographia Britannica*, Turnor (1806) and Biot. In addition, he claimed, he drew on some unpublished correspondence between Newton, S. Pepys and Millington, and the diary of Abraham Pryme. Thin stuff, perhaps, to be described as 'many new materials of considerable value' (1831, p. vi).

It was enough, however, to allow Brewster to defend Newton against Biot. The 'insanity' mentioned by Huygens becomes in Brewster a 'loss of tranquillity' caused by 'the destruction of his papers'. It lasted no longer than a month (1831, p. 229). Further, and also against Biot, Brewster went to some length to establish that Newton *had* undertaken serious scientific work well after his supposed breakdown (1831, pp. 244–5).

The *Life* is somewhat distorted by Brewster's own predominant interest in optics. Of the nineteen chapters (347 pages), seven of them (95 pages) deal exclusively with problems of optics, while the whole of Newton's mechanics is compressed into a single thirty-three-page chapter. A similar imbalance is maintained in the later *Memoirs* (1855), with a quarter of the book devoted to optics.

Aware that there was much more to be said and found out about Newton, Brewster approached the Portsmouth estate in 1837 and was given permission to inspect the papers in their possession. He had only a week at Hurstbourne Park and what he saw there was under the selection and guidance of H. A. Fellowes, brother of the mad third Earl of Portsmouth. This material was incorporated in the first volume of the *Memoirs* (1855). For the second volume Brewster never returned to Hurstbourne Park but was sent instead a 'collection of manuscripts and correspondence'.

Despite the limited access given Brewster to the PC his *Memoirs of the Life, Writings, and Discoveries of Sir Isaac Newton* (1855, 2 vols) contain an enormous amount of new material, much of it published in the forty-six appendices added to the book. The fourteen letters between Halley and Newton on the publication of *Principia* are here published for the first time, as are letters from the Abbé Conti, Pierre Varignon, Pepys, Bentley and several others. There is also a list of changes introduced into *Principia* (1726), the publication for the first time of several theological pieces, draughts of the General *Scholium*, and details of Newton's family.

There is much more in *Memoirs* than the simple publication of previously unknown material, for Brewster had seen for the first time what many people had previously suspected about Newton, that some elements of his thought were never revealed during his lifetime. Although much of this held no appeal for Brewster, he was too honest a man to ignore it. Thus he noted Newton's alchemy and conceded that Newton had indeed written about 'the transmutation and multiplication of metals . . . the discovery of the universal tincture'. How could, he asked, 'a mind of such power, and so nobly occupied with the abstractions of geometry . . . stoop to be even a copyist of the most contemptible alchemical poetry, and the annotator of a work . . . of a fool and a knave' (Brewster, pp. 374–5). Nor could Brewster refrain from offering excuses for Newton's strange behaviour. It could only have been 'a love of truth, a desire to make new discoveries in chemistry, and a wish to test the extraordinary pretensions of their predecessors' which led Newton into these studies.

Brewster went on to reveal Newton's Unitarian theology, his role in the publication of the *Commercium epistolicum*, his treatment of Flamsteed and his attitude to the apparently illicit relationship between Catherine Barton and Charles Montague. In each case Brewster found Newton quite blameless. Flamsteed was guilty of 'vulgar and offensive abuse'; Catherine 'never lived a single night under the roof of Lord Halifax'; while in the fluxions dispute, Brewster insisted, Newton's behaviour was 'at all times dignified and just'.

Such were Brewster's views, expressed freely and often. That today they appear naive and partisan is of little moment for it is from material first openly displayed by Brewster that we can at last see, clearly and precisely, how naive and partisan they are. As a later biographer put it, 'Brewster himself supplied the tools with which those who desired might tear down the image he set up' (Westfall, 1965b, p. xxxvii).

Editions have been surprisingly few, just the two Edinburgh editions of 1855 and 1860 and a New York Johnson Reprint of 1965. It is becoming increasingly hard to find an acceptable and modestly priced copy.

MORE

Brewster had done his job too well and he remained unchallenged for almost a century. This is not to deny that scholars like de Morgan (1885) and Rouse Ball (1893) produced monographs of great significance. Nor can the remarkable work of Ferdinand Rosenberger be ignored. His *Isaac Newton und seine physikalischen Principien* (1895) has turned out to be 'the only intellectual biography of Newton that exists' (Westfall, 1965b, p. xlii).

Outside these exceptions the biographical tradition continued to be dominated by Brewster. Thus the Newton article in the *Encyclopedia Britannica*, first written by Brewster for the seventh edition of 1842, remained substantially unchanged for nearly a century. Nor was Sir Richard Glazebrook's offer in the 1929 fourteenth edition any improvement; rather, with its reduced space and misprints, it was distinctly inferior.

It was thus left to the American physicist, L. T. More in 1934 to offer an alternative to Brewster's work. His attention had been called to our lack of 'any satisfactory critical biography' during the 1927 celebrations of the bicentenary of Newton's death. Brewster, despite his many virtues, More judged to be 'inadequate and untrustworthy'. As to his sources, More had access to the Portsmouth papers in the ULC. He did not examine the rest of the papers at Hurstbourne Park; instead, 'Blanche, Lady Portsmouth . . . sent their priceless collection . . . to the British Museum in order that I might examine and use it at my leisure'. Unfortunately More gives no indication of the extent of the papers delivered to him. It is unlikely that the entire Portsmouth Collection was moved to London for More's convenience.

There is a marked tendency for modern scholars to belittle More's efforts. Westfall has spoken of his 'annoying pomposity' and dismissed his work as an 'excessively long digest of previous scholarship' (1965b, p. xxxix). Manuel has complained of More's failure to divest himself 'of the conventional blinders of his predecessors' (1980, p. viii), while more recently Hall has described More as a 'reworked Brewster . . . from a quick glance at the Portsmouth family papers, and sauced . . . with his own prejudices' (1981, p. 172).

Yet, it must be said, More was at least available, while much of the 'previous scholarship' spoken of by Westfall could be found only in the libraries of collectors and universities. More was also generous in providing extracts from the manuscripts he examined, more generous in fact than Westfall in his even longer biography. Humphrey Newton's two letters to Conduitt, for example, are published by More in full (pp. 246–51). Nor was he as obsessed with optics as Brewster, and in consequence a fuller account is given of Newton's mechanics and other interests.

Yet it soon became clear that however much of the PC More had seen, he had used but a small portion of its riches. The Sotheby sale of 1936 showed how much more was to be done and that it would take decades rather than years. It was not, however, until after the Second World War that serious research could really begin. The first priority was to publish the more important of the papers; the biography would have to wait. Thus Whiteside began to prepare the mathematical papers for publication; Turnbull, Scott and Hall worked their way through the correspondence; while Cohen and Koyré started the work which eventually led to their critical edition of *Principia* (1972). It thus fell to Westfall to devote twenty years of his life to the preparation of the century's definitive biography of Newton. Long before this work was complete a study of a somewhat different kind was published by Manuel in 1968.

MANUEL

Manuel had already, in 1963, produced an impressive study of Newton's historical writings. His new book was described as a 'portrait' rather than a biography. Although it does tell the story of Newton's life, it is more concerned with the nature of his psyche. It omits much, and ignores all scientific detail. What remains is a controlled and detailed analysis of Newton's character, along with a bold attempt to identify the factors which produced that character.

The answers all lay in the relations between Newton, his mother, who apparently abandoned him as a child, the father he never knew, and the stepfather who stole his mother. Not only did such traumatic events shape Newton's personality, Manuel argued, they also moulded his science. Thus the fury he directed at rivals like Robert Hooke, Flamsteed and Leibniz who laid claims to his intellectual property was in reality aimed at those who had stolen his mother. Newton was in this way condemned to relive perpetually the anguish of this loss. Manuel further speculated on the state of mind of the young Newton, longing for his dead father and remarried mother. Could there not be, he mused, 'a relationship between this longing and a later intellectual structure in which a sort of an impulse or attraction is a key term descriptive of a force' (p. 83). Of all the seventeenth-century scientists, why was it Newton, Manuel asked, who put attractive forces so very much at the centre of his physics?

Few have followed Manuel in his analysis. Some have declared his work to be ill founded; others that, even if true, it is irrelevant to any real understanding of Newton and his work. More basically, Hall has charged, Manuel is over-reacting to the extreme hero worship of Brewster. Newton was admittedly no God, nor was he a devil (Hall, 1980, p. 220).

WESTFALL

In 1980 Westfall finally published his *Never at Rest*. Based on a full command of Newton's papers, correspondence and published work, it clearly aims to replace Brewster and to become, for the next generation at least, the definitive biography of Newton. Much more than any other previous biography it attempts to display the variety and complexity of Newton's work. Not only are the mathematics, optics and mechanics treated at some length, but equal space is provided for his alchemy, chronology and theology. It is undoubtedly, in Hall's words, 'the best biography' of Newton we have (1981, p. 172).

Westfall's picture of Newton has none the less been rejected by some as far too unattractive. Hall, for example, has found the description of Newton as 'solitary, bleak, self seeking, arrogant, fond of flattery, deceitful, self righteous' something of an exaggeration and certainly one sided.

SECONDARY BIOGRAPHIES

At the same time as Brewster, More and Westfall worked on their standard biographies, other scholars have been content to present their work in a briefer and more accessible form. There is little to choose between them apart from availability and price. All are derivative and based on secondary sources alone; all are brief and all attain their limited aims with a minimum of effort. None seems to be in print. They include the following.

1 Pullin, V. E. (1927) *Sir Isaac Newton, a biographical sketch*, London, Ernest Benn.

2 Brodetsky, S. (1927) *Sir Isaac Newton, a brief account of his life and work*, London, Methuen.

Both works were presumably written to catch the bicentenary of Newton's death. A second edition of Brodetsky appeared in 1929.

3 Vavilov, S. I. (1943) *Isaac Newton*, Moscow/Leningrad, Academy of Sciences. The first Russian biography. It has been translated into Roumanian (1947), German (1948), Serbian (1950), Polish (1952), Slovak (1952) and Italian (1954).

4 Pla, Cortes (1945) *Elogio di Newton*, Buenos Aires, Epasa-Calpe. The first (?) Spanish biography.

5 Andrade, E. N. da C. (1950) *Isaac Newton*, London, Max Parrish, Personal Portrait series.

6 Andrade, E. N. da C. (1954) *Sir Isaac Newton*, London, Collins, Brief Lives, Number 11. Essentially the same work as 5.

Both 5 and 6 were written as entries in popular biographical series. Andrade, with his knowledge of Newton's papers and his command of the physics of the period, was capable of something more ambitious.

7 Anthony, H. D. (1960) *Sir Isaac Newton*, London, Northumberland Press.

8 North, J. D. (1967) *Isaac Newton*, Oxford, Clarendon Press.
9 Ronan, C. A. (1969) *Sir Isaac Newton*, London, Butler & Tanner.
10 Rattansi, P. M. (1974) *Isaac Newton and Gravity*, London, Priory Press.

MISCELLANEOUS

A number of works, though not strictly speaking biographies, contain much biographical information and are too important to ignore. Amongst such works the following are essential elements in any analysis of Newton's biographical tradition.

1 Edleston, J. (1850) *Correspondence of Sir Isaac Newton and Professor Cotes*. With its 'synoptical view of Newton's life' (pp. xxi–lxxxi) it is a rich source for previously unpublished details of Newton's life. It is especially valuable on Newton's life in Cambridge and is available in a 1969 reprint.

2 de Morgan, A. (1885) *Newton: his Friend: his Niece*. The most detailed study yet made of the Barton affair. As with any other work of de Morgan, much valuable data on other topics is also included. It was reprinted in 1968.

3 de Morgan, A. (1914) *Essays on the Life and Work of Newton*. Amongst other items it contains de Morgan's 1856 biography of Newton contributed to *The Cabinet Portrait Gallery of British Worthies* and his long and important review of Brewster (1855) first published in 1856 in the *North British Review*.

4 de Villamil, R. (1931) *Newton, the Man*. As it contains the complete *Inventory* of Newton's estate, it remains an indispensable work. It also contains a valuable discussion of Newton's finances. It was reprinted in 1972.

Biot, Jean Baptiste (1774–1862)

After an early period as a gunner in the French revolutionary army, Biot spent the bulk of his life as a Professor of Physics at the *Collège de France* in Paris. His most important work concerned the optical activity of crystals and molecules.

Biot also made two notable contributions to Newtonian studies. In 1821 in the *Biographie universelle* he presented the first modern critical study of Newton's life and career. Later, in 1856, in collaboration with F. Lefort, he published a new edition of the *Commercium epistolicum* which included the variants between the first and second editions of 1713 and 1722.

See also Biography

Birch, Thomas (1705–66)

A self-educated historian, biographer, editor and pamphleteer, Birch was ordained in 1730 and served as secretary of the RS from 1752 to 1765. In this latter role he published a four-volume *History of the Royal Society* (1756–7) in which he transcribed the minutes of the Society and the Council up to 1687. He also reprinted many papers read before the Society but not printed in the *PT*; amongst these in vol. III, pp. 247–305 was the first publication of Newton's *An Hypothesis Explaining the Properties of Light* and the *Discourse of Observations*. Birch also published for the first time Newton's 1679 *Letter to Boyle* in vol. I, pp. 70–4 of his five-volume edition of *The Works of Robert Boyle* (1744), and Newton's *A Dissertation upon the Sacred Cubit of the Jews* in vol. II, pp. 405–33 in his edition of *The Miscellaneous Works of John Greaves* (Greaves, 1737). Birch also, in his contribution to the Newton entries in the *General Dictionary* (1738, vol. VII, pp. 776–802) and the *Biographia Britannica* (1760, vol. V, pp. 3210–44), laid down the main outlines of Newtonian biography and science to be followed by all other writers, until they were superseded a century later by the work of Sir David Brewster.

Blake, William (1757–1827)

The son of a London hosier and with no formal education, Blake was apprenticed to an engraver in 1771. Although he produced a substantial body of work – engravings, paintings and poetry – it was largely ignored by his contemporaries. Only the support of his friend John Linnell in commissioning some of his later work kept him from total poverty towards the end of his life. Later generations, however, have experienced less difficulty in appreciating the strange, powerful and uncommonly obscure vision proclaimed by Blake.

One thing clear in Blake is his consistent and total opposition to Newton and his work. Blake's objections were deeper and more powerfully felt than the better known Keatsian complaint that rainbows no longer look pretty after a course of Newtonian optics. Blake had a more complex and less clearly defined target. The newly emerging industrial machine, the primacy of reason, the claims of experience over innocence, of measurement over intuition, all became identified for Blake with the threatening figure of Newton. Art, he declared, 'was the tree of life', science 'the tree of death'.

Blake's most powerful representation of Newton can be seen in the Tate Gallery, London. A large monotype print, it dates from about 1795 when Blake produced a series of twelve prints, amongst which were the well known 'Newton' and the equally familiar 'Nebuchadnezzar'. The

'Newton' print is a mysterious object, the subject of much speculative interpretation. Newton is seen sitting naked on a rock, leaning forward to examine on the floor before him a diagram of a semicircle inscribed within a triangle. Hanging from his far shoulder a white cloth falls to the floor, joining imperceptibly with the scroll of paper on which the diagram has been drawn. He is staring intently at the ground, examining the diagram. One hand points to the figure while a pair of compasses held in the other hand are being used to measure the triangle's base.

The curious pose adopted by Newton is apparently taken from the figure of Abias, a supporter of a Persian sibyl, as drawn by Michelangelo on the Sistine ceiling. Beyond this all is speculation. The location of the scene has been variously placed as the bottom of a lake, Plato's cave, or any dark corner of the world suitable for optical experiments. The diagram itself seems to be unrelated to anything present in the *Opticks* or any other of Newton's works and is, presumably, no more than a random geometrical diagram. Gage (1971), however, has argued that it is based on diagrams from Book I, part I, of the *Opticks*, with the triangle representing a prism and the semicircle the passage of a ray of light, so shaped as to stand for the arc of the rainbow. On this interpretation the cloth becomes the white light from which the colours of the rainbow emerge. Alternatively, it has been seen as a reference to the 'Loom of Locke' taken from the Newton section in *Jerusalem* (Book I, line 15).

The symbolism of the compass, an image also appearing in the Blake print 'The Ancient of Days', has been investigated by Blunt (1938–9). Traditionally, stemming from Proverbs 8:27 ('When he set a compass upon the face of the depth'), it symbolised the imposition of order on chaos. By the time of the Renaissance, however, it took on a second meaning, standing indifferently for maths, science and philosophy. In Blake, Blunt has argued, compasses are seen as a sign not of God but of Urizen (your reason), the villain of Blake's *Prophetic Books*. Compasses are, thus, instruments for binding the Infinite, and for the destruction of the imagination.

It thus seems that the Newton/Urizen figure is displaying the poverty of his imagination by ignoring the heavens and staring, animal like, at the ground. Further, diverting his gaze from the wonders of God's creation, he concentrates instead on the measurement of an abstract object.

Newton also appears in the series of *Prophetic Books* published in the 1790s. The symbols adopted are numerous and also, somewhat confusingly, variable. The basic scheme, as presented in *Europe* (1794), saw the eighteenth century opening as a time in need of salvation. First, however, came Newton, the representative of Urizen, and with him all the errors of rationalism so apparent to anyone living in Blake's day. These errors were exposed and destroyed by Orc, the son of Los and

Enitharmon, the spirit of revolt as typified by the French and American Revolutions. Similar themes were pursued in *The Song of Los* (1795). Again there is a reference to the completion of the 'Philosophy of Five Senses' and the action of Urizen to put it 'into the hands of Newton & Locke'. The poem ends with the rise of Orc 'like a pillar of fire above the Alps'.

See also Poetic tradition

Boulliau, Ismael (1605–94)

A Catholic priest, Boulliau nevertheless supported Gassendi and Galileo. As a scholar he edited the first printed edition of Theon's *Arithmetica* while, as an observational astronomer working with Mira Ceti in 1667, he established for the first time the periodicity of a variable star.

His most influential work, however, was his *Astronomica philolaica* (1645), the text from which many astronomers derived their knowledge of Kepler's three laws. Whereas Kepler had sought for a physical cause for the elliptical orbits adopted by the planets, Boulliau insisted that geometry alone was sufficient. Planets, he declared, had an innate tendency to move in an ellipse and did so independently of any other body. Boulliau went on to reject Kepler's second area law which connected the orbiting planet to the sun sited at one of the ellipse's foci. The law was notoriously difficult to apply and also had the consequence of finding no use for the second of the ellipse's foci. Boulliau made the apparently empty second focus an equant point; that is, a point from which the planet in its orbit would appear to move with uniform motion. Boulliau modified his version of the second law in 1657 by adding to the equant an auxiliary circle taking as its diameter the major axis of the ellipse. Boulliau's versions of the area law became known to English astronomers, including Newton, through the derivative works of Seth Ward, Vincent Wing and Thomas Streete.

See also Ellipses and elliptical orbits; Kepler, Johann and Kepler's laws

Boyle lectures

Robert Boyle died in 1691. His will stipulated that rent of £50 from a property in London be used 'To settle an annual salary for some divine or preaching minister . . . To preach eight sermons in the year for proving the Christian religion against notorious infidels, viz, Atheists, Deists, Pagans, Jews, and Mahometans', without, Boyle prudently added, 'descending to any controversies that are amongst Christians themselves'. Four trustees were appointed: the diarist John Evelyn; the future Archbishop of Canterbury, Thomas Tenison; Sir Henry Ashurst; and Sir John Rotherham.

The lectures proved to be one of the main channels through which Newtonian science passed to the general public; from them, in turn, Newton's ideas were able to assume an unrivalled legitimacy and authority. The first lectures were delivered by Richard Bentley in 1692 under the title *A Confutation of Atheism*, and published in the following year. Bentley began by attacking the atheism of Spinoza and Hobbes but turned, in the final three lectures, to the demonstration of how Newtonian mechanics demanded the existence of an intelligent, omnipotent creator. While preparing the lectures for publication Bentley approached Newton for advice on a number of points and succeeded in extracting from him four important letters. They were eventually published as *Four Letters from Sir Isaac Newton to Doctor Bentley* in 1756.

Other well-known Newtonians followed. Samuel Clarke in 1704–5, William Whiston in 1707, and William Derham in 1711–12, for example, preached and wrote on the sound Newtonian principles adopted by God at the creation. Some of the published versions of the lectures became extremely popular, with Derham's *Physico-theology* (1714) reaching in 1768 an exceptional thirteenth edition. In 1739 the lectures already delivered were collected and published in three volumes. A full list of these and later lectures can be seen in Fulton (1961).

The lectures have recently been the subject of an important study by M. C. Jacob (1976) in which she has argued that for the Latitudinarian wing of the Church of England 'Newton's natural philosophy served as underpinning for the social ideology developed by the church after the Revolution' (p. 177). One of the main channels through which they sought to express such views, Jacob has argued, was the Boyle lectures.

Boyle, Robert (1627–91)

The son of the Earl of Cork, Boyle spent his life variously on the family estates in Dorset, in Oxford, and in London pursuing the life of a scientific virtuoso. Boyle's early influence on Newton is evident in numerous entries in the *Philosophical* and *Chemistry Notebooks* of the 1660s. A further sign of the respect accorded Boyle can be seen in the twenty-three works of Boyle, by far the largest holding of a single author, listed in Newton's library. Although several had been presented to Newton by the author, they show sufficient dog-earing to indicate wide use. They first met in 1675 when Newton attended his first meeting of the RS. Only two letters between the two scientists have survived. While Boyle's letter was a relatively trivial communication, Newton's letter to Boyle of 1679 contained important speculations about the nature of the ether and proposed a mechanism by which gravity could operate (*C*, II, pp. 288–95).

Newton and Boyle continued to correspond and to see each other throughout the 1680s. In 1687 Newton instructed Halley to present Boyle with a copy of *Principia*. He also seems to have attended Boyle's funeral in London some four years later.

See also Boyle lectures; Mechanical philosophy

Brattle, Thomas (1658–1713)

The son of a wealthy trader and landowner, Brattle was educated at Harvard. Using the 3½-ft telescope of Winthrop, he observed the 1680 comet. Details were printed in a 1681 almanac and sent to Flamsteed in Greenwich, who passed them on to Newton. The results were included in Newton's analysis of cometary orbits in Book III, prop. XLI of *Principia*. Brattle was not actually mentioned by name, but as 'the observer in New England' he became the first American to make a publicly acknowledged contribution to Newtonian mechanics. It might be thought that Brattle should share his position with an Arthur Storer from Maryland, whose observations are recorded in the same section of *Principia*. Storer, however, was no American but a nephew of Humphrey Babington and a friend of Newton's childhood.

See also Newton in America

Breakdown

Sometime in 1693 Newton undoubtedly suffered a nervous breakdown. Its cause, duration and severity are all matters of speculation; its existence, however, is openly revealed in the pages of the *Correspondence*. Thus to Pepys on 13 September 1693 he confessed that he was 'extremely troubled at the embroilment I am in, and have neither ate nor slept well this twelve month, nor have my former consistency of mind'. He went on to conclude that he must 'withdraw from your acquaintance, and see neither you nor the rest of my friends any more' (*C*, III, p. 279).

Pepys was sufficiently alarmed, or intrigued, to ask John Millington, a Fellow of Magdalene, Cambridge, to check on Newton. Millington reported on 30 September that he had seen Newton in Huntingdon. Newton, he reported, had expressed his concern for the Pepys letter, putting it down to a 'distemper that much seized his head, and that kept him awake for above five nights together'.

Locke also heard from Newton. On 16 September Newton wrote,

already emerging from the breakdown, apologising for having thought of his friend as endeavouring 'to embroil me with woemen', as being 'a Hobbist', and for 'saying or thinking that there was a designe to sell me an office'. In a further letter to Locke dated 15 October Newton once more sought the cause of his complaint.

> The last winter by sleeping too often by my fire I got an ill habit of sleeping and a distemper wch this summer has been epidemical put me further out of order, so that when I wrote to you I had not slept an hour a night for a fortnight together and for 5 nights together not a wink.

The breakdown seems to have been a relatively short affair. By September 1693 Newton was beginning to have some insight into his condition and shortly thereafter he was resuming his mathematical correspondence with Leibniz (16 October 1693), solving problems in probability theory for Pepys (November–December 1693), and discussing the text of Revelation with Mill (January 1694). If he was, therefore, cured by late 1693, when did the breakdown begin?

Newton was intellectually fit at the start of the year, as can be seen from his series of letters to Bentley, one of the most lucid expositions of his work he ever produced, which he completed on 25 February 1693. Thereafter there are only three Newton letters before the shock of the Pepys letter of September. Two of these, to Fatio de Duillier in March, were brief notes concerned with the payment of a £14 bill; the third, dated 30 May, to Otto Mencke, was equally trivial and concerned the receipt of a full run of *Acta Eruditorum* from 1682 to August 1692. There is no sign of any tension in Newton's style or thought. The third letter does end in mid sentence ('Quid'), but this was later explained by Newton when he completed the letter in November by his having mislaid the letter amongst his papers (C, III, pp. 291–2).

This would suggest that the breakdown can be restricted to the summer of 1693, and is marked by the absence of any letters. In June he was in London, possibly for as long as two weeks; he was also, according to his notebooks, working at his chemical experiments. As any breakdown in London must surely have been noticed, it can be safely assumed that it can only have become noticeable in July, August or September.

As to its cause there is Newton's own explanation of 'sleeping too often by my fire'. A modified form of Newton's poisoning theory has recently substituted the more potent mercury as the causative agent (Johnson and Wolbrasht, 1979, pp. 1–9). Confirmation of this view was offered by analyses of surviving samples of Newton's hair carried out by Spargo and Pounds (1979, pp. 11–32). Samples obtained from the Portsmouth family and TCC contained anything up to fifty times the normal level of mercury. Nor, they argued, should this cause any surprise. Newton was known to have used mercury in many of his chemical experiments and to have been none too careful about its handling. Further, it is claimed, the symptoms of the breakdown fitted well with clinical descriptions of mercury poisoning.

Against such claims Westfall has objected that Newton failed to show the characteristic symptoms of tremor, loss of teeth, and that, though mercury poisoning is thought to produce long-term effects, Newton had made a full recovery within a matter of a few months. An even more damaging review of the mercury hypothesis has been undertaken by Ditchburn (1980, pp. 1–16). Even if we could be sure that the hair did belong to Newton, the measurements recorded of mercury contamination are dismissed as valueless in giving any indication of its concentration in the central nervous system. Further, to account for a nervous breakdown in 1693, the hair would have had to be cut not too long after that date – an unlikely coincidence. In any case, Ditchburn concluded, as Spargo and Pounds had failed to include any controls in their analysis, or to exclude later sources of mercury contamination, their results were 'meaningless'. The evidence, such as it was, seemed to Ditchburn to be 'much more consistent with the very common disease of depressive illness than with the very uncommon one of mercurialism'.

Whatever the cause, the news of the event was soon known around Europe. Huygens had heard by mid-1694 and informed Leibniz. Soon English scholars like John Wallis were hearing from their Continental colleagues that Newton's friends had been forced to have him locked up.

Little more was heard of the event until Biot once more brought the issue up a century later. He added, however, a new touch. It was the breakdown of the 1790s, he declared, which accounted for Newton's lack of productivity in the last forty years of his life. All he was capable of were the trivial pursuits of theology and chronology and the occasional publication of work completed before the breakdown. Biot was, in fact, wrong on both counts.

The theological and chronological interests were far from new, but had both been the subject of much previous study over a period of twenty years or more. Further, while it is true that a book like the *Opticks* (1704) was based on earlier work, Newton did continue to work on new ideas. The many changes in the second edition of *Principia* and the work on his lunar theory are evidence enough of his continuing interest in science. If Biot's complaint is that Newton produced nothing new after 1693, it could be retorted just how many scientists over fifty *do* produce work of any originality? In this sense Biot's conclusion is supported by Westfall, who judges that in both theology and science Newton 'devoted the remaining thirty-four years of his life to reworking the results of earlier endeavours' (RSW, p. 540).

Brewster, Sir David (1781–1868)

The first and greatest biographer of Newton was born in Jedburgh, Roxburghshire, the son of a headmaster, and educated at Edinburgh University. Although he originally intended to enter the church, and was accordingly ordained in 1804, Brewster chose instead to make a career in science. It proved more difficult than he had any right to expect. Despite the backing of several leading figures, he failed to obtain the chair of maths at Edinburgh in 1805 or at St Andrews in 1807. Nor, twenty-five years later, with an established reputation in science, was he more fortunate in his applications for professorial positions.

Brewster was thus forced to finance his scientific work by his inventions and by his onerous editorial duties. From 1802 onwards he edited the *Edinburgh Magazine* and, beginning in 1807, he also found himself responsible for the eighteen volumes of the *Edinburgh Encyclopedia* as they appeared over the next twenty years. In addition he contributed over one hundred articles to the reviews of his day, wrote 315 scientific papers, published the two substantial works, *Treatise on the Kaleidoscope* (1819) and *Treatise on Optics* (1831), and was responsible for much other literary work. Recognition came late in life. In 1829 he was awarded a government pension of £100 a year, and in 1837 he received his first academic appointment, Principal of United Colleges, St Andrews.

As a scientist Brewster worked mainly in the field of optics and is best known for his work on polarisation and his discovery of the since-known Brewster's law. His career in optics is of some interest, for Brewster was one of the few who stood resolutely against the triumphant spread of the undulatory theory of light in the early years of the nineteenth century. He never seems to have wavered in his allegiance to Newtonian optics, with its commitment to a corpuscular view of light. This was not quite as reactionary as it might initially seem, as the undulatory theory, after its first success in describing the facts of interference, soon became distinctly less attractive when it failed to make much sense of the newly discovered phenomenon of polarisation. With, however, the demonstration by A. Fresnel in 1818 that light was transmitted not longitudinally but as a transverse wave, the corpuscular theory lost much of its remaining plausibility. Brewster responded with a restatement of Newton's theory of fits. It found little support.

A recent article in *New Scientist* in commemoration of the bicentenary of his birth was entitled 'Who remembers David Brewster?' (Cochran, 1981) It confined itself to Brewster's scientific research and could thus only answer historians of optics. In fact as a biographer of Newton, Brewster's work is regularly read, quoted and argued over. It is also still in print. His first attempt, *The Life of Sir Isaac Newton* (1831), turned into a trial run for his masterpiece, *Memoirs of the Life, Writings and Discoveries of Sir Isaac Newton* (1855, 2 vols; second edition, 1860).

Although Brewster set out to defend Newton against the apparently well-argued and documented attacks being made against both his character and work, he was far too honest a scholar to deliberately mislead his audience. His preferred method of defence was to be more knowledgeable than the critics and to this end he made the first careful examination of the unpublished papers of Newton in the PC. He continued to defend Newton against all attacks. Nowhere, however, did his work sink into the inane apologetics of so much Victorian biography.

Two features above all saved Brewster's work from such a disastrous fate. The first, already mentioned, lay in Brewster's honesty. Although he found much in the PC to worry him – Newton's interest in alchemy, for example, he found particularly hard to take – he none the less felt compelled to report what he found. It is thus from Brewster that readers first saw something of the complexity of Newton's personality and first glimpsed something of the enormous range of Newton's intellectual interests. Secondly, Brewster added to his text forty-six appendices containing some of the basic documents and letters about Newton's life and work. The result has been to make Brewster, though hopelessly out of date on many aspects of Newton, still a rich source of material.

See also Biography; Wave theory of light

Briggs, William (1642–1704)

In the period 1682–5 William Briggs, a physician at St Thomas's Hospital, London, entered into a correspondence with Newton on the subject of his new theory of vision. Although Briggs's part of the correspondence has been lost, three of Newton's replies have survived (*C*, II, pp. 377–8, 381–5, 417–19). They had been at Cambridge together as students and had apparently helped each other to dissect an eye. Briggs was anxious to hear Newton's comments on a paper he had published earlier in 1682.

The subject was binocular vision. Briggs proposed that the brain was connected to corresponding parts of the two retinas by nerves of exactly equal length and tension. They would thus present one impression to the mind, in the same way as two strings struck in unison appear to make a single sound. After Newton's usual coy beginning, that he was 'of all men grown ye most shy of putting pen to paper', he presented a detailed critique of Briggs's paper. He argued that the mind did not respond so much to identical retinal images, but to images which fell on the same retinal sites. As evidence he produced the experiments conducted on himself and described in the Chemistry Notebook in which he changed the shape of the retina by pressing a bodkin behind his eye.

Briggs replied to Newton's arguments in the *PT* (1683) and reprinted both papers in Latin translation in his *Ophthalmographia* (1685).

Brougham, Henry, 1st Baron Brougham and Vaux (1778–1868)

A leading jurist and politician of his day, Brougham had been involved with such important public events as the defence of Queen Caroline in 1820, the abolition of the slave trade in 1807, the founding of London University in the 1820s, and the passage of the great reform bill in 1832. He served as Lord Chancellor from 1830 to 1834.

Brougham was also a prolific writer. Educated at the University of Edinburgh, he qualified for the Scottish bar in 1800 and shortly afterwards in 1802 helped to found the *Edinburgh Review*. For the rest of his life he turned out scores of articles for the *Edinburgh* and other reviews of the period. In 1839, after the virtual end of his political career, Brougham published an edition of Paley's *Natural Theology* to which he added his own *Dissertations on Subjects of Science Connected with National Theology* (vol. II, pp. 243–480). The *Dissertation* was republished in 1855 as *Analytical View of Sir Isaac Newton's Principia*. It was, however, much revised by his collaborator E. J. Routh, who also extended the scope of the work to include material from Books II and III of *Principia*. The work, still the fullest analysis of *Principia* in English, is available in a facsimile reprint edited by Cohen (1972).

Earlier in his career Brougham had written extensively on optical problems, striving to preserve Newton's corpuscular theory of light against the objections of Thomas Young. Brougham's work thus did much to delay the acceptance in England of the undulatory theory of light. He himself sought to develop a system of optics more extreme than even Newton had ever contemplated. It demanded only the existence of attractive and repulsive forces, while firmly denying the need to assume any such medium as the ether. He argued, rather, that the properties of light could all be derived from the assumption that it was composed of particles of varying sizes.

In later life Brougham, presumably through his title and the high office he had once held, came to be seen as the senior Newtonian of the day. Consequently on such official occasions as the unveiling of the Theed statue in Grantham in 1858, Brougham was invariably to be found occupying the most prominent position and delivering the leading address.

Brouncker, Lord William (c.1620–1684)

Born in Ireland, Brouncker was educated at Oxford where he graduated in medicine. A founder member of the Royal Society, he served as its President from 1662 to 1677. He is best known, however, for his mathematical work. In particular he succeeded in expressing $\pi/4$ as a continued fraction; he also worked on the quadrature and rectification of various curves. It was perhaps news of the progress of Brouncker and others in the 1660s, fed to Newton by Barrow, that led him to prepare his own *De analysi* and to reveal it to selected friends.

Bruce, Jacob (1670–1735)

Of Scottish descent, the family had emigrated to Russia in 1647. Bruce was a courtier of Peter the Great as well as being an engineer. When Peter undertook in 1697 his remarkable trip to the West, he took Bruce with him and, presumably, charged him with the task of mastering as much Western science and mathematics as he could manage in the time available.

To this end he took lessons from a certain Ivan Kolsun (John Colson perhaps) and collected as much of the basic literature as he could find, both then and later. Much of this was, inevitably, Newtonian. An inventory published in 1759 shows that he had imported into Russia two copies of the *Opticks*, several *Principia*, including Motte's translation of 1729 and the Amsterdam edition of 1714, the *Universal Arithmetick*, *System of the World* and several volumes of the *PT*. In addition Bruce returned to Russia with a large number of secondary works by such authors as J. Rohault, D. Gregory and W. 'sGravesande. On his return home Bruce became the first to publish in Russian a book on Newtonian science. It was a translation of the *Cosmotheoros* (1696) of Christian Huygens. Not surprisingly, it was also Bruce who constructed the first Russian reflecting telescope.

See also Newton in Russia

Burnet, Thomas (1635–1715)

After a period at Cambridge, Burnet was appointed Master of Charterhouse in 1685. He was also the author of one of the most notorious books of the age, *Telluris theoria sacra* (1681–9, Sacred Theory of Earth). In it Burnet described an antediluvian world lacking mountains and seas, 'with not a wrinkle, scar, or fracture', and consequently spent much time seeking processes whereby the postdiluvian earth could emerge naturally from its initial state. Late in 1680 he sought the aid of Newton and asked him to comment on the completed manuscript.

Two letters from Newton to Burnet have survived (*C*, II, pp. 319, 329–34). In the course of the discussion Newton issued some general thoughts on the relation of earth history to scripture and to God. The description Moses had offered of creation was in no sense a literal one. Rather, it was expressed 'in a language artificially adapted to ye sense of ye vulgar'. On the difficult question of the origin of earth's rotation Newton confessed:

> I know no sufficient natural cause . . . Where natural causes are at hand God uses them but I doe not think them alone sufficient for ye creation and therefore may be allowed to suppose that . . . God gave the earth its motions by such degrees and at such times as was most suitable to ye creatures.

See also Age of the earth

C

Cajori, Florian (1859–1930)

Born in Switzerland, the son of an engineer, Cajori arrived in the US in 1875. He was educated at the universities of Wisconsin and Johns Hopkins and taught at Colorado College from 1889 until 1918, when he was appointed Professor of the History of Mathematics at the University of California.

The author of a large number of papers and books on the history of mathematics, his most original work is probably his *History of Mathematical Notation* (1928–9, 2 vols). He had almost completed his revision of Motte's English translation of *Principia* when he died in 1930. He aimed to 'render certain parts into modern phraseology . . . and to append historical and critical notes'. The work, seen through the press by R. T. Crawford in 1934, may have failed to realise Cajori's intentions. It remains none the less the standard available translation and is unlikely to face any competition in the near future.

See also Principia, Translations

Calendrical writings

There are few specifically calendrical, as opposed to chronological, writings in the Newton canon, and of these even fewer have been published. The only fully published work is:

1 'Form of the most ancient year', *Gentleman's Magazine*, 1755, vol. XXV, pp. 3–5.

Also known are a number of manuscripts.

2 *Considerations about rectifying the Julian Kalendar*, described by Brewster (1855, vol. II, pp. 311–12). There are two manuscript copies in the PC.

3 *Reguale pro determinatione Paschae*, described by Brewster (1855, vol. II, p. 312). There are two manuscript copies in the PC.

4 British Museum Add. MS 6489 contains four untitled and undated pages in Newton's hand on ancient calendars. Extracts were published in Edleston (1850, pp. 314–15). Included is the original of 1 above.

5 Yahuda Collection, Newton MS 24 contains similar material to 4 above.

There are also a couple of discussions of calendrical problems in published works.

6 *Chronology* (1728, pp. 71–81) repeats the substance of 4 above.

7 *Observations* (1733, Chapter xi) is concerned with the question of determining the exact dates of the birth and passion of Christ.

Caroline of Anspach (1683–1737)

The daughter of the Margrave of Brandenburg-Anspach, Caroline was brought up in various German courts before her marriage in 1705 to George Augustus of Hanover, the future George II of England. With the death of Queen Anne in 1714, Caroline and George Augustus, now Prince and Princess of Wales, left Hanover for London. In 1727, on the death of George I, she began her ten-year reign as one of England's more notable Queens.

Through her position in the courts of Hanover and London she had come to know and admire both Leibniz and Newton. It is in fact due to her intervention that the important correspondence between Samuel Clarke, her chaplain, and Leibniz began in 1715. It was also Caroline who succeeded in extracting from a reluctant Newton the notes which were eventually published as *A Short Chronicle*.

Caroline, if only for her sense of humour, must have been a somewhat incongrous figure amongst the grim and forbidding scientists of her day. When the Astronomer Royal, John Flamsteed, complained to her that Newton was 'a great rascal' who had stolen two of his stars, she could only respond with a fit of giggles.

See also A Short Chronicle; Leibniz–Clarke correspondence

Carter, Elizabeth (1717–1806)

One of the able but little-known woman scholars of the eighteenth century, she was a largely self-taught daughter of a clergyman. Although best known for her edition of Epictetus in 1758, she was sufficiently well-read in science to translate into English Algarotti's *Il Newtonianismo per le dame* (1737) under the title *Sir Isaac Newton's Philosophy Explained for the Use of Ladies*. It proved to be a popular work; two editions appeared in 1739 and four further editions in 1742, 1752, 1765 and 1772. A friend of Dr Johnson who, although he had judged that 'A man is generally better pleased when he has a good dinner on his table than when his wife talks Greek', had gone on to add that Elizabeth Carter 'could make a pudding as well as translate Epictetus, and work a handkerchief as well as compose a poem'.

Castillioneus, Johann (1704–92)

Born Giovanni Salvemini in Castiglione, Tuscany, he studied mathematics and law at Pisa before moving to Switzerland and adopting a new name taken from his birthplace. He remained in Switzerland until 1751 and subsequently spent thirteen years at the University of Utrecht in Holland before finally settling in 1764 at the Berlin Academy of Frederick the Great. It is sometimes supposed, in bookseller's catalogues for example, that Castillioneus published in 1744 an eight-volume edition of the collected works of Newton. The set, however, is a hybrid composed from the three-volumes of the Geneva *Principia* (1739–42), the 1740 *Optice*, Castillioneus's own edition of the *Arithmetica universalis* (1761), and his three-volume *Opuscula mathematica, philosophica, et philologica* (Lausanne and Geneva, 1744). The *Opuscula* contains the following works.

> *Tome* I Mathematica: *De analysi* (1711); *Methodis fluxionum* (1736); *De quadratura* (1706); *Enumeratio* (1706); *Methodus differentialis* (1711); solutions to the challenge problems of 1697 and 1716; excerpts from correspondence with John Wallis, John Chamberlayne, Abbé Conti, John Collins and Henry Oldenburg, including the texts of the *Epistola prior* and the *Epistola posterior* as they appeared in the *CE*.

> *Tome* II Philosophica: *De mundi systemate* (1731); *Lectiones opticae* (1729); papers from the *PT* (numbers 80–5, 86, 88, 96, 97, 110, 121, 128 on the subject of light and colour); *De natura acidorum* (1736); *Scala graduum caloris* (1701).

> *Tome* III Philologica: *A Short Chronical* (1728); *The Chronology of Ancient Kingdoms Amended* (1728); paper on chronology from *PT* (1725); *Observations Upon the Prophecies* (1737); *Dissertation upon the Sacred Cubit* (1737).

All works, whatever their original language, are in Latin. The dates in brackets refer to the edition from which the text was derived.

See also Horsley, Samuel

Cavalieri, Francesco Bonaventura (1598–1647)

A pupil and colleague of Galileo, Cavalieri served from 1629 onwards as Professor of Mathematics at Bologna University. In his best-known work, *Geometria indivisibilibus* (1635, The Geometry of Indivisibles), Cavalieri enunciated his principle of indivisibles in which he argued that a line was made up of an infinite number of points, a surface of an infinite number of lines, and a volume of an infinite number of surfaces. By its means Cavalieri was able to calculate the area and volume of a number of figures and thus introduced into mathematics new techniques of integration.

See also Fabri, Honoré

Centrifugal force

The term was introduced into physics by C. Huygens in 1673 in his *De vi centrifuga*. Huygens used the term to describe the tendency of some bodies to recede from the centre, as when a stone tied to a piece of string is swung around a central point. It was measured by Huygens by v^2/r, where v refers to the stone's velocity and r the radius of its orbit. The same result is to be found in papers of Newton dating from the 1660s. Newton went on in the 1684–5 period to model his introduction of the term centripetal force on the earlier usage of Huygens.

See also Centripetal force

Centripetal force

The term was coined by Newton and appeared first as definition I of *De motu corporum in gyrum*: 'I call centripetal that force by which a body is impelled or drawn towards any point which is regarded as a centre of force' (Herivel, 1965, p. 277). It was repeated in later manuscripts before appearing in its definitive form as definition V of *Principia*: 'A centripetal force is that by which bodies are drawn or impelled, or any way tend, towards a point as to a centre' (Cajori, p. 2). Examples of the force are gravity ('by which bodies tend to the centre of the earth'), magnetism ('by which iron tends to the loadstone'), and that force, whatever it may be, 'by which the planets are continually drawn aside from the rectilinear motions . . . and made to revolve in curvilinear orbits'. The following definitions VI–VIII dealt with the absolute quantity, the accelerative quantity, and the motive quantity of centripetal force, respectively.

The term had been clearly inspired by the expression centrifugal force, coined by Huygens in 1673 and meant to account for the tendency of certain bodies to flee from the centre. Centripetal forces were, in this way, forces which imposed on bodies a tendency to seek a centre. Newton himself described the origin of the term.

> Mr Huygens gave the name of vis centrifuga to the force by which revolving bodies recede from the centre of their motion. Mr Newton in honour of that author retained the name and called the contrary force vis centripeta. (COHEN, 1980, p. 237)

Huygens had defined centrifugal force as v^2/r, where v is the velocity of the orbiting body and r the radius of the orbit. Since the only difference between the two forces was one of direction, the same v^2/r relationship holds for both concepts. In the *Scholium* to prop. V of Book III of *Principia* Newton finally identified its true nature:

> The force which retains the celestial bodies in their orbits has been hitherto called centripetal force; but it being now made plain that it can be no other than a gravitating force, we shall hereafter call it gravity. (CAJORI, p. 410)

See also Centrifugal force

Chaloner, William (–1699)

According to Newton, Chaloner was 'A jappaner in clothes threadbare, ragged and daubed with colours, turned coiner and in a short time put on the habit of a gentleman'. He proved to be the best known coiner of his day and the one most remembered for his boldness in challenging the probity of Newton. He died on the Tyburn gallows on 22 March 1699. He was well enough known to warrant the publication of a popular biography, *Guzman Redivivus* (1699), in which it was claimed, with some justification, that scorning the 'petty Rogueries of Tricking single Men', he aimed rather at 'imposing upon a whole Kingdom'.

In addition to coining pistoles and guineas, Chaloner came to the attention of the authorities as an informer. He would first persuade printers to prepare Jacobite literature, only to inform on them, for a reward of £1,000, when they produced the documents. Arrested for coining and clipping, he escaped by informing on his former colleagues. Not satisfied with such spectacular successes, Chaloner seems to have formulated a plan to infiltrate the Mint. To this end he accused 'that Worthy Gentleman Isaac Newton Esqu' of conniving 'at many Abuses and Cheats' committed at the Mint. To a Parliamentary Committee meeting in 1697 Chaloner charged that the Mint actually engaged in counterfeiting and took insufficient care to prevent their own coins being forged. Some took him seriously and Chaloner began to dream of gaining high office in the Mint.

Newton was to prove unduly sensitive to any complaints made against his handling of the affairs of the Mint, and against such charges he would gather multiple drafts presenting his own case in formidable detail. Against Chaloner Newton responded by gaining as much information as he could from a whole string of informers about his background and plans. Arrested by Newton in 1697, Chaloner won his release. Newton continued to gather data and extract confessions from his colleagues.

Arrested once more in November 1698, it eventually became clear to Chaloner that Newton's persistence and the unreliability of his colleagues under pressure had allowed the authorities to build up a formidable case against him. At first, Newton noted, 'Chaloner hath feigned himself mad' but as the execution date approached he was reduced to making a final personal appeal to Newton. After presenting seven reasons why his trial was suspect, Chaloner concluded by begging for Newton's aid.

> O Dear Sr do this mercifull deed O my offending you has brought this upon me O for Gods sake if not mine Keep me from being murdered O dear Sr nobody can save me but you O God my God I shall be murdered unless you save me O I hope God will move your heart with mercy pitty to do this thing for me I am
> Your near murdered humble Servant   (*C*, IV, pp. 307–9)

Neither Chaloner's arguments nor his pleas had the slightest effect on Newton. His letter was carefully entered into the book of depositions without comment. Sixteen days later Chaloner was executed.

See also Mint, Counterfeiters and clippers

Chamberlayne, John (1666–1723)

Educated at Trinity College, Oxford, and Leyden University in Holland, Chamberlayne served thereafter as a courtier at the Courts of Prince George of Denmark, Queen Anne, and George I. He was elected to the RS in 1702.

Chamberlayne was one of the several figures who attempted to serve as mediator in the Leibniz–Newton priority dispute. He first wrote to Leibniz on 27 February 1714 offering 'my Poor Mediation' (*C*, VI, pp. 71–2). Leibniz replied on 17 April 1714 and was clearly in no mood for mediation. The *Commercium epistolicum* had just appeared, causing Leibniz to comment, with some justification, that the Royal Society had 'given judgement one side only being heard' and that Newton had

had the report printed for the express purpose of discrediting him. Chamberlayne showed the letter to Newton, who translated the letter from the original French and had it presented to the Society in May 1714 (*C*, VI, pp. 105–6). Chamberlayne was not present at the meeting and offered the mild complaint that he had not intended to have the letter 'expos'd to anyone's views, but your own' (*C*, VI, p. 140). To Leibniz he wrote apologetically confessing that the Society had paid not the slightest attention to Leibniz's complaints (*C*, VI, pp. 152–3). The end of Chamberlayne's brief peace offensive came in August 1714 with Leibniz's final letter to him. He seemed resigned to the response of the Royal Society and informed Chamberlayne of his intention to produce his own collection of letters and documents, a rival in fact to the *CE* (*C*, VI, pp. 173–4). Thereafter Chamberlayne left it to others to seek a settlement of the dispute.

Charleton, Walter (1619–1707)

Educated at Oxford, Charleton began his career in medicine in 1643 as physician to Charles I. He later became a leading figure in the College of Physicians, serving as its President from 1689 to 1691.

In 1654 he published his *Physiologia Epicuro-Gassendo-Charltoniana . . . upon the Hypothesis of Atoms, Founded by Epicurus, Repaired by Petrus Gassendi, Augmented by Walter Charleton*. Although far from original, being in large part a paraphrase of Gassendi's *Animadversiones* (1649), it remains the first work published in Britain to expound seriously the new atomism as an essential part of the mechanical philosophy. The well-known *De corpore* (1655, On Matter) of Hobbes appeared a year later.

Newton seems to have known the work well and quoted from it extensively in the *QQP* section of his Philosophy Notebook.

See also Atomism

Charlier, Carl Wilhelm Ludwig (1862–1934)

A Swedish astronomer and mathematician, Charlier served as Professor of Astronomy at Lund University and Director of the Lund Observatory from 1897 until 1927. He was the author of *Die Mechanik des Himmels* (1902–7) and well known for his work in mathematical statistics. He also published an impressive three-volume Swedish translation of *Principia* (1927–31). Further details can be found in Willy Hartner's review, *Isis*, 1936, vol. 26, pp. 176–7.

See also Principia, Editions

Charta volans

On 27 May 1713 Johann Bernoulli sent Leibniz an account of the *Commercium epistolicum*. It was a work, he told Leibniz, in which he was 'accused before a tribunal consisting of the participants and witnesses themselves, as if charged with plagiary, then documents against you are produced, sentence is passed; you lose the case, you are condemned' (*C*, VI, p. 3). Leibniz replied on 17 June 1713 from Vienna that he had not yet seen the book. He remained convinced, however, that Newton no more knew their calculus than 'Apollonius knew the algebraic calculus of Viète and Descartes'. He went on to complain of the swollen vanity of the English which led them to 'snatch' so often German things. In self-defence Leibniz chose to issue a fly-sheet giving his side of the case. Known as the *Charta volans*, it carries the date 29 July 1713. It was printed and circulated by Christian Wolf. It was also published in the *AE* (1713) and, in a French translation, in the *JL* (1713).

In the style of the time, the work is anonymous. Although by Leibniz, and known to all interested parties as being by Leibniz, it in no way prevented him from discussing, in the third person, the various wrongs supposedly inflicted upon him. It began with the crude fiction that Leibniz, apparently in Vienna, had not yet seen the *CE* and was therefore in no position to defend himself.

No one, it began, had yet denied Leibniz's priority of publication. At this stage Leibniz was prepared to believe Newton's work was developed independently of his own. However, quoting from Bernoulli's letter of 27 May 1713, it was now clear that 'the true way of differentiating differentials was not known to Newton until long after it was familiar to others'. Newton was thus accused of being 'neither fair nor honest', a feature of his character, Leibniz added, already noted by his colleagues Hooke and Flamsteed. Magnanimously, Leibniz concluded by advising that the 'vanity and injustice' of a few 'should not be imputed to the whole nation'. The whole text can be seen in full in both Latin and English in *C*, VI, pp. 15–21. Included in the text was the original letter from Bernoulli of 27 May. Leibniz introduced it, with no mention of Bernoulli, as 'the judgement of a leading mathematician most skilled in these matters and free from bias'. It was a reference Bernoulli would come to regret.

News of the fly-sheet reached Newton as copies of the *AE* and the *JL* arrived in England. Irritated by its tone, he wrote to Keill in April 1714 (*C*, VI, pp. 79–80), instructing him to prepare a reply. He would, he added, 'within a Post or two send you my thoughts upon the Subject'. Further, he told Keill, 'You need not set your name to it.' Keill's reply appeared in the *JL* (1714, pp. 319–58). It was not enough to satisfy Newton. He began to draft a lengthy reply to Johnson, editor of the

JL, in which he once more reviewed the whole dispute (*C*, VI, pp. 80–95). The letter seems not to have been sent.

See also Priority dispute

Chastellet, Gabrielle-Emilie, Marquise du (1706–49)

The daughter of the Baron de Breteuil, chief of protocol at the Court of Louis XIV, she was one of the most remarkable women of the century. In 1725 she married the Marquis du Chastellet, a soldier happy enough to pursue his military career away from his wife, and bore him three children. Well known for her love affairs with the Duc de Richelieu, de Maupertuis and Voltaire, she also developed in the 1730s a passion for mathematics and natural philosophy. In this she was fortunate in two of her lovers, for both Voltaire and de Maupertuis shared her interests and were happy to teach her what they knew and encouraged her to seek further illumination from others. Thus, to increase her mathematical powers, she turned to Clairaut.

In 1733 the Marquise, with Voltaire, retired to her chateau at Cirey in Champagne. Together they performed experiments, even entering the competition set by the *Académie* in 1737 on the nature of fire. They also worked on their separate projects, Voltaire on his *Élémens* of 1738 and the Marquise on her *Institutions de physique* which appeared in 1740. It was, surprisingly, an exposition of the physics of Leibniz.

Soon after she began work on the more ambitious project of translating *Principia* into French. To assist she recruited Clairaut. The translation was completed by 1746. There remained to be added an extensive commentary running to nearly 300 pages. This appears to have been completed and revised by Clairaut. Before the Marquise could finish the work herself she began a new affair with the Marquis de Saint-Lambert and in 1749 found herself pregnant at the age of 42. The delivery itself presented no problem. A few days later, however, she developed a fever and died shortly afterwards.

The *Principia* translation appeared posthumously in 1756 in a limited edition unavailable to the general public. It first went on sale to the public in the later edition of 1759.

See also Principia, Translations; Voltaire

Chastity

It has been held by a number of commentators that Newton led a life of complete chastity. Voltaire was the first to declare publicly, in 1733, that Newton 'had neither passion nor weakness; he never went near any woman' (Voltaire, 1980, p. 70). In justification he referred to Richard Mead and William Cheselden, 'the doctor and the surgeon who were with him when he died'. Later in the century Charles Hutton spoke of Newton's 'constitutional indifference' to women, while in the more robust language of today Manuel has declared quite bluntly, 'Isaac Newton died a virgin' (1980, p. 191).

In support of such views it has been pointed out that his aversion to sexual matters was such that he dropped an old and valued friend, the chemist J. Vigani, for repeating an indelicate tale about a nun. Again, in 1693, when Newton underwent a breakdown of some kind, the complaint he chose to level against John Locke was the purely fictitious one of endeavouring 'to embroil me with woemen' (C, III, p. 280).

Further evidence derives from the fact that throughout his long life Newton's name was linked romantically, and somewhat tenuously at that, with only two women. In the first case there is the recorded memories of the octogenarian Mrs Vincent in which she spoke of a love 'entertained . . . for her' in the 1660s. No other support is known for the story. In the second, even more implausible, case Newton is reported to have proposed marriage to Lady Norris sometime after 1702. The evidence of an undated letter in an unknown hand has, however, convinced few that the sixty-year-old Newton was contemplating marriage.

Nor is there any evidence of homosexual interests in Newton's life. It is true that he enjoyed the company of young men, that he went out of his way to further their career and even, in some cases, gave them money. The men he chose to support were invariably, unless they were kin, mathematicians and scientists. If they gained much from his patronage, he in turn reaped some fairly substantial benefits himself. They were used to copy manuscripts and, if competent enough, to undertake the editorial drudgery Newton seemed most unwilling to perform himself. They could also be used as messengers, translators and, where necessary, to defend him from his critics. Occasionally they might even be expected to publish under their own name material given them by Newton. There were thus any number of reasons of a quite practical kind, in addition to the adulation and friendship he no doubt enjoyed, to account for Newton's comparative accessibility to his younger colleagues. Nor, for that matter, did any of Newton's enemies, of whom there were a fair number, ever seem to consider that in such relationships there was anything worthy of comment.

Two other documents have been held as yielding some insight into Newton's sexuality. The fullest, quoted by Manuel (1974, p. 13) and presented by him as a 'transparently autobiographical piece', is concerned with the celibacy practised by the monks of the Eastern church (Yahuda MS 18). They apparently sought to avoid temptation by going ever further into the wilderness. But, Newton argued, with a freshness and insight seldom found in his theological writings, it was not isolation but industry which led to chastity. 'The way to chastity', he argued, 'is not to struggle with incontinent thoughts but to avert the thoughts by some imployment, or by reading, or by meditating on other things, or by convers.' Monks who fasted in isolation, he remarked, 'arrived to a state of seeing apparitions of women . . . and of hearing their voices in such a lively manner as made them often think the visions true apparitions of the Devil tempting them to lust'. Far from avoiding temptation, he concluded, 'these men ran themselves headlong into it'. Some have seen in this passage an explanation of much of Newton's own life-style. The endless drafts of unpublished manuscripts composed throughout the night – sixteen copies of chapter one of *Chronology* (1728) according to one source – have been taken by some as Newton's own way 'to struggle with incontinent thoughts'.

Another reference to incontinent thoughts, and perhaps even deeds, has been noted in the passages in Shelton shorthand recorded in the Fitzwilliam Notebook. Although Newton was prepared to admit to himself in the security of his notebook 'Having unclean thoughts words and actions and dreames', there were two following entries in which all he was willing to disclose was 'A relapse'. The thought must arise at this point that there were sexual lapses Newton found too painful to describe, lapses which could only be referred to obliquely. Whether these extended to anything more than 'thoughts . . . and dreames', or referred to anything beyond masturbation, is unlikely ever to be resolved; as is, despite the hints listed above, the true nature of Newton's sexuality. It is well to remember that we only know anything of the sexual fumblings of Samuel Pepys, or of Robert Hooke's incestuous couplings with his niece Grace, because both revealed such details in their remarkably frank diaries. In the absence of such diaries, historians could well have been forgiven for speaking of the relatively orthodox sexual lives of the two diarists and even have speculated about the chastity of the neurotic Robert Hooke. The unconfirmed gossip of a man's physicians may not, in fact, be the most reliable evidence about a patient's private life.

See also Norris, Lady; Vincent, Mrs

Chemical Dictionary

Described misleadingly in the Sotheby 1936 catalogue as a 'dictionary of terms, materials, and apparatus used in alchemy', it was bought by an American, R. V. Sowers, but is now to be found in the Bodleian Library, Oxford (MS Don.b.15).

Dating from the period 1667–8, it is one of Newton's earliest chemical compositions and shows him acquiring in the only way he knew how, by writing it down, some of the basic chemistry of his day; for the sixteen-page *Dictionary* of 7,000 words deals exclusively with chemical issues. Entries were listed on such straightforward topics as 'Amalgam', 'Crucible' and 'Sublimation'. Two apparently alchemical terms, *Sanguinis draconis* (the blood of the dragon) and *Magistery*, are in fact defined in unambiguously chemical terms.

Just how detailed Newton's descriptions could be can be seen in the 'Ffurnace' entry published by Dobbs (1975, p. 122) and Westfall (RSW, p. 284).

See also Alchemical papers

Chemistry and the Newtonian tradition

One consequence of the immense success of Newtonian dynamics was an emerging determination in other scientists to gain a comparable advance in their own discipline. What is more, success itself tended to be defined in Newtonian terms and judged by Newtonian standards. Only those scientists, therefore, who worked with attractive forces and based their experimental and theoretical work on some form of the inverse square law could be judged to have escaped from the confines of traditional thought. Further, it was no longer acceptable merely to describe the phenomena observed. The new standards demanded that results should be expressed quantitatively and that they should lead to clear and precise predictions.

Chemists had begun to move imperceptibly towards this model quite independently of Newton. They did not, however, speak of attractive forces, but of affinities. Thus E. F. Geoffroy drew up in 1718 one of the earliest table of affinities, which recorded such comparative facts that nitric acid had greater affinity for iron than it had for copper. Although it was easy enough to substitute 'attraction' for 'affinity', it was less easy to see how Geoffroy's language could be translated into a mathematical symbolism.

Inspiration for the new approach derived from the queries to the *Opticks*. In Query 31 he had proposed that there were agents in nature 'able to make the Particles of Bodies stick together by very strong Attractions'. It was the business of experimental philosophy 'to find them out'. One who took up the Newtonian challenge was the Comte de Buffon in his *Histoire naturelle* (1749–67, Natural History). The laws of affinity, he insisted, were the same with the 'general law by which celestial bodies act upon one another' (Thackray, 1970, p. 159). Buffon meant this quite literally and spoke of the same inverse square law as applying equally to motions in the heavens as to reactions taking place in the test tube.

It is, however, one thing to utter such generalities, and another to turn them into practical chemistry. Several chemists made the attempt none the less. Carl Wenzel, for example, in 1782, sought to infer the strength of the attractive forces between metals by measuring rates at which cylinders of the metals were dissolved in various acids. Another attempt, made by Guyton de Moreveau in the 1770s, involved measuring the force required to remove metal discs from a bowl of mercury; the results, Guyton hoped, would say something about the affinity of one metal for another. He was thus led to such conclusions as 'the affinity of mercury with gold is to the affinity of mercury with zinc as 446:204' (Thackray, 1970, p. 214).

Nearly a century of effort seemed, however, to get nowhere. Nor was this surprising. It was most unlikely that chemists who were just beginning to understand the notion of a chemical element would be able to speak quantitatively about complex chemical reactions. Disillusion began to set in. While Laplace, for example, could in 1797 look forward to a time when chemistry would be 'brought to the same degree of perfection, which the discovery of universal gravitation has procured to astronomy', when he heard in 1813 similar views coming from Humphry Davy he greeted them with 'a tone bordering on contempt' (Gjertsen, 1984, p. 275).

By this time the major breakthrough in chemistry had been made. It came from John Dalton, a good Newtonian, but one less committed to deriving his chemistry from the inverse square law. Dalton turned, as others before him had, to the *Opticks*, and accepted Newton's claim in Query 31 that God had made in the beginning matter 'in solid, massy, hard, impenetrable, movable particles'. He also, however, turned to *Principia* and found in prop. XXIII of Book II the proposal that elastic fluids could well be composed of particles which *repel* each. The two insights did not lead Dalton immediately to the atomic hypothesis; they were, however, essential steps on the way there.

Chemistry Notebook

The 283-page Notebook is to be found in the PC in the ULC (Add. MS 3975); details of its contents were first disclosed in the 1888 Cambridge *Catalogue* of the PC (pp. 21–4). The Notebook clearly begins as a continuation of QQP. The first twenty-two pages deal with the nature of colour and consist of notes taken from works of Robert Boyle, reports of experiments with prisms, a section on the 'effects of thin plates of air between glasses', and an account of internal reflection. This part of the

Notebook was first analysed by Hall (1955) and has been published in full in McGuire and Tamny (*QQP*, pp. 466–89).

The Notebook continues with further extracts from Boyle, notes on such topics as cold, heat, rarity, density, and reports on some experiments with fire. The truly chemical part of the Notebook begins on page 80 with the report of a number of chemical experiments. Some of the notes date from the mid-1670s while the final three pages carry a list of chemical prices for the years 1687 and 1693. The earliest recorded experiments date from 1669. Details of the experiments were first published by Boas and Hall (1958).

Pages 80–283 are very much in Newton's notebook style. Blank pages lie next to literal extracts from some text he had just read, and are followed in turn by several pages describing various chemical experiments. Examples of the experiments described are some 'on the action of distilled liquor of antimony on salts, of lead, iron, and copper', and on the 'preparation of regulus of antimony . . . and chlorides of mercury'. The experiments, according to Boas and Hall (1958, pp. 151–2), 'read like those of a rational experimental scientist'.

Clearly evident, however, is a distinct trend away from the straightforward chemistry of the early parts of the Notebook to the more obscure areas of alchemy presented towards the end. Thus, while the book may begin with extracts from Boyle, it concludes with extracts from George Starkey's *Pyrotechny*.

See also Alchemical papers; Chemistry and the Newtonian tradition

---

Cheselden, William (1688–1752)

A pupil of the London anatomist William Cowper, Cheselden was appointed assistant surgeon at St Thomas's in 1718. He was the author of a highly successful *Anatomy* (1713; 13th edition 1792) and went on to make his fortune as a surgeon by developing the lateral operation for the stone.

Newton probably first became aware of Cheselden when he was seeking in 1714 for someone willing to provide anatomical demonstrations before the Royal Society. Cheselden performed intermittently for the Society but presumably the rewards of a thriving surgical practice were too great to retain his services for long.

During his 1723 illness Newton consulted Cheselden and Mead. They diagnosed a stone. To this time there belongs a curious anecdote noted by Conduitt, similar to an earlier incident related about G. Cheyne. After a consultation Newton offered Cheselden a handful of guineas. An embarrassed Cheselden said he could take no more than one or two.

Newton found his reply amusing and responded, 'Why suppose I do give you more than your fee?'

Cheselden also examined Newton in August 1726 when he diagnosed 'a little Relaxation of the inward coat of the Gut' and suspected 'a Fistula'. He was also called in, with Mead, during Newton's final illness in early 1727. They diagnosed a stone, declared they could do nothing and that the outcome would be fatal.

Cheyne, George (1671–1743)

A pupil of Pitcairne, Cheyne began to practise medicine in London in 1702. In the same year he published his *New Theory of Fevers*, a work clearly in the iatro-mathematical tradition begun by his teacher Pitcairne. Thus, he dismissed the work of other physicians in uncompromising terms: 'All is nonsense, unless they first shew their systems . . . to be necessary corollaries from the known laws of motion.' As the 'known laws of motion' were Newton's laws it was therefore necessary to have a *principae medicinae theoreticae mathematicae* in which the method 'of that stupendously great Mr Newton' would be deployed.

Cheyne also tried to establish a reputation as a mathematician with his *Fluxionum methodus inversa* (1703). Cheyne declared that he had shown the work to Newton, who 'thought it not intolerable'. The story, however, is complicated by another account coming from Conduitt. Newton, according to this story, offered Cheyne a bag of money. Cheyne refused and Newton lost his temper, dismissed Cheyne and declined ever to see him again.

His mathematical work did however, according to Gregory, provoke Newton 'to publish his quadratures' in the first edition of his *Opticks* in 1704. The reference in the Advertisement to the work to his having 'met with some Things copied' from an early manuscript on 'squaring Curvilinear Figures' is therefore taken to be a reference to Cheyne. Whether fair or not, it was sufficient hint for Cheyne to give up his mathematical pretensions and return to medicine. He moved to Bath in 1720, wrote a book on gout and was later reported to have reached the immense bulk of 450 lb.

Chiron

Although traditionally Chiron the centaur was seen as the teacher of Asclepius and the father of medicine, Newton in his *Chronology* (1728) singled him out as the inventor of the primitive sphere. He had not always been Newton's choice, as in the New College manuscripts 'the cunning Palamedes' had been identified as the sphere's inventor.

Such was the euhemerism of the times that Newton and most other seventeenth-century chronologists naturally saw as astronomers anyone whose name in any myth was connected with the heavens. Atlas and Endymion were for Newton no less real, though more obscure perhaps, than Eudoxus and Hipparchus. Why, then, did he select Chiron?

In a lost work of Clement of Alexandria (150–215), *Titanomachia*, Chiron was reported to have taught men the *schemata olumpou*, a phrase translated by Newton as 'asterisms'. The evidence was no better and no worse than that capable of linking any one of dozen or more names with the asterisms of the primitive sphere.

See also Primitive sphere

Christ's Hospital

Founded in 1552, the Bluecoat school was originally intended for orphans and poor children. The buildings, on the site of the dissolved Greyfriars monastery in Newgate St, were damaged in the Great Fire but were sufficiently repaired by the 1680s to house nearly 800 pupils. The school was transferred to Horsham in Sussex in 1892.

In 1673 Pepys, then Clerk to the Admiralty, and several other interested parties persuaded Charles II to endow in the Hospital a school to train boys for the sea and the Royal Navy. A sum of £1,000 a year for seven years was promised to train forty boys in mathematics and navigation until they were old enough to commence their seven-year apprenticeship at sea. The first children were enrolled in 1675 in what became known as the Royal Mathematical School (RMS).

Newton's first contact with the Hospital arose when his advice was sought in 1682 about the appointment of a mathematics master. He recommended E. Paget, a Trinity colleague, as 'learned', 'sober and industrious' and a sound mathematician. Paget was appointed but, despite Newton's advice, turned out to be something of a drunkard and resigned in 1695. Again Newton's advice was sought and taken. He recommended three candidates; William Collins, John Caswell and the successful candidate, the unrelated Samuel Newton, who served in his post until 1708. Newton was also instrumental in getting H. Ditton appointed in 1706 to run a new mathematical school in the Hospital. The experiment failed to survive Ditton's death in 1715.

Earlier in 1694 Newton had been invited by Nathaniel Hawes, treasurer of the Hospital from 1683 to 1699, to comment on 'two schemes of learning' proposed to improve the quality of the mathematical teaching at the Hospital. The result was ten pages of detailed analysis (*C*, III, pp. 357–67). The present syllabus he dismissed as 'mean and of small extent', doing little more than teaching the use of instruments, and this, he objected, was done without any comprehension but 'by imitation, as a Parrot does to speak'. He went on to spell out the serious weaknesses implicit in such an approach:

> A Vulgar Mechanick can practice what he has been taught or seen done, but if he is in an error he knows not how to find it out and correct it, and if you put him out of his road, he is at a stand; Whereas he that is able to reason nimbly and judiciously about figure, force and motion, is never at rest till he gets over every rub. (C, III, pp. 359–60)

Chronological principles

Newton sought to establish his chronology not on some *ad hoc* basis but in terms of a number of precise and objective chronological principles. Classical chronology had begun with Timaeus of Tauromenium (*c.*356–260 BC) who established the concordance between the rulers of Sparta and the archons of Athens by Olympiads. The early work of Timaeus was built on by the later chronographers Eratosthenes and Apollodurus. This pagan material was extended and christianised by Eusebius (*c.*260–340 AD) who, using material of Julius Africanus, provided a *Chronicle* running from creation to about 300 AD.

The kind of argument Newton had to face ran as follows.

1 The time between the fall of Troy and the return of the Heraclidae was 80 years.

2 The time between the return of the Heraclidae and the first Olympiad was 328 years.

3 The first Olympiad began in 776 BC.

Therefore the fall of Troy can be dated to the year 1184 BC.

As it happened Newton found this conclusion unacceptable. The one unshakeable assumption behind all his chronology was the belief that Jewish civilisation had priority over Greek civilisation. Yet he had been able to place the founding of the Temple of Solomon no further back than the eleventh century BC, long after the fall of Troy. It was therefore very obvious to Newton that something was radically wrong with the traditional chronology. Consequently he set out to develop the chronological principles in terms of which a more accurate history could be established. Throughout his various chronological writings Newton appealed to four basic principles to justify his revisionist tendencies.

For his first principle Newton insisted that no reliance can be placed on oral evidence more than a century old; 'memory of such things as are not committed to writing', he declared, 'wears out in three or four generations'. Consequently, he went on, 'I allow no history of things done in Europe before Cadmus brought letters into Greece; no history of things done in Germany before the rise of the Roman Empire' (Manuel, 1963, p. 53). Nor could monuments erected much after the event be trusted. The Parian marble, for example, composed half a century after the death of Alexander, was unreliable evidence, Newton declared, for the reign of Cecrops some 1,200 years before.

Having rejected oral tradition, Newton sought to substitute for it something more objective and reliable. He noted that early king lists were often grossly unreliable. There was a tendency for all nations 'to raise their antiquities & make the lives of their first fathers longer than they really were' (Manuel, 1963, p. 211). The fundamental error committed by previous chronologists had been to equate reigns with generations and consequently reckon on about three reigns per century. Thus, he noted in *The Originall of Monarchies*, relying on oral traditions we have:

  7 Kings of Rome before the Consuls reigned 244 years: average regnal length 35 years

  14 Kings between Aeneas and Numitor reigned 425 years: average regnal length 30 years

  10 first Kings of Macedon reigned 353 years: average regnal length 35 years

  10 first Kings of Athens reigned 351 years: average regnal length 35 years

Newton went on to make a comparable survey of documented king lists. Typical examples are:

  15 Kings of Israel after Solomon reigned 259 years: average regnal length 17 years

  10 Kings of Persia after Cyrus reigned 208 years: average regnal length 21 years

  28 Kings of England after 1066 reigned 635 years: average regnal length 22½ years

  63 Kings of France after Pharamund reigned 1,224 years: average regnal length 19½ years

On the basis of the documented examples Newton proposed his second main chronological principle, the law of regnal length, in which he claimed that 'according to the ordinary course of nature kings reign one with another twenty years apiece' (Manuel, 1963, p. 212). Consequently, the traditional lists could be dismissed as fictitious.

With his new principle Newton could return to the problem of dating the fall of Troy. Greek chronology before the Persian invasion had been based on the widespread assumption of three kings to a century. But, he insisted, it was necessary that Greek history before the Persian invasion must be shortened 'in the proportion of about 19 to 33 or 4 to 7'. As a result he was able to place the fall of Troy long after Solomon had built his temple.

There was however a further principle, more accurate and more reliable than the study of regnal lengths. Thus for his third principle he observed that 'The surest arguments for determining things past are those taken from Astronomy' (Manuel, 1963, p. 66). Chronologists had long used calculated eclipses to date such events as the reign of Cambyses. There were, however, few records of eclipses. To extend the scope of astronomical dating Newton turned to the precession of the equinoxes. It was a radical step and one never contemplated before.

Since the time of Hipparchus, in the second century BC, it had been known that the equinoctial point precessed around the ecliptic. If the rate of precession was known, then, given also the present siting of the equinoctial points, any previous date whose equinoctial point was known could be calculated quite simply. Newton had calculated the annual rate of precession to be 50″, or 1° in 72 years (*Principia*, III, prop. XXXIX). He also claimed that Chiron had prepared for the Argonauts a stellar sphere on which the equinoctial and solstitial points fell 'in the middles of the constellations of Aries, Cancer, Chelae, and Capricorn'. Consequently it was easy to calculate that the equinoctial points had precessed 36° 44′ since then. At 50″ a year this would have required 2,646 years and placed the voyage of the Argonauts in the year 957 BC which, with some minor adjustments, became 937 BC, some three hundred years later than the traditional chronology. It did, however, have for Newton the advantage of coming long after the foundation of the Kingdom of Israel.

Newton's reasoning was impeccable; his data unfortunately were highly questionable. It is, to begin with, grossly anachronistic to suppose anyone in the tenth century had the slightest knowledge of the geometry of the celestial sphere. To suppose further that they could define and locate equinoctial points is absurd. No such knowledge can be found in Greek astronomy before the fifth century, with the figure of Euctemon.

Where then did Newton gain his information about the sphere of Chiron? He had picked up a reference in a work of Clement of Alexandria (150–215), the *Titanomachia*, referring to Chiron as the first to teach the *schematou olumpou* (asterisms in Newton's contentious translation). He also took a reference in Hipparchus (*c*.190–125 BC) to a sphere drawn by Eudoxus (*c*.390–40 BC), on which the colures had been fixed in the middle of Aries, Cancer, Chelae and Capricorn, as referring to the primitive sphere of Chiron. He assumed that as Eudoxus was unaware of the phenomenon of precession he would have followed the ancient astronomers in his siting of the equinoctial points.

Coming in at this point, and confirming his astronomical dating, is Newton's fourth principle, euhemerism. All the figures referred to in myths, epics, legends and whatever were, for Newton, ultimately based on some historical person. The descriptions of constellations were not exempt from this process. But, Newton argued, the names on the ancient sphere are not taken from the heroes of Theban or Trojan wars but from such figures as Perseus and Andromeda, who all relate to the voyage of the Argonauts. Consequently, he concluded, for he saw the process as a fairly rapid one, all the first constellations refer to the voyage, 'or rather about 20 or 25 years after when Jason, Hercules, Castor, Pollux, Orpheus, Aesculapius were newly dead and defied so that they might be honoured in ye Constellations' (Manuel, 1963, pp. 79–80).

Given such principles, Newton had little difficulty in establishing his desired chronological framework. Solomon's Temple had been founded in 1015 BC and the Argo had sailed in 937 BC; all else could be fitted around these dates to Newton's evident satisfaction. Not, however, to the satisfaction of a modern scholar, for whom the fall of Troy is more likely to have occurred in the thirteenth century BC, some two to three hundred years before Solomon and his Temple. As for the voyage of the Argo, the *Oxford Classical Dictionary* merely notes: 'If a real voyage underlies the tale, it is deeply buried.'

That Newton's chronology was grossly inaccurate is indisputable. It should not, however, be assumed from this that the underlying principles are baseless. Newton's total distrust of oral tradition was as misplaced as his commitment to euhemerism was excessive. More acceptable, and still in use amongst historians, are the principles of astronomical dating and the law of regnal succession. Newton's basic error was to think they could be used to establish a chronology. Used critically to demolish or control existing chronologies, such principles could be very effective. They could not, however, be deployed to create by themselves a new chronology, particularly, as with Newton, one which had been worked out in advance to satisfy quite non-historical beliefs.

See also The Chronology of Ancient Kingdoms Amended

Clairaut, Alexis-Claude (1713–65)

The leading French mathematical physicist of his day, Clairaut had been admitted to the *Académie des sciences* when only eighteen. Much of his career was spent in evaluating Newton's physics as presented in *Principia* and seeking to advance it further. To this end he was a member of de Maupertuis's expedition of 1736 to Lapland which helped to determine that the earth was shaped as Newton had predicted. In the 1740s he began to consider whether the lunar orbit could be analysed exclusively in terms of Newtonian principles. Was, for example, the inverse square law adequate? Aware that Newton had underestimated the motion of the lunar apsides by a factor of two (*Principia*, Book I, prop. XLV, cor.2; Cajori, pp. 146–7), Clairaut reconsidered the problem. His first response was that Newton had indeed been wrong. The inverse square law should be modified to include an extra term varying inversely as the fourth power of the distance. It was not, in fact, until 1749 that Clairaut realised that both he and Newton had been at fault and that, suitably corrected, the system of *Principia* could predict quite accurately the motion of the lunar apsides. A further intervention in 1758 enabled Clairaut to explain why the return of Halley's comet in 1759 was somewhat delayed.

Clairaut also collaborated with the Marquise du Chastellet on the French translation of *Principia*, adding much original work of his own.

Clark, Mr

Known simply as apothecary Clark, he was the Grantham chemist in whose house next to the George Inn Newton lodged during his schooldays, from 1654–60. Mrs Clark was a close friend of Newton's mother; there was also a brother, Dr Clark, who supervised Newton's mathematical training at his Grantham School. Also present in the house were the Storer children, Edward, Arthur and an unnamed sister who later, as Mrs Vincent, claimed to have shared a youthful romance with Newton.

Clarke, John (1682–1757)

The younger brother of Samuel Clarke, John was educated at Cambridge. In 1728 he was appointed to the Deanship of Salisbury Cathedral. He had earlier translated his bother's Latin translation of Rohault (1671) into English (*Rohault's System of Natural Philosophy*, 1732). He also published substantial extracts from *Principia* in his *A Demonstration of the Principal Sections of Sir Isaac Newton's Principles of Natural Philosophy* (1730).

Clarke, Samuel (1675–1729)

The son of a Norwich alderman, Clarke was educated at Cambridge where, after graduating in 1695, he was elected a Fellow of his college. He was ordained sometime after 1698 and entered immediately into the service of the Bishop of Norwich as his chaplain. In 1709 Clarke moved to London to the living of St James, Westminster. He also served as chaplain to Queen Anne. On the accession of the Hanoverians he became a familiar figure at Court through his friendship with the Princess of Wales, Caroline of Anspach.

Despite what appear to be very conventional connections with the hierarchy and the establishment, Clarke was in fact a heretic. Like his friends Whiston and Newton, he had come to deny the essential Anglican doctrine of the Trinity. In 1712 he went so far as to publish his doubts in his *The Scripture-Doctrine of the Trinity*. The Athanasian creed he declared to be unscriptural. His conclusion was based upon an analysis of 1,251 New Testament texts relating to the Father, Son and Holy Spirit. Only the terms 'God' and the 'Father' were used synonymously. The work provoked considerable opposition and led to Clarke being arraigned before the Lower House of Clergy of Convocation in 1714. Clarke compromised somewhat, issuing a recantation of his views. Although he found himself condemned nevertheless by the Lower House, the Bishops of the Upper House accepted his recantation and no further steps were taken. It did however involve Clarke in Trinitarian controversy for the rest of his life. Rumours that he had retracted his anti-Trinitarian views on his deathbed were later discounted by his son Samuel.

Described by Whiston, his biographer in 1730, as a 'bosom friend' of Newton, Clarke worked on three books important in the Newtonian canon. The first was his translation into Latin of the *Traité de physique* (1671) of Jacques Rohault. Published in 1697, and containing extensive footnotes, it became the main channel through which Cambridge undergraduates first heard of Newtonian mechanics. Rohault's text, as modified by Clarke, remained in use at Cambridge until the 1730s, when both the final English and Latin editions appeared.

It was also Clarke who was chosen by Newton to translate his *Opticks* of 1704 into Latin. He received £500 for his trouble. No correspondence has survived from the enterprise and it is therefore impossible to know how much of Newton and how much of Clarke is in the translation.

Much more is known about the third enterprise, the Leibniz–Clarke correspondence. When Clarke moved to London in 1709 his St James Rectory was within walking distance of Newton's home in St Martin's St. As a disciple of Newton in science, and agreeing with him in theology, it is likely that the two met regularly and perhaps, even, frequently. Newton was a member of the Board of Vestry of Clarke's church. Thus when Princess Caroline received in November 1715 a letter from Leibniz critical of Newton's natural theology it was natural that she should ask Clarke to answer the charge. It was also natural that Clarke should in turn approach Newton for guidance. Five letters were exchanged before Leibniz's death in November 1716. The correspondence was published first in 1717. No documentary evidence has survived of Newton's participation in the debate. There is, however, a report from Princess Caroline to Leibniz that Clarke's letters had been written with 'the advice of the Chevalier Newton' (RSW, p. 779).

On Newton's death in 1727 the post of Master of the Mint was offered to Clarke. He refused it.

Clavis (The Key)

One of the few alchemical manuscripts of Newton to have been published, the work itself is to be found in the Keynes collection and has been made available in both the original Latin and English translation in Dobbs (1975, pp. 251–5). Dobbs is careful to point out, however, that the work may not in fact be by Newton but merely a copy of someone else's manuscript (pp. 175–81). Figala (1977, p. 107) has not accepted the work as authentic; Westfall (RSW, p. 370), however, considers 'the evidence weighs in favour of authenticity'. Authentic or not, the manuscript itself dates from the late 1670s.

The subject of the work is the production of a philosophic mercury capable of dissolving all metals. The procedure involved forming a compound of antimony (star *regulus*), silver (the doves of Diana) and common mercury. If the procedure is followed accurately the result will be philosophic mercury. The importance of this substance was that it allowed metals such as gold to be fully dissolved and not, as happened with normal acids, simply broken down into atoms too small to be seen. The author claims to have successfully carried out the process described.

See also Alchemical principles and aims

Clement of Alexandria (*c.*150–*c.*216)

Born at Athens of pagan parents, Clement served from about 200 AD as head of the Catechetical School of Alexandria. He was forced to flee shortly afterwards with the beginning, in 202, of the Severan persecution. One of his few works to survive was the *Stromateis* (Miscellanies) which dealt at length with the inferiority of Greek to Christian philosophy. Newton owned a Greek–Latin edition of the works of Clement and it was from his *Stromateis* that he gained the dubious insight that Chiron was the creator of the primitive sphere of the Argonauts.

See also Chiron; Primitive sphere

Clepsydra

According to Stukeley, Newton made two clepsydras (water clocks) before he left Woolsthorpe for Cambridge. The first, four ft high, had a dial at the top with figures for hours; an index was turned by a piece of wood as it rose or fell with the level of water. A second device, of similar size, Stukeley reported to be 'famous for its exactness'. It was designed somewhat differently and operated by an hour rod descending as water escaped from the container. Both designs, Mills (1982) has argued, are based on plans published in Bate (1654).

Designing and building such devices was the kind of work Newton found most pleasing. He was clearly aware of the limitations of his clepsydras. Although he spoke of 'the exactness and usefulness of that kind of machine', he also noted that, to work accurately, the hole through which the water dripped must be small, otherwise, it was 'subject to be furr'd up by impuritys in the water'. If sand was used instead, it soon made the hole much bigger and necessitated the resetting of the clock.

See also Sundials

Clerke, Gilbert (1626–97)

The first informed response to *Principia* came from Clerke, a retired Presbyterian minister from Stamford, Lincs. He had served earlier as a mathematics don at Cambridge and was the author of *Oughtredus explicatus* (1682), a commentary on Oughtred.

In September 1687 he informed Newton that, perhaps because he was 'in ye evening of my declineing age', he was having difficulty following 'so much as your first three sections'. In particular, he asked, was there something wrong with prop.XVII; he could not follow the algebra. In response Newton wrote out his equations in full and concluded with the generous invitation that 'If there be anything else . . . pray do me ye favour of another letter, or two' (C, II, p. 488).

Clerke responded with three further letters (C, II, pp. 488–500). Amongst other points, he proposed that Newton should change some items of terminology and reformulate some of his equations; *Principia*, he added, was 'hard enough' without increasing its difficulty. Newton's response was sympathetic and helpful, in marked contrast to the hostile and intemperate reception offered to more public critics. Some of Clerke's proposals were in fact adopted by Newton, without acknowledgment, in the second edition of *Principia* (1713).

Cohen, I. Bernard (1914–   )

Apart from three years at the Carnegie Institute of Washington, Cohen has spent his entire academic career at Harvard. In 1947 he became the first American to receive a Ph.D in the history of science. Much of his professional life has been concerned with the study of Newtonian science. His first major study, *Franklin and Newton* (1956), traced the impact of the *Opticks* on eighteenth-century science. In the same year he conceived, with A. Koyré, the plan of preparing an edition of *Principia* with variant readings, a task finally completed in 1972. As a companion volume to the edition Cohen published his *Introduction to Newton's Principia* (1971) which, in conjunction with a score of his papers, has illuminated all aspects of *Principia*'s origin, composition, publication, argument and reception. The history of few seventeenth century works, after Cohen's labours, can be as well known as *Principia*.

Cohen has also sought to place Newton's work in a broader historical context. In *The Newtonian Revolution* (1980) he explored the ways in which scientific ideas are transformed during the upheavals of a scientific revolution. Much of the work seeks to identify and analyse Newton's extraordinarily ability to relate abstract mathematical constructs to physical systems.

Collins, John (1625–83)

Although less well-known than many other figures in seventeenth-century science, Collins is none the less one of the more interesting. No great mathematician himself, his work had a more profound impact on the discipline than the labours of many more talented workers. With little formal education, Collins was first apprenticed to an Oxford bookseller for three years before he appeared in London. Apart from 'seven years at sea, most of it in the Venetian service against the Turk', Collins spent his working life either at Court or as a clerk in one or other government office. It was far from ideal, affording him 'little or no leisure' and, often, little or no pay. Collins supplemented his income, no doubt, by the publication of a number of elementary textbooks such as his *Merchants Accompts* (1652) and *Geometricall Dialling* (1659).

Such pursuits were clearly for Collins all a sideline beside the more important task of the promotion and dissemination of mathematics. Condemned by, perhaps, lack of talent, and certainly by lack of education, Collins chose instead to be the impresario of British, and to some extent, European mathematics. This he did in a number of ways. First as a kind of publishers' agent, commissioning works, editing them, arranging for their translation and seeing them through the press. But he also began, through a formidable correspondence, to act more like a periodical, regularly transmitting the results of one mathematician around his favoured circle.

He first heard of Newton in 1669 when he sent Barrow a copy of Mercator's *Logarithmotechnica* (1668). Barrow replied that a Cambridge friend had a more general understanding than Mercator. Shortly afterwards he sent Collins a copy of *De analysi* and later still told him the name of the author. It was the first time the name of Newton would be heard outside the provincial world of Cambridge. Collins made his own copy of the tract and began informing his friends of Newton's results; James Gregory in Scotland, Richard Towneley and Thomas Strode in England, de Sluse in Holland, Borelli in Italy and Bertet in France, were all informed, as were others. It was a fact Newton would later pointedly emphasise in his *Recensio*.

Having discovered talent, Collins wished to exploit it further. He enquired about other results Newton may have, posed problems to him he knew mathematicians to be working on, and began to persuade Newton to write a book.

They met for the first in November 1669 when Newton made his second visit to London. Collins later reported to James Gregory on the meeting: 'I never saw Mr Isaac Newton . . . but twice viz somewhat late upon a Saturday night at his Inne, I then proposed to him the adding of a Musicall Progression, the which he promised to consider and send up . . . And againe I saw him the next day having invited him to Dinner' (*C*, I, p. 53).

Collins followed up the meeting by sending Newton a copy of Mercator's translation of Kinckhuysen's *Algebra*. The work needed to be revised and expanded. Would Newton, asked Collins, undertake the task? It says much for the charm and persistence of Collins that he could persuade a reluctant Newton to spend virtually the whole of 1670 working on Kinckhuysen. Through no fault of either Collins or Newton it proved to be impractical to publish the work. One of Newton's final words on the subject was to request Collins to please send him no more books (*C*, I, p. 68).

Yet Collins's prodding was not wasted. In July 1671 he heard from Newton that he had begun 'to new methodiz ye discourse of infinite series'. He had in fact started on his *Tractatus de methodis serierum et fluxionum*, the fullest account of his fluxional method so far attempted (*C*, I, pp. 67–9). Collins never saw the tract which, in any case, remained incomplete. In December 1672 Collins tried once more to gain information from Newton. He began by informing him of a method for drawing tangents worked out by René de Sluse. Newton responded with the casual news that the approach of de Sluse was only a 'Corollary of a General Method which extends it selfe without any troublesome calculation', not only to tangents but to 'the resolving other abstruser kinds of Problems about the crookedness, areas, lengths, centers of gravity of curves &c' (*C*. I, pp. 247–8). Newton, however, forbore to go further into the details of his 'General Method'. It is not difficult to imagine Collins's feelings at this point. What is not so clear is the attitude of Newton. Did he deliberately set out to tease Collins? Or, was he genuinely unaware how provocative such coy and partial unveilings could be? Newton may well have enjoyed games of intellectual strip-tease; Collins was less likely to have found them stimulating.

Whatever the cause, after December 1672 Collins received no further details of Newton's mathematical advances. Soon after, he informed James Gregory that Newton's interest had switched from mathematics to 'chimical studies' (*C*, I, p. 356).

If Collins could extract no additional material from Newton's unpublished work, he could at least distribute what he had already seen and copied. Newton himself would publish nothing until 1704; Collins filled the gap. Thus, when Continental mathematicians like Leibniz approached Henry Oldenburg, secretary of the RS, for news of advances in British mathematics, he turned for help to Collins. He drew up a lengthy summary, since known as the *Historiola*, which included details of Newton's letter of December 1672. Further, when Leibniz visited London in 1676 he showed to him the copy of the *De analysi* he had transcribed in 1669.

By this time Collins's health was beginning to fail. He complained in late 1676 of a 'scorbutic humour' and in the following years he was inflicted with itching, boils and an 'ebullition of the blood'. Although he lived another seven years, his mathematical correspondence no longer flourished. The last letter he received from Newton is dated November 1674.

In death Collins was allowed to make one further contribution to Newton's mathematical reputation. His papers had passed into the hands of William Jones. Consequently when, in 1712, Newton was seeking evidence for his claims of priority over Leibniz in the invention of the calculus, it was to the papers of Collins he turned. Their richness and detail proved, once more, to be very much to the advantage of Newton.

See also Commercium epistolicum; *De analysi*; *Historiola*

Colour

There are few things in the universe as pervasive as motion and light. Today we still see both in largely Newtonian terms. Equally Newtonian is our idea of colour.

Traditionally, Aristotelians had distinguished between apparent or emphatical colours and real or true ones. The latter were qualities of bodies while the former, seen in rainbows and prisms, were transient phenomena produced in some way by the modification of incident light. Thus it was quite common to explain the rainbow as arising from a weakening of light as it passed through or was reflected from an adjacent cloud. Real colour, in contrast, was actually in a body; it did, however, require the presence of light to illuminate it. In one early crude version, individual colours were identified with one of the four elements. Thus, according to Empedocles, if a body contained an abundance of fire it would be white. The other elements, water, air and earth, produced black, red and green bodies respectively. More sophisticated versions may have been offered by later philosophers; the basic structure of the theory remained, however.

Alternative views emerged in the seventeenth century with the development of the mechanical philosophy. If everything was dependent upon matter in motion there was no longer any place for colours as real properties of bodies. Consequently the traditional distinctions began to break down. Why, Boyle asked in 1664, should emphatical colours, as 'the proper and peculiar Objects of the Organ of Sight, and capable to Affect it as Truly and Powerfully as other Colours . . . be reputed but Imaginary ones'? (Newton, 1984, p. 4).

Colours, thus, for the mechanical philosophers became not qualities of bodies but modifications of light rays as they were reflected and refracted by various bodies. Descartes, for example, in a characteristically arbitrary fashion, sought to explain colour in terms of spin; light particles as they struck a body were either absorbed or reflected. If the former, the body was black; if the latter, they may acquire a rotary motion on reflection. If the acquired spin happened to be more rapid than the light's forward motion, the body would appear red; if it was less rapid it would appear green. Other modification theories were proposed by Robert Hooke and Christian Huygens.

Newton himself in his early notebooks was clearly attracted by such an approach. His first step to a different kind of theory came with his realisation, described in QQP, that different colours were refracted unequally.

> That ye rays wch make blew are rafracted more yn ye rays wch make red appeares from this experimnt. If one hafe of ye thred abc be blew and ye other red and a shade or black body be put behind it yn lookeing on ye thred through a prism one halfe of ye thred shall appeare higher yn ye other. & not both in one direct line, by reason of unequal refactions in ye differing colours.

At this time, 1664–5 most likely, Newton was not considering light itself. The discovery of unequal refrangibility was a major advance; it remained to deploy it effectively. So far Newton had only considered unequal refrangability as it applied to coloured bodies, and within this context he thought purely in mechanical terms.

The next major advance took place when Newton, early in 1666, for the first time examined sunlight as it passed through a prism and before it was reflected by a coloured body. Why he took this step is a matter of speculation. In the 1672 paper on *Light and Colors* he linked the step with his attempt to grind non-spherical 'Optick glasses'. This has led

Shapiro (Newton, 1984, p. 11), and others, to argue that such work drew his attention to the problem of chromatic aberration. At some point the significance of the early discovery of unequal refrangibility became apparent and consequently he began to reason:

> If . . . the sun's light directly as it comes from the sun, before it is reflected from any coloured body, consists of rays of different colour and degrees of refrangibility, then each colour would be bent a different amount and brought to a different focus. To test this conjecture, he for the first time passed a sunbeam directly through a prism to see if the spectrum was elongated rather than circular.

It was enough to set Newton off into a period of intensive experimentation. The results were reported in his 'New Theory about Light and Colors' in the *PT*. The essential point, supported by a wealth of experimental data, was simply that:

> Colors are not qualifications of light, derived from refractions or reflections of natural bodies . . . but original and connate properties . . . Some rays are disposed to exhibit a red color and no other, some a yellow and no other . . . and so of the rest . . . To the same degree of refrangibility ever belongs the same color, and to the same color ever belongs the same refrangibility.

The point was defended against attack in a series of papers he published in the *PT* during the period 1672–5; it was also developed at greater length in the *Lectiones opticae* (1729) and the *Opticks*. The idea is perhaps too familiar today to have any longer the power to startle. To recapture once more the initial excitement aroused by Newton's conception of light it is necessary to go to the poets of the eighteenth century who repeatedly struggled to express the import of his new insight in which:

> Even Light itself, which everything displays,
> Shone undiscovered, till his brighter mind
> Untwisted all the shining robe of day.
> (JAMES THOMSON, 1728, in HEATH-STUBBS and SALMAN, p. 139)

See also Aberration; *Experimentum crucis*; *New Theory about Light and Colors*

Colson, John (1680–1760)

The son of a clergyman, he was educated at Christ Church, Oxford, and taught mathematics at Sir Joseph Williamson's Free Mathematical School, Rochester. He later entered orders and obtained a living at Chalk near Gravesend. In 1739 he was elected to the Lucasian Professorship at Cambridge, despite competition from an ageing de Moivre.

He is best known today as the translator of the important Newtonian text *The Method of Fluxions*, first 'made publick' in Colson's English translation in 1736 and to which he added, 'A perpetual comment on the whole work consisting of annotations, illustrations and supplements'.

A possible early reference to Colson may be present in the papers of Jacob Bruce who accompanied Peter the Great on his visit to Britain in 1698. Boss noted a payment of 48 guineas on the 17 April 1698 to a certain Ivan Kolson (John Colson?) 'for training Jacob Bruce over a period of six months, as arranged by contract, including board and lodgings' (Boss, 1972, p. 29). If this was indeed Colson, then it was through him that Newtonian physics was introduced to Russia.

See also De methodis fluxionum; Newton in Russia

Comets

That comets played an important role in the development of Newton's dynamics is apparent from the most casual glance at *Principia*. Almost a third of Book III is devoted to their nature and orbit. Newton's first scientific interest in them appears in a long section in his QQP (pp. 410–18). He began with several observations of the comet of 1585 taken from Snell's *Descriptio cometae* (1619). His own observations were first recorded with the comet of 1664 which he observed intermittently from 9 December 1664 to 23 January 1665. Further observations of the comet were recorded on 1, 4 and 5 April. These reports were much more than casual references to strange phenomena in the heavens. Newton had learnt how to describe comets and how to record their daily position. Thus on 27 December 1664 he noted, amongst other things, that the comet was 28° 11' from Aldebaran and 38° 36½' from Rigel, its longitude was 37° 4' 13", its latitude was 10° 20' 47"S at 9.08 pm and the length of the tail was 11°.

Initially Newton accepted the orthodoxy of his day which declared comets to move rectilinearly through the solar system. Once seen, a comet would pass out of the system and should never appear again. This fitted in with its supposed nature as a transient, atmospheric phenomena. Of such objects no question of predicting their reappearance could ever arise. Consequently when, in November 1680, a comet appeared heading towards the sun, followed in December by a comet moving away from the sun, Newton assumed that he had observed two different comets. An alternative view was first heard in England from John Flamsteed. In a series of letters to Newton from December 1680 to March 1681 he argued that the sightings were of the same comet which, powered by some kind of magnetic attraction, passed, not around, but in front of the sun and returned in the same direction it had appeared. Newton resisted the idea strongly, insisting that two distinct comets had been observed. He had little difficulty in disposing of Flamsteed's arguments. How, for example, he objected, could the sun exercise such a magnetic attraction: 'A red hot loadstone attracts not iron.' Consequently, the sun, 'a vehemently hot body', would have lost all its 'vertue' (C, II, p. 341).

Newton had been so convinced that two comets were visible in 1680 because the motions observed seemed too paradoxical to fit a single body: 'its motion was thrice accelerated and retarded', he noted in obvious puzzlement (C, II, p. 342). After 26 December the comet's acceleration decreased continuously. Yet, despite his dismissal of Flamsteed, Newton seemed somewhat unsure of his own position. The appearance of a new comet in 1682, Halley's comet, allowed him to gather further observations. He also received from an old childhood friend, Arthur Storer, resident in Maryland, observations of the comets of 1680 and 1682.

Unpublished manuscripts of the time show Newton trying to work out, on the basis of four observations, the path of the 1680 comet (MP, V, pp. 524–31). The problem actually found its way into his Arithmetica universalis (MP, V, pp. 298–302). Also surviving, and dating from 1682, are notes on all recorded comets (Add.MS 3965.14). Some time shortly afterwards Newton abandoned the traditional notion that comets move in rectilinear paths. It was not, however, until September 1685 that he could bring himself to confess to Flamsteed: 'and taking that of 1680 into fresh consideration, it seems very probable that those of November and December were ye same comet' (C, II, pp. 419–20).

Consequently, when he came to write Book III of Principia a few years later, he could assert that 'comets move in some of the conic sections' and observe Kepler's area law (prop.XL). Further, in prop.XLI, he went on to demonstrate how the orbit of a comet moving in a parabola could be determined from three observations. It was, he began, 'a Problem of very great difficulty'. He actually did more than work out methods of computation; added to the proof was a detailed construction of the path of the 1680–81 comet (Cajori, pp. 507–21).

Newton's work on comets illustrates quite dramatically how hard it really was to formulate the concept of universal gravitation. Hooke and Halley by the early 1680s had some idea of the inverse square law and its connection with the elliptical orbits of planets; yet, it never seems to have occurred to either of them that comets could move any way except rectilinearly. Nor, initially, had it occurred to Newton that the planetary dynamics discussed with Hooke in 1679 could be applied to comets. The step was not taken before 1682.

There remained the question of the composition and function of comets. As long as they were seen as rare and one-time visitors, it must have been quite tempting to link their appearance with important terrestrial events. 'When beggars die, there are no comets seen', Shakespeare had written in *Julius Caesar*, and such views were still widely held in Newton's day. They failed, however, to tempt Newton. His account of comets was, accordingly, as in all other matters, unambiguously naturalistic.

Comets were, Newton declared in *Principia*, Book III, prop.XLI, 'solid, compact, fixed, and durable, like the bodies of the planets'. If not, he argued, they would be dissipated by the intense heat they encountered in their passage 'by the neighbourhood of the sun'. They also possessed a tail which was 'nothing else but a very fine vapour, which the head or nucleus of the comet emits by its heat'. Such vapour, scattered through the heavens, would little by little be attracted to the planets and, mixing with the atmosphere, would eventually drop down as rain. The value to earth of such cometary vapours, Newton went on to argue, could be considerable. It was this vapour, for example, which provided for the 'conservation of the seas, and fluids of the plants'; for if the seas were not replenished they must be 'in continual decrease, and quite fail at last'. A final suspicion, Newton confessed, was that 'it is chiefly from the comets that spirit comes . . . the smallest but the most subtle and useful part of our air, and so much required to sustain the life of all things with us' (Cajori, p. 530). Echoes of Newton's speculations can be heard in the writings of Fred Hoyle and C. Wickramsinghe (1978, 1979). Both life on earth and a number of terrestrial diseases originated in comets and have been subsequently brought to earth.

Halley judged in the introductory Ode to *Principia* that:

> Now we know
> The sharply veering ways of comets, once
> A source of dread, nor longer do we quail
> Beneath appearances of bearded stars.　　　　　(CAJORI, p. xiv)

Halley's optimism was misplaced. Despite Newton and *Principia*, the eighteenth century proved to be as credulous about comets as previous times.

Commercium epistolicum

The *CE*, the official report of the RS on the priority dispute between Newton and Leibniz, arose from Leibniz's statement of his case for the discovery of the calculus in a letter read to the Society, with Newton in the chair, on 22 March 1711 (*C*, V, pp. 96–8). Shortly afterwards John Keill drew Newton's attention to certain passages in the *AE* (1705) suggesting that Newton had, in *Principia* (1687), taken his method of fluxions from published papers of Leibniz. Keill was allowed to draft and to send in May 1711 a detailed reply to Leibniz in which not only was Newton's absolute priority of eighteen years vigorously affirmed, it was also claimed that Leibniz had had access to Newton's material and that 'it was not contrary to reason' to suppose that it was this material that had given him 'an entrance to the differential calculus' (C, V, p. 142). Leibniz replied in December 1711 demanding that the RS protect him from the 'empty and unjust braying' of such an 'upstart' as Keill (C, V, p. 208).

Newton's first response was to distance himself from the dispute. The controversy, he noted in a draft letter to the RS, was between Keill and Leibniz. Shortly after, however, a new policy was adopted and on 6 March 1712 the RS announced its decision to set up a committee to examine the relevant letters and papers and, presumably, evaluate the competing claims of Keill and Leibniz. Initially appointed to the committee were John Arbuthnot, Abraham Hill, Edmond Halley, William Jones, John Machin and William Burnet – solid Newtonians to a man. Later added to the committee were the further disciples of Newton, Francis Robartes, A. de Moivre, Francis Aston, Brook Taylor and the Prussian minister in London, Frederick Bonet.

The committee, described by Newton as 'composed of Gentlemen of several Nations', was ready to submit its report on 24 April 1712. It is difficult to believe that many of the committee's members could have had time to examine at all carefully much of the detailed and complex material assembled. Nevertheless, they found:

1 Leibniz had communicated, between early 1673 and September 1676, with John Collins who had been 'very free in Communicating . . . what he had received from Mr Newton and Mr Gregory';

2 Leibniz had been shown earlier by John Pell to have claimed 'Mouton's Method' as his own discovery;

3 Newton's discovery of the method of fluxions is clearly documented in manuscripts of 1669 and 1671;

4 the only difference between the method of fluxions and the differential method is their names and the 'Mode of Notation'.

Consequently, the committee concluded *nem con*: 'we reckon Mr Newton the first Inventor; and are of opinion that Mr Keill in asserting the same has been noways injurious to Mr Leibniz' (C, V, p. xxvi).

The work, with the full title *Commercium epistolicum D. Johannis Collins et aliorum de analysi promota* (The Correspondence of John Collins and others Relating to the Progress of Analysis), was published under the direction of Halley, Machin and Jones on 29 January 1713. It consisted of a brief report followed by the documentation on which the report supposedly rested. This in turn consisted of selections from the correspondence of Newton, Isaac Barrow, John Collins, James Gregory, John Wallis, John Keill, Henry Oldenburg, R. F. de Sluse and Leibniz. The book itself was never offered for sale. Instead it was issued free to interested parties, with twenty-five copies being sent to the Hague for distribution on the Continent.

Although, in Hall's words, 'The documents are fairly and accurately quoted' (C, V, p. xxvii), the CE remains as partial a document as ever a learned society is likely to issue. It is, of course, manifest that a committee constituted by disciples of Newton would be most unlikely to scrutinise at all critically evidence relating to the Society's President, even if they had been given sufficient time to do so. In any case, the material presented to them had been selected and assembled by one of the interested parties, Newton himself. Nor had the other interested party, Leibniz, been offered any opportunity to present his own evidence or to answer the charges brought against him.

There is, in addition, an even deeper degree of duplicity. Much of the report, documents would later show, had been drafted by Newton himself. His final draft is at present in private hands. Hall has shown, however, that virtually all the substantive parts of the published report are taken directly from Newton's draft, including such supposedly impartial judgments as 'the Differential Method is one and the same with the Method of Fluxions', and 'we reckon Mr Newton the first Inventor' (C, V, p. xxvi). 'No man', Newton would tell Leibniz in 1715, with an hypocrisy so monumental as to be scarcely credible, 'is a Witness in his own Cause' (he could also have added 'nor is he likely to prove a trustworthy judge'). As a final step Newton contributed a long, anonymous review of the CE, known as the *Account*, to the PT (1715).

The CE has proved to be a most unpopular work and is known in only the four following editions.

1 London, 1713, 122 pp.
2 London, 1722. Edited by John Keill, it contains also an *Ad lectorem* (6 pp., by Newton), the *Recensio* (a fifty-nine-page Latin translation of the *Account* of 1715), an *Appendix*, and various annotations, also by Newton and also as anonymous as all the other additions.
3 London, 1782. The CE and *Recensio* were included in vol.IV of Horsley, reprinted in a facsimile edition in 1964 in Stuttgart (Bad Cannstatt).
4 Paris, 1856. Edited by J. Biot and F. Lefort and with comments and the publication of much relevant material.

See also An Account . . .; Priority dispute

Conatus

Descartes spoke of a *conatus a centro*, an endeavour from the centre, possessed by such bodies as stones whirled around in slings. At the hands of Huygens it became the more familiar expression, centrifugal force. The term was used by Newton in his early manuscript *On Circular Motion* where he spoke, for example, of 'the conatus of the moon' as it endeavoured to recede from the earth's centre. Several years later, in a letter to Oldenburg dated 23 June 1673, Newton was still thinking in much the same way. Perhaps, he speculated, the reason why the moon always revealed the same side to the earth was because of 'the greater conatus of the other side to recede from it' (Herivel, 1965, p. 236; *C*, I, p. 290).

Surprisingly, long after he had abandoned the notion of centrifugal force, Newton continued to speak of the *conatus* of a body. It is to be found, for example, in def.IX of *De motu corporum in mediis regulariter ceedentibus*, dating from 1685, and in a draft for the Scholium to the definitions of *Principia* where, indeed, the term was retained (Cajori, p. 9). Cohen, however, has plausibly argued that such occurrences are simply 'examples of the persistence of forceful phrases that remain long after the concepts for which they originally stood have been rejected' (Cohen, 1980, p. 237). The issue is discussed at length in Herivel (1965, Chapter 3).

See also Centrifugal force

Conduitt, John (1688–1737)

Educated at Trinity College, Cambridge, and, though a man of substance, an MP from 1721, and the Master of the Mint from 1727, still remembered as the man who married Newton's niece, Catherine Barton. After leaving Cambridge, Conduitt seems to have spent several years serving in a civilian capacity with the British Army in Portugal and Gibraltar during the War of Spanish Succession. On his return to England he was a wealthy man. How much of this was inherited and how much acquired during his years abroad is not known.

He first came to Newton's attention through a communication submitted to the RS in late 1716 on the location of the Roman city of Carteia some few miles outside Gibraltar. Newton took the chair when Conduitt read the paper to the Society on 30 June 1717. Assuming this to be the first time Conduitt met Newton and Catherine, events moved quickly thereafter. A few weeks later, in August, the twenty-nine year old Conduitt married the thirty-eight year old Catherine Barton. Conduitt owned a country house, Cranbury Park, Hampshire, where he and Catherine spent some time. When in London they stayed with Newton.

Conduitt clearly enjoyed the role of nephew-in-law to Newton. While Newton's attitude to Conduitt is unknown, the undiluted hero worship offered him by Conduitt is likely to have formed the basis for an agreeable relationship. There was more to Conduitt, however, than simple hero worship. On two occasions in particular, without the intervention of Conduitt, much of the recorded evidence of Newton's life would have been irretrievably lost.

Shortly after Newton's death he wrote to a number 'who had so great a share in his esteem' and asked them to record their memories of Newton. Amongst those invited to cooperate were John Machin, John Craig and A. de Moivre. The initial cause was to collect material for the *éloge* to be delivered in Paris by Fontenelle. It is clear, however, that Conduitt was planning also to compose a memoir of Newton. The results were a forty-two-page manuscript on Newton's life before going to Cambridge, sixteen pages on his life and work at Cambridge, seventeen pages of miscellaneous anecdotes, an equal amount on his character, and a page or two each on his manual dexterity and his final illness. Much of this, edited by Conduitt, was copied and sent to Fontenelle. Although the bulk of Conduitt's material, as the primary source of much of Newton's early life, has been used and used again by writers on Newton, the full text of his collection has never been published. Almost all of it is to be found in the Keynes Collection in KCC. The actual material sent to Fontenelle was published by Turnor (1806, pp. 158–67).

It was also largely due to Conduitt that the integrity of Newton's papers, as the PC, was initially maintained. In the final agreement with Newton's uterine kin drawn up in 1727 it was decided that Conduitt 'shall have such papers which shall not be thought proper to be printed'. In return he was forced into guaranteeing any outstanding debts left by Newton at the Mint. The commitment was unlimited, while in return he received no more than thousands of pages dismissed by the experts as unprintable. However it seems reasonably clear that if Conduitt had not stepped in at this time the bulk of the material now making up the PC would have been destroyed.

One further responsibility discharged by Conduitt is to be seen in Westminster Abbey. It was Conduitt who commissioned the artists William Kent and Michael Rysbrack to work on the sarcophagus to Newton's tomb, and it was also Conduitt who apparently designed the monument (Haskell, 1970, p. 305). At the same time he commissioned from Rysbrack the portrait bust of Newton still in the possession of the Portsmouth family. He also commissioned in the 1720s three portraits of Newton.

Although Conduitt did succeed Newton as Master of the Mint, the nomination did not come from Newton. He had apparently wished the post to go to Samuel Clarke (Ferguson, 1976, p. 158). Clarke, however, was not interested. On being appointed to the post Conduitt showed his gratitude to Clarke by giving his son £1,000.

On his death a memorial plaque was placed in Westminster Abbey. Characteristically it records before all else his relationship to Newton.

See also Barton, Catherine; Biography; Fontenelle, Bernard

Conduitt, Kitty/Catherine (b.1718)

The only child of Catherine Barton and John Conduitt, Kitty married John Wallop, Viscount Lymington, and eldest son of the first Earl of Portsmouth, in 1740. They had five children, with her eldest son becoming in 1762 the second Earl of Portsmouth. It is thus through Kitty that Newton's papers passed into the hands of the Portsmouth family. Kitty also inherited from Newton a £4,000 estate in Kensington.

See also Family; Portsmouth Collection

Considerations upon Rectifying the Julian Kalendar

Unpublished, although Brewster (1855, vol. II, pp. 311–12) included a brief summary of the work. He dated it to 1699 and noted that there were two copies in the PC.

After describing the Julian, Egyptian and Gregorian years, Newton went on to propose what he took to be the best form of the solar calendar. Introduced in 1582, the Gregorian calendar reduced the Julian calendar by ten days and consequently restored the date of the vernal equinox to March 21. To prevent any future equinoctial drift, three out of every four centurial years – those not divisible by 400 (1700, 1800 and 1900, for example) – would drop their leap day. The consequence of such an apparently minor change was to provide a mean length for the calendar year of 365.2425 days as opposed to 365.2422 days for the tropical year – a difference of only twenty-six seconds a year. The idea originated with Aloisius Lilius, a physician at the University of Perugia, who published the details of his new calendar in his *Compendium novae rationis restituendi kalendarium* (1576). Newton proposed a somewhat neater system (Brewster, 1855, vol. II, pp. 311–12).

> To divide it by the four cardinal periods of the quinoxes and solstices, so that the quarters of the year may begin at the equinox and solstice as they ought to do, and then to divide every quarter into three equal months, which will be done by making the six winter months to consist of thirty days each, and the six summer months of thirty one days each, excepting one of them, suppose the last, which in leap years shall have thirty one days, in the others only

thirty days. At the end of every hundred years, omit the intercalary day in the leap year, excepting at the end of every five hundred years. For the rule is exacter than the Gregorian, of omitting it at the end of every hundred years, excepting the end of every four hundred years, and thus reckoning by five hundreds and thousands of years is rounder than the other by four hundred, eight hundred and twelve hundred. And this I take to be the simplest, and in all respects the best form of the civil year that can be thought of.

How did the various systems compare in practice? Over a period of 2,000 years the Julian, Gregorian and Newtonian calendars would produce the following results:

Julian: 2,000 years of 365 days plus 500 leap days – 730,500 days
Gregorian: 2,000 years of 365 days plus 485 leap days – 730,485 days
Newtonian: 2,000 years of 365 days plus 484 leap days – 730,484 days

As 2,000 tropical years equal 730,484.4 days, the Newtonian calendar is marginally more accurate than the Gregorian. Or, to compare the results in a slightly different way, the length of a year in each system works out at:

Tropical year   – 365.2422 days
Julian year   – 365.25 days
Gregorian year – 365.2425 days
Newtonian year – 365.242 days

See also Calendrical writings

Conti, Abbé Antonio-Schinella (1677–1748)

Usually described as a Venetian nobleman, Conti was first heard of in Paris in 1713 seeking out such leading figures of French science as Malebranche and Fontenelle. By 1715 he had moved to London and could be seen dining with Newton and attending Caroline, Princess of Wales.

Conti chose, perhaps at the suggestion of Caroline, to make yet one more attempt to resolve the long-standing dispute between Leibniz and Newton on their contributions to the development of the calculus. The result was a brief correspondence between Newton and Leibniz, directed at all times to Conti, over the period April 1715 to April 1716 (*C*, VI, pp. 215, 250–3, 285–8, 304–12). Far from achieving any reconciliation, the correspondence seems, if anything, to have extended the dispute into new areas. Newton published the correspondence, together with his *Observations* (*C*, VI, pp. 341–9), in the second edition of Raphson's *History of Fluxions* (1718).

In 1716 Conti accompanied George I to Hanover. He arrived too late, however, to meet Leibniz, who had died on 4 November. Accordingly he wrote to Newton later in the month informing him that 'M. Leibniz est mort; et la dispute est finie' (*C*, VI, p. 376). He also seems to have acquired at this time a number of Leibniz's manuscript letters and papers relevant to the dispute. They later appeared in des Maizeaux's *Recueil* (1720).

Conti returned to London in 1717. He left soon after in 1718 for Paris, taking with him a copy of Newton's *A Short Chronicle*. His decision to show the work to the scholars of Paris and to allow in 1725 its unauthorised publication was seen by Newton as an intolerable betrayal of his trust. While in England, Newton complained, Conti had 'pretended to be my friend' but thereafter he was guilty of the grave offence of 'engaging me in new Disputes' (RSW, p. 811). Conti replied by noting that Newton himself had been quite happy to print, without permission, a letter from Leibniz. In any case, he added, he held such work in no greater esteem than 'the quadrille or hunting'.

He did, however, go out of his way to publicise a rival and, at the time, little-known work, the *Scienza Nuova* of Giambattista Vico. First published in an obscure edition of 1725, Conti had drawn the attention of French scholars to the work and encouraged Vico to produce in 1730 a second and more available edition. Such, claimed Manuel (1963, p. 34), was the 'relentless tenacity' with which Conti pursued Newton even after his death.

See also *A Short Chronicle*; Priority dispute

Corpuscular theory of light

Light, Newton repeatedly emphasised, travels in straight lines. In contrast, waves 'bend manifestly'. Sounds can be heard from the other side of a hill; the cause of the sound will remain out of sight behind the mound of earth. From such a simple and basic observation Newton drew the conclusion that light, whatever it was, could not possibly be a wave.

Of what then are rays of light composed? Are they not, he answered in Query 29, 'very small Bodies emitted from shining substances?' The suggestion was taken up and developed by later writers. Robert Smith, for example, in his *Compleat System of Opticks* (1738), declared that the 'properties and effects of light are exactly similar to the properties and effects of bodies of sensible bulk'. Light was, he concluded, nothing other than 'a very small and distinct particle of matter' (Steffens, 1977, p. 35).

Such a view was not without its difficulties, and the initial problem facing the Newtonians was to demonstrate that the corpuscular theory could cope with such difficulties. The most obvious problems turned on the supposed mass of light. If light particles really were small hard bodies, how could light beams intersect without destroying each other? Surely, also, it was argued, bodies like the sun should be diminishing regularly as vast numbers of light particles were emitted; as the mass of the sun decreased, its attractive power would weaken, and planetary orbits would enlarge. No such effect, however, had been noticed. Thirdly, it was asked, how could a delicate structure like the eye withstand the constant bombardment from energetic particles of light?

The basic defence of the Newtonians to such objections was to insist upon the minuteness of light particles. So small were they, in fact, according to one calculation, that the massive daily output of solar energy amounted to no more than a loss of mass of two grains. Not small enough, however, for their momentum to remain undetected. As a result, several scholars attempted to demonstrate experimentally the momentum of light. The best-known such experiment, performed by John Michell in the 1750s, involved focusing sunlight on a copper plate suspended in a torsion balance. He found that light rays struck the plate and moved it about an inch. Using Michell's data, Joseph Priestley went on to calculate, on the assumption that the sun was as dense as water, that the solar diameter would decrease by about 2in a century. Newton's own answer to the supposed wastage of the sun was somewhat different. Allowing that the sun did indeed lose mass by the emission of light, he argued that it could be replenished by collisions with comets.

One further set of arguments concerned the immutability of light, for if light did consist of the 'solid, massy, hard, impenetrable, moveable Particles' of Newton, then it should be subject to neither change or decay. One difficulty in this view was presented by the phenomenon of phosphorescence. Certain substances, it was argued, absorbed light of one colour and emitted light of a quite different colour. The experimental evidence for this view, however, was sufficiently confusing as to allow Newtonians like Joseph Priestley to quote it in their favour.

A final property demanded of light was that, like other material bodies, it should respond to gravitational attraction. One who set out to detect and measure the effect of gravity on light was the indefatigable John Michell. Light emitted from stars more massive than the sun should be, Michell argued, somewhat retarded. This reduction in velocity should be detectable as an increased refractive index. The effect was unsuccessfully sought for by the Astronomer Royal, Nevil Maskelyne. Perhaps, Michell mused, the negative result showed that there were no stars significantly more massive than the sun; or, again, it could be that light was rather special and was not affected by gravity as other bodies. Whatever the reason, there were clearly too many unknowns in Michell's work to allow anyone to claim readily that his failure had disproved the corpuscular theory of light.

A second argument advanced by Newton against the wave theory lay in its seeming inability to explain the phenomenon of double refraction. No such weakness was to be met with in the corpuscular theory. When, however, the phenomena of interference and polarisation were discovered early in the nineteenth century, it soon became clear that the wave theory was much more adaptable to such new phenomena than the rather restricted corpuscular theory. Although a few English physicists continued to reject the wave theory, an extensive report presented to the British Association in 1834 by Humphrey Lloyd on *The Present State of Physical Optics* came out strongly against them. Thereafter, in the words of Steffens, 'The Newtonian system of optics did not suffer defeat in England in the 1830s, it simply failed to attract new adherents' (p. 150).

See also Double refraction; Wave theory of light

Correspondence

Items from Newton's considerable correspondence had begun to appear during his life. The *Algebra* (1699) of John Wallis, and Newton's own *Analysis per quantitatum series* (1711), for example, contained extracts from letters to Henry Oldenburg, John Collins and Wallis himself. Several other items appeared throughout the century. The *Biographica Britannica* (1760) published extracts from the 1686–7 correspondence with Halley on the publication of *Principia* (1687), along with material taken from letters to Flamsteed, Collins and Oldenburg. The *Four Letters to Bentley* appeared in 1756, while the various letters on light from the 1670s were included in Castillioneus (1744, *Tome* II). Similar selections appeared in Birch (1756–7) and Horsley.

In the nineteenth century further details of the Halley correspondence, together with several other items, were added by Rigaud (1838), Brewster and Ball (1893). Four new collections appeared: the Flamsteed–Newton letters in Baily (1835); the correspondence with Collins in Rigaud (1841); thirteen letters to John Covel were edited by Dawson Turner (1848); and the impressively prepared correspondence between Newton and Cotes was published by Edleston (1850).

Despite such valuable collections, by 1900 less than a quarter of the correspondence had been published. Against this, Continental editors were already hard at work on collected editions of the works of such important figures as Descartes, Galileo, Huygens and Euler. The first sign that anything comparable was being planned for Newton came in 1904 with the announcement from the Cambridge Philosophical Society of their decision to publish a complete edition of Newton's scientific works and correspondence. As editor, the astronomer R. A. Sampson was chosen. The choice was far from wise. Too concerned with the satellites of Jupiter, Sampson confessed later in 1924 that he had had no time to devote to Newton's papers. Despite further calls in 1924 from the astronomer, J. L. E. Dreyer, and the then Secretary of the Royal Society, Sir Joseph Larmor, nothing more was actually done before 1938. No doubt wishing to avoid the embarrassment of having nothing to show at the impending tercentenary of Newton's birth in 1942, a committee was set up under the chairmanship of Sir Charles Sherrington 'to discuss the question of the publication of the Newton letters'. H. C. Plummer was appointed editor, but the intervention of the War years, and Plummer's own declining health, allowed little to be done except to work out the editorial principles to be followed and to begin to assemble the actual materials to be collected. After the Second World War, and Plummer's death in 1946, a new committee was set up in 1947 under the chairmanship of E. N. da C. Andrade. The historian of mathematics, H. W. Turnbull, was appointed as editor.

The great achievement of Plummer had been to adopt from the start very generous principles of inclusion. Not only were all letters to and from Newton to be published *in extenso*, but, also to be included were 'extracts from contemporary letters referring to Newton' and 'shorter memoranda illustrating the life of Newton, particularly minor and hitherto unpublished manuscripts of Newton'. Further, all letters originally in Latin would be translated into English. The first volume dealing with the period 1661–75 appeared in 1959. Turnbull managed to complete two more volumes before his own health forced him to resign in 1959. He was succeeded by J. F. Scott, his assistant editor. Scott, however, survived only long enough to edit vol. IV in 1967. The last three volumes were consequently edited by A. R. Hall and Laura Tilling, with the final seventh volume appearing in 1977.

The *Correspondence* contains 1,553 items plus a further 225 'additions and Corrections to Earlier Volumes' published in vol. VII. Of this total, about 430 are letters written by Newton himself, a quarter of which had already been published in some form or other. A further thirty letters turned up in 1982. They had been sold as Lot 129 during the Sotheby sale of 1936 to Dr Erik Waller. They were eventually located in the University of Uppsala and were published, often abbreviated, in English translation by Hall (1982, pp. 7–34). They consist 'mostly of compliments from foreign Scholars (in Latin)' (*C*, VII, p. 357).

The *Correspondence* is most often consulted as the repository of a number of relatively self-contained series of letters. Especially significant are the series with the following individuals.

  1 John Collins (vol. I–II), in which Newton first revealed his mathematical genius to the outside world. It is also a correspondence full of character and dramatic interest. Collins was keen to get as much of Newton's material as he could and to disseminate it as

widely as possible. The conflict this approach produced when it met the reticent personality and unpredictable moods of the young Newton make a fascinating study.

2 Henry Oldenburg (vol.I–II), in a more official capacity, did for Newton's optics what Collins had done for his mathematics. The results were similar and equally fascinating.

3 E. Halley (vol.II). These letters tell the remarkable story of the publication of the first edition of *Principia* (1687).

4 John Flamsteed (vol.II–VI). The longest running correspondence and, in many ways, the most interesting. It is certainly the most complex and presents the story of two strong-willed, bad-tempered and intolerant philosophers who needed each other's services but, despite some genuine efforts on both sides, found each other impossible to get on with.

5 Robert Hooke (vol.II); a correspondence in which Newton's first public attempt to understand celestial motions was cruelly exposed.

6 Fatio de Duillier (vol.III); a short-lived but, by Newton's standards, intense and enigmatic correspondence.

7 John Locke (vol.III–IV); a not very extensive correspondence, but revealing never the less.

8 Richard Bentley (vol.III). Four important letters on the interpretation of Newtonian science.

9 John Covel (vol.III). Newton's official reports to his Parliamentary seat of events in the Convention Parliament.

10 Roger Cotes (vol.IV–V); follows the numerous changes and revisions introduced into the second edition of *Principia* (1713).

11 Priority dispute (vol.V–VII).

12 Henry Pemberton (vol.VII); preparations for the final edition of *Principia* (1726).

There is, of course, much more of interest besides. It is surprising, for example, to see from vol.IV onwards just how much of Newton's time was taken up by Mint affairs. Equally, the reader is made aware throughout the correspondence that family matters and estate affairs were seldom long absent from Newton's thoughts. A further item of interest was the willingness shown by Newton to respond to the casual correspondent. Although he might refuse to prolong a polemical issue with one of his colleagues, to any who seemed merely curious, or in need of information, he would respond politely, helpfully and promptly.

A full analysis of the correspondence is yet to be made. The claim of Hall (*C*, VII, p. xlv), for example, that 'In not one of his extant letters does he show humour or affection, or forbearance of the failings of others, unless in his allusion to his grand-niece Kitty' is clearly a judgment requiring further consideration.

Also needing further analysis is the actual style of the correspondence.

CORRESPONDENCE

The first impression gained is one of unvarying formality. This is a world in which even brothers begin their letters to each other with a 'Sir', and in which Halley and Newton, colleagues of forty years, could still conclude their letters to each other in terms of 'Your most humble servant Isaac Newton', and 'Your most faithfull servt Edm:Halley' (*C*, VII, pp. 294 and 302). It was a convention Newton and his correspondents scrupulously followed. The furthest he seemed able to move from such conventional courtesies was with Fatio, to whom he became 'Your most affectionate friend' (*C*, III, p. 263), and to his niece Catherine he concluded his only surviving letter to her 'Your very loving Unkle' (*C*, IV, p. 349). Catherine did not respond in similar terms, signing herself in later life as 'Your most dutiful niece and most obliged servant' (*C*, VII, p. 74).

After formality, the next impression gained is one of great seriousness. Not only is the correspondence marked by an almost total lack of humour, it is also unrelieved by anything as light as gossip or anecdote. Letters for Newton were thus primarily a means of conducting business or conveying information and only secondarily, if at all, a permissible form of social exchange. Many family letters have survived. None, however, seems to be concerned with the mere exchange of family news; all, rather, are written in the performance or acknowledgment of some item of business.

A final impression conveyed by the correspondence is of great variety. All Newton's interests, be they mathematical, chemical, theological, historical, physical, political, financial, or whatever, are amply represented. There is also a tremendous range of correspondents. At one end of the scale there are letters to such powerful noblemen as the Earls of Halifax and Oxford; at the other there are pleas of mercy from those in Newgate awaiting their execution for counterfeiting. Along with a fair number of seemingly standard begging letters, there can be found the intensely personal and dramatic signs of Newton's 1693 breakdown; while, in terms of length, there are letters of a few words reporting the dispatch of a barrel of oysters, and letters of several thousand words on topics of more durable value. There is even a letter from an otherwise unknown 'D.S.' asking the President of the Royal Society to settle a 'considerable wager' on whether a ball dropped from the top of a ship's mast in harbour would fall 'perpendicular to some exact Poynt beneath as if ye Shipp were in its swiftest Motion' (*C*, VI, p. 371). The reply should be sent to 'Toms Coffee House, Cornhill'.

There remains the question of forgeries. A large number, 622 to be exact, emerged in the 1860s, authenticated by Michel Chasles (1793–1880), a leading mathematician of the day, including a number from Pascal. Few can have been taken in by such crude forgeries, apart from Chasles himself. More accessible is a supposed letter from Newton to a Dr Law and published first in *Nature* (12 May 1881); it can also be seen in Lodge (1960, pp. 201–2). With its brash style and jocular manner it is most un-Newtonian. Hall is convinced, however, that no forgeries have made their way into the *Correspondence* (*C*, VII, p. 386).

Coste, Pierre (1668–1747)

Born at Uzes in the Languedoc, Coste was one more Huguenot refugee who left France after the revocation of the Edict of Nantes, settling first in Amsterdam, where he survived by writing, translating and teaching. In 1697 he was appointed tutor to the son of Francis Masham and went to stay with the family at Oates in Suffolk, the house which already had John Locke as a resident. During his stay he translated Locke's *Essay Concerning Human Understanding* into French. Later, helped by Desaguliers, he made the first French translation of the *Opticks* (1704), 'par l'ordre d'une grande Princesse', presumably Princess Caroline (*Traité d'optique*, 1720). It was revised by Varignon in a second edition published in 1722. Coste was unhappy with the manner in which this work was produced. He wrote to Newton in August 1721 (*C*, VII, pp. 147–9) complaining that he had been 'used coarsely' as he had not been shown the 'corrections of Mr. de Moivre before they were printed', his own corrections were ignored, and he was having to face 'the slanders of Mr. Des Maizeaux'. Newton's reply has not survived.

Cotes, Roger (1682–1716)

Educated at St Paul's and TCC, Cotes was soon spotted by R. Bentley as a man of talent, and under his patronage was elected a Fellow of Trinity in 1705 and the first Plumian Professor of Astronomy in 1706. While several members of Newton's immediate circle of disciples saw themselves as editors of the planned second edition of *Principia*, the post went to Cotes. The first indication that Newton was doing anything more than planning an edition of *Principia* appeared in a letter to him from Bentley dated 10 June 1708 (*C*, IV, pp. 518–19). Bentley had already had a 'specimen of the first sheet' printed but, as yet, there was no mention of Cotes. At this point Bentley himself seemed firmly in charge of the new edition. Yet, a few months later, in March 1709, Newton was sending Cotes, via Bentley, a corrected copy of *Principia* as editor of the proposed new edition. While it can be readily appreciated why Newton would have been unhappy to have Bentley, with his lack of mathematics and willingness to alter an author's text as editor, nothing has survived to indicate why Cotes was selected for the task.

Whatever the reasons, the results were, in Cohen's phrase, 'extremely fortunate' (1971, p. 227). Cotes was, Cohen has pointed out, not only able enough to see where *Principia* could be improved but also 'able to criticise Newton and correct his errors without ever anatagonising him – no mean feat'. When he first began his duties and informed Newton of some errors he had found in the second corollary of prop.XCI of Book I he was politely but firmly told by Newton not to bother with such details. It would be labour enough, he argued, 'corrcting only such faults as occurr in reading over the sheets' (*C*, V, p. 5). Cotes was, however, too conscientious, too persistent and, as soon became apparent, too much concerned with the reputation of Newton to allow himself to become a mere proof-reader. Newton soon came to recognise the quality of Cotes's work and before long he was sending him such comments as 'The corrections you have made are very well & I thank you for them, and am glad that the Theory of the resistance of fluids does not displease you provided the XXXVIth Proposition be true, as I think it is' (*C*, V, p. 70); and, in his next letter to Cotes, 'I received both your Letters and am sensible that I must try three or four Experiments before I can answer your former' (*C*, V, p. 75); or, 'I have read over and considered your alterations, and like them very well and return you my thanks' (*C*, V, p. 164).

Despite Newton's respect for and willingness to cooperate with Cotes, there were still the inevitable delays suffered by all Newton's editors. Initially, progress was rapid. In September 1709 Cotes received copy for *Principia* up to prop.XXXIII of Book II. By 15 April 1710 Cotes was informing Newton that he had printed 'so much of ye Copy You sent us yt I must now beg of you to think of finishing the remaining part as soon as You can with convenience' (*C*, V, p. 24). This had taken the work as far as prop.VII of Book II. At this point Cotes found the remainder of Book II full of obscurities, difficulties, and even several errors. He informed Newton accordingly, after which progress was much slower. Newton was thus forced, Cohen has judged, to undertake a far more drastic revision of Book II than he had originally planned (1971, p. 231). The first 296 pages of the eventually 448-page work had been printed by 30 June 1710; Cotes received the rest of the copy on 13 September 1710. Nothing else, however, was printed until June of the following year.

Delays continued. In July 1711 Cotes raised some queries about prop.XLVIII of Book II. Newton replied shortly afterwards that he had been 'so taken up with other affairs that I have had no time to think of Mathematicks' (*C*, V, p. 179). It was not in fact until the February of 1712 that he responded to the queries of Cotes over prop.XLVIII. There then began a detailed discussion on several propositions of Book III. 'I fear I give you too much trouble with my Letters' Cotes apologised on 3 May 1712, but persisted none the less. However, despite the further queries pressed by Cotes, Newton remained helpful, cooperative and, on the whole, prompt in his replies. Thereafter progress was rapid and in November 1712 Cotes informed Newton that the work was complete, 'excepting about 20 lines' (*C*, V, p. 356).

His confidence, however, was misplaced. By this time Newton had heard from Nicolas Bernoulli that his uncle, Johann, had discovered an error in prop.X of Book II. It was not until 6 January 1713 that Newton was able to send to Cotes 'the tenth Proposition of the second book corrected' (*C*, V, p. 361). One final item, the General *Scholium*, was sent to Cotes on 2 March 1713.

At this point Cotes, who had spoken with candour and force to Newton on the contents of *Principia*, became conspiratorial and submissive over the question of the Preface. Would Newton prefer him to attack Leibniz, he asked Bentley; or, he went on, would it not be better if Newton used the Preface to mount such an attack under the cover of Cotes's name (*C*, V, p. 389). Newton, however, at this time, was reluctant to provoke Leibniz further and accordingly sent instructions via Bentley that he 'spare ye *Name* of Leibniz, and abstain from all words or Epithets of reproach'. Cotes should write the Preface himself. When he tried to clear the matter with Newton and to ask what questions he should discuss, he was told simply to get on with it. 'I must not see it', Newton added, 'for I find that I shall be examined about it' (*C*, V, p. 400). Such scruples, it should be pointed out, had not prevented him, for example, in interfering in the far more delicate matter of the *Commercium epistolicum* (1713).

Consequently, the Preface was sent to Samuel Clarke, not Newton, for a final check. Suggestions made by him were incorporated willingly by Cotes into the final version. Just as remarkable, in its own way, is the Preface contributed by Newton to the volume. Unlike the Preface to the first edition, with its handsome acknowledgment of Halley's contribution, and to the later third edition, with its generous reference to the 'care' shown by Henry Pemberton, no reference to Cotes, let alone expressions of gratitude, are to be found in Newton's Preface of 1713.

Newton had not, however, completely forgotten Cotes. Two years later, on 8 November 1715, he wrote to him to see if he would be interested in the post of Master of Charterhouse, recently fallen vacant through the death of Thomas Burnet and worth £200 a year plus 'lodgings meat drink and fire and the maintenance of one or two servants' (*C*, VI, p. 248). If Cotes could assure him of his 'firmness to the present government under King George', then Newton was sure he could obtain the post for him. Cotes's reply has not survived, but his continued presence at Cambridge suggests that he found the offer unattractive.

In any case Cotes had little more than six months to live. On 5 June 1716 he died 'upon a Relapse into Fever attended with a violent Diarrhoea and consyant Delirium' (Edleston, 1850, p. lxxvi). On his death Newton bestowed on Cotes the tribute he had denied him in his life:

'If He had lived we might have known something', he declared to Robert Smith, Cotes's cousin and successor in the Plumian chair. Smith also provided more permanent monuments to Cotes by arranging for the posthumous publication of his *Harmonia mensarum* (1722) and *Hydrostatical and Pneumatical Lectures* (1738). Smith also commissioned the Scheemakers' bust of Cotes which can still be seen in TCC.

See also Principia, Origin and production, and Cotes's Preface to the second edition of 1713

Covel, John (1638–1722)

Covel entered Newton's life through his service as Vice-chancellor of Cambridge University in 1689, the year Newton represented the University in the Convention Parliament. Newton reported to Covel any proceedings in Parliament relevant to the University's interests and went on to advise Covel how the University should respond. The fourteen letters sent by Newton have survived and can be seen in *C*, III, pp. 10–25). The correspondence was first published by Dawson Turner in 1848.

Covel had earlier served as Chaplain to the Levant Company, spending the period 1670–6 in Constantinople, and the two following years travelling throughout the Near East. Before returning to England he served as Chaplain to the Princess of Orange at the Hague from 1681 to 1685. In 1688 he was appointed Master of Christ's College, Cambridge.

See also Thirteen Letters from Isaac Newton to John Covel; Turner, Dawson

---

Craig, John (d.1731)

Little is known of Craig's background. A pupil of David Gregory, he published two early mathematical treatises on the calculus, *Methodus figarum . . . quadraturas determinandi* (1685, The Method of Determining the Quadratures of Figures), and *Tractatus . . . de figarum curvilinearum quadraturis* (1693, Tract on the Quadratures of Curved Figures).

In 1685 Craig visited Newton in Cambridge and is thought to have seen some of the developing *Principia* manuscript. He was also shown some of Newton's work on the calculus and on infinite series. Details of this work were conveyed to David Gregory, Archibald Pitcairne, Colin Campbell and, no doubt, other Edinburgh colleagues.

Craig was also the author of one of the strangest works to appear under the influence of Newton, *Theologiae christianae principia mathematica*

(1699, *Mathematical Principles of Christian Theology*). It sought to use mathematical reasoning, in the manner of Newton, to establish the time of Christ's return. It thus began with three laws, the first of which, almost in parody of the law of inertia, reads: 'Every man endeavours to prolong pleasure in his mind, to increase it, or to persevere in a state of pleasure.'

Craig's basic insight derived from Luke 18:8: 'when the Son of Man cometh shall he find faith on earth?' But we know, Craig insisted, that the degree of belief we are prepared to assign written history diminishes with time. If we could only work out the rate at which our credibility fades we should be able to calculate precisely when the probability accorded to the Gospels will fall to zero. This in turn, given the truth of Luke 18:8, would yield an upper bound for Christ's return. Using such lemmas as 'Velocities of suspicion produced in equal periods of time increase in arithmetical progression', and equations of ever-growing complexity, Craig finally concluded that the second coming must take place before the year 3150 AD.

In later life Craig produced a further mathematical tract, *De calculo fluentes* (1718, On the Calculus of Fluents). He had been elected to the RS in 1711. His own career was in the church in which he served as a Prebendary first, from 1708, at Durnford, near Salisbury, and after 1726 at Gillingham in Dorset.

Crell, Samuel (1660–1741)

A member of an old Polish Socinian family, Crell came to England in 1726. He was working on a book which would demonstrate the corrupt nature of all texts in St John's gospel which suggested the divinity of Christ, a topic of perennial interest to Newton and one on which, in his *Two Corruptions* (1754), he had written at length himself. The work, *Initium Evangelii S. Johannis Apostoli* (1726), is to be found in Newton's library.

Crell somehow made contact with Newton and has left a valuable and independent account of Newton's state of mind during the last few months of his life. Writing in July 1727, Crell noted: 'I also conversed at different times with the illustrious Newton . . . He read manuscript without spectacles . . . still reasoned acutely.' Crell also confirmed the report of John Conduitt that 'a few weeks before his death he threw into the fire many manuscripts written in his own hand' (Brewster, vol. I, p. 390).

Croker, John (1670–1741)

Born in Dresden, the son of a woodworker, Croker was apprenticed to a goldsmith. He came to England in 1691 and in 1697 was appointed assistant engraver at the Mint; later in 1705 became the Mint's chief engraver, a post he occupied until his death in 1741. As the engraver of all dies for gold and silver coins throughout the reigns of Anne and George I, and during the first fourteen years of George II, Croker literally put his stamp on the British coinage of his generation. He also designed many commemorative medals. It was also Croker who in 1731 engraved the Mint medal of Newton.

Crownfield, Cornelius

A Dutchman, Crownfield worked as a Cambridge bookseller from 1698 to 1743. He also served as printer to the University from 1706 to 1740 and in this capacity was commissioned by Richard Bentley to print the second edition of *Principia* in 1713.

Cycloid

Also known as a roulette, a trochoid and, because of its power to incite quarrels amongst mathematicians, the Helen of geometry; it is in fact the curve traced by a point on a circumference of a circle rolling along a fixed straight line. Unknown to the Greeks, it was described first by Charles Bouvelles in 1501; it was not, however, until the seventeenth century that mathematicians began to investigate intensively the curve's properties. Included amongst these properties were the following.

1 Area. G. P. de Roberval demonstrated in 1634 that the area under the cycloid's arch was three times the area of the generating circle. The result was independently worked out and published for the first time by E. Torricelli in 1644.

2 Tangent. De Roberval also demonstrated in 1638 how to draw tangents to cycloids; similar results were obtained by Fermat and Descartes.

3 Length. The rectification of the cycloid was worked out by Christopher Wren in 1658 to be four times the diameter of the generating circle.

4 Tautochrone. Christian Huygens was aware that the swing of a pendulum in a circular arc was not strictly isochronous. What curve, he asked, would yield oscillations of an exactly equal period? In 1658 he demonstrated that balls placed anywhere inside an inverted

cycloid would all reach the lowest point of the bowl in exactly the same time. The cycloid was thus the curve of equal descent, more formally known as the tautochrone. Huygens at once set about attempting to introduce his discovery in his newly invented pendulum clock.

5 Brachistochrone. In 1696 Johann Bernoulli posed the following problem. Given two points A and B, such that B is below but not directly below A, what is the curve connecting A to B along which a ball with travel, under the influence of gravity alone, in the shortest possible time? Bernoulli issued the problem as a challenge to the mathematicians of Europe. He and Leibniz had previously solved the problem. On receiving the problem late one night in January 1697 Newton had shown within a matter of hours that the curve of quickest descent, the brachistochrone, was in fact the cycloid (see diagram). He published the solution anonymously in the *PT* for February 1697.

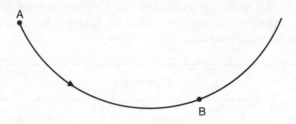

Other writings of Newton on the cycloid include *Gravia in trochoide descendentia* and *Principia*, Book I, pp. XLVIII–LIII.

See also Bernoulli's problems

D

Dahl, Michael (1659?–1743)

Dahl left his native Sweden in 1682 for London, where he worked initially as an assistant to Kneller. He spent the period 1685–8 on the Grand Tour and on his return to London in 1689 began his successful career. He is perhaps best known for the 'Petworth Beauties', portraits of ladies of the Court of Queen Anne, which hang at Petworth. He is also reported to have painted a portrait of Newton 'in his hair' in the 1720s. The portrait is lost but has been identified by some with the National Portrait Gallery portrait (RSW, p. 831). Another possibility is the Heffer portrait (RSW, p. 847). There is no conclusive evidence either way.

See also Portraits, medals, busts and statues

Dallin, Cyrus Edwin (1861–1944)

Born in the frontier settlement of Springville, Utah, and the son of a farmer, Dallin worked first in the local mines. He began his artistic career modelling busts in clay. In 1882 he opened his first studio in Boston. As a sculptor he specialised in large equestrian groups on Indian themes. He is also known as the sculptor of the only Newton statue in the US. It stands in the Library of Congress, Washington, overlooking the main reading room, and dates from 1897. It can be seen displayed in Brasch (1928).

See also Portraits, medals, busts and statues

Dary, Michael (1613–79)

A self-taught mathematician and a protégé of John Collins. He worked for sometime as a gauger for the Excise in Bristol and Newcastle before joining Collins in London. At the prodding of Collins, Dary entered into a correspondence with Newton in 1673 on questions of algebra (*C*, I, pp. 319–20, 326, 332–3).

Davis, William (1771–1807)

A London bookseller and mathematician. He published a number of important texts, like Maclaurin's *Fluxions* (1801), and wrote himself such elementary texts as *Treatise on Land Surveying* and *The Use of Globes*. In 1803 he published a revised version of Motte's *Principia* (1729). No further English translation would appear for another 131 years.

See also Principia, Translations

De aere et aethere (On the air and ether)

This brief work is to be found in the PC in the ULC as a sheet of double foolscap, folded and written on all four sides in Newton's hand. It has been published, for the first and only time, in both its original Latin and English translation, by the Halls (pp. 214–28). They assign it to the period 1673–5. Westfall, however, who has developed a quite different chronology, places it after the 1679 *Letter to Boyle*.

The title of the work derives from the two chapter headings of what soon became yet one more abandoned and unpublished treatise of Newton. The first chapter began by asking how the rarefaction and condensation of air could so readily take place. He answered in terms of 'expansion, compression, heat and the proximity of bodies'. While the first two factors are quite familiar, the reference to 'the proximity of bodies' is less so.

It was part of Newton's view of matter that bodies seek to avoid mutual contact. Examples he cited at this point include the ability of flies to walk on water with dry feet, the avoidance from each other of particles of powder floating in liquid, and the difficulty of pressing two surfaces together. Nor was this observed to hold only for 'bodies'. It was also true of air, Newton insisted, that it tended to avoid bodies. From this fact Newton was able to explain capillarity. As air 'seeks to avoid the pores . . . between the parts of . . . bodies', it will be rarer in narrow pipes than the surrounding atmosphere and will consequently allow water to rise when the pipes are placed in water. For this reason also, 'water creeps little by little up the sides of vessels, the air withdrawing from their sides'.

Air was thus, for Newton, parts of bodies torn off by some such process as friction or fermentation. In this way there were 'as many kinds of air as there are substances on the Earth'. Within this multiplicity Newton distinguished three main kinds of air: the least permanent and lightest arising from liquids; a middle kind of particle arising mostly from the vegetable kingdom; and 'air properly so called whose permanence and gravity are indications that it is nothing else than a collection of metallic particles which subterranean corrosions daily disperse from each other'.

The second chapter, 'De aethere', presented Newton's case for the existence of the ether. Its origin lay in the particles of air already described but now broken down into particles subtle enough 'to penetrate the pores of glass, crystal and other terrestial bodies'. Evidence for the existence of such 'a spirit of air' was of three kinds. There was first the experiments of Boyle showing that metals heated in a sealed vessel could actually gain weight. It was clear to Newton that they had absorbed 'a most subtle saline spirit . . . coming through the glass'. Secondly, he pointed to the failure of a pendulum to continue oscillating in a vacuum. Again, this demonstrated that there was something much more subtle than air dampening the bob's motion. For a third reason Newton began to point to certain magnetic and electrical phenomena, when the manuscript abruptly ends in mid-sentence.

See also Ether

De analysi per aequationes numero terminorum infinitas

De analysi, the work which established Newton's reputation outside the walls of Trinity College, was first heard of in a letter from Barrow to Collins dated 20 June 1669. 'A friend of mine', Barrow wrote, 'brought me the other day some papers, wherein he hath sett downe methods of calculating the dimension of magnitudes like that of Mr Mercator concerning the Hyperbola; but very Generall; as also of resolving equations' (*C*, I, p. 13). The manuscript, with Newton's permission was sent to Collins on June 31. The author's name was revealed to Collins on 20 August, when Barrow wrote that the author was 'Mr Newton, a fellow of our College, and very young . . . but of an extraordinary genius and proficiency in these things' (*C*, I, pp. 14–15).

Not only was Collins the first outside Cambridge to see important work of Newton; he had also, although inadvertently, provoked the work. In the early months of 1669 he had sent Barrow a copy of

Mercator's *Logarithmotechnia* (1668), a work which contained the series for log $(1+x)$. Barrow was aware that Newton had worked out for himself a general method for infinite series some two years before. Mercator's book warned Barrow, and through him Newton, that others were working along similar lines. Newton's reaction was to write, probably in a few summer days of 1669, his treatise *De analysi* which showed, by its generality, how far ahead he was of all other rivals.

Collins, like Barrow, had no difficulty in recognising the originality and power of Newton's technique and, consequently, brought up the question of publication. An appendix to Barrow's forthcoming optical lectures seemed a suitable place. Newton revealed, however, for the first time, his ability to frustrate even such skilled and persistent suitors as Collins. Immediate publication was rejected out of hand; thereafter Newton deployed a variety of excuses: a need to revise the work, a desire to add further material, the pressures of other business and, as a last resort when demands became too pressing, he simply failed to reply. As a result *De analysi* remained, with a good deal more of Newton's early mathematical work, unpublished for half a century.

Newton's reluctance to publish did not prevent Collins from copying and distributing the work. One copy was found by Jones in 1709 and is now to be seen in the Royal Society. Another copy was sent to John Wallis, at some point passed to David Gregory, and is at present in the Gregory papers at St Andrews. Others who heard from Collins of Newton's work were James Gregory, de Sluse and, above all, Leibniz. In October 1676 Leibniz visited London, saw Collins, and was allowed to read *De analysi*. He took thirteen printed pages of notes, an event construed by Newton as undoubted evidence of Leibniz's reliance upon the discoveries of others in his mathematical development.

The work, Newton began, would present a general method 'for measuring the quantity of curves by an infinite series of terms'. To this end, three rules were formulated.

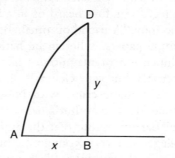

The first rule, given the curve ABD in the diagram in which AB = x and BD = y, stated: If $ax^{m/n} = y$, then $\dfrac{an}{m+n} x^{m+n/n}$ will equal the area of ABD, where a,b,c are 'given Quantities' and m and n whole numbers. In the simplest example considered by Newton, if $x^2 = y$, where $a = 1 = n$, and $m = 2$, then the area of ABD will be $1/3x^3$.

The second rule simply stated: If the value of y is compounded of several terms of that kind the area also will be compounded of the areas which arise separately from each of those terms. Thus, to take Newton's own example once more, if:

$$x^2 + x^{3/2} = y$$

and if:

$$x^2 = y. = .1/3x^3$$

and:

$$x^{3/2} = y. = .2/5\, x^{5/2}$$

then:

$$x^2 + x.^{3/2} = .1/3x^3 + 2/5\, x^{5/2}. = . \text{ABD}.$$

Proofs were offered of both rules (*MP*, II, pp. 243–5).

In the third rule, which took up the bulk of the work, Newton considered cases where 'the Value of Y, or any of its Terms' were so compounded as to require a reduction into more simple terms. This was done variously by division, by the extraction of roots, and by the resolution of affected equations. Thus, if the curve was a hyperbola, and the equation was $y = \dfrac{1}{1 + x^2}$, Newton began by dividing 1 by $(1 + x^2)$, which yielded:

$$y = 1 - x^2 + x^4 - x^6 + x^8 \text{ etc.}$$

Rule 2 was applied at this point and the area of the parabola was seen to be equal to:

$$x - 1/3x^3 + 1/5x^5 - 1/7x^7 + 1/9x^9 \text{ etc.}$$

The series, Newton noted was an infinite one and therefore carried on indefinitely. What, then, of the area of the hyperbola? No matter, Newton somewhat complacently responded, as 'a few of the initial Terms are exact enough for any Use'.

There was more in *De analysi*, historians have noted, than the manipulation of infinite series. When at the conclusion of the paper Newton set out his proof of Rule 1, he revealed at the same time details of his method of fluxions. The proof required the use of 'infinitely small' areas (later to be called 'moments'). It was, Boyer (1968, p. 434) has noted, 'the first time in the history of mathematics that an area was found through the inverse of what we call differentiation', and thus made Newton 'the effective inventor of the calculus', for his ability 'to exploit the inverse relationship between slope and area through his new infinite analysis'.

Newton's failure to establish his priority at this point by following the advice of Barrow and Collins would later involve him, and many others, in much distress and in considerable polemical effort.

De analysi, excluding reprints, is known in the following nine editions.

1 London, 1711. Included in Jones (1711), forty-two years after its composition; it was reissued in Amsterdam in 1723, both separately and bound with a reprint of *Principia*.

2 London, 1713. Newton included *De analysi* as a vital piece of evidence in the *Commercium epistolicum*; as such, it was reissued in 1722 and 1856.

3 Lausanne and Geneva, 1744. Included in Castillioneus, *Tome* I.

4 London, 1745. The first English translation prepared by John Stewart and published by him together with *De quadratura* in his *Isaac Newton's Two Treatises*.

5 London, 1779. Included in Horsley, vol. 1, and reprinted in a facsimile edition in Stuttgart and Bad Cannstatt in 1964.

6 Moscow–Leningrad, 1937. Included in a Russian translation of 3 above, prepared by D. D. Mordukay-Boltovskoy.

7 Dresden, 1954. A German translation by Max Miller.

8 New York, 1964. Included in Whiteside's *Newton's Mathematical Works*, vol. 1, in Stewart's 1745 translation.

9 Cambridge, 1968. The definitive text with English translation included in *MP*, II, pp. 206–47.

Accessible extracts can be found in Midonick (1968, vol. 2).

See also Fluxions, fluents and moments; Priority dispute

Death

Newton seems to have lived until the age of eighty in remarkably good health. During the last five years, however, he complained of gout, the stone, incontinence, and inflammation of the lungs. Apart from acute attacks they seemed not to interrupt unduly his normal way of life. He attended meetings of the Royal Society regularly and he continued working on his *Chronology* until a few days before his death.

He attended the Royal Society for the last time on 2 March 1727. Shortly afterwards he fell ill and was in considerable pain. His physicians Richard Mead and William Cheselden were summoned; a stone was diagnosed. There was clearly little anyone could do.

According to Conduitt there were 'violent fits of pain with very short intermissions; and though the drops of sweat ran down his face with anguish, he never complained or cried out'. He seemed a little better on the 18 March, 'read the papers, and held a pretty long discourse with Dr Mead'. But the same evening, a Saturday, he collapsed about 6 p.m. and never regained consciousness before his death between 1 a.m. and 2 a.m. on the morning of Monday 20 March 1727. No last words were recorded.

Deborah

Newton's bedmaker at TCC was called Deborah. When Newton left Cambridge in 1697, Deborah served Bentley until his death in 1742; thereafter she worked for W. Walker, a Vice-master of the college, and 'in whose service she died' (Edleston, 1850, p. xliv). According to Richard Cumberland, Bentley's grandson, 'she was much in request for the many entertaining circumstances she could narrate of Sir Isaac Newton, when she waited upon him as his bedmaker'. The stories seem not to have been recorded. Edleston also noted that Deborah was illiterate, yet, with her sister Betty, another bedmaker, improved 'their capital by loans to their master'. It is doubtful if Newton ever needed the services of the Baxter sisters.

De computo serierum

Having abandoned his *Matheos universalis specimina* in July 1684, Newton began, in his usual manner, to rework the same material into a new draft. The polemical references to Gregory and Leibniz were dropped, but just three chapters were drafted before Newton once more abandoned the project. Presumably the visit of Edmond Halley to Cambridge in August led Newton to drop everything and to consider anew the dynamical problems which would eventually lead him to the composition of *Principia*.

The three drafted chapters were entitled:

1 How equations are to be resolved into infinite series;
2 On the transformation of series;
3 On the interpolation of series.

Chapter 1 is in private hands while, as Add.MS 3964.3, the remaining two chapters are to be found in the PC in the ULC. They have been published for the first and only time in *MP*, IV, pp. 590–616 in both the original Latin and, as *On the Computation of Series*, in English translation.

See also Matheos universalis specimina

De constructione problematum geometricum

In late 1706 Newton began to rework the *Problems for construing aequations* (*MP*, II, pp. 450–516) of the early 1670s. The results have been published in both the original Latin and English translation for the first and only time in *MP*, VIII, pp. 200–19. 'Once written', Whiteside has noted, 'the tract vanished straight into the disordered limbo of Newton's private papers, leaving no external recorded trace' (*MP*, VIII, p. 200).

See also Problems for construing aequations

De gravitatione et equipondio fluidorum (On the gravity and equilibrium of fluids)

IN THE PC, and now in the ULC (MS 4003), there is a calf-bound notebook in which there is written, in Newton's hand, a continuous work running from page 4 to page 23. No other entries are included in the notebook. The Halls, on stylistic grounds, and on the evidence of the handwriting, judge it to date from between 1664 and 1668; Westfall (RSW, p. 301), however, judges it to have been written not earlier than 1668. The work itself has been published in full, in both the original Latin and in English translation, for the first and only time by the Halls (pp. 89–156). Extracts were later included in Herivel (1965, pp. 219–35).

Although the work begins as a treatise on 'the science of gravity and of the equilibrium of fluid and solid bodies', Newton was diverted within a page or two to the evaluation of several basic Cartesian assumptions he had met with in the *Principia philosophia* of Descartes. And so he continued for another twenty-five pages before noting: 'I have already digressed enough; let us return to the main theme.'

He began with a critique of the Cartesian analysis of space, motion and matter. His aim, in particular, was to dispose of the relativism explicitly proclaimed by Descartes. Having accepted the universe as a plenum, Descartes was forced to define the motion of a body in terms of the change of place it undergoes 'from the vicinity of those bodies that immediately touch it, and that are considered at rest, to the vicinity of others'. Thus Descartes could conveniently proclaim the earth to be at rest since it was not translated 'from the neighbourhood of the contiguous ether' (Halls, 1962, p. 126).

Against this view, Newton insisted that there was a 'physical and absolute motion' which was to be defined on other grounds than a 'merely external' translation (p. 128). One such ground proposed by Newton, and later developed in *Principia* (1687), was that of space itself. As a 'motionless thing', local motions could be defined by reference to it' (p. 131). Another consideration distinguishing real from relative motion lay, as expressed in definition 5, in the fact that 'Force is the causal principle of motion and rest.' In this way the tendency shown by the earth and other planets to recede from the sun can be recognised as a real motion.

Newton also launched a major attack against the rigorous distinction drawn by the Cartesians between mind and matter. In the Cartesian identification of extension and body Newton managed to detect 'a path to Atheism'. As extension was clearly not created but had existed eternally, it could have an existence independently of God. Further, if body and mind were completely independent of each other, then, Newton concluded 'God does not eminently contain extension within himself and therefore cannot create it; but God and extension will be two substances separately complete, absolute, and having the same significance' (p. 143). Consequently, Cartesianism, by denying the basic dependence of the world on God became, for Newton, equivalent to atheism.

To avoid this possibility Newton developed a much more robust account of body. He defined it as a determined quantity of extension which the omnipresent God had endowed with the properties of motion, impenetrability and the power to excite various sense perceptions (p. 140). Having thus purified physics from any atheistic incursions, Newton returned in the final pages to his account of fluid dynamics.

See also Descartes, René

Deism

Often traced back to Lord Herbert of Cherbury (1583–1648), the brother of the poet George Herbert, Deism is an ill-defined term which encompasses a wide variety of opinions. Herbert, in his De veritate (1625, On Truth), argued that 'universal consent (which can only be arrived at by divine providence) is the sole criterion of truth' in religion (Willey, 1972, p. 115). Beware the Church, Faith and Prelates, Herbert warned; they can lead us into 'a false religion' as readily as into 'the true one'. He claimed to have found five features common to all religions, of which 'That there is a supreme power' and 'That this sovereign power must be worshipped' were the first two.

One strand of this tradition, exemplified by such works as Locke's The Reasonableness of Christianity (1695) and John Toland's Christianity not mysterious (1696), was that the truths of religion could be sustained by reason alone and that, consequently, faith and revelation were secondary phenomena.

Wishing to stress the supreme role of reason in matters of religion, Deists tended to dismiss as naive, arguments from revelation and prophecy. It would thus be misleading to describe Newton as a Deist. He certainly accepted part of the Deist case that God's existence could be seen in the operations of Nature. His frequent insistence, however, of the vital role played by divine prophecy in religion conflicts strongly with the main Deistic programme.

de l'Hopital, Marquis (1661–1704)

After an early career as an army officer, de l'Hopital sought fame as a mathematician and subsequently achieved his aim with the publication of the first book on the differential calculus, *Analyse des infiniment petits* (1696, Analysis of infinitely small quantities), a work which has since gained a certain notoriety amongst mathematicians.

In 1691 de l'Hopital met the young Johann Bernoulli, who impressed him with his ability to determine the curvature of any curve given him. De l'Hopital invited Bernoulli to stay with him and, for a handsome fee, to teach him his powerful new techniques. The result a few years later was de l'Hopital's *Analyse* of 1696. Bernoulli's role in the affair was conclusively established in 1921 when the manuscript of the material he had revealed to de l'Hopital was discovered in Basle.

De l'Hopital was one of the five mathematicians credited with having solved Bernoulli's challenge problem of 1696. Newton, however, according to David Gregory, and with some justification, found it hard to believe 'that the Marquis . . . could have discovered the curve . . . unaided' (*C*, IV, p. 267). The Marquis had no such doubts about Newton. 'Does he eat and drink and sleep? Is he like other men?' he is reported to have asked John Arbuthnot in the late 1690s.

De methodis fluxionum et serierum infinitorum

On 20 July 1671 Newton wrote to Collins that 'partly upon Dr Barrow's instigation, I began to new methodiz ye discourse of infinite series' (*C*, I, pp. 65–6). It began with the material of the *October 1666 Tract* and *De analysi* and sought to produce a comprehensive treatise on the new mathematical techniques he had developed in the late 1660s. Although, according to Hall (1980, p. 19) it 'might have effected a mathematical revolution in its own day', it remained incomplete and unpublished until its posthumous appearance in 1736.

He referred to the work in the *Epistola posterior*, noting that it was incomplete and that 'nor has my mind to this day returned to the task of adding the rest' (*C*, II, pp. 133–4). In fact, he confessed in the earlier *Epistola prior* (1676): 'I write rather shortly because these theories long ago began to be distasteful to me, to such an extent that I have now refrained from them for nearly five years' (*C*, II, p. 39). However, this did not prevent Newton from allowing the manuscript to circulate fairly freely amongst his mathematical colleagues and friends. On this issue Raphson reported in 1691 that he and Halley had been lent the manuscript and that it was 'much worn by having been lent out' (*MP*, III, p. 33). Collins had been informed of the work in May 1672 but shown no part of it. In July he was told by Newton that he was unsure 'when I shall proceed to finish it' (*C*, I, p. 215). In fact, apart from a few later additions and corrections, Newton seems to have abandoned the manuscript at this point.

The manuscript itself is in the PC in the ULC (Add. MS 3960.14) and consists of fifty sheets folded and sewn to produce 200 pages. Of these, sixty pages are blank. The opening page of the manuscript has been lost and consequently it is unknown what title, if any, Newton gave to the work. Its present title was awarded by John Colson (1736). An abridged version was made by David Gregory in 1693, while a transcript by William Jones, now in private hands, was made in about 1710. Jones gave it the title *Artis analyticae specimina sive geometrica analytica* (A specimen of the art of analysis or analytic geometrica).

After three editions in four years *De methodis* has received no further separate publication and has since appeared only as a part of a larger work. It has appeared in the following eight editions.

1 London, 1736, 140 pp. 'Translated from the author's Latin original not yet made publick to which is subjoined . . . annotations, illustrations and supplements in order to make this treatise a compleat institution for the use of learners . . . by John Colson.' Colson based his text on a copy of Newton's original manuscript made by William Jones. Jones's copy was none too accurate and lacking its first page, as did the original manuscript, Newton's title being unknown; the title *De methodis* . . . originates with Colson.

2 London, 1737. A second and independent translation; anonymous.

3 Paris, 1740. *Les methodes des fluxions*, French translation by G. L. le Clerc, better known as the Comte de Buffon, the celebrated naturalist. Reprinted in facsimile in 1966.

4 Lausanne and Geneva, 1744. Included in Castillioneus, *Tome* I, a translation back into Latin from Colson's English translation.

5 London, 1779. Included in Horsley, vol. I. Horsley worked from three manuscripts: Newton's holograph draft (Add. MS 3960.14); the copy made by Jones; and a copy, now lost, made from Jones's copy by James Wilson. He rejected Colson's title and adopted instead the title *Geometrica analytica sive specimina arto analytica*. It was reprinted in 1964 (Stuttgart–Bad Cannstatt).

6 Moscow/Leningrad, 1937. Russian translation by D. D. Mordukay-Boltovsky in his Russian edition of Castillioneus, *Tome* I.

7 New York, 1964. Nearly two centuries later *De methodis* was finally

reprinted in a facsimile edition of 1 above in vol. I of Whiteside
(Newton, 1964–7).
8 Cambridge, 1969. Newton's three-hundred-year-old original
manuscript was finally published in both Latin and English translation in *MP*, III, pp. 32–353.

In his preface to the first English edition of the work, Colson (1736)
noted:

> The chief Principle, upon which the Method of Fluxions is here
> built, is . . . taken from the Rational Mechanicks; which is, That
> Mathematical Quantity, particularly Extension, may be conceived
> as generated by continued local Motion; and that all Quantities . . .
> may be conceived as generated after a like manner. Consequently
> there must be comparative Velocities of increase and decrease
> during such generations, whose Relations are fixt and determinable,
> and may therefore . . . proposed to be found.

Thus, a line or a curve was seen as generated by a continuously moving
point, a surface by the motion of a line and a solid by the motion of a
surface. After defining fluxions, fluents and moments, Newton went on
to show how, within this framework, significant results could be
derived. Following an introduction in which it was shown how equations could be solved with the use of infinite series, seven major problems were considered.

1 From the Following Quantities (fluents) given to find their
  Fluxions.
2 From the given Fluxions to find their Flowing Quantities.
3 To determine Maxima and Minima of Qualities.
4 To draw Tangents to Curves.
5 To find the Quantity of Curvature in any Curve.
6 To find the Quality of Curvature in any Curve.
7 To find any number of Curves that may be squared.

The tract remained safely in Newton's custody until his death, and when
it did finally appear in 1736 it was of little more than historical interest.

See also Fluxions, fluents and moments; Mathematical development

---

de Moivre, Abraham (1667–1754)

The son of a surgeon and a Huguenot, de Moivre fled France after the
revocation of the Edict of Nantes in 1685 and arrived in England in
1688. He worked as a mathematics tutor. At the home of one of his
pupils, a son of the Duke of Devonshire, he saw a copy of *Principia* and,
'surprised to find it beyond the range of his knowledge', he bought a
copy. But 'since the lessons he had to give forced him to travel continu-

ally, he tore out the pages in order to carry them in his pocket and study them during his free time'. He soon became part of the Newton circle, making himself, if not indispensable, certainly very useful to Newton in a number of ways.

De Moivre saw the *Opticks* (1704) through the press, served on the 1712 committee of the Royal Society investigating the priority dispute with Leibniz, and was always on hand to translate any of Newton's anonymous pieces into French for the Continental journals or to translate into English any articles of interest to Newton. Also, through his contacts with Continental scholars in his extensive correspondence, de Moivre was able to keep the scholars of Europe and England aware of each other's work.

Unlike most others of Newton's circle, de Moivre seems not to have benefited from Newton's patronage. Although he was interested in a number of academic posts, they always seemed to go to other Newtonians. They remained, never the less, on good terms and in later years when approached about his work Newton would frequently direct the enquirer to de Moivre who, he claimed, 'knows these things better than I do'.

One further service rendered by de Moivre was to record for Conduitt in November 1727 his recollections of Newton. It contains the fullest account extant of the genesis of *Principia*. One of the few biographical pieces to escape Keynes, it is at present in the hands of Joseph Halle Schaffner of New York City. A transcript was made by H. R. Luard in the nineteenth century and can be seen in ULC (MS 4007). More conveniently, the parts dealing with the origin of *Principia* are printed in Cohen (1971, pp. 297–8).

De Moivre established an independent reputation as a mathematician through his *Doctrine of Chances* (1718), dedicated to Newton, and one of the founding works of probability theory.

---

de Monmort, Pierre Remond (1678–1719)

A pupil of Malebranche and a man of private means, de Monmort is best known as a mathematician who, in his *Essai d'analyse sur les jeux de hasard* (1708, Essay on the Analysis of Games of Chance), made important contributions to the development of probability theory. He met Newton on a visit to London in 1700. Contact was maintained, with Monmort presenting Newton with a copy of his *Essai* in 1708 (*C*, IV, pp. 533–4) and printing in 1709 copies of Newton's *De quadratura* (1704) for distribution to the mathematicians of France.

De Monmort visited London once more in 1715 as a member of the mission sent by the *Académie* to observe the solar eclipse. Newton was keen to impress the mission. De Monmort was invited to Newton's home, was introduced to several of the young Newtonians, and fell under the spell of Catherine Barton. On his return to France he arranged for fifty bottles of champagne to be sent to Newton and 'la belle bouche de Mademoiselle Barton' (Brewster, vol. II, p. 491). Newton must have responded with some kind of gift, for in February 1717 de Monmort was offering elaborate expressions of thanks for some 'ornaments' chosen by Catherine for his wife (*C*, VI, p. 380).

Newton took advantage of such visits to seek allies in his priority dispute with Leibniz and Bernoulli. While de Monmort was willing to serve as a channel of communication between Bernoulli and Newton, he appeared reluctant to adopt anything like a partisan position. Newton, he agreed, was the inventor of the calculus; Leibniz and Bernoulli had, however, promoted its adoption (*C*, VII, pp. 21–2).

---

de Morgan, Augustus (1806–71)

Born in Madras, the son of an Indian Army colonel, de Morgan was educated at TCC where he graduated as fourth wrangler in 1827. After a brief period at the Bar he was appointed in 1828 Professor of Mathematics at the newly founded London University. He resigned in 1831 on the grounds of professorial independence but, reappointed in 1836, he held the chair until his retirement in 1866. In addition to a number of technical works in the fields of logic and mathematics, de Morgan also produced the memorable, illuminating and unclassifiable *Budget of Paradoxes* (1872).

He was also the author of a number of penetrating studies on Newton's life, personality and work. In 1846 he published a brief biography of Newton which, complemented by his lengthy review of Brewster, make together, despite their age, one of the best introductions to Newton ever produced. Victim of neither the hagiography of his own age nor the obsessive iconography of later times, de Morgan's work has a freshness and balance found in few studies of Newton. De Morgan also made the first critical study of the behaviour of Newton and his followers in their dispute with Leibniz. It was de Morgan, for example, in 1852, who first clearly demonstrated that Newton was the author of the anonymous *Account*. Much of the above work was collected in the unfortunately long-out-of-print *Essays on the Life and Work of Newton* (1914).

Further work of de Morgan, largely pursued in the pages of *Notes and Queries*, concerned the relationship between Catherine Barton, Newton's niece, and his patron, Charles Montague. The material was eventually worked up into the comprehensive survey *Newton: his Friend: his Niece* (1885 and 1968).

See also Barton, Catherine

De motu

After the visit of Halley to Newton in August 1684 a number of references are met with to a treatise which can be seen in retrospect as the first draft of *Principia* (1687). A document of some sort was sent to Halley in November 1684, while on December 10 he informed the Royal Society that Newton had lately shown him 'a curious treatise *De motu*', which he had promised 'to be sent to the Society to be entered upon their Register'. A document of this kind had been so entered by 23 February 1685, when the fact was recorded in Newton's correspondence (*C*, II, p. 415). All three references are, according to Cohen (1971, p. 57), to this latter work, 'although not necessarily to one and the same state or version'. Five versions of *De motu* are known.

1 The document entered in the RS Register sometime before 23 February 1685 was first published by Rigaud (1838) under the title *Propositiones de motu*, and reprinted by Rouse Ball (1893). It is little more than a copy of 2 below.

2 (B) In Newton's own hand, it is the earliest of the three versions from the PC in the ULC (MS 3965, ff. 55–62), and is entitled *De motu corporum in gyrum*. The full text in both Latin and English has been published by Herivel (1965, pp. 257–89). It consists of three definitions, three hypotheses, four theorems and seven problems.

Definition 1 contains the first reference to 'centripetal force', introduced as that force 'by which a body is impelled or drawn towards any point which is regarded as a centre'. Although Newton's first law of motion is stated (hypothesis 2), there is as yet no sign of the other two laws. Also present, as definition 2, is the notion of the innate force or inertia of a body. In hypothesis 3 Newton found it necessary to assume the parallelogram of forces.

Theorems 1–3 are similar respectively to prop.I, prop.IV and prop.VI cor.I of Book I of *Principia* (1687). The first five problems are concerned with relating together the orbits of bodies in circles and ellipses to the centripetal force directing them. The remaining two problems deal with the motion of bodies in a 'uniformly resisting medium'.

Westfall claims to have identified 'a series of internal contradictions' in this version of *De motu*. Newton was operating with three quite different conceptions of force: 'impulses which produce discrete increments of motion ($f = \Delta mv$), or continuous forces which produce uniform acceleration ($f = ma$)', together with a third concept 'of force as an internal propulsion which maintains a uniform velocity ($f = mv$)' (RSW, p. 413). Newton could not, Westfall noted, 'have built *Principia* on a foundation so uncertain'.

3 (C) In Halley's hand and also in the PC (MS 3965, ff. 63–70), the manuscript is untitled. It is little more than a copy of 2 above. There are, however, some differences. A fourth hypothesis has been added and the concluding two problems on motion in a 'uniformly resisting medium' have been omitted. Other differences are listed in Herivel (1965, pp. 292–4).

4 (D) The final and latest version from the PC (MS 3965, ff. 40–54) is in the hand of Humphrey Newton and carries the title *De motu sphaericum corporum in fluidis*. It has been fully published in the Halls (pp. 243–92) in both the original Latin and English translation.

It is by far the fullest version and contains a number of significant developments. The title 'hypothesis' had been dropped in favour of 'law'. Two new laws appear, one of which, law 2, was the first statement in the various versions of *De motu* of Newton's second law. A second change concerned the parallelogram of forces, a hypothesis in 2 and 3, but now derived as the first lemma. Also added were two long passages. The first occurs at the end of the *Scholium* to theorem 4 and is concerned with 'the whole space of the planetary heavens'; the second was added after problem 5 and sought to demonstrate that the resistance offered by pure ether to planetary motion was 'excessively small'.

5 A fifth copy, as yet undescribed, is known to be in the Macclesfield Collection at Shirburn Castle.

Most scholars date Halley's first Cambridge visit to Newton to August 1684 and have dated the various versions of *De motu* accordingly. An alternative chronology, however, has been proposed by Herivel (1965, p. 97), in which Halley first visited Newton in May 1684, for which date there is some documentary evidence. Consequently, Herivel has proposed that 2 was composed 'around June and July 1684' and 4 'even possibly before October 1684'.

There remains the question of the significance of *De motu* in the development of Newton's dynamical thought. Cohen (1971, p. 61) has judged it to be 'only one small step towards Newton's *magnum opus*', with 'no hint of the grandeur to come'. Missing completely from the tract is any sign of the third law and with it the realisation that attraction between revolving planets and the focal sun is mutual. Also missing is any awareness of the perturbations introduced into planetary orbits by the presence in the solar system of other celestial bodies. Newton was, however, becoming aware of these problems, as can be seen by the following addition to 4.

The orbit of any one planet depends on the combined motions of all the planets, not to mention the action of all these on each other. But to consider simultaneously all these causes of motion and to define these motions by exact laws allowing of convenient

calculation exceeds, unless, I am mistaken, the force of the human
intellect. (HERIVEL, 1965, p. 301)

It was, however, precisely Newton's attempt to tackle such 'combined
motions' which distinguished the various drafts of *De motu* from the
completed manuscript of *Principia*.

De motu corporum: definitiones

A single sheet in Newton's hand from the PC in the ULC (MS 3965,
f. 21), it consists of definitions of the following five terms: the quantity
of matter; the quantity of motion; the innate force (*vis insita*) of matter;
impressed force; and centripetal force. These are in fact preliminary
drafts of the first five definitions of *Principia* (1687). The three additional
Principia definitions, concerned with the absolute quantity, the accelerative quantity and the motive quantity of centripetal force, are all incorporated into the definition of centripetal force.

The manuscript was first printed by the Halls (pp. 239–42) in both
its original Latin and in an English translation. It is also included, again in
both Latin and English, in Herivel (1965, pp. 315–20). He has, however,
added a number of definitions taken from MS 3965, f.25, arguing that
they continue from f.21 described above. They are numbered from 6 to
14 and cover density, heaviness, quantity of motion, the exercised force
of a body, and, as headings only, position, rest, motion, and velocity.
There is no definition 13. Cohen (1971, p. 93), on textual grounds, has
argued against Herivel's proposal.

See also Principia, Origin and production

De motu corporum in gyrum (On the motion of revolving bodies)

The earliest of the three versions of *De motu* in the PC. It has been
published by Herivel (1965, pp. 257–89) in both its original Latin and
in English translation.

See also De motu; Principia, Origin and production

De motu corporum in mediis regulariter cedentibus (On the motion of bodies in regularly resisting media)

The manuscript, in the hand of an amanuensis, is in the PC in the ULC
(MS 3965, ff.23–6) and is incomplete. It consists of eighteen definitions,

six laws of motion and one lemma. It was published for the first and only time, in the original Latin and English translation, in Herivel (1965, pp. 304–15). The work is generally held to be intermediate between *De motu* and the Lucasian lectures.

A number of crucial innovations have been identified in the present text. It is here for example that the *Principia* terminology of *Leges motus* for its laws of nature is finally adopted. Earlier manuscripts had spoken of hypotheses or *leges*. Also seen for the first time as law 3 is the third law of *Principia*, stated in the form: 'As much as any body acts on another so much does it experience in reaction. Whatever presses or pulls another thing by this equally is pressed or pulled.' A final innovation concerns the important distinctions between absolute and relative time (definitions 1 and 2), absolute and relative space (definitions 3 and 4), and absolute and relative motion (definition 9). The distinctions would eventually appear in the *Scholium* following definition VIII of *Principia* (1687).

See also Principia, Origin and production

De motu corporum, liber primus

The manuscript, in the hand of Humphrey Newton, was deposited in the ULC (MS Dd 9.46) as the lectures delivered in 1684 in compliance with the regulations governing the Lucasian chair held by Newton. It is in fact a draft of Book I of *Principia* and will be referred to as *LL-I* to distinguish it from the *De motu corporum, liber secundus* (*LL-2*), also supposedly given as Newton's Lucasian Lectures. Cohen has distinguished two major sequences of the manuscript. The first, *LLa*, consists of the definitions, laws of motion and the rest of Book I up to prop.XXIV. The second, much closer to the actual manuscript of *Principia*, runs from the corollary to prop.XVI to prop.LIV. Both sequences contain annotations in Newton's hand and end in mid-sentence. The manuscript undoubtedly went much further and probably included, Cohen (1971, pp. 92–1) has argued, the remainder of Book I and maybe even some of the material of Book II.

The manuscript begins with the date October 1684. It is unlikely, however, that Newton actually delivered the text or even the substance of *LL-I* as Cambridge lectures at this date. As it is a considerable advance on *De motu* it would make no sense to suppose that in November 1684 Newton sent a crude version of his dynamics to the Royal Society while delivering a more sophisticated account to Cambridge audiences a little before. It is likely therefore to have been composed sometime between February 1685, when *De motu* was registered with the Royal Society, and April 1686, when the manuscript of Book I was presented to the Society.

LL-I is the first document to present Newton's three laws of motion and only those three laws. They carry the same title, '*Axiomata sive Leges Motus*', as that adopted in *Principia* and are phrased in similar terms. Although initially *LL-I* contained two extra definitions to the eight to appear in *Principia* (II *Axis materiae*; III *Centrum materiae*), Newton crossed out the supernumerary pair and adopted the number sequence later found in *Principia*.

See also *Principia*, Origin and production

De motu corporum, liber secundus

Principia was originally intended to be composed of two books, the first dealing with the principles of motion, drafted in *LL-I*, and the second dealing with the system of the world and the subject of *De motu corporum, liber secundus*, referred to henceforth as *LL-2*. Two manuscript versions are known. One, from the PC in the ULC, is in the hands of both Newtons, Humphrey and Isaac, with extensive revisions in Newton's hand. The first twenty–seven sections are numbered, the remainder unnumbered. At the end of section 27 there is the marginal note 'finis anni 1687' altered to 'ffinis Lectionum annis 1687'. It is not, however, divided into lectures. A second copy in the hand of Humphrey Newton (MS Dd 4.18), covering the first twenty–seven numbered sections of the first manuscript, is divided into five lectures, the first of which bears the date 'Sept 29 Praelect.1'. A copy of this was made by Roger Cotes and is in TCC Library, while a further copy is in Clare College Library, Cambridge.

When was the full version of *LL-2* in the PC completed? At some point Newton decided to expand *Principia* to three books. He further decided that *LL 2* was not sufficiently mathematical to include and too likely to lead to disputes. As, according to a letter to Halley on 20 June 1686, Newton was working on his new, more technical version of Book III in autumn 1685, it is plausible to suppose that *LL-2* was completed before this date.

He did not, however, abandon all the material. Cohen (1971, p. 110) has identified fourteen paragraphs of *LL-2* which were used 'almost verbatim' in Book III of *Principia*. Other material was used less directly.

The manuscript itself, as found in the PC, was first published in 1728 as *De mundi systemate*. Thus, though first planned as Book II of *Principia*, later changed to Book III, the work in fact only appeared posthumously in 1728.

See also *Principia*, Origin and production; *The System of the World*

De motu sphaericorum corporum in fluidis (On the motion of spherical bodies in fluids)

The fullest and latest of the three versions of *De motu* in the PC. It has been published by the Halls (pp. 243–92) in both its original Latin and in English translation.

See also De motu; *Principia*, Origin and production

De natura acidorum

In 1692 Alexander Pitcairne visited Newton in Cambridge. While there he was shown a manuscript of the incomplete *De natura acidorum* and allowed to take it away with him back to Edinburgh. Pitcairne actually added to the text a couple of notes and the final five lines. They were included in a copy of the work made by David Gregory. In 1710 Newton authorised its publication, making it the only one of his chemical works to appear in his lifetime.

The text is brief. It begins with a series of notes on the nature of acids. They are coarser than water and therefore less volatile, but finer than earth and consequently not as fixed. The key property of acids, however, lay in their 'great attractive force' whereby they were enabled to 'dissolve bodies and affect and stimulate the organs of the senses'. He continued with further details of the chemistry of acids. While the text so far, as Harris the first editor noted, appears to be a 'continued Discourse', what follows is little more than a set of loosely connected notes. There are thus such unrelated propositions as 'Dizziness is caused by the quivering motion of the eyes,' and 'All black things grow hot more quickly and strongly.'

More interesting than any such casual jottings are Newton's thoughts on the possibility of transmutation. Can metals, for example, he asked, be turned into other metals, in the same way 'as common Nourishment is turn'd into the Bodies of Animals and Vegetables?' The possibility of such a process was suggested to Newton by the ability of mercury and aqua regis to pervade something as seemingly solid as gold. Bodies, he speculated, could therefore be made of mutually attractive particles. These were combined to form 'Particles of the *first Composition*', which in turn could be formed into 'Particles of the *Second Composition*'. If the particles of either these compositions 'could be separated', then the metal 'might be made to become fluid, or at least more soft. And if gold could be brought once to ferment and putrefie, it might be turn'd into any other body whatsoever.' Transmutation for Newton was thus, though speculative, a process which fell entirely within the domain of chemistry.

Two manuscripts are known. The original autograph manuscript belonging to Newton is in private hands. A copy made by David Gregory, together with the notes added by Pitcairne, is in the library of the RS.

The following editions are known.

1 London, 1710. It first appeared in both the original Latin and an English translation in John Harris's *Lexicon technicum* II (1710). The translation, according to Harris, had been 'supervised and approved by the Illustrious Author'. It was included in the introduction under the title 'Some Thoughts about the Nature of Acids; by Sir Isaac Newton'. In the later editions of 1716, 1725 and 1736 it appeared simply under the heading 'Acids'. Pitcairne's notes were not fully published.

2 Lausanne, 1744. Included in *Tome* II of Castillioneus, in Latin.

3 London, 1782. Included in Horsley vol. IV, in Latin. Like 1 above, only parts of Pitcairne's notes were included. Facsimile reprint 1964 (Stuttgart and Bad Cannstatt).

4 Cambridge, Mass., 1958. Included in *PLNP*, a facsimile of both the Latin and English text of 1 above. Reprinted 1978.

5 Cambridge, 1961. Published in both English and Latin in *C*, III, pp. 205–14, including for the first time Pitcairne's notes in full.

Derham, William (1657–1735)

Derham, an Oxford graduate, was ordained in 1682 and shortly afterwards, in 1689, was appointed to the living of Upminster in Essex. He is best known for his experimental investigations into the determination of the velocity of sound. On 28 February 1705 he climbed the tower of his Upminster church to observe the flash of cannons being fired twelve miles away across the river at Blackheath. By timing the interval between the flash and the roar of the cannon he was able to calculate the velocity of sound as 1,142 feet per second. His results were published in the *PT* (1708) and proved to be inconsistent with results published earlier by Newton in *Principia* (1687).

Derham was also the author of two immensely popular works, *Physico-theology* (1713) and *Astro-theology* (1715). Delivered initially as the Boyle lectures of 1711–12, they aimed to show that Newtonian mechanics and cosmology were convincing evidence of 'the being and attributes of God'.

See also Boyle lectures; Velocity of sound

Desaguliers, John Theophilus (1683–1744)

As the son of an Huguenot refugee, Desaguliers was brought over to England when he was two. Educated at Christ Church, Oxford, he remained in Oxford as the successor in 1710 to John Keill, lecturer in experimental philosophy at Hart Hall. He soon, however, abandoned Oxford for London where in 1714 he followed Francis Hauksbee as 'Curator and Operator of Experiments' at the RS. In this role he was often called upon to demonstrate aspects of Newton's work. Some, even, found their way into *Principia* (1726). Thus, experiment 14 of the *Scholium* to prop.XL of Book II describes experiments carried out by Desaguliers in 1719 in which a number of blown up hogs' bladders and lead weights were dropped 272 feet from the top of a church. The times of their descent were taken and, by assuming the density of air to water to be 1:860, Newton was able to conclude that 'the resistances of bodies, moving in any fluids whatsoever . . . are, other things being equal, as the densities of the fluids'. It is quite clear that the work was carried out at the suggestion and under the direction of Newton.

He first gained Newton's confidence in 1714 when, in response to often expressed Continental scepticism, he took up the challenge of repeating 'before several Gentlemen of the Royal Society' nine optical experiments taken from Book I, part I of Newton's *Opticks* (1704). The results were published in the *PT* (1717). He was later, in 1715, called upon to repeat several of these experiments before visiting scientists from Holland and France. These were by no means idle exercises and went a long way in persuading such scholars as de Monmort and 'sGravesande of the validity of Newtonian optics. They, in turn, returned to France and Holland and began the long process of converting their colleagues to what had for so long been dismissed as purely speculative views.

Having played a key role in the confirmation of Newtonian philosophy, Desaguliers spent much of his later life involved in its dissemination. This was achieved partly by his demonstrations and lectures given 'at Mr. Brown's, Bookseller, Temple Bar', and partly by writing. His *Course in Experimental Philosophy* (2 vols., 1730–4; 3rd corrected edition 1763) made his lectures available to a wider public and sought, in a way which would be much imitated, to demonstrate experimentally what Newton had proved mathematically. He was also responsible for the first English translation of 'sGravesande's *Introductio ad philosophiam Newtoniam* (2 vols., 1720–1) which, as *Mathematical Elements of Natural Philosophy*, would prove even more popular than his own work.

Desaguliers was also a poet and consequently commemorated Newton's death with a remarkable poem: *The Newtonian System of the World, the Best Model of Government* (1729). It inevitably sought to raise

[168]

Newton above all other scientists and so claimed for him the discovery of all truths:

> His Tow'ring Genius, from its certain Cause
> Ev'ry Appearance *a priori* draws,
> And shews th' Almighty Architecht's unalter'd Laws.
>
> (Nicolson, 1966, p. 136)

There was, however, more to the poem than eulogy. He pursued a political analogy in which the manner whereby the sun rules the solar system is mirrored in the political domain by a limited monarch like George II:

> And reigning thus with limited Command
> He holds a lasting Sceptre in his Hand.

In seeing in both systems a number of checks and balances,

> His pow'r coerc'd by Laws, still leaves them free,
> Directs, but not Destroys, their Liberty.

Some have claimed to see, as the 'logical culmination' of Newton's dynamics, nothing less than 'the Constitution of the United States' (Meadows, 1969, p. 148).

Descartes, René (1596–1650)

Certainly the first modern philosopher, Descartes can also make a fair case to be considered the first modern scientist. As a scientist and mathematician Descartes was probably the single most important influence on the intellectual development of Newton.

The son of a lawyer, he was educated at the Jesuit College at La Flèche, in Anjou. He left La Flèche in 1614 and spent the next fourteen years travelling around Europe. In 1619 while at Neuberg on the Danube on 10 November he underwent the visionary experience which inspired him to refashion the thought of his day. When in 1628 he abandoned his travels and settled in Holland, he also began, in his *Le Monde, ou Traité de la Lumière* (The World, or a Treatise on Light), to present his views in a comprehensive scientific treatise. In 1633, when news of Galileo's condemnation by the Inquisition for declaring his support for Copernicus reached Descartes, he decided to suppress the work. 'It is not my temperament to set sail against the wind', he later commented. Much of the work, however, was incorporated in his *Principia philosophiae* (1644, The Principles of Philosophy). By this time Descartes had already published his *La Géométrie* (1637), a work which transformed mathematics, and his *Discours de la Méthode*, one of the most innovative of all philosophical works.

[169]

Descartes abandoned his Dutch retreat in 1649 for the court of Queen Christina in Stockholm. Four months later, after one of his regular 5 a.m. tutorials with the Queen, he contracted pneumonia and was dead within a matter of days. Descartes' specific influence on Newton can be seen in the fields of mathematics, mechanics and optics.

MATHEMATICS

Newton possessed two copies of Descartes's *Geometry*, both in Latin. Divided into three books, it opens with the claim that 'Any problem in geometry can easily be reduced to such terms that a knowledge of the lengths of certain lines is sufficient for its construction.' In this spirit Book I is concerned with 'Problems which can be constructed by the aid of circles and straight lines.' The highlight of Book I is the solution, by algebraic means, of the problem, outstanding since the time of Euclid, of the four-line locus (Turnbull, 1952, pp. 97–100). Book II contains a little-used classification of curves, and Descartes's method of drawing tangents. The final Book III deals with the solution of higher-order equations, as well as Descartes's rule of signs.

There is little of the familiar language and formalism of analytic geometry to be found in Descartes. The terms 'coordinate', 'abscissa' and 'ordinate' originate with Leibniz; nor can the coordinate axes be found in the form they are presented in the textbooks of today. The truth is that Descartes, as he admitted to Mersenne, had deliberately set out to make his work needlessly obscure. The book remained, nevertheless, a timely production. As Hall (1970, p. 91) has noted, physical problems, especially those of mechanics, tended to present themselves in spatial terms. At last, with the appearance of Descartes's techniques, such problems could be 'subjected to the flexible and solvent attack of algebra'. Descartes had thus 'rendered possible the later achievements of seventeenth-century mathematical physics'.

Newton described his first contact with the work as: 'in the year 1664 a little before Christmas . . . I bought Van Schooten's *Miscellanies* and Descartes *Geometry* (having read this Geometry . . . above half a year before)'. He read it, according to Conduitt, slowly, and with some difficulty, before eventually making himself 'Master of the whole without having the least light or instruction from any body' (RSW, p. 99). His copy of Van Schooten has survived and contains, untypically, several expressions of disagreement. 'Error' occurs eight times, 'non probo' twice, and 'non est Geom' a further three times.

In later life Newton came to object strongly to the Cartesian approach, calling it 'the Analysis of the Bunglers in Mathematicks' (Hiscock, 1937, p. 42). He argued in the *Geometria curvilinea*, for example, to those who:

Eager to add to the discoveries of the ancients, have united the arithmetic of variables with geometry . . . Progress has been broad and far-reaching if your eye is on the profuseness of output, but the advance is less of a blessing if you look at the complexity of its conclusions. For these computations . . . often express in an intolerably roundabout way quantities which in geometry are designated by the drawing of a single line. (*MP*, IV, p. 421)

MECHANICS

Cartesian mechanics rested upon the basic principle of Cartesian philosophy that body consisted only of extension. While it was a restrictive step, which imposed insuperable barriers to the development of a coherent physics, it was also a bold and imaginative step which at the same time expelled forever from physics much extraneous nonsense; for, if bodies had no properties other than extension, the only features they could possess were the quantifiable ones of shape, size and motion. Consequently, earlier appeals to occult qualities and substantial forms could no longer be accepted. For Descartes this meant, also, the elimination from physics of all talk of force, gravity, attraction and other dubious concepts.

Because matter and extension were co-extensive there could be no void. Nor, given the unlimited divisibility of any extended body, could there be any such thing as the atoms of antiquity. What there could be, and all there could be, was extended matter completely surrounded by more extended matter, in motion. Motion itself came from God and was conserved. Consequently, all cases of motion must consist in the transference of motion from one body to another. From this consideration Descartes was able to derive his first law of motion, that bodies, whether in a state of rest or motion, remain in those states until acted upon by other bodies. The law was to form the model for Newton's own first law; it also introduced him to the concept of inertia.

Descartes's second law, equally innovative, broke with the tradition of two millennia in declaring the dependent nature of circular motion: 'Any particular part of matter . . . is never inclined to prosecute motion in any curved lines, but only in straight lines' (Herivel, 1965, p. 45). It remained to Newton to explain just how and why bodies did enter into motion in a 'curved line'.

No concessions were allowed by Descartes when he came to consider celestial phenomena. Here, too, the only factors he allowed were matter in motion. How, in particular, did the circular motion of planets begin? How was it preserved? In a plenum a particle can only move by participating in a general circular motion. Descartes thus envisaged the universe to consist of an immense number of vortices made up of particles of various shapes and sizes. In time, friction produces a fine dust which, gathering at the centre of the vortex, becomes a luminous star like our own sun. Some of the fine dust will settle on the sun's surface as sunspots. These, in turn, will either dissolve or enlarge until they cover the entire surface. The star will then move from one vortex to another as a comet, or find a vortex with a compatible velocity in which it can settle as a planet.

Newton clearly placed considerable attention on the basic physical assumptions of Descartes. His *De gravitatione* of the late 1660s, beginning as a treatise on hydrodynamics, soon turned into a radical appraisal of Cartesian physics. The identification of extension and matter was dismissed as atheistic as it implied that something, extension or body, could have an existence independent of God. Consequently, Newton lacked any similar need to reject the existence of either atoms or the void.

Initially he seems to have found vortices quite acceptable. Whiston, for example, noted how Newton in the 1660s called upon vortices to help explain the lunar orbit (Herivel, 1965, p. 65). By the time he came to write section IX of Book II of *Principia* (1687), however, he had developed a powerful critique against their existence. They remained attractive, none the less, to Pierre Varignon, Christian Huygens and Leibniz.

Newton proved to be more sympathetic to general Cartesian ideas concerning motion. The principle of inertia was perhaps Descartes's most important contribution to Newtonian mechanics. There were others. It has, for example, been suggested that the very title of *Principia*, *Philosophiae naturalis principia mathematica*, was taken directly from the *Principia philosophiae* of Descartes.

LIGHT AND COLOUR

As the universe was a plenum it was inevitable that Descartes should seek to explain the spread of light by the pressure of one particle on another.

> And I desire you to think that light is nothing else in bodies which we call luminous than a certain movement or action very prompt and liveley which passes to our eyes by the agency of the air or other transparent bodies, in the same fashion as the movement, or the resistance of bodies encountered by a blind man passes to his hand by means of his stick. (*La Dioptrique*, 1637; Scott, 1952, pp. 32–3)

The issue was discussed and promptly dismissed by the young Newton in his *QQP*:

> Light cannot be by pression . . . for yn wee should see in the night

a wel or better yn in ye day we should see a bright light above us
because we are pressed downewards . . . there could be no refraction
since ye same matter cannot presse 2 ways . . . A man goeing or
running would see in ye night . . . The whole East would shine in
ye day time & ye west in ye night.

Nor, he added, as pressure could be transmitted through solids as readily
as through a fluid, should eclipses ever take place.

When Descartes moved on to consider colour he conveniently
dropped his earlier account and spoke of light as particles emitted by
luminous bodies. As Descartes was constrained in no other way, it was
a relatively simple task to identify, quite arbitrarily, some aspect of the
particles' motion with the colour produced by the light. He chose to
concentrate on the particle's spin. As the particle struck an object various
things could happen. It could be stopped, in which case the body would
look black. It could also be reflected and gain in the process a rotary
motion: 'If the rotary motion is very rapid compared with the direct,
the body appears red; if it is less so, it appears blue or green' (Scott,
1952, p. 33). Despite its arbitrariness Westfall (1971a, p. 56) has still
greeted Descartes's work at this point as 'a major event in the history
of optics. Not only did he abolish the distinction between real and
apparent colours, placing them all on the same ground, but he was also
responsible for incorporating the phenomena of colour into the science
of optics.'

In general terms Descartes had accounted for colour by proposing a
mechanism for modifying the original, pure, white light as it passed
through the medium to the observer. In this he was followed by most of
his contemporaries. Grimaldi, Hooke and Boyle, though all proposing
different mechanisms, followed the basic Cartesian assumption that
pure, unmodified light was white and that only when it had been altered
in some way did colours appear. It was left to Newton to turn this
entire structure on its head and produce, not so much a true account of
the nature of colour, as a theory based indisputably in experience and
controlled by experiment and observation.

One of the key aspects of Newton's approach derived from experiments with prisms. Descartes some years before had worked with
prisms. In his *Les météores* (1637), while considering the nature of the
rainbow, he noted how sunlight passing through a prism produced the
colours of the rainbow. Unlike Newton, however, he failed to notice
the peculiar dispersive power of the prism and, consequently, was in no
way led to query the basic assumptions of his optics.

de Sluse, René (1622–85)

A Dutch mathematician, actually a Walloon, de Sluse served for much of his life as a canon in Liège. He is best remembered as a mathematician for his discovery of an improved method of drawing tangents. Although worked out in the 1650s, it was first published in the *PT* of 1673 under the title *A Short and Easier Method of Drawing Tangents to all Geometrical Curves*. It was the method Newton later claimed in his account of the *annus mirabilis* to have discovered for himself in May 1665. De Sluse's work was first drawn to Newton's attention by John Collins in December 1672. Once more Newton acknowledged the method to be identical to his own (*C*, I, pp. 247–8). Consequently, Newton's charge that Leibniz must have derived his tangent rule from Newton's letter of December 1672 to Collins is difficult to understand. The same rule had become public property with the appearance in 1673 of the paper of de Sluse.

des Maizeaux, Pierre (1673–1745)

Des Maizeaux, a Huguenot, fled with his family from France after the revocation of the Edict of Nantes in 1685. After studying theology in Geneva and after various travels des Maizeaux settled in England in 1699. He remained in England for the rest of his life, working as a writer, publisher and businessman. He made the acquaintance of Charles Montague and, possibly through him, he was introduced to Newton. His most important contact with Newton came through his publication of his *Recueil de divers pièces sur la philosophie* (Amsterdam, 1720, 2 vols; re-issued 1740 and 1759).

The first volume was innocuous enough, consisting mainly of the Leibniz–Clarke correspondence already published. The second volume, however, contained several of the letters between Leibniz, Conti, Chamberlayne and Newton. Although some of the correspondence had been published in Raphson and elsewhere, other letters were being published for the first time. The proofs were sent to Newton some time in 1718 for his comments. Although initially he was prepared to cooperate, raising no objections and pointing out errors, his attitude seems to have changed by the end of 1719. In November he wrote to des Maizeaux begging the favour to delay publication until next Lady Day and offering the bookseller twelve guineas compensation (*C*, VII, pp. 73–4). Although Newton gave no reason for his request, it has been generally assumed that as the text revealed Bernoulli to be the 'eminent mathematician' of the *Charta volans* (1713) its publication would provoke him to further correspondence. If this was Newton's fear, and despite doubts expressed in the *Recueil* on the identity of the mathematician, it was well founded. The *Recueil* did serve to initiate the final round of the long-standing priority dispute, with Bernoulli as the leading protagonist and Newton as a weary accomplice.

See also Bernoulli, Johann; *Charta volans*

---

d'Espagnet, Jean (1564–1637)

A French magistrate and author of the influential *Enchyridion physicae restitutae* (1623 (?)), Summary of physics recovered). Newton owned the French edition of 1651. Some of his Neoplatonism, Dobbs suspects, in its alchemical guise, was taken up by Newton. Like Sendovigius, he argued for the presence of certain bodies which, like magnets, attracted into themselves new powers capable of transforming their hosts. Newton saw antimony performing a similar role in alchemy and consequently spent many years working on its chemistry.

See also Sendovigius, Michael

Determination of the form of the solid of least resistance

The problem is discussed in prop. XXXIV of Book II of *Principia* (1713 and 1727); it had appeared in the first edition as prop. XXXV. It consists of a demonstration that in a rare medium with 'equal particles freely disposed at equal distances from each other', and given a globe and a cylinder described with equal diameters and moving with equal velocities, then 'the resistance of the globe will be but half as great as that of the cylinder' (Cajori, p. 331). In the following *Scholium* it is shown how 'figures may be compared together as to their resistance'. John Craig claimed in his annotated copy of *Principia* (1687) that 'The occasion for this afterthought I myself provided, when in Cambridge I proposed to the celebrated Author the problem of finding the most suitable outline for ships' (1971, p. 204). Newton did in fact note in the *Scholium* that 'This Proposition I conceive may be of use in the building of ships' (Cajori, p. 333).

The *Scholium*, however, was presented without demonstration; the lapse was made good in a letter to David Gregory dated 14 July 1694 (*C*, III, pp. 380–3). The letter was first published in the 1888 Cambridge *Catalogue* of the PC (pp. xxi–xxiii) and can also be seen in Cajori (pp. 657–9).

De vi electrica

The holograph manuscript of the text is to be found in the *Opticks* papers of the PC in the ULC. It is, however, more closely related to *Principia* and arguments developed in the concluding General *Scholium* of the second edition of 1713. On the basis of material included in the paper, it can be assigned to the period 1711–13. It has been published, in both the original Latin and English translation, for the first and only time (in *C*, V, pp. 362–9).

The paper relies very heavily on experiments carried out by Francis Hauksbee during the period 1705–12 at the RS. Newton began by supposing 'there is some spirit hid in all bodies, by means of which light and bodies act upon each other mutually' (*C*, V, p. 365). It was used to explain the reflection, refraction and inflection of light, the transmission of nervous impulses and the attraction bodies have for each other at short distances. On this last topic, and using experiments of Hauksbee on capillary attraction (*PT*, 1712), Newton attempted to calculate the strength of such short-range forces. It proved to be quite substantial; sufficient, he concluded, to account for the cohesion of bodies, and also, he noted, to effect 'remarkable results in fermentation, putrefaction and chemical reaction' (*C*, V, p. 368).

Similar material is to be found in Query 31 of the *Opticks*.

See also Hauksbee, Francis

de Villamil, Richard (1850–?)

With nothing recorded in the *DNB* or *Who's Who*, and with no obituary in the London *Times*, little is known of de Villamil's life. He was gazetted lieutenant in the Royal Engineers in 1870 and rose to the rank of lieutenant-colonel before retiring from the Army in 1896. Nothing is thereafter known of him before the 1920s other than that he published a number of technical works, amongst which were his *ABC of Hydrodynamics* (1912), *Motion of Liquids* (1914) and *Resistance of Air* (1917).

When approaching eighty, in 1928, de Villamil discovered the remains of Newton's library, 860 volumes, in the hands of the Wykeham-Musgrave family at their home in Barnsley Park in Gloucestershire. Equally impressive, and just as revealing, was his discovery, by a 'lucky accident', in the records of the Prerogative Court of Canterbury at Somerset House, of the full inventory of Newton's estate at the time of his death. So complete was it, de Villamil noted, 'that we could easily re-furnish every room in Newton's house . . . as it was at the time of his death'. The inventory, together with much other important data, was published by de Villamil in his invaluable *Newton: the Man* (London, 1931; reprinted New York, 1972).

See also Inventory; Library

---

de Witt, Jan (1625–72)

The son of the Burgomaster of Dordrecht, de Witt was educated at the University of Leyden, where he was a student of F. van Schooten. After a brief career in mathematics he entered politics, was appointed Grand Pensionary of Holland in 1653, and was finally murdered by the mob in 1672.

De Witt's *Elementa curvarum* (*c*.1650, The Elements of Curves), first published in van Schooten's edition of the *Geometrie* (1659–61), has been described as the first elementary treatise on analytic geometry. It was the first text, after Euclid, recommended by Newton for those like R. Bentley who wished to provide themselves with sufficient mathematics to be able to read *Principia* (*C*, III, pp. 155–6).

Diamond

One of the most often repeated anecdotes about Newton concerns his dog Diamond, 'the constant but incurious attendant of his master's researches'. The dog 'threw down a lighted candle, which consumed the almost finished labours of some years. Sir Isaac returning too late, but to behold the dreadful wreck, rebuked the author of it with an exclamation "Oh Diamond! Diamond! thou little knowest the mischief done"' (Edleston, 1850, p. lxiii). The single source for the story is Thomas Maude, writing in the third edition of his *Wensley-Dale; or, Rural Contemplation* (1780). He claimed the story to be 'authenticated by a person now living'.

There are ample reasons for dismissing Maude's story as baseless. Why are there no descriptions of the dog Diamond in the recollections of Humphrey Newton, David Gregory, or anyone else who knew Newton in the 1680s and 1690s? No trace of the creature can be found in any surviving letter or in any of the recollections assembled by Conduitt. There is also something implausible about Maude's informant. How could he, in 1780, authenticate an event of the late 1670s or early 1690s? Not from his own personal experience. But if his authority derives from another's report, why could not the source have been revealed to Maude?

While contemporary biographers either dismiss or ignore the story, poets and playwrights and novelists have continued to find it attractive.

Shaw (1939), Banville (1982) and Noyes (1937), for example, all refer to the story. The fullest account is Noyes (p. 97), who noted that the dog was:

Named Diamond, for a black patch near his tail.

See also Fire

Diet

According to Humphrey Newton, who served as his amanuensis in the 1680s, Newton 'ate sparingly', and often forgot to eat at all. He only ever drank 'wine, ale, or beer . . . at meals, and then but very sparingly'. Two details he did remember were that, 'in winter time he was a lover of apples', and that 'sometimes at night he would eat a small roasted quince'.

Another source was Catherine Conduitt, who noted that Newton, in later life, had become a vegetarian. Whiston reported that his reluctance to eat such foods as black puddings was because they were made of blood. However it was rather, Catherine reported, a hatred of the cruelty involved in the slaughter of animals that led Newton to his views. In contrast, Conduitt who also noted that Newton ate 'little flesh, and lived chiefly upon broth, vegetables, and fruit, of which he always eat very heartily', seemed to suggest that such a diet was adopted in the 1720s in response to an attack of the stone. A third witness to the Newton of the 1720s, William Stukeley, described his modest breakfast of sweetened orange peel boiled in water, and bread and butter.

Neither did Newton take snuff or smoke tobacco; his grounds were that 'he would make no necessities to himself'.

Discourse of Observations

In February 1672 Newton published in the *PT* his *New Theory about Light and Colors*. It provoked an immediate reply from Robert Hooke, with a detailed defence of his modification theory of colour. Newton, in turn, began to prepare a reply using material taken from his *Lectiones opticae*, to which he added some additional results on the phenomenon of thin films. From this material Newton eventually extracted the reply to Hooke published in the *PT* in November 1672.

By 1675 Newton had begun to tire of the controversy excited by his initial paper of 1672. Unwilling, he told Oldenburg, 'to put pen to paper any more on yt subject', he did have, 'one discourse by me of yt subject written when I sent my first letters to you about colours', and this he was prepared to release to the RS (*C*, I, p. 358). On 7 December 1675 Newton sent a revised version of the 1672 manuscript, transcribed by John Wickins, to Oldenburg. It was read to the Society on 20 January and the 3 and 10 February 1676. The *Discourse* consists of:

1 twenty-four observations on thin transparent bodies;
2 remarks on the above observations;
3 nine propositions on 'how the phaenomena of thin transparent plates stand related to those of all other natural bodies'.

Oldenburg was ordered by the Society to publish the entire *Discourse*. On 25 January 1676, however, Newton instructed Oldenburg that 'the printing of his observations about colours might be suspended for a time, because he had some thoughts about writing such another set of observations for determining the manner of the production of colours by the prism' (*PLNP*, p. 210). It was a long suspension. Shortly afterwards Newton's interests changed somewhat and he began to work intensively in the areas of chemistry and alchemy. The *Discourse* was eventually published, virtually word for word and comma for comma, in 1704 as parts I, II and III of Book II of the *Opticks*. The original *Discourse* itself was first published in vol. 3 of Thomas Birch's *History of the Royal Society*, pp. 272–305, and can be seen in this form in *PLNP*, pp. 202–35.

Ditton, Humphrey (1675–1715)

Although without a university education, Ditton was a competent mathematician respected by Newton. Two of Ditton's works, *General Treatise on the Laws of Nature and Motion . . . Being a Part of the Great Mr Newton's Principles* (1705) and *An Institution of Fluxions . . . According to Sir Is.Newton* (1706) had so impressed Newton, as they may well have been designed to do, that he obtained for Ditton a post of mathematics teacher at Christ's Hospital.

Ditton is better remembered for his collaboration with William Whiston on their pamphlet *A New Method for the Discovery of the Longitude at Sea* (1714). The method consisted of anchoring ships along the trade routes at known positions. At an agreed time each day they would fire a rocket. In 1714 Newton gave evidence before a House of Commons Committee on this and other proposals. Newton commented on the project that 'this is rather for keeping an Account for the Longitude at Sea, than for finding it, if at any time it should be lost'. It also had the disadvantage, he continued, that whenever ships are to sail over very deep seas, 'they must sail due East or West, without varying their Latitude' (Howse, 1980, pp. 50–1).

See also Christ's Hospital

Double refraction

In 1669 Erasmus Bartholin published his *Experimenta crystalli islandica disdiaclastici* in which he explained the curious behaviour of light as it passed through the crystal known as Iceland spar (calcium carbonate). One light ray would enter, two rays would emerge. Newton described the phenomena in Query 25 of the *Opticks*. While one ray of light passed through the crystal perpendicularly, 'as it ought to do by the usual Laws of Opticks' (the ordinary ray), the second ray (the extraordinary ray) 'by an unusual Refraction' diverged from the perpendicular by about 6 2/3° (*Opticks*, p. 357).

Such anomalous phenomena play a vital role in science. They constantly challenge the exactness of the theorist's understanding of nature. Only if his comprehension is deep enough and accurate enough can he hope to handle an unending sequence of challenging problems. If such cases do not arise naturally, theorists spend their time inventing their own puzzles with which they can impress their patrons and embarrass their rivals. Iceland spar proved to be just such a case.

Huygens, in his *Traité de la lumière* (1690), took up the matter first and endeavoured to show how the problem could be incorporated into a wave theory of light. Initially he met with some success. As there were two different refractions, he argued, there must also be 'two different emanations of waves of light'. Some of the waves, with a spherical form, travelled through the ether and produced the ordinary rays. Others were transmitted by both the particles of the ether as well as the particles of the crystal in the form of spheroidal waves with different velocities and in different directions and so produced the extraordinary rays. The model, although completely speculative, did contrive to yield the desired effect.

There was, however, a further effect noted by Huygens. He allowed the two rays produced by a crystal of Iceland spar to fall on a second crystal. To his surprise Huygens found that the ordinary ray continued in the same direction as an ordinary ray, while the extraordinary ray continued to be refracted as an extraordinary ray. No further division of the light rays occurred. Why, precisely, they behaved so differently from the ray entering the first crystal was, Huygens confessed, quite beyond him. His inability to resolve the point was held by many – Newton for one – to be absolute evidence of the inadequacy of the wave theory.

Newton's own solution was advanced in Queries 25–6. The effect was due, he insisted, to an 'original difference in the Rays of Light' and not to 'new Modifications impress'd on the Rays at their first Refraction'. Otherwise, he argued, further modifications would have been imposed on the light rays as they passed through the second crystal. To follow through his claim, Newton was committed to describing an 'original' property of light which would permit the complex behaviour observed when it passed through crystals of Iceland spar.

He answered in Query 26 that light rays have 'several sides endued with several original properties'. This did not mean that there were 'two sorts of Rays differing in their nature from one another'; rather, there was one kind of ray only which, depending on its position, would be refracted in an ordinary or an extraordinary manner. Newton went on to show how, on this assumption, he could account much better than Huygens for the facts of double refraction.

Although Newton offered no details concerning what he meant by the notion of a side of a light ray, he did, in Query 29, speak of 'some kind of attractive virtue lodged in certain Sides both of the Rays, and of the Particles of the Crystal', and went on to compare the sides with the poles found in magnets. It was for this reason that Etienne Malus, a century later in 1808, when he discovered yet one more oddity about Iceland spar, sought to explain it by assigning to light a property he termed polarisation. Looking back with hindsight after Malus, Newton's extraordinary physical intuition is revealed yet again. What he wrote in Queries 25–6 was sketchy and speculative and, for a century, led nowhere. Despite this, it contained the essential insight into the nature of double refraction, and provided the basic physical understanding which would eventually permit the explanation of much more besides.

See also Polarisation; Wave theory of light

E

Edleston, Joseph (1816–95)

In 1850 Edleston, a Fellow and senior bursar of TCC, published his invaluable *Correspondence of Sir Isaac Newton and Professor Cotes including Letters of Other Eminent Men*. It contained, in addition to the correspondence, a vast amount of detail culled from the Trinity archives about Newton's life in Cambridge, as well as much biographical data of a more general kind. Amongst this material Edleston included:

1. a twenty-page 'Synoptical view of Newton's life' supplemented by forty pages of notes;
2. the dividends received by Newton as a Trinity fellow from 1668–1702;
3. Newton's exits and redits from Trinity over the period 1668–96;
4. the weekly buttery bills of Newton from 1686–1702;
5. tables of the lectures Newton supposedly delivered as Lucasian Professor.

Much of this material was new and has since served as the primary source of many a later biography.

The heart of the book, however, remains the eighty-four letters between Newton and Cotes dating from August 1709 to May 1715 dealing mainly with the publication in 1713 of the second edition of *Principia*. The letters had passed via Cotes's executor, Robert Smith, a later Master of TCC and cousin to Cotes, and the Reverend Edward Howkins, to Trinity in 1779. Edleston had noted that the collection lacked about twenty or thirty letters written by Newton to Cotes and 'borrowed from Smith by Conduitt' (p. xvii). He expected them to turn up in the PC. No such hoard has in fact been found. The definitive *Correspondence* uncovered only five letters from the PC unknown to Edleston, all from Cotes to Newton, and dated 5 October 1710 (*C*, V, pp. 73–4), 26 October 1710 (*C*, V, pp. 74–5), 31 March 1711 (*C*, V, pp. 107–10), 4 June 1711 (*C*, V, pp. 152–3) and 25 October 1711 (*C*, V, p. 202). Additional correspondence relating to *Principia* (1713) between Cotes, William Jones, Richard Bentley, John Keill and several others

was also included by Edleston. An appendix contained yet further correspondence between Newton, Henry Oldenburg, John Locke, Robert
Hooke, John Wallis *et al.* on a variety of topics.

The entire work is available today in a facsimile reproduction published
in 1969 by Frank Cass as vol. 12 in the Cass Library of Science Classics.

Ekins family

A number of Newton's chronological and theological manuscripts,
eleven items in all, were sent in the 1750s to A. A. Sykes for him to
evaluate their suitability for publication. After his death in 1756 they
were passed on to his friend the Reverend Jeffrey Ekins of the parish of
Barton-Seagrave, Northamptonshire, an executor of Lady Lymington
(Kitty Conduitt). They must have remained with the family for over a
century, handed down from father to son, until in 1872 another
Reverend Jeffrey Ekins presented them to New College, Oxford. They,
in turn, deposited them in the Bodleian Library where they can now be
found as New College 361/1–4. Brewster saw copies of them in 1855.

See also Portsmouth Collection

Ellipses and elliptical orbits

An ellipse, a conic section, is the locus of points, the sum of whose
distances from the two foci A and B is constant; its main features can
be seen in Fig. 1.

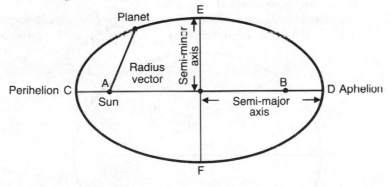

Fig. 1

The line C–D, the longest axis, is known as the major axis; seen
astronomically as joining aphelion to perihelion, it is known as the line
of apsides. The line E–F, the shortest axis, is known as the minor axis.
The line joining a planet in its orbit to the sun, located at one focus, is

known as the radius vector. The point C, where the radius vector is shortest, is known as perihelion; the point D, where the radius vector is longest, is known as aphelion. The eccentricity of an ellipse can be expressed as the ratio between the distance between A and B and the major axis C–D, i.e. A–B/C–D. If the eccentricity is 0 the figure has become a circle; if, however, the eccentricity is 1 the figure has opened up into a parabola.

According to Kepler's first law, every planet moves in an ellipse with the sun placed at one of the foci. The second law claims that a straight line joining the sun and a planet, a radius vector, sweeps out equal areas in equal times. Thus in the ellipse in Fig. 2 X–Y represents the line of

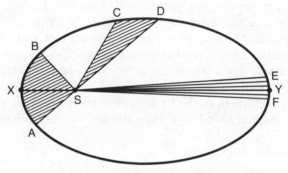

Fig. 2

apsides and the point S the sun located at one focus. According to Kepler's area law, if the times taken by a planet in its orbit around the sun to travel from A–B, C–D and E–F are all equal, then the shaded areas, marked out by the radius vectors, will all be equal. Planets thus travel faster at perihelion than at aphelion.

The area law proved difficult to operate in practice. Consequently astronomers tended to use a simplified form (see Fig. 3). In this construc-

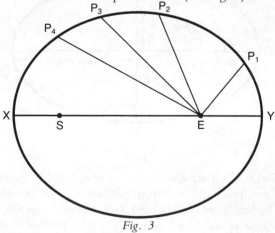

Fig. 3

[184]

tion a radius vector is assumed to rotate uniformly, not about the sun but about the empty focus. Although a geometrical rather than a physical construction, and although less accurate than the area law, it proved to be a fair enough approximation to be acceptable to most astronomers.

Ellis, John (n.d.)

Ellis was one of the three figures named by Humphrey Newton, amanuensis to Newton in the early 1680s, as a regular visitor to Newton's rooms in TCC. A Fellow of Caius College from 1659, he was appointed Master in 1703, and Vice-Chancellor of the University in 1705. In this latter post he was knighted, together with Newton and James Montague, by Queen Anne in TCC in 1705.

The only contact between them to be found in the *Correspondence* concerned a matter of patronage and was a simple request for Newton to recommend a mathematician for Christ's Hospital (*C*, II, pp. 373–6).

See also Friends

Éloge de M. Newton

Written by B. Fontenelle, *secrétaire-perpétuel* of the *Académie des Sciences*, and published in 1727 in the *Histoire de l'Académie Royale des Sciences* (pp. 151–72), it was based on material collected by John Conduitt, *Memoirs Relating to Sir Isaac Newton sent by me to Monr Fontenelle in Octr 1727*, now in the Keynes Collection, KCC. The work was much in demand when issued separately. Two issues appeared in Paris in 1728 and no less than five in London in an English translation. It was also translated into Italian (Venice, 1757; Naples, 1765). In all some eighteen editions appeared in the eighteenth century. An English translation, *The Elogium of Sir Isaac Newton by Monsieur Fontenelle* (London, 1728) has been reprinted in facsimile in *PLNP* (pp. 444–74).

See also Biography; Fontenelle, Bernard

Emerson, William (1701–82)

The son of a schoolmaster, Emerson managed to devote his life to the study of mathematics with the aid of an inherited income of about £70 a year. Beginning with his *Fluxions* (1749), the British Museum Catalogue lists some twenty-two of his elementary mathematical textbooks. Two of these short works, *A Short Comment on the Principia* and *A*

Defence of Newton, were included in William Davis's 1803 edition of the *Principia*. In the latter text Emerson defended Newton against Leibniz's attack on the General *Scholium*, against points raised by Johann Bernoulli and, above all, against the 'vortex mad Euler' who could not 'even account for the rising of the tides without vortices'.

See also Principia, Translations

Enumeratio linearum tertii ordinis

Although the Greeks had made a fairly comprehensive study of the conic sections – circle, ellipse, parabola and hyperbola – they paid scarcely any attention to the higher plane curves. In fact, only two such curves were identified: the cissoid of Diocles ($y^2(2a-x) = x^3$), a cubic curve described by Geminus in the first century BC; and the conchoid of Nicomedes ($k^2x^2 = (x-a)^2(x^2+y^2)$), a quartic described in the second century BC by Pappus. Nor was much more interest displayed by the mathematicians of the medieval period and the Renaissance. Four further cubics were identified in the seventeenth century before Newton began to take an interest in the problem: two by Descartes in the 1630s, the folium ($x^3 + y^3 = 3axy$) and the trident ($xy = ax^3 + bx^2 + cx + d$); the cubical parabola by Wallis ($y = kx^3$); and the semi-cubical parabola by William Neile ($y^2 = kx^3$).

Newton first worked on the problem in 1664 but made little progress. Thereafter he returned to the problem on several occasions before presenting his definitive analysis in 1695. The first determined attempt at the problem was made in the period 1667–8.

1 *Enumeratio curvarum trium dimensium* (Add. MS 3961.1). Newton made three separate attempts at the work (*MP*, II, pp. 10–18, 18–36, 36–85) before abandoning it for other problems. In the final manuscript he had got as far as identifying sixteen species of cubic curve. He went on to list the sixteen curves in a further manuscript, *Nomina curvarum in sexdecim speciebus* (*MP*, II, pp. 86–9). Some of the more figurative names of the manuscript, such as the 'mussell shell' and the 'endeal' (ivy leaf) would not survive into later classifications.

Newton returned to the problem in the period 1678–9.

2 In an untitled manuscript (Add. MS 3961.4, 3961.1), *Revised Analytical Investigation of the General Cubic Curve* (*MP*, IV, pp. 354–81) to adopt Whiteside's title, Newton increased the number of species to fifty-three.

Newton's final attempt on the problem was made in the early 1690s.

3 He began with a manuscript (Add. MS 3961.4) which simply listed the sixty-nine species he had succeeded in identifying (*MP*, VII,

pp. 579–87). By 1695 he had extended the number to seventy-two and was ready to begin the final draft of what he then called *Enumeratio linearum tertii ordinis* (Add. MS 3961.2; *MP*, VII, pp. 588–645). It was shown to Gregory who noted in 1698 that 'There are sixteen species of curve of the second class, and 76 curves. Newton has written a treatise on them, which he will communicate to me for me to publish' (*C*, IV, p. 277). Newton actually hung on to the *Enumeratio* for a further six years before finally publishing it as an appendix to the *Opticks* (1704).

In the work itself Newton had argued that all cubic curves could be reduced to one of the following four equations:

(a) $xy^2 + ey = ax^3 + bx^2 + cx + d$
(b) $xy = ax^3 + bx^2 + cx + d$
(c) $y^2 = ax^3 + bx^2 + cx + d$
(d) $y = ax^3 + bx^2 + cx + d$

He went on to identify nine cases which he subdivided into sixteen genera and seventy-two species. For the most part classification was made in terms of the properties of the diameters and asymptotes of the curves. The nine cases distinguished with the number of species in brackets were: redundant hyperbola (32); defective hyperbola (13); parabolic hyperbola (11); hyperbolisms of a hyperbola (4); hyperbolisms of an ellipse (3); hyperbolisms of a parabola (2); parabolic trident (1); divergent parabola (5); cubical parabola (1). Each of the species was clearly illustrated by a line diagram.

In some ways the *Enumeratio* is the most original of all Newton's mathematical work. It had no predecessors, met with no rivals claiming to have anticipated his results, or few even who acknowledged its results. No mention of the work appeared in the *PT* before 1715, while Bernoulli, writing to Leibniz in 1714, commented 'I have not yet been able to bring myself to examine this matter, since I do not willingly embroil myself with intricacies of that sort, utterly useless as they are indeed' (*MP*, VII, p. 572).

As there are in fact seventy-eight and not seventy-two cubic curves, it remained for others to complete Newton's programme. James Stirling added a further four in his edition of the *Enumeratio* in 1717, while the remaining two were identified by Francois Nicole and Nicholas Bernoulli in the 1730s.

Newton also stated, without proof, a general theorem about the generation of cubic curves. It is well-known that all conics (circle, ellipse, parabola and hyperbola) can be represented as the shadows cast by a circle. Newton sought for a similar way of representing cubics and proposed that all such curves could be seen as the shadows cast by the curve known as the divergent parabola and represented by the equation:

$$y^2 = ax^3 + bx^2 + cx + d$$

It was proved first by F. Nicole and A. C. Clairaut in 1731 and subsequently, and more rigorously, by Murdoch in 1740.

Although, in Hall's phrase, the *Enumeratio* 'held no fascination for either British or German mathematicians' (1980, p. 137), it has in fact turned out to be one of the most frequently issued of Newton's mathematical works and is known in the following thirteen editions.

1 London, 1704. Included in the first edition of *Opticks*; also present in the first Latin edition of 1706 but omitted from all subsequent editions.

2 London, 1710. The first English translation, made by John Harris, appeared in his *Lexicon technicum* under the heading *Curves*. It was retained in the second edition of 1723.

3 London, 1711. Included in William Jones (1711) and the reprint in the Amsterdam *Principia* (1723).

4 Oxford, 1717. Edited by James Stirling in his *Lineae tertii ordini Newtonianae*. Sterling added four further cubics to the seventy-two already distinguished by Newton.

5 Lausanne and Geneva, 1744. Included in Castillioneus, *Tome* I.

6 London, 1779. Included in Horsley, vol. I; re-issued in 1964 in a facsimile edition (Stuttgart–Bad Cannstatt.)

7 Paris, 1797. Edited by J. R. Lottin.

8 London, 1856. Included in C. R. M. Talbot's *Sir Isaac Newton's Enumeration of Lines of the Third Order*; reprinted in 1860.

9 Moscow–Leningrad, 1937. A Russian translation of 5 prepared by D. D. Mordukay-Boltovskoy.

10 Dresden, 1953. A German translation prepared by M. Miller.

11 Bologna, 1957. An Italian translation prepared by I. Bertoldi.

12 New York, 1967. A reprint of 2 in vol. II of Newton, 1964–7.

13 Cambridge, 1967. The emerging manuscript tradition of *Enumeratio* can be followed in *MP*, II, pp. 10–85, *MP*, IV, pp. 354–81 and *MP*, VII, pp. 579–645.

See also Stirling, James

Epistola prior and *Epistola posterior*

The two lengthy letters were sent to Leibniz in 1676 to acquaint him with the main lines of Newton's mathematical development. The former was dated 13 June and was actually dispatched to Leibniz on 26 July through the agency of Samuel König, a visiting German mathematician from Bratislava; it was received by Leibniz on 16 August. Four copies are known.

1 A copy in the PC in the ULC in Newton's hand.

2 Another copy in the ULC in an unknown hand with a few corrections in Newton's hand.

3 A copy made by John Collins, corrected by David Gregory (Gregory Collection, St Andrew's).

4 The copy made by Oldenburg and sent to Leibniz (Leibniz Collection, Hanover).

The second letter, dated 24 October, was only dispatched to Leibniz in the following May and was received on 11 June 1677. Four copies are known.

1 Newton's autograph text in the BM.

2 A transcript in an unknown hand in the PC in the ULC.

3 A copy made by John Collins (Gregory Collection, St Andrew's).

4 The copy sent to Leibniz by Oldenburg (Leibniz Collection, Hanover).

The letters were fully published for the first time in vol. III of Wallis's *Algebra* (1699). Both are readily available today, in both the original Latin and in English translation, in C, II, pp. 20–47, 110–61.

Epistola prior, beginning with the binomial theorem, went on to describe Newton's work on series. Throughout, the tone was friendly and respectful. Although much was presented openly and freely, Newton did indicate that he had additional material which he lacked sufficient time to explain. His new mathematical techniques developed in such works as *De analysi* and *De methodis* were displayed in use rather than expounded in detail.

The second letter also contains much discussion on infinite series. It is best known, however, for Newton's reference to powerful and general methods he had developed for the drawing of tangents, the determination of maxima and minima, and the quadrature of curves. These, he added, he preferred to conceal within a quite insoluble anagram. A second, and even longer, anagram concealed Newton's claim to be able to solve fluxional equations. The solution to the first anagram was revealed to Leibniz in a letter from Newton dated 16 October 1693 (C, III, pp. 285–9). The solutions to both were publicly disclosed by Wallis (1699).

Newton made it clear to Oldenburg, with the completion of the *Epistola post*, 'that he had no further interest in pursuing the correspondence. He had 'other things in my head' and he would not be willing 'to write any more about this subject' (C, II, p. 110). The 'other things' demanding Newton's attention in the 1670s were alchemy and chemistry, subjects he found much more appealing than the optics and mathematics Collins and Oldenburg kept forcing upon him.

See also Anagrams; Priority dispute

Ether

The idea of an omnipresent medium has considerable attractions for the scientist. It enables him, for example, to explain how such familiar phenomena as light, heat, sound and magnetism can operate over great distances and travel through a seemingly empty space. One of the earliest ether theories was developed by the Stoics, in classical times. They spoke not of an ether but a *pneuma* which, amongst other things, allowed sound to spread like waves in water. With the emergence of modern science in the early seventeenth century similar theories inevitably reappeared. Descartes, who set the tone of much of modern science, denied the void and filled space with a transparent *matière subtile*, a proposal followed by most of his successors.

Newton was as susceptible to the appeal of ether theories as any other physicist and throughout his life he continued to explore ways in which they could be adapted to account for the essential properties of light and gravity. His various writings on ether, with their changes of view, can be listed as follows.

1 In a number of works in the 1670s – *De aere, An Hypothesis* and the *Letter to Boyle* – Newton argued for the existence of an air 'subtle enough to penetrate the pores of glass, crystal, and other terrestial bodies'. He called it 'the spirit of air, or the aether' (Halls, p. 227). The evidence for its existence was twofold. He noted, in *De aere*, that 'in a glass empty of air a pendulum preserved its oscillatory motion not much longer than in the open air'. Clearly, Newton concluded, 'there remains in the glass something much more subtle which damps the motion of the bob'. Secondly, Newton pointed to certain experiments of Boyle in which 'metals, fused in a hermetically sealed glass', when calcinated, 'become heavier'. The increase could only have come, Newton insisted, from a subtle spirit passing through the pores of the glass.

   Where did the ether come from? In *De aere* he proposed that, just as 'bodies of this Earth by breaking into small particles are converted into air, so these particles can be broken into lesser ones by some violent action and converted into yet more subtle air' (Halls, p. 227).

   Newton also found a number of uses for the ether. In the *An Hypothesis* of 1675 he looked to an interaction between the ether and light to explain reflection and refraction. More ambitiously, in the *Letter to Boyle*, he sought to use the lack of homogeneity in the ether to explain the facts of gravity.

2 In the 1680s Newton seems to have become dissatisfied with the ether. In the opening definition I of *Principia* (1687) Newton had expressly excluded from his definition of mass 'a medium if any

such there is, that freely pervades the interstices between the parts of bodies'. His main worry appears to have been that a pervasive ether would disturb the motion of heavenly bodies. Thus, in an undated manuscript, *A Theory of the Moon* (*C*, IV, pp. 1–6), written before 1702, he argued: 'all the planets are ruled by gravity, and that not only are solid spheres to be resolved into a fluid medium, but even this medium is to be rejected lest it hinder or disturb the celestial motions that depend upon gravity' (*C*, IV, p. 3).

In the General *Scholium* to section VI of Book II of *Principia*, Newton sought to test experimentally 'the opinion of some that there is a certain etherial medium extremely rare and subtile, which freely pervades the pores of all bodies' (Cajori, pp. 325–6). But detailed experiments with pendulums revealed that the resistance of the ether was 'either nil or completely insensible'. It would still, of course, be possible to talk about an ether so subtle that its effects were indiscernible. Such a medium, however, would be of little use to anyone hoping to use it to explain gravity and other phenomena.

3 Despite such experimental evidence, Newton could be found a few years later in 1693 writing to Bentley about the absurdity of supposing that a body could act upon another at a distance 'without the mediation of anything else' (*C*, III, p. 254). At the same time he was telling Leibniz that 'some very fine matter seems to fill the heavens' (*C*, III, p. 287).

4 Further commitment to the ether is to be found in the General *Scholium* added to the second edition of *Principia* (1713). Once more he spoke of 'a certain most subtle spirit which pervades and lies hid in all gross bodies' (Cajori, p. 547). It was in terms of this spirit, Newton continued, that we could best understand light, heat, sensation, attraction, coherence, and much else. How precisely all this worked Newton did not reveal, commenting instead that such things 'cannot be explained in a few words'.

5 Newton's final published views on the ether were revealed in the additional eight queries (Q.17–Q.24) added to the second English edition of the *Opticks* (1717). Once more Newton had new experimental support of the ether's existence. In Q.18 he described how thermometers were placed in two sealed glass vessels, one of which had had the air pumped out. The result, he declared, was that 'the Thermometer in vacuo will grow warm as much, and almost as soon as the other Thermometer'. Did this not mean, Newton asked, that heat was conveyed by a medium 'more rare and subtile than air'.

In Q.21 and Q.22 Newton returned to the problem of gravity and the ether and reproduced the speculations of nearly forty years before. The medium, he proposed, was 'much rarer within the dense Bodies of the Sun, Stars, Planets, and Comets, than in the empty celestial Spaces between them' (Q.21). In this way gravitational attraction becomes a case of 'every Body endeavouring to go from the denser parts of the Medium towards the rarer'.

Newton also considered the question of why the ether should be so 'rare and elastick'. Ether particles are exceedingly small, Newton answered; they also repel each other. Further, attractive and repulsive forces were stronger in small bodies than in large ones in proportion to their bulk. The result, Newton commented would be a 'Medium exceedingly more rare and elastick than Air, and by consequence exceedingly less able to resist the motion of Projectiles, and exceedingly more able to press upon gross Bodies, by endeavouring to expand itself' (Q.21).

The concept of a pervasive ether continued to attract physicists long after Newton. Indeed, the physicist of the nineteenth century was presented with a bewildering variety of alternative ethers. For some, like Fresnel, the ether was stationary; others, like G. G. Stokes, argued that the earth dragged the ether along as it rotated daily and annually orbited the sun. A rigid luminiferous ether was proposed to explain the transverse propagation of light, and a 'magneto-electric medium' consisting of a fluid filled with rotating vortex tubes was put forward by Maxwell as an accurate description of the electro-magnetic field. As physics became more sophisticated and as phenomena multiplied, ethers also advanced in both number and complexity. Until, that is, 1905 when Albert Einstein in his special theory of relativity argued that physics could dispense with the concept entirely.

Euhemerus (fl.300)

The Mediterranean peoples of the third and second centuries BC had seen the deification of Alexander the Great and, after his death in 323 BC, a similar apotheosis took place amongst the ruling Seleucids and Ptolemies. Some who witnessed this process were inclined to reverse it and see in the Gods of their day the rulers of the past.

One such was Euhemerus of Messene who, in his lost *Sacred Scripture*, described an imaginary voyage to Panchaea, an island in the Indian ocean. On the island he found statues and monuments recording the deeds of their past kings, Uranus, Chronos and Zeus. Translated into Latin by Ennius (239–169 BC), it had more impact in Rome than in Athens. It also proved a tempting position for the early church fathers who, like Clement of Alexandria, much studied by Newton, could turn round to the pagans and insist: 'Those to whom you bow were once men like yourself.'

It was a view Newton found attractive and useful in his chronological writings. Once euhemerism had lost its early polemical bite it became no more than a widely used historical assumption.

See also Chronological principles

Experimentum crucis

When in 1672 Newton first published his account of the nature of light and colour he referred to an 'experimentum crucis' he had performed (*PLNP*, p. 50). The experiment has since been recognised as one of the turning points in optics, as well as also being a powerful demonstration of the new experimental technique. The term itself became part of the language of science with, over the centuries, the call for other crucial experiments to enable scientists to choose between alternative, competing theories.

The concept, though not the terminology, goes back to Francis Bacon. In his *Novanum organum* (1620) Bacon spoke rather of an *instantiae crucis*, or crucial instance, which, like a sign-post located at a cross-roads, will unambiguously point to the true path. It was Robert Hooke in the *Micrographia* (1665) who first used the more familiar expression when he referred to the generation of colours by thin plates as 'a Guide or Land-Mark', and 'Experimentum Crucis', with which we could 'search after the true cause of Colours' (Hooke, 1961, p. 54).

The actual experiment is described somewhat sketchily (*PLNP*, pp. 50–1). The question facing Newton was why the coloured spectrum produced by the passage of light through a prism was of oblong and not circular shape. The experiment was described but not illustrated in the original 1672 paper. Light was passed through a prism (A) and subsequently directed through a hole in a board on to a second prism (B). By adjusting A, Newton found that he could direct any part of the spectrum on to B. The result, he noted, was:

> That the light, tending to that end of the Image, towards which the refraction of the first Prisme was made, did in the second Prisme suffer a Refraction considerably greater than the light tending to the other end. And so the true cause of the length of that Image was detected to be no other, then that Light consists of Rays differently refrangible, which, without any respect to a difference in their incidence, were, according to their degrees of refrangibility, transmitted towards divers parts of the wall.

The point Newton was seeking to make, and one on which he would later choose 'to lay the whole stress of' his case before Hooke (*PLNP*, p. 134), was that the rays of light fell on prism B with an equal angle of incidence. The image produced, however, varied considerably in refrangibility. Thus the refrangibility of colours was independent of the angle of incidence, or, as he put it later to Hooke, differently-coloured rays 'consider'd apart, do at *Equal* incidences suffer Unequal *Refractions* without being split, rarified, or any ways dilated' (*PLNP*, p. 134).

How original was the *experimentum crucis*? The subject has been exhaustively examined by J. A. Lohne (1968). It appears that Robert Boyle, Marci and Grimaldi all performed very similar experiments. There is, however, no reason to believe that Newton was aware of any of this work. Further, the experiments tended to be included amongst large numbers of closely-related experiments. Unnoticed by their author they were only too likely to be passed over by even the most diligent of readers. Unlike his contemporaries, Newton described a mere handful of experiments in the 1672 paper and went on to emphasise their significance. It may not have been necessary to agree with Newton; it was impossible, however, to fail to see he was making important claims.

When did Newton first enact the *experimentum crucis*? The 1672 paper begins with the observation that 'in the beginning of the year 1666' he procured a prism 'to try therewith the celebrated phenomena of colors'. The first written description of the experiment is to be found in the notebook *Of Colours* (ULC, Add. MS 3975). There he wrote:

> Refracting ye rays through a Prisme into a darke roome . . . And
> holding another Prisme about 5 or 6 yards from ye former to
> refract ye rays againe I found first yt ye blew rays did suffer a greater
> Refraction by ye second Prisme, then ye Red ones.

The manuscript is undated but is thought to come from the period 1666. The experiment is also to be found described in the lectures delivered in Cambridge in 1670, the *Lectiones opticae* (Lohne, 1968, p. 180). In the *Opticks* (1704) the term *experimentum crucis* is not to be found. Newton did, however, describe similar two-prism experiments (*Opticks*, Book I, part I, exp. V, pp. 46–7).

Later Newton chose to emphasise not the double prism experiment but a prism–lens experiment. It was this variety he urged J. T. Desaguliers to perform publicly in 1713 to justify his work. It was also this experiment that he selected as a head-piece to each part of the second French edition of the *Opticks* (1722). It appears first as experiments XI and XII of Book I, part I of the *Opticks* (1704).

The experiment itself came under attack from Newton's various critics in the ensuing controversy in the PT. Hooke argued that, while he accepted Newton's account of the experiment, it was far from crucial, being 'solved by my hypothesis as well as by his' (*PLNP*, p. 111). Others chose to object specifically to the *experimentum crucis*. Beginning with Ignace Pardies in 1672 and followed by Franciscus Linus in 1675, A. Lucas in 1676, Mariotte in 1679 and de la Hire some time after 1707, many who tried to repeat the experiment failed utterly. It was thus, surprisingly, a considerable time before the supposedly crucial experiment was accepted as a genuine effect. Final acceptance seemed to depend on successful public demonstrations of the experiment, before a committee of the RS in 1676, before visiting scholars to London in 1716 and before members of the *Académie* in Paris in 1719. By the 1720s, but not before, a half century after its first publication, the *experimentum crucis* finally became acceptable as an accurate and significant result.

See also Colour; *New Theory about Light and Colours*; Prisms

F

Fabri, Honoré (1607–88)

A Jesuit, and a minor mathematician of the period, Fabri became widely known in his day as a plagiarist. In his *Synopsis geometrica* (1669, Synopsis of Geometry), he had begun with a work of Francesco Cavalieri and, merely by substituting a different terminology, claimed to have developed a new method. When Leibniz came to review Newton's *De quadratura* in 1705 (*AE*) he noted that Newton used the language of fluxions rather than differentials, just as, he added, 'Honoré Fabri . . . substituted the advance of movements for the method of Cavalieri'. Although Leibniz later denied any intention to accuse Newton of plagiary, there were few British mathematicians prepared to agree with him.

See also Priority dispute

Family

Newton, through ties of affinity and birth, was a member of the Newton, Smith and Ayscough families. The exact relationships can best be seen in Figs 1, 2 and 3.

1 Newton's immediate family, and ultimately his heirs, consisted mainly of his step-siblings and their descendants (see Fig. 1). The eight underlined names are the heirs who shared between themselves the £31,821 16s 10d Newton left on his death.

2 He was also related, through his mother, to the Ayscough family (see Fig. 2).

3 There is, finally, Newton's paternal kin (see Fig. 3). The underlined John of Colsterworth inherited the Manor of Woolsthorpe on Newton's death in 1727.

See also Ancestry; Heirs

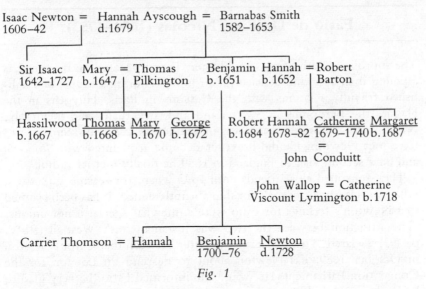

Isaac Newton = Hannah Ayscough = Barnabas Smith
1606–42   d.1679   1582–1653

Sir Isaac   Mary = Thomas   Benjamin Hannah = Robert
1642–1727   b.1647 Pilkington   b.1651   b.1652   Barton

Hassilwood Thomas Mary   George   Robert Hannah   Catherine   Margaret
b.1667   b.1668 b.1670 b.1672   b.1684 1678–82 1679–1740 b.1687
                                                        =
                                              John Conduitt

                                      John Wallop = Catherine
                                      Viscount Lymington b.1718

Carrier Thomson = Hannah   Benjamin   Newton
                             1700–76   d.1728

Fig. 1

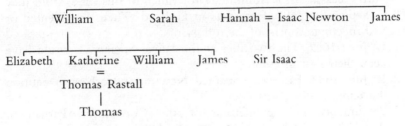

James Ayscough = Margery Blyth of Stroxton

William   Sarah   Hannah = Isaac Newton   James

Elizabeth   Katherine William   James   Sir Isaac
            =
Thomas Rastall

Thomas

Fig. 2

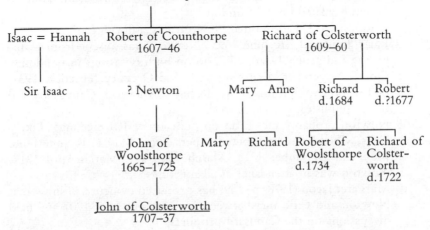

Robert of Woolsthorpe 1570–1641

Isaac = Hannah   Robert of Counthorpe   Richard of Colsterworth
                  1607–46   1609–60

Sir Isaac   ? Newton   Mary   Anne   Richard   Robert
                                                d.1684   d.?1677

                John of   Mary   Richard Robert of   Richard of
                Woolsthorpe   Woolsthorpe Colster-
                1665–1725   d.1734   worth
                                                          d.1722

                John of Colsterworth
                1707–37

Fig. 3

[197]

Fatio de Duillier, Nicolas (1664–1753)

The son of a wealthy Swiss landowner, Fatio appeared on the scene as a young man as a kind of scientific groupie. Touring Europe, he established friendly relations with the Cassinis in Paris, Huygens in the Hague, the Bernoullis in Switzerland and, eventually and inevitably, Newton in Cambridge. Fatio was in London in 1687 but seems not to have met Newton. He did however become acquainted with *Principia* and on a second visit to England in 1689 he finally met its author.

They remained close friends until 1693 when, for reasons unknown, what was clearly a close relationship abruptly ended. It has been claimed that Newton's feelings for Fatio were somewhat special if not unique. 'The attraction between the two was instantaneous', Westfall (RSW, p. 493) declared. The first surviving letter between them, from Newton in October 1689, has Newton about to descend on London for the Convention Parliament. He would, he informed Fatio 'be very glad to be in the same lodgings with you' (C, III, p. 45). Thereafter they are known to have met only seldom, perhaps on five or six other occasions, before the break in 1693. Admittedly for much of this time, from June 1690 to September 1691, Fatio was in Holland. Their documented or suspected meetings consist of the following.

1 12 June 1689. The two met at the Royal Society. It could have been their first meeting.

2 10 July 1689. Fatio accompanied Newton and others to petition the King.

3 Presumably in the lifetime of the Convention Parliament (Jan.1689–Jan.1690) there were occasions for the friends to meet.

4 March/April 1690. Newton met Fatio in London.

5 12–19 September 1691. Following Fatio's return from Holland Newton visited him in London.

6 Autumn 1692. Fatio visited Newton in Cambridge.

7 Early June and late June 1693. Newton was absent from Cambridge and probably visited Fatio on both occasions in London.

8 On 15 November, according to David Gregory (Hiscock, 1937, p. 14), Newton promised 'Mr Robarts, Mr Fatio, Capt Hally and me to publish his Quadratures'.

9 Newton probably met Fatio on occasion at RS meetings. Likely dates, when Fatio contributed papers, were May 1704, June 1706, May and December 1714, March 1716 and March/April 1717. Newton was in attendance at all meetings.

10 Margaret Jacob (1978, p. 139) has produced evidence to show that Newton and Fatio met between January and May 1707 and held discussions on the Camisard prophets.

Evidence, however, for the intensity of their relationship, it has been held, lies not in the frequency of their meetings but elsewhere. There is, firstly, the correspondence. Newton, according to Westfall (RSW, p. 531), was at one time 'frantic with concern' when he heard from Fatio in September 1692 that he had 'got a grievous cold, which is fallen on my lungs' (C, III, p. 230). Newton's reply began: 'I have ye book & last night received your letter wth wch how much I was affected I cannot express. Pray procure ye advice & assistance of Physitians before it be too late & if you want any money I will supply you' (C, III, p. 231). As Fatio had written as if he was on the verge of death, a gross exaggeration, Newton's concern would best be described as genuine rather than frantic. When Newton heard in January 1693 that Fatio's cold persisted he invited him to stay with him in Cambridge where the air was thought to be better. Fatio's response was to ask Newton, rather obscurely, to be 'plain' (C, III, p. 243). Was Fatio angling for a chair? Newton went into greater detail in March telling Fatio: 'The chamber next me is disposed of; but that which I was contriving was . . . to make you such an allowance as might make your subsistence here easy to you' (C, III, p. 263). Fatio replied that he had an estate in his country large enough to keep him as long as he lived, 'provided I go there again' (C, III, p. 391). He was none the less grateful for Newton's offer of financial help. Also, if it had been possible, he would have wished 'to live all my life, or the greatest part of it, with you'.

The final letter from Fatio came on 18 May 1693 (C, III, pp. 267–70). It is a strange document. In it Fatio speaks of becoming a physician, of a friend who had prepared a menstruum capable, amongst other things, of curing smallpox; Fatio saw himself curing thousands by it and making his fortune. He concluded by expressing the hope that he would be able to confer with Newton. It seems that Newton could have visited Fatio in London shortly afterwards. If he did so, no record of their conversation has survived. All that is known is that it marked the end of the close relationship between Fatio and Newton.

If the letters between Fatio and Newton were different to all his other correspondence, so too was the manner of Fatio's talk about Newton different from the talk of all other disciples. While Newton was prepared to accept disciples, assistants, editors and scribes, he never at any point sought for a collaborator. Yet Fatio, in the early days of their relationship, spoke often of the problems they would tackle, the theories they would construct and, even, how Newton had been influenced by his work. Newton must have heard of Fatio's posturing yet never seems to have responded critically. He even went so far in De Quadratura to acknowledge Fatio's contribution, not to editorial duties, but to the work itself: 'This rule, or one like it, was communicated to me some while ago by Mr Fatio' (MP, VII, p. 79). Westfall has commented that one will look in vain 'for a similar passage elsewhere in Newton's mathematical papers' (RSW, p. 516).

As a scientist Fatio is largely remembered for two works. The first, *De la cause de la pesanteur* (On the Cause of Weight), was read to the Royal Society in 1688 and finally published in 1949 (B. Gagnebin, 1949). He explained gravity in terms of violent agitations of the ether. His view, he claimed, was embraced by Huygens. He also claimed that Newton had written that Fatio's account was the 'one possible cause of gravity'. His second work, *Lineae brevissimi* (1699, Line of Quickest Descent), benefited Newton little; this was the text which began the exhausting and time-consuming debate with the Leibnizians on the origins of the calculus.

After the break with Newton, Fatio's career seems not to have flourished. He spent some time as a tutor of the Duke of Bedford's children and also gave lessons in mathematics. In 1707, however, he was reported to have been placed in the pillory at Charing Cross. He had apparently become an initiate of the Cévennes prophets, a group of French protestant refugees who became possessed, held seances, and spoke in tongues in the streets of Central London.

Newton and Fatio did make contact again. In 1717 Fatio confirmed by letter an arrangement to make for Bentley a £15 watch. He also included a note for Halley on 'the Sun's excentricity' (*C*, VI, pp. 391–2). One final letter from Fatio is known. Dated 1 April 1724, it sought Newton's permission to use his name to advertise the value of jewelled pivots in watches, a design Fatio was trying to develop commercially. Newton's response is unknown.

Fauquiere, John Francis (d.1726)

Thomas Neale, Newton's predecessor as Master of the Mint, appointed Fauquiere, a director of the Bank of England, to be his deputy in the final years of his reign. Fauquiere served Newton in the same post until his death some six months before Newton's own death.

Relations between Newton and Fauquiere must have been good. Fauquiere, a Huguenot refugee, was a man of substance, able to invest £26,000 in the Bank of England in 1709. He stood surety for Newton in his post of Master for a sum of £1,000 in 1702 and 1718, and also seems to have served as a financial agent to Newton. Thus, Newton instructed his 1713 dividends from his 'south sea stock' to be paid directly to his deputy (*C*, VI, p. 27); in 1720 he was to be found instructing Fauquiere to 'subscribe for me and in my name the several annuities you have in your hands belonging to me' (*C*, VII, p. 96). Two months earlier he had granted a power of attorney to Fauquiere. A further sign of the closeness of the relationship was that Fauquiere was one of the fifty selected to receive presentation copies of the largest paper edition of *Principia* (1726).

Filmer, Sir Robert (1588–1653)

A political writer, knighted by Charles I, Filmer was the author of *Patriarcha* (1680) in which he argued that the divine right of kings was ultimately derived from the divine right of a father to rule his children. Filmer also argued that it was from the 'distinction of families' that kingdoms had originated. His views were attacked by Locke in his first *Treatise* (1689). Newton was more sympathetic and echoes of Filmer's views can be found in his *The Original of Monarchies*.

Finances

Newton died an extremely wealthy man with an estate valued at £32,862, despite having given away fairly substantial sums in his later years. There is also a possibility that he lost heavily in the South Sea Bubble. The source of his wealth breaks down into four areas: earnings at Cambridge; earnings at the Mint; income from his estates; and earnings from investments.

CAMBRIDGE

There was clearly a comfortable living but no fortune to be made here. His earnings break down as follows.

1 Minor Fellow (October 1667–July 1668):

Wages	£2 – 0 – 0 p.a.
Livery allowance	£1 – 6 – 8 p.a.
Dividend	£10 – 0 – 0 p.a.
TOTAL	£13 – 6 – 8 p.a.

In addition he was assigned a room in college which, if he chose to live elsewhere, he could rent out. Newton was known to have done this in the summer of 1668 when he received a rent of £1 11s 0d.

2 Major Fellow (1668–1696):

Wages	£2 – 13 – 4 p.a.
Livery allowance	£1 – 13 – 4 p.a.
Dividend	£25 – 0 – 0 p.a.
Pandoxator's dividend	£5 – 0 – 0 p.a.
TOTAL	£34 – 6 – 8 p.a.

In addition Newton received food and lodgings to the value of £25.

The Pandoxator's dividend refers to the profits paid to the resident Fellows from the College's brewery and bakery; the dividend drawn from the college estate and investments was a means by which the wages of Fellows, controlled by statute, could be raised to more reasonable levels. Newton also earned money by taking tutorial pupils. Newton's salary as Fellow, including allowances, is therefore likely to have been £60 p.a. Serving as a Fellow for 28 years would thus have brought him a sum of at least £1,680.

3 Lucasian chair (1669–1701). Barrow had taken care to so draft the statutes for the chair that its incumbents could continue to draw their professorial salary of about £100 a year in addition to any income derived from their Fellowship. Newton must thus have earned in his thirty-two years as Lucasian professor a sum of at least £3,100.

Newton's total earnings from Cambridge would therefore have been about £4,800, giving him an average income from this source of about £150 p.a.

FAMILY ESTATES

Newton inherited from his father the family lands at Woolsthorpe. He also received in due course his mother's dowry of lands at Sewstern and property from his stepfather, Barnabas Smith, in North Witham. A number of estimates have been recorded of the value of some or all of Newton's estate. Unfortunately it is never clear whether the figures quoted refer simply to the Woolsthorpe Manor or also include Newton's additional property. Stukeley gave a figure of £80 p.a. for the Woolsthorpe Manor and the Sewstern estate; the Rev. Benjamin Smith gave the higher figure of £105 p.a. for the entire Woolsthorpe estate, while Newton himself spoke of a value of £100 p.a. for his inherited estate.

If it is assumed that Newton received a figure of £100 p.a. after the death of his mother in 1679 then his gross income would increase by a further £2,800.

Thus from Cambridge and his inheritance Newton was earning from 1669 an income of £150 p.a. and from 1679 of at least £250 p.a. To put this in some kind of perspective, Westfall has pointed out that Pepys lived with a wife in London on a salary of £50 p.a., while a labourer's pay was only £20–£30 p.a. (RSW, p. 181). For the bachelor Newton, living in free lodgings, with food provided, an income of £250 a year was very comfortable indeed. It was not, however, the stuff of £30,000 fortunes, the sum Newton left on his death. This must therefore have come from his years at the Mint.

MINT (1696–1727)

Newton served as Warden of the Mint from 1696 to 1699 at a salary of £400 p.a. In 1699 he was appointed Master at a salary of £600, plus another £60 p.a. as Assay Master. He would thus have earned:

Warden (1696–9) at £400 p.a.	£1,200
Master (1699–1727) at £600 p.a.	£16,800
Assay Master (1699–1727) at £60 p.a.	£1,680
TOTAL	£19,680

In addition, Newton also received a poundage based on the coinage minted. It was paid at a rate of 1s 10d for each pound weight of gold minted, and 3¼d for each pound weight of silver. The Inventory taken at his death assigned to Newton for the period 1 January 1727 to March 20 1727 a poundage of £303 17s 6d for gold and £3 5s 9¾d for silver. If this was at all typical then, as de Villamil pointed out, in a full year Newton would have received a poundage of about £1,400, providing him with an annual Mint salary of £2,000 and increasing his Mint earnings by a further £40,000 to almost £60,000.

Could Newton have saved £30,000 from this sum? This depends very much on whether Newton's speculative ventures were profitable or not.

INVESTMENT

In the Inventory sums of £28,000 are noted; £18,000 invested in Bank of England stock and £10,000 in various South Sea funds. Just how well did Newton fare with these? According to Catherine Barton her uncle had lost £20,000 through rash speculation in the South Seas. De Villamil has argued against Catherine on this issue on the simple ground that Newton never had a sum of this size to lose. Earnings balance quite neatly with money he is known to have spent, given away and saved. Catherine was unlikely to have been completely misled, de Villamil argued. She could have meant that Newton lost funds in the sense that profits made from a small investment were not realised and eventually collapsed. His loss was no real loss but only a failure to maximise his profits by cashing in his investments at the right time.

Against this, Westfall (RSW, pp. 860–1) and Hall (C, VII, pp. 96–7) have argued that Newton's involvement in South Seas stock was over a longer period and far more complex than de Villamil appreciated. Both seem inclined to accept that Newton may well have lost substantial sums of money.

See also Inventory

Fire

There are a number of stories claiming that at some time a fire in Newton's Trinity rooms destroyed some important manuscripts. Just when this fire took place, what was destroyed and the effect of the accident on Newton are all areas of some doubt.

The earliest source is an entry in 1692 in the diary of Abraham de la Pryme, a student of the adjacent St John's College.

> 1692, February 3rd. What I heard today I must relate. There is one Mr Newton . . . that is mighty famous . . . but of all the books that he ever writt there was one on colours and light, established upon thousands of experiments, which had been twenty years of making, and which had cost him many a hundred of pounds. This book which he valued so much . . . had the ill luck to perish and be utterly lost . . . after this manner. In a winter morning, leaving it amongst his other papers on his studdy table, whilst he went to chappel, the candle which he had unfortunately left burning there too catchd hold by some means or other of some other papers, and they fired the aforesayd book, and utterly consumed it and several other valuable writings.

It was first published by Brewster (1831, pp. 228–9).

The story, although with a different date, was confirmed by Huygens. He noted that on 29 May 1694 a Scotsman, M. Colin, informed him that 'eighteen months ago' Newton had lost 'by fire, his chemical laboratory and several manuscripts'. This would put the date of the fire to about November 1692.

Newton himself, in conversation with Conduitt in 1726, reported:

> When he was in the midst of his discoveries he left a candle on his table amongst his papers and went down to the Bowling green and meeting someone that diverted him from returning as he intended, the candle set fire to his papers and he could never recover them. I asked him whether they related to his opticks or to the method of fluxions and he said he believed there were some relating to both.

The question is, what period would Newton have in mind by the phrase 'in the midst of his discoveries'? Hardly the early 1690s.

That the fire was earlier than the 1690s was confirmed by Humphrey Newton who wrote: 'As for his *Optics* being burned, I knew nothing of it but as I had heard from others, that accident happening before he writ his *Principia*' (More, 1962, p. 247). There is also a fair amount of evidence that suggests that the fire took place in the late 1670s. It was then that David Loggan drew Newton's picture for a book on light and colours and in late 1677 Newton referred to the work in a letter to

Hooke (*C*, II, p. 239). Indeed part of the work in printed sheets was discovered by Derek Price in 1960 in the binding of a book. It would thus seem incontrovertible that Newton was intending to publish such a work in 1678. It also seems fairly clear that the reason why it did not appear was a fire some time in 1678 which destroyed the manuscript.

What then of the accounts of de la Pryme and Huygens? In support of this possibility Westfall has noted that a number of Newton's papers of the 1690s have badly charred edges (RSW, p. 538n). Unfortunately, though, several of them date from 1694 and 1695 and suggest they are the result not of Huygens and de la Prynne's fire but of some later accident.

Two pieces of folklore have attached themselves to the supposed fire of 1692. One suggestion, first raised by J. B. Biot in 1821, was that the fire led to a nervous breakdown of such severity that Newton never again undertook serious scientific research. While it is true that Newton did have a breakdown at this time, its cause must be sought for elsewhere. Nor was the breakdown severe enough to destroy completely Newton's scientific interests.

The second myth concerns the 'the little dog, called Diamond' who by knocking over a candle destroyed the 'almost finished labours of some years'. As the story is unknown before 1780 and emerges from a single source, it can be easily discounted.

See also Breakdown; Diamond

Fits of easy reflection and fits of easy transmission

In Book II, part III, props.12–20 Newton presented his theory of fits to account for the phenomena of periodicity observed as light passes through thin films. A plane glass and a convex glass were pressed together, as in the diagram, so that they were separated by a thin film

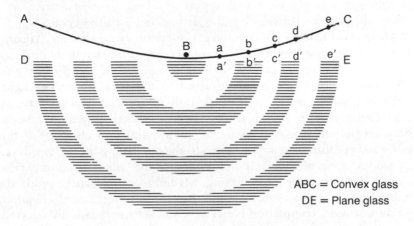

ABC = Convex glass
DE = Plane glass

of air of variable thickness. As the glasses were pressed closer together, coloured rings appeared, similar to those seen today in oil slicks on any road, encircling a central, dark area. If monochromatic light was used alternate dark and bright rings were produced. What feature of light could possibly produce the alternate dark and bright bands? Put slightly differently, why should some light particles be entirely transmitted and other seemingly identical particles entirely reflected?

At this point Newton put forward a quite uncharacteristic proposal. Light rays, as they were emitted by luminous bodies, Newton speculated, alternated between being disposed to be reflected and disposed to be refracted. Consequently, when a light ray met a transparent medium or glass then, depending on its disposition, it would be reflexted or refracted. The two dispositions he termed 'Fits of easy Reflexion, and . . . Fits of easy Transmission' with the space a light ray travels between changes of state described as 'the Interval of its Fits' (*Opticks*, p. 281). The process should be conceived as taking place continuously and extremely rapidly. The interval, for example, for yellow and orange light was put at '1/89,000 th part of an inch' (*Opticks*, p. 285).

On this basis Newton could at last offer an explanation of the periodic phenomena produced by thin films. As the light rays reached the point B in the diagram, allow them to be in a fit of transmission; they will all accordingly be transmitted and the area will appear dark. Imagine, next, a set of light rays falling on point b and that the distance between b and b' is equal to the interval; then all particles in fits of easy transmission at b will have returned to the same disposition at b'. If, again, the distance between d and d', and e and e', is two and three intervals respectively, the same effect will be produced.

What, however, happens at a? Allow the distance between a and a' to be half an interval. All light in a fit of easy reflection at a will of course be reflected. Transmitted light at a, however, will be reflected at a', and transmitted after travelling a whole interval on its return to a. In this way a bright band will appear at a and, for that matter, at c where the distance between c and c' is one-and-a-half intervals.

There is no denying the ingenuity of Newton's proposed mechanism. It remains unusual within the Newtonian corpus for two quite different reasons. In the first place it is the one section of the *Opticks* in which Newton seemed to be at all attracted to the wave theory of light. Substitute wave for fits, and wavelength for interval, and we have an explanation familiar to the reader of any modern physics textbook. Newton himself was well aware of his proximity to Huygens at this point and compared the action of fits to the undulating motion produced by stones falling in water. He also compared the 'vibrations thus excited . . . in the refracting or reflecting Medium or Substance', with the 'vibrations . . . propagated in the Air for causing Sound' (*Opticks*, p. 280). It was a comparison Newton, elsewhere, emphatically rejected.

As he also rejected what he termed, elsewhere, 'incongruous surmises'. Thus in the *Account* he insisted that, unlike Leibniz, he did not fill his work 'with Opinions which cannot be proved by Phenomena'. Indeed, he continued, in his philosophy 'Hypotheses have no place, unless as Conjectures or Questions proposed to be examined by Experiments' (Hall, 1980, p. 222). Yet the theory of fits was, as Newton conceded in *Opticks* (pp. 280–1), undoubtedly a 'Hypothesis'. And one moreover for which he had no experimental evidence at all. Nor, a century later, did Sir David Brewster (1831, pp. 74–5) when he spoke of making the theory of fits 'intelligible'. To do so he proposed that light particles possess 'two attractive and two repulsive poles at the extremities of two axes at right angles to each other'. Against such 'incongruous surmises' Newton was normally quite dismissive. Why, in this case, did he prove to be more charitable? Westfall (1970, p. 93) has noted that when Newton finally composed the *Opticks* in the mid-1690s he had abandoned belief in the ether and inclined to explain everything in terms of attractive forces rather than etherial pressures. Attractive forces, however, unlike the ether could not be made to vibrate periodically. Consequently, Newton adopted a position similar to that maintained about the nature of gravitational attraction: 'I content my self with the bare Discovery, that Rays of Light are by some cause or other alternately disposed to be reflected or refracted' (*Opticks,* p. 281). Why then, Westfall has asked, have historians of science greeted so enthusiastically 'Newton's positivism applied to gravity', yet reacted with 'pained bewilderment when they face exactly the same distinction applied to fits of easy transmission' (Westfall, 1970, p. 97).

What, finally, of the unusual word 'fit'? Westfall has commented that it was taken from the medical usage of Newton's day in which it referred to 'one of the recurrent attacks of a periodic or constitutional ailment' (Westfall, 1970, p. 96).

See also Ether

Fitzwilliam Notebook

In the catalogue of the PC there is a reference to 'A bound manuscript containing at one end memoranda of Newton's expenses at College, and at the other a short outline of Trigonometry and Conic sections in Newton's hand'. The Notebook is to be found in the Fitzwilliam Museum, Cambridge. It is in fact the most revealing of all Newton's notebooks.

It contains Newton's Cambridge accounts for the period 23 May 1665 to April 1669. The most surprising feature of the accounts is their revelation of Newton's presumably profitable career as a money lender.

There are several references of the form 'lent Wilford 1s', 'Dew from John Evans . . . 1s 10d' and the careful recording of his outstanding debt, 'Dew to me . . . £3 5s 10d'.

The Notebook also records Newton's growing interest in chemistry. There were purchases of chemicals, a furnace (8s), and the *Theatrum chemicum* for £1 8s 0d in April 1669. Other books bought were T. Sprat's *Hystory of ye Royall Soc.* for 7s and 'Gunter's book & sector' for 5s.

Some entries indicate that Newton was not yet the obsessive scholar portrayed by later witnesses. He lost 15s 'at cards twice' and spent 3s 6d 'at the tavern twice'. But, in so far as it is possible to reconstruct Newton's expenses from incomplete accounts, and bearing in mind that much of this time was spent at home in Woolsthorpe, it seems that Newton lived on the £10 a year he received from his mother. Out of this sum Newton had to pay during the years 1665–7 fees of £10 to his tutor.

The strangest part of the Notebook, however, and sufficient in itself to remind us that we are dealing with a seventeenth-century puritan and not a contemporary mathematician, is a carefully composed list of sins. It is divided into those committed before Whitsuntide 1662, forty-nine in all, and the nine committed afterwards. Prudently, Newton transcribed his sins in Shelton 'short writing', the system of shorthand favoured by Pepys in his famous diary of the same period. It was not until 1962 that Westfall published a plain text version of Newton's list and revealed in the process the strange obsessions tormenting the twenty-year-old Newton.

Some, of course, simply reflect the puritan's concern with the Sabbath and the name of God. There are thus plenty of sins like 'Using the name "God" openly', 'Missing chapel' and 'Eating an apple at Thy house'. Others seem mere reports of meschievous behaviour. Was it really a sin to go swimming, or to squirt water?

More suggestive is anxiety expressed in 'Having unclean thoughts words and actions and dreames', one of the few references to Newton's sexuality in the thousands of pages he devoted to all kinds of other subjects. Two other consecutive items, 'A relapse', 'A relapse', suggest there were sins which even the security of Shelton's short writing would not allow Newton to disclose or even hint at.

All other lapses are openly declared. Even the oft-quoted declaration 'Threatening my father and mother Smith to burne them & the house over them' and the following 'Wishing death & hoping it to some' could be openly expressed.

The Notebook also contains some mathematical annotations from the works of W. Oughtred, R. Descartes, F. van Schooten and de Witt. They have been published in *MP*, I, pp. 25–46. A final item concerns a single sheet, presumably an exercise, translating Hebrew words into Latin.

See also Notebooks

Flamsteed, John (1646–1719) and the Flamsteed affair

Newton engaged in numerous scientific disputes throughout his career. Two of these disputes, both long and bitter, were little concerned with matters of substance and more with a man's rights over his own intellectual property. In the most famous of the disputes, with Leibniz, the issue debated was the very fundamental one of what constituted ownership of an intellectual property; the second related dispute, with Flamsteed, took the matter a little further and, assuming there were no disputes over ownership, went on to ask what rights the owner retained over his property.

Scientists frequently adopt a somewhat protective attitude to their work. Astronomers are no exception. Long hours, often spent in cold and uncomfortable conditions, does not prepare them for the often casual, frequently dismissive, and invariably unacknowledged, treatment bestowed on their observations by a patronising theoretician. Above all, the theoretician will be impatient and selective in his demands. Observers, in return, will insist that only a lengthy and comprehensive approach can ever yield the precise and accurate results the theorist needs. The conflict between theorist and observer is one of the most often encountered of all scientific disputes. Sometimes, as with the case of Newton and Flamsteed, it can reach epic proportions.

One reason for the intensity of the dispute lay in the equally strong-willed and bad-tempered personalities of the participants. Flamsteed, no doubt, had ample excuse for his bad temper. Born a somewhat sickly child at Denby, near Derby, Flamsteed's condition seems to have worsened in 1660 by what sounds like an attack of rheumatic fever. He was taken away from school and devoted himself to the study of mathematics and astronomy. A visit to Ireland in 1665 to be touched by Vincent Greatrakes, a famous healer of the day as a seventh son of a seventh son, had no effect upon his health. Shortly afterwards, however, his work began to be noticed by a number of Fellows of the RS. Amongst these was Sir Jonas Moore, who was considering building a private observatory for Flamsteed. It proved unnecessary, for in 1675 Flamsteed was appointed to be the first Astronomer Royal by Charles II. As the first holder of the post, Flamsteed was responsible for the building and organisation of the new observatory at Greenwich. He also found that on a salary of £100 a year he was expected to engage and pay his own staff, and to provide his own instruments. Although some instruments were donated by Moore and others, Flamsteed still found it necessary to spend £120 of his own money on a mural arc. Made and divided by Abraham Sharp it was ready for use in September 1689. As a result of this expenditure, all observations made after 1689 seemed to Flamsteed to be unarguably his own property, and his to do with as he willed.

He met Newton for the first time in Cambridge in 1674. The first substantial issue between them arose over the nature of the comet of 1680–1. Newton was convinced that two comets were present and in letters to Flamsteed argued so at length (C, II, pp. 340–7, 358–62). Flamsteed, however, insisted only one comet was present, a position Newton finally accepted in September 1685 (C, II, pp. 419–20). Relations remained cordial and in 1687 Flamsteed was one of the few scholars selected to receive a presentation copy of *Principia*. It contained, he noted, only 'very slight acknowledgements' to his Greenwich observations.

On 1 September 1694 Newton paid his first visit to Greenwich. He spoke with Flamsteed about the moon. Newton was keen to examine Flamsteed's lunar data in order to correct and improve the lunar theory presented in *Principia*. Flamsteed offered to loan Newton 150 'places of the moon' on two conditions: firstly, that Newton would not show the work to anyone else; secondly, and more unreasonably, Newton would have to agree not to reveal any results derived from Flamsteed's observations to any other scholar. It was the beginning of an ill-tempered dispute which would last until Flamsteed's death. His own version of the quarrel is contained in his *History of his own Life and Labors* published in Baily (1966, pp. 7–105). It is a most bitter document.

None of Newton's proposals found favour with Flamsteed. The offer in November 1694 'to gratify you to your satisfaction' brought the answer that he was not tempted with 'covetousness' and the lament that Newton could have ever thought so meanly of him (C, IV, p. 58). An offer in 1695 to pay Flamsteed's scribe two guineas for his transcriptions brought an equally forthright rejection. It was enough, Newton was told, to offer 'verball acknowledgements'; a 'superfluity of monys', he found, 'is always pernicious to my Servants it makes them run into company and wast their time Idly or worse' (C, IV, pp. 157–8). If Newton asked for 'your Observations only' (C, IV, p. 134), Flamsteed complained of being treated like a drudge; if, however, calculations were asked for as well, Flamsteed would respond that such work required all kinds of tedious analysis for which he had little time.

When all else failed Flamsteed fell back on the excuse of his no doubt genuine headaches. They were a regular theme of the correspondence, with Flamsteed keeping Newton informed of the various cures he tried. Sweating, he found, brought some relief (C, IV, p. 138), as did 'waters and exercise' (C, IV, p. 153). The pain was bad enough apparently to prevent Flamsteed from working for much of the day. In May 1695 he was complaining to Newton that he had been so much troubled 'with paines in my head' that he had made no calculations of the moon's place for three months (C, IV, p. 122). Newton's interest in a medical problem took over and in July he was able to inform Flamsteed that he had a 'certain cure'. Flamsteed should 'bind his head strait with a garter till ye crown of his head nummed'. In this way his head would be cooled by retarding the circulation (C, IV, p. 152). Flamsteed thanked Newton for his consideration but seemed to have some doubts as to whether such a cure was really suitable in his case.

Over the period 1694–5 Newton received another 150 observations. They were, however, none too reliable, having been made with the help of a stellar catalogue constructed with the help of a sextant alone. By this time Flamsteed was beginning to resent Newton's somewhat imperial tone. 'But I did not think myself obliged', he complained, 'to employ my pains to serve a person that was so inconsiderate as to presume he had a right to that which was only a courtesy' (Baily, 1966, p. 63). Consequently, he returned to his own work, leaving Newton to work through the observations he had already received.

The two continued to see each other and to discuss Flamsteed's lunar observations until January 1699. This part of the correspondence ends with Flamsteed lecturing Newton on pride and humility. His own humility, he proudly told Newton, allowed him to 'excuse small faults in all mankind', and to 'bear great injurys without resentment' (C, IV, p. 303).

The second stage of the dispute began on 11 April 1704 with a visit by Newton to Greenwich. Newton had yet to complete his lunar theory and could scarcely have looked forward to the prospect of another prolonged quarrel with Flamsteed. He seems to have decided to attempt to resolve the problem in a more direct manner. Using his position as President of the Royal Society, and his connections at Court, he sought to pressurise Flamsteed into publishing his long-awaited catalogue, thus putting all his observations into the public domain. The approach was rejected. Newton, Flamsteed noted, was too obviously someone who 'would be my friend no further than to serve his own ends . . . spiteful, and swayed by those that were worse than himself' (Baily, 1966, p. 66).

Newton went over Flamsteed's head and gained the backing of Prince George, husband to Queen Anne, for the project. Scientists in the eighteenth century did not reject the offer of royal patronage. Consequently, Flamsteed in November drew up an estimate of his three-volume catalogue. The work would be 1,450 pages long and the printing of the first volume could begin immediately (C, IV, pp. 420–3). Unwilling to leave the task to Flamsteed, Newton arranged instead for a Committee of Referees to examine Flamsteed's papers and to oversee publication. The members of the Committee were either, like Francis Aston and David Gregory, Newton's men or, like Sir Christopher Wren, too old and busy to concern themselves with such a task. Newton also extracted from Prince George the sum of £863 to finance the project.

It soon became clear that Newton and Flamsteed had different visions of the planned work. Flamsteed had hoped to present his work within a detailed historical context by including in the third volume, along with his own stellar catalogue, all important earlier catalogues from Ptolemy to Hevelius. He also wished to add a celestial atlas consisting of sixty large star-charts. Newton's aim was much more restricted and consisted of no more than completing and publishing Flamsteed's observations.

Flamsteed could do little more than delay the project. In this he was quite successful as by 1708, when Prince George died, the first volume was still incomplete. With the death of Prince George the Referees no longer had control over Flamsteed's text. Newton's response was to have himself, as President of the RS, appointed in 1710 a 'constant Visitor' to the Greenwich Observatory, with access to all observations and the right to direct the work of the Astronomer Royal. Shortly afterwards Flamsteed heard that the Queen had commanded him to hand over all outstanding material and so allow the work to be finally completed.

It finally appeared in 1712, edited by Halley, as *Historia coelestis* (History of the Heavens). It was not to Flamsteed's liking, seeming to him to be no more than a parody of the work he had once dreamed of publishing. Equally distressing to him was the fact that it had been produced by Halley, a man he despised as an atheist, a libertine and a plagiarist (Baily, 1966, p. xxxi).

With the accession of George I in 1714 Flamsteed found that at last he had friends at Court. Flamsteed's case was listened to and it was decided to hand over to him the outstanding 300 copies of his work in the hands of the printer. He extracted anything prepared by Halley and 'made a Sacrifice of them to Heavenly Truth' (Baily, 1966, p. 101). The three volumes of the *Historia* appeared posthumously in 1725 in the form Flamsteed had originally planned. They constitute, with the Atlas, one of the great landmarks of modern observational astronomy.

Although Flamsteed did eventually have his way, Newton fared less well. He never did get the observations he wanted; nor did he ever succeed in working out his lunar theory as comprehensively as he had wished. Also to suffer has been his reputation. It was, declared Westfall, 'the most unpleasant episode in Newton's life' (RSW, p. 696). The dispute, none the less, typifies much of the conflict met with in science, and deserves closer study.

Meetings between the two were seldom productive. Flamsteed took some grim pleasure in his special power to break down Newton's self-control and provoke him into a rage. On one occasion, for example, Flamsteed reported that when 'told calmly of his faults' Newton 'could not contain himself' (Baily, 1966, p. 264). Another ploy adopted, and one Newton could have seldom met before, was for Flamsteed to tell him how little he thought of his work. Thus, in 1704, Newton presented Flamsteed with a copy of the *Opticks*. Some time later, Flamsteed reported, they met in Greenwich.

> My discourse, about the faults of Mr. Newton's *Opticks* and
> corrections of my lunar numbers, brought the subtle gentleman
> down . . . I thanked him for his book: he said that he hoped I
> approved of it. I told him truly, no . . . This point would not bear
> discussion: he dropt it. (BAILY, 1966, pp. 216–17)

On another occasion Flamsteed went out of his way to inform Newton
of some faults he had found 'in the 4th book (?) of *Principia*'. But,
Flamsteed noted, 'instead of thanking me for, he resented ill' (Baily,
1966, p. 73). With such provocation it is hardly surprising that Newton
at one time, again in Flamsteed's words, 'dared to ask "why I did hold
my tongue"' (Baily, 1966, p. 73).

The most dramatic and public confrontation took place when Flamsteed was summoned in 1711 to the RS by Newton. Present also were
Sir Hans Sloane and Richard Mead. In Flamsteed's description of the
meeting:

> The President ran himself into a great heat, and very indecent passion
> . . . I complained then of my catalogue being printed by Halley,
> without my knowledge, and that I was *robbed of the fruits of my labors*.
> At this he fired, and called me all the ill names, puppy &c, that he
> could think of. All I returned was, I put him in mind of his passion,
> desired him to govern it, and keep his temper: this made him rage
> worse: and he told me how much I had received from the
> Government in 36 years I had served. I asked what he had done
> for the £500 per annum that he had received ever since he settled in
> London. This made him calmer.

Clearly pleased with himself, Flamsteed met Halley on the way out and,
he continued, 'drank a dish of coffee with him, and told him, still
calmly, of the villainy of his conduct, and called it blockish' (Baily,
1966, pp. 294–5).

Fluxions, fluents and moments

Although long since discarded by mathematicians, Newton's method of
fluxions remains still his best known contribution to mathematics. The
method itself dates from the summer of 1665 and can be found discussed
in the October 1666 Tract. It received, however, its fullest treatment in
De methodis fluxionum of 1670–1.

The basic idea conceived geometrical magnitudes to arise from a
continuous motion. A line or curve was, in this manner, generated by
the continuous motion of a point, a surface from the motion of a line,
and a solid by the motion of a surface. Thus, to take the simplest case,
a line was thought to be a flowing quantity and was termed accordingly

a *fluent*. The rate at which it flowed, the point's velocity, was named the line's *fluxion*. In Newton's later work fluxions came to be represented by dotted letters. If, for example, x and y are given as fluents, their fluxions will be $\dot{x}$ and $\dot{y}$ respectively. These, in turn, could be taken as fluents and lead to the formation of the higher-order fluxions $\ddot{x}$ and $\ddot{y}$. Fluents themselves were shown most simply as $\overset{,}{x}$ and $\overset{,}{y}$, with higher-order fluents becoming $\overset{,,}{x}$ and $\overset{,,}{y}$. The two are clearly related: the velocity of the point will determine the nature of the curve, and a curve of a given nature can only be generated by a point with a certain velocity. Two problems thus arose: how, given a relationship between fluents, can the corresponding relationship between fluxions be determined; and, the inverse problem, to determine fluents on the basis of fluxions. The two processes are better known today as differentiation and integration respectively.

To tackle the problems Newton first introduced the notion of a *moment*. This was the 'indefinitely small' part by which fluents grew in 'indefinitely small' periods of time, and was represented by the sign o. The moment of the fluent x would therefore be $\dot{x}$o, and of the fluent y, $\dot{y}$o. In this way, it follows that quantities x and y will become in an indefinitely small interval $x + \dot{x}$o and $y + \dot{y}$o.

Consider, at this point, two curves (x and y) related by the equation:

$$x^3 - ax^2 + axy - y^3 = 0$$

To determine how the fluxions which generated the two curves are related, Newton began by substituting $x + \dot{x}$o for x and $y + \dot{y}$o for y:

$$(x + \dot{x}o)^3 - a(x + \dot{x}o)^2 + a(x + \dot{x}o)(y + \dot{y}o) - (y + \dot{y}o)^3 = 0$$

which becomes:

$$(x^3 + 3\dot{x}ox^2 + 3\dot{x}^2o^2x + \dot{x}^3o^3) - (ax^2 + 2a\dot{x}ox + a\dot{x}^2o^2) +$$
$$(axy + a\dot{x}oy + a\dot{y}ox + a\dot{x}\dot{y}o^2) - (y^3 + 3\dot{y}oy^2 + 3\dot{y}^2o^2y + \dot{y}^3o^3) = 0$$

At this point Newton eliminated the initial equation and divided all remaining terms by o. He also argued that as o was supposed to be 'infinitely little', any term multiplied by it will be 'nothing in respect to the rest' and can be safely eliminated. There remained:

$$3\dot{x}x^2 - 2a\dot{x}x + a\dot{x}y + a\dot{y}x - 3\dot{y}y^2 = 0$$

The relation between the fluxions can, therefore, be expressed as:

$$\frac{\dot{y}}{\dot{x}} = \frac{3x^2 - 2ax + ay}{3y^2 - ax} = \frac{dy}{dx}$$

Newton could also solve the inverse problem. That is, beginning with the fluxions:

$$3\dot{x}x^2 - 2a\dot{x}x + a\dot{x}y + a\dot{y}x - 3\dot{y}y^2 = 0$$

he was able to integrate the terms to derive the fluents:

$$x^3 - ax^2 + axy - y^3 = 0$$

The examples are taken from problems I and II of *De methodis* (1736).

See also Mathematical development

F., Mr

On the alchemical manuscript *Manna* a note is appended in Newton's hand: 'Here follow several notes and different readings . . . communicated to Mr F. by W.S. in 1670, and by Mr F. to me in 1675.' Dobbs (1975, pp. 111–12) has identified Mr F. with Ezekiel Foxcroft, a Fellow of KCC from 1652 until 1675, and a possible source of supply of the various unpublished alchemical manuscripts Newton endlessly copied. Foxcroft himself seems to have been a Cambridge Platonist and to have translated the Rosicrucian tract, *The Chymical Wedding*.

See also Alchemical papers

Folkes, Martin (1690–1754)

Born in London, the son of a lawyer, Folkes was educated at Cambridge. An antiquarian rather than a scientist, he served none the less as Vice-president of the Royal Society under Newton during the period 1722–3 and succeeded Sir Hans Sloane as President in 1741, holding the office until 1753.

Folkes helped Conduitt prepare Newton's *Chronology* (1728) for the press. He also donated to the Royal Society the 1726 Vanderbank portrait which still hangs in the Society's rooms.

Fontenelle, Bernard le Bovyer de (1657–1757)

A nephew of Corneille, Fontenelle began his career as a dramatist and essayist. He turned to more serious topics and in his *Entretiens sur la pluralité des mondes habités* (1686, Conversations on the Plurality of Inhabited Worlds) he published one of the first attempts to present the main details of the Copernican and Cartesian systems in a modern language. He was also something of an iconoclast and in his *Histoire des oracles* (1686, History of Oracles), one of the century's most seminal works, he sought to overthrow much of the superstition, both clerical and secular, so endemic in the thought of his day. He was, however, less radical on scientific questions. Fontenelle remained a Cartesian throughout his long life, even publishing at the age of ninety-seven in his *Théorie des toubillons* (1752, Theory of Vortices), the last serious defence of vortex theory.

In 1697 he had been appointed *secrétaire-perpétuel* of the reformed *Académie des sciences* and for the next half century Fontenelle found himself responsible for the *éloges* of its members. Consequently, in 1727, it fell to Fontenelle, the leading Cartesian of the day, to compose Newton's *éloge*. Using material provided by John Conduitt, it in fact revealed little of Fontenelle's own convictions, and those only came to the front in the concluding passages.

A number of letters have survived between Newton and Fontenelle. They consist, however, of nothing more than 'humble' offers from Newton to the *Académie* of such 'small gifts' as *Optice* (1719), with Fontenelle's 'trés humblement' accepting them (*C*, VII, pp. 72, 216).

See also Biography; *Éloge*

'Form of the most ancient year'

Published just once, in the *Gentleman's Magazine*, 1755, vol. XXV, pp. 3–5, its full title ran to: 'A Letter from Sir Isaac Newton to a Person of Distinction, who had desired his opinion of the learned Bishop Lloyd's Hypothesis concerning the Form of the Most Ancient Year'. One manuscript of the work is known, British Museum MS 6489, although holograph drafts are to be found in the Yahuda Collection. Edleston (1850, pp. 314–15) published a draft summary of the manuscript. Although the letter has never been reprinted since its appearance in 1755, similar arguments are to be found in Newton's *Chronology* (1728, pp. 71–81).

The occasion of the letter was a discussion some time in 1713 between Humphrey Prideaux, the Dean of Norwich, and William Lloyd, Bishop of Worcester, on the nature of the ancient calendar. Lloyd maintained that an uncorrected calendar of 360 days had been widely used in the ancient world. At some point Newton's opinion must have been sought. He could not agree with Lloyd, he declared, that 'any ancient nation used a year of 12 months and 360 days, without correcting it from time to time by the luminaries'. Showing his characteristic command of the literature, Newton briefly surveyed the various calendars adopted by the Greeks, Egyptians, Chaldeans, Phoenicians and other ancient peoples, and concluded:

> I met with no other years among the antients than such as were either luni-solar, or solar, or lunar . . . a practical year of 360 days

is none of these. The beginning of such a year would have run around the four seasons in 70 years, and such a notable revolution would have been mentioned in history, and is not to be asserted without proving it.

See also Calendrical writings

Fourier, François Marie Charles (1772–1837)

Fourier was a social theorist who, like many of his contemporaries who had lost their businesses and been imprisoned under the Terror, began to entertain fantasies of a more harmoniously ordered society. His initial insight was generated by his contemplation of Newtonian attraction. Newton had only been concerned with the material world; Fourier proposed to extend it to the industrial world, where 'passionate attraction' was as fixed as 'physical attraction' in the material world. Fourier pursued his Newtonian analogies. To the 'four curves in the cone there corresponded four groups of passionate attraction', while to the seven colours of the rainbow there corresponded 'seven primitive passions of the soul'.

Such naive analogies suggested to Fourier in ways too obscure to comprehend the blueprint for a more harmonious society. His ideas were actually implemented in the US, although the longest surviving community, located in Monmouth County, New Jersey, lasted only a dozen years.

See also Attitudes to Newton

Four Letters from Sir Isaac Newton to Dr Bentley containing some arguments in Proof of a Deity

Koyré has described the correspondence as 'one of the most precious and important documents for the study and interpretation of Newtonian thought' (1965, p. 202). They are known in the following editions.

1 London, 1756. Published without preface or comment by R. Cumberland, Bentley's grandson. 35 pp.
2 London, 1782. They were included in Horsley, vol. IV; facsimile reprint, 1964.
3 London, 1822. As part of *Literary History of the Eighteenth Century*, vol. IV, edited by John Nichols.
4 London, 1836. They were included in *The Works of Richard Bentley*, vol. III, edited by A. Dyce (reprinted in New York, 1966).

5 London, 1842. In *The Correspondence of Richard Bentley*, edited by Christopher Wordsworth.

6 New York, 1953. Included in Thayer.

7 Cambridge, Massachusetts, 1958. Included in *PLNP*; reprinted 1978.

8 Cambridge, 1961. (In *C*, III, pp. 233–41, 244–5, 253–6).

In 1692 Bentley was prebendary and chaplain to the Bishop of Worcester. He had been invited to deliver the first Boyle lectures in St Martin-in-the-Fields, London, late in 1692. He chose to lecture on 'A Confutation of Atheism' and before publishing the lectures Bentley thought it best to check with Newton that he had not misunderstood his ideas. Consequently he posed to Newton, in a missing letter, four problems. Newton replied on 10 December 1692 in the first of the four letters (*C*, III, pp. 233–8).

The first letter began with Newton's expression of satisfaction that his system was being used to support 'the beliefe of a Deity'. He soon introduced a persistent theme of the correspondence, namely that he found it impossible to explain many celestial phenomena by natural causes. Such mysteries were, he declared, due to 'ye counsel and contrivance of a voluntary Agent'. For example, how is it that the planets 'move ye same way and in ye same plane without any considerable variation?' There can be no 'naturall cause' of this effect for comets 'move all manner of ways'. The regular motions of the planets must therefore arise from 'an intelligent agent'. After several other examples Newton dismissed the idea that 'ye inclination of ye Earths axis' helped in proving the existence of God. Newton concluded the letter with the cryptic remark: 'There is yet another argument for a Deity wch I take to be a very strong one, but till ye principles on wch tis grounded be better received I think it more advisable to let it sleep.'

Bentley's reply is lost. He must, however, have raised the problem of the fate of 'matter eavenly diffused through a finite space not spherical'. Newton replied on 17 January 1693 (*C*, III, pp. 238–41). The issue was whether, given mechanical principles, such a distribution of matter was sufficient to account for the 'frame of the world' as we know it. Newton supposed that it would 'convene by its gravity into one or more great masses'; the alternative solution, that all particles of matter 'be so accurately poised one among another as to stand still in a perfect equilibrium', he took to be implausible.

This however would only lead to the existence of great masses. But one of the features of the solar system as we known it is the orbital motion of planets. Of this 'transverse motion' Newton insisted that he knew no 'power in nature wch would cause this . . . motion without ye divine arm'.

Newton concluded the letter with the famous and oft-quoted passage in which he chided Bentley for speaking of gravity as 'essential and inherent to matter'. 'Pray do not ascribe that motion to me', he continued. 'The cause of gravity' he concluded, was something he did not 'pretend to know'.

On 11 February 1693 Newton returned, in the third letter, to 'the frame of the world' (C, III, pp. 244–5). He repeated the point that 'ye diurnal rotations of the Planets could not be derived from gravity but required a divine power to impress them'. All gravity could produce was 'a motion of descent towards the Sun'. This left the 'transverse motions by wch they revolve in their several orbs' which required the 'divine Arm'.

Bentley's reply to this letter has survived. Dated 18 February 1693, it raised once more the nature of gravity. Again, in his final reply, dated 25 February 1693, Newton sought to formulate his views on the nature of gravity and attraction. 'It was inconceivable', he declared, 'that inanimate brute matter should (without ye mediation of something else which is not material) operate upon and affect other matter without mutual contact.' Newton went on to emphasise the point:

> That gravity should be innate inherent & essential to matter so yt one body may act upon another at a distance through a vacuum without the mediation of anything else by and through wch their action or force may be conveyed from one to another is to me so great an absurdity that I beleive no man who is in philosophical matters any competent faculty of thinking can ever fall into it. Gravity must be caused by an agent acting constantly . . . but whether this agent be material or immaterial is a question I have left to ye consideration of my readers.

Whether gravity acted through the mediation of a material ether or through the operation of an immaterial force, Newton was not prepared to say. The trouble was he was attracted to both views, and throughout his life could never take the decisive step of abandoning either.

Four-line locus

In Book III of the *Conics*, Apollonius referred to a problem first raised by Euclid and known to later generations of mathematicians variously as the four-line locus, the three-line locus, the Pappus problem and the *locus solidus*. Given three of four lines in the plane, the problem was to find the locus of points from which three or four lines can be drawn to the given lines, meet the lines at the same angle, and were such that the product of the lengths of two of the lines is proportional to the square of the third line (three-line locus), or to the product of the other two lines (four-line locus). The loci, Apollonius demonstrated, form conic sections.

The mathematicians of antiquity had, however, found it difficult to generalise their work to apply to more than four lines. The problem was taken up by Descartes in his *Geometrie* (1637) almost as a test of the power of his new analytical methods. Within a few pages, and almost effortlessly, Descartes was able to show that if no more than nine lines were involved the relationship could be expressed by equations no higher than the fourth degree, and if no more than thirteen lines were involved, equations no higher than the sixth degree would suffice.

The problem attracted Newton's attention some time around 1680. Part of the problem's attraction for Newton lay in his unremitting conviction that the geometrical techniques of antiquity were superior to the modern algebraic innovations of Descartes. The problem was tackled in several incomplete tracts, all quickly abandoned and now visible only in the pages of *MP*, IV, pp. 230–320. Some of this work surfaced, however, in *Principia*, Book I, section V.

Newton's unpublished writing on this issue is accordingly full of praise for the 'elegance' of the ancient geometers, and of complaints against the 'tedious and entangled' work of the Cartesians. Yet, beneath the rhetoric, Whiteside has argued, Newton employed techniques as modern as any displayed by Descartes; indeed, Whiteside maintains that his work was one of 'pioneering modernity' (*MP*, IV, p. 226).

Francis, Alban (–1715)

Francis became a Benedictine monk in Hanover in 1670 with the name Placid. Imported back to England by James II, he returned to Hanover on the accession of William. Many years later Francis was sent to his order's English mission and thus died in his native land in 1715.

On 9 February 1687 John Peachell, Vice-chancellor of Cambridge, was instructed by the King to admit Father Francis to the degree of MA without first requiring him to take the oath of allegiance to the Church of England. Although such dispensations had been granted in the past, usually to non-christian visitors, Francis's case was clearly different and was seen as part of James's long-term policy to undermine the established church.

By this time Newton must have completed *Principia*. A few difficulties remained; the task of seeing the work through the press had been assigned to Halley. Newton was thus free to devote all his energies to fighting this new Catholic threat. On this issue he sought no cover from front men, and expressed his views openly rather than confining them to unsent letters and private memoranda. 'If his Majesty be advised to require a Matter which cannot be done by Law, no Man can suffer for neglect of it', he declared and acted accordingly. Halley was informed that until further notice all problems to do with solar parallax would have to wait (*C*, II, p. 464), and Newton began to consult his law books.

Advised by the University that his instructions were 'illegal', James simply renewed them, adding that any who chose to ignore them would do so 'at their peril'. The Cambridge Senate met on 11 March and chose Newton as one of its two representatives to inform Peachell that it remained illegal to admit Francis on James's terms. By this time James had had enough of letters and consequently summoned Peachell and his colleagues to appear before the Court of Ecclesiastical Commission in London. At this point there were many in Cambridge willing to compromise with James and it was suggested that Francis be admitted but on the understanding that his case should not be used as a precedent. According to Conduitt it was Newton who had successfully led the opposition to the proposed compromise.

As a result, on 21 April Newton stood with Peachell and several other Cambridge colleagues before Judge Jeffreys, best known to history for his work in the 'bloody assize' of 1685. Jeffreys' strategy seems to have been to attempt to panic the delegation into submission. Peachell, never an impressive figure to begin with, was ridiculed by Jeffreys and at a hearing on 7 May removed from office. Far from panicking, as Jeffreys presumably expected, the remainder of the delegation began to state and argue their case far more effectively than Peachell could ever have managed. Five drafts of the defence can be found in Newton's papers. The delegates were called before Jeffreys once more on 12 May. 'Go your way, and sin no more', he told them, 'lest a worse thing come unto you.' The threat was unmistakeable. While it is today clear that James's powers were limited, that he had far more important problems to concentrate on, that, in fact, his own days were numbered, to someone standing before Jeffreys the issue cannot have looked so favourable. It must have seemed to Newton and his colleagues that they were taking genuine risks; that, if not their lives, certainly their careers were in some jeopardy. As it happened a determined and united opposition was sufficient to persuade James to abandon his campaign. Within two years Jeffreys was in the Tower, James was in exile, and Newton could rest assured that the institutions of England would remain closed to Catholics for many years to come.

Franklin, Benjamin (1706–90)

Printer, publisher, politician and revolutionary, Franklin was also the first American scientist to gain widespread European recognition. In 1753 he became the first person 'out of the nation' to be awarded the Royal Society's Copley medal, and was himself elected to the Society in 1756; he also became, in 1772, an *associé étranger* of the *Académie des*

Sciences. His classic work, *Experiments and Observations on Electricity* (1751), went through five English editions, and was translated into French (twice), German and Italian, well before the end of the century.

To what extent was Franklin a Newtonian? By the time he began serious scientific research in the 1740s, Franklin had already been long exposed to Newton's works and ideas. As a boy he had attended Cotton Mather's Newtonian sermons, and read of Newton's genius in the Boyle lectures of such disciples as Richard Bentley, William Derham and Samuel Clarke. In 1724 he visited London for the first time and, although he failed to meet Newton himself, he learnt much about his work from direct contact with such leading Newtonians as Henry Pemberton and J. T. Desaguliers. He rapidly became, in Cohen's words, 'a Newtonian scientist' (Cohen, 1956, p. 209).

He was not, however, a totally uncritical Newtonian, and in 1769 produced a number of telling arguments against Newton's conception of light. Even the smallest particle of light, Franklin argued, would have 'a force exceeding that of a twenty-four pounder discharged from a cannon'. Yet, such particles seemed incapable of turning aside 'the least and lightest dust they meet with'. Further, Newton's claim in Query 30 of the *Opticks*, that 'gross bodies and light' were 'convertible into one another', led to the objection that the mass of the sun would have been so reduced that the planets, instead of drawing nearer to the sun, would have receded through the 'lessened attraction' (Cohen, 1956, pp. 318–19).

Franklin's most important work, however, was concerned with the nature of electricity. It had been argued that electricity was a fluid and came in two distinct varieties, described by Charles du Fay in the 1730s as the vitreous and the resinous. For Franklin, the 'electrical fire' was a 'species of matter, not *created* by the friction, but *collected* only'. As such there was only one kind of electricity, and electrical effects were accordingly produced by bodies electrified positively or negatively. Cohen (1980, p. 168) has argued that Franklin's introduction of the concept of an 'electrical matter' at this point was 'a transformation of the Newtonian concept of aether'.

Freind, John (1675–1728)

The son of a clergyman, Freind was educated at Oxford. After some time in Leyden he settled in London at the turn of the century and became one of the growing number of scholars seeking to apply Newtonian principles to nature. In his *Emmenologia* (1703) he argued for a mechanical medicine, while his *Praelectiones chymicae* (1709), dedicated to Newton, aimed at reducing chemistry to mechanics. His basic assumption was that the short-range attractive forces discussed by

Newton in his *Opticks* could do for chemistry and physiology what centripetal forces had done for mechanics and astronomy.

Freind's work was reviewed anonymously in the *Acta Eruditorum* (1710) and dismissed as a return to 'fantastic scholastic philosophy'. He replied in the *PT* and defended the legitimacy of the concept of attraction in chemistry. Thus, while the priority dispute about the calculus was waging between Newton and Leibniz, almost as a sub-plot Freind and the Leibnizians argued in the same journals over whether 'attractive virtues' had a role to play in chemistry. It was a view which received a more favourable response in France and did indeed point the way in which French eighteenth-century chemistry would develop.

In later life Freind turned to politics, being elected Tory MP for Launceston, Cornwall, in 1712. In 1722 he was imprisoned for his supposed complicity in Bishop Atterbury's plot to restore the Stuarts. According to one tradition he was released under pressure from his colleague Mead, who refused to treat the prime minister Walpole as long as Freind was imprisoned.

See also Chemistry and the Newtonian tradition

Freret, Nicolas (1688–1749)

Freret was elected to the *Académie des Inscriptions et Belles-Lettres* in 1714. Shortly afterwards he published a controversial account of the origin of the Franks which earned him a spell in the Bastille. By 1743 Freret had regained sufficient orthodoxy to be appointed secretary of the *Académie*.

Some time in the early 1720s he had been shown and allowed to copy the manuscript of Newton's *Short Chronicle*, brought to Paris by the Abbé Conti. Freret went further, translated the manuscript into French and began to consider its publication. Although Freret was aware that Newton had forbidden publication of the manuscript, he arranged none the less for the printer Guillaume Cavelier to add the short twenty-page manuscript as a supplement to French edition of Prideaux's *The Old and New Testament Connected* (1725).

Freret did more than simply translate the *Short Chronicle*. He added 'observations', querying all the key assumptions of Newton's chronology. Even his priority was questioned. Newton replied in the *PT* (July/August 1725) but it was against Conti that he directed his rage; Freret, the 'Observator', he dismissed condescendingly as undertaking 'to translate and to confute a Paper which he did not understand'. Against Freret's duplicity in publishing his translation, Newton savagely exposed the absurdity of the French position by asking whether 'any Man could be so foolish as to consent to the publishing of an unseen

Translation of his Papers, made by an unknown Person, with a Confutation annexed, and unanswered at their first Appearance in Publick'.

See also A Short Chronicle

Friends

It is no straightforward matter to identify at a distance of three hundred years, from amongst a man's colleagues, acquaintances and staff, those he would be prepared to call his friends. Newton, for example, knew Edmond Halley for well over forty years. Did they, however, see each other as friends? Mutual respect, common intellectual interests, official duties, and several other factors, no doubt are sufficient to explain their continued relationship. Another scholar Newton saw much of was David Gregory. At no time of their relationship, if the surviving correspondence is an accurate guide, did they ever address each other in anything but formal terms. It is a salutary experience to read the correspondence of Newton and Darwin, side by side. With Darwin, expressions of affection are regularly recorded; none such are seen anywhere in the entire Newton *Correspondence*.

Newton would thus seem to be one who little needed a wide circle of friends. Above all, as Humphrey Newton recorded, 'He always kept close to his studies' (More, 1962, p. 247). He also kept close to his family. Consequently, for much of his life Newton seemed quite content to devote himself to his work and his family. It would, however, be too extreme to cast Newton in the role of friendless recluse. Although not, like a Darwin or an Einstein, surrounded by friends, there were some in Newton's life, never the less, who were more than colleagues.

From Newton's undergraduate days two names suggest themselves: Francis Aston and John Wickins. Contact seems to have been maintained with Aston until his death in 1715, while Newton and Wickins shared rooms in Trinity for several years. There is no record, however, of any contact with Wickins after he left Trinity in 1684 for a living in Monmouthshire. Another source for Newton's Cambridge life is Humphrey Newton, who spent some five years in the 1680s as his amanuensis. Newton 'very rarely went a visiting', he noted. As for visitors, 'he had as few'. Excepting, Humphrey added, 'two or three persons, Mr Ellis, Mr Laughton of Trinity, and Mr Vigani, a chemist, in whose company he took much delight and pleasure at an evening when he came to wait upon him' (More, 1962, p. 249). Laughton gained a further mention from Humphrey as having 'resorted much to his chamber' (More, 1962, p. 249). Newton's pleasure with Vigani's company, however, did not persist. Catherine Barton reported that all contact between the friends was broken after Vigani had told Newton a loose story about a nun.

Two further friendships, perhaps the closest Newton ever formed, began in the 1690s with John Locke and Fatio. Evidence of the strength of the relationships can be seen in the untypical invitations to visit him in Cambridge offered by Newton to Fatio and to Locke, and from the even less characteristic willingness on Newton's part to visit them in London and in Sussex.

Locke, however, died in 1704, by which time Fatio's growing religious obsessions had taken him into other circles. Although for the rest of his life Newton seems to have been active socially, entertaining visitors to the Royal Society and attending Court, for example, no one seems to have taken the place of Locke or Fatio. A possible exception was Hopton Haynes, a Mint official, described by Whiston as Newton's 'intimate friend'. Nothing of any such intimacy can be seen, however, in their surviving correspondence.

Two other figures Newton saw much of in the last decade of his life were John Conduitt, his nephew-in-law, and William Stukeley. It remains doubtful whether or not the relationship between an eminent octogenarian and his much younger prospective biographers could be properly described as one of friendship.

Fundamentum opticae

Located in the PC in the ULC and dating from the 1690s is a draft of Book I of the *Opticks* (1704). It is described briefly by Westfall (RSW, pp. 520–4), and referred to by Lohne (1968, pp. 187–8). David Gregory saw some of this material in 1694 and reported that Newton intended to publish it 'within five years after retiring from the University' (*C*, III, p. 339). Despite being badgered by Wallis, and pressure from the RS, Newton clearly had second thoughts and hung on to the material until it finally appeared in 1704 as part of the *Opticks*.

Funeral

Newton died in the early morning of Monday 20 March 1727 in his home in Kensington. He was 84. On Tuesday March 28 the body lay in state in the Jerusalem Chamber of Westminster Abbey. He was buried on April 4. The coffin was supported by the Lord Chancellor, the Dukes of Roxburghe and Montrose, and the Earls of Pembroke, Sussex and Macclesfield. The service was performed by the Bishop of Rochester and the chief mourner was Sir Michael Newton.

The sarcophagus seen today in the nave of the Abbey was erected in 1731.

G

Gandy, William (1660–1729)

Little is known about Gandy. He painted Newton's portrait in 1706. The actual portrait itself is lost and is known only from an 1848 lithograph by G. B. Black. It can be seen in the D. E. Smith collection at Columbia University, New York (RSW, p. 588).

The print shows a blank-faced Newton, quarter length, in his own hair, looking vacantly ahead.

See also Portraits, medals, busts and statues

Gascoigne, William

A British Jesuit in Liège, and a pupil of Franciscus Linus, Gascoigne intervened briefly in late 1675 in the dispute, provoked by Newton's first paper of 1672 on light and colour, and pursued in the pages of the *PT*. On 15 December 1675 he wrote to Oldenburg informing him of the death of Linus. He went on to assure Newton that Linus, without any success, had tried the *experimentum crucis* 'again and again'. Gascoigne and his colleagues could not be 'more confident' on the validity of their experiments. Unless there was some overlooked difference between the Liège and Cambridge experiments then, Gascoigne concluded, 'Mr. Newton's Experiment will hardly stand' (*PLNP*, p. 155).

Extracts from Gascoigne's letter were included in Newton's reply of 10 January 1676. Newton could do little more than describe the experimental set-up in ever-increasing detail and to propose that sceptics should try once more. At this point Gascoigne confessed that he was 'wanting convenience to make the Experiment' and handed over the case to yet another British Jesuit, Anthony Lucas.

See also Experimentum crucis; Linus, Franciscus; Lucas, Anthony

Gassendi, Pierre (1592–1655)

Ordained in 1617, Gassendi spent the bulk of his life teaching philosophy and science at Aix and, after 1645, at the Collège Royal in Paris. Although brutally dismissed by Koyré (1965, p. 176) as 'a not very good physicist, a bad mathematician . . . and a rather second-rate philosopher', Gassendi remains an important figure in seventeenth-century science. His main role was as a polemicist and propagandist for atomism and its incorporation in the new mechanical philosophy. In this endeavour he had to battle against both the traditional Aristotelians and the rival Cartesians. Beginning with his *Exercitationes paradoxicae adversus Aristotelos* (1628, Paradoxical Exercises against Aristotle) and culminating in his *Animadversiones* (1649, Observations), Gassendi sought to present the atomism of Epicurus and Lucretius in a manner acceptable to the seventeenth-century mind. It was not, he insisted, an atheistic doctrine, as it required God to have created the atoms and to have endowed them with their various properties of hardness, gravity and motion. Gassendi's atomism, as it was introduced into England by Walter Charleton, proved to have a lasting impact on the thought of Newton.

Gassendi also, in his *De motu* (1641, On Motion), considered the problem of gravitational attraction. Something of the measure of Newton's achievement in *Principia* can be seen when it is realised that some forty years earlier Gassendi could propose that bodies fall downwards because they are attached to strings connecting them to the earth.

See also Atomism

Generosity and gifts

While it has become customary in recent years to concentrate on some of the less pleasant aspects of Newton's personality – his deviousness, ruthlessness, unforgiveness and self-righteousness, for example – it should not be forgotten that he also possessed a number of more attractive attributes. Outstanding amongst these was Newton's generosity. 'He was very charitable', observed his amanuensis of the 1680s, Humphrey Newton; 'few went away empty handed from him'. Stukeley also spoke of Newton's free ways with money: 'He was generally present at the marriage of his relations . . . He generally made a present of £100 to the females, and set up the men to trade and business' (Stukeley, 1936, pp. 68–9).

There were others, outside Newton's family, who benefitted. Editors of his various works tended to be rewarded with cash. Thus Samuel Clarke in 1706 received £500 for translating the *Opticks* (1704) into Latin, while Henry Pemberton was given 200 guineas for his work on the third edition of *Principia* (1726). Doctors who attended Newton could be startled by being offered handfuls of guineas. Institutions also received substantial sums. To TCC Newton donated £40 in 1676 for the construction of a new library, and a further £50 in 1708 for the purchase of a pendulum clock. The Royal Society was given about £120 in the period 1709–10 and a further £70 in 1718. Towards the end of his life Newton subscribed £12 in 1725 for the erection of a gallery in Colsterworth church and, in the following year, £3 was provided for repairs to the floor.

Tenants of Newton's estates seem to have been treated generously. As an example the case of E. Buswell, a tenant in some financial difficulty in 1694, can be considered. Newton wrote to him in June expressing his willingness 'to order my concerns so as to stay for ye money'. Although, he claimed, he needed the rent, he agreed to wait until January rather than seeing Buswell 'straitened' (*C*, III, p. 374). A second letter from about the same time, and probably to Buswell's brother, speaks with no great concern, of rent 'now 3 years and almost ½ behind hand' (*C*, III, p. 393).

Perhaps, however, the purest expression of Newton's generous spirit is to been seen in his treatment of the young mathematicians he befriended. If money was needed to help them in their career, Newton was willing to provide it. He paid in 1724 for James Stirling to return from Venice, and in 1725 offered to pay Colin Maclaurin a salary of £20 a year until a post fell vacant at Edinburgh. Earlier, in the period 1719–20, the astronomer James Pound received two payments of £52 10s, recorded by Pound himself as 'a free gift' and a 'gift' respectively.

Nor was it simply money that was dispensed by Newton. Visiting scientists like David Gregory, John Colson, Alexander Pitcairne and others were allowed to see many of Newton's unpublished manuscripts. Often they were allowed to take them away, copy them, show them to others, and even, occasionally, publish them. It is difficult not to believe that Newton was as liberal with his ideas in conversation with his younger colleagues as he had been with his manuscripts.

Against such numerous examples of generosity there stands just one dissenting voice. In 1725 the Abbé Alari, Louis XV's tutor, dined with Newton. The meal, he declared, was 'detestable'; Newton was a miser, serving only wines of Palma and Madeira presented to him (Edleston, 1850, p. lxviii).

Geographia universalis

A work of physical geography by Bernhard Varenius, published in Amsterdam in 1650, it was reissued in Cambridge in 1672 under the editorial direction of Newton. It was in fact the first time Newton's name ('Varenius ab Isaaco Newton Math. Prof. Lucasiano') appeared on the title page of any published work.

The book itself is divided into the following three parts.

1 *Pars absoluta* – the shape, size and astronomical position of the earth.

2 *Pars relativa* – the relations between the earth and the heavens.

3 *Pars comparativa* – methods of determining longitude and the location of a number of well-known places.

A second edition containing further revisions by Newton appeared in 1681.

The work proved successful. It was first translated into English by William Dugdale in 1733 and reissued in 1734, 1736 and 1765. In addition to the six Latin editions of 1650, 1672, 1681, 1693, 1712 and 1715, it was also translated into Dutch (1750), French (1755) and Russian (1790).

Why Newton undertook such editorial duties is unknown. Dugdale noted in his edition of 1736:

> The reason why this great man took so much care in correcting and publishing our author, was because he thought him necessary to be read by the audience while he was delivering lectures upon the same subject from the Lucasian chair. (MORE, 1962, p. 152n)

As no other reference has ever been made to such lectures, Dugdale's comment carries little weight.

Newton's actual contribution to the text seems to have been minimal. Hall (1960) has noted that in addition to some verbal changes, and the correction of a few mathematical errors, his role was 'little more than a careful review of the original text and reading the proofs of the new'. The book, he concluded, 'left his hands almost as exactly as it came to them', and 'no word of comment, explanation or observation' from Newton himself can be detected anywhere in the text.

See also Varenius, Bernhard

Geometria curvilinea

A typical piece of Newtonian mathematics; a well-worked-out draft, summarily and for no apparent reason abandoned and unread for almost two centuries. The manuscript is in ULC, Add. MS 3968, and was published for the first and only time in *MP*, IV, pp. 420–84 in both its original Latin and English translation. On handwriting evidence alone Whiteside has assigned the work a date of 1680.

It was originally planned in four chapters.

1 General theory and its application to algebraic, geometric and trigonometric magnitudes.

2 Maxima and minima, normals and tangents.

3 Inverse method.

4 Curves in general.

Only the first chapter is anything like complete.

It contains a number of critical points directed against Cartesian analysis, a system which may well have led to a 'broad and far-reaching' progress but only at the price of 'the complexity of its conclusions' and its 'intolerably roundabout' computations. He therefore proposed to develop further the methods introduced in *Methodus fluxionum* and to show their superiority over Cartesian techniques. Thus, by fluxion he meant 'the swiftness of growth' as, for example, the speed of a point that generates a line'. Differentiation was handled by the use of 'nascent and ultimate ratios'. Consequently, 'Fluxions of quantities are in the first ratio of their nascent parts or, what is exactly the same, in the last ratio of those parts as they vanish by defluxion' (*MP*, IV, p. 427).

Whiteside has proposed that it was the comet of 1680 which drew Newton away from his incomplete tract.

Geometriae libri tres

In the 1690s Newton made several attempts to present his views on geometry in the form of a substantial treatise. The results of this endeavour can be seen in the papers of the PC. Whiteside has extracted from this confusing mass of material and pieced together several substantial fragments of this proposed work which, typically, exist in a number of drafts. Amongst this material he has identified and published in *MP*, VIII:

1 *Proemium* (Preface), pp. 248–76;

2 *Geometriae liber primus*, pp. 286–338, 352–82;

3 *Geometriae liber secundus*, pp. 382–400.

Also present is a *Geometriae libri duo* with parts of the two books restored as:

4 *Liber primus*, pp. 402–506;

5 *Liber secundus*, pp. 508–61.

In addition, effort was also directed to restore the lost books of Euclid's *Porismata*.

The persistent theme of this work, and lying behind all the technical effort, was a determination to show that the Greeks had developed the same algebraic and analytical skills available to Newton and his contemporaries.

Giants and pebbles

If I have seen further it is by standing on ye shoulders of Giants.

I don't know what I may seem to the world, but, as to myself, I seem to have been only like a boy playing on the sea shore, and diverting myself in now and then finding a smoother pebble or a prettier shell than ordinary, whilst the great ocean of truth lay all undiscovered before me.

The two statements above are among the most frequently quoted of all Newton's pronouncements. They are generally held to be expressive of Newton's innate modesty and of his awareness of his dependence upon his illustrious predecessors. 'What a lesson to the vanity and presumption of philosophers' intoned Brewster (1831, p. 328), while Alfred Noyes chose to begin the Newton section of *The Torch-bearers* (1937, p. 88) with the lines:

'If I saw further, 'twas because I stood
On giant shoulders,' wrote the king of thought,
Too proud of his great line to slight the toils
of his forbears.

In fact neither pronouncement is expressive of modesty, humility, ancestral veneration, or anything else. Both expressions are purely conventional, with one of them, at least, having become by the seventeenth century the kind of sentiment the great and good were expected to make. The first statement, thanks to a remarkable *tour de force* by Robert Merton (1965), is now well documented. Merton succeeded in tracing the basic idea back to the twelfth century when Bernard of Chartres claimed: 'Nos esse quasi nanos gigantium humeris insidientes' (We are as dwarfs sitting on the shoulders of giants). And indeed, precisely this sentiment is to be found illustrated in the windows of the south transept of Chartres Cathedral, where the evangelists can be seen sitting on the shoulders of the prophets Ezekiel, Daniel, Isaiah and Jeremiah. The image is also displayed in Bamberg Cathedral, on a baptismal font at Meresburg and on a carved pillar in a church in Payerne.

Merton has listed at least twenty-six writers who, between Bernard and Newton, expressed their modesty in this manner. Included are Marin Mersenne, Robert Burton, John Donne and Thomas Sprat. After Newton it can be found, amongst many others, in the writings of J. S. Mill, Friedrich Engels and Sigmund Freud. Even Frank Harris could find an occasion for its deployment.

Newton himself used the expression in a letter of 1676 to Robert Hooke (*C*, I, p. 416). It was precisely the moment when Newton had become so exasperated by a seemingly endless correspondence imposed upon him by the various critics of his 1672 paper on light and colour that he was telling anyone who would listen that he wanted no more of natural philosophy; she was a far too 'litigous lady'. He went on in the 1676 letter to suggest that Hooke deferred 'too much to my ability for searching into this subject'. He then went on to throw at Hooke, as a denial of any originality in his work, the reference to standing on giant's shoulders. It thus seems that, far from being an expression of any modesty on Newton's part, it was a deliberate lie intended to discourage Hooke from pursuing the discussion any further. On this issue Newton knew that, unlike other aspects of his work, the 1672 paper was as original as any scientific paper is ever likely to be. There were no debts to be paid here, nor any giant required to provide a better view.

It has been suggested that Newton's statement was also intended as a deliberate snub. Hooke, with his dwarfish and twisted body, could hardly fail to notice that Newton was claiming the assistance of giants, figures markedly different from his own stunted growth. If a snub was intended it is likely to have been an unconscious one. The whole tone of the letter is conciliatory and respectful, suggesting someone anxious to end rather than prolong a dispute.

No Merton has yet been tempted to trace the history of the second statement. It derives from Joseph Spence (1699–1768) and was first published in his *Anecdotes* (1820) as anecdote 1259. It was reported to have been made 'a little before he died' and the source is given as Andrew Michael Ramsay (1686–1743), better known to his contemporaries as the Chevalier de Ramsay. The son of a Scottish baker, he had served in France as secretary to Fénelon and as the tutor of the Young Pretender in Rome. He was in London in 1730 and probably picked up the story from such friends of his as Samuel Clarke, Fatio de Duillier, or even John Conduitt, who had recorded an almost identical judgement.

It is clearly a prepared comment, the kind of expression eminent men feel is expected of them. Nor does it contain the kind of images which might naturally have sprung to Newton's mind. As far as is known he had never even seen the sea or ever walked on a beach. His entire life was spent between Grantham, Cambridge, and Woolsthorpe, and he is unlikely ever to have stood by anything grander than the Thames.

A possible source for the imagery was proposed in 1820 by S. W. Singer, who noticed the following passage in John Milton's *Paradise Regained* (Book IV, lines 337–8), in which someone 'shallow in himself is described', someone who:

> trifles for choice matters, worth a sponge,
> As children gathering pebbles on the shore.

It should be noted that Newton possessed a copy of the 1720 edition of Milton's *Poetical Works*.

Glover, Richard (1712–85)

The author of many now-unread blank verse plays with such titles as *Boadicea* (1753) and *Medea* (1763), Glover was also, from 1761 to 1768, MP for Weymouth in Dorset. 'Newton demands the Muse', Glover wrote shortly after Newton's death and went on to contribute one of the first poetic eulogies, *A Poem on Newton*, to Henry Pemberton's *A View of Sir Isaac Newton's Philosophy* (1728).

See also Poetic tradition

God

Newton's clearest expression of his own personal conception of God is contained in the General *Scholium* added to the second edition of *Principia* (Cajori, 1713, pp. 543–7). There is nothing here, however, of God as the loving father, nor is there any talk of the God of love. God is rather the Pantocrator or universal ruler; he has Dominion, he is Lord and we worship and adore him, not as trusting children, but as servants.

Such views were formed by Newton long before 1713. They can, in fact, be seen clearly expressed in the early Fitzwilliam Notebook. Included in the list of sins are the significant items: 'Not fearing Thee so as not to offend Thee. Fearing man above Thee' (Westfall, 1963, p. 14). Whatever his attitude, it did not entail frequent visits to church. Humphrey Newton, the amanuensis of the 1680s, noted of Newton that 'He very seldom went to the chapel', and indeed, 'that he scarcely knew the house of prayer'. His only church attendance seems to have been on Sunday afternoon at St Mary's (More, 1962, p. 248).

His reluctance to attend church could well have been, as Humphrey suggested, due to the pressure of his chemistry experiments. It could also, however, have been linked with his own deep Unitarianism. On this last issue Newton expressed his own creed in an unpublished manuscript in the Yahuda Collection (RSW, pp. 823–4):

> We are forbidden to worship two Gods but we are not forbidden to worship one God & one Lord: one God for creating all things & one Lord for redeeming us with his blood. We must not pray to two Gods but we must pray to one God in the name of one Lord.

And should we give 'the Son all that worship which is due to the father we should make two creators & be guilty of polytheism'. Christ could be honoured and blessed as 'the Lamb of God'; he rose from the dead and ascended into heaven, he is 'exalted to the right hand of God', and he shall come 'to judge the quick and the dead'. All this, and more, was true of Christ. But at no point does it add up to Christ as creator, and consequently he cannot be, with God, 'first author of all things by the almighty power of his will'. In support of this view Newton could, and frequently did, quote Biblical texts by the score.

So much is a matter of record. Manuel (1974, 1980) has sought to make a less easy-to-document point. Newton, he declared, 'was conscious of his special bond to God', and that he had been 'destined to unveil the ultimate truth about God's creation' (Manuel, 1974, p. 19). It remains a speculative point and one which has found little support.

Godolphin, Sidney, first Earl of (1645–1712)

The son of a prominent landowner, Godolphin began his long political career in 1662 as a page at the Court of Charles II. He held various government posts before being appointed Lord High Treasurer by Queen Anne in 1702. As such he was responsible for financing Marlborough's wars. When Anne in 1710 turned to the Tories, Godolphin left the Treasury and with his departure from office his political career of half a century came to an end.

Although thirty-four letters from Newton and the Mint to Godolphin have survived (*C*, IV–V, *passim*), all are formal and all are concerned with Newton's official duties. At no point in the correspondence is there any suggestion that a less formal relationship may have existed.

Goethe, Johann Wolfgang von (1749–1832)

The son of a lawyer, Goethe trained initially for the law before embarking upon his well-known literary career. He also showed, in the manner of the times, a deep interest in geology and natural history. It was an interest which extended to chemistry and physics. Goethe, however, was not a man content merely to read and absorb the works of the scientists of his day. He wanted both to make discoveries of his own and to evaluate supposed scientific truths on the basis of his own philosophical assumptions.

One such assumption was that light, the simplest and most elementary of all phenomena, could not possibly be composed of anything more basic. He had looked through a prism at a white wall and found, as he expected, that it remained white; colour only appeared at such dark boundaries of the wall as window frames and doors. Colour was thus claimed to be the result of some supposed tension between the basic realities of light and dark. One was as likely to discover the nature of light by forcing it through a prism as to find the secret of life by tearing a butterfly to pieces:

Friends, avoid the darkened prisons
Where they pinch and tweak the light
And in pitiful decisions
Bow to rays distorted quite.

Goethe published his views at considerable length in his *Zur Farbenlehre*
(1810, On the Theory of Colour). It is a work little thought of by
modern historians of science, being dismissed, for example, by Gillispie
(1960, p. 196) as presenting no more than 'the painful spectacle of . . .
a great man, making a fool of himself'.

'sGravesande, Wilhelm Jacob (1688–1742)

Described by the *DSB* as 'the earliest influential exponent of Newtonian
philosophy in continental Europe', 'sGravesande began as a lawyer. In
1713 he helped to found, and edited for some years, the *Journal Littéraire
de la Haye*, to which the English Newtonians regularly contributed.
Closer contact was made with this group when he was appointed in
1715 Secretary of the Dutch Mission sent to London to congratulate
George 1 on his accession. 'sGravesande stayed in London for about a
year. While there he met Newton and established relations with such
leading Newtonians as Desaguliers and John Keill.

On his return to Holland he was appointed in 1717 to the chair of
mathematics and philosophy at Leyden. He also began to prepare his
Introductio ad philosophiam Newtoniam (Introduction to Newtonian Philosophy) which, after its publication in 1720, would appear, in one form
or another, in twenty-four editions before 1760. It was a work which
emphasised the experimental rather than the mathematical side of
Newton's thought and as such must have introduced many throughout
Europe to the basic principles of the new science. 'sGravesande also
edited the first Continental edition of Newton's *Arithmetica universalis*
(Leyden, 1732).

Three letters from 'sGravesande to Newton have survived. One of
these, dated 7 August 1721 (*C*, VII, pp. 143–6), contains a sympathetic
description of a supposedly perpetual motion machine he had examined.
He could find no power source and seemed willing, although somewhat
guardedly, to accept the reality of the machine. No reply from Newton
has survived.

Gravia in trochoide descendentia (The descent of heavy bodies in cycloids)

The editors of the 1888 Cambridge PC *Catalogue* thought the manuscript
to be one of Newton's early papers. It consists of a double-folded sheet

in Newton's own hand and is to be found in the ULC. First published by the Halls (pp. 170–80), in both the original Latin and English translation, it can also be seen in Herivel (1965, pp. 198–207). Whereas the Halls considered there to be no evidence to suggest 'its writing preceded the publication of Christian Huygens' *Horologium oscillatorium* in 1673', Herivel has argued that it could be the manuscript written before 1669 dealing with 'the principle of equal times of a pendulum suspended between cycloids' seen by David Gregory in 1694.

The paper lists a number of well-known features of the cycloid. They are described in terms of a body moving in an inverted cycloid and cover such features as the fact that 'if a body oscillates in a cycloid all oscillations whatsoever will occupy the same time'. Newton himself drew attention to what he considered to be 'the outstanding fact' of the piece, namely 'that given the time in which the pendulum vibrates a given distance, there follows the time in which a heavy body falls through a given depth'. The Halls have noted that at this point Newton could have gone on to calculate the gravitational constant. This he seems not to have done and when, in *Principia*, Book III, prop.IV, he needed a figure for g, he simply adopted the 30.16 Paris feet worked out by Huygens.

See also Cycloid

Gravity

TRADITIONAL THEORY

Gravity was not something discovered or invented by Newton. He did, however, endow it with a number of novel properties. Traditionally, the term had been conveniently used to describe the behaviour of bodies as they fell to earth. It did not need Newton to tell his colleagues that apples dropped out of trees. For earlier thinkers, however, gravity was not a universal property of matter. While it was true that most bodies possessed gravity, it was equally true that other bodies, air and smoke for example, possessed the attribute of levity and, accordingly, rose into the heavens.

Nor was there any comprehension of the uniqueness of the gravitational force. For scholars like Copernicus or Kepler, each planet would have its own gravity. That is to say, pieces of earth would be attracted to earth, and pieces of Mars to Mars; there is no reason to suppose, on this view, that a piece of Mars would ever be attracted by terrestrial gravity. The view had been expressed in antiquity by Plutarch. He referred to the fact that bodies, thrown in the air, returned to earth as due to their 'having a certain community and natural kinship with the earth'. But, he continued, 'if any body has not been allotted to earth from the beginning', as with the moon, 'what is there to prevent its existing separately and remaining self-contained, compacted and fettered by its own parts' (Sambursky, 1956, pp. 206–7). Something similar is to be found in the writings of Copernicus, Galileo and Kepler, and was clearly expressed by William Gilbert:

> All that is earthly unites itself with the earth's globe; in the same way all that is of the same substance as the sun tends towards the sun, all the moon's substance towards the moon, and the same for the other bodies which make up the universe.   (HESSE, 1965, p. 128)

The occult causes of traditional science did not survive long into the seventeenth century. Attempts were soon made to substitute for appeals to 'natural kinship', a more mechanical picture of gravitational attraction. The results could be no less crude. Thus, the leading mechanist, Pierre Gassendi, writing in 1641, proposed a scheme in which bodies were connected to the earth by thin strings. Larger bodies, in this way, would weigh more than smaller bodies because they were connected to the earth by far more strings. Others, such as Kepler, argued that the planets were held in their solar orbit by the magnetic attraction exerted by the sun.

For many, of course, the very idea of gravity as an attractive force was absurd. Descartes, for example, with his denial of the void, attributed gravity to the presence of a small vortex, rotating with the earth and reaching to the moon. In essence, though not in detail, he was followed in his claim by Huygens and Leibniz.

The first major advance in the theory of gravitation came in the work of Robert Hooke. Why, he asked in 1666, should the planets move around the sun. There were no solid orbs or visible strings to constrain them. Bodies, he argued, unless affected by special conditions, moved in straight lines. Hooke answered: 'Circular Motion, is compounded of an indeavour by a direct motion by the Tangent and of another indeavour tending to the Center' (Koyré, 1965, p. 181). Hooke also, a little later in 1670, began to make claims for the universality of gravity:

> Not only the Sun and Moon have an influence on the body and motion of the Earth, and the Earth upon them, but that Mercury, Venus, Mars, Jupiter and Saturn also . . . have a considerable influence upon its motion, as . . . the corresponding attractive power of the Earth hath a considerable influence upon every one of their motions also.   (KOYRÉ, 1965, p. 182)

Hooke further saw that these attractive powers weaken with distance. He was not aware in 1670, however, precisely at what rate the attraction diminished. Some time later in the 1670s he had worked it out that the force should decrease inversely as the square of the distance, and so he informed Newton in a letter dated 6 January 1680. At this point Hooke could go no further; attempts to derive the elliptical orbits of the planets from the inverse square law had all failed. It remained for him to propose one more mechanical model of attraction and to await the advances of others.

NEWTONIAN THEORY

Three early accounts have survived of Newton's discovery in 1666, independently of Hooke, of the principle of universal gravitation. Newton's own account describes how in 1666 he began to think of 'gravity extending to the orb of the Moon'. From this he deduced that the forces keeping the 'Moon in her Orb' varied inversely as the square of the distance. He had also 'compared the force requisite to keep the Moon in her Orb with the force of gravity at the surface of the earth, and found them answer pretty nearly' (Herivel, 1965, p. 67). Why then did he wait twenty-one years before publishing his results?

One answer was provided by a report in 1749 by William Whiston of a 1694 conversation with Newton. Taking 1° to be 60 miles, and using the inverse square law, Newton found to his disappointment that 'the Power that restrained the Moon in her Orbit . . . appeared not to be quite the same that was to be expected, had it been the Power of Gravity alone' (Herivel, 1965, p. 65). A similar story, derived from conversations with Newton in the last years of his life, was given by Henry Pemberton (1728). Being absent from books in Woolsthorpe he took the common estimate of 60 miles to 1 degree instead of the more accurate figure of 69.5 miles. The inevitable result was that 'his computation did not answer expectation'. Consequently, Newton 'laid aside for that time any farther thoughts upon this matter' (Herivel, 1965, p. 66).

Herivel has calculated that if Newton did take 1° = 60 miles, and if he had also taken 1 mile = 5,000 ft, and the lunar orbit = 27 days 8 hours, then the moon would fall in her orbit in 1 minute by 13.2 ft, against a true figure of 16 ft per minute. After his disappointment Newton seems to have spent little further time considering the matter before late 1679, when the topic was brought up once more by Robert Hooke. It was from this correspondence that Newton first heard that the motions of the planets could be compounded from an attractive motion towards the sun and from a direct motion tangential to the orbit.

Hooke, on 17 January 1680, raised a final problem. What path, he asked Newton, would a planet follow if it was attracted by the sun with a force which varied inversely as the square of the distance? Newton apparently worked out that such planets would move in ellipses; he did not, however, bother to inform Hooke of his results.

Four years later Edmond Halley posed the same question to Newton.

At Halley's invitation he agreed to write up his results for the RS. It was while working through the results established in 1679–80 that Newton must have begun to realise the inadequacy of his earlier analysis. Renewed work led him in early 1685 to the principle of universal gravitation. Two specific items were absent from the earlier analysis. There was no mention of the universal nature of gravity; instead it seems to have been assumed that such a force was a monopoly of the central sun as it exercised its control over the planets. Nor had it been realised that gravitational attraction was mutual; thus, not only did the sun attract the earth but the earth attracted the sun. But, given also the universal nature of the force, there would be more bodies than the sun and the earth mutually attracting each other. All the planets would in their turn be influencing both the sun and the earth, both of which would be exerting their own influence over the planets.

Signs of the increasing sophistication of Newton's views can be seen in the various *De motu* manuscripts. In the final version (D), *De motu sphaericorum corporum in fluidis*, there can be found the first reference to the many-body problem: 'The orbit of any one planet depends on the combined motion of all the planets, not to mention the action of all these on each other' (Herivel, 1965, p. 301). Shortly afterwards, in *De motu corporum in mediis regulariter cedentibus*, the third law is met with for the first time: 'As much as any body acts on another so much does it experience in reaction' (Herivel, 1965, p. 312).

The broad operations of gravity in the solar system were spelt out at the beginning of Book III of *Principia*. In prop.IV Newton returned to the moon test he had abandoned in disappointment in 1666. This time he had more accurate data. Taking the moon to be 60 earth diameters distant, it followed by the inverse square law that the attraction exerted on the moon by the earth would be $1/60 \times 60$ times weaker than the force exerted by the earth on a body at its own surface. Newton found that if 'we imagine the moon, deprived of all motion, to be let go, so as to descend to the earth', we will find that it will fall 15 1/12 Paris feet per minute. Consequently, a body falling at the surface of the earth should do so with a speed of $60 \times 60 \times 15$ 1/12 Paris feet per minute, or 15 1/12 Paris feet per second. Such a figure, Newton pointed out, had been recorded by Huygens on the basis of precise pendulum measurements. Therefore, he concluded, 'the force by which the moon is retained in its orbit is that very same force which we commonly call gravity' (Cajori, p. 408).

CAUSE

Given that gravity was a universal force and that it operated over vast areas of empty space, the question inevitably arose as to how any force could act at a distance. For many, such as Descartes, Leibniz and

Huygens, the answer was clear. Nothing, they insisted, could act at a distance and to talk of gravity in this way was to talk of fictitious occult causes. Newton was acutely aware of the difficulty and, at various times, attempted to weaken its force.

Gravity was not, he insisted to Bentley in 1693, 'essential and inherent to matter' (*C*, III, p. 240). Nor, he emphasised, could it ever act at a distance.

> Tis unconceivable that inanimate brute matter should (without ye mediation of something else wch is not material) operate upon & affect other matter without mutual contact . . . That gravity should . . . act . . . at a distance through a vacuum without the mediation of anything else . . . is to me so great an absurdity that I believe no man who has in philosophical matters any competent faculty of thinking can ever fall into. Gravity must be caused by an agent acting constantly according to certain laws, but whether this agent be material or immaterial is a question I have left to ye consideration of my readers. (*C*, III, pp. 253–4)

In addition to his general claim that gravity had an unknown cause and operated through an unknown medium, Newton also responded in two further ways.

Occasionally Newton was tempted to propose possible mechanisms for the operation of gravity. The earliest such speculations are to be found in the 1675 *An Hypothesis Explaining the Properties of Light*. He spoke, in general terms, of the 'continual condensation' of an etherial spirit as causing 'the gravitational attraction of the earth' (*PLNP*, pp. 180–1). This was followed in the 1679 *Letter to Boyle* by a further conjecture on 'the cause of gravity'. Again, it was expressed in terms of the ether. This time the ether was considered to be of variable density, 'in such a manner, that from the top of the air to the surface of the earth . . . the aether is insensibly finer and finer' (*PLNP*, p. 253). In this way, bodies would fall to the earth in the same manner as corks rise in water.

Both the above pieces remained unpublished in Newton's lifetime. When he did discuss it publicly, as in the General *Scholium* (1713), he shunned speculation and merely noted: 'I have not been able to discover the cause of those properties of gravity from the phenomena, and I frame no hypotheses' (Cajori, p. 547). Such a gap did not unduly worry Newton. It was clear to him that the properties of gravity, as opposed to its cause, had been 'deduced from the phenomena' and 'rendered general by induction'; it was enough that 'gravity does really exist and act according to the laws . . . and abundantly serves to account for all the motions of the celestial bodies' (Cajori, p. 547). The point was repeated in the *Account* (1715).

It is not the Business of Experimental Philosophy to teach the Causes of things any further than they can be proved by Experiments. We are not to fill this Philosophy with Opinions which cannot be proved by Phaenomena. (HALL, 1980, p. 312)

Was it a crime, he asked against the Leibnizians, to be content 'with Certainties and let Uncertainties alone'. The same message was to be found in Query 31 of the *Opticks*. Attraction, Newton noted, with a show of indifference, 'may be perform'd by impulse, or by some other means unknown to me'. The word was being used 'to signify . . . any Force by which Bodies tend towards one another, whatsoever be the Cause' (*Opticks*, p. 376).

Greaves, John (1602–52)

The son of a clergyman, Greaves was educated at Oxford, becoming a fellow of Merton college in 1624 and Professor of Geometry at Gresham in 1630. He is best remembered for his studies of the metrology of the ancient world. As a mathematician and with a knowledge of both classical and oriental languages, Greaves was well-prepared to undertake detailed fieldwork. In 1637 he set off for Rome with a brass foot-ruler divided into 2,000 parts. By measuring instruments depicted on Roman tombs he was able to establish the length of the Roman foot as 1,994/2,000 a British foot. A visit to the Parthenon enabled Greaves to calculate the Roman foot to be 24/25 of the Greek foot.

In 1638 Greaves moved on to Egypt to attempt to derive the length of the Egyptian cubit from the dimensions of the Great Pyramid, using a 10-foot masonry rod sub-divided into 10,000 parts. On his return to England Greaves published his results in two works, *A Discourse of the Roman Foot* (1647) and *Pyramidographia* (1646), both of which are to be found in Newton's library. Such basic data was of some significance to Newton in his quest to establish the dimensions of Solomon's Temple. The results of this work can be seen in his *A Dissertation upon the Sacred Cubit of the Jews*.

Greaves himself was appointed to the Savilian Professorship of Astronomy in 1643, only to be dismissed in 1649 for his royalist sympathies.

Greene, Robert (c.1678–1730)

Educated at Clare Hall, Cambridge, Greene was awarded an MA in 1703 and remained a Fellow of his college for the rest of his life. Eccentric, verbose, and something of an egomaniac, Greene was one of the first British scientists to seek to dismiss Newtonian physics and to substitute for it alternative foundations. The result was a 927-page treatise on *The Principles of the Philosophy of the Expansive and Contractive Forces* (1727) in which he claimed to have developed a 'Greenian' philosophy which was 'truly English . . . Cantabrigian . . . and Clarensian' (Edleston, 1850, pp. 44–5).

In Greene's physics, bodies were composed of forces: a 'centripetal, gravitating or attractive force'; and a 'centrifugal, elastic or expansive force'. His work was too prolix, disorganised and indifferent to the problems it raised to exercise any real influence over his contemporaries. Similar views, expressed in a clearer and sharper form, would be raised later in the century by R. J. Boscovich, and would exercise a deep and lasting influence on those who were seeking to develop alternative views of matter.

Greenwood, Isaac (1702–45)

Born in Boston, Mass., the son of a merchant, Greenwood studied at Harvard under Thomas Robie from 1717 to 1721. He spent the period 1723–6 in England where he studied Newtonian physics under John Desaguliers. While in England he met Thomas Hollis, who was so impressed by him that he proposed that Greenwood should be the first to hold the Hollis Professorship of Mathematics and Natural Philosophy he had founded at Harvard in 1727. In 1737 Greenwood was censured for drinking and ordered to stay sober for five months. A relapse in 1738 led to his dismissal and his replacement by John Winthrop IV.

Greenwood introduced into Harvard the Newtonian science he had acquired during his stay in England. He was the first to lecture on fluxions in America; he also gave an 'experimental course' on mechanical philosophy in which, in the style of Desaguliers, he attempted to demonstrate the validity of the Newtonian system experimentally.

See also Newton in America

Gregory, David (1661–1708)

The nephew of James Gregory, the mathematician, and the son of the Laird of Kinnairdie, Banffshire, Gregory was educated at the University of Edinburgh where he was later appointed to the chair of mathematics in 1683. Soon after his appointment Gregory began his long and complex relationship with Newton.

In 1684 Gregory sent Newton his *Exercitatio geometrica* (Geometrical Exercises), a fifty-page pamphlet in which, using unpublished material of his uncle, he applied the method of infinite series to a variety of problems. He had heard of Newton through references in Collins's letters to his uncle. Would Newton, he asked, allow him his 'free thoughts and character of this exercitation' (C, II, p. 396). The letter stimulated Newton sufficiently for him to begin work on a planned treatise in six chapters, *Matheseos universalis specimina*.

Gregory next approached Newton in 1687 to send him a letter of praise for the recently published *Principia*. It was not, however, until the summer of 1691 that Gregory's attempts to establish some kind of relationship with Newton were rewarded when the two met in London. Gregory must have impressed Newton, for shortly afterwards, on 27 July 1691, Newton wrote a letter recommending Gregory for the post of Savilian Professor of Astronomy at Oxford, despite the fact that none other than Edmond Halley had also applied for the chair. Gregory, Newton wrote, was 'prudent sober industrious modest and judicious and in Mathematiques a great Artist' (C, III, pp. 154–5). Gregory was appointed and Halley, who had done so much for Newton, was forced to wait a few more years before he too benefited from Newton's patronage.

It is far too crude a view to suppose that Gregory cultivated Newton simply to advance his career. In all his dealings with Newton he showed him enormous respect. He always referred to him, even in private memoranda, as Mr Newton or, eventually, Sir Isaac. No query of Newton was too trivial to be ignored. Thus, a request about Scottish universities brought in August 1691 a long report on the 'contrivance of the Coledges' and the 'methode of teaching in them' (C, III, pp. 157–63). It would, in fact, be truer to say that Newton used Gregory and that if Gregory did receive the Savillian chair as a reward, it would be a reward he would be forced to earn.

Fortunately for later scholars, Gregory so admired Newton that he was unwilling to allow his words to pass unrecorded. Consequently, Gregory frequently took notes of their conversations held in the 1690s, of the manuscripts he was shown, and of the often unrealised projects Newton was contemplating. The results can be seen in the following surviving memoranda.

1. London, 28 December 1691. *Varia astronomica et philosophica* (C, III, pp. 191–2). A six-page text of discussions with Fatio, Halley and others. Fatio was reported to be designing 'a new edition of Mr Newton's book in folio'.

2. Leyden, 30 June 1693. Report of conversations with Huygens (C, III, pp. 272–4).

3. Cambridge, 4 May 1694. *Adnotata phys et math cum Neutono* (C, III, pp. 311–22).

4. Cambridge, 5, 6, 7 May 1694. *Adnotata math ex Neutono* (C, III, pp. 327–31).

5 Cambridge, 5, 6, 7 May 1694. *Adnotata math ex Neutono* (*C*, III, pp. 331–3).

6 Cambridge, 5, 6, 7 May 1694. *Adnotata phys math et theol ex Neutono* (*C*, III, pp. 334–40). It contains a reference to Newton's desire to exhibit the agreement between his own work and that of 'the Antients'.

7 Undated (?May 1694). *Problema* – To find a circle equally curved with a conic section at a given point (*C*, III, pp. 340–4).

8 Undated (? May 1694). Random jottings on Newton's thoughts (*C*, III, pp. 344–8).

9 London, 16 May 1694. *Adnotata phys et math ex Fatio* (*C*, III, p. 355).

10 ? July 1694. In the new edition of Newton's Philosophy these things will be done by the Author (*C*, III, pp. 384–9).

11 1 September 1694. Brief account of visit to Greenwich (*C*, IV, pp. 7–8).

12 September 1694. A sketch of our method of fluxions (*C*, IV, pp. 17–20).

13 3 February 1695. It consists of a brief reference to Newton's tables of stellar refraction (*C*, IV, p. 82).

14 20 February 1698. Miscellaneous (*C*, IV, pp. 265–8).

15 ? July 1698. *Adnotata phys et math ex Newtono 1698 particulatim de refractione* (*C*, IV, pp. 276–8).

16 21 May 1701. Miscellaneous (*C*, IV, pp. 354–6).

The memoranda defy summary, often leaping from a sentence on a mathematical problem to an adjoining one on theology. A theme running through them, however, is Newton's plans for a revised *Principia*. Gregory did much not only to announce Newton's intention, but also to circulate many of the changes he was contemplating. He clearly had himself in mind as the editor of the work. To this end Gregory had begun in 1687 his *Notae in Newtoni Principia*; when completed in 1694 they had grown to a manuscript of 213 pages. By this time he had become, according to Cohen, more familiar with *Principia* than anyone other than Halley and Newton himself. He even began to entertain the hope that Newton would allow the notes to be published with the new edition of *Principia*, 'interspersed everywhere on the same page' (*C*, III, p. 386). Newton's comments on the suggestion have not been recorded.

If Newton showed no interest in publishing his disciple's notes, Gregory was more than willing to publish any notes of Newton. Thus his *Astronomiae physicae et geometricae elementa* (1702, 2 vols) contained Newton's Classical *Scholia*, unacknowledged, and his *Theory of the Moon's Motion*.

As for Gregory's dream of editing the second edition of *Principia*, his death in 1708 came some time after Richard Bentley had optimistically, and temporarily, assumed the role. Instead, the faithful Gregory found himself appointed by Newton to the uncongenial task of overseeing the minting in Edinburgh of the Union coinage.

Gregory's reputation today probably rests on his edition in 1703 of the complete works of Euclid, published in both Greek and Latin. It remained the only such edition until the late nineteenth century. One further work of Gregory, an 188-page manuscript, was found in September 1935 in a cupboard in the library of Christ Church, Oxford. As edited and published by W. G. Hiscock (1937) under the title *David Gregory, Isaac Newton, and their Circle, Extracts from David Gregory's Memoranda 1677–1708*, it provides a vivid picture of the scientific community of his day.

Gregory, James (1638–75)

The uncle of David Gregory, and like him a son of the manse, he was educated at Marischal, Aberdeen, and, from 1664 to 1668, in Italy at the University of Pisa. On his return to Scotland in 1669 he was appointed Professor of Mathematics at St Andrews. He moved to Edinburgh University in 1674 but died shortly afterwards at the age of thirty-seven, having first gone blind.

Of British mathematicians of the seventeenth century, Gregory was only excelled by Newton. Although somewhat isolated in St Andrews, he was kept in touch with developments elsewhere through the letters of the faithful John Collins. From 1668 until his death Gregory received about one hundred letters from Collins and replied with some forty letters of his own. Gregory also published two important mathematical texts, both of which were owned by Newton: *Vera circuli et hyperbolae quadratura* (1667, The True Quadrature of the Circle and Hyperbola); and *Geometriae pars universalis* (1668, Universal Part of Geometry). The full power of Gregory's mathematical genius was only revealed with the publication in 1939 by H. W. Turnbull of the *Tercentenary Memorial Volume*.

See also Telescopes

Grimaldi, Francesco Maria (1618–63)

Grimaldi, a Jesuit, was appointed in 1648 to the chair of mathematics at his order's college in Bologna. There appeared after his death the results of his lifetime's experimental work in optics, *Physico-mathesis de lumine, coloribus, et iride* (1665). Presented in two books, the first considered the case for the 'substantiality of light' while in the second book Grimaldi upheld 'the Peripatetic teaching of the accidentality of light'.

Grimaldi spoke of light as not only being propagated directly, refracted and reflected but also transmitted in a 'fourth mode', namely, the process of diffraction. When he had passed a narrow beam of light through small holes in a screen he had noticed that the spots formed on the other side were somewhat larger than geometry should have allowed. He also noted that each spot was surrounded by faint coloured fringes. It was thus yet one more phenomena to challenge competing theorists of the wave and corpuscular theory of light. Newton acknowledged and discussed Grimaldi's work in Book III, part I of the *Opticks*.

H

Hall, Alfred Rupert (1920–   )

Hall belongs to the first generation of professional historians of science to emerge in Britain after 1945. He served until 1959 in Cambridge as Curator of the Whipple Museum and lecturer in the history of science. As such he proved to be ideally placed to explore the then still unexamined riches of the PC, much of which was preserved in the ULC. It was thus Hall's 1948 paper on 'Sir Isaac Newton's notebook, 1661–1665' which not only drew attention to the importance of the *QQP* in the development of Newton's thought but also, in exploiting the PC so publicly, opened the Collection to all. Newtonian studies had finally entered its modern phase and would never be the same again.

Hall followed his first paper with several other pioneering studies. A 1958 joint study with Marie Boas, later to be Marie Boas Hall, provided the first detailed analysis of the Chemistry Notebook, while in their *Unpublished Scientific Papers of Isaac Newton (1962)* they selected from the PC numerous items showing early advances made by Newton in mathematics, mechanics, the theory of matter and dynamics.

From 1963–80 Hall served as Professor of the History of Science and Technology at Imperial College, London. He continued to work on Newton. After the death of J. F. Scott in 1971 he undertook to edit the final three volumes of Newton's correspondence (*C*, V–VII), a task finally completed in 1977. This was followed by a detailed study on the priority dispute with Leibniz, *Philosophers at War* (1980).

In addition to Hall's numerous publications on Newtonian topics he has also done much to illuminate the background of late seventeenth century science with his, in cooperation with Marie Boas Hall, eleven-volume edition of *The Correspondence of Henry Oldenburg* (1963–75).

Hall, Thomas (d.1718)

Hall was appointed to the Mint in February 1696 to assist the Master, Thomas Neale, in the great recoinage. He was described by a Parliamentary Committee as 'a very careful diligent officer' who 'doth almost the whole business of the Mint in Mr Neale's absence'. He left the Mint with the completion of the recoinage but returned in 1702 to serve as Chief Clerk to Newton, a post he occupied until his death in 1718. In 1700, 1702 and 1718, Hall had stood surety for Newton for the sum of £1,000 in his appointment as Master of the Mint. In return, Newton and Hopton Haynes were appointed executors in 1718 of Hall's sizeable estate of £42,000.

Halley, Edmond (1656–1742)

A major figure in his own right in the science of the seventeenth and eighteenth centuries, Halley's life and career from 1684 onwards became closely linked with the name of Newton. Without Halley it is most unlikely that *Principia* would have appeared as and when it did. He was born in London, and according to Aubrey was 'the eldest son of . . . a Soap-boyler, a wealthy Citizen of the City of London'. He quickly established his scientific reputation when, at the age of sixteen, he showed how to determine the main features of a planet's orbit given only three observations. His theoretical success was followed by his appointment in 1676 to command an expedition to St Helena to map telescopically for the first time the stars of the southern hemisphere. Halley's talents were immense and spanned not only areas of theoretical and observational science but extended also to scholarship. Working from Greek, Latin and Arabic texts, Halley published the *editio princeps* of the *Conics* of Appolonius in 1710.

Surprisingly, for someone so closely connected with Newton, Halley was attacked by several of his contemporaries as a libertine and an atheist. Aubrey coyly noted how he was accompanied on his voyage to St Helena by 'a woman and her husband who had no child in several yeares'. But, before she arrived back in London, 'she was brought to bed of a child'. Others were less indirect in their complaints. Thus, Flamsteed complained to Newton in 1692 about Halley's 'ill manners', his 'ingratitude and foolish prate', his plagiarism, and his 'infidel companions'. Not even Christ, were he to walk abroad today, would be spared the 'calumnies' of their 'venomous tongues' (C, III, p. 203). The charges seem to have stuck and were still being made a generation later, with Berkeley directing his *Analyst* (1734) against Halley as an 'infidel mathematician'.

Newton himself was reported to have found it necessary to rebuke Halley on religious matters. Catherine Barton noted, for example, that Newton 'was often angry with Dr Halley on that score'. On another occasion when Halley reportedly spoke disrespectfully of religion, Newton rebuked him with the phrase 'I have studied these things – you have not.'

Libertine and infidel or not, it was Halley who visited Newton in Cambridge in 1684 and asked him what kind of curve would the planets follow on the assumption that gravity diminished as the square of the distance. Halley, according to Conduitt, was struck with 'joy and amazement' when Newton answered that he could demonstrate that the curve would be an ellipse. For much of the next three years Halley's life would be directed towards ensuring that Newton's insight was made public. He seems to have begun simply as an intermediary between Newton and the Royal Society. In January 1686, however, Halley had been elected to the paid post of Clerk to the Society. Consequently, in May the Society instructed its Clerk to arrange for the publication of *Principia*. The difficulty hiding behind this simple instruction was that the Society was virtually bankrupt. Unable to pay Halley his salary of £50, it was reduced to offering him fifty copies of Francis Willoughby's *Historia piscium* in lieu.

This meant that Halley not only had to edit the work but also would be forced to finance its publication. It also meant that he had to deal with an increasingly unpredictable Newton. The editorial duties were clearly very demanding. Proposition XLV of Book I, he reported, gave him 'extraordinary trouble', while the 'correction of the press', he noted, was giving him 'a great deal of time and paines'.

By this time Halley was no longer the wealthy figure of his youth. His father had died in 1684 and, with a family of his own to support and an employer who seldom paid its staff, Halley was in no position to subsidise Newton. The details of the publication of *Principia* can be followed in the letters which passed between Halley and Newton during the period 22 May 1686 to 5 July 1687. The main problem facing Halley was to prevent Newton from deciding at the first sign of criticism not to publish after all. On 22 May 1686 Halley had told Newton about claims already being made by Hooke to have anticipated Newton's discovery of the inverse square law. On 20 June Newton replied that rather than consorting with the 'impertinently litigious Lady' of philosophy, he would suppress the contentious Book III. At this point Halley made what could 'just have been', in Cohen's words, 'his most significant contribution to *Principia*' (1971, p. 134). On 29 June Halley appealed, successfully, to Newton 'not to let your resentment run so high, as to deprive us of your third book'. It was this book, he reminded Newton, which would render the work 'acceptable to those that call themselves philosophers without Mathematicks'. Whether it was really the force of Halley's appeal which changed Newton's mind cannot now be known with any certainty. By 1686 Newton was showing signs of wearying of a Professor's life. He may well have realised that *Principia* was his key to something higher and that he would be well advised in his own self-interest not to hinder its chance of success. In any case, after Halley's letter of June 29 Newton spoke no more of dropping Book III.

On 5 July 1687 Halley could finally write to Newton that he had 'brought your Book to an end'. He had added to the work an impressive Ode to Newton and, as the publisher, found himself involved in the distribution of the work. It is unknown whether Halley covered his investment in *Principia*, or whether, even, he may not have made a profit. As the edition sold out reasonably quickly it can be assumed safely that Halley at least covered his costs. Two further public duties to *Principia* remained for Halley to complete. It fell to him, as editor, to review *Principia* anonymously in the *PT* (no.186). It also fell to Halley some time in 1687 to present to James II a copy of *Principia*, together with a treatise on *The True Theory of the Tides*, supposedly designed to help the King in his study of Newtonian mechanics.

In return for his labours Newton, who not always behaved so, acknowledged his debt to Halley in the handsomest of terms.

> In the publication of this work the most acute and universally learned Mr Edmund Halley not only assisted me in correcting the errors of the press and preparing the geometrical figures, but it was through his solicitations that it came to be published.
>
> (CAJORI, p. xviii)

It might be thought that Halley had earned the right to expect more from Newton than a public acknowledgment of his gratitude. Yet when in 1691 he sought the post of Savilian Professor of Astronomy at Oxford, Newton chose to support David Gregory, a weaker candidate with no special claims on Newton's patronage. At first sight it seems an act of inexplicable ingratitude. It can hardly have been due to any reluctance on Newton's part to becoming too closely involved with Halley, the well-known atheist. He had publicly confessed his gratitude in the Preface to *Principia* four years before. Further, in 1696, Newton, as Warden of the Mint, saw to it that Halley was appointed Deputy Comptroller at the Chester Mint during the period of the great recoinage. One possible reason for Newton's unwillingness to support Halley in 1691 could have been his realisation that Halley stood no chance in the election. The powerful figure of John Tillotson, Archbishop of Canterbury, opposed his election and, ever the realist, Newton threw his weight behind a more plausible candidate. When, in 1704, Halley was appointed to the Savilian Professorship of Geometry at Oxford, he revealed no resentment against Newton, going out of his way to eulogise him in his inaugural lecture. By this time Tillotson and Bishop Stillingfleet, Halley's two most eminent foes, were both dead.

Despite continuing to pursue his own productive research, Halley also continued to serve Newton as and when he was called upon. His loyalty seems to have been absolute, with no available source even hinting at any resentment Halley might have felt to Newton. The most prolonged demand for his services arose from the Flamsteed affair. Seeking for an editor of Flamsteed's star catalogue in 1712, Newton assigned the task to Halley. Earlier, in 1704, when Newton wanted someone to acknowledge and present his *Opticks* to the Royal Society, Halley was the obvious choice. Or, again, if Newton wished to see his calculations of 1694 on atmospheric refraction published, then Halley was on hand in 1721 to arrange for it to appear as *Tabula refractionum siderum ad altitudines apparentes* in a longer paper of his own (*PT*, no. 31).

Even after Newton's death Halley was still willing to see that Newton's work, however peripheral, was suitably defended. Thus in 1727 Halley became the first in print with his *Remarks upon some Dissertations lately publish'd at Paris by the Rev.P.Souciet, against Sir Isaac Newton's Chronology* (*PT*, No. 34) followed, in the next issue, with his *Some further remarks*.

There remains one further aspect of Halley's work which did much to secure the durability of Newtonian theory. Mature successful scientific theories survive by demolishing challenges. Two important ones emerged from the work of Halley. The first, and the event which won him greatest fame, was his identification of the comet since named after him and visible once more in 1985. In his *Astronomiae cometicae synopsis* (1705), using Newtonian constructions, Halley predicted that the comet of 1682 would return at Christmas 1758. The accuracy of Halley's prediction was seen widely as a crucial test of Newtonian theory. Another problem for Newtonian theory arose out of the so-called long inequality of Jupiter and Saturn. Halley had reported in 1695 that it was necessary to introduce into the tables for Jupiter a regular acceleration, while the tables for Saturn demanded an appropriate deceleration. Halley suspected, rightly, that the anomalies were the result of gravitational interactions between Jupiter and Saturn. It is one thing to harbour such a suspicion, it is another to show in detail that the observed inequalities followed exactly from the first principles of Newtonian mechanics. It took a further century of work, in which some even began to doubt the validity of the inverse square law, before Laplace in 1784 could finally confirm Halley's suspicion and remove a persistent doubt about the soundness of the Newtonian programme.

See also Principia, Origin and production, Halley's Ode, Reviews, James II, Observational tests and problems

Harris, John (*c*. 1666–1719)

A member of Newton's circle of mathematicians, through whom his own views were published and defended. Harris was educated at Oxford, took orders and was eventually appointed a prebend of Rochester cathedral. He also, in the manner of the mathematicians of the day, gave mathematical classes at his home and at a coffee house. He was Boyle lecturer in 1698 and served as Secretary of the Royal Society for the year 1709 to 1710.

He is best known for his *Lexicon technicum, a universal dictionary of arts and sciences explaining not only the terms of the art, but the arts themselves* (1704) and subsequent editions in 1708, 1710, 1716, 1725, 1736 and a 1744 supplement. Common now, Harris's work was one of the earliest such dictionaries ever to appear. In the various entries Harris expounded Newtonian doctrines while, beginning with the 1710 edition, he published for the first time a number of Newton's papers.

See also Lexicon technicum

Hartsoeker, Nicolas (1656–1725)

A Dutch physicist and friend of Huygens, Hartsoeker remained a Cartesian throughout his life. In 1712 he engaged in a public correspondence with Leibniz in which Newton's conception of gravitational attraction was analysed and dismissed. Newton drafted but did not publish a detailed reply (*C*, V, pp. 298–300). Hartsoeker's opposition to Newtonian ideas persisted and were displayed at length in his *Recueil de plusiers pièces de physique où l'on fait principalement voir l'invalidité du système de Mr.Newton* (1722, A Collection of Several Physical Tracts . . . on the Invalidity of the Newtonian System). Hartsoeker also managed to revive the flagging priority dispute between Newton and Johann Bernoulli by bringing yet again Bernoulli's embarrassing description of himself as an 'excellent mathematician' (*C*, VII, pp. 218–23).

See also Bernoulli, Johann

Hauksbee, Francis (1670–1713)

Little is known about Hauksbee's background. A student of Robert Boyle, he was first noted at the RS in late 1703 experimenting with an air pump. Although he never, apart from his election in 1705 to a Fellowship, held any official position with the Society, he served there as a demonstrator from 1703 until his death. For this he was paid a gratuity. The experiments were collected and published in his *Physico-mechanical experiments* (1710). He appears to have been treated somewhat casually by Newton. One night in 1705, for example, he was called upon to demonstrate before some unexpected visitors: 'I will give him 2 guineas for his pains', Newton promised (*C*, IV, pp. 446–8).

Hauksbee was, however, far more than a lab. assistant noted for his dexterity. Two series of experiments, in particular, proved to be sufficiently stimulating as to be quoted by Newton. In the first series Hauksbee rotated a glass globe from which the air had been evacuated. When he rubbed his hands against the globe lights flashed within and sparks were made to fly outside. In his *De vi electrica*, Newton argued that the electric spirit described by Hauksbee was responsible for, amongst other things, the manner in which 'bodies attract each other mutually at short distances' (*C*, V, pp. 366–7).

In a second series of experiments in 1712 Hauksbee succeeded in showing that capillary phenomena could be observed *in vacuo*. Clearly, Newton's previous explanation of capillarity in terms of the lower air pressure found in narrow tubes was inadequate. Further experiments, described in Query 31 of the *Opticks*, were performed and suggested that the same phenomena could be explained by attractive forces. The great value of Hauksbee's work was that it allowed these forces to be measured. It was found that 'where the distance is exceedingly small, the Attraction must be exceedingly great' (*Opticks*, p. 393).

See also De vi electrica

Hayes, Charles (1678–1760)

A lawyer and mathematician who published the first work in English on Newton's calculus, *A Treatise of Fluxions: or, an Introduction to Mathematical Philosophy* (1704). In later life Hayes worked on chronology, spending much time in arguing in his *Chronographia asiatica and aegyptica* for the compatibility of the history of both east and west with the Septuagint, a very Newtonian exercise.

Haynes, Hopton (1672–1749)

Haynes entered the service of the Mint in about 1687 and, apart from two brief periods of absence, spent the rest of his career there. Newton, on his own arrival at the Mint in 1696, must have come quite quickly to recognise Haynes' ability and the two crypto-Unitarians seem to have formed a genuine friendship. Under Newton's patronage Haynes was appointed Weigher and Teller in 1701 and promoted in 1723 to the post of Assay Master. Newton's reference for Haynes, in which his 'integrity sobriety good humour & readiness in business' as well as his 'steady hand' are described, has survived and can be seen in *C*, IV, pp. 375–6.

Outside his normal Mint duties Haynes wrote his *Brief Memoires Relating to the Silver and Gold* (1700) in which he described the recoinage, finding much to praise in Newton's contribution. He translated into Latin Newton's *Two Notable Corruptions* and published, usually anonymously, a number of theological tracts.

For Haynes was a committed Unitarian. He did not go as far as Whiston and openly declare his belief. He did, however, go further than Newton by refusing to stand up at certain points in the church service. An unlikely story, emerging only after the death of both men, claims that Haynes castigated Newton for not daring to lead a new Reformation.

Described by Whiston as Newton's 'intimate friend', Haynes named his fourth son Newton Haynes. Nothing of this comes over in the few surviving letters of Haynes. All are concerned exclusively with Mint business and in all of them Haynes has adopted an elaborate, almost fawning, style.

Health

'He was blessed with a very happy and vigorous constitution', Conduitt noted of Newton. It was not in fact, if we exclude the 1693 breakdown, until the 1720s that reports of serious illness are met with. Five years before he died, Conduitt observed 'he was troubled with an incontinence of urine' and, in 1724, 'he voided without any pain, a stone about the bigness of a pea'. In the following year he developed gout, and the more serious symptoms of a 'violent cough and inflammation of the lungs' also appeared (Turnor, 1806, p. 165).

Newton's life-style seems not to have been particularly healthy. He took no exercise, worked all hours of the day, and spent much time in confined laboratories, breathing toxic fumes and tasting poisonous mixtures. He was, however, conscious of his diet, taking, for breakfast, 'orange peel boiled in water' as he thought 'it dissolves phlegm'. He also seems to have dosed himself regularly with a nostrum called Leucatello's balsam. Basically turpentine, he drank it by the pint, and claimed it as a cure for measles, plague, smallpox, wind, colic, bruises and the 'biting of a mad dog'.

It was also something he brought to the attention of his family and friends. Nor was his advice restricted to Leucatello's balsam. Indeed, one of the persistent themes of his correspondence is his eagerness to prescribe a range of dubious cures to almost anyone who would listen.

Thus for a swelling in his half-brother Benjamin's wife's breast he recommended a fomentation and 'Sowes' (a kind of porridge). Being pregnant, she apparently found the 'Sowes' difficult to take but, Benjamin respectfully informed Newton, 'shee is resolved to try' (*C*, IV, p. 187). His niece Catherine Barton was advised to try, for her smallpox, 'warm milk from ye Cow' (*C*, IV, p. 349).

Something more elaborate was reserved for the Astronomer Royal, John Flamsteed, with his repetitive complaints of headaches. He should, Newton told him, 'bind his head strait with a garter till ye crown of his head was nummed. For thereby his head was cooled by retarding the circulation of the blood' (*C*, IV, p. 152).

See also Death; Diet

Heirs

Newton died intestate. He left, in addition to the Manor of Woolsthorpe and other lands in Sewstern, Woolsthorpe and Buckminster, assets valued at £31,821 16s 10d. With no children of his own, the Manor and other lands were inherited by John Newton (1707–37), the great-grandson of his father's brother, Robert of Counthorpe (1607–46).

The remainder of his estate passed to the eight surviving children of his half siblings, Benjamin Smith, Hannah Barton and Mary Pilkington. The eight heirs, who received something of the order of £4,000 each, were: Thomas, Mary, and George Pilkington; the Smith children, Benjamin, Newton, and Hannah (Tompson); and the two Barton children, Catherine (Conduitt) and Margaret (Warner).

There remained one further asset, namely Newton's papers and manuscripts. In a complex trade-off of assets within the family they passed to the Conduitts and hence, through their daughter, to the Portsmouth family.

See also Family; Inventory

Hessen, Boris Mikhailovich (1883–1937)

In his 'The social and economic roots of Newton's philosophy' published in *Science at the Crossroads* (1931, pp. 147–212) Hessen presented what readers in the West took to be the official Soviet line on Newton.

Hessen was actually a philosopher rather than a historian of science, and his main work was directed towards the compatibility of Einstein with Marx. He supported A. M. Deborin in claiming there was no conflict between the two theories and that, in fact, a consistent use of dialectical materialism led to relativity theory. In the 1930s such views became increasingly unpopular and Hessen, a victim of the Great Terror, simply disappeared.

With regard to the seventeenth century Hessen argued that it was only then that science ceased to be 'the humble servant of the church' and passed instead into the hands of the bourgeoisie. Newton was not a 'learned scholastic divorced from life', Hessen declared, and produced in evidence the letter to Aston (*C*, I, pp. 9–13). He went further and tried to show that *Principia* was really a survey and resolution of the problems facing the economy of his day. Hence his concern with tides, the pendulum, hydrostatics, hydrodynamics and the motion of bodies through a resisting medium – all problems, Hessen declared, connected with such commercial activities as navigation, ballistics, shipping and mining.

While Hessen's work lacked the historical insight and documentation to prove anything, his proposals were sufficiently intriguing to excite the interest of more formidable scholars. The most important of these was Robert Merton (1938), who assembled a formidable mass of material on the relationship between science and society in the seventeenth century.

Extracts from Hessen can be found in Bassalla (1968, pp. 31–9).

Hieroglyphics and zoolatry

Newton had decided views on a topic much discussed by eighteenth-century thinkers. In *The Original of Monarchies* he argued that hiero-glyphics were, in part, descriptive of the achievements of the kings they named: Ammon had conquered the sheep-rich Libya; he is therefore represented by ram's horns; Osiris had introduced the ox and plough and consequently takes the ox as his symbol.

The 'Birds, Beasts, and Fishes' worshipped by the Egyptians were thus simply symbols of their early kings. Zoolatry, for Newton became one more example of his view that early men had worshipped 'their founders and first kings and that this worship was older than Moses and even as old as the idolatry of Egypt' (Manuel, 1963, p. 219).

Historiola

In his *An Account* (1715) Newton reported that after the death of James Gregory in 1675:

> Mr Collins, at the request of Mr Leibniz and some other of the Academy of Sciences, drew up Extracts of his Letters, and the

Collection is still extant in the Hand Writing of Mr Collins with this
Title; Extracts of Mr Gregory's Letters, to be lent to Mr Leibniz
to peruse, who is desired to return the same to you [Oldenburg].
And that they were sent is affirmed by Mr Collins in his Letter to
Mr David Gregory . . . dated August 11 1676.

(HALL, 1980, p. 276)

The extracts drawn up by Collins, fifty quarto pages of notes, still exist
and are to be found in the library of the Royal Society. The collection
is known to historians of mathematics as the *Historiola*. They were not,
in contradiction to Newton's claim above, sent to Leibniz. Oldenburg
instructed Collins to draw up a six-page summary, since known as the
Abridgment, which was sent to both Leibniz and Tschirnhausen on 26
June 1676. Newton knew of the *Abridgment*, agreed to its transmission,
and even made a couple of alterations of the text.

The *Abridgment*, according to Hall, 'condensed to a few uninformative
lines' Newton's letter to Collins of December 1672 (Hall, 1980, p. 181).
Leibniz, to complicate the story still further, did have access to the
Historiola during his visit to London in 1676. Thus, while Newton's
Account is wrong in detail, it is true in general. The implications to be
drawn from Leibniz's exposure to the two documents is another matter.
The tangent rule described in the 1672 letter to Collins was public
property by 1676 and Leibniz could thus have gained nothing from the
Abridgment about Newton's work which he did not already know. As
to the *Historiola*, this contained details of the work of James Gregory
and could, therefore, in no way have compromised Newton's own
priority.

Extracts from the *Historiola* and the *Abridgment* have been published
in *C*, II, pp. 18–20 and 47–50 respectively.

Hooke, Robert (1635–1703)

Hooke has seldom received a good press. From the beginning, critics
along with friends have emphasised the unattractiveness of his form.
John Aubrey, for example, a close colleague, presented Hooke in his
Brief Lives as 'of middling stature, something crooked, pale faced . . .
his eie full and popping'. Richard Waller, his first biographer in 1705,
was even more brutal, describing him as 'in person but despicable, being
crooked and low of stature, and as he grew older more and more
deformed'. His temper, Waller added, was 'melancholy, mistrustful, and
jealous'. Such a view of Hooke's personality was confirmed by another
member of the RS, Sir Thomas Molyneux, who dismissed him as 'the
most ill-natured, conceited man in the world, hated and despised by
most of the Royal Society, pretending to have all other inventions when

once discovered by their authors to the world' (Lyons, 1944, p. 97). Even Hooke's pitiful sex life has been cruelly exposed by the publication in 1935 of his diary for the years 1672–80. Against such imperfections it must be recorded that Hooke's contributions to optics and his mechanics, along with his technical inventiveness, were surpassed in his day by Newton alone.

Hooke's tendency, identified by Molyneux above, to claim all discoveries for himself, ran all the way through his relationship with Newton. Thus when, on 11 January 1672, details of Newton's newly-invented telescope were recorded in the *Journal Book* of the RS, the announcement was accompanied by the further note: 'The Curator said he did endeavour to make such a telescope himself.' Such comments were mere irritants; on three other occasions, however, Hooke's interventions were substantial and consequential.

In 1665 Hooke published his *Micrographia* (Small Drawings) in which he presented (observation LVIII) his theory of colour. When Newton's own theory was read to the RS on 8 February 1672 Hooke was in the audience and, as Curator, was instructed to 'peruse and consider' it. His *Considerations* were presented to the Society a week later. The observations, he somewhat condescendingly reported, were accurate, as he had 'by many hundreds of trials, found them so'. Newton's conclusions were dismissed as unsubstantiated, with Hooke going on to restate the position of the *Micrographia* that 'light is nothing but a pulse or motion, propagated through an homogeneous, uniform, and transparent medium' (*PLNP*, p. 111). Not all the coloured bodies in the world, he emphasised, could ever be combined to make a white light. Colour was not, he emphasised, 'an original and connate' property of light, but a modification of light as it was reflected and refracted by various bodies. Throughout the paper Hooke spoke in tones of great complacency as if his mere dismissal of an opposing view was sufficient to demonstrate its absurdity.

Hooke was also on hand in 1675 when Newton sent his *An Hypothesis* and *Discourse of Observations* to the RS. The *Journal Book* noted on 16 December Hooke's by-now-expected comment: 'The main of it was contained in his Micrography, which Mr. Newton, in some particulars, had only carried further.' The reference provoked from Newton the reply, in a letter to Oldenburg, that Hooke had taken his hypothesis straight from Descartes. Newton's own material, he insisted, was quite different and was nowhere to be found in the *Micrographia* (*C*, I, p. 406). Some of this material found its way into the *Journal Book* of the RS in the 20 January 1676 entry (Turnor, 1806, pp. 182–3). Soon afterwards Hooke wrote to Newton directly, offering him praise for his 'excellent Disquisitions' and inviting him to enter into a private correspondence on philosophical matters. Others, he feared, were seeking to embroil them in public controversy (*C*, I, pp. 412–13). Newton replied in equally fulsome terms and expressing his willingness to continue the correspondence (*C*, I, p. 416). This is the letter in which Newton made his much quoted claim: 'If I have seen further it is by standing on ye shoulders of giants.' Neither Hooke nor Newton seemed in fact to have made any move to continue the correspondence they had both earlier expressed their eagerness to pursue.

The second clash between the two philosophers began with a letter from Hooke, newly appointed Secretary of the RS on the death of Oldenburg, to Newton on 24 November 1679. Hooke expressed the hope that they would be able to work together and informed Newton, as in the manner of Oldenburg, of items of scientific interest emerging from France. In his reply Newton took up some of the points Hooke had raised and added 'a fancy' of his own on the path taken by a body as it fell to a diurnally rotating earth. Such a body, Newton argued, would fall in 'a spiral line' to the east of its initial position; 'A gross blunder', according to Westfall (RSW, p. 384) and one Hooke, despite his earlier offers of a private correspondence, lost no time in publishing. On the 11 December 1679 he reported to the RS that the curve 'would not be a spiral line, as Mr. Newton seemed to suppose, but an excentrical elliptoid, supposing no resistance' (Koyré, 1965, p. 246). So angry was Newton with the breach of confidence that, he later confessed to Halley, he could 'scarce persuade' himself to answer. He replied none the less, with the correspondence struggling on into 1680.

There was more to the correspondence than the public embarrassment of Newton. In the first letter of 24 November Hooke had asked Newton to comment on his hypothesis that the orbit of a planet was compounded from 'a direct motion by the tangent and an attractive motion towards the central body' (Koyré, 1965, pp. 229–30). It was Newton's introduction to the idea which would later figure prominently in his mature mechanics. Hooke also went on to propose, on 6 January 1680, that the centripetal attraction varied inversely as the square of the distance. What kind of curve, Hooke asked in his final letter of the correspondence on 17 January, would such an attractive force produce? The problem was beyond Hooke. Newton had more success in working out the curve to be an ellipse. Having solved the problem to his own satisfaction he did not bother to pass on any details to Hooke, nor even to work any further on the problem himself. The issue was only taken up once more when Edmond Halley chose to visit Newton in Cambridge in August 1684.

It was this visit which led ultimately to the publication of *Principia* (1687); it also led to the final clash between Newton and Hooke. When Hooke became aware in May 1686 what *Principia* was going to contain, he approached the editor, E. Halley and, with the details of 1679 correspondence in mind, asked that this work should be acknowledged. Newton's response was quite uncontrolled and suggests that he considered Hooke to be seeking not so much an acknowledgment as an abdication of his priority.

Newton's first response was to search his papers and date his own discovery of the inverse square law to pre-1679. Dissatisfied with this, he began to argue that, even granting Hooke's priority, he had merely formulated the law.

> Now is this not very fine? Mathematicians that find out, settle and do all the business must content themselves with being nothing but dry calculators and drudges and another that does nothing but pretend and grasp at all things must carry away all the inventions as well of those that were to follow him as those that went before.

As for Hooke's personal behaviour, Newton continued:

> Should a man who thinks himself knowing, and loves to show it in correcting and instructing others, come to you when you are busy, and . . . press discourses upon you . . . and then make use of it, to boast that he taught you all he spake and oblige you to acknowledge it and cry injury and injustice if you do not, I believe you would think him a man of strange unsociable temper. (C, II, pp. 435–40)

Rather than grant Hooke the acknowledgment he desired, Newton turned to his text and changed a reference to 'Clarissimus Hookius', first to 'the very distinguished Hooke', and eventually to the bare 'Hooke'.

Hooke's own view of his work, 'the greatest Discovery in Nature that ever was since the World's Creation', was recorded by John Aubrey. Aubrey also claimed that *Principia* contained 'some other Theories and experiments of Mr Hooke's without acknowledging from whom he had them'.

After the appearance of *Principia* Newton and Hooke had little to do with each other. As Newton had stopped contributing to the *PT* there was nothing new for Hooke to comment on. Newton seemed to remain content for many years, despite the complaints of several of his colleagues, to pass his manuscripts around his disciples without bothering to publish them. Nothing of substance appeared after *Principia* until the publication of the *Opticks* in 1704. Although there is no hard evidence on the issue, it is widely assumed that Newton's decision to publish this material, long complete, was stimulated by the death of Hooke in 1703. It was also Hooke's death in May 1703 which allowed Newton to run in November for the post of President of the RS. Against these traditional claims it must be pointed out that from the mid-1690s onwards Hooke could have been no threat to anyone. Declining health and increasing poverty had so incapacitated him as to make him indifferent to the work of others. In his last years he was, according to Waller, blind, isolated and 'rendered sordid by penury'. It is difficult to see how such a tragic figure could hold any threats for the powerful figure of Newton.

See also Principia, Origin and production, Hooke in *Principia*

Horsley, Samuel (1733–1806)

Born in London, the son of a clergyman, Horsley was educated at Trinity Hall, Cambridge, before succeeding in 1759 to his father's living of Newington in south London. He later served as Bishop, first of St David's (1788–93) and subsequently of Rochester (1793) and St Asaph (1802–6). He is, however, best known for his five-volume *Isaaci Newton opera quae existant omnia* (1779–85), the closest thing yet to appear to a complete edition of Newton's works. All items appeared in their original language or in the language 'in which it appeared in the latest edition made in the Author's life'.

Included in the five volumes are the following works.

1 London, 1779.
   (a) *Arithmetica universalis.*
   (b) *Tractatus de rationibus primis ultimisque* (Tract on the method of first and last ratios). Newton had never written such a work and the text is taken from the mathematical lemmas, I–XI, with which he began section I of Book I of *Principia*.
   (c) *De analysi.*
   (d) *Excerpta . . . epistolis.* Extracts from letters to Oldenburg, Wallis and others on fluxions and series.
   (e) *De quadratura.*
   (f) *Geometria analytica sive specimena artis analytica.* The first Latin edition of *Methodus fluxionum.*
   (g) *Enumeratio.*
   (h) Horsley also included two of his own works, quite clearly identified as such: *Logistica infinitorum* and *Geometria fluxionum.* They brought from a later editor, R. A. Sampson, the charge of 'ineptitude' for including 'his own lucubrations under the same covers and on a par with Newton's writings' (C, I, p. xv).

2 London, 1779.
   (a) *Principia*, 1726, Books I and II.

3 London, 1782.
   (a) *Principia*, 1726, Book III.
   (b) *De mundi systemate.*
   (c) *Theoria lunae.*
   (d) *Lectiones opticae.*
   (e) *De viribus centralibus* (Concerning Central Forces). Yet another work by Horsley.

4 London, 1782.

  (a) *Opticks.*

  (b) Letters.

     (i) Relating to reflecting telescopes and addressed to Oldenburg and Collins from the period 6 January 1672 to 9 April 1673.

    (ii) Relating to the theory of light and colour and addressed to Oldenburg from the period 6 February 1672 to 18 August 1676.

   (iii) Relating to the excitation of electricity in glasses, taken mainly from the minutes of the RS from the period 9 December 1675 to 13 January 1676.

   (iv) On gravity, addressed to Robert Boyle and dated 28 February 1679.

  (c) *De natura acidorum.*

  (d) *Tabula refractionum* and the *Scala graduum caloris.*

  (e) Letter to Montague dated 30 January 1697 on two problems of Johann Bernoulli.

  (f) *Propositions for determining the motion of a body urged by two central forces.* A work composed by William Jones.

  (g) Four letters to Richard Bentley from the period 10 December 1692 to 25 February 1693.

  (h) *Commercium epistolicum*, plus the *Recensio* and, taken from Raphson's *Historia fluxionum*, letters from Leibniz, Newton, Wallis and Fatio on the priority dispute.

5 London, 1785.

  (a) *Short Chronicle.* Two versions.

  (b) *The Chronology of Ancient Kingdoms Amended.*

  (c) *Observations upon the Prophecies.*

  (d) *Two Notable Corruptions.*

Horsley's work is far from complete. The point remains true even when restricted to texts already in print by 1779, or available to him in manuscript. He failed, for example, to publish Newton's *A Dissertation upon the Sacred Cubit*, available in print since 1737, or *De motu*, widely known to be in manuscript in the library of the RS. Even more surprising was his failure to use any material from the PC. Horsley was, in fact, one of the few scholars allowed access to the collection. Writing in September 1777 he noted: 'I intend to go into Hampshire in about ten days, to visit a repository of manuscripts Sir Isaac Newton left behind him, to which I have with great difficulty procured access. I may perhaps stay there ten days' (*MP*, I, p. xxv). He spent the period 15–26 October 1777 at Hurstbourne Park and, with the aid of W. Mann Godschall, drew up a catalogue of what he had seen. The only use made of the material was to enable Horsley to correct some of the already-published texts and to include in his vol.4 extracts from Newton's correspondence with Oldenburg.

Despite such *lacunae*, the edition is still the most convenient source for Newton's chronological and theological works. Anyone in search of other material from the Newtonian opera is, however, more likely to seek elsewhere. The full *Opera* has been reprinted just once, in a facsimile edition published in 1964 in Stuttgart–Bad Cannstatt.

In addition to his editorial duties, Horsley also entered into the polemical debates of his day in defence of Newton's optics and dynamics. Thus, in his *Difficulties in the Newtonian Theory of Light, considered and removed* (*PT*, 1770, pp. 417–40), he sought to defend Newton's corpuscular theory of light against several detailed objections raised by an ever-growing number of critics.

One such objection was that if light was corpuscular then the sun must be shrinking as a result of the prodigious amount of material it was emitting. Consequently, the force it exercised over the planets would diminish and they would recede. Horsley's response was to argue that particles of light were so small that the sun annually lost no more 5×10^{-15}th of its mass and could therefore survive for many millions of years before its diminishing mass would be felt in the solar system.

See also Castillioneus, Johann; Wave theory of light

Hudde, Jan (1628–1704)

The son of a merchant, Hudde was educated at the University of Leyden where he studied under F. van Schooten. He worked only briefly as a mathematician, for the period 1654–63, after which he devoted himself to politics, serving as Burgomaster of Amsterdam from 1672 onwards.

Hudde is best known for two rules included under his name in van Schooten's edition of the *Géométrie* of Descartes (1659, vol. I). The first rule concerned the solution of equations with double roots, the second described a new and improved method of drawing tangents. Newton read of Hudde's work in the early 1660s in the pages of van Schooten. The rules were soon mastered and extended.

Humour

Did Newton have a sense of humour? There has been a long and consistent tradition holding that Newton was totally humourless. It started with Humphrey Newton, who claimed that in their five years together he had seen Newton laugh only once. This singular occasion arose when an unknown acquaintance to whom Newton had loaned a copy of Euclid asked him what use its study would be to anyone, 'Upon which Sir Isaac was very merry.'

William Whiston confirmed Humphrey's judgment when he declared in 1719 that a particular anonymous work could not have been by Newton for it contained a jest. There is also the story, related by his niece Catherine Barton, that Newton broke off all relations with a close friend, John Vigani, when he told a loose story about a nun. This, however, could merely reflect Newton's prudery.

Against such accounts there stands the testimony of William Stukeley, who admittedly only knew him in later life, but noted none the less that he had often seen Newton merry and that he was 'easily made to smile, if not to laugh' (Stukeley, 1936, p. 57).

There remains, for what it is worth, the testimony of Newton's works and correspondence. Far from dull, and often written with a controlled savagery and vividness of phrase, they do not sparkle with their wit. Newton never went out of his way to search for a pleasing or humorous anecdote. But nor, for that matter, have many other scientists and mathematicians. Figures like George Gamow (1904–68), a modern physicist, who enliven their technical physics with jokes and conundrums are rare indeed and it is not surprising that Newton was not one of them.

Hutton, Charles (1737–1823)

A self-educated son of a colliery worker, Hutton, after working as a private tutor and as the author of mathematical textbooks, was appointed in 1773 to the Professorship of Maths at the Royal Military Academy, Woolwich. He is remembered today for his *Mathematical and Philosophical Dictionary* (1795–6, 2 vols), a work which published Thomas Pellett's 1727 rough catalogue of Newton's papers (vol. II, pp. 155–7).

In 1869 Francis Galton (1822–1911) made the intriguing claim that Newton and Hutton were related. He quoted the engineer C. B. Vignoles (1793–1875), Hutton's grandson: 'The mother of James Hutton and the mother of Dr. Charles Hutton were sisters; and his grandmother and the mother of Sir Isaac Newton were also sisters' (Galton, 1962, p. 273). As Galton pointed out, if the 'his' above is taken to refer to Charles Hutton, then the ninety-five years separating the births of Newton (1642) and Hutton (1737) would have to fit into just one generation. It is just possible if Newton's mother bore him while very young and Hutton's mother and grandmother both conceived in their forties.

Galton proposed, however, that a phrase had been omitted and that the passage should have read: 'The mother of Dr. James Hutton and the mother of Dr. Charles Hutton were sisters [they were children (or ?

grandchildren) of Mr. Hutton;] and his grandmother and the mother of Sir Isaac Newton were also sisters.' The relationship would thus be represented not by Fig. 1 but by Fig. 2. In this way Hutton is no longer a second cousin of Newton, a relationship he would have been likely to recall, but a more distant fourth cousin (great-grandchild of a first cousin).

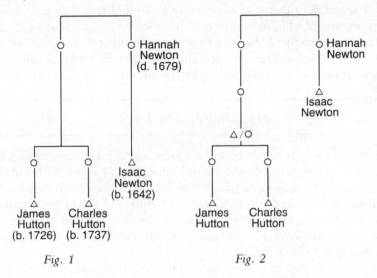

Fig. 1   Fig. 2

Huygens, Christian (1629–95)

Coming from a family of diplomats, and a man of independent means, Huygens was educated at the University of Leyden where he studied under van Schooten. Thereafter he worked at home until 1666, when he joined the staff of the newly-founded Paris *Académie des Sciences*. In 1681, however, because of sickness and the deteriorating relations between Holland and France, Huygens returned home to the Hague. Huygens visited London on a number of occasions and on his final visit in 1689 met Newton at the RS.

Huygens was the leading Continental mathematical physicist of his day. He is often spoken of as the scientist who, in the absence of Newton, would have been most likely to have duplicated his work. Could Huygens, however, have ever formulated the key Newtonian insight of universal attraction? Given his later-expressed reaction to *Principia*, it seems unlikely. In his *De la cause de la pesanteur* (1690, On the cause of gravity), Huygens rejected the notion of universal attraction on the grounds that 'such an attraction is not explainable by any of the principles of Mechanics, or of the rules of motion'. Seeking a mechanical explanation, Huygens elected, under the influence of Descartes, for a system of vortices. They were necessary, Newton notwithstanding, because without them 'the earth would run away from the sun'.

Huygens also dissented, in his *Traité de la lumière* (1690), from Newton's corpuscular view of the nature of light. Like Descartes, he found it difficult to conceive how light particles could collide without affecting each other; nor did he see how they could ever gain the vast speeds required of them. Consequently he sought to develop an undulatory theory capable of accounting for the rectilinearity of light. To this end he introduced the idea of a wave front; it remained obscure, none the less, how such an idea allowed light to move rectilinearly without imposing a similar restriction on sound.

Hypotheses non fingo

One of the most quoted of Newton's judgments, it first appeared in the General *Scholium* added to the second edition of *Principia* (1713). Since the publication of Motte's translation in 1729 it has been commonly translated as 'I do not frame hypotheses' (Cajori, p. 547). In the Marquise du Chastellet's French translation this became 'Je n'imagine pas d'hypothese', while the German translation of Wolfers adopted the form 'Hypothesen erdenke ich nicht.'

Koyré (1965, pp. 35–6) has objected to the translation. Newton could not have denied so clearly that he framed hypotheses for there are several places in his work where they are in fact asserted without any comment or defence. For example, prop. X of Book III of *Principia* is followed by 'Hypothesis I. That the centre of the system of the world is immovable' (Cajori, p. 419). Newton was insisting, Koyré has argued, that he did not 'make use of fictions . . . use false propositions as premmisses or explanations'. The correct word for this procedure is 'feign' not 'frame' and this is exactly the word used by Newton when he expressed himself in English on the same issue in his *Opticks* in query 28: 'Whereas the main business of natural Philosophy is to argue from Phaenomena without feigning Hypotheses.'

Koyré has also pointed out that as a simple matter of Latin, a language Newton knew well, 'fingo' means 'feign' and not 'frame'. Consequently, when the passage quoted above was translated into Latin the verb 'confingere' was used.

Further insight can be gained from early drafts of the General *Scholium*. Newton had first tried 'Hypotheses non sequor' and 'Hypotheses fugio', meaning respectively that he did not strive after hypotheses, that he shunned them. Both were rejected in favour of 'fingo' because, presumably, neither carried the implication that the hypotheses thus adopted were either false or speculative.

I

Iatrophysics

For a brief period at the beginning of the eighteenth century it appeared to many practising physicians that, just as mathematical analysis had succeeded in accurately describing and predicting celestial phenomena, a similar approach would be equally successful with medicine and physiology. One of the earliest to argue in this way was Archibald Pitcairne of Edinburgh and Leyden. Others who followed him, and who were all connected in some way with Newton, were George Cheyne, Richard Mead, John Freind and James Keill.

Some, like Cheyne, spoke as if the facts of physiology and medicine could be derived from the laws of motion directly. Others, however, followed the Newton of the *Opticks* and sought instead to derive the facts of life from the operation of short-range attractive forces on the particles of the body. Nor was there any doubt of the source of their inspiration. All, without exception, would go out of their way to declare their aims and allegiance. A similar movement could be seen in the chemistry of the period.

The history of iatrophysics was brief. It soon became apparent that it suffered from two fatal weaknesses. The first was its failure to deliver any theories of significance or value. There was much talk of motion, of force, of mass, but only at a general level; theorists seemed incapable of linking their general theoretical concepts with any new, interesting and unexpected observations. A good deal of effort was spent in translating the well-known into a new, technical and unfamiliar language. The new language, however, proved to be sterile, incapable of generating fresh problems or solutions.

Its second weakness arose from the growing awareness that it was not as easy as it initially seemed to deduce all celestial phenomena from the laws of motion. A number of recalcitrant phenomena, the orbits of Jupiter and Saturn for example, fitted only roughly into the Newtonian scheme. If Newton's laws and mechanical assumptions could not cope adequately with the planets, it seemed grotesque to suppose that the same laws could be applied with any confidence to the motion of blood through our veins.

Immortal dinner

At 3 p.m. on Sunday 27 December 1817 there began, in the studio of the painter Benjamin Haydon, the so-called 'immortal dinner'. Over the dining table there hung an unfinished picture by Haydon showing Christ's entry into Jerusalem. The faces of Keats, Wordsworth, Hazlitt, Voltaire and Newton could be seen on figures in the crowd.

Present at the dinner were Keats, Wordsworth, Lamb and Thomas Monkhouse. A drunken Lamb began to speak about Voltaire, whose works Wordsworth, in his *Excursion*, had described as 'the dull products of a scoffer's pen'. A toast was drunk to Voltaire. Lamb then turned his attention to Newton. Haydon should not have used him in the painting, Lamb protested; he was 'a Fellow who believed nothing unless it was clear as the three sides of a triangle'. Lamb and Keats then agreed that Newton 'had destroyed all the Poetry of the rainbow by reducing it to a prism', a proposition the poets of the eighteenth century would have found hard to comprehend. As a final toast, 'Newton's health and confusion to mathematics' was drunk.

After dinner they were joined by John Kingston, Deputy Controller of the Stamp Office. 'Don't you think Newton a great genius?' he asked his companions. The name of Newton must have woken the drunken Lamb, who inconsequentially asked Kingston to show him his 'phrenological development' and interrupted all attempts by Kingston to reply with the nursery-rhyme refrain 'Diddle, diddle dumpling, my son John, went to bed with his britches on.'

The account of the dinner suggests something more than the obvious truth that wits as well as oafs can become boorish when drunk. It reveals the profound change in the general attitude to nature and science brought about by the Romantic movement. Lamb and Keats were not alone.

Haydon's painting can be seen in the Philadelphia Art Gallery.

See also Blake, William; Goethe, Johann Wolfgang von; Keats, John; Poetic tradition

---

Index chemicus

Described in the 1888 Cambridge *Catalogue* of the PC as an 'elaborate Subject-index to the literature of alchemy', in its final form it runs to

113 pages and 20,000 words. It was bought by J. M. Keynes and is now part of the Keynes collection in KCC.

Begun in the early 1680s, it listed 115 headings on eight pages. The headings began to collect references in the style of: 'Calcinatio Scala p 82 83 84 1.37. Ludus puer p 128 1.II Ripl p 126. Intr. ap. p 85.' However the *Index* continued to grow until it reached 251 entries and could hold no more. Newton began again with a twenty-four page *Index* but again it expanded until, with 714 entries, it was once more completely full.

In the early 1690s Newton began to reconstruct his *Index* for the last time. It contained 879 separate entries, referred to 150 different alchemical works from which it noted some 5,000 page references. The *Index* remains the most obvious testament to Newton's interest in and command of the alchemical literature. Nothing like it has ever been compiled before or since.

See also Alchemical papers

Inertia

Newton's first law of motion, also known as the law of inertia, states that 'Every body continues in its state of rest, or uniform motion in a right line, unless it is compelled to change that state by forces impressed upon it' (Cajori, p. 13). It is, in many ways, the principle which most clearly marks the great divide between the mechanics of antiquity and modern times. Neither the law, nor the concept, however, originate with Newton.

Classical physicists had taken motion to be a process, something which required the operation of an external agency for both its initiation and its continuation. In contrast, rest was taken to be not a process but a state. Bodies could be in and remain indefinitely in a state of rest without the operation of any external agency whatsoever. One of the first to attempt to break away from this traditional view was Galileo in the early seventeenth century. He did not in fact use the term 'inertia', nor did he succeed in formulating the concept. On the basis of experiments conducted by rolling balls down inclined planes, Galileo argued that once a body had been put into motion, it would continue forever unless it was affected by an external resistance of some kind. Such motion, however, Galileo insisted, was always circular motion. Balls moving horizontally would move in the same plane forever; but, in so doing on the earth, they would inevitably be moving in a plane which is at all points equidistant from the centre, or, in fact, in a circle. Galileo had failed to see that the same principle could be extended to uniform rectilinear motion.

The crucial step was taken by Descartes in his unpublished *Le Monde* of 1629–33, and was first revealed in the *Principia philosophiae* (1644): 'The first law of nature: that everything whatever – so far as depends on it (quantum in se est), – always perseveres in the same state; and thus whatever once moves always continues to move.' Descartes went on to emphasise that the law applied to bodies at rest as well as bodies in motion, to rectilinear but not to circular motion. He also attempted to justify the law by appealing analogically to the facts of experience. We are aware, Descartes argued, that objects do not naturally increase or decrease in bulk unless something is added to or taken away from them; equally, objects do not change their shape unless modified by external agencies. Nor, he insisted, are bodies, whether in motion or at rest, any more likely to suffer a spontaneous change of state.

Newton's first statement of the principle is to be found in the Waste Book and probably dates from the period 1665–6:

> Axiom 1. If a quantity once move it will never rest unlesse hindered by some externall caus.
> Axiom 2. A quantity will always move on in the same streight line (not changing the determination nor celerity of its motion) unlesse some externall cause divert it. (HERIVEL, 1965, p. 141)

The term 'inertia' was first used by Newton in *De gravitatione* where, as definition 8, he defined inertia as 'the internal force of a body' (*vis interna corporis*) which resists change (Halls, p. 148). The word itself was introduced into science by Kepler and referred to the supposed tendency of all bodies to come to rest and stay at rest. The term had been picked up by Jeremiah Horrox and was recorded by him in the *Opera posthuma* (1678), a copy of which had been presented to Newton by Collins.

It is now fairly clear that Newton had taken the concept from Descartes. The key evidence for the claim has been presented by Cohen (1964) and derives from the distinctive phrase 'quantum in se est' used in Descartes' statement of the law. Exactly the same phrase, a far from common Latin expression, and meaning very little, is to be found in definition III of *Principia*: 'The vis insita, or innate force of matter, is a power of resisting by which every body, as much as in it lies (quantum in se est), continues in its present state, whether it be of rest, or of moving uniformly forwards in a right line' (Cajori, p. 2).

Although derived initially from Descartes, Newton went on to transform the principle in a quite radical way. Linguistically he changed the innate force (*vis insita*) of the definition into inertia (*vis inertiae*); conceptually, he made it 'always proportional' to the mass of the body. In this way inertia became something more than an element in some philosophical analysis of motion. By making it proportional to mass, Newton had shown at a stroke how to incorporate the concept into any equations and calculations arising out of the motions of bodies. Further simplification was achieved by the claim (*Principia*, Book II, prop. XXIV, cor. VII) that 'by experiments made with the greatest accuracy, I have always found the quantity of matter in bodies to be proportional to their weight' (Cajori, p. 304).

Inflection

The term widely used in the seventeenth and eighteenth centuries to refer to what is today commonly known as diffraction. Grimaldi, the discoverer of the phenomenon, actually used the term diffraction in his posthumously published *De lumine* (1665). It was left to Robert Hooke in his *Micrographia* (1665) to talk in observation LVII of 'a new Property in the Air . . . named Inflection' and went on to illustrate it by the appearance of the sun and moon seen through a telescope near the horizon when they lose 'that exactly-smooth terminating circular limb which they are observed to have when situated nearer the Zenith'.

Although Newton discussed Grimaldi's work in the *Opticks* (Book III, part I), he chose to use the terminology of Hooke. The very title of the work speaks of the *Opticks* as a 'Treatise on the Reflections, Refractions, Inflections . . .', while in the body of the text reference is invariably made to inflection rather than diffraction. The same terminology was adopted in *Principia* in the *Scholium* to proposition XCVI of Book I. Yet, despite Newton's authority, it was the term diffraction which became part of the general scientific vocabulary.

See also Grimaldi, Francesco

Interference

The supporters of the wave theory of light and of the corpuscular theory of light were both presented with the same problem. How, they were asked, could light beams intersect without destroying each other? How, to use a popular example of the day, could two people ever look each other in the eye? The same answer was given by both parties and consisted of no more than insisting that the particles or waves were so minute as to render collisions extremely unlikely. For this reason Newton failed to recognise interference effects. When he did discuss them, as with his account of thin films in Book II of the *Opticks*, he saw them as special cases of complex patterns of reflection and refraction. Interference, as such, only became apparent to physicists in the late eighteenth century when the term entered the English language with anything like its modern scientific sense.

In this sense interference arises when two or more waves combine in such a way that the trough of one wave meets the crest of another wave, destroying them both; alternatively, two crests could meet and produce an enlarged wave. The first to detect and to see the great importance of such phenomena was Thomas Young.

It was in May 1801, Young reported, while reflecting on 'the beautiful experiments of Newton', that he formulated 'the general law of the interference of light'. It agreed, he found, 'most accurately with the measures recorded in Newton's *Opticks* relative to the colours of transparent substances' (Steffens, 1977, p. 116). The law itself, as stated in 1802, read: 'When two Undulations, from different Origins, coincide . . . in Direction, their joint effect is a Combination of the Motions belonging to each.' More particularly, 'the joint motion may be the sum or difference of the separate motions accordingly as similar or dissimilar parts of the undulations are coincident' (Steffens, 1977, p. 171). Young indicated that his ideas had derived from his earlier work on sound waves and from Newton's account of the tides in the Port of Batshaw (*Principia*, Book III, prop.XXIV).

In this context Young went on to demonstrate two important effects. The first, the two-slit experiment, though not considered to be particularly significant by Young himself, turned out to be one of the most important experiments of the century. Young passed light through two pin-holes in a card on to a screen. What he saw on the screen was alternate layers of light and dark looking exactly as the rippled pattern produced when water waves meet. Heroic steps of the imagination would be called for when Newton's followers attempted to see precisely how light corpuscles could produce such an effect.

Young also proposed an extremely neat and plausible mechanism whereby the colours seen in thin films could be seen as an interference effect. Newton, in his theory of fits, had offered an explanation. The theory, however, proved too speculative and implausible to have more than a limited appeal. In contrast, Young was able to argue that once light was accepted as a wave phenomena, for colour to appear in thin films could be seen as a simple and direct interference effect. For example, in the diagram consider the behaviour of the two light rays,

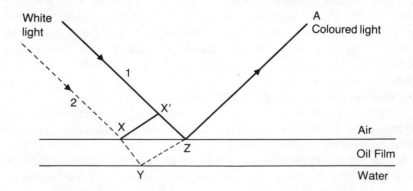

1 and 2, as they strike a thin film of oil on water. At XX' the two rays are in phase. Ray 1 is reflected from the oil surface and passes to the observer at A; ray 2, however, makes the longer journey and when it reaches the observer is likely to be out of phase with 1. For a certain wavelength and distance the two waves will cancel each other. If, for example, the wavelength eliminated is that of green light, the observer will see a purple colour. Appropriate wavelengths and paths will automatically produce the other colours. Young had thus managed to produce effortlessly, from the single assumption of the undulatory nature of light, what Newton had been able to derive in an admittedly artificial and suspect manner.

See also Wave theory of light; Young, Thomas

Interpretation and purpose of prophecy

Newton had thought long about, and wrote much upon, the nature and meaning of divine prophecy. Throughout his numerous writings on the subject he frequently emphasised the following four points.

1 Prophecies were meaningful and meant to be understood. 'If they are never to be understood, to what end did God reveal them?', Newton repeatedly asked (Manuel, 1974, p. 107).

2 Prophecies carried a special authority. Other institutions, synods, councils, bishops and popes were all human; prophecy, by contrast, was divine. Consequently, Newton declared, if an angel were to preach any doctrine incompatible with prophecy, he would be accursed. To reject prophecy was to reject Christianity.

3 The purpose of prophecy, however, was not 'to gratify mens' curiosities by enabling them to foreknow things', but rather to demonstrate the role of providence in the world. For when the modern reader looks back at the things 'predicted many ages before', and sees their fulfilment, he will have been given 'a convincing argument that the world is governed by Providence' (Horsley, V, p. 449).

4 We are all under a strong obligation to consider the prophecies of God, not because this will allow us to foretell the future but because it will enable us 'to discern the signes of the times'. The Jews, Newton argued, rejected the Messiah through their ignorance of the prophecies; we, in turn, through a simlar ignorance, could fail to recognise Antichrist (Manuel, 1974, pp. 108–9).

How then could the prophecies be understood? 'He that would understand a book written in a strange language', Newton began, 'must first learn the language' (McLachlan, 1950, p. 119). It was, indeed, a single language. John had not written in one language, Daniel in another and

Isaiah in a third. Further, it was a clear language, as certain and definite in its signification as 'any vulgar language of any nation whatsoever'. Nor was it a language confined to the prophets of the Bible. Familiarity with it could be found, for example, in the writings of the Chaldean prophets, interpreters of dreams, and other mystical writers of the Near East.

What, then, of the detailed process of interpretation? The key, Newton revealed in Chapter 11 of *Observations of the Prophecies*, was the realisation that the language of prophecy was taken 'from the analogy between the world natural, and an empire or kingdom' (Horsley, V, p. 306). He went on to show how such analogies operated. Beginning with the heavens ('thrones and dignities'), and the sun ('the whole species and race of kings'), he went on to consider meteorological conditions ('tempestuous winds . . . for wars'), animals and vegetables ('a forest for a kingdom'), and more abstract concepts (righteousness by white and clean robes, wickedness by spotted and filthy garments).

Newton was acutely aware that his interpretation, and indeed, any interpretation, could be accused of arbitrariness. Any number of different interpretations were possible; why should support be given to any one particular system? Similar objections, Newton realised, could be raised against *Principia*. Consequently, just as he had in his scientific work laid down rules of philosophical reasoning (*Regulae philosophandi*, *Principia*, Book III), comparable rules were proposed for the interpretation of prophecy (*Rules for Interpreting the Language of Scripture*). Following these rules involved considering all texts, not just a selected few, assigning a single meaning to symbols, respecting the 'prophetique stile', and adopting the most natural and simplest of interpretations. If these rules were followed, Newton claimed, consistent and accurate interpretations could be derived from prophecy. In the same way 'an excellent Artificer', surveying the parts of an engine, 'readily believes that the parts are set right together when he sees them joyn truly with one another notwithstanding that they may be strained into another posture' (Manuel, 1974, p. 98).

Some of the strengths and weaknesses of Newton's approach can be seen in his discussion of John's use of the frog symbol in Revelation 16:13: 'And I saw three unclean spirits like frogs come out of the mouth of the dragon, and out of the mouth of the beast, and out of the mouth of the false prophet.' He began with Artemidorus, for whom frogs, as they appeared in dreams, were identified with impostors. The image was then traced in works of Ovid, Aristophanes, Origen, Grotius, Aristotle, Tzetzes and the sixteenth-century commentator, Benedictus Montanus. All of them, Newton claimed, supported the original interpretation. Who, then, was the impostor John had in mind? At this point Newton's plausible methodology and impeccable scholarship broke down and he turned instead to the 'private imagination' he had dismissed earlier in the *Rules* (Manuel, 1974, p. 116). Impostors were identified with idolators, who were, in turn, inevitably seen by Newton as none other than papists.

It can still come as something of a shock to the young scientist of today when he first discovers that Newton devoted so much of his time to the study of ancient prophecy, especially if he is tempted to equate Newton's labours with the kind of current work he sees pouring off the presses on the prophecies of the *I Ching*, Nostradamus, or any other witless text an enterprising author can get his hands on. Against this natural reaction, two points should be made. Such an interest was of course part of the times and it is naive to suppose Newton could somehow have been free to stand outside the intellectual climate of the period. Also, it should be emphasised that throughout Newton's work on the prophecies he displayed a totally rational, historical and textual approach. The methods and standards he applied to nature in *Principia* were, in his own mind, and with some justification, applied to Daniel and John in his writings on the prophecies. Modern biblical scholars may or may not accept his conclusions; they are hardly like to diverge markedly in their own work from his methodology. If a modern analogue to Newton's work on prophecy is wanted, it can be seen, not in recent attempts to decipher Nostradamus, but in the efforts of a scholar like C. Lévi-Strauss in his *Mythologiques* (1964–71) to understand the mythology of the American Indians.

See also Observations upon the Prophecies

Inventory

De Villamil (1931) noted that Maude's *Wensleydale* had mentioned the taking of an 'inventory' of Newton's estate. He began to search for it. 'By a lucky accident', he reported, 'I found that this inventory had been taken by the order of the Prerogative Court of Canterbury; and on inquiry at Somerset House, I was informed that the Records of the Court were in their keeping . . . on a search being made, the "True and perfect Inventory" was, to my great joy, at last found.' It is a most revealing document listing every item found in Newton's household, every book in his library, and every pound owed or invested by him. The three-storey house in St Martin's St, London, consisted of eight rooms plus a kitchen, wash-house and stable. The items listed in the various rooms and the value assigned them can be briefly summarised as follows.

Fore garret – mathematical instruments, 'chymical £5-0-0
glasses', furniture

Back garret – various beds, curtains, rugs, furniture,   £3-0-0
      1 picture, 6 prints

On the first floor three rooms were listed as:

Workroom – cabinet and writing desk, 6 cases of shelves £22- 4-0
      (Newton's bookcases presumably), 210
      prints (?), 40 articles in Dutch (litho-
      graphs?), 2 small pictures, furniture,
      glassware

Newton's bedroom – 'crimson mohair bed compleat £81- 2-6
      with case curtains of crimson
      Harrateen', crimson mohair
      hangings, 3 pictures, 6 chairs

Mrs Conduitt's bedroom – furniture, curtains, clock   £38-18-6

There were three living rooms on the ground floor:

Fore parlour – tables, chairs, 7 maps, 3 prints   £5-15-0

Back parlour – crimson easy chair, 6 crimson cushions, £8-13-0
      13 India prints, 1 map

Dining room – tables, chairs, 11 pictures and 'a figure £75- 5-6
      cut in ivory of Sir Isaac in a glass frame'

Also mentioned separately are the domestic areas:

Kitchen – spits, plate warmers, gridirons, 4 dozen plates £13- 9-6
Wash house   £2-15-0
Stable – sedan chair   £10-12-0

Other items were entered not by location but by their nature:

Medals – 39 silver, 1 copper, 6 lead, foreign coins, gold £106-14-6
      bars

Wines – wine and cider in bottle   £2-15-0
China – 40 plates, 10 dozen glasses, 6 chocolate cups £5-12-0
Linen – 24 ells of New Holland, 11 pair of old sheets, £11-16-6
      6½ dozen napkins

Plate – 3 silver dishes, 1 coffee pot, 12 knives, forks, £101-15-0
      spoons, 2 silver urinals
      370 ounces at 5s 6d an ounce

Books – 362 folio, 477 quarto, 1,057 octavo together £270- 0-0
      with about 1 cwt of pamphlets and Wast
      books

Manuscripts – *Short Chronicle*, 12 pp in folio   £250- 0-0
      Chronology, 90 pp in folio, 5 chapters
      Observations on Prophecies, 88 pp in folio,
      10 chapters

Also described but not valued were 'manuscripts in a box sealed up at the house of John Conduitt Esq.' and 'several boxes at Sir Isaac Newton's house wherein are contained many loose papers and letters, relating to the office of the Mint . . . two small parcels of papers in the box att the house of John Conduitt Esq.'

There were finally to be considered Newton's more liquid assets listed under ten headings.

£14,000 principal stock of the Bank of England valued at 126 2/3%, plus a 3% dividend due on Lady Day, 1727	£18,130- 0-0
£5,000 Capital Stock in the South Seas Company at 104	£5,200- 0-0
£5,000 South Sea annuities at 97½ with a 2½% dividend due	£5,000- 0-0
Cash with Conduitt	£1,711- 0-1
Salary due from Mint	£117-11-2
Salary as Assay Master	£15- 0-0
1s 10d per lb for 3,315 lb weight of gold	£303-17-6
3¼d per lb for 243 lb weight of silver	£3- 5-9¾
Cash found in the Scruters	£78- 9-3¼
Promissory notes from various friends and relatives	£201- 4-0
TOTAL	£31,821-16-10

To this sum there should be added the amounts estimated as the values of the books, manuscripts and contents of the house:

Books	£270- 0-0
Manuscripts	£250- 0-0
House contents	£520- 6-6
FINAL TOTAL	£32,862- 3-4

See also Finances; Library; Residence

Inverse square law

In general terms an inverse square law indicates the manner in which a force, such as gravity or magnetism, varies with distance. Thus, to say that the force attracting A to B varies as $1/r^2$ indicates that the greater the distance between A and B, the weaker the force; the closer the distance, the stronger the force. More precisely, the force will vary as the *square* of the distance. Consequently, if C and D are two and three times further than A from B, the force attracting them to B will be a quarter and a ninth as strong, respectively, as the force between A and B. It could also be said that the force between A and B is four times stronger than the force between C and B and nine times stronger than the force between D and B.

Newton maintained that gravity obeyed an inverse square law. He also maintained, however, that more than distance was involved. Gravity also varied as the product of the masses of the bodies involved. Thus, all other things being equal, if A was twice as massive as B it would exercise twice the gravitational force of B, and if it was three times as massive its gravitational potency would have also increased threefold. Given the above, it is possible to describe the gravitational attraction between any two bodies A and B as being proportional to $m'm''/r^2$, where m' and m'' represent the masses of A and B, respectively, and r is the distance between them. Newton, in fact, derived the inverse square law from Kepler's third law and the definition of centripetal force in the following manner. Given:

1 Kepler's third law that for every planet:

$$r^3/T^2 = k$$

where r is the distance from the sun, T the time of the orbital period, k a constant;

2 the definition of centripetal force as v^2/r where v is the velocity of the orbiting body, and r the radius of the orbit;

it is a relatively easy matter to derive the inverse square law. Thus, given a body in a circular orbit around the sun, its centripetal force will be:

3 v^2/r. But velocity is distance over time (T). In this case, distance is simply the circumference of the circle ($2\pi r$). Making the appropriate substitutions in v yields:

4

$$\left(\frac{2\pi r}{T}\right)^2 \frac{1}{r} = \frac{4\pi^2 r^2}{T^2} \times \frac{1}{r}$$

Multiplying the left hand of the product by r/r yields:

5

$$\frac{4\pi^2 r^3}{T^2 r} \times \frac{1}{r} = 4\pi^2 \times \frac{r^3}{T^2} \times \frac{1}{r^2}$$

But, by 1 above, $r^3/T^2 = k$. 5 can therefore be rewritten as:

6

$$4\pi^2 k \times \frac{1}{r^2}$$

But 6 is merely an expanded version of the definition of centripetal force (v^2/r), and as the expression $4\pi^2 k$ in 6 above contains only constant terms, the centripetal force felt by a body in circular orbit will vary inversely as the square of the distance ($1/r^2$).

The inverse square law was an important step along the long road which would eventually lead Newton to the principle of universal gravitation. Newton seems to have been aware of the law in the late 1660s. As he recalled some fifty years later of the period 1665–6, 'I deduced that the forces which keep the Planets in their Orbs must [be] reciprocally as the squares of their distances from the centers about which they reveolve.'

The law itself first appeared in writing in an untitled manuscript first published by Hall (1957) and later reprinted by Herivel (1965, pp. 192–8) under the title *On Circular Motion*. There he concluded:

> Since in the primary planets the cubes of their distances from the Sun are reciprocally as the squares of the number of revolutions in a given time (Kepler's third law): the endeavours of receding from the Sun will be reciprocally as the squares of the distances from the Sun. (HERIVEL, 1965, p. 197)

Herivel assigns the manuscript a date of 1665–6.

Such an insight, however, central though it may be, marked only the beginning of Newtonian mechanics. Much remained to be done before Newton could demonstrate in Book I, props XI–XIII of *Principia* (1687) that the motion of bodies in eccentric conic sections is governed by a law of centripetal force that varies inversely as the square of the distance.

Irenicum: or ecclesiastical polity tending towards peace

The treatise is known in seven autograph drafts and is to be found in KCC as Keynes MS 3. Brewster (vol. I, pp. 407–11) published a version divided into twenty 'theses'. A second version was included in McLachlan (1950, pp. 28–43) but was confusingly composed of some four drafts; the result was, according to Westfall (RSW, p. 820), the selection 'of the least typical parts'.

The thesis of the *Irenicum* is a radical one. All nations originally subscribed to a common religion. It consisted of two precepts: love God with all your might; and love your neighbour as yourself. Such beliefs Newton traced to the 'sons of Noah'. They descended through Abraham, Isaac, Jacob and Moses to the Israelis and thereafter were disseminated to other nations by such figures as Pythagoras, Confucius, Socrates and Cicero. A scheme so simple must inevitably become corrupted. Later prophets like Christ came not to add to the original precepts but to recall a forgetful people to the already-established truths.

It followed from Newton's scheme that those who sought to add further items of belief, like the Trinitarians of the fourth century, were in fact corrupting an already-established religion. The basis of this religion was reason, not revelation. It was also available to and had been widely accepted by the bulk of mankind – by, in fact, 'the sons of Noah'.

It is hardly surprising that none of the eighteenth-century scholars who examined the *Irenicum* was inclined to advise on its publication.

Isaac Newton Telescope

At the tercentenary celebrations of Newton's birth, held by the Royal Society somewhat belatedly in 1946, the President announced approval from the Treasury for the construction of a large new telescope. The cost was estimated at £250,000. It was decided to site the telescope at Herstmonceaux Castle, Eastbourne, E. Sussex, under the control of the Royal Greenwich Observatory. The 2.5-metre (98 in) telescope was opened by the Queen in 1967. By this time astronomers were less interested in large, bright stars than in the newly-discovered quasars and distant, faint galaxies. The skies of Sussex and the neighbouring towns made Herstmonceaux of little use for these purposes. Consequently, at a cost of £10,000,000, the telescope was closed down and removed to the 2,400-metre peak Roque de los Muchachos, on the island of La Palma in the Canaries. In place of the original 98-inch pyrex mirror a slightly larger 100-inch (2.54 metre) mirror made from low-expansion zerodur was substituted. New light was obtained in February 1984 and regular observing began in May of that year.

J

Jacquier, Francis (1711–88)

A friar of the order of Minims, Jacquier served as Professor of Physics at Rome from 1746, apart from a period in the 1760s spent in Parma with Condilliac supervising the education of the infant Don Ferdinand. As a scientist he worked on the lunar orbit and published a textbook on the integral calculus. He remains best known, however, as the editor with Le Seur of the inappropriately-named Jesuit edition of *Principia* (1739–42, 3 vols). Reissued five times, the Jesuit edition so dominated the market that no new Latin edition of *Principia* appeared between the publication of the third edition in 1726 and the appearance of the *variorum* edition of Koyré and Cohen in 1972 (Newton, 1972).

See also Principia, Editions

Jervas, Charles (*c*.1675–1739)

An Irish painter and a pupil of Kneller, whom he succeeded as Principal Portrait Painter to the King in 1723. His portrait of Swift hangs in the National Portrait Gallery.

In 1703 he completed a portrait of Newton. It carries the inscription 'D.Isaacus Newton Eques, Reg.Societatis Praes. Anº 1703.' It could well have been commissioned to portray the newly-elected President of the Royal Society. He is shown sitting, three-quarter length, bewigged and very formally dressed – 'the reigning monarch of the philosophic world' (RSW, p. 682).

In 1717 Newton presented the portrait to the Royal Society, where it hangs today in the Council Room. It presumably indicates how Newton was happy to see himself; but if so, why the fourteen-year delay between the completion of the portrait and its presentation in 1717?

See also Portraits, medals, busts and statues

Jones, William (1675–1749)

The son of a small Welsh farmer, Jones, under the patronage of a local landowner, was first employed in the counting house of a London merchant. Like so many young men with scientific pretensions in the circle around Newton, he earned his living teaching mathematics. One of his pupils later became the Earl of Macclesfield and in due course took Jones upon his staff at Shirburn Castle, Oxfordshire.

In 1708 Jones somehow obtained the bulk of the papers and correspondence of John Collins. Amongst them was Collins's transcription of Newton's *De analysi* and other of his mathematical papers. By this time Jones was known to Newton. His attention had been drawn to Jones through the publication of his *Synopsis palmariorum matheseos* (1706), a work which, incidentally, introduced the symbol π to refer to the ratio between the circumference and the diameter of a circle. Jones was keen to publish the papers of Newton he had acquired. For once this suggestion suited Newton. With the priority dispute showing no signs of dying away, it was clearly to Newton's advantage to have some of his earlier mathematical writings in print for all to see the justice of his claim. Consequently Newton allowed Jones to go ahead and publish the *Analysis per quantitatum series* (1711), the first major collection of his mathematical papers. Jones dutifully recorded in the introduction his opinion, undoubtedly suggested by Newton, that the bulk of the results had been established by 1665 and 1666. Jones further aided Newton in his priority dispute with Leibniz by serving on the committee set up by the Royal Society in 1711 to determine to whom the honour of the invention of the calculus really belonged. Inevitably, Jones agreed with his colleagues that Newton's work was far the earlier.

The papers of Collins collected by Jones have remained at Shirburn Castle in the hands of the Macclesfield family, where they have been, with the exception of S. P. Rigaud in the nineteenth century, inaccessible to scholars.

In 1730 Jones was approached by Thomas Birch for details of Newton's mathematical works for inclusion of a biographical sketch of Newton he was preparing for the *General Dictionary*. Jones actually produced a twenty-four-page tract covering Newton's work from 1663 to 1686, which contained, in Whiteside's phrase (*MP*, VIII, p. xxii), 'lengthy verbatim extracts' from several early manuscripts. The document, 'a loose compilation of half-understood excerpts' (*MP*, VIII, p. xxiii), has never been published. It somehow found its way into the PC and is today in the ULC.

K

Keats, John (1795–1821)

The poet Keats was present at the so-called immortal dinner held by Benjamin Haydon in 1817. With Charles Lamb, he drank a toast to 'Newton's health and the confusion of mathematics'.

Shortly afterwards Keats wrote *Lamia* (1819). It contains the famous lines in which he tried to articulate as vividly and clearly as possible the precise objection of the Romantic poets to the Newtonian description of nature.

> There was an awful rainbow in heaven:
> We know her woof, her texture; she is given
> In the dull catalogue of common things.
> Philosophy will clip an Angel's wings,
> Conquer all mysteries by rule and line,
> Empty the haunted air, and gnomed mine –
> Unweave a rainbow.　　　　　　　　(*Lamia* II, lines 231–7)

See also Poetic tradition

Keill, James (1673–1719)

The brother of John Keill, he was educated at Paris and Leyden. Keill set up his medical practice in Northampton, from which base he was able to give anatomy classes at both Oxford and Cambridge.

In his *Animal Secretions* (1708) he sought to deploy the short-range attractive forces described by Newton in his *Opticks* to problems in physiology. How could such secretions as gall, bile and sperm arise from the blood, Keill asked. Arguing that 'the attractive force varies, according as the particles are cones, cylinders, cubes, or spheres', he went on to conclude that 'a few different sorts of particles variously combined, will produce great variety of fluids'.

Keill, John (1671–1721)

Born in Edinburgh, the brother of James Keill and a pupil of David Gregory, Keill accompanied Gregory to Oxford in 1694 where, as a lecturer in experimental philosophy, he gave some of the earliest lectures and demonstrations of the new Newtonian science ever delivered at a British university. The lectures were published in 1701 as *Introductio ad veram physicam* (Introduction to the True Physics), probably the first textbook of Newtonian physics ever to appear. It was translated into English in 1720 and was joined by a similar work, *Introductio ad veram astronomiam* (1718).

Having failed to succeed Gregory in 1708, Keill accepted the post of Treasurer to the Palatines and was thus responsible for the administration of the fund subscribed to aid the Palatine refugees. He also served briefly as, according to Kahn (1966, p. 169), a 'totally incompetent' cryptographer to Queen Anne. In 1712, however, Gregory's old Oxford chair once more fell vacant and this time, with the support of Newton, Keill was elected.

When and how Keill met Newton is not known. The introduction was more than likely made through David Gregory. Thereafter, until his death in 1721, Keill was Newton's man, ever willing to do his bidding. In the dispute with Leibniz over the invention of the calculus, Keill was Newton's first line of defence and attack. Unwilling, as ever, to engage his critics directly, Newton chose the pen and name of Keill to defend his own position and to attack his enemies. Keill would be provided with drafts, letters and manuscripts to aid him in his work. The results would be edited by Newton and, depending on the state of the dispute, either hardened or softened. As an example of Keill's malleability there is his note to Newton in May 1714: 'I leave my whole paper to You and Dr Halley to change or take away what you please' (*C*, VI, p. 142); or, in October 1715: 'I here send you the first part wch I intirely submitt to your Judgement to change and alter as you think fitt, If you doe not like the Title I desire you may give it another' (*C*, VI, p. 245).

Keill was thus deeply involved in the priority dispute. His main contributions include the following items.

1 *De legibus virium centripetarum* (*PT*, 1708; actually appeared 1710; Concerning the Laws of Centripetal Force). Keill's paper was probably written without Newton's knowledge. It contained the following provocative statement: 'All these laws followed from the very celebrated arithmetic of fluxions which, without any doubt,

Dr Newton invented first . . . yet the same arithmetic afterwards under a changed name was published by Dr Leibniz in the *AE.*' It brought complaints from Leibniz to the RS.

2 *Lettre de Londres* (*JL*, 1713). An anonymous account by Keill of the invention of the calculus taken from the *CE*. Leibniz replied later in the year in the *JL* with his *Remarques.*

3 *Réponse de M.Keill . . . aux auteurs des Remarques* (*JL*, 1714; Mr Keill's Reply to the Authors of the Remarks). Keill broadened his attack to cover Leibniz's dynamical essay, *Tentamen* (1689). 'I cannot bring myself to make a reply to that crude man ("homo impolito") Keill' Leibniz confessed to Wolf (*C*, VI, p. 211).

4 *Defense du Chevalier Newton par M.Keill contre M.Bernoully* (*JL*, 1716; Keill's Defence of Newton against Bernoulli). A reply to Bernoulli's charge that Newton had not really solved the inverse problem of central forces.

5 *Lettre à Bernoulli* (*JL*, 1720; Letter to Bernoulli). The letter was actually composed in 1716 and constituted Newton's reply to the *Epistola pro eminente mathematico* of Bernoulli. Keill sent the letter to Newton in 1716. He held on to it for two years before, during a resurgence of the dispute, releasing it in the *JL.*.

6 In October 1718 Keill posed to Bernoulli a challenge problem. It asked for 'the curve a Projectile describes in the air in the most simple supposition of gravity and the density of the medium being both uniform: but the resistance in duplicate proportion of the velocity' (*C*, VII, p. 11). Bernoulli had little difficulty in solving the problem, in the course of which he referred to 'A certain individual of the Scottish race who has become no less notorious among his own people for his immorality than odious everywhere to foreigners.' Keill complained in a report read to the RS (1720) against such 'scurrilous language' and called upon the Society 'to shew their Dislike of such foul proceedings' (*C*, VII, p. 13). No action was taken.

Keill's participation in the dispute did nothing to enhance his reputation. Described in his day as 'Newton's toady', later scholars have been no more respectful. Some have seen in the 'crude and abrasive' Keill a figure with the will and motive to prolong the dispute. As long as Newton was under attack from foreign mathematicians, there would be a role for Keill to play; whenever Newton seemed to tire of the exercise, Keill would be on hand to draw his attention to some particularly biting jibe. Thus in May 1711 he was to be found drawing Newton's attention to 'pag 39' of the 'Acta Lipsiae' where it was suggested by Leibniz that Newton could not deal with the foci of second-order and higher curves (*C*, V, p. 115). Later he could be seen informing Newton how amazed he was at the 'the impudence of Bernoulli' and, a little later, that he should be made 'to beg your pardon publickly' for such impudence (*C*, VI, pp. 385, 447). With such an adviser and colleague it is not surprising that Newton found himself embroiled in the dispute until 1722, the year after Keill's death.

See also Bernoulli, Johann; Priority dispute

Kent, William (1685–1748)

Born in Yorkshire, Kent began his career as an apprentice coach painter in Hull. While studying painting in Rome he met Lord Burlington, under whose patronage he became one of the most important painters, architects and landscape gardeners of his day. Together they worked on Burlington's Chiswick Villa and the Earl of Leicester's Holkham Hall in Norfolk. It was in fact largely due to their enthusiasm that Palladianism became such a force in British eighteenth-century architecture.

But Kent could also work in a more baroque tradition, as can be seen in the sarcophagus he designed for Newton's tomb. Sculpted by M. Rysbrack under the supervision of John Conduitt, it was completed by 1731 and can still be seen in the nave of Westminster Abbey, to the left of the pulpit.

See also Public monuments

Kepler, Johann (1571–1630) and Kepler's laws

Kepler's life is readily available in the vivid account presented in Arthur Koestler's *The Sleepwalkers* (1959). To Newton he was known as the author of the following three basic laws of planetary motion.

1 Planets move around the sun in ellipses, with the sun located in one focus of the ellipse (elliptical law).

2 The radius vector joining each planet to the sun sweeps out equal areas in equal times (the area law).

3 There is a constant ratio between the square of a planet's orbital period and the cube of its solar distance (harmonic law).

In the first law Kepler had described the shape of an orbit; the second law accounted for the varying speed of a planet, the manner in which it moved quickest at perihelion and slowest at aphelion; and the third law related the size of the orbit to the orbital period.

How did Newton come to know the laws? The only work of Kepler he owned was the optical text *Dioptrice* contained in Gassendi's *Institutio astronomica* (1682). It is thus very likely that Newton had no direct access to Kepler's astronomical works. He certainly never quoted from them.

The first law was widely acknowledged by Newton's day and was therefore to be found in almost any astronomical text he cared to consult. Prop.XI of *Principia* took the first law much further by asking: 'If a body revolve in an ellipse; it is required to find the law of centripetal force tending to the focus of the ellipse.' Newton answered that 'the centripetal force is . . . inversely as the square of the distance' (Cajori, pp. 56–7).

The harmonic law was probably derived from Thomas Streete's *Astronomia carolina* (1661, Caroline Astronomy), a work from which Newton quoted in his *Philosophical Notebook*. The law was made use of in Book III of *Principia*. Newton first demonstrated in some detail that the law was observed by the satellites of Jupiter (Phen.I) and Saturn (Phen.II), by the five planets (Phen.III) and by the earth (Phen.IV). He also commented in Phenomena IV that: 'This proportion, first observed by Kepler, is now received by all astronomers.' (Cajori, p. 404). Newton then went on to demonstrate that the law was observed by the satellites of Jupiter (phen.I) and Saturn (phen.II), by the five planets (phen.III), and by the earth (phen.IV).

The area, or second law, was less well-known and more troublesome. Despite its formulation by Kepler in 1609, the law appears not to have been recorded in an English work before it was referred to by John Wallis in his *Tractatus duo* (1659). There is no reference to the law, for example, in the works of Streete. He could, however, have obtained the law from Nicolaus Mercator's *Institutionum astronomicarum* (1676), a work he possessed and which contains 'extensive astronomical notes by Newton' (Harrison, 1978, p. 191).

Despite the use made of Kepler's work, he received little acknowledgment from Newton. Book I of *Principia* ignores him completely. Book II went further and in the concluding *Scholium* to prop.LIII attributed the elliptical law to Copernicus (Cajori, p. 395)! Why Newton should make such a perverse attribution, one he knew to be false, remains a mystery. The earlier text, *De motu*, had correctly spoken of Kepler as the discoverer of both elliptical and the area laws. The reader of *Principia*, however, would have seen him only as the author of the harmonic law.

Newton also sought to distance himself from Kepler's account of inertia. In his own copy of *Principia* he had noted, as if for inclusion in a later edition: 'I do not mean the Keplerian force of inertia by which bodies incline to rest, but a force of remaining in the same state of rest or motion' (1971, p. 27). It was not, however, incorporated in later editions of *Principia*.

See also Boulliau, Ismael; Ellipses and elliptical orbits

Kersey, John (1616–77)

A self-taught mathematician, born near Banbury, he taught maths in London and was well-known to John Collins. In 1673 he published an *Algebra* in two volumes. 'There never was a duller book writ; and . . . there was never a man who pretended to write of Algebra that understood the design of it less', judged John Craig to Bentley. A later and less-biased scholar commented that it was 'too elaborate to meet with great success' (Smith, 1951, vol. I, p. 414). Nevertheless, its appearance made the printers of London and Cambridge most reluctant to risk publishing a comparable text like Newton's *Kinckhuysen*.

See also Observations on Kinckhuysen

Keynes, John Maynard (1883–1946)

Keynes won fame, and is still largely remembered, by his work in economics, both theoretical and practical. As the author of *The General Theory of Employment, Interest and Money* (1936) he was responsible for the Keynesian policies followed by much of the Western world for the last fifty years, while, at Bretton Woods shortly before his death, he did much to establish the institutions and framework within which the contemporary economy developed. If the world owes much to Keynes, he in turn owed much to Cambridge. The son of a don, he was educated at King's College and remained connected with the college, whether as student, Fellow or bursar, for the rest of his adult life.

As a young man in Cambridge he was a regular customer of the stall of Gustave David, doyen of Cambridge booksellers. In 1905 David bought for 4d from a barrow in London a copy of the third edition of *Principia* with the book-plate of the Duke of Sussex. He sold it to Keynes for 4s 0d. It was the start of what would eventually become one of the finest collection of the works of Newton ever held by an individual. He later acquired a further copy of the third edition, Fontenelle's copy, 'ex dono auctoris'. Keynes also owned two copies of the first edition. One copy, the two-line imprint, had previously belonged to Martin Folkes and Sir Robert Peel; the other copy, an uncut Smith belonging to J. L. E. Dreyer, was bought in 1936 for £85. He also owned two copies of the second edition.

The most important part of the Keynes collection, however, lay in its manuscript holdings. In 1936 he accompanied his brother, the noted bibliographer and surgeon, Geoffrey Keynes, to the Sotheby sale of the Portsmouth Collection of Newton's books and papers. He bought thirty-eight of the 329 lots. More important, he later reported:

Disturbed by the impiety, I managed gradually to re-assemble about half of them, including nearly the whole of the biographical portion, that is, the 'Conduitt papers', in order to bring them to Cambridge where I hope they will never leave. The greater part of the rest were snatched out of my reach by a syndicate which hoped to sell them at high prices, probably in America, on the occasion of the recent tercentenary. (KEYNES, 1947, p. 34)

At a cost of £3,000 and the pursuit of numerous dealers, Keynes managed to increase his holdings of the Portsmouth Collection from thirty-eight to 130 lots.

Included in the Keynes collection are the following items.

Alchemy – although Keynes bought only seven items at the sale he managed eventually to collect fifty-seven out of the original 120 lots on offer. A full list of his holdings is provided in Dobbs (1975, Appendix A).

Correspondence – sixty-nine letters addressed to Newton, eleven autograph drafts and eighty-four transcripts not in Newton's hand.

Theology – eleven lots, including the *Morals of Athanasius*.

Chronology – *The Original of Monarchies*.

Personal – various lots on Newton and Cambridge University. Of the Conduitt papers on offer Keynes managed to obtain eight of the nine lots.

Keynes left the entire collection to King's College, Cambridge, where it can be seen today.

Keynes was no mere collector. Despite failing health and numerous official duties, Keynes made a careful study of his collection and, incidentally, became one of the first scholars to gain an insight into the full range of Newton's intellect and interests. His views were expressed in a paper delivered posthumously by his brother at the Royal Society tercentenary celebrations in 1947 under the title, 'Newton, the man'. The Newton Keynes spoke of was an unfamiliar figure. In Keynes's oft-quoted description he was:

Not the first of the age of Reason. He was the last of the magicians . . . the last great mind which looked out on the visible and intellectual world with the same eyes as those who began to build our intellectual inheritance rather less than 10,000 years ago. Isaac Newton . . . was the last wonder-child to whom the Magi could do sincere and appropriate homage. (KEYNES, 1947, p. 27)

Kinckhuysen, Gerard

A Belgian mathematician of the mid-seventeenth century who published a work in Dutch, *Der Grondt der Meet-kunst* (1660, The Foundations of

Geometry). As it proved too difficult for most readers, he provided a companion and introductory volume with his *Algebra* (1661). It was this work that John Collins arranged to have translated into Latin by Nicolaus Mercator in 1669 and then tried, with less success, to publish it with annotations and additions by Newton. The result, *Observations on Kinckhuysen*, was eventually published 300 years later in *MP*, II, pp. 295–447.

Kit-Kat Club

The Kit-Kat was a Whig club numbering amongst its members Steele, Addison, Congreve and Vanbrugh. It met in the house of Christopher Cate, a pastry cook famous for his mutton pies, appropriately named Kit-cats, in Shire Lane near Temple Bar. The portraits of all forty-two members were painted by Kneller in a uniform series which now hang in the National Portrait Gallery.

It was a custom of the Club to engrave the name of a lady, known for her beauty and wit, on a toasting glass. In 1703, Charles Montague, also a member, had the name of Catherine Barton inscribed on one of the club's glasses. Part of the verse reads:

> Beauty and Wit strove each, in vain,
> To vanquish Bacchus and his Train;
> But Barton with successful Charms
> From both their Quivers drew her Arms;
> The roving God his Sway resigns,
> And awfully submits his vines.

See also Barton, Catherine; Montague, Charles

Kneller, Sir Godfrey (1646–1723)

Born in Lübeck, Kneller studied painting in Amsterdam under F. Bol, a pupil of Rembrandt. He travelled in Italy before settling in England in 1676. Kneller soon established himself as the leading portrait painter of his day and in 1688 he was appointed Principal Painter to the Court. Knighted in 1692, he became in 1715 the first painter to receive a baronetcy. Included amongst the 6,000 portraits attributed to him are ones of Charles II, James II, William and Mary, George I, Louis XIV, Peter the Great and Charles VI of Spain. He is, perhaps, better known for his forty-two portraits of the Kit Kat club hanging in the National Portrait Gallery.

Kneller must have painted Newton five times at least. Four portraits survive, with a wigged portrait reported by Stukeley to have been painted in Newton's old age apparently missing. Stukeley has also left an account of a 1720 sitting given by Newton to Kneller, at which he was an eager witness.

> Both Sr.Isaac & Sr.Godfry desired me to be present at all the sittings. It was no little entertainment to hear the discourse that passed between these two first of men in this way. Tho it was Sr.Isaacs temper to say little, yet it was one of Sr.Godfrys arts to keep up a perpetual discourse, to preserve the lines and spirit of a face. (C, VII, p. 106)

It was on this occasion that, when asked if he would allow Kneller to paint him in profile, Newton replied, 'What . . . would you make a medal of me', and refused the request.

The four surviving portraits consist of the following.

1 1689 – the earliest known portrait of Newton. It was described in the late-nineteenth century as hanging in the hall of Hurstbourne Park, home of the Portsmouth family, with whom it remains. It portrays Newton with his own shoulder-length grey hair, wearing a white open-neck shirt covered by an academic gown. Standing out sharply from the darkness of his gown and the background are long, tense, spidery fingers emerging from his right sleeve and the delicately-shaped face staring ahead as if in concentration. He looks much younger than his forty-seven years.

   In many ways the most impressive of all the Newton portraits, it has inevitably been widely reproduced and can be seen in Westfall (RSW, p. 482) and Manuel (1980, p. 172).

   It was also used as the frontispiece to the first volume of the *Correspondence*.

   Why Newton commissioned the work is unknown. It would not have been a cheap exercise. The result must have pleased him, though, for he retained the painting throughout his life. A second, less well-known version, is in the Royal Collection at Kensington Palace.

2 1702 – described as once hanging in the billiard room at Hurstbourne Park, it was auctioned at the Sotheby sale in 1936. Bought by Peter Rosenbach for £800, it was presented to the National Portrait Gallery where it hangs today. It shows a half-length Newton in a shoulder-length wig. Once more he is gowned and in an open-necked shirt. It is a little more formal than the Kneller of 1689, but still quite different in style from the lordly portraits to come. Once more he looks much younger than his sixty years, although his face has become much heavier, with signs of a double chin (RSW, p. 578; Manuel, 1980, p. 239).

3 1720 – in 1715, through the Abbé Conti and de Moivre, Pierre

Varignon had asked for a portrait of Newton. Sympathetic to the request, Newton arranged in 1720, after a fair delay, to sit once more for Kneller. The result is very much Newton the nobleman, shown in full wig, holding a pair of gloves and wearing a sword.

On receiving the portrait Varignon commented that the seventy-six-year-old Newton seemed no older than fifty and that his appearance was 'frais & vigoureux'. Present with him at the time was Brook Taylor who told him that it was a good resemblance. In a letter to Newton Varignon described his immediate and extravagant response.

> I tore open the parcel at once, wanting so much to look at you, and when the canvas had been unrolled your most high and lofty intellect together with the dignity of your aspect seemed to me as if it were alive in the countenance and forehead and eyes of this likeness . . . A few days afterwords Mr Taylor came to see me . . . who assured me . . . that it was certainly most like you, which delighted and still delights me. (C, VII, p. 105)

Varignon continued in much the same strain for a further 300 words, concluding with profuse gratitude for the news he had just received from de Moivre that Newton would in return accept a portrait of Varignon.

The original Kneller of 1720 was acquired by Lord Egremont some time in the eighteenth century and now hangs at Petworth House, Sussex. The portrait is used as the frontispiece of vol. VII of the *Correspondence*; it can also be seen in Westfall (RSW, p. 786).

4 1723 – a half-length portrait showing a seated Newton with his own thinning and unruly hair. One of the few portraits in which Newton is shown looking an old man. It is one of two commissioned by Conduitt, the other being lost. It remains the property of the Portsmouth Estate and can be seen in Westfall (RSW, p. 855).

Knighthood

On 16 April 1705 Queen Anne knighted Newton in the Master's Lodge at Trinity College, Cambridge. As the brother of Lord Halifax, a patron of Newton, was also knighted on the same occasion, the source of the honour is not hard to find. Indeed, it has been suggested that the award was so timed to help Newton's electoral chances in the 1705 Parliamentary elections. It was certainly an honour which brought Newton considerable satisfaction. He lost no time in tracing his ancestry at the College of Heralds.

Whether knighted for political service, for his work at the Mint or, even, for his scientific achievements, Newton thus became the first scientist to be knighted, however indirectly, for his scientific attainments. It proved no precedent for it was not until 1781 that another scientist, Joseph Banks, would be equally honoured. Nor was this repeated before 1812, when Humphrey Davy was knighted. The major change came in the 1830s when, through the influence of Lord Brougham, the government began regularly to recognise and formally honour the leading scientists of the day. Another fifty years had to elapse, however, before peerages were awarded to Kelvin and Playfair in 1892.

The official report of the ceremony, published in the *London Gazette*, number 4116, is reprinted in *C*, IV, p. 444.

Koyré, Alexandre (1892–1964)

Born in Russia, Koyré studied classics in Rostov, mathematics and physics at Göttingen and philosophy at the Sorbonne. In France he taught for most of his career at the *École pratique des hautes études* while, in later life, also holding an appointment at the Institute of Advanced Studies, Princeton.

Koyré's main field of study was the physics and astronomy of the seventeenth century. Beginning with the now classic work *Études Galiléennes* (1939), Koyré sought to teach his colleagues two lessons. The first was the primacy of the text or, if necessary, the manuscript. Nothing could be taken for granted or assumed. No less than classical texts, works of science were items to be pored over, dissected and analysed. Secondly, in reaction to the crude positivism of his day, Koyré insisted that science was much more than a series of observations and experiments; it was, above all else, an intellectual creation, with ties closer to philosophy than to technology.

Both aspects of Koyré's approach can be seen in his work on Newton. In his *Newtonian Studies* (1965) he sought to show the nature, the roots and the interconnections of Newton's thought. The result was certainly the most elegant work ever produced on Newton's thought and, in many ways, the most satisfying. He had also been working since 1956 with I. B. Cohen on an edition of *Principia* with variant readings. The textual part of the edition was more or less complete at the time of Koyré's death in 1964 and was finally published in two volumes in 1972 (Newton, 1972). The accompanying *Introduction* (1971), planned by both Koyré and Cohen, had to be written by Cohen alone.

Krylov, Aleksei Nikolaevich (1863–1945)

The son of an artillery officer, Krylov graduated from the Maritime Academy, St Petersburg, in 1890. He remained there for half a century, teaching mathematics and engineering. Krylov was a leading Soviet scientist who was much honoured and who served in a number of important consultative and administrative roles during his long career. In 1915 he published the first, and still the only Russian translation of *Principia*.

See also Principia, Translations

L

Landor, Walter Savage (1775–1864)

A poet and essayist, Landor is best remembered today for the five volumes of *Imaginary Conversations* published between 1824 and 1829. It is a form often attempted, although seldom with illuminating or entertaining results. Among Landor's imagined dialogues, for example between Elizabeth and Cecil, Henry VIII and Anne Boleyn, Diogenes and Plato, he chose to include one between Newton and Barrow.

Landor's imaginative approach seems so strange and inadequate that the contemporary reader must keep on reminding himself that it is indeed Newton who is supposedly speaking. It opens with a fearful Newton confessing to Barrow his dread of the coming examinations: 'Oh, sir! forbear, forbear! I fear I may have forgotten a good deal of what you have taught me.' After a dull discussion on whether Newton should choose a scientific or a political career, an even duller discussion is pursued on the comparative merits of Bacon and Cicero. Throughout Newton seems timid, unsure, even skittish, while Barrow doles out ponderous maxims such as: 'Never try to say things admirably; try only to say them plainly' and 'Do not fear to be less rich in the productions of your mind at one season than at another.'

The 'conversation' concludes with Newton asking Barrow a most unlikely question: 'Sir! in a word – ought a studious man to think of matrimony?' Barrow's reply, ponderous as ever, was that 'Painters, poets, mathematicians never ought; other studious men, after reflecting for twenty years upon it, may.'

Languages

How good a linguist was Newton? What languages did he speak and read? He clearly wrote and read Latin almost as fluently as English. Some 40 per cent of his library, 707 volumes, were in Latin, as against

41 per cent in English. So familiar was he with Latin that in reading a Latin text, any marginal annotations would normally be in Latin. If called upon to do so, as at official receptions of the Royal Society, he could deliver extempore speeches in Latin. Presumably, also, he would converse in Latin with any Continental visitors who were uncomfortable in English.

His Greek was less good, although quotations in Greek in his work are reported as generally correct. Only twenty-five books in his library were in Greek alone; many more were joint Greek/Latin texts. Newton could thus read Greek, but not well enough to prefer an original text if an alternative Latin version was available.

Less impressive was Newton's French and, although his library contained 152 volumes in French (8 per cent), it is unlikely that he ever tackled a non-mathematical French text on his own. Fatio was obviously aware of this limitation and, when asked to deliver Huygens's *Traité de la lumière* (1690) to Newton in 1690, asked Newton whether he should send the volume to Cambridge or, he tactfully added, 'It beeing writ in French you may perhaps choose rather to read it here with me' (*C*, III, p. 390).

As for German, Newton seemed to lack all knowledge. 'I am told that the word Reichs or Rycks Thaler signifies Imperial Dollar. But I am not skilled in German language', Newton wrote to the Treasury in 1726. Neither he nor Locke possessed a single German volume in their libraries. Nor, for that matter did Adam Smith later in the century, other than three presentation volumes. German seems to have been ignored by scientists and scholars before the Romantic movement.

Newton also had some knowledge of Hebrew. Early notebooks show him learning the alphabet and doing elementary exercises. Five Hebrew books were in his library, the same number as Locke owned, mostly dictionaries and grammars. Newton's aim seems to have been no more than to equip himself with sufficient expertise to be able to check the meaning of any word found in the Bible or other sacred writings.

Latin Exercise Book

The 1936 Sotheby *Catalogue* lists 'A Latin phrase-book, under the heads of English words in alphabetical order, the first word abate, the last conduct. At the other end are extracts from Epiphianus, S. Augustine, etc.' It contains possibly the oldest writing in Newton's hand and consists of about 350 phrases in English and Latin in parallel columns.

Manuel (1980, p. 11) has suggested that they were not copied from some long-forgotten textbook but made up by the fifteen-year-old Newton himself. If so, Manuel claims, the phrases chosen by Newton contain 'frequent expressions of self-disparagement and of a sense of insignificance'. Examples quoted by Manuel include 'There is noe roome for mee to sit', 'I am sore affraide', 'No man understands mee' and 'What will become of me. I will make an end. I cannot but weepe. I know not what to doe' (Manuel, 1980, pp. 58–9).

Whether invented by Newton, copied from a book, or whatever, the phrases seem to take on a life of their own, suggesting, probably with no authority, an almost narrative link. What, after all, can we make of the sequence: 'You are sure to be punisht. Hee should have been punished. At this age I went not a-wenching'?

The notebook is in the hands of a Los Angeles private collector.

See also Notebooks.

Laughton, Richard John (1668–1723)

Sometime Librarian and Chaplain of TCC, Laughton was one of the three colleagues who, according to Humphrey Newton, regularly visited Newton in his college rooms. Writing of the early 1680s, Humphrey noted: 'Mr. Laughton who was then the library keeper . . . resorted much to his chamber' (More, 1962, p. 249). The basis of the friendship is unrecorded. It was reported, however, that Laughton set, some time before 1710, a Cambridge examination paper on Newtonian questions.

There are just two references to Laughton in the Correspondence, both concerning patronage (C, III, pp. 184–5; C, IV, p. 196). In 1717 Laughton was appointed Prebendary of Worcester Cathedral.

See also Friends

Laws of motion

One of Newton's more persistent claims to fame is his statement in Principia (1687) of his three laws of motion.

LAW 1

'Every body continues in its state of rest, or uniform motion in a right line, unless it is compelled to change that state by forces impressed upon it.' In support he offered three illustrations: the motions of projectiles, spinning tops and planets.

The law itself is not of Newton's creation. It was first formulated by Descartes in his Principia philosophiae (1644).

If [a body] is at rest we do not believe it is ever set in motion, unless it is impelled thereto by some [external] cause. Nor that there is any more reason if it is moved, why we should think that it would ever of its own accord, and unimpeded by anything else, interrupt this motion. (HERIVEL, 1965, pp. 44–5)

Newton himself, in a fragment in the PC (MS 3970, f.652a), was inclined to trace the law of inertia back to classical times and attributed versions of the law to Anaxagoras, Aristotle and Lucretius (Halls, pp. 310–11).

Newton's own formulation first appeared in the Waste Book of the 1660s where axioms 1 and 2 state the following.

1 If a quantity once move it will never rest unlesse hindered by some externall caus.

2 A quantity will always move on in the same streight line (not changing the determination nor celerity of its motion) unlesse some external caus divert it. (Herivel, 1965, p. 141)

As it stood at this point the law was incomplete, dealing only with the case of moving bodies. A similar incompleteness can be seen in the version of the law adopted in the early version of *De motu* (B) where it appears as hypothesis II: 'Every body under the sole action of its innate force moves uniformly in a straight line unless anything extraneous hinders it' (Herivel, 1965, p. 277). Nor had it changed much in the final version of *De motu* (D). Although described for the first time as a law, it still merely states: 'Law 1. By its innate force alone a body will allways proceed uniformly in a straight line provided nothing hinders it' (Herivel, 1965, p. 299). It is not until the appearance of *De motu corporum in mediis regulariter cedentibus* that a recognisable draft of the final version of the law is seen: 'Law I By reason of its innate force every body preserves in its state of rest or of moving uniformly in a straight line unless in so far as it is obliged to change its state by forces impressed upon it' (Herivel, 1965, p. 312).

LAW 2

'The change of motion is proportional to the motive force impressed; and is made in the direction of the right line in which that force is impressed.' A brief note adds that force and motion are directly related, and that motions can be added, cancel each other and form new oblique motions.

The law is first found hinted at in Newton's writings in the Waste Book where axiom 120 declares: 'A body must move that way which it is pressed' (Herivel, 1965, p. 159). It is next met with in *A Demonstration* (the draft sent to Locke), where hypothesis 2 notes: 'The alteration of motion is ever proportional to the force by which it is altered' (Herivel, 1965, p. 246). The law, however, is absent from early versions of *De motu* ((B) and (C)) but finally appears in version (D) as law 2:

'The change in the state of movement or rest [of a body] is proportional to the impressed force and takes place along the straight line in which that force is impressed' (Herivel, 1965, p. 299).

LAW 3

'To every action there is always opposed an equal reaction: or, the mutual actions of two bodies upon each other are always equal, and directed to contrary parts.' The law is illustrated by references to pressing stones with fingers, horses pulling stones tied to a rope, and colliding bodies. It is pointed out that if a horse pulls a stone, then the horse will in turn 'be equally drawn back towards the stone'.

As applied to collisions, the third law can be found stated in the Waste Book (definitions 7 and 8, axioms 119 and 121). After that it is not met with again until it is found expressed as law 3 of *De motu corporum in mediis regulariter cedentibus*: 'As much as any body acts on another so much does it experience in reaction. Whatever presses or pulls another thing by this equally is pressed or pulled' (Herivel, 1965, pp. 312–13).

Laws of nature

The idea that there are a set of laws governing the behaviour of bodies in the natural world was a peculiarly seventeenth-century innovation. They are not to be found described in N. Copernicus, Sir Francis Bacon, Galileo, William Gilbert or Kepler. While today we may speak casually of Kepler's laws, it was not a phrase Kepler himself ever adopted. The first two of his 'laws' were simply enunciated, while the third was introduced as a theorem.

Earlier thinkers had inevitably spoken of law, both natural and divine, and its operation in the world. The Stoics, for example, had spoken of a universal law (*koinos nomos*), while the occasional reference can also be found in such writers as Plato, Aristotle and Cicero. It was equally evident to later generations of scholastic philosophers that the universe was ruled by law. No more, however, was meant by this than that, in the words of Aquinas, 'all things are directed towards their proper ends'. It was thus seen as part of the divine providence that planets move in a certain way, and that falling bodies move in a different manner. Absent from this perception was the idea of a number of specific laws, the laws of motion for example, or the gas laws, each operating within its own specific domain.

The OED notes the first appearance of such a conception in English in the year 1665. Earlier occurrences are evident long before. Descartes, in his *Principiae philosophiae* (1644), had spoken both of 'rules of nature' and 'laws of nature'; the French translation of 1647, however, spoke exclusively of 'laws of nature'. It also took some time for Newton's own terminology to evolve. The Waste Book of the 1660s listed a large number of 'axioms'. This was replaced in the early *De motu* tracts of the 1680s with the term 'hypothesis'. The term 'law' did not appear until the later tract, *De motu sphaericorum corporum in fluidis*, which listed five laws. The terminology was modified by the time of *Principia* (1687) with its three 'Axioms or Laws of Motion'. Yet, by the *Opticks* (1704) Newton had reverted to the language of the 1660s and began the work not with laws, but with five axioms. Thus, instead of speaking of Snell's law, as in the modern style, Newton introduced it as 'Axiom V'.

Le Clerc, Jean (1657–1736)

Born in Geneva, Le Clerc became Professor of Philosophy at the Remonstrants' Seminary in Amsterdam. The Remonstrants were, though members of the Dutch Reformed Church, Arminians. Le Clerc himself was best known during his day for his Bible commentaries.

In 1691 he was approached by his friend, John Locke, to have an anonymous work on some textual corruptions in the Bible translated into French and published. When the author, Newton, changed his mind about publication, Le Clerc sensibly preserved the manuscript in the library of the Remonstrants. They remained there until, re-discovered, they were eventually published in 1754.

Leibniz–Clarke correspondence

ORIGIN

Leibniz had long made it clear that he found the fundamental assumptions of Newtonian science quite unsound. In a letter to Newton, via the hands of the Abbé Conti, in November 1715, Leibniz listed his objections. Newton was, however, more interested in the priority dispute and in his reply in February 1716 he did little more than note Leibniz's comments. At the same time Leibniz had sent to his former pupil, Caroline, the Princess of Wales, a similar set of objections. She accordingly commanded Samuel Clarke to reply to the charges raised by Leibniz. The correspondence which resulted lasted from November 1715 to 29 October 1716 and involved the exchange of five letters each. Before Leibniz could reply to Clarke's fifth letter he died on 14 November.

Caroline was retained throughout the dispute and it was, in fact, through her that the actual exchange of letters was made.

ARGUMENT

Leibniz chose to attack Newton on five specific issues. His objections, together with Clarke's replies, are listed below. Page references are to Alexander (1956); individual letters are referred to by the appropriate initials, with L.I and C.I standing for the first letters of Leibniz and Clarke respectively.

1 'Sir Isaac Newton says, that space is an organ, which God makes use of to perceive things by. But if God stands in need of any organ to perceive things by, it will follow, that they do not depend altogether upon him, nor were produced by him' (L.I; p. 11). Leibniz was referring to Query 28 of the *Opticks* (1717) and Newton's comment that:

> Does it not appear from Phaenomena that there is a Being incorporeal, living, intelligent, omnipresent, who in infinite space, as it were in his Sensory, sees the things themselves intimately . . . and comprehends them wholly by their immediate presence to himself.

The argument turned on what Newton had, or had not, said. Clarke denied that Newton had claimed space to be an organ 'which God makes use of to perceive Things by'. It was, he insisted, no more than a statement of God's omnipresence (L.II; pp. 12–13). Leibniz, in turn, responded that Newton, without any qualification, had declared 'space is the *sensorium* of God' and the term 'sensorium hath always signified the organ of sensation' (L.II; pp. 16–17). Thereafter, the dispute turned upon the precise meaning of the term 'sensorium', with Leibniz triumphantly appealing to the *Dictionarum philosophicum* (1613) of Goclenius (L.III; p. 28) and Clarke stubbornly insisting that the issue was not 'what Goclenius, but what Sir Isaac means by the word sensorium' (C.III; p. 33).

There is some evidence that both Leibniz and Clarke were arguing at cross purposes. In Clarke's copy of the *Opticks* Newton did speak of 'space, *as it were* [tanquam]' as the sensory of God. An earlier state of the text lacked the 'tanquam' and spoke simply of space as 'the sensorium of God'. It seems likely that Leibniz possessed one of these earlier states (see *Opticks*, Editions).

2 On a second problem of natural theology Leibniz complained that the Newtonians had:

> A very odd opinion concerning the work of God. According to their doctrine, God Almighty wants to wind up his watch from time to time otherwise it would cease to move. He had not, it seems, sufficient foresight to make it a perpetual motion. (L.I; p. 11)

The charge was a just one. In the *Letters to Bentley* and in Queries 28 and 31 of the *Opticks*, Newton had spoken quite unambiguously of the various ways in which God's intervention was needed to preserve the stability of the heavens. Clarke took up Leibniz's analogy of the clockmaker and insisted:

> The notion of the world's being a great machine, going on without the interposition of God . . . is the notion of materialism and fate, and tends . . . to exclude providence and God's government in reality out of the world.

Further, Clarke argued "tis not a diminution, but the true glory of his workmanship, that nothing is done without his continual government and inspection' (C.I; p. 14). Thereafter, although Clarke and Leibniz continued to pursue the implications of their analogy of God as clockmaker, neither had anything of substance to add to their opening position.

3 As it was in the nature of 'free body' to recede 'from a curve in a tangent', Leibniz argued, only a miracle could cause 'a body to move free in the aether round about a certain fixed centre' (L.III; p. 30). Further, Leibniz added, "Tis also a supernatural thing, that bodies should attract one another at a distance, without any inter-mediate means' (L.IV; p. 43). Against such charges Clarke offered the traditional Newtonian reply. The sun did attract the earth and all were free to search for a cause of this attraction: 'But if they cannot discover the cause; is therefore the effect itself, the phenom-enon . . . ever the less true?' (C.V; p. 118).

4 Leibniz objected to the existence of the vacuum on two grounds: 'for, the more matter there is, the more God has occasion to exercise his wisdom and power. Which is one reason . . . why I maintain there is no vacuum at all' (L.II; p. 16); and, further, "tis impossible there should be any principle to determine what proportion of matter there ought to be, out of all the possible degrees from a plenum to a vacuum, or from a vacuum to a plenum' (L.IV; p. 44).

Clarke rejected the theological implications of the arguments. We might just as well argue that God requires an infinite number of men 'to exercise his power and wisdom' (C.II; p. 21). Clarke also presented to Leibniz a wealth of experimental data designed to show the existence of the vacuum (C.IV; pp. 46–7).

5 Leibniz dismissed the Newtonian claim that space and time were absolute and argued instead for a relational view. The subject came to dominate the latter half of the correspondence. Leibniz argued that any absolute theory imposed absurd constraints on God's freedom (L.III; p. 26) and led to all kinds of contradictions. Clarke also sought to identify contradictions in his opponent's position. In

addition he advanced some of the experimental evidence produced by Newton in *Principia* (C.IV; p. 48).

NEWTON'S INFLUENCE

To what extent were the replies of Clarke controlled by Newton? Koyré (1968, p. 301) has argued that it is 'unthinkable' that Newton could have remained a spectator while he was being accused of atheism. Caroline had admitted as much in a letter to Leibniz dated 10 January 1716: 'You are right about the author of the reply; they are not written without the advice of Chev. Newton' (Alexander, 1956, p. 193). Clarke's letters are thus seen by Koyré 'as representing *literally* the metaphysical views of Newton'. Koyré and Cohen (1961, p. 560) have further argued that 'the source of Clarke's replies . . . was Newton himself'. Westfall, however had judged Newton's degree of participation in the correspondence to be still 'an open question' (RSW, p. 778).

EDITIONS

The correspondence has proved to be of lasting interest and is known in the following editions.

1 London, 1717. The whole correspondence was published in both English and French, with the letters of Leibniz translated into English by Clarke and the English letters of Clarke translated into French by de la Roche.

2 Frankfurt and Leipzig, 1720. A German translation by H. Köhler with an introduction by C. Wolff, and a reply to Clarke's fifth letter proposed by L. P. Thümmig; reissued in 1740.

3 Amsterdam, 1720. A French edition was included by des Maiseaux in vol. I of his *Receuil*; reissued in 1740 and 1759.

4 London, 1738. English and French editions were included in vol. IV of *The Works of Samuel Clarke*.

5 Groningen, 1740. The first Latin translation, prepared by N. Engelhard.

6 Geneva, 1768. A French edition was included in vol. II of L. Dutens's edition of Leibniz's *Opera omnia*; reissued in 1789.

7 Berlin, 1840. A French edition was included in vol. II of Leibniz's *Opera philosophica* edited by J. E. Erdmann.

8 Paris, 1842. A French edition was included in Leibniz's *Oeuvres* edited by A. Jacques; reissued in 1844 and 1847.

9 Paris, 1866. A French edition was included in Leibniz's *Oeuvres philosophiques* edited by P. Janet.

10 Hanover, 1884. A French edition was included in vol. XI of O. Klopp's *Die Werke von Leibniz*.

11 Berlin, 1890. An edition of the correspondence with Clarke's

letters in English and Leibniz's in French was included in vol. VII of C. J. Gerhardt's *Die philosophischen Schriften von G. W. Leibniz*.

12 Leipzig, 1903. A German edition translated by A. Buchenau and edited by E. Cassirer was included in their *G.W.Leibniz, Hauptschriften zur Grundlagen der Philosophie*; reissued in 1924.

13 Manchester, 1956. The first complete English edition since 1738, edited, with introduction and notes, by H. G. Alexander; reissued in 1976, 1978 and 1984.

14 Paris, 1957. An edition based on the original manuscript text, edited by A. Robinet.

Leibniz, Gottfried Wilhelm (1646–1716)

The son of a professor of philosophy, and a Protestant, Leibniz chose a diplomatic rather than an academic career and in 1667 he entered the service of the Elector of Mainz. He spent the period 1672–6 in Paris. They were to prove the most creative years of his life. Under the influence of Huygens, also based in Paris, and other scholars he met in France, London and the Hague, Leibniz was exposed to the major problems facing the mathematicians, scientists and philosophers of his day. Thereafter, Leibniz returned to Germany and the service of the Dukes of Brunswick in Hanover. Intellectually isolated, he spent much of his time in Hanover working on a history of the House of Brunswick. One consolation was the presence after 1705 of Caroline of Anspach, wife of George Augustus, the future George II of England and eldest son of the Duke. With the accession of the Duke in 1714 to the throne of England, Leibniz hoped to accompany him to London where he still had a number of friends in the Royal Society. It was not to be. With the departure of Caroline he found himself even more isolated, working supposedly on his never-to-be-completed history of the House of Brunswick.

Leibniz was a man of extraordinary genius, with a great vision concerning the systematisation of thought. It would involve a reform of language, the production of a *characteristica universalis*, and would eventually consist of a calculus capable of eliminating all controversy and solving all problems in all disciplines. Much of Leibniz's work was misguided; much, however, remained genuinely prophetic and it is possible, looking back, to identify in his writings ideas which have seen their fruition in such typically twentieth-century 'creations' as the binary system, symbolic logic and the computer.

Ironically, for one who worked towards the elimination of controversy, much of Leibniz's own life was spent pursuing relatively unrewarding intellectual quarrels. The most famous of these, and possibly the most famous quarrel in the entire history of science, concerned his dispute with Newton over their respective claims to have discovered the calculus. In the *CE* (1713) the claim was made that Newton was undoubtedly 'first inventor' of the 'Differential Method', with claims going back to the 1660s. It was further claimed that, before Leibniz had revealed any knowledge of any 'Differential Method', he had been given access to various items of Newton's correspondence containing details of his 'Method of Fluxions'. The implication – that Leibniz had derived his own differential method from Newton's fluxional method – was clear to all. Was it, however, a fair and accurate inference?

Brewster concluded in 1831 that:

By the unanimous verdict of all nations, it has been decided that Newton invented fluxions at least ten years before Leibniz. Some of the letters of Newton which bore reference to this great discovery were perused by the German mathematician; but there is no evidence whatever that he borrowed his differential calculus from these letters. Newton was therefore the *first* inventor, and Leibniz the *second*. (BREWSTER, 1831, p. 216)

Intensive research in recent years by Westfall (RSW), Hall (1980) and Whiteside in the final volume of the *MP* (1981), in which they have had access to all relevant documentation, has thrown much light on the characters and motives of the participants in the dispute. It has not, however, seriously challenged Brewster's judgment of 150 years ago.

Leibniz's own contributions to the dispute involved the following public items.

1 In a number of early works (*see* Priority dispute) Leibniz acknowledged the work of and the claims being made by the Newtonians. At this stage he did little more than insist on the priority of his own publication and indicate that he did not accept, without reservation, any of their claims.

2 In 1710 there appeared in the *PT* John Keill's *The Laws of Centripetal Force* in which Leibniz was charged with having published material originating with Newton. Leibniz, Keill declared, had changed only 'the name and symbolism'.

3 In both February (*C*, V, pp. 96–7) and December (*C*, V, pp. 207–8) 1711 Leibniz, as a Fellow of the Royal Society, wrote to the secretary, Sir Hans Sloane, complaining of the abusive treatment he was receiving from the Newtonians. Newton responded shortly afterwards by setting up a committee of the RS to examine the entire dispute. The committee's report, the *CE*, was published in January 1713.

4 Leibniz's response to the *CE* was his anonymous fly-sheet, the *Charta volans* (*C*, VI, pp. 15–21) dated 18 July 1713. At this stage Leibniz was prepared to accept Newton's words on the calculus

that 'such things had come to him from his own ingenuity'. He still insisted, however, on his own priority of publication.

5 In a second anonymous publication, *Remarques sur la different entre M.de Leibniz, and M.Newton* (*JL*, Nov.–Dec. 1713; *C*, VI, pp. 30–2, Remarks on the dispute between Leibniz and Newton), he took a much harder line. Newton's account of his method of fluxions, Leibniz insisted, contained nothing which had not previously appeared in his own published work. It was also clear to him that Newton had been ignorant of the differential calculus in 1687 when he had published his *Principia*. While previously he had been willing to grant Newton the independent discovery of the main principles of the calculus, it was becoming more and more clear to him that Newton had done little more than to express Leibniz's own results in fluxional terms.

6 The charge was repeated, in essence, in a letter to John Chamberlayne dated May 1714 (*C*, VI, pp. 105–6). In words intended as much for Newton as for Chamberlayne, Leibniz insisted that 'it appears now that there is great room to doubt whether he knew my invention before he had it from me'.

7 In a letter to Conti dated 25 November 1715 (*C*, VI, pp. 250–5) Leibniz posed a problem to the English mathematicians, first set by Bernoulli in 1694. Bernoulli and Leibniz expected the Newtonians, by their failure to find a general solution to the problem, to reveal their lack of understanding of the principles of the calculus.

8 In a second letter to Conti dated 29 March 1716 (*C*, VI, pp. 304–12) Leibniz prepared a long review of the course of the dispute. Newton replied at some length in his *Observations* (*C*, VI, pp. 341–52).

9 The whole story was repeated a few days later in a letter to the Baroness von Kilmansegge, the mistress of George I (*C*, VI, pp. 324–30).

10 On several occasions Leibniz noted his intention to publish a collection similar to the *CE* in which his own case would be fully and fairly presented. The result was his *Historia et origo calculi differentialis* (History and Origin of the Differential Calculus). As with many another of Leibniz's projects, the work was started and quickly allowed to drop. It remained unpublished until Gerhardt included the text in vol. V, pp. 392–410 of Leibniz's *Mathematische Schriften* (1849–63); an English translation was made available in Child (1920).

Running alongside the priority dispute, and often overlapping, lay an equally bitter controversy on the subject of Newtonian mechanics, its validity and foundations. Leibniz's *Tentamen* (1689) presented a physics based on vortices and quite incompatible with the system of *Principia*

(1687). At the height of the priority dispute Leibniz chose, in such pieces as the *Apostille* (*C*, VI, pp. 250–5), to broaden the dispute by challenging Newton on such issues as gravity, the void, atomism and the stability of the universe. Newton responded with an unpublished highly critical analysis of the *Tentamen* (*C*, VI, pp. 116–22), and with a public reproof in the *Account* on Leibniz's physical assumptions. Such incidents can now be seen as no more than skirmishes. The real battle would be waged between Leibniz and, on Newton's behalf, Samuel Clarke. The results were first published in 1717 and are widely known today as the Leibniz–Clarke correspondence.

It is difficult not to sympathise with Leibniz in his final years. Hanover must have seemed a lonely place with the departure of the brightest members of the Court to London in 1714. While Newton – knighted, a high government official, President of the Royal Society, wealthy, respected at Court and venerated by many of his contemporaries – must have seemed to Leibniz completely successful in all walks of life, his own lot was very different. Isolated in a provincial Court, committed to trivial works of domestic history, he must have realised very clearly how ill his lot compared with that of Newton. As a final burden he was forced to contend with Newton's aggressive young disciples, seemingly determined to rob him of his remaining prestige. If the dominant theme of much of Newton's correspondence during the priority dispute is one of rage, Leibniz's contributions are marked more by feelings of bitterness.

See also Leibniz–Clarke correspondence; Priority dispute

Le Seur, Thomas (1703–71)

A friar of the order of Minims, Le Seur served as Professor of Mathematics at the Collège de la Sapience in Rome. He is best known, however, as editor, with Francis Jacquier, of the inappropriately-named Jesuit edition of *Principia* (1739–42, 3 vols).

See also Jacquier, Francis; *Principia*, Editions

Letter to Robert Boyle (1679)

On 28 February 1679 Newton wrote to Boyle a highly speculative letter in which he developed further some of the views contained in *De aere* and the 1675 *An Hypothesis* on the subjects of the ether and gravity. Newton began in his usual self-conscious manner apologising for sending such 'indigested' thoughts and went on to set down five suppositions.

1 'There is diffused through all places an etherial substance, capable of contraction and dilatation, strongly elastic, and, in a word, much like air in all respects, but far more subtle.'

2 Although all-pervasive, Newton's ether was not conceived of as being an homogeneous medium. Instead, he supposed it 'to stand rarer in the pores of bodies than in free spaces'. This was why, for example, 'the parts of all bodies cohere'.

3 The gradation between the rarer ether within bodies and the denser without was gradual and continuous.

4 As two bodies approach each other the ether between them becomes rarer.

5 When bodies 'come so near together that the excess of pressure of the external ether which surrounds the bodies, above that of the rarefied ether which is between them, is so great as to overcome the reluctance which the bodies have from being brought together, then will that excess of pressure drive them with violence together and make them adhere strongly to one another'.

After illustrating his suppositions Newton added that he would 'set down one conjecture more' which had only come into his mind while writing the letter.

6 Could a variable ether be the cause of gravity?

Newton concluded his letter with the inevitable apology and disclaimer that he took such speculations seriously. It was only Boyle's encouragement that had moved him to such conjectures.

The letter remained unpublished until 1744, when it appeared in Thomas Birch's *The Life of Boyle*, pp. 70–4. Thereafter it has been frequently anthologised and can be seen readily today in Brewster, Thayer (1953, pp. 112–16), *C*, II, pp. 288–95 and *PLNP*, pp. 250–4.

See also Ether; Gravity

Leucatello's balsam

A medicine Newton prescribed for himself and others. Its principal ingredient was Venus or Venice turpentine. Newton recommended it for 'measell, plague, or smallpox, a half ounce in a little broth; take it warm and sweat after it'. It was also of use against 'wind, cholic . . . bruises'. Even poison and the 'biting of a mad dog' could be treated with the balsam, in the latter case by local application.

Newton's commitment to the balsam was sufficient to so stick in the mind of John Wickins as to be one of the few stories of his 'chamber fellow' recalled by his son Nicolaus. Newton, suspecting himself 'inclining to a consumption', would apparently drink about a quarter pint of it at a time (More, 1962, p. 206).

See also Health

Lexicon technicum

One of the first technical dictionaries ever to be published, the *Lexicon*, edited by John Harris, appeared in 1704. An enlarged two-volume edition followed in 1710, while further editions are known from 1716, 1725 and 1736. The first edition of 1704 contained 8,200 terms and attracted 900 subscribers. Although Newton was a subscriber, no copy of the *Lexicon* is listed in any of the surviving catalogues of his library.

As a good Newtonian, Harris took the opportunity to expound Newtonian principles. In the edition of 1710 he went a step further and included an English translation of the previously unpublished *De natura acidorum*. He also gave English translations, under the heading *Curves*, of the two mathematical treatises, *De quadratura* and *Enumeratio*, first published in Latin in *Opticks* (1704).

See also Harris, John

Library

HISTORY

Listed amongst the official inventory of Newton's goods drawn up after his death in 1727 were the following items: '362 folio books, 477 quarto, 1057 octavo', plus '1 cwt of pamphlets and Wast books'. The collection of books was quickly valued at £270, a rough catalogue was compiled and the 1896 books were sold as a single lot to John Huggins, Warden of the Fleet Prison, for £300. They were wanted by his son, Charles Huggins, for whom he had bought in 1723 for £2,000 the living at Chinnor, near Oxford. Charles died in 1750, when the living was bought by the Reverend Dr James Musgrave, who also bought, for £400, the still-intact library. Both owners added book plates and press marks while, in 1776, Musgrave compiled a second catalogue of the collection. The books were last heard of at Chinnor in 1775 when a visiting Swedish scholar, Jacob Björnståhl, noted how richly annotated were some of Newton's works. Musgrave died shortly afterwards in 1778 and his library was transferred to Barnsley Park, Gloucester, to his family home and his son.

Nothing more of the books is heard of until 1920. By this time the

Musgraves had become Wykeham-Musgrave, with another house at Thame Park, Oxfordshire. Wishing to sell the house, they decided also to add to the sale some 3,000 volumes of 'miscellaneous literature' taken from Barnsley Park. Neither the Wykeham-Musgraves nor the auctioneers, Hampton and Sons of London, could have had the slightest idea of the provenance of many of these books, for about 1,000 of them came from Newton's library and were sold in such lots as 'Theology (Old), calf, etc, 173 volumes' for derisory amounts. The whole collection fetched only £170.

If Hampton and Sons had been unaware of what they were selling, the same cannot be said of the London book trade. Before long works bought at the Thame sale started to appear at more-to-be-expected prices in the catalogues of Sotheran. The most expensive such volume was the *Euclid* (1655) given to Newton by I. Barrow and priced at £500. It was still, however, unsold in 1943. The bulk of works sold in 1920, unlike the *Euclid*, have disappeared without trace.

But if only 1,000 or so were sold at Thame, about 800 remained at Barnsley Park. They remained there until 1927 when the remarkable Richard de Villamil, 'by a series of lucky accidents', located them at the Wykeham-Musgraves. Finally aware of the treasures in their possession, they put the surviving 858 volumes into the hands of Sotheran's, who offered the collection intact for £30,000. By 1936, when J. M. Keynes showed interest in the library, he was told that the owners 'are now willing to sell it for £5,000 net'. But Keynes was still uninterested, as were, despite further adverts in 1940, all other private buyers.

It was finally bought, at the suggestion of G. M. Trevelyan, the historian and Master of TCC, by the Pilgrim Trust in 1943 at a price of £5,500. This included Barrow's *Euclid*. Having bought the collection, the Trust was stuck with the problem of where to locate it. Keynes strongly advised against the British Museum where, he argued, it would be 'sunk and buried without trace'. His own inclination was for the Royal Society, followed by TCC. He preferred the Royal Society because Newton 'is their tutelary god, their one god – there is a bit more polytheism in Trinity'.

In the end the Trust decided on Trinity and on 30 October 1943 Lord Macmillan, Chairman of the Trust, handed over the 858 volumes purchased from the Wykeham-Musgraves plus Newton's copy of Barrow's *Euclid* and a Greek Old Testament containing Newtonian annotations. The 860 volumes were located in the Wren Library, where they still remain. They all contain, in addition to the Huggins and Musgrave book plates, a special Trinity plate designed by R. A. Maynard.

Of the missing 1,000 volumes, some are no doubt destroyed. Others are in private hands, while a third group float around the secondhand book trade until someone identifies their original owner. Thus in 1975 a work from the library, *Opera* (1631) of Optatus, was bought in Cambridge for £4. Some of the missing works could be of considerable interest. Thus, Sotherans sold in 1926 for £50 Newton's *Theatrum chemicum* (1659–61, 6 vols) by L. Zetzner. It contained copious Newtonian annotations but has, none the less, disappeared completely.

CATALOGUES

So far four catalogues have been issued. The first was the sale catalogue of 1727, the so-called Huggins list. It lists only 969 works by title (1,442 volumes); the rest are described under some such heading as '3 Dozen of small chymical books'. A second ninety-one-page catalogue was compiled by Musgrave in about 1776. It is, however, a catalogue of Musgrave's collection, and consequently contains works which have no connection with Newton. It lists 1,601 titles in 2,385 volumes and is therefore much fuller than the Huggins list. Of these 1,601 titles, however, 161 refer to works published after Newton's death; at the most, therefore, only 1,440 titles (2,029 volumes) could have been Newton's property. To the 1,896 volumes of the 1727 catalogue Musgrave must had added at least a further 133 volumes of his own. The Musgrave catalogue was reprinted by de Villamil (1931, pp. 62–110); books also noted in Huggins were starred while those listed in Huggins only were listed separately. It was not free from error.

A final and definitive catalogue has been published by Harrison (1978). It lists 1,763 titles, indicating in each case basic bibliographical data, shelf marks, location if known, details of any annotations and catalogue listings. It is a superb and engrossing study, containing an enormous amount of information about all aspects of Newton's library and from which most of the data contained in this entry have been gratefully derived.

CONTENTS

Harrison has analysed the composition of the library and broken it down into the subjects shown in the first table; comparable figures for the library of John Locke taken from Harrison and Laslett (1965) are also provided. In terms of languages, the works of the two libraries break down into the following categories shown in the second table. Neither library contained a single work in German.

The spread of subject matter covered by the libraries of Newton and Locke speak for themselves and need no further comment. A few other points are less apparent and yet show something of Newton's interests.

Robert Boyle was by far the most popular author in the library, with some twenty-four separate works present; the same is true of Locke, who had thirty-four works in his collection. Also startling to the modern

Subjects covered in the libraries of Newton and Locke

	Newton (1752 titles)		Locke (3,641 titles)	
	Number of volumes	Proportion (%)	Number of volumes	Proportion (%)
Scientific works	538	30	644	18
Non-scientific works	1,214	70	2,977	82
Alchemy	138	8	–	–
Chemistry	31	1.5	48	1.3
Physics/optics	52	3	69	1.9
Astronomy	33	1.5	9	0.3
Medicine/physiology	57	3	402	11
Geography/travel	76	4.5	275	7.6
Theology/Bible	477	27.5	870	23.8
Mathematics	126	7	–	–
Classics	149	9	366	10
History	143	8	187	5
Reference	90	5	201	5

Languages used in the libraries of Newton and Locke

	Newton (1752 titles)		Locke (3,641 titles)	
	Number of volumes	Proportion (%)	Number of volumes	Proportion (%)
English	722	41	1,426	39
Latin	707	40	1,326	36
Greek and Greek/Latin	138	8	84	2.3
French	152	8.5	669	18.3
Hebrew	5	0.2	5	0.1

reader is the large number of Bibles both scholars possessed. Allowing for separate editions of the old and new testaments, Newton had some thirty Bibles to Locke's fifty-five.

Though rich in Bibles and the works of Boyle, there are no signs in Newton's library of any great interest in literature. He had a *Hamlet* and *Tempest* of Shakespeare, a *Tempest* of Dryden, the *Poetical Works* of

Milton, Matthew Prior's *Poems* and Butler's *Hudibras*. In all, Harrison (1978, p. 70) attributes forty works (2 1/3 per cent) to the domain of contemporary literature, a figure which compared favourably with other known collections. Harrison warns, however, that some of these works may well have belonged to Catherine Barton or have been added later by James Musgrave.

There can be no such doubt about the 149 works of classical literature present in the library. It should not be assumed that the presence of the works of Catullus, Horace, Ovid, Virgil, Aristophanes, Terence, Pindar and Homer showed much concern with classical verse. They were there mainly because of Newton's interest in ancient chronology, and were read in the hope of finding some hints on the dating of such events as the Argonauts' expedition, the fall of Troy and the rise of Egypt.

SIZE AND USE

Newton was in no sense a collector. The 2,000 volumes of his library were working books, augmented by a few presentation copies. However it still remained a large library by the standards of his day. Admittedly collectors like John Evelyn with his 5,000 volumes and Samuel Pepys with his 3,000-plus exceeded Newton in size, but compared with Isaac Barrow's 992 volumes, J. Flamsteed's 200 in 1685 and Adam Smith's 1,100 a century later, Newton's collection was a substantial one.

Evidence for the use of the books is contained by Newton's annotations, which are found in eighty-four of the 900 books examined by Harrison (1978, pp. 15–24). A further indication is provided by Newton's unusual system of page marking. Rather than scar the text he used to turn up or down the nearest page corner so that it pointed to the precise part of the text he wished to note. Harrison has noted such precision dog-earing in 274 of the 862 volumes in the Wren Library.

It should also be remembered that for the period 1661 to 1696 Newton was resident in TCC, with its library of about 4,000 volumes on his doorstep. There can be little doubt that Newton actually used its resources, for in his *Theological Notebook* a number of works are listed with the library's shelf marks.

LEIGH AND SOTHEBY SALE 1813

On 22 March 1813 there began a five-day sale of 'the Library of the late Mrs. Anne Newton, containing the Collection of the Great Sir Isaac Newton'. Twelve works were listed as bearing Newton's autograph, although only one of these is listed in the Huggins catalogue and that was sent to Barnsley Park in the late eighteenth century. Harrison (1978, pp. 268–9) has plausibly argued that the signatures 'were those of Sir John Newton (1651–1734), rather than of his distant kinsman Sir Isaac, and . . . that "the late Mrs. Anne Newton" was Anne Newton . . . who died in June 1811, widow of Michael Newton, nephew and heir of Sir John's son Michael'.

Life, career and works of Newton

1642 April. Marriage of Hannah Ayscough and Isaac Newton.
     October. Death of Newton's father, Isaac.
     December 25. Birth of Newton.
1643 January 1. Newton's baptism.
1646 January 27. Marriage of Hannah Newton (née Ayscough) to Barnabas Smith.
1653 August. Death of Barnabas Smith and return of mother to Woolsthorpe.
1655 Attends Free Grammar School of King Edward VI, Grantham; lodged with Apothecary Clarke.
1659 Recalled from school to Woolsthorpe by his mother.
1660 Began Morgan Notebook.
     Autumn. Returned to school in Grantham; lodged with Headmaster Stokes.
1661 June 5. Admitted into TCC as subsizar.
     July 8. Swore matriculation oath.
1663 Bought Euclid at Stourbridge Fair.
     Lucasian Chair founded.
1664 April 28. Elected scholar.
     Began mathematical entries in Waste Book; began *QQP*.
1665 January. Takes BA degree; entered *Of Reflections* in Waste Book.
     May 1665 Tract.
     August. Left Cambridge because of the Plague and moved to Woolsthorpe.
     November 1665 Tract.
1666 March 20. Returned to Cambridge.
     May 14 Tract; May 16 Tract.
     June. Returned to Woolsthorpe.
     Lawes of Motion; Vellum MS; October 1665 Tract; *Of Colours* entered into Chemistry notebook.
1667 April. Returned to Cambridge.
     October 2. Elected minor Fellow of TCC.
     Composed *Enumeratio curvarum*.
     Spent period from December 4 at Woolsthorpe.
1668 March 16. Elected major Fellow of TCC.
     July 7. Awarded MA.
     August 5. Made first visit to London; returned to Cambridge, via Woolsthorpe, by September 29.

1669 February 23. Reflecting telescope described in a letter to Oldenburg.

July 31. *De analysi* sent to John Collins.

October 29. Elected Lucasian Professor of Mathematics.

November. Second visit to London; meets Collins.

1670 January. Delivered the first of his *Lectiones opticae*.

Much of the year spent working on *Observations on Kinckhuysen*.

1671 Composed *De methodis*.

December. Sends reflecting telescope to Royal Society.

December 21. Proposed by Seth Ward for election to the Society.

1672 January 11. Elected FRS.

February 6. Sent to Oldenburg first letter on *Light and Colors*, read to Society on February 8, printed in the *PT* on February 19.

March 25. Account of new reflecting telescope published in *PT*; a further seven optical papers appeared in the *PT* throughout the year.

Composed *Discourse of Observations*; edited Varenius.

December 10. Letter to Collins on method of tangents.

1673 October. Began to lecture on mathematics.

1674 August. Visited London for the installation of the Duke of Monmouth as Chancellor of Cambridge University.

1675 February 18. Attended first meeting of Royal Society.

March. Attended further meetings of Royal Society and met Robert Boyle.

April 27. Patent granted by Crown to excuse Lucasian Professor from taking orders.

December 9–16. *Hypothesis explaining the Properties of Light* read to Royal Society.

1676 January 20–February 10. *Discourse of Observations* read to Royal Society.

June 13. *Epistola prior* sent to Oldenburg.

October 20. *Epistola posterior* sent to Oldenburg.

Composed *Regula differentiarum* and *Methodus differentialis*.

1677 September. Death of Oldenburg.

1679 February 28. Letter to Boyle.

June 4. Burial of Newton's mother at Woolsthorpe, where he spent much of the year.

November 24. Start of correspondence with Hooke on planetary motion.

1680 January 17. Conclusion of Hooke correspondence.

December 12. Began observing comet.

Composed *Geometria curvilinea*.

1681 Observed comet until March; corresponded with Flamsteed on the nature of the comet.

1682 December. Observed Halley's comet.

1683 Deposited lectures on arithmetic and algebra in ULC.
November 10. Death of Collins.
1684 August. Visit from Halley and start of work on *Principia*.
October. Began to lecture on *De motu corporum, liber primus*.
November. The tract *De motu* sent to London; Halley's second Cambridge visit.
December 10. Acknowledgment of *De motu* by Royal Society.
Composed *De composito serierum* and *Matheseos universalis*.
Publication of *Novus methodus*, Leibniz's first publication on the calculus.
1685 February 23. By this date *De motu* had been entered in Register of Royal Society.
1686 April 28. *Principia*, Book I presented to Royal Society.
May 19. Royal Society decided to publish *Principia*.
May 22. Halley began to correspond with Newton on *Principia*.
June 2. Halley instructed by Royal Society to publish *Principia*.
June 30. *Principia* licensed by Pepys as President of Royal Society.
1687 March 1. Book II of *Principia* sent to Halley.
April 4. Book III of *Principia* sent to Halley.
April 11. Appointed by Cambridge Senate as one of the eight representatives in the Francis affair.
April 21. Appeared before Ecclesiastical Commission.
July 5. Completion of Newton–Halley *Principia* correspondence; publication of *Principia*.
September 28. Began lecturing on *De mundi systemate*.
1689 January 15. Elected to Convention Parliament by Cambridge Senate.
January 22. Parliament assembled.
Sat for Kneller.
First met Locke.
1690 February 6. Parliament dissolved.
March–April. In London with Fatio.
November 14. Sent Locke *Two notable corruptions*.
1691 January. Visited Locke at Oates.
August. First meeting with David Gregory in London.
September. Visited Fatio in London.
1692 January. In London for funeral of Robert Boyle.
January 26. Asks for return of *Two notable corruptions*.
March 2–3. Visited in Cambridge by A. Pitcairne who is shown and allowed to copy *De natura acidorum*.
Autumn. Visited in Cambridge by Fatio.
December 10. First letter to Bentley.
1693 Three further letters to Bentley: January 17, February 11 and March 14.
January–February. Visited in Cambridge by Fatio.

May–June. Visited Fatio in London.

September 13 and 16. Letters to Locke and Pepys revealing breakdown.

November 23 and December 16. Letters advising Pepys on probability theory.

Composed *Praxis* and *De quadratura*.

Wallis published his *Opera* vol.II with an account of fluxions.

1694 May 11. Charles Montagu appointed Chancellor of Exchequer.

May. Visited by David Gregory in Cambridge; he compiled several memoranda on Newton's plans and on his unpublished writings.

September 1. Visited Flamsteed at Greenwich.

1695 Reworked *Enumeratio curvarum*.

Composed *Tabula refractionum*.

1696 March 19. Offered appointment of Warden of the Mint by Montagu.

April 20. Left Cambridge to take up Mint appointment.

August. Moved into Jermyn St house.

1697 January 30. Received and solved Bernoulli's problem. Details of solution read anonymously to Royal Society on February 24.

1698 December 4. Visited Flamsteed.

1699 February 21. Elected Foreign Associate of the *Académie des sciences*.

November 30. Elected to Council of Royal Society.

Completion of Great Recoinage.

Publication of Fatio's *Lineae brevissimi* and start of the priority dispute with Leibniz.

1700 February 3. Appointed Master of the Mint.

1701 January 27. William Whiston began to lecture at Cambridge as Newton's deputy.

May 28. *Scala graduum caloris* read anonymously to Royal Society.

November 26. Elected to Parliament by Cambridge Senate.

December 10. Resigned Lucasian chair.

1702 July 2. Parliament dissolved.

Autumn. Visited Locke at Oates.

Sat for Kneller.

Published *Lunae theoria*.

1703 March 3. Death of Robert Hooke.

November 30. Elected President of Royal Society.

Sat for Jervas.

1704 February. Published *Opticks*.

April 12. Visited Flamsteed at Greenwich.

December 7. Visited Prince George.

1705 January 23. Recommended to Prince George the publication of Flamsteed's *Observations*.

April 16. Knighted by Queen Anne in Cambridge.

May 17. Unsuccessful candidate in Parliamentary elections.

1706 Publication of first Latin edition of *Opticks* with its seven new queries.

1707 Publication of *Arithmetica universalis*.

April 15. Visited Greenwich with David Gregory.

November. Began Union Recoinage.

1709 Autumn. Moved to house in Chelsea.

October 11. Began correspondence with Cotes on the second edition of *Principia*.

1710 September. Moved to house in St Martin's St.

Adverse trial of the pyx.

De natura acidorum, *Enumeratio* and *De quadratura* published in *Lexicon technicum*.

Sat for Thornhill.

1711 Publication of *Analysis per quantitatum*.

1712 March 6. Committee set up by Royal Society to examine the priority dispute between Newton and Leibniz.

April 24. Committee's report read to Royal Society.

September. Visited by N. Bernoulli who raised problems about Book II, prop.X.

1713 January. Publication of *Commercium epistolicum*.

July 11–14. Publication of the second edition of *Principia*.

August 1. Visited Greenwich with Halley.

1714 June 11. Gave evidence to House of Commons committee on the longitude problem.

1715 February. Anonymous publication of *Account*.

May 19. Death of Montague.

November. Beginning of Leibniz–Clarke correspondence.

Visit by *Académie* delegation to observe solar eclipse.

First meeting with Conti.

1716 June 5. Death of Cotes.

November 14. Death of Leibniz.

1717 May 16. Presents portrait to Royal Society.

September 21. Published *State of Gold and Silver Coyns*.

December 22. Devaluation of guinea.

Marriage of John Conduitt and Catherine Barton.

Publication of second English edition of *Opticks* with eight new queries.

1718 Sat for Murray.

1719 Publication of second Latin edition of the *Opticks*.

1720 Publication of first French edition of *Traité d'optique*.

Publication of the first English edition of *Universal Arithmetick*.

Sat for Kneller.

August. Visited Oxford with John Keill.

1721 Publication of third English edition of *Opticks*.
Publication in *PT* of *Tabula refractionum*.
1722 Publication of second French edition of *Traité d'optique*.
Publication of second edition of *Commercium epistolicum* with the addition of the *Recensio*.
Attack of the stone.
1725 March 7. Conversation with Conduitt.
May 27. Refused to allow publication of *Short Chronology*; published, none the less, later in the year. Anonymous reply in *PT*.
Inflammation of the lungs.
Moves to Orbell's Buildings, Kensington.
1726 March 31. Publication of third edition of *Principia*.
1727 March 2. Attended Royal Society for last time.
March 18. Final collapse. Publication of second Latin edition of *Arithmetica universalis*.
March 20. Died between 1 and 2 a.m.
March 28. Body lay in state in Westminster Abbey.
April 4. Buried in Westminster Abbey.
1728 Publication of *Chronology of Ancient Kingdoms Amended*, *Short Chronicle*, *The System of the World*, *Optical Lectures* and *Universal Arithmetic*, *De mundi systemate*.
1729 Publication of *Lectiones opticae*.
Publication of Motte's English translation of *Principia*.
1731 Unveiling of monument at Westminster Abbey.
1733 Publication of *Observations on the prophecies*.

Lineae brevissimi descensus investigatio geometrica duplex (Twofold geometrical investigation into the line of briefest descent)

The *Lineae brevissimi*, published in 1699, of Fatio was the immediate cause of the long priority dispute between the Newtonians and the Leibnizians on the origins of the calculus. As Newton had not met Fatio for six years, it is unlikely that the work was even known to Newton, let alone inspired by him. Fatio informed the world that he had invented the calculus in 1687 and, while he was willing to cede his priority to Newton, the rights of Leibniz appeared to him to be more dubious. Whether Leibniz had actually borrowed anything from Newton, he would not himself judge but leave to those who had seen Newton's manuscripts. But, he added, he had seen the manuscripts and was consequently unimpressed by the 'active exertions of Leibniz in everywhere ascribing the invention of the calculus to himself' (RSW, p. 714).

Leibniz complained to the Royal Society and published both a signed reply and an anonymous review in the *AE* (November 1669, pp. 510–13; May 1700, pp. 198–208) and thereafter the issue dragged on for another quarter of a century.

See also Fatio de Duillier; Priority dispute

Linus, Franciscus (1595–1675)

Also known as Francis Hall and Francis Line, Linus, as he became when he entered the Jesuit order, spent most of this career teaching mathematics and Hebrew at his order's English college in Liège.

In 1675 Linus published two papers in the *PT* critical of Newton's *New Theory about Light and Colors* (1672). He began by questioning the very basis of the 1672 paper. Newton's crucial observation that, under certain conditions, a ray of light passing through a prism adopts an oblong form was dismissed by Linus as a trivial meteorological effect. He too, he announced, had observed such phenomena but, he added, only on a cloudy day. The effect was thus due to clouds 'making a far greater Angle of Intersection . . . than the true rays of the Sun do make' (*PLNP*, p. 149). Newton replied briefly and to the point: 'the Experiment . . . was tryed in clear days' (*PLNP*, p. 150).

This, however, was not enough for Linus. In his second *PT* paper he insisted, amongst several other misunderstandings, that the experiment 'was not made in a clear day' (*PLNP*, p. 151). Newton's initial answer was brief and curt. The dispute, he noted, was no longer 'about any ratiocination but my veracity in relating an Experiment'. Such an issue could not be resolved by further discourse but by a 'new tryal of the Experiment' (*PLNP*, p. 153).

Two months later in January 1676 Newton was informed that Linus was dead. His pupil, William Gascoigne, went on to relate that shortly before his death the seventy-nine-year-old Linus had tried once more to repeat Newton's experiments and once more failed. 'Mr. Newton's Experiment will hardly stand', he concluded (*PLNP*, p. 155). Nor did the matter rest with the death of Linus. Yet another English Jesuit from Liège, Anthony Lucas, appeared to express comparable doubts about the reliability of Newton's 1672 experiments.

Linus had earlier won a limited kind of fame by publishing views on the atmosphere which provoked Robert Boyle to perform a series of experiments in 1662 which would lead him to the discovery of the now familiar Boyle's law.

Lloyd, William (1627–1717)

Lloyd served successively as Bishop of St Asaph, Lichfield, and Coventry before taking in 1700 the see of Worcester. Earlier, in 1688, he had been imprisoned by James II in the Tower as one of the seven Bishops who had protested against the Declaration of Indulgence which would have allowed Catholics to hold public office. He was tried and acquitted.

Like many of his contemporaries, Lloyd was deeply interested in chronology. He formed the opinion that a calendar of 360 days was common in the ancient world. Such views were discussed in correspondence with Humphrey Prideaux, Dean of Norwich, some time in 1713. Lloyd's views were passed on to Newton, stimulating him to prepare a draft of his own opinions on the subject. The draft was eventually published in the *Gentleman's Magazine* (1755) under the title 'Form of the most Ancient Year'.

See also Calendrical writings

Locke, John (1632–1704)

The son of a lawyer, Locke was educated at Oxford. He began his career as a physician and in 1667 entered the service of Ashley Cooper, later to become the first Earl of Shaftesbury, and with whom he remained, whether in government or exile, until Shaftesbury's death in 1683. Locke spent the period 1683 to 1689 once more in exile, in Holland, and shortly after his return to England in 1689 he joined the family of Sir Francis Masham at Oates, Essex, with whom he remained for the rest of his life.

Locke was one of the first major figures of European thought to recognise the genius of Newton. His most important work, the *Essay Concerning Human Understanding* (1690), the founding document of modern empiricism, made clear his commitment to Newton. 'It is ambition enough', he declared, 'in an age that produces . . . the incomparable Mr Newton . . . to be employed as an under-labourer in clearing the ground a little, and removing some of the rubbish that lies in the way to knowledge.' Locke made a considerable effort, despite his lack of mathematics, to understand 'the incomparable' Mr Newton's work. He sought advice from Huygens about how best to approach *Principia*, becoming in due course, in Desaguliers's phrase, 'the first Newtonian philosopher without the help of geometry'.

The two probably met some time soon after Locke's return to England from exile in Holland in 1689. Judging by Newton's surviving letters to Locke, the relationship between them was one of the freest and relaxed to be found in the whole correspondence. The letter of 3 May 1692 beginnning:

Now the churlish weather is almost over I was thinking within a Post or two to put you in mind of my desire to see you here where you shall be as welcome as I can make you. I am glad you have preventd me because I hope now to see you ye sooner. You may lodge conveniently either at ye Rose Tavern or Queen's Arms Inn. (C, III, p. 214)

This is about as informal and conversational as Newton's letters ever became.

Another, and for Newton quite untypical, sign of the esteem he held Locke in was his willingness, eagerness even, to visit him at the Masham house in Sussex. It should be remembered that apart from visits to London, journeys home to Woolsthorpe, and one visit to Oxford, Newton spent his life at his two places of work, Cambridge and London. Yet he chose to visit Locke in January 1691 and in the autumn of 1702. There was also talk on other occasions of visits which failed to come off. Only Fatio amongst the Newton circle seems to have warranted special visits. Also, like Fatio, he was offered and accepted an invitation to visit Newton in Cambridge. Again, it is difficult to think of others who received personal invitations to visit Newton. Unlike his relationship with Fatio, Newton's friendship with Locke ended only with his death in 1704.

One obvious reason for the continuing friendship was its base in a number of common interests. Eighteen letters from Newton to Locke have survived and clearly reveal their interest in biblical scholarship and chemistry. It was their common interest in the first subject which led Newton to seek Locke's advice on the publication of his *Two Notable Corruptions of Scripture*. Through his contacts in Holland, Locke sought to accommodate Newton and with the help of Jean le Clerc would undoubtedly have had, without the inevitable change of mind on Newton's part, the manuscript translated and printed in 1692. The letters of 1691–2 also reveal much discussion about a certain 'red earth' of Boyle's and a recipe for the extraction from it of pure mercury. Newton seemed reluctant to undertake any actual experimental work himself on this issue, but remained willing to discuss the matter with Locke.

One further theme running through the correspondence was the need to find Newton a suitable post. In late 1691 the posts of Master of Charterhouse, Controller of the Mint and Provost of King's College, Cambridge were being discussed. Locke, with his political contacts, enlisted the aid of Charles Mordaunt, a leading Whig politician. Nothing however came of their plans. When Newton, in 1696, was appointed to the Mint as Warden, Locke was serving as Commissioner at the Board of Trade, and the two friends consequently found themselves working together. One letter has survived from this period and reveals the two leading philosophers discussing the weights of Spanish Pistols, French Crowns and Cross Dollers (*C*, IV, p. 282).

The best-known letter, however, sufficiently famous to become the basis of a novel and film by John Banville, remains the letter of 16 September 1693 in which Newton, recovering from a breakdown of some kind, confessed to Locke that: 'Being of the opinion that you endeavoured to embroil me with woemen – by other means I was so much affected with it as that when one told me you were sickly and would not live I answered twere better if you were dead. I desire you to forgive me this uncharitableness' (*C*, III, p. 280). The letter must have come as a considerable shock to Locke. He replied on 5 October as best he could. He hoped he had 'not lost a freind' he so much valued and went on to assure Newton that 'I am more ready to forgive you than you can be to desire it'. After some more awkward discussion, Locke, with some clear relief, went on to talk about the forthcoming new edition of his *Essay*.

Logan, James (1674–1751)

The son of a Quaker schoolmaster, Logan sailed with Penn in 1699 and served as his secretary in Pennsylvania. Trading in land and furs brought him a fortune, with which he assembled at his house in Stenton one of the finest libraries in the New World. In about 1708 he imported the first copy of *Principia* into America. On his death his library went to the Library Company of Philadelphia, a subscription library started by Benjamin Franklin in 1731.

See also Newton in America

Loggan, David (1635–1700)

Born in Danzig, Loggan arrived in Britain some time before 1653. In 1669 he was appointed engraver to Oxford University and produced shortly afterwards his *Oxonia illustrata* (1675) with its forty plates. This was followed by twenty-six views of Cambridge, drawn between 1676 and 1688 and printed in his *Cantabrigia illustrata* (1690). Loggan's latter work contains the only contemporary engraving of Trinity College. It shows very clearly the Great Gate, the front of the college with the rooms probably occupied by Newton, the stairs down to his garden and his laboratory. The print has been frequently reproduced and can be seen in RSW (p. 255), Manuel (1980, p. 174) and Rattansi (1974, p. 72).

Loggan was also reported to have drawn Newton's portrait in 1677 for a planned book on light and colour (*C*, II, pp. 200–1). It has not survived, nor was the book ever completed.

Longitude

The problem of the determination of longitude in a practical and simple manner persisted throughout much of the eighteenth century. It became official after an horrific error in 1707 by Admiral Sir Cloudesley Shovell, in which he mistook the Scilly Islands for the English Channel and ran four ships on to the Gilstone Ledges with a loss of 2,000 lives. Petitioned by seamen and merchants alike, the House of Commons appointed a committee in 1714 to investigate the problem and to evaluate a number of proposed solutions. For help on technical matters they called upon, amongst others, Newton, Halley and Flamsteed.

Newton's evidence, given before the Committee on 11 June 1714, was first published in the *House of Commons Journal*, vol. 17. He discussed four proposed solutions. The first, by keeping exact time with a watch, awaited the development of an instrument able to cope with 'the Motion of a Ship, the Variation of Heat and Cold, Wet and Dry, and the difference of Gravity in different Latitudes'. The second method involved observing eclipses of Jupiter's satellites, a task too difficult to perform on a moving ship with a long telescope. Thirdly, Newton dismissed relying on lunar observations as they were too inaccurate to produce 'a Longitude within Two or Three Degrees'. Against the proposal of Humphrey Ditton, which involved siting vessels at known intervals along the trade routes from which they would fire midnight flares, Newton went into greater detail. It too, he declared, would be impractical and was really a method 'for keeping an account of the Longitude at Sea, than for finding it'.

The Committee, with Newton's support, recommended the setting up of a Board of Longitude empowered to award a prize of £20,000 to anyone who could determine longitude at sea with an accuracy of half a degree. Newton, as President of the Royal Society, found himself an *ex officio* member of the Board for the rest of his life. Thereafter Newton was often invited by the Board to evaluate the proposals and instruments that the inventors of Europe sent to London. Consequently his correspondence after 1714 contains several of his careful judgments on the solutions put before him. Thus as late as 1725 at the age of eighty-three Newton was to be found testing the 'hour glasses of Mr Rowe made with sand of Tin and reporting to the Lords Commissioners of his Majties Admiralty' that 'its greatest errors in running too fast or too slow did scarce exceed a minute in an hour' (*C*, VII, pp. 330–2). There are signs that Newton, though ever conscientious in his official duties, was beginning to find them somewhat irksome. Consequently in 1721 he drafted the proposals that clocks should not be submitted to the Board before being examined and tested at sea, while astronomical theories should be first examined by astronomers and sea-captains of Trinity House (*C*, VII, p. 173).

Newton's own view that 'without Astronomy the longitude is not to be found' (*C*, VI, p. 211) seems not to have changed. Clocks may, he conceded, enable the navigator to keep the longitude once having found it by other means but, in his final published words on the question, 'the Longitude will scarce be found at sea without pursuing those methods by which it may be found at land. And those methods are hitherto only two: one by the motion of the Moon, the other by that of the innermost Satellit of Jupiter' (*C*, VII, p. 330). But these methods, he judged, as he had done in 1714, were neither exact enough nor practical enough for regular use.

Newton's evidence was read to the Board and his draft has survived in the PC in ULC. It has been published twice in recent times: *C*, VI, pp. 161–2 and Howse (1980, pp. 80–1).

Lowndes, William (1652–1724)

Lowndes joined the staff of the Treasury in 1679 and served there from 1695 until 1724 as its Permanent Secretary, a post which brought him into regular contact with Newton. He also served from 1695 until 1722 as a Member of Parliament.

In 1695 Lowndes was invited to give his views on the state of the coinage. They were presented in his *Essay for the Amendment of the Silver Coin* (Shaw, 1935). He argued that the simplest way to restore confidence in the currency would be to raise the face value of the coins, with a half crown becoming 3s 1½d, and a pound weight of silver yielding 75s rather than the customary 60s. Newton expressed similar views. A 25 per cent devaluation was deemed to be unacceptable and the government approved instead the more difficult and far costlier proposal of John Locke to recoin at the old standard.

Although twenty-one letters between Newton and Lowndes have survived, the bulk of them do little more than inform Newton of a forthcoming meeting, or advise him of the need to submit a report on some official matter to the Treasury. There is nothing in the exchanges of a quarter century to suggest that relations between the two were ever anything more than official and formal.

Lowndes's name can be found in dictionaries of quotations as the originator of the familiar phrase 'Take care of the pence and the pounds will take care of themselves.'

See also Mint, Recoinage

Lucas, Anthony (1633–93)

A British Jesuit from Durham, Lucas served from 1672 at his order's English college at Liège as Professor of Theology. He moved later in 1687 to Rome to head the English College and in 1693, shortly before his death, he was appointed Provincial of the order.

At Liège he had observed the failure of his colleague Franciscus Linus to repeat the experiments reported by Newton in his 1672 paper, *New Theory about Light and Colors*. After the death of Linus in 1675, Lucas came forward to present the Liège case. He began by conceding that on a clear day he had indeed found 'the length of the coloured image', as it emerged from the prism, 'considerably greater than its breadth' (*PLNP*, p. 164). But, whereas Newton had reported an image five times as long as it was broad, Lucas could only achieve a ratio of three-and-a-half. He went on to report the results of nine experiments, called by him 'Experimental Exceptions', which, he hoped, would not be 'unwelcome' to Newton.

Newton's reply in the *PT* largely ignored the nine experiments, 'For it is not number of Experiments, but weight to be regarded', he insisted, 'and where one will do, what need many?' (*PLNP*, p. 174). His main concern was to insist on the accuracy of his 1672 report that images were elongated by a factor of five, not the three-and-a-half claimed by Lucas. Once more he went into details of his experimental arrangement, giving for the first time exact measurements of the prisms used, the length of the room and the images formed.

By this time, September 1676, Newton could call on the RS to support him. In April 1676 his experimental work of 1672 had been publicly performed and confirmed by the officers of the Society. By this time, also, Newton had begun to tire of the dispute; 'For I see a man must either resolve to put out nothing new or to become a slave to defend it', he wrote to Oldenburg shortly after receiving yet one more letter from Lucas. At one point it seems that Newton was considering printing all the correspondence and leaving it to interested readers to make up their own minds. A fire and the destruction of vital papers at this time may well have delayed the project long enough to divert Newton's interests to other fields.

Further letters, however, continued to come from Lucas throughout 1677 and 1678. At first Newton simply ignored them. Finally, on 3

March 1678 he sent to Lucas the most brutal and dismissive letter he was ever to compose.

> Do men use to press one another into Disputes? Or am I bound to satisfy you? It seems you thought it not enough to propound Objections unless you might insult over me for my inability to answer them all . . . But how know you yt I did not think them too weak to require an answer and only to gratify your importunity complied to answer one or two of ye best . . . I hope you will consider how little I desire to explain your proceedings in public. (C, II, p. 263)

Quite incredibly Lucas persisted with his correspondence. Newton's final comment is contained in a letter to John Aubrey dating from June 1678: 'I understand you have a letter from Mr Lucas for me. Pray forbear to send me anything more of that nature' (C, II, p. 269). Nothing more would be published by Newton on these issues until the appearance in 1704 of the *Opticks*.

Lucas, Henry (d.1663)

Educated at St John's College, Cambridge, Lucas served as secretary to the Earl of Holland, the Chancellor of the University. He was briefly, in 1639–40, M.P. for Cambridge. In response to the Savilian chairs at Oxford, founded in 1619 by Sir Henry Savile, Lucas directed his executor to purchase lands of sufficient value to bring in £100 a year with which to endow a new chair at Cambridge.

See also Lucasian chair of mathematics and the Lucasian lectures

Lucasian chair of mathematics and the Lucasian lectures

When Henry Lucas instructed his executors to raise £100 a year to finance a Cambridge chair, it was the first new chair created since Henry VIII in 1540 founded his five Regius professorships. Barrow had a large say in the drafting of the statutes and conveniently laid it down that holders would be entitled to retain their Fellowships, to hold non-pastoral church appointments and to lecture on 'some part of Geometry, Astronomy, Geography, Optics, Statics or some other Mathematical discipline' each week during the three terms. Ten lectures had to be deposited each year in the University library. The first five occupants of the chair, all of whom were connected with Newton in some way, were:

1 Isaac Barrow, 1663–9;

2 Isaac Newton, 1669–1701, although Newton actually left Cambridge for London in 1696;

3 William Whiston, 1701–10; he was dismissed for his Unitarian views;

4 Nicolas Saunderson, 1711–39, blind through an attack of smallpox at the age of one;

5 John Colson, 1739–60, editor and translator of Newton's *Method of Fluxions*.

The details of Newton's lectures during his tenure of the Lucasian chair are as follows.

1 *1670–2*. He lectured on optics and in 1674 deposited the lectures in the University library. They were eventually published as *Lectiones opticae* (1728).

2 *1673–83*. He lectured on mathematics. The lectures were deposited in the year 1683–4 and were eventually published as *Arithmetica universalis* (1707).

3 *1684–5*. Newton lectured on the material which eventually became part of *Principia* (1687), Book I. It was deposited in the library under the title *De motu corporum, liber primus*.

4 *1687*. Lectures entitled *De motu corporum, liber secundus* were eventually published as *De mundi systemate* (1728).

No record has survived of what Newton did in 1686 and between 1686 and 1696 when he took up his appointment at the Mint. Did he simply not lecture? Or did he merely fail to deposit his lectures? A more complex question is just how reliable are the deposited lectures as a record of Newton's behaviour. Did he deliver the lectures as deposited? And if so did he continue to deliver them over a period of time?

Cohen has argued that they are a far-from-accurate record. They are, rather, 'finished treatises', 'revised, rewritten and polished versions, prepared by Newton . . . *after* they had been delivered' (*PLNP*, p. 305). Cohen thought, none the less, that the deposited lectures did represent the subjects Newton lectured on at the relevant times.

One further query concerns Newton's audience. Who were they? And how many? According to Humphrey Newton, 'so few went to hear him . . . oftentimes he did . . . for want of Hearers, read to ye Walls'. Although he was supposed to lecture for thirty minutes, he had often returned to his rooms in much less time. Substance is added to Humphrey Newton's claim when actual auditors at the lectures are sought for. Westfall has claimed to have detected only three students who, during Newton's twenty-seven-year occupancy of the chair, actually heard him lecture. They were his successor William Whiston, and the obscure figures of Henry Wharton and Sir Thomas Parkyns (RSW, p. 210).

Although Newton retained his chair as a sinecure long after he had left for London, it had earlier looked at one time as if he would have to resign the post. In January 1675 he wrote to Oldenburg that 'ye time draws near yt I am to part with my Fellowship' (*C*, VII, p. 387). The trouble was Newton's failure to take orders, in violation of the rule that after several years Fellows either did so or resigned. Someone must have intervened behind the scenes, for on 27 April 1675 a Royal Patent exempted the Lucasian Professor from the rule.

It is a common belief that Newton obtained the chair when its incumbent, his tutor Isaac Barrow, first appreciated the unparalleled genius of his young pupil. Against this traditional story it must be realised that Newton was never Barrow's pupil and that, secondly, Barrow was keen to give up the chair and devote his time to theological activities, a not uncommon priority in the late seventeenth century. Further, Barrow was ambitious to gain the Mastership of the College, a post he could not hold while still occupying the Lucasian chair. There were thus ample grounds for Barrow's resignation. Having once decided to resign, he was then free to recommend as his replacement his young colleague whose mathematical genius he was one of the first to recognise.

Lunar apogee and nodes

The apogee, as opposed to the perigee, is the point in a satellite's orbit of greatest distance from the earth. It is not a fixed point. Because of the pull of the sun the whole lunar orbit slowly revolves in its own plane. As a result the lunar apogee progresses around the plane of the moon's orbit in about nine years. In *Principia*, Book I, prop. XLV Newton calculated the rate of the progression to be 1° 31′ 28″ a month; the actual rate, he also noted, was 'twice as swift' (Cajori, p. 147). The discrepancy was finally cleared up by Clairaut in 1749 with his detection of several terms apparently neglected by Newton. Once incorporated into lunar theory they yielded the desired results. It has, however, been claimed that Newton had in fact succeeded in correcting the error himself without bothering to publish his new results in the final edition of *Principia* (1726). The evidence is to be found in the Cambridge *Catalogue* of the PC (1888), and is discussed by Ball (1893) and Cajori (pp. 648–51).

The two places where the moon's orbit cuts the ecliptic are known as the nodes, ascending and descending respectively. Only when the moon is close to a node can an eclipse occur. Like the apogee and perigee, the nodes are not fixed, but regress around the ecliptic. Ptolemy in the second century AD had calculated the nodes to regress completely around the ecliptic in 6,729.26 days (18.6 years). The problem was discussed by Newton in *Principia*, Book III, props. XXX–XXXIII. He also added immediately afterwards an alternative account prepared by John Machin.

Newton calculated the mean motion of the lunar nodes in a sidereal year to be 19° 18′ 1″, just about the same 18.6 years worked out by Ptolemy long before. Machin's comparable figure was 19° 20′ 31″.

M

Machin, John (1680–1751)

Little is known of Machin's early background. He clearly impressed Newton, who described him as the man who 'understood his *Principia* better than anyone'. Elected to the RS in 1710, he was first to serve Newton in 1712 as a faithful member of the RS committee appointed to investigate the priority dispute between Newton and Leibniz. In the following year he was appointed Professor of Astronomy at Gresham College on Newton's recommendation. Machin was, Newton informed the electors, 'studious, sober, and learned in the Latin tongue, and in Mathematicks . . . a great Master' (*C*, V, p. 408).

Contact was maintained between the two for the remainder of Newton's life. With Newton as President of the RS from 1703, and Machin as Secretary from 1718–47, regular meetings between the two mathematicians are likely to have taken place during the last decade of Newton's life. One sign of this was the choice of Machin to see Newton's own edition of *Arithmetica universalis* (1722) through the press. Conduitt reported that Newton had intended 'to give him 100 guineas but made him wait 3 years for a preface and then did not write one'.

Machin himself seems to have worked mainly on lunar theory, producing a large but incomplete work never yet published. Two pieces which did appear were his account of *The Motion of the Moon's Nodes* and *The Laws of the Moon's Motion according to Gravity*. The former was incorporated by Newton into the third edition of *Principia* (Cajori, pp. 464–7), and the latter was added to Motte's English translation of *Principia* (1729).

His name remains linked with *Principia* by a ludicrous misprint. Initially introduced as 'Mr. Machin, Gresham Professor', the title became misplaced in the Davis edition of 1803 with the result that the nebulous figure of a 'Professor Gresham' can be found following Machin's name. The error has been retained in the various Cajori editions and can still be seen in the *Scholium* following prop. XXXIII of Book III.

Maclaurin, Colin (1698–1746)

The youngest son of a clergyman, Maclaurin was educated at Glasgow University where he came to the attention of the Euclid scholar, Robert Simson. He began his career as Professor of Mathematics at Marischal College, Aberdeen in 1717 and as such first met Newton on a visit to London in 1719. In 1725 Newton wrote of Maclaurin, in support of his application for a post at Edinburgh: 'I reccon him well skilled in Arithmetic, Algebra, & Astronomy & Opticks . . .& abundantly sufficient for a Professor.' The Chair was held by James Gregory, brother of David Gregory. Consequently Newton offered 'to contribute twenty pounds per annum towards a provision for him till Mr Gregories place becomes void if I live so long' (*C*, VII, p. 338). Gregory retired shortly afterwards on health grounds. He was succeeded by Maclaurin, who held the chair until his death in 1746.

Maclaurin was the author of two important works on Newtonian philosophy and mathematics. The first, *An Account of Sir Isaac Newton's Philosophical Discoveries*, though complete in 1728 and intended to be part of Conduitt's intended memoir of Newton, was published posthumously in 1748. It has been described by Cohen (1956, p. 209) as one of the three 'most outstanding popular introductions to Newtonian science of the eighteenth century'.

The second and more substantial work, *A Treatise of Fluxions*, 2 vols (1742), was translated into French (1749) and was re-issued in 1801 in a second English edition. Maclaurin had taken seriously the objections raised by the philosopher George Berkeley against 'modern Analysis'. He did not, however, seek, as others would do, to make sense of Newton's ultimate ratios in terms of limits, but rather he sought to validate Newtonian procedures by rigorous geometrical proofs. The result was unfortunate for British mathematics, which became narrowly Newtonian, geometrical and insular. It was not until the nineteenth century that it rejoined the mainstream of European mathematics and introduced the study of the differential calculus into the Cambridge curriculum.

As a pure mathematician, Maclaurin's name is preserved by the Maclaurin series, a special case of the Taylor series.

See also Berkeley, George; Fluxions, fluents and moments; Taylor, Brook

McSwiney, Owen

McSwiney had been a theatrical manager, actor and impresario before abandoning London for Venice in 1711 to escape from his creditors. In

Venice he awarded Canaletto his first British commission in 1722 and went on to sell the results to the Duke of Richmond, grandson of Charles II and Louise de Keroualle. Many of them can still be seen at the Richmond country house of Goodwood in Sussex.

A further venture, begun in the mid-1720s, involved commissioning several leading Venetian painters to produce a number of elaborate, allegorical paintings of the 'Tombs' of 'British Worthies who were bright and shining Ornaments to their Country'. The initial plan was to have 'a principal Urn' supposedly containing 'the Remains of the deceased Hero'. It would be surrounded by 'Statues and Basso Rilievo's' alluding to 'the Imployments, or to the Learning and Science of the Departed' (Haskell, 1970, p. 307). Twenty-four such paintings were originally planned, Levey (1980, p. 82) has noted, and, of those completed, ten were bought by the Duke of Richmond and hung at Goodwood. Engravings of nine of the completed tombs by a group of French painters headed by François Boucher, including that of Newton, were published in Paris in 1741 under the title *Tombeaux des Princes grands capitaines et autres hommes illustrés*. Two of the tombs, those belonging to William III and the Duke of Devonshire, can be seen displayed in Borenius (1936) and Levey (1980) respectively.

Newton's tomb was painted by Giovanni Pittoni and the Valeriani brothers, Domenico and Giuseppe. The original picture is inaccessible in a private collection in Rome. The 1741 engraving, however, can be seen displayed in Haskell (1970, p. 310). The engraving shows Minerva and the Sciences being led weeping to the Urn. Above it an inscribed pyramid shows a beam of light passing through a prism, while various figures stand around in the manner of Raphael's 'School of Athens'. The painting was completed by 1729 and sold to a Sir William Morice.

From correspondence between John Conduitt and McSwiney, published in Haskell (1970, pp. 311–16), it seems that a second painting was commissioned, one intended to meet the particular demands of Conduitt. The urn has been replaced by the Westminster Abbey monument, the prism has been removed and the scene much simplified. Although Conduitt had paid £50 in advance for the painting, it seems that McSwiney was unable to complete the commission to Conduitt's satisfaction and the picture went elsewhere. Haskell prints what he terms 'a bad photograph' of the original (1970, p. 315).

Magirus, Johannes

As a Cambridge undergraduate of the 1660s, Newton's introduction to physics was through the *Physiologiae peripateticae* (1642, Peripatetic Physics) of Magirus. Notes taken from the work were entered into his *Philosophy Notebook*. The work itself, as the title indicates, is Aristotelian and clearly reveals how little Newton can have gained from his undergraduate education. If the notes are a reliable guide to the extent of his reading, Newton would seem not to have finished the book.

Manley, Mary de la Rivière (1663–1724)

Born in Jersey, Mrs Manley is best known for her *New Atlantis* (1709), and as the successor to Swift as editor of *The Examiner*. In 1710 she published the *roman à clef*, *Memoirs of Europe*, a work supposedly written by Eginardus, secretary to Charlemagne. The Constantinople of the book, of course, represents London and provides ample opportunity to present the gossip and scandal of her day camouflaged as eighth-century events.

One character described is Julius Sergius with a mistress, La Bartica, 'ever a proud slut', on whom he had 'lavish'd Myriads'. Besides demanding marriage, she had also gained for her 'worthy ancient Parent a good Post'. Newton's attitude to the work, assuming he was aware of it, is unknown.

See also Barton, Catherine

Manuel, Frank Edward (1910–   )

A noted American historian of ideas, Manuel served for many years as Professor of History at Brandeis University. He has written extensively on utopian themes in European thought, producing finally with his wife, Fritzie Manuel, their definitive study *Utopian Thought in the Western World* (1979). He has also published three important books on Newton's life and work.

The first such work, *Isaac Newton, Historian* (1963), displayed considerable originality. Before Manuel, no one had been prepared to take seriously or to work intensively upon any aspect of Newton's non-scientific writing. Manuel not only surveyed all Newton's chronological work, and firmly located it in its own historical context, he also published for the first time a couple of Newton's historical manuscripts. A second monograph, *The Religion of Isaac Newton* (1974), much less detailed, did little more than attempt to mark out the main areas of Newton's religious concerns; once again, however, Manuel took the opportunity to publish for the first time a number of Newton's manuscripts.

Manuel's best-known work on Newton remains his *A Portrait of Isaac Newton* (1968; British edition, 1980). Meant neither as an orthodox biography, nor as a survey of Newton's scientific achievements, it sought instead to identify and to exhibit the rich and varied character of Newton. Further, and with less success, Manuel made a bold attempt to relate Newton's work, scientific and otherwise, to the character he had so vividly portrayed. Although few have been prepared to follow Manuel in his detailed presentation of Newton's portrait, many have, none the less, sought in his manner to portray Newton in a more realistic light.

See also Biography

Marat, Jean Paul (1743–93)

The great revolutionary leader, slain in his bath by Charlotte Corday, had earlier studied medicine at Bordeaux. He spent some time in Britain, practising medicine in London, gaining in 1775 an M.D. from St Andrews, and publishing, in English, *An Essay on Gleets* (1775), an early study of chronic gonorrhoea. Marat was also a philosopher and consequently, in the manner of the times, conducted experiments on light, heat and electricity. His most durable work in science was a new French translation of Newton's *Opticks* (1787, 2 vols). It was published anonymously as 'par M---' and, ironically, 'Dédiée au Roi'. It is 'an excellent translation', according to Gillispie (1980, p. 320), a 'free rendering' but nowhere 'inaccurate'.

In addition, and less successfully, Marat sought to develop an original theory of light. In his *Découvertes sur la lumière* (1779) (Discoveries about light), and other writings, he argued that Newton was wrong to insist that colours were produced by the refraction of light. They arose, he claimed, by diffraction and consequently proposed the science of 'perioptics' for its study.

Marci, Johann (1595–1667)

A Bohemian, Marci was educated at the University of Prague where he obtained his M.D. in 1625 and where he served for much of his life as Professor of Medicine. He also served as physician to the Emperors Ferdinand III and Leopold I.

Marci is sometimes described as having anticipated Newton's key insights into the composite nature of light first publicly announced by him in 1672. Marci, however, in his much earlier work, *Thaumantias, liber de arcu coelisti* (1648, Thaumantias, the celestial arc), had announced the following results.

Theorem XII: Different colours are produced by different refractions.

Theorem XVIII: The same colour cannot proceed from two different refractions, and the same refraction cannot produce more than one colour.

Theorem XX: If a coloured ray is refracted, this does not change in colour. (Lohne, 1968, p. 175)

Even more startling, it has been claimed, is a clear description in the work of Newton's *experimentum crucis*.

Missing from Marci's work, however, was the further step taken by Newton in demonstrating that the various coloured rays could be reconstituted into white light. Also missing was any special emphasis assigned to the results. Whereas, with Newton, the importance and significance of his insights and conclusions were repeatedly declared, Marci simply presented the equivalent theorems as three amongst many. Consequently, while this allows the modern reader to identify anticipations of Newton, the contemporary reader, without the benefit of hindsight, would have found it less easy to recognise such crucial developments amongst the multiplicity of Marci's theorems.

There is no evidence that Newton had ever read or was aware of Marci's views.

Mariotte, Edme (1620–84)

A priest and prior, Mariotte is best known to British scientists for his independent discovery in 1676 of what is known in Britain as Boyle's law. He was, however, one of the earliest practitioners of experimental physics in France. The work which had most impact on the reception of Newton's views in France was Mariotte's *De la nature des couleurs* (1681) in which he described his unsuccessful attempts to repeat Newton's *experimentum crucis*.

Mariotte passed light through a prism and then directed the violet light from the resulting spectrum through a second prism. He found, unlike Newton, that the violet rays which emerged from the second prism were mixed with rays of red and yellow. Consequently, Mariotte concluded, 'the ingenious hypothesis of Mr.Newton should not be admitted'. It led to French scientists effectively ignoring Newton's work on light and colour for another thirty years.

See also Experimentum crucis; Newton in France

Mathematical development

It is widely recognised today that mathematicians, like musicians and chess players, sometimes display quite remarkable talents when young. Contrary to popular legend, Newton revealed no such precociousness.

When he left Grantham in 1661 for Cambridge, Newton had yet to show any special skills other than his mechanical ingenuity and dexterity. When, in 1947, the windows were opened in the north bedroom of Newton's childhood home for the first time in almost 250 years, considerable excitement was aroused when several geometrical figures were discovered carved in the stone (Richardson, 1947, pp. 34–5). Analysis of them by Robinson (1947) soon showed them to be without mathematical interest. The signs, Whiteside (1964) has argued, would require 'the blindness of maternal love' before they could ever be seen as examples of 'mathematical precocity'.

Newton's own account of his mathematical development, as related to de Moivre, began with a visit in 1663 to Stourbridge fair and the purchase of a work on judicial astrology. Finding the diagrams hard to understand he was led, via works on trigonometry and Euclid, to the texts of such contemporary mathematicians as Descartes, Oughtred and Wallis. From his notebooks he was able later to establish that towards the end of 1664 he bought 'Schooten's Miscellanies and Cartes's Geometry . . . and borrowed Wallis's works'. Oughtred's *Clavis* and the *Geometrie* of Descartes had in fact been read, he added, 'above half a year before'.

Although Newton came to higher mathematics at a relatively late age, his progress was extraordinarily rapid. Within two years he had found the method of infinite series, the binomial theorem, the method of tangents and the direct method of fluxions. He had also computed 'the area of the Hyperbola . . . to two and fifty figures'. Such exercises in computation give some idea of the intensity with which Newton must have pursued his mathematical researches at this time. Also present in the early papers are several attempts to calculate logarithms to fifty-five places.

Such progress as Newton did make derived entirely from his own resources. Stimulated by the books he read, and quite independently of any teachers or friends, he began in 1664 to reshape the mathematics of his day. The process was virtually completed by 1672. Its main stages can be followed in the three works October 1666 Tract, *De analysi* (1669) and *De methodis* (1670–1). Thereafter, much of Newton's mathematical effort was spent not so much in developing his great insights of the 1660s but in seeking to present them in an acceptable form. Such works of the 1680s, for example, as *Geometria curvilinea*, *Mathesos universalis* and *De computo* were not in fact new works but Newton's attempts to rework earlier material into a publishable treatise. Other interests intervened to prevent their completion. Newton's final views on the problems of the 1660s were expressed in his draft of *De quadratura* composed in 1691–2 and published several years later as an appendix to the *Opticks* (1704).

From this point onwards Newton's mathematical energies were

directed towards defending the priority of his achievements of the 1660s against the claims of the Continental mathematicians, and the preparation of the second edition of *Principia* (1713). Once it is appreciated that, by this time, Newton was approaching 70, such behaviour can in no way be seen as unusual.

Mathematical notation

In the matter of orthodox mathematics, Newton inevitably adopted the conventional notations of his day, many of which are still in current usage. When, however, he began to set down in the 1660s his newly-invented calculus, he was immediately presented with the problem of how to represent such original concepts as fluxions, fluents and moments.

Fluxions – the rate at which a quantity was generated – were represented by dotted letters. Thus, for the fluxion of x, Newton wrote $\dot{x}$. Fluents – the actual quantities generated – were denoted variously by ⊠, [x] or, more commonly $\dot{x}$. Higher-order fluxions and fluents were formed on the same pattern, yielding $\ddot{x}$, $\dddot{x}$ and $\overset{..}{x}$, $\overset{...}{x}$ respectively. Moments, the indefinitely small amounts by which quantities grow, were represented by o. Equating fluxions with their modern equivalent, $\dot{x}$ and $\dot{y}$ become dx/dt and dy/dt, respectively, and $\ddot{x}$ and $\ddot{y}$ appear as d^2x/dt^2 and d^2y/dt^2.

Dotted letters first appeared in print in 1693 in the extracts taken from Newton's manuscript of *De quadratura* and published by Wallis in vol. 2 of his *Algebra*. They first appeared in print in a work published by Newton himself in 1704 in the revised version of *De quadratura* appended to the *Opticks*. The issue of their first appearance in a manuscript has become somewhat complicated by the anachronistic tendencies of later editors. John Colson, for example, in his 1736 English translation of the *De methodis* manuscript dating from 1670–1, attributed to Newton the convention of representing fluents by the letters v, x, y and z and fluxions by the dotted letters $\dot{v}$, $\dot{x}$, $\dot{y}$ and $\dot{z}$. Whiteside (*MP*, III, pp. 72–3) has shown, however, that in the original manuscript Newton designated fluxions with the letters l, m, n and r. While the dot notation thus dates only from the *De quadratura* manuscripts of the 1690s, the use of o to stand for infinitesimal quantities can be found in manuscripts of 1665 and 1666. For the process of integration or quadrature Newton adopted, once again in the *De quadratura* manuscript of 1691, the symbol Q.

It is thus clear that Newton has exercised little influence on the calculus notation found in the textbooks of today. This in fact, with the d expressing differentiation and $\int$ expressing integration, originated with Leibniz. It was first used by him in manuscripts dating from late 1675, and first appeared in print in 1684 in his *Nova methodis pro maximis et minimis*.

Nor was it until well into the nineteenth century that Leibniz's differential notation became acceptable to British mathematicians. Though widely used by Continental mathematicians throughout the eighteenth century, no echo can be found in any significant British text of the period. The first such British work to adopt the differential notation was Robert Woodhous's *Principles of Analytical Calculation* (Cambridge, 1803). Six years later the notation was used for the first time in an article in the *PT*; a further landmark was the appearance of the notation for the first time in 1817 in a Cambridge examination paper. It caused, William Whewell noted, 'a considerable outcry'. While modernists like Charles Babbage and his colleagues could welcome their new freedom to accept 'the d's instead of those rotten dots', traditionalists reasserted their authority and in the 1818 examinations all questions were posed in the fluxional notation. When, however, the influential Whewell used the new symbolism throughout his *Elementary Treatise on Mechanics* (1819), it was clear to all that dotted letters would soon be items of historical interest only.

Mathematical patronage

There were few official posts open to British mathematicians of the eighteenth century. The only available academic jobs were the chairs available at Oxford and Cambridge (two each), at the three Scottish universities of Glasgow, Edinburgh and Aberdeen, and in London at Gresham College and the Mathematical School at Christ's Hospital. There was also a certain amount of patronage, whether royal, as at the Greenwich Observatory, or private, as exercised by George Parker at Shirburn Castle. Without one of these posts, mathematicians were forced to work as private tutors, like de Moivre; to seek full-time employment elsewhere, with the church and the civil service being the most likely employers; or, like a John Kersey and a William Emerson, to resort to the writing of textbooks.

Newton's influence extended most readily to the universities and related colleges. Consequently, it was to these institutions that he tended to look first to find posts to meet the needs of his young mathematical disciples. At one time it seemed as if every British mathematical chair was occupied by a Newtonian and that most of these appointments had been made on his specific recommendation. Details of the chairs and their holders are as follows.

1 Cambridge.
  (a) Lucasian chair.
     (i) W. Whiston (1703–10). Appointment made on Newton's recommendation.
     (ii) N. Saunderson (1710–39). Newton had supported, with

Bentley and Cotes, the candidature of Christopher Hussey (*C*, VII, p. 479). Saunderson won by six votes to four.

    (iii) J. Colson (1739–60). Translator of *Method of Fluxions* (1736).

(b) Plumian chair.

    (i) R. Cotes (1706–16). Appointment made by Bentley and Newton.

    (ii) R. Smith (1716–68). Author of a Newtonian work on optics (1738).

2 Oxford.

  (a) Savilian chair of geometry.

    (i) J. Wallis (1649–1703).

    (ii) E. Halley (1703–20). Editor of *Principia* (1687).

  (b) Savilian chair of astronomy.

    (i) D. Gregory (1692–1708). Recommended by Newton (*C*, III, pp. 154–5).

    (ii) J. Caswell (1709–12). A pupil of Wallis.

    (iii) J. Keill (1712–21). Disciple of Newton.

3 London.

  (a) Christ's Hospital.

    (i) E. Paget (1682–95). Recommended by Newton (*C*, II, pp. 375–6).

    (ii) S. Newton (1695–1708). Recommended by Newton (*C*, IV, pp. 93–4).

    (iii) H. Ditton (1708–15). Post obtained by Newton.

  (b) Gresham College (astronomy).

    (i) J. Machin (1713–   ). Recommended by Newton (*C*, V, p. 408).

4 Scotland.

  (a) Edinburgh.

    (i) D. Gregory (1684–91).

    (ii) J. Gregory (1692–1726).

    (iii) C. Maclaurin (1726–45). Recommended and supported by Newton (*C*, VII, p. 338).

  (b) Aberdeen.

    (i) C. Maclaurin (1717–26).

It is clear that Newton was not always successful. In addition to the failure to obtain the Lucasian chair for Hussey in 1710 already mentioned, Newton also failed to have William Jones appointed in 1709 to Christ's Hospital and to gain for John Keill the succession in 1709 to the Savilian chair of geometry at Oxford. There were, however, Newtonians elected to chairs much further afield. Thus the first two occupants of the Hollis chair at Harvard, Isaac Greenwood (1727–38) and John Winthrop IV (1738–79), were both declared Newtonians. It would thus be true to say that for a brief period in the eighteenth century all the available chairs of maths/astronomy in the English-speaking world were held by disciples of Newton.

Mathematical works

Finding a way through Newton's mathematical papers without easy access to a bibliography and the expensive volumes of the *Mathematical Papers* can be a difficult and time-consuming exercise. Published, if at all, in different formats and under a variety of titles, it is not always immediately apparent that, for example, the *Geometrica analytica* published by Horsley (1779) is in fact the same work as *The Method of Fluxions* translated and published by John Colson in 1736. Consequently an attempt will be made here to provide a checklist, presented in chronological sequence and with basic bibliographic data included, of all significant mathematical works of Newton. Each work also has a separate entry under its title elsewhere in the text; there the contents of the work are described and its significance in the development of Newton's mathematical thought indicated.

It should perhaps be added that, for the mathematician, the riches of the *MP* edited by Whiteside and colleagues are freely available. The aim here will be to indicate what is to be found and where it can be located. The details of the works and their analysis will remain the monopoly of Whiteside.

COLLECTIONS

The numbers in the *Contents* column refer to the numbered items listed under 'individual works' below.

Title	Date	Language	Editor	Contents
1 *Analysis per quantitatum series*	1711	Latin	William Jones	6,12,18,19, plus selected correspondence
2 *Opuscula: I Mathematica*	1744	Latin	Castillioneus	6,12,8,18,19, plus selected correspondence
3 Two *Treatises*	1745	English	John Stewart	6,18
4 *Opera omnia, vol. I*	1779	Latin	Samuel Horsley	6,12,8,18,19,10, plus selected correspondence
5 *Mathematical Works*, 2 vols	1964	English	D. T. Whiteside	6,12,8,18,19,10
6 *Mathematical Papers*, 8 vols	1967–81	Latin/English	D. T. Whiteside	Exhaustive

INDIVIDUAL WORKS

	Title	Composed	Published	Editor	English trans.	Editions	MP
1	20 May 1665 Tract	1665	1967	D.T.W.	—	1	I, pp. 272–80
2	13 November 1665 Tract	1665	1838	S. Rigaud	—	2	I, pp. 382–90
3	14 May 1666 Tract	1666	1967	D.T.W.	—	1	I, pp. 390–2
4	16 May 1666 Tract	1666	1967	D.T.W.	—	1	I, pp. 392–4
5	October 1666 Tract	1666	1962	Halls	—	2	I, pp. 400–48
6	De analysi	1669	1711	W. Jones	J. Stewart (1745)	11	II, pp. 206–47
7	Observations on Kinckhuysen	1670	1968	D.T.W.	—	1	II, pp. 295–447
8	Methodis fluxionum	1670–1	1736	J. Colson	J. Colson (1736)	6	III, pp. 32–353
9	Letter to Collins 10 December 1672	1672					
10	Arithmetica universalis	1673	1707	W. Whiston	J. Raphson (1720)	15	V, pp. 54–491
11	Regula differentiarum	1676	1927	D. C. Fraser	D. C. Fraser (1927)	2	IV, pp. 36–50
12	Methodis differentialis	1676	1711	W. Jones	D. C. Fraser (1918)	9	VIII, pp. 244–55
13	Epistola prior 13 June 1676	1676	1699	J. Wallis	C, II		—

Title	Composed	Published	Editor	English trans.	Editions	MP
14 Epistola posterior 24 October 1676	1676	1699	J. Wallis	C, II		—
15 Geometria curvilinea	1680	1971	D.T.W.	D.T.W. (1971)	1	IV, pp. 420–84
16 Mathesos universalis specimina	1684	1971	D.T.W.	D.T.W. (1971)	1	IV, pp. 526–90
17 De computo serierum	1684	1971	D.T.W.	D.T.W. (1971)	1	IV, pp. 590–616
18 De quadratura curvarum	1693	1704	S. Clarke	J. Harris (1710)	17	VII, pp. 24–129; VIII, pp. 92–159
19 Enumeratio linearum	1695	1704	S. Clarke	J. Harris (1710)	17	VII, pp. 588–645
20 Letter to Montague 30 January 1697	1697	1967	J. F. Scott	J. F. Scott (C, IV)		VIII, pp. 72–9
21 Geometria libri tres	1690s	1976	D.T.W.	D.T.W. (1976)	1	VII, pp. 248–400
22 De constructione problematum geometricum	1706	1981	D.T.W.	D.T.W. (1981)	1	VIII, pp. 200–19
23 Account	1715	1715	—	—	4	—
24 Bernoulli's second problem	1716	1716	—	D.T.W. (1981)	1	VIII, pp. 424–34

MODERN SELECTIONS

Again, the numbers in the *Contents* column refer to the works listed under 'Individual works' above.

Title	Date	Language	Editor	Contents
1 *A Source Book in Maths*	1929	English	D. E. Smith	Extracts on the binomial theorem and fluxions
2 *A Source Book in Maths, 1200–1800*	1969	English	D. J. Struik	Extracts from 10,19,18, *Principia* and letters to Oldenburg
3 *Treasury of Mathematics*, 2 vols	1965	English	H. Midonock	Extracts from 6,18, *Principia*

WHITESIDE'S MATHEMATICAL PAPERS OF ISAAC NEWTON, 1967–81

Useful as the above collections were, they are all incomplete. They also often had to rely upon inaccurate texts and provided the minimum of editorial information. It remained for Whiteside, in a major work of scholarship, to remedy such defects. Working, wherever possible, from original manuscripts, Whiteside has collected the results of his immense labours into the definitive *MP*. They contain the following items.

Vol. I, 1664–6 (1967).

1 Annotations from Oughtred, Descartes, Schooten, Huygens, Viete and Wallis.
2 Researches in analytical geometry and calculus, including the various tracts of 1665 and 1666 and much material from the Waste Book and the Mathematical Notebook.
3 Early work on geometrical optics including the paper *On Refractions*.

Vol. II, 1667–70 (1968).

1 Pure and analytical geometry, cubic and other curves.
2 Calculus, *De analysi*.
3 Algebra, *Observations on Kinckhuysen*.
4 Problems for Construing Equations.

Vol. III, 1670–3 (1969).

1 Fluxions and infinite series, *De methodis*.
2 Miscellaneous geometrical texts.
3 Geometrical optics.

Vol. IV, 1674–84 (1971).

1 Algebra, number theory, trigonometry, *Regula differentiarum*.

[344]

Throughout, where appropriate, English translations accompany the original Latin texts. Also printed are many secondary documents which are otherwise not readily available. Typical examples are the regulations governing Newton's Lucasian chair, extracts from Conduitt notes and reviews of Newton's major mathematical works. In addition, details are provided of Newton's mathematical correspondence, drafts of various works are presented and analysed, and very full bibliographic data is offered.

Mathesos universalis specimina

In 1684 Newton received from David Gregory a copy of his fifty-page tract *Exercitatio geometria*, containing material similar to that recorded earlier in his *De analysi*. It must have been immediately clear to Newton that his work was under threat and to preserve his claim to priority he would have to publish a fairly full account of his early discoveries.

He began by noting: 'A certain method of resolving problems by convergent series devised by me about 18 years ago had, by my very honest friend Mr. John Collins, around that time been announced to Mr. James Gregory . . . as being in my possession.' Extracts were then quoted from various letters to Oldenburg from the period 1676–7 to justify Newton's claims. The text itself is divided into five chapters.

  1 On the roots of affected equations.

2 On the properties of series.

3 The broad expanse of analysis by infinite equations is revealed.

4 A method of resolving problems by means of the fluxion of quantities is expounded. It contains the solution to the fluxional anagrams of the *Epistola*.

5 A more general method.

Although Newton abandoned the project, he must originally, at least, have intended to publish it. Surely, he could not have gone to such lengths to justify his priority claims to himself? Nor is it hard to find reasons why the project should have been dropped. The visit of Halley later in the year diverted Newton's interest into preparing the manuscript which eventually became *Principia*.

The text itself is in the PC in the ULC (Add. MS 3964.3). It was published for the first and only time in *MP*, IV, pp. 526–90 in the original Latin and, as *Specimens of a Universal Mathematics*, in English translation.

See also De computo serierum

Maude, Thomas (1718–98)

Described by the *DNB* as a minor poet and essayist, Maude began his career as a physician, but from 1765 onwards he served as steward of the Yorkshire estates of the sixth and last Duke of Bolton. Much of his verse was about the Yorkshire dales, with his best-known work being *Wensleydale, or Rural Contemplations, a Poem* (1772). It was in the third edition of this work, published in 1780, that Maude first published the since discredited story of Newton and his dog Diamond. A second work, *Viator, a poem; or, A Journey from London to Scarborough by the way of York* (1782) contained an appendix on *Illustrations on the character of Sir Isaac Newton*. He reported the claim of an elderly relative of Newton to have been told directly by Newton himself that he had led a life of chastity. As Maude seemed mistakenly to believe that Newton's father was called John and not Isaac, the accuracy of much of the other material he collected in Lincolnshire can easily be doubted.

See also Chastity; Diamond

Maupertuis, Pierre Louis Moreau de (1698–1759)

Maupertuis was educated privately and in Paris, where he studied mathematics and music. In 1728 he visited London, becoming converted to Newtonian mechanics. He also visited the Bernoullis in Basel and on his return to Paris he began to work with Clairaut. Soon after he published his *Discours sur les différentes figures des astres* (1732, Discourse on the Different Figures of the Stars), a work widely recognised as the first unequivocal Newtonian text to come from a Frenchman. In it he objected to Cartesianism on the ground that it was unable to explain why Kepler's laws should hold. He in turn was attacked for attempting to re-introduce into science such outmoded occult qualities as attraction. Maupertuis replied that attraction at a distance was no more occult than impulsion by contact. 'Is it more difficult', he asked, 'for God to make two separate bodies endeavour the one towards the other, than to delay moving a body until it has been struck by another.'

In 1736 Maupertuis and Clairaut travelled to Lapland. Their main aim was to measure as accurately as possible the length of a degree of longitude. At the same time La Condamine had sailed to Peru with the object of making similar measurements. When the two measurements were compared it would be possible to decide just how the earth was shaped. The results of the expeditions, that the earth was flattened at the poles and was, in fact, an oblate spheroid, were published in his *La figure de la terre* (1738, The Shape of the Earth).

Maupertuis moved to Berlin in 1745 to become Vice-president of Frederick the Great's Berlin Academy. It was not a placid time. In 1744 he had formulated the principle of least action which soon brought him into conflict with one of his colleagues, Samuel König, who claimed the principle to have been stated earlier by Leibniz. He also quarrelled with Voltaire. The result was a biting satire in which Maupertuis became a Docteur Ahahia Micromegas.

Maupertuis finally abandoned Berlin in 1756 and returned home to France where he died three years later.

Mead, Richard (1673–1754)

The son of a clergyman, Mead was educated privately and at the University of Leyden, where he came under the influence of Pitcairne. He went on to Padua, where he obtained his M.D. in 1695, before returning to London to set up his practice. One of his patients was Newton.

With such a work as *The Mechanical Account of Poisons* (1702), Mead indicated that it was not just Newton's health that he served. As an iatrophysicist, he confidently proclaimed that in a short time physicians would be distinguished from quacks by their 'mathematical learning'. A later work *Of the Power and Influence of the Sun and Moon on Humane Bodies; and of the Diseases that Rise from Thence* (1712) has nothing to do, despite the title, with astrology but was rather an attempt to show that the gravitational force exercised by the sun and the moon influenced not only the flow of tidal waters but the fluids of the body.

As Newton's physician, Mead had little to do. He was, however, with W. Cheselden in attendance on Newton during his final illness in 1727.

Mechanical inventions

There is an early tradition of Newton's evident mechanical skill. The tradition begins with Stukeley, who first noted Newton's preference for 'making nick-nacks and models of wood' to 'playing with other boys'. Specific items mentioned by Stukeley include a wooden clock, a model windmill, two water clocks, paper kites and sundials.

The skill is evident later in life, when it was directed to more serious ends. Thus, when in 1671 Newton sent to the Royal Society a reflecting telescope, he was sending something he had entirely made himself. He was in fact an inventive and competent experimentalist. Whether grinding lenses, manipulating chemical equipment or fiddling with pendulums, Newton is far removed from the comic stereotype of the scientist so out of tune with ordinary life as to be incapable of boiling water. It would be more in keeping with Newton's interests and character if he were to be described as designing and building the furnace with which to boil the water.

See also Clepsydra; Sundials; Telescope

Mechanical philosophy

The mechanical philosophy, also referred to as the corpuscular philosophy, arose basically as the response of seventeenth-century science to the vacuity of traditional modes of explanation in terms of occult causes and qualities. Though its roots were complex, the new system of thought matured throughout the century in the works of Descartes, Gassendi and Boyle.

In its ideal form the mechanical philosophy insisted on explaining all phenomena in terms of matter and motion. Thus, Boyle, writing in 1674, insisted that if any process 'be intelligible and physical, it will be reducible to matter' (Crosland, 1971, p. 56). But as, for Boyle, there was one universal matter, it followed that 'the diversity of bodies must necessarily arise from somewhat else'. And, as there 'could be no change in matter at rest', Boyle went on to propose that there is a 'necessity of motion to discriminate it'. Boyle added to the two basic ideas of matter and motion the further assumption that 'matter must actually be divided into parts' and that each of these parts, whether sensible or not, had magnitude and shape. With just such principles the mechanical philosopher set out to explain all the observed phenomena of the natural world. Those who sought to bring in other factors found themselves dismissed as appealing to long-since-discredited occult causes.

In the mechanical universe motion tended to take place by the pressure of contiguous bodies. The cause of motion, Thomas Hobbes insisted, must always be 'some external body'. An example of a mechanical explanation, showing the strengths and weaknesses of the programme, is provided by the Cartesian explanation of colour. When a particle of light strikes an object and is reflected back it may acquire spin. If the spin is rapid relative to the forward motion, the body appears red; if, however, the particle's spin is slower than the forward motion, the body appears blue or green. In this way colour could, indeed, be explained in terms of matter and motion alone. It remains obvious, none the less, that the explanation is as speculative and as little based in reality as any appeal to the occult qualities of bodies. The mechanical philosophy became a victim of its own success. Capable of explaining anything by an appropriate selection of motions, the system began to appear too arbitrary and too little based on experience to satisfy the demands of the newly-emerging experimental science.

Newton himself, apart from some occasional flirting with mechanism, as in the 1679 *Letter to Boyle*, had little sympathy with the mechanical approach. To the basic concepts of matter and motion, Newton added the third notion of force. Unlike his contemporaries, however, he resolutely refused to construct mechanical hypotheses to explain the attractive and repulsive forces he had introduced into his physics. The cause of gravity, Newton declared on several occasions, was something he did not 'pretend to know'. He would not even be drawn, in the *Letters to Bentley*, on whether the cause was 'material or immaterial' (C, III, p. 254). Hypotheses, Newton insisted in the General *Scholium*, 'whether metaphysical or physical, whether of occult qualities or mechanical, have no place in experimental philosophy' (Cajori, p. 547).

See also Occult causes and qualities

Mechanics

WRITINGS

Title	Found in
1 *Of Violent Motion* (QQP, 1664)	Herivel, 1965, pp. 120–7.
2 *Of Reflections* (Waste Book, January 1665)	Herivel, 1965, pp. 132–6.
3 Definitions (Waste Book, 1665)	Herivel, 1965, pp. 136–40.
4 Axioms and propositions (Waste Book, 1665–6)	Herivel, 1965, pp. 140–82.

Title	Found in
5 *Vellum manuscript (PC, 1665–6)*	C, III, pp. 46–54; Herivel, 1965, pp. 183–91.
6 *On Circular Motion* (PC, 1666–9)	Hall, 1957, pp. 62–71; C, I, pp. 297–303; Herivel, 1965, pp. 192–8.
7 *Gravia in trochoide descendentia* (PC: pre-1669 (Herivel); 1673 (Halls))	Halls, pp. 170–80; Herivel, 1965, pp. 198–207.
8 *The Lawes of Motion* (PC, 1666–9)	Halls, pp. 157–64; C, III, pp. 60–6; Herivel, 1965, pp. 208–18.
9 *De gravitatione et aequipondio fluidorum* (PC, pre-1672)	Halls, pp. 89–156.
10 *De aere et aethere* (PC, 1672–3)	Halls, pp. 214–28.
11 *Letter to Boyle* (1679)	C, II, pp. 288–95; *PLNP*, pp. 250–4.
12 Correspondence with Hooke (1679–80)	C, II; Koyré, 1965, pp. 221–60.
13 *A Demonstration that the Planets by their Gravity towards the Sun may move in Ellipses* (PC, early 1680s)	Halls, pp. 293–301; C, III, pp. 71–7; Herivel, 1965, pp. 246–56.
14 *De motu corporum in gyrum* (PC, 1684)	Herivel, 1965, pp. 257–92; *MP*, VI.
15 *De motu sphaericorum corporum in fluidis* (PC, 1684–5)	Halls, pp. 243–92.
16 *De motu corporum, definitiones* (PC, 1685)	Halls, pp. 239–42; Herivel, 1965, pp. 315–20.
17 *De motu corporum in mediis regulariter cedentibus* (PC, 1685)	Herivel, 1965, pp. 304–15.
18 *De motu corporum, liber primus* (ULC, 1685–6)	Unpublished; extracts in Herivel, 1965, pp. 321–6 and *MP*, VI; it is extensively discussed in Cohen, 1971.
19 *De motu corporum, liber secundus* (ULC, 1685–6)	As *The System of the World* it is readily available in Cajori, pp. 549–626.
20 *Principia* (RS, 1687, 1713, 1726)	Cajori; Koyré and Cohen.
21 *Conclusio* (PC, 1687)	Halls, pp. 320–47.
22 *Elements of Mechanicks* (PC, post-1687)	Halls, pp. 165–9.
24 *Four Letters to Bentley* (1692–3)	*PLNP*, pp. 279–312; C, III, pp. 233–41, 244, 253–6.
25 *Scholium generale* drafts (PC, 1712–13)	Halls, pp. 348–64.
26 Correspondence with Cotes on revisions to *Principia* (1710–13)	C, V.
27 Correspondence with Pemberton on revisions to *Principia* (1723–6)	C, VII.

CLASSICAL

Classical mechanics began with the plausible assumption that bodies move only insofar as they are pushed or pulled by other bodies. Motion was accordingly, for someone like Aristotle, a process imposed on a body by external factors. It soon became apparent, however, that three very common forms of motion could not be analysed in this way. Planets moved around the heavens, bodies fell in straight lines to earth and projectiles moved in complicated curves through the air; in no case, however, were there any other bodies pushing or pulling them.

To overcome these difficulties two crucial distinctions were introduced. The first distinguished between natural and violent motion. Each of the four elements – earth, air, fire and water – belonged in its own natural place. If removed from its natural place it would return there, unless restrained, immediately and directly. In this way a stone dropped from a hand did not need to be continuously pushed in order to fall to the earth. Natural motion needed no external cause, it happened of itself. For a body to be moved violently, however – that is, away from its natural place – it needed to be pushed all the way. A body might fall of its own accord to the earth; there was no such way it could leave the earth.

A second distinction maintained a radical division between motion in the heavens and motion on the earth. Whereas natural motion on the earth was always rectilinear motion, in the heavens it invariably adopted a circular form. There was, accordingly, no need to seek for any agent responsible for the fall of bodies to earth, as long as they followed a straight-line path, or for the circular orbits adopted by celestial bodies.

There remained the case of projectiles. They were to prove much more troublesome and, despite a thousand years' effort, were never comfortably absorbed into either classical or medieval mechanics. As a projectile moves neither in a circular orbit nor in a rectilinear path, it cannot be said to move naturally. Therefore it must move violently. In this case there would have to be an external body pushing or pulling the projectile as it moved through the air. Despite the ingenuity of centuries, no satisfactory or plausible agent was ever proposed.

One suggestion originating with Aristotle argued that there was a general 'mutual replacement' of air. By this he meant that the air displaced by the moving projectile could somehow travel to its rear and give it a needed push. It was precisely this doctrine that was considered by Newton in his first written note on mechanics, entitled *Of Violent Motion* and contained in QQP (Herivel, 1965, pp. 121–5).

It was to prove remarkably simple to destroy this particular proposal of Aristotle. Philoponus, for example, in the sixth century, argued that if a projectile could be maintained in motion by the movement of air behind it, then it should prove possible to move a stone by fanning it.

By this time it was clear to all that no material cause of the motion of projectiles was ever going to be found. The response of the medieval physicist was not, however, to reject the classical account of motion, but to seek instead for an immaterial cause. Consequently there arose the doctrine of impetus. In this way it was claimed that the string of the bow imparted to the arrow as it began its flight an impressed force (impetus) which served as its motive power during its passage through the air. The suggestion was to prove sufficiently fertile to allow the traditional account of motion to survive for several further centuries. To the new generation of scientists of the seventeenth century, however, such concepts appeared more as scholastic occult qualities. As such, they were sterile and had to be expelled from the language of science, along with a number of other scholastic concepts. In their place scientists turned to more mechanical ways to describe the facts of motion.

CARTESIAN

The first major break with the classical tradition came from Descartes. There was, he insisted, no radical distinction between motion in the heavens and on earth; both celestial and terrestial bodies obeyed one and the same set of laws. Further, he argued, motion was not a process but a state, as also was rest. Consequently:

> And as that which is at Rest will never of itself begin to move,
> unless something move it; so that which is once in Motion, will
> never of itself cease to move, unless it meet with something that
> retards or stops its Motion. And this is the true Reason why a
> Stone continues to move after it is out of the Hand of him that
> throws it. (*Le Monde*, Koyré, 1965, p. 73n)

From this point of view Aristotle had been asking the wrong question. He had assumed that motion was a mysterious complex for which causes were needed. In contrast, Descartes was claiming that motion was something bodies just did. For this, no cause was needed and no explanation need be sought. Descartes was, of course, at this point, only talking about uniform rectilinear motion. Wherever a body moved otherwise, explanations would then be called for.

Here Descartes was less radical. The Cartesian world was a plenum. Consequently, all motion other than rectilinear motion could only be caused by the pushes and pulls of surrounding bodies. Within such a world Rohault demonstrated how bodies would begin to move in vortices.

> Because the World is full, a Body moving in a straight Line, must
> of Necessity push another, and that a Third, but it ought not to
> go on thus infinitely; for some of thosee which are thus pushed, will

be forced to turn out of the Way, in order to take the Place, of that which was first moved, that being the only Place where they can go, and which is free for them. Wherefore when any Body is moved, a certain Quantity of Matter must always necessarily be moved in the form of a Ring or a Circle. (KOYRÉ, 1965, p. 72n)

The cause of motion was God. Further, he insisted, the quantity of motion was conserved. On the basis of his conservation principle, Descartes set out to develop the laws of impact. They were taken up and advanced by Newton in some of the dynamical entries in the Waste Book (Herivel, 1965, pp. 133–9).

See also Inertia; Vortex theory

NEWTONIAN

Newtonian mechanics displays a number of features missing from the work of such predecessors as Descartes. To begin with, it was a genuinely experimental science. Wherever possible, Newton sought to justify his conclusions by appealing to the experimental results of others or by reporting upon his own investigations. The very first page of *Principia* (Cajori, p. 1) begins with the claim that 'by experiments on pendulums' he had found that a body's mass is proportional to its weight, and thereafter throughout the text appeals to experimental results are frequently advanced.

Secondly, the world in which Newton's mechanics operated was seen by him as largely void. Again, the argument was mainly experimental. Gold, he argued, must contain 'more Pores than solid parts' for only then would it allow water to squeeze through it (*Opticks*, p. 267). In addition to the void, the universe contained matter composed of 'solid, massy, hard, impenetrable, moveable Particles' (*Opticks*, p. 400).

The main aim of Newton's mechanics was thus to explain how bodies could and did move in such a universe. Whereas Aristotle had operated within a universe in which different bodies moved in ways appropriate to their nature, and whereas for Descartes the motion of one body was invariably the result of a prior motion of another body, Newton presented a third alternative in which bodies moved under the influence of a force. Together with the Cartesian concept of inertia, it enabled Newton to develop his revolutionary system of mechanics while at the same time exposing him to the charge of attempting to reintroduce into philosophy the rightly-abandoned occult causes of Renaissance science.

Bodies left to themselves, Newton saw, would continue in their state, whether it be of rest or of uniform motion in a right line, indefinitely. So much Newton had learnt from Descartes. Any variation from this state, however, whether of acceleration, deceleration or a change of

[353]

direction, could not be explained so readily in Cartesian terms. Newton's great insight, stated clearly in the first law, was simply that whenever such a change of state did take place, a force was both present and responsible for the change. This is Newton at his most imaginative. Many before Newton had tried to break away from the traditional mechanics of antiquity, but none before had achieved the scope and simplicity of his proposals. Some like Galileo had, for example, failed to see that the principles of mechanics apply just as readily to celestial bodies as they did to terrestrial projectiles. Against this there is the opening of Newton's first law with its simple yet immensely significant reference to 'Every body'.

Newton had not, of course, invented the concept of force. For Descartes and his contemporaries, however, force had been seen as 'the pressure of crowding of one body upon another'. Newton substituted for this primitive concept a more abstract notion. Its pivotal role in his mechanics can be seen most clearly by its appearance in six of the eight definitions and two of the three laws with which *Principia* opens. It is no accidental act of piety that the S.I. derived unit of force is named the newton.

Having introduced the concept, Newton set out to show how it operated and how it could be measured. He identified a universal force operating upon bodies. To measure its strength, it was only necessary to observe a body's 'change of motion' to which it was proportional (second law: $f = ma$). As it operated between bodies, it varied inversely as the square of the distance between them, and directly as their masses

(*Principia*, Book III, prop. VII; Cajori, pp. 414–15; $f \alpha \frac{m_1 m_2}{r^2}$. Little imagin-

ation is required to see how such principles could be applied to cases of rectilinear motion. What, though, of bodies such as the planets, moving in elliptical orbits? Newton's answer, derived from Hooke in 1679, was that such motion could be seen as complex, compounded from inertial and centripetal components. Thus, with the parallelogram of forces (*Principia*, Book I, corollary I to axioms; Cajori, p. 14), Newton was able to complete his programme by showing how curved motion could be handled just as readily in his system as the apparently more straightforward case of rectilinear motion.

See also Attractive and repulsive forces; Inertia; Inverse square law; *Principia*, Book I, props XI–XIII

Mede, Joseph (1586–1638)

A Fellow of Christ's College, Cambridge, from 1613, Mede, in his *Clavis apocalyptica* (1627, Key to the Apocalypse), developed a radically new approach to Biblical prophecy. Newton, who possessed a copy of Mede's *Works* (3rd edition, 1672), in an unpublished manuscript on Revelation spoke of the 'judiciously learned and conscientious Mr Mede who . . . I have for the most part followed' (Manuel, 1974, p. 114). There are few such expressions of dependence in the writings of Newton.

Mede argued that the sequence in which images and symbols are presented in a work like Revelation was not necessarily the correct chronological sequence. An event predicted by the Second Seal, for example, could occur before those predicted by the First Seal. Mede also insisted that the language of prophecy was uniform throughout the ancient Near East. It was thus possible to construct a dictionary from which symbols could be read out as and when they were needed. With these insights Newton could claim that 'as Mr Mede layed the foundation . . . I have built upon it'.

Mercator, Nicolaus (1620–87)

The son of a school teacher, Mercator was born in Holstein, then part of Denmark, and educated at the University of Rostock. He arrived in England in 1653 and began work as a mathematics tutor. An early member of the RS, he published a number of mathematical works, of which the most important was his *Logarithmotechnia* (1668) in which he stated the series:

$$\log (1 + x) = x - \frac{x^2}{2} + \frac{x^3}{3} - \frac{x^4}{4} + \ldots$$

It could be used to calculate logarithms. More importantly, when news of the series was conveyed in 1669 to Newton, it stimulated him to write down an account of his own much more general method of infinite series. The result was *De analysi*, the paper which brought Newton's mathematical talents to the attention of the outside world.

Mercury poisoning

In 1979 two scholars, L. W. Johnson and M. L. Wolbarsht, argued that the most likely cause of Newton's 1693 breakdown was mercury poisoning. As mercury was a common ingredient of many of the compounds Newton worked with in his chemical experiments, and as he seemed indifferent to all safety precautions, it has been claimed to be more than likely that over a period of time mercury levels in Newton's body reached toxic proportions. The excitability, irritability, paranoia and tremulous handwriting so much in evidence in Newton's behaviour in 1693 were thus diagnosed as symptoms of mercury poisoning.

Evidence for the diagnosis was provided by P. E. Spargo and C. A. Pounds (1979, pp. 11–32). Several supposed samples of Newton's hair have survived, two locks in the possession of the Portsmouth family and two others in TCC. The four samples, when analysed by Spargo and Pounds, were found to contain mercury levels, in parts per million, of 7.2, 43, 54 and 197, as against the 5.1 parts found in the average contemporary hair. Also found were unnaturally high levels of arsenic, lead and other metals.

The diagnosis itself has been queried by Westfall (RSW, pp. 537), while the analytical procedures of Spargo and Pounds have been subjected to a highly critical review by Ditchburn (1980, pp. 1–16).

See also Breakdown

Methodis differentialis

In the *Epistola posterior* (1676) Newton referred to work on, and important results derived from, the problem of interpolation. No details of the work were given. Instead he sought to express his ideas in a brief treatise, *Regula diffentiarum*, and to develop them somewhat further in a passage in the Waste Book (82^r–84^r) entered some time after October 1676. Both items can be seen in *MP*, IV, pp. 36–59. The *Methodis differentialis* itself first appeared in Jones (1711). Although the manuscript of the work is lost, the sole manuscript of a major mathematical text not to have survived, a transcript made by William Jones in 1710 has remained intact in the Macclesfield Collection. Whiteside has noted that the published version consists of four 'minimally restyled' propositions taken from the 1676 entries in the Waste Book, to which two further propositions had been added (*MP*, VIII, p. 244).

The work, began, as did so many of Newton's mathematical papers, with a query. A certain John Smith working on a table of square and higher roots, at the suggestion of John Collins, sought Newton's advice in 1675 on ways to reduce the immense computational labours involved. Newton advised Smith to pursue methods of interpolation and, more importantly, began to consider himself how such methods could be generalised. The *Methodis*, at its most general, sought to show how 'Given some number of terms of any series whatever arranged at given intervals, to find any intermediate term you will with close approximation' (*MP*, VIII, p. 251). Something of this work also emerged in *Principia* in Book III, lemma V, where it was demonstrated how 'To find a curved line of the parabolic kind which shall pass through any given number of points' (Cajori, pp. 499–500).

Modern workers, Duncan Fraser noted in 1927, had only just struggled up to the level reached by Newton in 1676. Whiteside was equally impressed by the work, claiming that 'During the years 1675–76 . . . Newton laid down the . . . modern elementary theory of interpolation by finite differences but . . . diffidently kept back his insights and discoveries therein for nearly forty years more' (*MP*, IV, pp. 7–8).

Newton's work at this point has been fully surveyed and analysed in Duncan Fraser's 'Newton and interpolation' published in Greenstreet (1927, pp. 45–69).

The work has been published in the following twelve editions.

1 London, 1711. Included in Jones (1711) and the 1723 Amsterdam edition of *Principia*.

2 Lausanne and Geneva, 1744. Included in Castillioneus, *Tome* I.

3 London, 1779. Included in Horsley, vol. I and the 1964 reprint (Stuttgart–Bad Cannstatt).

4 Leipzig, 1917. First German translation by A. Kowalewski.

5 London, 1918. D. C. Fraser, published in the *Journal of the Institute of Actuaries*, vol. 51, the first English translation (pp. 94–101), together with a facsimile reprint of 1 above (pp. 85–93). The two pieces were further reprinted in 1919 by C. & E. Layton in a fifty-two-page offprint costing 1s.

6 London, 1927. Fraser's English translation was re-issued by C. & E. Layton in his *Newton's Interpolation Formulas*, prepared as a presentation copy for members attending the VIII Congress of Actuaries held in January 1927 in London.

7 Moscow/Leningrad, 1937. A Russian translation made by D. D. Mordukay-Boltovsky and published in his translation of Castillioneus (1744), *Tome* I.

8 Dresden, 1954. A second German translation, made by Max Miller.

9 Bologna, 1957. An Italian translation made by I. Bertoldi and published in *Periodico di Mathematiche*, vol. 35 (pp. 14–43).

10 Bologna, 1962. A second Italian translation made by Ettore Carrucio.

11 New York, 1967. Fraser's translation was included in vol. II (pp. 165–73) of Whiteside (Newton, 1964–7).

12 Cambridge, 1971/1981. Included in *MP*, IV, pp. 52–69, in both Latin and English translation, is the original entry from the Waste Book dating from October 1676. *MP*, VIII, pp. 245–55 contains, also in English and Latin, the transcript made by William Jones from Newton's now lost manuscript of the remodelled 1676 Waste Book entry.

Mill, John (1645–1707)

The Principal of St Edmund Hall, Oxford, Mill had spent thirty years collating nearly 100 manuscripts before finally publishing in 1707 his Greek New Testament. Inevitably, Newton had a copy. The surviving correspondence between Mill and Newton gives some indication of Newton's standing as a Bible scholar amongst professionals like Mill.

Some time in 1694 Mill visited Cambridge and left with Newton a manuscript of his New Testament for Newton to check against his own collation of Revelation. Newton returned the manuscript in January 1694 with apologies for his delay (C, III, pp. 303–4). He included some collations of his own. Mill replied in February (C, III, pp. 305–8) with a highly technical discussion of the readings proposed by Newton, clearly taking the suggestions seriously.

Mint

APPOINTMENT AND CAREER

By 1690 Newton had begun to seek public office. In 1691 he was soliciting Locke to recommend him for the 'controulers place of ye M.' (C, III, p. 152). This early approach proved unsuccessful. In late 1695, however, Charles Montague, a former pupil and a close friend of Newton, was appointed Chancellor of the Exchequer. On 19 March 1696 he wrote to Newton that at last he could give 'a good proof of my friendship' with the offer of the post of Warden of the Mint. It was worth at least £500 a year and, Montague informed Newton, the office 'has not too much bus'nesse to require more attendance than you may spare' (C, IV, p. 195). Montague's intentions to offer Newton a sinecure were revealed further in his comment that 'he would not suffer the lamp which gave so much light to want oil'. He was clearly unaware that Newton was incapable of taking any such duties less than seriously.

Initially, as the King's representative, the Warden had been a figure of some importance in the Mint's affairs. Until its abolition in 1666, the Mint was financed by the practice of seignorage, the imposition of a tax under the authority of the Warden on the actual process of coining. Thereafter the Mint was financed by direct taxes on liquor. The Warden's role thus took on a nominal aspect. Newton was so informed on his appointment by Thomas Fowle, a Mint official. Earlier Wardens, like Sir Anthony St Leger (1660–80), for example, 'came very seldom to the place and did not anything of service more than to come and ask how the affairs of the Mint were'.

Newton's inclinations were somewhat different. The Mint in 1696, with the great recoinage to push through, needed all the help from its officials it could get. As Warden, Newton was responsible for the buildings and consequently he found himself involved in the construction of new Mints at Norwich, York, Chester, Bristol and Exeter. Some £13,000 was placed at Newton's disposal. Halley was found a place at the Chester Mint as Deputy Comptroller, at a salary of £90 per annum.

Newton was clearly dissatisfied with his position. He resented serving under Neale as Master and, shortly after his appointment, he was writing to the Treasury complaining that his salary 'suffices not to support the authority of his Office' (C, IV, p. 206). A study he made of the constitution and history of the Mint convinced him that it was the office of Warden which held highest authority and he began to write about the need to restore the 'ancient constitution' (C, IV, p. 208).

Another duty assigned to the Warden was the fight against counterfeiters. Whereas previous Wardens had been happy to leave such unpleasant pursuits to their clerks, Newton took complete responsibility himself and pursued his duties in his normally thorough manner. 'Boxfuls' of testimony, Conduitt reported, were burnt by Newton; 'boxfuls' have also survived.

In December 1699 the Master, Thomas Neale, died. Shortly afterwards Newton was appointed to succeed him, despite the fact that his patron, Montague, was no longer in office. Nor was it customary for Warden to follow Master. In fact, in the Mint's long history, it was a succession without precedent and was never repeated. One problem Newton immediately faced was the need to find securities. Neale had posted a bond of £15,000. Newton argued in a letter to the Treasury that this figure was something of an exception and that a security of £2,000 had been more commonly demanded (C, IV, p. 348). His petition was accepted on 1 July 1700 and shortly afterwards Montague and Thomas Hall stood security for sums of £1,000 each. With the accession of Anne in 1702 a new bond was called for and this time Thomas Hall and Francis Fauquiere made similar guarantees, as they did in 1718 for the same sum of £1,000 each when the Indenture of George I's reign was passed.

The Indenture, the document which laid down the Master's commission and the standards he would have to meet, made Newton a rich man. The main source of the wealth was the 1s 5½d he received for every pound of silver minted. Although the bulk of this went to the moneyers, the craftsmen who converted silver bars into coins, there remained 3¼d per pound weight for the Master. It was sufficient to bring Newton, on average, and in addition to his salary of £600 a year, a further £1,000 per annum.

Newton remained in his post until his death in 1727. On the basis of the surviving correspondence he seems to have remained in control until his final illness. In August 1726 he was to be found considering the appointment of an assistant engraver; a few weeks later Hopton Haynes was advising him he should attend the Mint to witness the breaking of some ingots (*C*, VII, pp. 350–2). He was succeeded as Master by his nephew-in-law, John Conduitt.

Individual problems of Newton's administration will be discussed under their separate headings below.

RECOINAGE

On his appointment in 1696 as Warden of the Mint, Newton found himself caught up in one of the most dramatic events in the history of British coinage. All English coins before the mid-seventeenth century had been produced by hammering a die against a specially prepared blank. From the time of Charles II, however, machinery designed by Pierre Blondeau was used which not only produced a clear impression but added to the coin a milled edge. Around some of the more valuable coins the legend *Decus et Tutamen* (A Decoration and a Safeguard), revived on the current British £1 coin, was inscribed.

Both hammered and milled coins were allowed to circulate. As the old coins, without a clearly-defined edge, were easy to clip and counterfeit, their weight and validity became ever more suspect over the years. No one would willingly surrender a full-weight milled coin if he could pass instead a hammered coin with perhaps a third less silver in it. The problem was compounded by the Mint's obligation to coin any bullion brought them free of charge. Consequently, in Craig's words, 'The new machine-struck coins were reserved for illegal export or melting pot; the hammer-struck served as hitherto the needs of circulation, and bore all the burden of the day' (Craig, 1953, p. 167).

The consequences of dealing in clipped coins were spelt out by William Lowndes, Secretary to the Treasury:

> Great contentions do daily arise among the King's Subjects, in Fairs, Markets, Shops . . . Persons before they conclude in any Bargains, are necessitated first to settle the Price of Value of the very Money they are to Receive for their Goods; and if it be in Guineas at a High Rate, or in Clipt, or Bad Moneys, they set the Price of their Goods accordingly. (CUNNINGHAM, 1912, p. 435)

Coins, in fact, were weighed before use, and the guinea, a gold coin, rose in value from £1 1s 6d to 30s.

To this very clear demonstration of Gresham's law the government responded in 1695 by seeking advice from its own Treasury and such outside scholars as John Locke, John Wallis, Christopher Wren and Newton. Two general policies were proposed. Both recommended recoinage, but disagreed on the terms of its operation. Lowndes proposed to devalue the silver coinage by issuing the new coins with 25 per cent less silver content; but, rather than mess around with weights, he argued, it would be simpler to raise the face value of coins with, for example, a half crown becoming 3s 1½d and a £1 becoming 25s.

Newton submitted a short essay on the *Amendmt of English Coyns*, in which he agreed, in principle, with Lowndes. He disagreed with Lowndes, however, on the point that awkward denominations like 3s 1½d were impractical; the same effect could be gained by reducing the weight of the coin and leaving its face value unchanged.

Against the Lowndes–Newton line, John Locke argued that no change in the silver content of the new coinage could be tolerated. He was, however, prepared to accept the proposal that old coins should be accepted by the Mint at their bullion value. Neither position was adopted entirely by the Treasury. On 30 December 1695 Parliament authorised a compulsory recoinage in which all silver coins, whatever their bullion content, and as long as they were used to pay taxes or as loans to the government, would be exchanged at face value. The old fineness of 62s to a pound weight of silver would be retained. The minting of old coins began on 22 January 1696.

Thus, when Newton was appointed Warden of the Mint in May 1696, not only had the decision to recoin already been made, but the principles for its implementation had also been worked out. Newton could, therefore, have contributed to no more than the efficiency of the plan. His first specific duty was to arrange for the construction of five temporary Mints at Norwich, York, Chester, Bath and Bristol, to meet the demand for the new coins. Whatever the value of Newton's role, the task was complete by mid-1698. Some £9.6 million had been accepted by the Mint and some £6.8 million of new coins issued.

Evidence of Newton's role, of a less than partial kind, came from Montague and Hopton Haynes. Montague insisted that he could not have carried out the recoinage without the help of Newton (RSW, p. 557), and a similar point was made by Haynes (RSW, p. 561).

COPPER COINAGE

The first official copper coins – halfpennies and farthings – appeared in 1672, with Frances Stewart, Charles II's mistress, appearing as Britannia. After some years experimenting with tin coins the Treasury turned once more to copper coins in 1694. During the next seven years private contractors supplied the Mint with over 700 tons of copper blanks for stamping. The quality was not good but, when production stopped in 1701, some £137,000 of halfpennies and farthings had been put into circulation.

No new copper coins appeared for a further sixteen years. Newton resisted the private contractors, who continued to press for additional licences. There was even talk of a bribe of £6,000 being offered. Against them he argued that there was sufficient base currency in circulation.

He also insisted that in future such coins should be the responsibility of the Mint itself. In this way quality could be preserved and the fineness of the currency guaranteed.

Newton actually wanted to go further and buy copper in ingots and cast, roll and cut it himself. He experimented on the project in late 1713, with far from satisfactory results. The metallurgy of copper proved to be less well understood than that of gold and silver, and when it was decided finally in 1717 to issue new copper coins, Newton put out tenders for rolled copper fillets. Between January 1718 and January 1719 he issued £30,288 17s 2d worth of halfpennies and farthings.

UNION COINAGE

With the union of the Kingdoms of England and Scotland in 1707 came the decision that 'the coin shall be of the same standard and value throughout the United Kingdom as now in England'. To serve this end 'a mint shall be continued in Scotland under the same rules as the Mint in England'. It was a venture that demanded Newton's close personal attention. By 12 April 1707 (C, IV, pp. 485–7) he was writing to Godolphin about the equipment needed for the Scottish Mint. Later he was to be found instructing the officials on how to keep their accounts and on such details of procedure as that 'the money thus counted be put into baggs' and that 'A Melting house . . . be provided with two fire holes for two iron melting potts' (C, IV, pp. 502–3).

The declared policy was to establish a uniform coinage. The Edinburgh officials, however, declined Newton's invitation to train at the London Mint. Consequently he arranged for his faithful disciple, the mathematician and astronomer David Gregory, to go to Edinburgh to oversee the introduction of London techniques wherever practical. Gregory took with him three moneyers, a variety of equipment and a clerk. Recoinage took from November 1707 to December 1708 and yielded a little over £320,000.

The surviving correspondence between Gregory and Newton suggests that nothing was done without the Master's agreement and often without his initiation.

TIN

In 1703, for purely political reasons, the government agreed to buy a set amount of Cornish tin each year at over the market price. The Mint was instructed to store and sell the tin. As much more was bought than could be sold, it became in time one more administrative problem for Newton. The agreement was to purchase 1,600 tons of Cornish tin at a price of £70 a ton. In this way did Queen Anne hope to gain the allegiance of Cornish M.P.s. At the end of seven years the contract was renewed for a further seven, with an increase by 2,000 tons of the amount bought. Only the death of Queen Anne in 1714 seems to have freed the Mint from its burdensome obligation. Even so, it was not until the 1720s that the Mint finally got rid of its last load of tin. It brought Newton £150 a year.

GUINEAS

One of the persistent problems facing Newton was how to preserve the integrity of the coinage against the temptations offered merchants by variations in the rates for gold and silver. The guinea, minted from gold derived from the Guinea coast, had been introduced by Charles II in 1663 with a value of 20s. By the time of Newton's appointment to the post of Master in 1699 the guinea was valued at £1 1s 6d. In accordance with the Mint's indenture, one pound weight of gold yielded 44½ guineas, giving a pound of gold the value of £47 16s 9d. By the same indenture a pound of silver yielded 62 shillings and was thus worth £3 2s 0d. The gold–silver ratio was thus 15.43:1. The catch in this scheme was that if anyone could exchange a pound of gold for more than 15.43 pounds of silver, or if they could gain a pound of gold with less than 15.43 pounds of silver, they would do so. The price to be paid for such transactions was that the under-valued metal would disappear, to be converted into the over-valued metal and consequently no longer be readily available to serve as currency.

Newton pondered long on this problem, writing extensively both for himself and to his political masters at the Treasury. He identified three particular areas of abuse and sought persistently to check them. The first problem arose over what became known as 'come again guineas'. Such was the standard of minting in Newton's day that, while a pound of gold would indeed yield 44½ guineas, some would be heavier by a grain or two than the intended 129.4 grains and some proportionately lighter. Inevitably the heavier coins would be culled and returned to the Mint to be recoined. It was estimated that fifty-two guineas could be converted in this way into fifty-three guineas and that so widespread were such coins that one-fifth of 'Of all gold coin issued returned in this way to the Mint' (Craig, 1953, p. 212). Newton's remedy was to ensure that guineas were coined in a more standard manner. The removal from the moneyers of a handy little profit line caused no little resentment at the new Master's regime.

A second problem arose from the presence in Britain of foreign gold coins. *Pistoles*, for example, though valued at the turn of the century at 17s 6d, contained, according to Newton (*C*, IV, pp. 352–3), gold worth only 17s 0½d. No one with any sense would use guineas when *pistoles* and other equally profitable foreign coins could be passed instead. Newton argued to the Treasury that foreign coins were bullion and should be treated as such. Consequently, he recommended that *pistoles* be valued at 17s 0d. On 5 February 1701 the Government issued a Proclamation announcing the change, and thereafter foreign gold coins began to flow into the Mint to be turned into guineas. A similar reaction to an abundance of Portugese *moidores* was seen in 1714, when they were reduced in value from 28s to 27s 6d.

The most persistent problem, however, concerned the loss of silver overseas. Between 1700 and 1717 the East India Company alone shipped out some 22½ million ounces of silver. The reason was clear to all. Gold in the Far East could be bought for 10 ounces of silver rather than the 15.43 ounces demanded in London. Huge profits could be made by melting silver down, shipping it to India and buying gold, which was then returned to London to buy more silver. A similar trade took place with Europe, where profits, though not as large, could still be made by converting silver into bullion and buying gold. Newton raised the problem with Godolphin in a letter dated 7 July 1702 (*C*, IV, pp. 388–90). Gold, he noted, was higher in Britain than in France, Holland, Germany and Italy. The importation of great amounts of silver from Latin America had inevitably depressed the price of silver. 'Gold', he concluded, 'is therefore at too high a rate in England by about 10d. or 12d. in the Guinea.' Consequently, he recommended that the way to preserve silver was to reduce the price of the guinea by a corresponding amount.

Similar sentiments were still being expressed by Newton in 1717 in a report to the Treasury on the *State of the Gold and Silver Coyns of this Kingdom* (*C*, VI, pp. 415–18). 'Silver in Bullion exportable is usually worth 2d. or 3d. per ounce more than in coyn', he told them. Consequently, almost as a law of physics, 'silver flows from those places where its value is lower in proportion to gold . . . and that Gold is most plentiful in those places in which its value is highest in proportion to silver'. If left alone the situation would remedy itself, as gold would fall 'of it self by the want of silver money'. The Treasury could, however, choose to act and reduce the value of the guinea by 10d or 12d. Even a reduction of 6d 'would dimimish the temptation to export or melt down the silver coyn'.

This was the advice the Treasury accepted and on 22 December 1717 they reduced the guinea from £1 1s 6d to £1 1s 0d. It is consequently due to Newton that the guinea, so attractive to gamblers and professional men alike, came to have its distinctive value of 21s. More immediately, it failed to have the effect predicted and Newton seems to have been no more prescient in financial affairs than the many lesser minds following him. Silver did not fall in price and remained throughout the century in short supply. Newton's change did not, Conduitt noted in 1730, 'bring an ounce of silver to the Mint' (Craig, 1953, p. 218). After 1717 less than £600,000 worth of silver was minted during the rest of the century, while for the same period well over £70 million of gold coin was produced.

COUNTERFEITERS AND CLIPPERS

As Warden of the Mint from 1696 to 1700, part of Newton's duties was the detection, capture and prosecution of 'Clippers and Coyners'. Earlier Wardens had left their clerks to pursue such duties, but Newton, unwilling to delegate and incapable of taking his duties lightly, undertook their direction himself. He began by complaining to the Treasury that the duties brought him little but calumnies, overwork and, at the end of the day, juries had become most reluctant to convict. Consequently, he prayed 'that this duty may not be annexed to the Office of the Warden of his Majts Mint' unless, he went on, revealing the true intent of his letter, he was granted the facilities to enable him 'to go through with it with safety credit and success' (C, IV, pp. 209–10). A few weeks later Newton was granted the assistance of an extra clerk.

There can be no doubt of the seriousness and thoroughness with which Newton undertook his duties. Manuel (1980, pp. 234–5) has even argued that the work, allowing Newton to 'rage at prisoners and their wives and mistresses with impunity', was of therapeutic value and, by releasing the 'inexhaustible font of rage in the man', saved him from breakdowns comparable to that experienced in 1693. Even if true, it should however be appreciated that the work was not of Newton's choosing and, if he did pursue it with a seriousness not to be found in any of his predecessors, this must in part have reflected his inability to take any matter less than seriously. In any case, within the context of the period, it was a serious matter; after 1697 the mere possession of counterfeiting tools was sufficient to attract the death penalty.

Newton thus moved into a strange new world. He frequented taverns to take depositions, came to know Newgate and other London prisons, and interrogated at the Mint several hundred coiners, clippers and informants. Between June 1698 and Christmas 1699 he examined 200 witnesses on 123 occasions. Conduitt reported that Newton later burnt boxes full of depositions and evidence. Under his regime nineteen criminals were executed at Tyburn in 1697 and a further eight in the following year. Pleas of mercy seem to have moved him not at all. Only the willingness to provide evidence incriminating others was likely to cause Newton to drop a case. Thus in 1724, when asked about the otherwise unknown Edmund Metcalf, a counterfeiter convicted at Derby, he replied: 'I am humbly of opinion that it is better to let him suffer, than to venture his going on to counterfeit the coin and teach others to do so until he can be convicted again, For these people very seldom leave off. And its difficult to detect them' (C, VII, p. 289). 'They are like dogs', he elsewhere commented, 'ever ready to return to their vomit.'

Evidence of his labours can be seen in such documents as this request of his to the Treasury on 1 October 1699: 'The prosecution of Coyners during the three last years having put me to various small expenses in coach-hire & at Taverns and Prisons & other places of all wch it is not possible for me to make accompt on oath' (*C*, IV, p. 317). He went on to claim expenses of £120 which the Treasury authorised in November. After 1700, with his elevation to the Mastership of the Mint, and with the completion of the recoinage, counterfeiters and clippers played a less central role in Newton's life.

See also Chaloner, William

TRIAL OF THE PYX

It had been customary since the reign of Henry II (1154–89) for the Exchequer regularly to test the quality of its coinage. By Newton's day it had become the practice to select at random each year a number of newly-minted coins and to place them in a locked box known as the pyx. Every three or four years the box was opened and the coins assayed in the presence of the king's representatives. From time to time a trial plate of a certain fineness was struck, against which the current coinage could be judged. A certain leeway was allowed. Known as the Master's remedy, it consisted in Newton's day of 48 grains per pound of silver and 40 grains per pound of gold. (A grain is 1/7,000 lb, or 0.0648 grams.)

The actual procedure was described by Newton in a memorandum of 1701 (*C*, IV, pp. 371–3). A jury was summoned and sworn in before the Lord Chancellor. The pyx was then opened.

> And when they have told out every Species of Gold or Silver monies
> so much as should make a pound . . . they weigh it and melt it
> into an Ingot and weigh ye Ingot and ye grains . . . Then the Jury
> draw up and signe their Verdict expressing the weight and Tale of
> all the monies in ye Pix and how much they make in the pound
> weight and that they are agreeable to standard or better or worse.

Few reports, Craig has noted, were ever adverse (1953, pp. 405–6). The first in 1318 was followed by a second in 1349 and a third in 1534. Newton's early trials, beginning with the pyx of 1701, presented no problems. Difficulties arose, however, with a new trial plate struck in 1707. It turned out to be '2½ parts in 1,000 finer than the preceding gold plate' (Craig, 1953, p. 216). Inevitably, when Newton's own gold pieces were measured against this new standard, they were found to be significantly light. When, at the trial of 1710, Newton produced coins struck to the standard of the 1688 plate, the jury reported them to be a quarter of a grain below standard.

Newton responded by informing the Treasury that 'the present indented trial piece is . . . finer than the last trial piece by about a quarter of a grain' (*C*, V, pp. 82–3). At the same time he began to prepare a memorandum on *Of the assaying of Gold and Silver, the making of indented Triall-pieces, and trying the moneys in the Pix* (*C*, V, pp. 84–90). Some eight drafts of the memorandum have survived. Once more, he charged, the plate was too fine. It was used just once more, in the trial of 1713. Thereafter Newton ensured that all future trials, beginning with the pyx of 1718, should be based on the plate of 1688. It remained in use until 1829.

WRITINGS AND DOCUMENTS

1 *Concerning the Amendmt of English Coyns*, 1695. Unpublished proposals for the recoinage; they are to be found in Goldsmith's Library, University of London.

2 *Appointment as Warden of Mint*, 13 April 1696 (*C*, IV, p. 200).

3 *The State of the Mint*, June 1696. A brief account of the Mint's officers and their duties (*C*, IV, pp. 207–8).

4 *An Account of the Mint in the Tower of London*, early 1697. A fuller account of the Mint's officers and their duties (*C*, IV, pp. 233–5).

5 *Observations Concerning the Mint*, 1697. A technical account of the assaying, melting and making of coins (*C*, IV, pp. 255–8).

6 *An Answer to Mr Chaloner's Petition*, early 1698. A reply to the counterfeiter's charges that officers of the Mint were corrupt and incompetent (*C*, IV, pp. 261–2).

7 *Appointment as Master of the Mint*, 3 February 1700 (*C*, IV, pp. 320–1).

8 *Directions about the Triall of the Monies of Gold and Silver in the Pix*, July 1701. A detailed account of the procedure to be followed at the Trial of the Pyx (*C*, IV, pp. 371–3).

9 *The Values of Several Foreign Coyns . . . and Ways of Preserving the Coyn*, 7 July 1702. Newton's first proposal to lower the price of gold (*C*, IV, pp. 388–90).

10 *Securities*, 16 October 1702. Proposals of Thomas Hall and J. F. Fauquiere as sureties of £1,000 each (*C*, IV, p. 392).

11 *Design for Queen Anne coronation medal*, 1702 (RSW, pp. 621–2).

12 *Design for Union of Scotland medal*, 1707 (*C*, IV, pp. 508–9).

13 *Of the Assaying of Gold and Silver, the Making of Indented Triall-pieces, and Trying the Moneys in the Pix*, 1711. Newton's response to the adverse Pyx trial of 1710 (*C*, V, pp. 84–8).

14 *Memorandum Concerning a Copper Coinage*, 1713. Guidelines to be followed during the coinage of copper (*C*, V, pp. 415–16).

15 *Observations on the Copper Coinage*, 1714. As above (*C*, VI, pp. 99–100).

16 *State of the Gold and Silver Coyns of the Kingdom*, 21 September 1717. Newton's repeated recommendation of the devaluation of gold (*C*, VI, pp. 415–18).

17 *Memoranda on the Copper Coinage*, July 1718. Problems involved in minting and assaying copper (*C*, VI, pp. 451–4).

18 *Observations upon the State of the Coins of Gold and Silver*, 20 October 1718. Arguments against the revaluation of gold (*C*, VII, pp. 8–10).

19 Mint Papers. Sold at Sotheby's in 1936, they are now to be found in the Public Records Office as Mint/19, I–III.

Montague, Charles, first Earl of Halifax (1661–1715)

A student, colleague, patron and friend of Newton, Montague was born the fourth son of a younger son of the first Earl of Manchester. Educated at Westminster School and TCC, where he first made contact with Newton, he was intended along with many other younger sons for the church. He chose instead, by an equally traditional route, a political career with the necessary aid of a wealthy marriage. In 1687 Montague married Anne, a widow in her sixties of the third Earl of Manchester with an income of at least £1,500 a year. In the same year, in collaboration with Matthew Prior, he published *The Town and Country Mouse*, a satire on Dryden's *Hind and Panther* (1687). It was sufficient to make the name of the lowly Montague widely known in London society. His political career flourished. A member of the Convention Parliament of 1689, he was appointed Chancellor of the Exchequer in 1694 and continued to hold the post until 1699. By this time the days of the Whigs and Montague were over. Although he became Lord Halifax in 1700, he had already lost office. During the rule of the Tories, under Queen Anne, he found himself out of office and, in 1704, impeached on charges of corruption. With the succession of the Hanoverians and the return of the Whigs to office, Montague once more, although only briefly, served as Chancellor. His political career ended in 1715 with his premature and sudden death from pneumonia.

Newton met Montague as a Cambridge student. He spoke in 1685 of an attempt they had made to form a philosophical society in Cambridge and shortly afterwards was speaking of Montague as his 'intimate friend' (*C*, II, p. 464). They also served together in 1689 as members of the Convention Parliament. Something seems to have disturbed the relationship, for in January 1692 Newton was to be found complaining to Locke: 'Montague upon an old grudge wch I thought had been worn out, is false to me, I have done with him' (*C*, III, p. 193). The nature of the 'grudge' is unknown. Whatever its cause, Montague cannot have allowed his 'grudge' to persist, for in 1696 he made his most important intervention in Newton's life by offering him the position of Warden of the Mint (*C*, IV, p. 195) – 'a good proof of my friendship', he emphasised to Newton. For the next few years, with the pressures of the Great Recoinage, Newton and Montague seemed to have worked well together; Montague is in fact on record with the claim that he could not have carried out the recoinage without the help of Newton (RSW, p. 557).

Further contacts were likely to have arisen through Montague's service from 1695–8 as President of the Royal Society. It is also likely that Newton's reluctant participation in the Parliamentary elections of 1701 and 1705 owes something to Montague's political ambitions.

The crucial aspect of the relations between Montague and Newton is, however, neither political nor scientific but domestic. The charge, first raised publicly by Voltaire in 1757, was that Montague had taken Catherine Barton, Newton's niece and housekeeper, as a mistress. Further, Newton not only knew of and tolerated the relationship but sought to benefit from it. The issue is a complex one and, though much discussed, remains to be resolved.

See also Barton, Catherine

More, Henry (1614–87)

More was born in Grantham, the site of Newton's schooldays, and educated at Eton and Christ's College, Cambridge, where he became a Fellow in 1639 and where he remained for the rest of his life, refusing all preferments. More knew Newton and has left an account of a discussion with him on the ever-familiar topic of 'Apocalyptical Notions'. He noted that, while Newton had a 'singular Genius to Mathematicks' and was a 'good serious man', they could not agree on the meaning of such symbols as the 'seven Vials' and the 'seven Trumpets'.

More was a member of the group of philosophers known as the Cambridge Platonists. It has long been suspected that the young Newton was much influenced by More and his friends. J. E. McGuire (1966, 1968, 1970, 1977), in particular, has stressed his contribution to Newton's work; Koyré (1957) too has identified More as a source for several of Newton's key ideas. Thus, Koyré (1957, p. 126) has argued that More gave 'to the new science', despite his 'unbridled phantasy' and 'amazing credulity', some of the most important elements of its metaphysical foundations. Two such ideas are echoed in much of Newton's thought. One was his claim, against the Cartesians, of the existence of an infinite void space. More also objected to the mechanical world of the Cartesians in which bodies moved only under the impact of other bodies. More argued for, in addition, the need to allow for a number of active principles in nature. Although Newton made little use of such principles in *Principia* (1687), they can be seen more clearly in such later pieces as the Queries, *Scholium generale*, and the suppressed *Conclusio* and Classical *scholia*.

More, Louis Trenchard (1870–1944)

Trained as a physicist, More served for much of his life from 1900–40 as Professor of Physics at the University of Cincinnati. His move to scientific biography began in 1927 with his realisation that on the bicentenary of Newton's death 'no satisfactory critical biography of the man' could be found. Brewster's biography of 1855 he dismissed as uncritical and incomplete. His own effort, published first in 1934, is little thought of today. The work is not, however, without its virtues. It is readable, quotes extensively from a number of unpublished manuscripts and pays due attention to Newton's previously-ignored writings on theology and history. Unfortunately for More, shortly after the publication of his work the Portsmouth Collection was put up for public auction. Once the dimensions of the Collection had become apparent, works like More's biography began to look somewhat thin. Whatever its merits and defects, More's work remained the most accessible and detailed biography of Newton until it was finally replaced in 1980 by Westfall's definitive study.

See also Biography

Morgan Notebook

Conduitt had referred to a notebook of Newton's 'to which he had put his name & 1659' and which contained 'Rules for drawing and making colours'. Although Brewster searched for it in the PC he failed to find any trace of it. It was not until the 1920s that D. E. Smith announced that he had found the book in the Pierpoint Morgan Library, New York, where it had been, he declared, 'for a long time'.

After the Latin Exercise Book, the Morgan Notebook is probably the oldest of the notebooks. It carries an initial inscription: 'Isaacus Newton hunc librum possidet. teste Edvardo Secker: 2d. ob 1659' ('This book is owned by Isaac Newton, witnessed by E. Secker, obtained for 2d. in 1659'). Smith argues for a date of 1655–62 for the Notebook, although most other scholars have argued for a later opening date.

The Notebook is basically divided into three sections.

1 Under the running heading *Of drawing*, entries are mainly concerned with the preparation of colours. Thus, to make yellow, Newton instructed: 'Take yellow berries, and bruse ym & steepe ym a quarter of an hower in allum water'. These entries are followed by the new running heading *Extravagants*, which includes such miscellanea as how 'to catch crows and ravens', 'a salve for sores' and 'an excellent Plaister of his for cornes'. Under the final heading *Certaine trickes* we learn how to turn water into wine, and other trivial tricks. There is finally a six-page section on Newton's reformed spelling scheme.

Andrade (1935) has shown that much of this first section was copied from a book of recipes popular at the time, *The Mysteries of Nature and Art* (1634; 3rd ed. 1654) by John Bate.

2 The second section was derived from yet another work, *Nomenclatura brevis* (1654) by Francis Gregory. Nomenclators were books containing lists of words, usually classified into simple groupings like animals, minerals, drinks, etc. Newton had filled forty-two pages with 2,400 words arranged into sixteen chapters.

> 1. Artes, trades, sciences. 2. Birdes. 3. Beastes. 4. Cloathes. 5. Of a Church. 6. Of Diseases. 7. Of the Elements. 8. Of Ffishes. 9. Of Hearbs & Woodes & fflowers. 10. Of a House and Housald-stuffe. 11. Of Husbandry. 12. Instruments and things belonging to Artes. 13. Of Kindred, & Titles. 14. Of Man, his Affections, & Senses. 15. Of Meate & Drinke. 16. Of Mineralls.

The chapters are clearly in alphabetical order but, for whatever reason, Newton went no further than the letter M.

In Newton's choice of items for the nomenclator Manuel claims to detect signs of his hostility to his mother and step-father. Thus in Chapter 13 the following sequences are selected by Manuel, with words not found in Gregory underlined:

W – Wife, wedlock, wooer, widdow, widdower, whoore

F – Father, fornicator, flatterer

B – Brother, bastard . . . Benjamite

M – Marriage, mother . . . manslayer (Manuel, 1980, pp. 27–34)

   3 The middle of the book contains a more technical set of notes. It includes five pages on the solutions of triangles, two pages on dialling, two pages on the Copernican system, and an ecclesiastical calendar for the period 1662–89 that runs to six pages.

It is clear from the Notebook that Newton's habit, so apparent in his manuscripts, of copying items that interested him from books was a long-standing one traceable to his schooldays. Also apparent is the wide range of Newton's interests. From the development of a universal language to a cure for toothache, from the production of various pigments to the design of a sundial – the practical and the theoretical, the pure and the applied, the strictly scientific and the frankly dubious, all were already in the young Newton's mind.

Significant extracts from the Morgan Notebook have been published in Smith (1927). Newton's design for a system of reformed spelling has been published with a commentary by Elliot (1954).

See also Notebooks

Morton, Charles (1627–   ?)

Born in Cornwall and educated at both Cambridge and Oxford, Morton was ordained in 1652, but with the Restoration he turned to school teaching. In 1686 he emigrated to New England, taking with him his *Compendium physicae*, a work completed in about 1680.

According to Morison (1936, vol. I, p. 238), the *Compendium* was adopted as a Harvard textbook of physics before Commencement 1687, and remained the foundation of instruction in natural science at the College for some forty years. The rise of science at Harvard was thus 'kindled by the Mortonian candle rather than the Newtonian sun' (p. 249). It was, for example, the work used by the young Benjamin Franklin in the 1720s.

In content the *Compendium* was a mixture of traditional Aristotelian physics, modified by newer Cartesian mechanics.

See also Newton in America

Moschus

In his attempts to show that the main doctrines of seventeenth-century science had their classical roots, Newton chose in his *Classical scholia* to trace the origins of the atomic hypothesis to Moschus the Phoenician, a figure described by Strabo as 'older than the Trojan war'. As Moschus is no more than a name, little was to be gained by such an identification. Other scholars identified Moschus with Moses.

Moses

It was a common claim of Renaissance scholars that Moses had been aware of the main details of the science of his day. Had not Plato been called, Pico della Mirandola asked, the Greek Moses? Other scholars, such as Ralph Cudworth, sought to identify Moses with the Phoenician Moschus, and thus claim for him the discovery of the atomic hypothesis. But, if Moses was scientifically sophisticated, did this mean that the account of creation presented by Moses was scientifically accurate? Newton answered the point in his letter to Thomas Burnet.

> As to Moses, I do not think his description of the creation either philosophical or feigned, but that he described realities in a language artificially adapted to the sense of the vulgar . . . his business being, not to correct the vulgar notions in matters philosophical, but to adapt a description of the creation as handsomely as he could to the sense and capacity of the vulgar. (*C*, II, p. 331)

See also Moschus

Motte, Andrew (d.1734)

Virtually nothing is known of Motte's life. There is no *DNB* entry. He was described in the *Gentleman's Magazine* as an engraver. Although he held no official position at Gresham College, he was described as having 'delivered' certain 'Discourse' there. He remains well-known, however, as the author of the first, and still the only, English translation ever made of *Principia*. First published by his brother, Benjamin Motte, in 1729, it has remained the basis for all subsequent English editions.

See also Principia, Translations

Murray, Thomas (1666–1724)

He was a pupil of John Riley (1646–91), Principal Painter, with Kneller, to William and Mary. Murray produced portraits of the royal family, and of Sir Hans Sloane and E. Halley, both of which hang in the Royal Society.

He painted one portrait of Newton; dated 1718, it hangs in TCC. The occasion for the portrait is quite unknown. An undistinguished piece, it shows a three-quarter length, standing, bewigged Newton (RSW, p. 695).

See also Portraits, medals, busts and statues

N

Neale, Thomas (? –1699)

Neale was the Master of the Mint at the time of Newton's appointment as Warden in 1696. He had served as Master since 1686 and had earlier been appointed to the Court of Charles II, where he held the office of Groom Porter. The office was responsible for controlling and servicing gambling within the Court. It also held the lucrative power to license gaming houses.

In his term of office at the Mint, Neale was responsible for the £1 million lottery of 1694 and the great recoinage. By all accounts he was not up to the latter project and was far more concerned with his own speculative investments. Consequently, on assuming office in 1700, Newton inherited, in Westfall's phrase (RSW, p. 612), an 'administrative mess'. It took up to two years to sort out Neale's accounts, and even then there were items no amount of scrutiny would ever explain.

'New Theory about Light and Colours'

Newton's most important scientific paper, and the paper on which our modern conception of light is based, was published in the *PT* early in 1672. It was also Newton's first published work. The brief paper has been much anthologised and is readily available today in Thayer (1953, pp. 68–81), *C*, I, pp. 92–102, M. B. Hall (1970, pp. 250–61) and *PLNP* (pp. 47–59).

The starting point of the paper is the spectrum cast by a ray of light as it passes through a prism. Such a phenomenon had, of course, been described and analysed often enough before. Classical writers like Seneca, medieval authors like Witelo and Theodoric of Fribourg, and such seventeenth-century scientists as Descartes, Boyle, Marci and Grimaldi, had all described the familiar coloured spectrum. None, however, had noted the simple point which so puzzled Newton and led him to propose a startlingly original theory on the nature of light and colour.

Light coming through a small hole in the 'window shuts' was directed on to a prism which, in turn, was refracted on to the opposite wall some 22 feet away. To his surprise the image took on 'an *oblong* form; which, according to the received laws of refraction, I expected should have been *circular*'. Why, Newton asked, should refracted light produce a coloured spectrum some five times longer than its breadth? If others had observed this aspect of the spectrum they had ignored it. More likely, it has been suggested, earlier writers had collected the image formed by the refracted beam on a screen held close to the prism – too close, in fact, to allow the dispersion of the beam to become evident. Thus, instead of an elongated image, they were presented with a circular blob fringed with red-orange on one side and blue-violet on the other.

Newton's first concern was to show that the effect was a real one and not produced by irregularities in the prism or some other idiosyncracy of the experimental set-up. Convinced, finally, of the genuineness of the observations, he went on, through the *experimentum crucis*, to establish that 'light consists of rays differently refrangible'.

The implications of this central insight were emphasised in a series of numbered propositions and include the following.

1 'Colours are not *qualifications of light . . . but original and connate* properties.' With this simple claim Newton broke away sharply from all previous Western theories of light and colour.

2 'To the same degree of refrangibility ever belongs the same colour, and to the same colour ever belongs the same degree of refrangibility.'

3 'The species of colour . . . is not mutable by refraction, nor by reflection.'

5 'There are two sorts of colours. The one original and simple, the other compounded of these.'

7 The colour white is 'ever compounded, and to its composition are requisite all the aforesaid primary colours'. The point was demonstrated by a final experiment in which light was first spread out into its constituent rays by a prism, and immediately reconstituted into the original white source by being passed through an accompanying convex lens.

As a practical consequence of his theoretical insights Newton pointed out a limit to the perfection attainable by telescopes. Any glass, he argued, so 'exactly figured as to collect any one sort of rays into one point', would not thereby be capable of collecting at the same point all other rays. It led him 'by degrees' to the development of a novel kind of instrument, the reflecting telescope, with which he could discern Jupiter's satellites and Venus's phases.

Newton concluded his first paper with the hope that others would try his experiments. If anything seemed defective in them, he added, he would be very glad to be so informed in order that he could either give 'further directions' or acknowledge his error. Six years later he would feel very differently and refuse to consider any further correspondence whatsoever on the issue.

For Newton's paper was not greeted with the respect and recognition accorded it today. Many simply ignored it. The *Mémoires* of the *Académie des sciences*, for example, contain before 1699 just one reference to Newton and that was an account of his 1672 report on his reflecting telescope written by Huygens. Those who did bother to read Newton's paper usually rejected it on one or another of three grounds.

Many simply denied the experimental facts. Mariotte in 1679, Pardies in 1672 and Linus in 1675 all claimed that they had failed to replicate the basic experiments described by Newton. Unwilling to enter into detailed argument, Newton responded by asking his critics to repeat carefully his experiments. They did and without success.

One cause of such repeated failures was the sparse description of his experimental procedures originally offered in the 1672 paper. Not only was no diagram of the *experimentum crucis* provided but basic measurements were lacking as well. Newton did in fact respond with further details. It was left, however, for Oldenburg to make the crucial breakthrough with his suggestion in March 1676 that 'now the sun and season being likely to serve for making Mr Newton's experiment called in question by Mr Linus, an apparatus might be prepared for that purpose; Mr Hooke said he had an apparatus ready to make the experiment, when the Society should call for it'. The experiment was indeed successfully performed in April 1676 before a committee of the RS and was accordingly so reported by Oldenburg to the sceptics of Liège. A similar public demonstration was needed in London in 1716 and in Paris in 1719 before French scientists could be persuaded to take Newton's theories seriously.

Other critics, like Hooke, accepted the experimental details but went on to query Newton's interpretation of them. They claimed the published facts could be incorporated comfortably into one or other of the various modification theories on offer.

A third response, offered by Huygens in 1673 (*PLNP*, pp. 136–7), simply found Newton's account inadequate. 'Different refrangibility' was no more than an accidental property of light. Only a mechanical account of colour, Huygens emphasised, could ever be completely acceptable. In the absence of any such explanation coming from Newton, Huygens chose to ignore his work in his influential *Traité de la lumière* (1690).

Against objections of this type, answers are seldom available. Newton could not, nor ever wished, to provide a mechanical account of light. Nor, even, was he anxious to devote time and effort to a critical analysis of Hooke's theory. Reluctant to engage in polemics, he could do no more than build up the experimental base of his own position. This he did, mainly in the 1670s and again in the 1690s, with the results eventually appearing in the *Opticks* (1704).

Newton's original manuscript of the paper has long been lost. Surviving, however, in the PC in the ULC is a copy in the hand of John Wickins.

See also Colour, *Experimentum crucis*

---

newton

The lower case n is no misprint but the correct way to write the unit of force in the *Système Internationale* (SI). It is defined as the force that provides a mass of one kilogram with an acceleration of one metre per second per second. It is equivalent to 10^5 dynes.

The convention of absolute units began in the nineteenth century with the mathematician C. F. Gauss (1777–1855). In 1852 he devised, with W. Weber (1804–91), the so-called Gaussian system based on the millimetre, milligram and second. In 1873 the British Association for the Advancement of Science accepted the metric system but adopted as basic units the centimetre, gram and second (CGS system). The unit of force adopted was the dyne, proposed by Professor Everett of Belfast.

In 1900 the further suggestion was made that 100,000 dynes should be known as a large dyne. This was followed in 1904 by the proposal, made by D. Robertson in *The Electrician* (24 April), that it would be more appropriate and convenient to term 100,000 dynes a newton. Little attention was paid to Robertson's suggestion until 1935, when it was revived by L. Hartshorn and P. Vigoreux in *Nature*. The name was authorised by the International Electrotechnical Commission in 1938 and formally adopted by the *Conférence Générale des Poids et Mesures* in 1948.

Newton as experimentalist and observer

In popular imagination Newton is seen, and rightly so, as the greatest of all theoretical thinkers who, shunning hypotheses, laid down the mathematical principles through which nature operates. Less well-known, however, is the quality and extent of Newton's experimental work. It is, of course, widely known that Newton first established his reputation through experiments on light performed with prisms; thereafter Newton is generally thought to have devoted himself to less direct assaults on nature. In fact substantial parts of both *Principia* and

Opticks are devoted to reporting in detail the results of Newton's own experimental labours. They include the following.

1 *Principia*.
   (a) Eperiments with pendulums to demonstrate the conservation of momentum (*Scholium* to axioms; Cajori, pp. 22–5).
   (b) To find 'the resistance of mediums by pendulums oscillating therein' (*Scholium* to sect. VI, Book II; Cajori, pp. 316–26).
   (c) 'To find the motion of water running out of cylindrical vessel through a hole at the bottom' (Book II, prop. XXXVI; Cajori, pp. 337–45).
   (d) 'To find by experiment the resistance of a globe moving through a perfectly fluid compressed medium' (Book II, prop. XL; Cajori, pp. 353–5).
   (e) The resistance of fluids (Book II, *Scholium* following prop. XL; Cajori, pp. 355–66).
   (f) The velocity of sound (Book II, *Scholium* following prop. XL; Cajori, pp. 382–4).
   (g) Experiments to determine the rate at which very hot bodies cool (Book III, prop. XLI; Cajori, pp. 521–2).

2 *Opticks*. The *Opticks* is so saturated with experimental data that any attempt to list them would involve providing a summary of the entire work. In very broad terms, however, three distinct types of experiments were discussed.
   (a) In Book I there are details of innumerable prism experiments in which all aspects of the varying refrangibility of the rays of light are considered.
   (b) Book II is more concerned with examining the behaviour of light as it passes through or is reflected by thin plates, or as it falls on various kinds of bodies.
   (c) Book III attempts to explore experimentally diffraction phenomena produced in the shadows formed by light as it passes through pin-holes, or slits formed by knife blades.

3 Details of other experimental investigations are contained in several other works of Newton. They include the following.
   (a) Reports of Newton's extensive chemical and alchemical experiments are contained in the Chemistry Notebook, Queries, *De natura acidorum* and the alchemical papers.
   (b) *De vi electrica* reports the results of capillarity experiments.
   (c) *Scala graduum caloris* describes detailed experiments on the melting points of various metals.
   (d) The optical papers make it clear that Newton's reflecting telescope was the result of a prolonged investigation into the property of mirrors, lenses and other materials.

It should also be emphasised that Newton's experimental work was prolonged, often intensive, and pursued with the same rigour and seriousness he brought to any topic. Writing of the 1680s, for example, Humphrey Newton noted that 'He very rarely went to bed till two or three of the clock', at a time when the laboratory fire scarcely went out 'night or day' (More, 1962, p. 247). Westfall has illustrated the thoroughness of Newton's procedure. Finding an error in his work on coloured rings of less than 1/100 inch 'he refused to ignore it but stalked it relentlessly until he found that the two faces of his lens differed in curvature . . . No one else in the seventeenth century would have paused for an error twice that size' (RSW, p. 217). Or, as an example of commitment, there is little to equal the sickening experiments reported in *QQP* in which he slipped 'betwixt my eye and ye bone' a bare bodkin.

As an observer Newton was not in the same class as professionals like John Flamsteed and Edmond Halley. His own personal observations reported in *Principia* and elsewhere are few. He observed the comet of 1680 and recorded the results in his notebook; he also presented them in *Principia* (Book III, prop. XLI; Cajori, p. 508). They were made with a 7-ft telescope fitted with a micrometer and housed, presumably, in TCC.

Although Newton may have used few of his own observations in his published works, it did not stop him calling on the work of others. Book III of *Principia*, in particular, is rich in the deployment of the observations of others used to demonstrate the power of the new Newtonian system. Two topics, comets and tides, were selected against which to test the theoretical assumptions and capacities of *Principia*. Thus, prop.XXXVII contained details of the tides at Bristol, Plymouth, Chepstow, the Magellanic Straits, etc.; more data was presented in prop.XXIV, with particular attention paid to the port of 'Batshaw' in the Gulf of Tongkin. Ever richer in observational data are props XLI–XLII in which Newton tried to determine the orbit of the comet of 1680–1 on the basis of material supplied by Flamsteed, Halley, Pound, Ponthio (Rome), Montenari (Padua), Arthur Storer (Maryland), Hooke (London), Gallet (Avignon), Ango (La Flèche), 'a young man' (Cambridge), Halley (Boston, New England), Zimmerman (Nuremberg), Cellio (Rome), Kirch (Saxony), Valentin Estancel (Brazil), Saxon Chronicle (1106), Simeon of Durham, Mathew of Paris, Aristotle, Auzout, and Bradley (1723). The seventeenth-century scientist, if he so wished, could hardly complain of a lack of essential data. Newton, with his customary thoroughness, ignored nothing. The bulk of *Principia* may well consist of abstract mathematical reasoning, but only in parts; wherever possible Newton sought to apply his work and to ground it in experience. Unlike Descartes, his work was not a physics of declaration but one of experiment and observation.

Newton, Humphrey

The unrelated Humphrey Newton went up to Cambridge from Grantham in the 'last year of King Charles II' to serve as sizar to his namesake. He remained as assistant and amanuensis for about five years, from 1685 to 1690.

It was Humphrey who actually wrote *Principia* down, although according to Newton he 'understood not what he copied'. He also copied out for Newton his Lucasian lectures for 1685–6 and his *De mundi systemate*.

Soon after Newton's death Humphrey recorded for Conduitt his recollections of his life in Cambridge. It is from this document, now in the Keynes Collection at King's College, Cambridge, that many of the later, traditional images of Newton originate. Absent minded, humourless, single-minded in his devotion to his work, abstemious, industrious and an imsomniac – such were the characteristics noted by Humphrey and repeated by biographers ever since.

It is also to Humphrey that the picture of Newton as the obsessive chemist originates. Although, he confessed, he had no idea of Newton's aims, he could still report that 'About 6 weeks at spring and 6 at the fall, the fire in the elabatory scaracely went out'. Humphrey also left a valuable account of Newton's Cambridge lectures and, in fact, provided many vivid details of Newton's life, character, work and appearance at this time. His letters to Conduitt can be seen in More (1962, pp. 246–51).

Humphrey returned to Grantham after his five years at Cambridge. He was still there in the late 1720s when Stukeley went to live there. Stukeley described him as a 'physician and manmidwife'. In 1728 he had a son whom, Stukeley reported, he named Isaac 'in honour to the memory of Sir Isaac'.

Newton in America

In late seventeenth-century New England there had arisen a tradition of astronomical observation and mechanical speculation. John Winthrop (1606–76), a Governor of Connecticut, began the construction of large telescopes and some time in 1672 presented one to Harvard. With it Thomas Brattle observed the comet of 1680. His observations were referred to by Newton in *Principia* (1687). Brattle, Winthrop and others were in touch with European science and published their results, mainly observational, in the *PT*.

There was little sign, however, that the theoretical principles of Newtonian science had been absorbed widely or deeply at this stage. No copy of *Principia*, for example, is known in the colonies before 1708, when James Logan imported the first-known copy. A further copy of the second edition, together with a copy of the 1706 *Opticks*, arrived at Yale in September 1714, gifts from Newton himself. Earlier, the standard text at Harvard had been, and continued in use well into the 1720s, Morton's *Compendium*, a work which looked no further than Aristotle and Descartes for illumination.

There were, however, signs of a new attitude emerging as the eighteenth century broke. The first chair of science in an American college was founded in 1711 at William and Mary College, Virginia, followed by the creation in 1727 at Harvard of the Hollis Chair of Mathematics and Natural Philosophy. By a curious coincidence the initial occupants of both chairs, Lefevre at William and Mary, and Greenwood at Harvard, were dismissed for drunkenness. It was also about this time that scientific literature began to arrive in the colonies in quantity and with some regularity. Yale, for example, hired Jeremiah Dummer, a Harvard graduate and the London agent of Massachusetts and Connecticut, to purchase books for their new library. Consequently, late in 1714 nine cases of books, including works of Newton, arrived in Boston. Further, actual contact was established between the scientists of America and the scholars of Europe. Both Greenwood and Benjamin Franklin, for example, visited London in the 1720s and mixed with Newtonians like Desaguliers and Derham. They attended their lectures, read their books and, on their return to New England, initiated similar courses of their own.

The first book to appear in America, written by an American, to show some comprehension of Newtonian mechanics was probably *The Christian Philosopher* (1720) by Cotton Mather, a Harvard graduate, physician and puritan divine. And so the new philosophy spread. The science of Newton, written about by Mather and taught by Greenwood, reached Yale in 1739 when Thomas Clap, a Harvard graduate, was appointed President. One who studied the *Principia* at Yale and lectured on its contents was Samuel Johnson. He, in turn, took the new science to New York when he was appointed Principal of King's College, founded in 1754, and later to become Columbia University.

By the mid-eighteenth century, however, American scientists were no longer content merely to digest and repeat the science of Newton and Europe. Thus, Cadwaller Colden (1689–1776) in his *First Causes of Action in Matter* (1745) engaged in the popular eighteenth-century game of seeking the cause of gravity and, like many before and after him, sought to locate it in an attractive ether. Another scholar, John Winthrop IV, spent much of the 1740s and 1760s checking the accuracy of Newtonian mechanics against the various transits of Venus and Mercury visible in North America.

The first American, however, to develop Newtonian theory into significantly new areas was Benjamin Franklin (1706–90). Franklin's inspiration derived from the *Opticks* rather than *Principia*, from Newton the experimentalist as opposed to Newton the mathematical physicist. In his account of his 1749 experiments on the 'Properties and Effects of the Electrical Matter', Franklin applied the notion of a Newtonian aether composed of repulsive particles in order to yield some insight into the puzzling behaviour of charged particles. It enabled him to formulate the principle of the conservation of electrical charge, one of the earliest novel scientific insights to emerge from the American colonies.

Newton in France

If published material alone were consulted, Newton would appear in French seventeenth-century science as a very minor figure. The data are unequivocal. Thus between 1666, the date of its foundation, and 1699, the date of Newton's election to the *Académie*, he gained just one mention in the *Mémoires*, and this was simply a brief note by Huygens on the reflecting telescope. Nor was the *Journal des sçavans* any more forthcoming, with just a brief review of *Principia* in 1688. No further mention of gravitation can be found before the 1715 review of the second edition of *Principia*.

Nor were the French scientists impressed by Newton's early papers on light and colour. In short, they dismissed it as false. Consequently, when Malebranche published his *Réflexions sur la lumière et les couleurs* (1699) he never even mentioned Newton. Malebranche could be so casual because, like all French physicists, he was familiar with the work of Mariotte, *De la nature des couleurs* (1681), in which he reported on his attempts to replicate Newton's experiments. In particular he had tried to reproduce the *experimentum crucis*. When, however, he passed supposedly violet rays through a second prism he found, not the unchanged violet Newton had claimed to perceive, but violet tinged with red and yellow. He concluded that light was modified by its passage through the media and that 'light receives different colours as a result of different modifications'. Newton's work could thus be ignored.

In 1704 copies of the *Opticks* were sent by Sir Hans Sloane to E. F. Geoffroy. He prepared extracts in French which he read to the *Académie* between August 1706 and June 1707. The Latin *Optice* (1706) was, in turn, summarised in the *Journal des sçavans*. Yet, despite such publicity, French scientists, with a few exceptions, continued to ignore Newton's work. They were further confirmed in their attitude by the failure of Phillipe de la Hire in 1708 to repeat Newton's experiments.

The first signs of a change in attitude appeared in 1715. On 22 April a total solar eclipse would be visible in London. To observe the eclipse, and to pay its respects to the newly crowned George I, the *Académie* sent to London a delegation consisting of Remond de Monmort, C. J.

Geoffroy, de Louville and the Abbé Conti. Some time during their stay Desaguliers demonstrated before them certain experiments 'concerning colours reported in Mr Newton's book of optics'. News of Desaguliers' success must have been taken back with them to Paris, for a year or two later a number of books sympathetic to Newton's theory of light began to appear.

It remained for someone to repeat the experiments in Paris itself. In his preface to the first French edition of the *Opticks* (1720), Pierre Coste reported that Jean Truchet, also known as Pére Sebastien, a Carmelite friar, replicated the experiments before an audience consisting of Fontenelle, Varignon and other leading members of the *Académie*. Shortly afterwards Truchet enthusiastically informed Newton of his success (C, VII, pp. 111–16). By this time there was sufficient interest in Newton's work on light and colour to warrant a second French edition of the *Opticks* (1722). Thereafter French optics was basically Newtonian and seems to have become so before Fontenelle composed his *éloge* to Newton in 1727.

The same, however, cannot be said of the French reception of Newtonian mechanics. Voltaire in his 1734 *Letters* noted the contrast.

> A Frenchman arriving in London finds things very different . . . He has left the world full, he finds it empty. In Paris they see the universe as composed of vortices of subtle matter, in London they see nothing of the kind . . . For your Cartesians everything is moved by an impulsion . . . for Mr Newton it is by gravitation. In Paris you see the earth shaped like a melon, in London it is flattened on two sides. (VOLTAIRE, 1980, p. 68)

Thus in Paris in the 1730s there were genuine alternatives to the physics of *Principia*. While two French editions of the *Opticks* could appear during Newton's lifetime, there was no such demand for a comparable French edition of *Principia* for another thirty years. The first distinctively Newtonian work to appear in France was Maupertuis's *Discours sur les différentes figures des astres* (1732). There were of course earlier Newtonians and some of these – Malebranche, Varignon, Dortous de Mairan and others – have been identified by Guerlac (1981, pp. 41–74).

What, however, convinced the majority of scholars were the successful extensions of Newtonian theory brought about by Maupertuis, Clairaut and others in the 1740s and 1750s. Their derivation from basic Newtonian principles of the shape of the earth, the return of Halley's comet, the motion of the moon and the inequalities observed in the orbits of Jupiter and Saturn, as they became confirmed one by one, proved too powerful for most younger scientists to resist. An ancient Fontenelle in his ninety-sixth year in 1752 could perhaps produce a final work on vortices, *Théorie des tourbillons*; it remained, however, very much the end of the line. It was also followed, in 1756, by the posthumous publication of the Marquise du Chastellet's French translation of *Principia*.

Newton in Italy

The detailed history of the spread of Newtonian ideas in Italy remains to be written. Two candidates have so far been proposed as the first to introduce Newtonian ideas into Italy. The first, Guido Grandi (1671–1742), entered the religious order of the Camaldolese in 1687. He is known to have studied *Principia* while serving in his order's monastery in Florence. In 1700 he entered the service of the Medicis, becoming eventually mathematician to the Grand Duke and Professor of Mathematics at the University of Pisa. Whether he taught Newtonian mechanics in Pisa is not clear. He did, however, in a treatise published in 1703, introduce the calculus into Italy.

As a rival contender there is Jakob Hermann (1678–1733), a Swiss mathematician and pupil of Jakob Bernoulli, who served as Professor of Mathematics in the University of Padua from 1707 until 1713. A third source of Newtonian ideas was Francesco Bianchini (1662–1729), an astronomer based in Rome. After receiving a copy of the *Optice* (1706) in 1707 he successfully repeated Newton's optical experiments. Bianchini was in London in 1713. He met Newton, attended meetings of the Royal Society and was elected to a Fellowship. From Newton he received several copies of the *CE* (1713) and the *Optice* to distribute amongst his Italian colleagues. On his return to Italy he is known to have given Grandi a copy of *CE* and to have deposited in 1714 a copy of the *Optice* in the Vatican Library.

Further news of Newton's reputation in Italy comes from two letters from Alexander Cunningham, envoy to Venice, dating from February and May 1716 (*C*, VI, pp. 278–80, 330–2). 'The learned seldom omit asking about you Sir and assure you of the high esteem they have for you', he wrote to Newton. Also, he continued, they found 'ye commercium is unanswerable'. In Padua, he had heard from Giovanni Poleni (1683–1761), Professor of Astronomy and Physics there and yet another Italian FRS, 'that your book of principles has inflamed about 20 or 25 of his acquaintance into the study of Nature and Mathematics, and yt they altogether follow your way'.

By the time of Cunningham's visit to Venice, Italian science was no longer the dominating force it had been in the days of Galileo. Italy had declined, both as a political and a commercial power. Consequently, few copies of *Principia* found their way to eighteenth-century Italy, nor was any attempt made to provide a vernacular edition. The demand for Newtonian science must have been met for the most part by Francesco Algarotti, whose *Il Newtonianismo per la dame, ouvero dialoghi sopra la luce e i colore* (1737) was published in some twelve Italian editions before its final appearance in 1832.

Newton in Japan

Newtonian theories were first introduced into Japan by Shizuki Tadao (1760–1806). He spent twenty years translating Johan Lulof's translation of John Keill's *Introductiones ad veram physicam* (Amsterdam, 1741) from Dutch into Japanese. It was published in 1802 as *Rekisho Shinsho* (New Treatise on Astronomical Phenomena) and contained a discussion of universal gravitation, the laws of motion and the inverse square law.

Principia itself had to wait a further century before it appeared in Japanese. In 1930 Kunio Oka issued a complete translation under the title *Purinshipia* by Nyu Ton.

Newton in Russia

In 1697 Peter the Great paid a famous visit to the West. He was accompanied by Jacob Bruce, an army engineer of Scottish origin. Bruce was instructed to learn as much of Western science as he could manage and to acquire as comprehensive a scientific library as he could obtain. On the return of the mission, Bruce set up in 1701 a Navigation School. In 1703 he handed the School over to an Aberdeen import, Andrew Farquharson, who was supported in his work by Stephen Gwyn and Richard Grice, two graduates from Christ's Hospital. It would be reasonable to suppose that, bearing in mind their origin, all three were Newtonians.

Russian science, at a higher level, really begins with the inauguration in 1726 of the St Petersburg Academy, and was largely pursued by visitors. Amongst the founder members of the Academy were Christian Wolf and Georg Bilfinger, a Leibnizian and a Cartesian respectively. Consequently the Academy tended to adopt a truculently anti-Newtonian attitude and to refer dismissively to the 'vulgar hypothesis' of gravitation. The tradition persisted. The first outstanding Russian-born scientist, Mikhail Lomonosov (1711–65), argued in 1743 that 'there is no such thing as pure attraction', and went on to claim that 'Newton did not accept the force of attraction in his own lifetime, but became its involuntary champion owing to the excessive zeal of his followers' (Boss, 1972, p. 174). Later in the century the Academy's leading member, the mathematician L. Euler, launched in his *Letters to a German Princess* (1768–74), in both Russian and French versions, a formidable and comprehensive attack on Newtonian science and philosophy. It proved to be a popular work, appearing in five Russian and four French editions over the following forty years.

There were, of course, exceptions among the academicians. Daniel Bernoulli, for example, an early member of the Academy, defended Newton against the attacks of Bilfinger. It was not, however, until the reign of Catherine the Great (1762–96), that Newtonian philosophy, under the influence of Diderot and Voltaire, became widely accepted in Russia.

See also Bruce, Jacob

Newton, Isaac (1606–42)

Newton's father. He inherited the manor of Woolsthorpe from his father, Robert, shortly before his marriage in April 1642 to Hannah Ayscough. He died soon afterwards and was buried in Colsterworth graveyard on 6 October 1642, some months before the birth of his son. In his will he left, excluding land and the Woolsthorpe house, goods and chattels to the value of £459 12s 4d. This included 234 sheep, 46 cattle and crops worth £140 – a sizeable estate which, via his mother, would eventually go to Newton.

Virtually nothing is known about Isaac's character. A report describing him as 'wild, extravagant and weak' dates from the late eighteenth century, but its reliability is impossible to check. It is, however, known from the 'X marke' on his will, that he was illiterate.

Newton, John (died *circa* 1544)

The founding father of the Newton family, John Newton of Westby, was supposedly descended from the Newtons of Lancashire. His eldest son, also named John (d.1562) had eleven children. It was from his third son, Richard of Woolsthorpe (d.1588), that Newton traced his own descent.

Newton, John (1707–37)

The great-grandson of Newton's uncle Robert, and heir to Newton. Described by Stukeley as 'an idle fellow', he soon dissipated his inheritance and in 1733 was forced to sell the estate to a Thomas Alcock. His unusual death was described by Maude: 'dying about his thirtieth year in 1737, at Colsterworth, by a tobacco pipe breaking in his throat, in the act of smoking, from a fall in the street, occasioned by ebriety.'

Newton, Robert (*c.*1570–1641)

The paternal grandfather of Newton, who bought the manor of Wool-sthorpe, then valued at £30 per annum, in 1623. He was buried in Colsterworth churchyard on 20 September 1641, a year before his grandson's birth. Before this, in 1639, he had settled his estate on his eldest son, Isaac.

There were several other Roberts in the family, including a brother of his father and two cousins. There was also a second cousin, Robert (d.1734), for whom Newton in his last years purchased a farm valued at £30 per annum.

Newton, Sir John (1629–99)

Made a baronet in 1661, Sir John was a distant descendant of the same John Newton of Westby to whom Newton traced his own ancestry. Newton in fact discussed the question of descent with Sir John's son, a second Sir John (1651–1734). It was this second Sir John's son, Sir Michael Newton, who served as chief mourner at Newton's funeral in Westminster Abbey.

Newton's rings

In observation IX of his *Micrographia* (1665) Robert Hooke described the colours produced in thin sheets of muscovy glass (mica), in soap bubbles, in blown glass, on tempered steel and by pressing together two glass plates. Amongst other things, Hooke found that when he took a thin plate of mica and examined it under the microscope, coloured rings were observed: 'The consecution of these Colours from the middle . . . outward being Blew, Purple, Scarlet, Yellow, Green; Blew, Purple . . . and so onwards, sometimes, half a score times repeated'. Similar phenomena had been described by Robert Boyle in his *Experiments and Considerations touching Colours* (1664). Despite, however, the clear priority of Boyle and Hooke, the phenomena has been known ever since as Newton's rings.

He first considered them briefly in his *Of Colours* and at more length in *Of ye Coloured Circles*, *Discourse of Observations*, *Lectiones opticae* and, in their final form, the *Opticks*. Above all they reveal Newton as one of the finest experimental scientists of his day.

The basic experimental set-up is described in *Opticks*, Book II, part I, obs.4.

I took two Object-glasses, the one a Plano-convex for a fourteen Foot Telescope, and the other a large double Convex for one of about fifty foot; and upon this, laying the other with its plane side downwards, I pressed them slowly together to make the Colours successively emerge . . . and then slowly lifted the upper Glass from the lower to make them successively vanish. (*Opticks*, p. 197)

The basic set-up and the resulting rings can be seen in Figs 1 and 2.

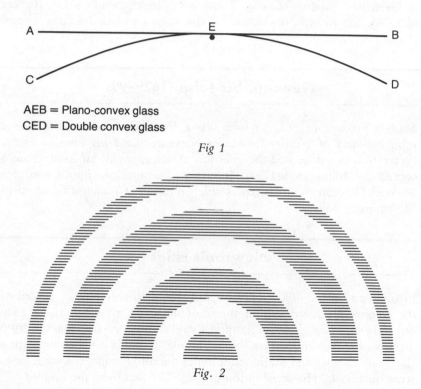

AEB = Plano-convex glass
CED = Double convex glass

Fig 1

Fig. 2

It was clear to Newton, as it had been to Hooke before, that the coloured rings were caused by and related to the varying thickness of air separating the two glasses. Hooke, however, had advanced no further; Newton, in contrast, began a long series of observations and experiments, often working to accuracies of less than one hundredth of an inch, to uncover the range and nature of the phenomena. Westfall has noted that, in so far as it is possible to compare his results with modern observations, 'his final figures do not appear to diverge from modern measurements' (RSW, p. 218).

Newton's most suggestive finding was contained in obs.5 of Book II, part I.

I measured the Diameters of the first six Rings at the most lucid parts of their Orbits, and squaring them, I found their Squares to be in the arithmetical Progression of the odd Numbers, 1,3,5,7,9,11 . . . I measured also the Diameters of the dark or faint Rings between the more lucid Colours, and found their Squares to be in the arithmetical Progression of the even Numbers, 2,4,6,8,10,12.

(*Opticks*, p. 200)

Newton had thus introduced into optics for the first time a periodic property of light. Similar rings, only this time of black and white, were produced when monochromatic light was directed on to the two glasses. The effect was clearly a function of the two glasses and the thin film separating them. Substituting water for air made no essential difference to the observed progressions, and nor did changes in the angle of the light.

Having clearly demonstrated the presence of periodicity, Newton sought to explain it. To this end he presented in Book II, part III, props XII–XX of the *Opticks* his little-thought-of theory of fits.

See also Fits of easy reflection; Interference

Nicaea

Somewhere between 250 and 300 bishops met in 325 AD at Nicaea, modern Isnik in Turkey. Almost all were Greek and under strong pressure from the Emperor, Constantine, to achieve church unity. Emerging from the Council came the creed, anti-Arian in intent and since known as the Nicene creed, with its declaration that the Son is of one substance (*homoousios*) with the Father. It was also declared to be an anathema to maintain the Son to be created, or to be either metaphysically or morally inferior to the Father. Such conclusions were totally unacceptable to Newton and consequently he returned regularly to the analysis and evaluation of the proceedings at Nicaea.

Norris, Lady

Elizabeth Read of Bristol, as she was born, was married three times. Her first husband, Isaac Meynell, was a goldsmith, while her second, N. Pollexfen, was a London merchant. Her third husband, Sir William Norris, had been a Fellow and colleague of Newton at Trinity. He also served as M.P. for Liverpool and Ambassador to the Great Mogul. He died in 1702.

Having survived three wealthy husbands, Lady Norris was a very desirable match. A letter from Newton to his niece Catherine Barton in 1700 chiding her that 'My Lady Norris thinks you forget your promise to write her and wants a letter from you' (C, IV, p. 349) suggests a friendship between the families.

Brewster, however, found a much stranger letter in the PC. 'It is in the handwriting of Mr. Conduitt . . . and is entitled, in the same hand, 'Copy of a Letter to Lady Norris by ____' while on the back is written in another hand, 'A Letter from Sir I.N. to ____.' It carries no date, (Brewster, vol. II, p. 211). The letter itself is a rather tedious and elaborate proposal of marriage. The suitor, however, cannot bring himself to ask the simple question but speaks through a real or fictitious intermediary who, after commenting on the miseries of widowhood, speaks of the suitor and concludes by requesting that 'you will give him leave to discourse with you about it'.

Brewster accepted it as a genuine proposal from the sixty-year-old Newton, but only because he could think of no other explanation to account for the letter's existence. Neither de Morgan, More or Manuel have followed Brewster's lead. The evidence of authorship is dismissed as too flimsy or, it is maintained, to be too improbable to suppose that Newton could have acted so uncharacteristically. De Morgan thought the letter could have been sent by Lady Norris to 'Mrs Conduitt (as an old letter which turned up) to amuse her, and that Conduitt copied it' (de Morgan, 1885, p. 144). The letter itself, de Morgan continued, came from 'some coxcomb of a suitor' shortly after 1702 but never reached Newton's house until after 1717, when Conduitt joined Newton's household. De Morgan made the further point that the style of the letter was more akin to that adopted by the 'young bucks in the *Spectator*' than by such 'a man of feeling' as Newton.

See also Chastity

Notebooks

Throughout much of his life Newton was accustomed to recording his thoughts in a series of notebooks. While some of the notebooks were general catch-alls, others were more specialised and devoted themselves exclusively to such topics as alchemy or theology. Although none of the notebooks has so far been published in its entirety, substantial extracts from some of the more important texts have appeared, and most have been described. The following notebooks have been identified.

Newton's Notebooks

Title	Location	Contents
Latin Exercise Book	Private collection, Los Angeles	350 Latin phrases
Morgan Notebook	Pierpoint Morgan Library, New York	1 Notes on drawing, etc. 2 2,400-word nomenclator 3 Miscellaneous mathematical and astronomical notes
Fitzwilliam Notebook	Fitzwilliam Museum, Cambridge	1 One sheet of Hebrew/Latin 2 Personal accounts, 1665–9 3 List of 51 sins in Shelton shorthand
Trinity Notebook	TCC	1 Latin word list 2 Personal accounts
Philosophical Notebook	ULC, Add. MS 3996	1 Extracts and notes from textbooks 2 QQP
Waste Book	ULC, Add. MS 4004	1 Mathematics 2 Dynamics
Theology Notebook	KCC, Keynes MS 2	Theological notes, biblical and patristic
Chemistry Notebook	ULC, Add. MS 3975	1 Of Colours 2 Chemistry notes 3 Alchemy notes
Mathematics Notebook	ULC, Add. MS 4000	1 Annotations 2 Early writings on calculus
Alchemy Notebook	Yahuda Collection, Jerusalem	Alchemical headings
Index chemicus	KCC, Keynes MS 30	Survey of alchemical literature

Noyes, Alfred (1880–1958)

The author of such well-known poems as *Drake* and *The Highwayman*, Noyes was one of the more popular English poets of the pre-1939 period. In his *The Torch-bearers* (1922–30, 3 vols) Noyes tackled, at considerable length, less conventional themes. In the 422 pages of the 1937 one-volume edition he set out to write an epic poem on the history of science. Beginning with Copernicus, Part I pursued the history of astronomy as far as Sir John Herschel (1792–1871). Other long sections were devoted to eighteenth-century geology, as represented by Jean Guettard, the taxonomy of Linnaeus and the evolutionary biology of Lamarck and Darwin. It is a poem quite without precedent in English poetry. In the course of writing the poem Noyes, in 1927, entered the Catholic Church. Not surprisingly, therefore, he was determined to show:

> What is all science then
> But pure religion, seeking everywhere,
> The true commandments.   (*The Torch-bearers*, 1937, p. 107)

Part I contains (1937, pp. 88–108) a long section on Newton. He had clearly read Brewster and, within that limitation, he was well informed. In addition to accounts of Newton's work on light and gravity, there is an imagined letter from Newton to the supposed fiancée of his youth, Mrs Vincent, written on his eightieth birthday, an account of the Barton affair and a description of Newton delivered by Halley to Catherine Barton. Throughout the section are references to the traditional stories of the dog Diamond, the apple tree, Newton's battle with the bully, his absent-mindedness and his sundials.

There are few, if any, memorable lines. The main interest of the work is to see in it, once more, many of the themes pursued so relentlessly by the poets of the eighteenth century. After, for example, the roll of the colours (p. 89) and other familiar material, Noyes concluded the Newton section, echoing Halley:

> He rose at last so near
> The Power divine that none can nearer go;
> None in this age! To carry on his fire
> We must await a mightier age to come.
>   (*The Torch-bearers*, 1937, p. 108)

Nutshell theory of matter

'Bodies are much more rare and porous than is commonly believed', Newton had written in 1704. As evidence he noted that:

> Water is nineteen times lighter, and . . . rarer than Gold; and Gold is so rare as very readily and without the least opposition to transmit the magnetick Effluvia . . . to admit Quicksilver into its Pores, and to let Water pass through it . . . From all of which we may conclude, that Gold has more Pores than solid parts, and by consequence that Water has above forty times more Pores than Parts. (*Opticks*, Book II, part III, prop. VIII)

Joseph Priestley, later in the century, vividly expressed Newton's insight in the striking claim 'all the solid matter in the solar system might be contained within a nut-shell' (Thackray, 1970, p. 53).

Precisely how matter would have to be organised internally to permit these effects Newton considered in material added to the second English edition of the *Opticks* (1718).

> Now if we conceive these Particles of Bodies to be so disposed amongst themselves, that the Intervals or Empty Spaces between them may be equal in magnitude to them all; and that these Particles may be composed of other Particles much smaller, which have as much empty Space between them as equals all the Magnitudes of these smaller Particles.

And so on, with these smaller particles in turn composed of even smaller particles and equal empty spaces. If this third sub-particle were to be solid then, Newton calculated, the initial body will have 'seven times more Pores than solid Parts'. But if it required six stages of sub-particles before solid matter was reached, then 'the Body will have sixty and three times more Pores than solid Parts'.

Such a view of matter presented Newton with an important problem. How could water be 'so rare and yet not be capable of compression'? The answer, Newton came to see, lay in the existence of repulsive forces.

Echoes of Newton's views on this point can be found in the writings of his disciples. Thus, Henry Pemberton in 1728 reported that the whole universe was compounded of no more matter 'than might be reduced into a globe of one inch only in diameter, or even less'. Similar views are to be found expressed by John Keill, James Keill and John Freind.

At the same time it brought forth the scorn of the Leibnizians. Newton, Leibniz reported, held that 'matter fills up only a very small part of space'. Against this view he argued, in the second letter to Clarke, that 'the more matter there is, the more God has occasion to exercise his wisdom and power' (Alexander, 1956, p. 16).

Observations

On 29 March 1716 Leibniz wrote a long letter to Conti, for the attention of Newton, stating once more his position on the priority dispute (*C*, VI, pp. 304–14). It brought forth from Newton the even longer *Observations* (*C*, VI, pp. 341–52). They appeared first in Raphson (1718) and date from May 1716. It is unlikely that they were ever seen by Leibniz, who died six months later in November.

Coming shortly after his anonymous *Account* (1715), the work contains few novelties. It is, however, rich in hypocrisy. Leibniz, for example, was chastised for publishing his *Charta volans* in a 'clandestine, back-biting manner . . . without the Name of the Author'. Bernoulli was similarly dressed down for his tendency to issue challenge problems, as if 'a Duel, or perhaps a Battel with his Army of Disciples' were more appropriate ways to determine the truth 'than an Appeal to ancient and authentick Writings'.

See also Priority dispute

Observations Concerning the Medium through which Light passes, & the Agent which emits it

One of the puzzling questions of Newtonian bibliography is why in the second English edition of the *Opticks* (1718) Newton introduced at the beginning of Book III the heading 'Part I', when no other parts follow. The answer was revealed by Henry Guerlac when in 1967 he discovered in the ULC the above manuscript, Add. 3970, folios 623–9, which carried the heading 'The Third Book of Opticks. Part II'. It is undated but Guerlac assigned it to the period 1715–17.

The aim of the work was, Guerlac has argued, 'to marshal experimental evidence for his aether theory'. But before he had completed the task 'Newton's customary caution won out: he changed his plan and cast this material . . . in the form of those new or altered Queries with which we are familiar' (Guerlac, 1967, p. 47). The 'Part I' must already have been printed when Newton changed his mind.

As it now stands, Book III consists of eleven observations on diffraction, followed by thirty-one queries. Guerlac has proposed that Newton intended to add to these Observations a further five, and had numbered them in the manuscript appropriately observation XII to observation XVI. They cover mainly experiments performed by Francis Hauksbee designed to throw light on the ether. At some point Newton became dissatisfied with this initial scheme and added two more observations which he numbered observation I and observation II and renumbered the additional five observation III to observation VII.

The bulk of the observations were distributed amongst the already-existing queries and formed the basis for much of the seven additional queries first presented in 1718.

Observations on Kinckhuysen

Few works of Newton have a simple publishing history. Even their non-publication, as in the case of *Kinckhuysen*, could involve years of indecision, frequent changes of plan and the ultimate withdrawal from the project.

Kinckhuysen's *Algebra* had appeared in 1661. It had sufficiently impressed John Collins for him to arrange to have Nicholas Mercator translate the work into Latin. In early 1669 Newton's colleague at Trinity, Isaac Barrow, suggested that Newton should revise and annotate Mercator's translation. The task had been completed by the summer of 1670 and the result sent to Collins in London. If Collins intended to print the text, then would he make sure, Newton asked him, that his work would not be acknowledged by name. If something had to be put to note Newton's contribution then it should be no more than the anonymous *ab alio Authore locupletata* ('enriched by another author', *C*, I, pp. 30–1).

Having obtained some cooperation, Collins began to ask for more. Would not Newton enlarge the work? Extend it to cover surds? For once Newton agreed, and the rest of 1670 seems to have been spent in Cambridge completing the text. It was finished by Christmas. By now, however, a further problem had arisen. Moses Pitt, a leading London publisher of mathematical texts, was already committed to printing John Kersey's *Algebra* and could see no sense in competing against himself by releasing a similar text. Newton even offered to add to *Kinckhuysen* his own *De analysi*, on the ground that if his name were to be associated with the project then he would rather it was for 'something wch I may call my owne and which may be acceptable to Artists as well as the other to Tyros' (*C*, I, pp. 67–9). Pitt remained uninterested and sold his interest in the work to Newton for £4.

At this point Newton seemed uncharacteristically keen to see the work in print and spent some time trying to interest Cambridge printers. They, however, aware of the impending Kersey, were no more interested than Moses Pitt. Newton's last reference to the work was in a letter of September 1676 when it was noted that 'It is now in the hands of a Bookseller here' (*C*, II, p. 95). Nothing came from the 'Bookseller' nor, for that matter, from anyone else for almost another 300 years.

The revised Mercator text seems to have passed at some stage to John Wallis and through him to the Bodleian Library. There it remained, ignored, until it was found by C. J. Scriba in the early 1960s. The revisions and annotations were eventually published, together with Mercator's text, for the first and only time in *MP*, II, pp. 295–447.

Observations upon the Prophecies of Daniel and the Apocalypse of St John

---

The *Observations* was formed after Newton's death by joining together two manuscripts and adding to this a further three chapters; 1 and 2 of part I, and chapter 1 of part II. It has not been well-received in recent times and is either ignored or dismissed by scholars like Westfall as 'the meandering products of an old man', made even more unmanageable by Newton's 'suppression of their real argument' (RSW, p. 819).

The work itself is a substantial volume of 323 pages and is divided into two parts, containing the following chapters.

PART I

1 Concerning the compilers of the books of the Old Testament.
2 Of the prophetic language.
3 Of the vision of the image composed of four metals (Daniel 2:32–3: head = gold = Babylon; breast = silver = Persia; belly/thighs = brass = Greece; feet = iron/clay = Rome).
4 Of the vision of the four beasts (Daniel 7:4–7: lion with eagle wings = Babylon and Media; bear = Persian empire with the three ribs in its mouth standing for Sardis, Babylon and Egypt; leopard = Greek empire with its four heads representing the kingdoms of Cassander, Ptolemy, Lysimachus and Seleucus; the fourth beast with ten horns = Roman empire).
5 Of the kingdoms represented by the feet of the image composed of iron and clay (Gothic tribes).
6 Of the ten kingdoms represented by the horns of the beast (Daniel

7:20: Vandals and Alans, Suevians, Visigoths, Alans of Galia, Burgundians, Franks, Britons, Huns, Lombards, Ravenna).

7 Of the eleventh horn of Daniel's fourth beast (Daniel 7:20: Church of Rome).

8 Of the power of the eleventh horn to change times and laws (Daniel 7:25). The reference is to the growth of and change in the nature of the power of the bishop of Rome. The edicts of Gratian and Valentinian gave him *spiritual* supremacy over the provincial charges. With, however, the subjection of the Franks in the fifth century, the Goths in the sixth century and the Lombards in the eighth century, he assumed political dominion also. In Newton's words, 'he reigned with a look more stout than his fellows, and times and laws were henceforward given unto his hands'.

9 Of the Kingdoms represented by the ram and the goat (Daniel 8:3–10: ram = Medes and Persians; goat = Greeks).

10 Of the prophecy of seventy weeks (Daniel 9:24–27). Newton followed the traditional interpretation of taking one week as seven years, which consequently yielded a period of 490 years. This he took to be the time from the seventh year of Artaxerxes Longimanus (457 BC), when Ezra led a body of Jews from Babylon to Jerusalem, to the death of Christ in 33/34 AD.

11 Of the times of the birth and passions of Christ (*see also Regulae pro determinatione paschae*).

12 Of the prophecy of the scripture of truth (Daniel 10:21; 12:4, 9). Daniel was instructed to 'shut up the words, seal the book, even to the time of the end'.

13 Of the king who doeth all according to his will (Daniel 11:36–45: Constantinople).

14 Of the Mahuzzims honoured by the king who doeth according to his will (Daniel 11:38–39). The Authorised Version speaks of 'a God of forces: and a god whom his father knew not' as a translation for the term 'Mahuzzim'; Newton preferred the term 'guardian'. By it he meant the souls, images and relics of the dead first worshipped in the Eastern Empire and eventually to spread into the West.

PART II

1 Concerning the time when the Apocalypse was written. It has generally been supposed that the text of St John dates from the reign of the Emperor Domitian (81–96). Newton, however, favoured an earlier date from the reign of Nero (54–68).

2 Of the relations which the Apocalypse of John hath to the Book of Moses, and the worship of God in the Temple.

3 Of the relation which the prophecy of John hath to those of Daniel; and the subject of the prophecy.

The symbolism of John is far too rich and complex to allow any easy summary as in the manner of Daniel above. The work itself was considered by Newton to be of the highest importance. There is no other book, he had declared in the 1670s, 'so much recommended and guarded by providence as this' (RSW, p. 319). Consequently, it was discussed at length in an unpublished manuscript located in the Yahuda Collection, Jerusalem (Yahuda MS 1.1–1.4).

In summary, the prophetic parts of Revelation begin with the book 'sealed with seven seals' and their opening (5:1–8:1). The opening of the final seal was followed by 'a silence in heaven about the space of half an hour' (8:1). This, in turn, was followed by seven angels with seven trumpets which they proceeded to blow (8:2–11:15). The final chapters deal with the war in heaven (12–14), the Beast (13), the seven angels with seven plagues (15–16), the destruction of Babylon (17–18), the final triumph of God (19–22:5) which began with the casting of the dragon into the pit and the 1,000 year reign of Christ (20:1–20:6), and was interrupted after the 1,000 years had expired by the rebellion of Satan (20:7–10).

Traditional Protestant interpretation saw Revelation as a rather obscure history of the church. The triumph of Roman Catholicism at the Council of Constantinople in 381 was identified by Protestants with the opening of the seventh seal. From there until the defeat of anti-Christ a 'time times and a half time' must elapse. This was generally taken to stand for a year, two years, and half a year, or, assuming a year of 360 days, 1,260 days. Allowing a day to stand for a year gave a time of 1,260 years for the reign of Rome and conveniently located its end in the middle of the seventeenth century. Having established the basic parameters of Revelation, it remained for the student of prophecy to show how the subsidiary details fitted into his overall scheme.

Newton's account in the early Yahuda manuscripts differed somewhat from this interpretation. By no means sympathetic to Rome, he saw in Trinitarianism an even greater evil. The year 381 was therefore, for Newton, the triumph of the 'fals infernal religion' of Trinitarianism. He chose, however, to date the beginning of the 1,260 years not with 381 and the opening of the seventh seal, but with the year 607 and the blowing of the fourth trumpet, a time he saw Trinitarianism to have been at its most influential. One consequence of Newton's revised chronology was that, unlike many of his contemporaries, he still saw the millennium as a distant nineteenth-century event.

Little of this is apparent in the final manuscript of *Observations* published after his death in 1733. Whether half a century of fiddling with and adding to Newton's original drafts had obscured the initial simplicity of his thought, or whether he had deliberately expunged all traces of his anti-Trinitarianism, is impossible to say at this point. The result remains, according to Westfall, a work without point (RSW, p. 321).

EDITIONS

The work is known in the following editions.

1 London, 1733. When Newton's papers were examined, after his death, by the appraisers Comins and Ward, they set no value on the 'Prophecies they being imperfect'. They were also examined by Thomas Pellet who thought the 'prophecies' should be considered for publication. As no publisher could be found to buy the work, it was finally prepared for the press and published by Benjamin Smith, the nephew Newton had formerly found it necessary to chastise. It was published simultaneously in Dublin.

2 Amsterdam, 1737. A Latin translation prepared by M. Sudeman and reissued in 1738.

3 Lausanne and Geneva, 1744. Sudeman's translation also appeared in *Tome* III of Castillioneus.

4 Göteborg, 1760. A Swedish translation of Daniel prepared by G. A. Beijer.

5 Leipzig, 1765. A German translation of Daniel prepared by C. F. Grohmann.

6 Leipzig, 1765. A German translation of John prepared by A. G. Rosenberg and reprinted in 1770.

7 London, 1785. Included in vol. V. of Horsley and in the facsimile reprint of 1964.

8 Taunton, 1808. A new English edition edited by I. Norris.

9 London, 1831. A further English edition prepared by Peter Borthwick.

10 Retford, 1832 (?). An English edition of John prepared by Thomas Turvey. It was also published as a supplement to vol. I of *The Investigator, or Monthly Expositor*, edited by J. W. Brooks, 1832–3.

11 Petrograd, 1915. A Russian translation prepared by A. S. Suvorin.

12 London, 1922. An English edition of the full text prepared by Sir William Whitla and published with 'an introductory study of the Nature and Cause of Unbelief, of Miracles and Prophecy', in order 'to restore to the Biblical student Sir Isaac Newton's valuable study of the Babylonian prophet'.

See also Interpretation and Purpose of prophecy

Occult causes and qualities

At any particular moment in the history of science certain approaches, attitudes and techniques are likely to be judged so baseless as to be unworthy of consideration. The mere detection of any such fault in a work is alone sufficient to warrant its dismissal. Thus, at one time or another, it has been enough to call a zoologist a Lamarckian, a mathematician a Platonist, a physiologist a vitalist, or a geologist a catastrophist, to deny their work any scientific merit.

In the world of seventeenth-century physics a comparable charge could be raised by claiming to detect in a rival's work occult causes or qualities. Occult causes were typically sought to account for the power of one body to affect another. The earth had the power to attract falling bodies, opium to put people asleep, magnets to attract iron, and fire to melt iron. It was tempting to attribute to the appropriate body a specific property which would account for the precise response. Thus bodies fell to the earth because they possessed the quality of gravity, opium put people to sleep because it had a dormative power, magnets attracted through their magnetic power, and fire transformed by its plastic power. The process was endless, effortless and, as became apparent, quite pointless. All things, whatever their behaviour, could be automatically embraced by such a technique. If a body fell to earth it had gravity, if it rose from the earth it had levity. All problems dissolved at the magical touch of language.

With the rise of the new science in the seventeenth century, and as part of the general manifesto of the movement, a conscious decision was taken to shun such explanatory forms from the domain of science. Consequently, when Newton in *Principia* (1687) began to speak of the force which 'retains the celestial bodies in their orbits' as gravity, it appeared to many as a retrograde step. Thus Leibniz in 1715 specifically described Newton's concept of gravity as a 'qualité occulte Scholastique' (*C*, VI, p. 251). The point was made by numerous other critics of Newton.

Newton was well aware of the charge and repeatedly attempted to deal with it. It is, for example, discussed in the concluding paragraphs of the *Account* (Hall, 1980, pp. 222–4), the General *Scholium* (Cajori, pp. 543–7) and the *Letters to Bentley*. The fullest answer, however, is to be found in Query 31 where, speaking of the forces of gravity, cohesion and fermentation, he insisted:

> These principles I consider, not as occult Qualities, supposed to result from the specifick Forms of Things, but as general Laws of Nature . . . their Truth appearing to us by Phaenomena, though their Causes, be not yet discover'd. For these are manifest Qualities,

and their Causes only are occult . . . To tell us that every Species of Things is endow'd with an occult specifick Quality by which it acts . . . is to tell us nothing. But to derive two or three general Principles of Motion from Phaenomena, and afterwards to tell us how the Properties and Actions of all corporeal Things follow from these manifest Principles, would be a very great step . . . though the Causes of these Principles were not yet discover'd. (*Opticks*, pp. 401–2)

See also Gravity; Mechanical philosophy

October 1666 Tract: *To Resolve Problems by Motion*

The manuscript, to be found in the PC in the ULC (Add. MS 3958), consists of eight sheets of paper folded into a small booklet of thirty-two pages; twenty-four pages are written upon. There is another copy, in the hand of John Wickins, in a private collection. The work was known to and described by Brewster; it was, however, first printed by the Halls (pp. 15–64) and has been reprinted in *MP*, I, pp. 400–48. It has been described by Whiteside as 'the first comprehensive tract on flexions' (MP, I, p. 154), while Westfall (RSW, p. 137) has seen it as 'a virtuoso performance that would have left the mathematicians of Europe breathless in admiration, envy, and awe'.

It is divided into three sections.

1 Eight propositions are presented for resolving problems by motion. Throughout the Tract Newton took the terms of an equation to be represented by lines generated by points moving with variable velocities over the same period of time. Although the term does not appear in the Tract, the velocities of the points would later be described by Newton as fluxions. The key advances of the Tract were presented in:

> Proposition 7. Haveing an Equation expressing ye relation twixt two or more lines x,y,z, &c: described in ye same time by two or more moveing bodys A,B,C, &c [see diagram]: the relation of their velocitys p,q,r, &c may bee thus found . . .

> Proposition 8. If two Bodys A & B, by their velocitys p & q describe ye lines x & y. & an Equation bee given expressing

ye relation twixt one of ye lines x, & ye ratio q/p of their
motions q & p; To find ye other line y.

Hall has noted that 'the seventh proposition explains a method
which is virtually differentiation; the eighth, the reverse process of
integration' (Halls, p. 6).

2 The former Theorems Applyed to Resolving of Problems. Some
thirteen problems were considered including:

  (i) To draw tangents to crooked lines.

  (iv) To find the points at which lines are most or least crooked.

  (xii) To find the length of any given crooked line, when it may be
done.

3 Five further problems were discussed concerned with finding 'ye
center of Gravity in rectilinear plainefigures'.

One further feature of the Tract was Newton's attempt to introduce a
new notation. A special symbol, □, equivalent to the modern $\int$, was
introduced as the integral sign. It can be found in other works of
Newton. Not so, however, with the symbol ·X, used to signify 'those
terms ordered according to ye dimensions of y, & yn multiplyed by any
Arithmeticall progression'. It was abandoned, along with several similar
operations, shortly afterwards.

The Halls final judgment on the Tract was that it shows Newton in
possession of methods of 'great power', limited by his adoption of
'clumsy and laborious processes'.

See also Fluxions, fluents and moments; Mathematical notation

---

Of an Universal Language

Sold by Sotheby's in 1936 to H. J. Halle of New York, the thirty-five
page manuscript has been published just once, by R. W. V. Elliott in
the *Modern Language Review*, 1957, vol. LII, pp. 2–18 under the title
'Isaac Newton's "Of an Universal Language"'. Elliott assigns the piece
a date of 1661. It is now in the University of Chicago Library.

The quest for a universal language was a common seventeenth-century
pursuit. Two general approaches were adopted. The first noted that
numerical signs were understood throughout Europe by speakers of
many different languages. Surely it would be possible, it was argued, to
introduce equally comprehensible words. The second approach, deriving
from Chinese ideograms, called for the introduction of 'real characters'
which would refer directly to things or ideas rather than to words or
letters.

Newton adopted the former approach. He began by constructing, 'an
Alphabetical Table of all substances . . . and to let ye names of ye same

sort of things begin with ye same letter: As of instruments with s; Beasts with t; the Soules passions with b and c'. Thereafter more information was fed into the name by a system of conventional prefixes, infixes and suffixes. For example, the 'number' of things would be shown by adding one of the following prefixes to the basic root: *uw*, very many; *ow*, many; *aw*, few; *ew*, very few; *w*, one or more; *iw*, more than one. Thus *ben*, Newton's proposed term for man, could be expanded to *owben* and *awben* to mean many and few men respectively.

The category 'number of things' Newton termed a 'conjugation'. Other conjugations he proposed were degree, action, state, mood, time, quality and epithet. Some of these were less easy to work out than the simple conjugation of number. For action he proposed, amongst others, the following suffixes: *v*, remote cause; *f*, mediating cause or instrument; *r*, the action or abstract form; *k*, the terminus *a quo*. Thus, beginning with the root *tol*, painter, Newton went on to construct the complex forms: *tolv*, the persuasion, moving the artist to paint; *tolf*, cloth, pencils; *tolr*, his painting action; *tolk*, unpainted cloth. Conjugations could, of course, be iterated. Thus, if from *tol*, *tolf* could be formed to refer to pencils, then from *tolf*, *owtolf* could be formed to refer to many pencils.

There is nothing especially original in Newton's approach. He may well have been familiar with a work like George Dalgarno's *Ars signorum* (1661), in which a universal language was constructed out of twenty-three irreducible categories. Each category was distinguished by a separate initial letter, with further data conveyed, as with Newton, by the addition of further letters.

The thirty-five page manuscript consists of a draft (pp. 3–7), followed by the actual paper itself (pp. 9–21). Some pages are blank. There is also a genealogical tree of Newton's descent (p. 1) and an English–Latin phrase list (pp. 25–34).

See also A Scheme for Reformed Spelling

Of Colours

The Chemistry Notebook, to be found in the PC in the ULC (Add. MS 3975), begins with a twenty-two-page section entitled *Of Colours*. Its contents were briefly described in the PC *Catalogue* of 1888; it was only, however, with the publication in 1955 of Hall's initial survey of the text that scholars began to realise how crucial the work was in fully understanding the early development of Newton's optical thought. It has been published in full in McGuire and Tamny (QQP, pp. 466–89).

The work carries on from the entries on light and colour in QQP. It shows a familiarity with and quotes from the *Micrographia* (1665) of Robert Hooke, and Robert Boyle's *Experiments and Considerations touching*

Colours (1664). Unlike Hooke and Boyle, and even the Newton of *QQP*, Newton at this point seems to have discarded finally all modification theories of colour. He noted in section 10 on 'Experiments with ye Prisme' that 'blew rays suffer a greater refraction yn red does'. He also noted (section 7) that light refracted through a prism adopted an oblong form 2 inches broad and 7–8 inches long. There is even, in section 44, a brief description of the *experimentum crucis*.

> Refracting ye Rays through a Prisme into a darke roome . . . holding another Prisme about 5 or 6 yards from ye former to refract ye rays againe I found first yt ye blew did suffer a greater Refraction by ye second Prisme, than ye Red ones. (*QQP*, p. 478)

The description differs from the 1672 report, Lohne has judged, only in the 'less important details' (Lohne, 1968, p. 180).

Other topics discussed included thin films (sections 27–43), the rainbow (section 53) and the physiology of vision. On this latter topic Newton described this quite horrifying experiment: 'I tooke a bodkin & put it behind my eye & ye bone as near to ye backside of my eye as I could: & pressing my eye with the end of it . . . there appeared severall white darke and coloured circles' (*QQP*, p. 482).

It is thus clear that the essential features of Newton's first paper of 1672 on light and colours were to be found in the Chemistry Notebook. On the basis of material included in the work, it cannot have been composed before 1665. Perhaps it was the text Newton had in mind when he began his 1672 paper with the reference to work carried out on 'the celebrated phenomena of colors' at the beginning of 1666.

See also Colour; *Experimentum crucis*; Philosophical Notebook

---

Official appointments

It is clear that by the late 1680s Newton was keen to find some kind of official, and presumably more senior, appointment. He would soon be fifty and have occupied the Lucasian chair for over twenty years. *Principia* was finished and perhaps it was time, he may have thought, to redeem some of his reputation for a position with more status and power. There were few, if any, ties of friendship to keep him in Cambridge, nor did he seem to find the life of a teacher especially attractive. Although he made no direct moves himself, he encouraged a number of friends to act for him.

The first hint of Newton's interest emerged in 1689 when the Provost of King's College, Cambridge, died. John Hampden approached William III on Newton's behalf. But, contrary to statute, Newton was neither in orders nor a Fellow of the college. It was too much to expect the newly-crowned William to go against all precedent and statute for no obvious advantage to himself.

Newton next turned his attention to the Mint and in May 1690 he heard from his solicitor, Henry Starkey, that the posts of Master, Warden and Comptroller were 'very good places'. A year later he was soliciting the aid of Locke in obtaining the position of Comptroller. Although Locke seemed unable to help, he continued to lobby on Newton's behalf and late in 1691 was discussing with him the merits of the Mastership of the Charterhouse. Newton, however, was not interested: 'I see nothing in it worth making a bustle for', he told Locke. 'Besides a Coach wch I consider not, its but £200 per an wth a confinement to ye London air and to such ways of living as I am not in love with' (C, III, p. 185).

Locke enlisted the aid of Charles Mordaunt, the first Earl of Monmouth, but to no effect. Newton seemed convinced that the influential figure of Charles Montague bore him a grudge and 'is false to me' (C, III, p. 192). Consequently he told Locke that he intended 'to sit still' and that he would not trouble Monmouth further (C, III, p. 195).

He wrote more than once in this fashion in 1692. Nothing more is heard of any official posts until March 1696, when Newton was denying to Halley the rumour that he was about to receive preferment at the Mint. Five days later Montague informed Newton that 'the King has promised Me to make Mr Newton Warden of the Mint' (C, IV, p. 195). Newton's eagerness for the position can be seen in the haste with which he abandoned his home of the previous thirty-five years. Informed of the offer on 19 March 1696, he was officially appointed on April 13 and left Cambridge on April 20.

Newton remained at the Mint for the rest of his life, as Warden until 1700 and Master thereafter. The translation, both from Cambridge to London, and from academic to public life, has been seen by many as the end of Newton's scientific life. The point is something of an exaggeration. The *Opticks* (1704) and the second edition of *Principia* (1713) were yet to appear. In addition, de Morgan claims to have detected a deterioration in the 'moral intellect' of Newton during his London period. It is far from obvious, however, that Newton would have been more productive, or behaved in a significantly different manner, if he had spent the rest of his life as Lucasian professor in TCC.

Of Reflections

Included in Newton's Waste Book (folio 10) and dated 'Jan 20th 1664' (1665 NS), is a brief study of the collision of two perfectly inelastic bodies. It has been published in Herivel (1965, pp. 132–6). It contains, in section 5, Newton's first statement of the supposed law of the conservation of motion; it appeared later as corollary III to the axioms of *Principia*. Whereas for Descartes the quantity of motion in a body had been proportional to its size and speed, Newton spoke instead of the mass and velocity of a body. It was thus momentum, not motion, that was conserved.

Of Refractions

Contained in Newton's Mathematical Notebook (ULC Add. MS 4000), on pages 26r–33v, are a series of optical notes. They were first described and published in part by Hall (1955, pp. 36–43). Hall noted that two leaves were missing and that the work itself was of no great 'profoundity'. The missing leaves were located at Shirburn Castle by Whiteside and published by him, together with the rest of the text omitted by Hall, in *MP*, I, pp. 559–76.

The entries deal with the grinding of hyperbolic and elliptical lenses. It was well known that spherical lenses, though easy to grind, would not refract parallel rays of light to a single focus. Spherical aberration, as the phenomenon was termed, seemed to be an essential feature of a spherical lens. Such a drawback, Descartes had shown, would not be found in hyperbolic or elliptical lenses. They were, however, considerably more difficult to grind. Newton, the enthusiastic mechanic, set about devising instruments capable of overcoming such difficulties. They can be seen illustrated in RSW, p. 162.

Why, Westfall has asked, did not Newton proceed further and actually grind the lenses? Presumably because, even with such lenses Newton must have begun to realise, chromatic aberration would have been sufficient to produce even larger errors. On this last point it is perhaps significant that the two missing pages described a compound lens composed of two different materials, supposedly capable of eliminating chromatic aberration. Once more Newton advanced no further. It is unclear, however, whether this was due to technical problems or new theoretical insights.

See also Aberration

Of Violent Motion

The heading is an entry taken from *QQP* (f. 98; p. 113). It has been published by Herivel (1965, pp. 121–7) and is included in the edition of *QQP* edited by McGuire and Tamny (1983).

The entry obviously derives from Newton's undergraduate reading of the Aristotelian, Johannes Magirus. It is consequently of some interest to see the young and inexperienced Newton considering Aristotle's claim that violent motion, that of a projectile for example, is 'continued by the aire'. Surely not, he objected, 'since the aire crowds more uppon the thing projected before, than behind, and must therefore rather hinder it'. Further, he noted of objects moving in water that 'the water is moved very slowly from behind'.

Nor, he continued, could a projectile continue to move 'by a force impresst'. For, if it did so, Newton asked, how was the force communicated from 'the mover into the moved-? If by some corporeal intermediary, then this merely leads to an infinite regress; but, if an incorporeal 'efflux', how could this 'be so easily united to the body'?

Consequently, he concluded, it must be moved, 'after its separation from the mover by it one gravity'.

Oldenburg, Henry (1615–77)

Born in Bremen, Oldenburg was educated at his local gymnasium and at the University of Utrecht. Little is known of his early life, but a fluency in German, French, Italian and English suggests some fairly extensive travel. He was first heard of publicly in 1652 when he was appointed representative of Bremen in London. The appointment cannot have lasted very long, for in 1656 Oldenburg was reported to be tutoring Robert Boyle's nephew. After a tour around Europe with his pupil from 1657 to 1660 Oldenburg returned to London, at which point the real work of his life began.

In 1663 he was appointed, with John Wilkins, secretary to the newly-formed Royal Society, a post he continued to hold until his death. In addition to such trivial duties as attending meetings and taking minutes, Oldenburg also corresponded with, in several languages, 'at least fifty persons' throughout Europe. He acted, in fact, as a clearing house for the scientific ideas of Europe. On 27 March 1665 he took the further step of presenting his correspondence in the more public forum of the *Philosophical Transactions*, the first scientific periodical ever to appear. The *PT* was basically Oldenburg's own private news-sheet. It was often Oldenburg who initiated the correspondence and who controlled its direction. His profit from his labours, for Oldenburg was financially as well as editorially responsible for the *PT*, he complained to Boyle, was a mere £50 a year. From its beginning in March 1665 to his death in 1677 Oldenburg was responsible for 136 issues.

Newton first appeared in the *PT* and in correspondence with Oldenburg in early 1672. Between 6 January 1672 and 28 November 1676 Oldenburg wrote to Newton forty-eight times; sixteen of Newton's replies have survived. During this period Newton contributed seventeen papers to the *PT*, a level of productivity never matched in later life, and partly a tribute to Oldenburg's persistence and diplomacy.

Some have claimed to see Oldenburg as a disruptive figure, seeking to prolong and even provoke disputes. Thus Andrade has claimed that the trouble between Hooke and Newton was caused by Oldenburg and that 'the whole matter might have been dropped if Oldenburg had not, as always, done his best to stir up controversy' (*C*, I, pp. xxi–xxii). Certainly Oldenburg saw to it that Newton's work became more widely known. Thus, when he sent Huygens a copy of the *PT*, he directed his attention to Newton's paper on light contained in the issue. Did he, however, do more than simply draw the attention of scholars to work he thought would be of interest to them? Hooke seemed to think so, and spoke in his diary of Oldenburg's 'fals suggestion' leading to a quarrel with Newton (Hooke, 1935, p. 213). It must however be pointed out that characters like Hooke and Newton seemed to have no difficulty in finding issues to quarrel about long after Oldenburg's death.

See also Philosophical Transactions

On Circular Motion

The actual manuscript (Add. MS 3958 ff. 87, 89 in the ULC) is untitled. It was first published by Hall (1957, pp. 62–71) in both the original Latin and English translation and thereafter in *C*, I, pp. 297–303 and Herivel (1965, pp. 192–8). The title *On Circular Motion* derives from Herivel.

The manuscript is important in that it contains Newton's first reference to the inverse square law. Using Kepler's third law, and a crude notion of centrifugal force, he established that, with regard to the planets, their 'endeavours of receding from the Sun will be reciprocally as the squares of the distances from the Sun' (Herivel, 1965, p. 197). Cohen (1980, p. 236) dates the manuscript to the period 1667/8.

Newton referred to the manuscript in a letter to Halley dated 20 June 1686 (*C*, II, p. 436). Anxious to demonstrate his knowledge of the inverse square law before his correspondence with Hooke in 1679, he referred Halley to 'one of my papers writ . . . about fifteen years ago' in which he spoke of the way 'the proportion of the forces of the planets from the sun, reciprocally duplicate to their distances from him'.

See also Gravity; Inverse square law

One pound note

In 1970 the Bank of England began to issue pictorial banknotes. Designed by Harry Ecclestone, the first to appear was the £20 Shakespeare on 9 July 1970. It was followed by the £5 Duke of Wellington on 11 November 1971 and the £10 Florence Nightingale on 20 February 1975. The £1 Newton was issued on 9 February 1978.

The obverse shows a medallion of Britannia, a vignette with caduceus, cornucopia and olive branch, and the Queen's head. One distinctive feature of the note is the presence of only one serial number, placed at the bottom right-hand corner. The reverse shows a portrait of Newton, sitting bewigged, and holding a large book, presumably *Principia*, balanced upon his knees. Behind him apple blossom can be seen, while, to his right, standing on a table are those other familiar Newtonian icons, a prism and a reflecting telescope. The portrait itself is a composite study, with the head and wig taken from Kneller's 1702 portrait in the National Portrait Gallery.

Dominating the left side of the note is a representation of the solar system, with the sun shining brightly in the centre. Overlying the solar system is the diagram from *Principia*, Book I, prop. XI: 'If a body revolves in an ellipse; it is required to find the law of centripetal force tending to the focus of the ellipse' (Cajori, p. 56). Because, however, of the alignment of the two diagrams it appears as if the sun (C) occupies the centre of the ellipse, when it should of course have been located at the focus (S) of the ellipse.

The notes issued have carried the signatures of two chief cashiers, J. B. Page and D. H. F. Somerset. No further notes have been issued since December 1984, when the process of the withdrawal from circulation of the 600 million or so notes began.

Optical Lectures (1728)

Even though published posthumously, the provenance of Newton's *Optical Lectures* has proved to be as complex as any work published during his life. Appointed in 1669 to the Lucasian Chair of Mathematics at Cambridge, he was obliged by the statutes of the post to lecture and to deposit the lectures in the University Library. For the period 1670–2 Newton lectured on optics and deposited the lectures in the ULC in October 1674. At one time Newton seemed to be contemplating publishing the lectures together with the mathematical work *De methodis*, but by May 1672 he had decided otherwise and wrote to Collins: 'I have now determined otherwise of them; finding already by the little use I have made of the Presse, that I shall not enjoy my former serene liberty till I have done with it' (*C*, I, p. 161). Consequently, although Newton used some of the material from the lectures in other works, the lectures themselves remained unpublished until after his death. He did, however, in his usual fashion, allow various of his young disciples access to the manuscript. In this way a number of manuscript copies have survived. A copy made by Roger Cotes is in TCC, while a copy given by Newton to David Gregory is now in private hands. Other copies can be found in the British Museum, Clare College, Cambridge, and the University of Keele.

Following Newton's death in 1727 it was decided by his family and followers to publish the lectures in both the original Latin and English translation.

1 London, 1728, 212 pp. '*Optical Lectures* read in the Publick Schools of the University of Cambridge AD 1669 by the late Sir Isaac Newton . . . Never before printed. Translated into English out of the original Latin.' The actual translator is unknown. Although the manuscript of the lectures is divided into two parts, Part I dealing with 'The Refraction of Light Rays' and Part II with 'The Origin of Colours', only Part I was translated and published. It was claimed that the second part 'was left imperfect' and, in an improved form, had already been published in the *Opticks* (1704).

2 London, 1729, 291 pp. *Lectiones opticae*, the Latin *princeps* issued complete. It was prepared initially from the copy belonging to David Gregory. Errors, however, were noted when the manuscript was compared with the original in the ULC and publication was consequently delayed to allow for corrections to be made. The work is divided into thirty-one lectures, the first of which is dated January 1670.

It was re-issued six times in the eighteenth century.

3 Lausanne and Geneva, 1744. Included in Castillioneus, *Tome* II.

4 Graz, 1747. Published with the *Opticks*; reprinted 1765.

5 Padua, 1749. Published with the *Opticks*, reprinted 1773.

6 Horsley, 1782. Included in Horsley, vol. III; reprinted in 1964 (Stuttgart–Bad Cannstatt).

Since then it has appeared in only one new edition.

7 Cambridge, 1984. The definitive text and translation edited by Alan Shapiro as vol. I of the *The Optical Papers of Isaac Newton* (Newton, 1984).

One translation is known.

8 Moscow/Leningrad, 1946. *Lekcii po optike*, translated and edited by S. I. Vavilov.

In 1963 R. S. Westfall discovered in the ULC, where it had been ignored since 1888, a second manuscript of the work. It is in Newton's own hand and had been handed over with the rest of Newton's scientific manuscripts as part of the PC. Like 2 above it is divided into two parts, but is some 30 per cent shorter. It has also reversed the order of the parts, beginning with colours and ending with refraction. Divided into eighteen lectures it is an earlier version of 2. As with 2, the first lecture is dated January 1670. It has been published just once, in facsimile.

9 Cambridge, 1973. *The Unpublished First Version of Isaac Newton's Cambridge Lectures on Optics*, edited by D. T. Whiteside (Newton, 1973).

Newton drew on the *Optical Lectures* for his *Discourse of Observations* presented to the Royal Society in 1675. Much of it also appeared in Book I of the *Opticks* some thirty years later in 1704. Missing from the *Opticks*, however, are the specifically mathematical sections of the *Optical Lectures*.

Opticks

PREHISTORY

In the Advertisement to the first edition of the *Opticks* (1704) Newton noted:

> Part of the ensuing Discourse about Light was written at the Desire of some Gentlemen of the Royal-Society, in the year 1675, and then sent to their Secretary, and read at their Meetings, and the rest was added about twelve Years after to complete the Theory; except the third Book, and the last Proposition of the Second, which were since put together out of scatter'd Papers.

The reason for the delay of thirty years Newton gave as his reluctance to become 'engaged in Disputes about these Matters'. Why, then, had he decided to publish at last? Because, he replied, he had been prevailed upon by the 'Importunity of Friends'. Such, then, was Newton's official account of the origin of the *Opticks*.

Of the earlier part of Newton's account there is ample confirmation. The *Discourse of Observations* had been composed in 1672 and sent to the Royal Society in 1675. It was, in fact, an almost verbatim draft of parts I, II and III of Book II of the *Opticks* (1704). There is also some evidence that Newton had actually decided round about 1676 to publish the work. Only, he felt, would a detailed and comprehensive treatise free him from the inane and repetitive queries Oldenburg passed to him from the readers of the original article. The artist D. Loggan prepared a drawing of Newton to be included in the book, and Robert Hooke, secretary of the Royal Society, seems to have been told of the planned work. Further, Derek Price reported in 1960 his discovery of what he took to be a few printed sheets of the book. It is thought that a fire about this time could have destroyed enough of the relevant papers to discourage any further work on the project.

Book II part IV seems to have been drafted in 1681. It involved Newton in further detailed optical experiments, the last such work he would undertake. Material used in query 31 was also drafted in the 1680s for inclusion in a planned, but never used, *Conclusio* to *Principia* (1687).

Newton is also known to have turned to optical questions after the publication of *Principia*. At this stage the planned *Opticks* consisted of four books, with the final book showing the relevance of optical phenomena to the problem of action at a distance. Yet when the *Opticks* was first heard of, in 1694, in a comment of David Gregory, it had been reduced to 'Three Books of Optics' intended for publication by Newton 'within five years after retiring from the University' (*C*, III, pp. 338–39). Shortly afterwards the Journal Book of the Royal Society for 4 July 1694 'Ordered that a Letter be written to Mr Issac Newton, praying that he will please to Communicate to the Society in order to be Published his Treatise of Light and Colours.' Another who had heard of the completed work was John Wallis, who wrote to Newton on 10 April 1695 that he would be glad to see the work 'abroad'. It was followed on 30 April 1695 by a stronger letter refusing to admit 'by no means . . . your excuse for not publishing your Treatise' (*C*, IV, p. 116).

Yet if, as he declared in the Advertisement, his reason for publication was the 'Importunity of Friends', why did it take ten years for the importunities of Wallis and others to have any effect? The record is silent. Unlike *Principia*, virtually nothing is known about the preparation of the *Opticks* for the press. As late as 1701 Gregory was unaware of any plans to publish the work and was scheming 'To endeavour to gett his book of Light and Colours, & to have it transcrib'd if possible' (*C*, IV, p. 355).

One reason for the lack of detail at this point is that, unlike most other works of Newton published in his lifetime, the *Opticks* appeared from the hands of the author and not through the cover of a variety of editors, assistants and front men. Consequently, there is no Halley-type correspondence between Newton and his editor. For the only time in his life he appears to have been his own editor. Thus the *Opticks* appeared unheralded when, on 16 February 1704, the newly elected President of the Royal Society presented from the chair the work of three decades ago. Halley was asked to examine and summarise the work which finally appeared a few weeks later on 1 April 1704.

If it was not, then, the 'Importunity of Friends' which persuaded Newton to release his work, what else could have moved him? One common suggestion is that the death of Newton's old critic, Robert Hooke, in 1703 was the crucial factor. Such an answer, however, ignores the fact that from the mid-1690s onwards Hooke was so concerned with his declining health and increasing poverty as to be quite indifferent to the work of others. Hooke's condition was public knowledge. The cause of Newton's long delay in publishing the *Opticks* must, therefore, be located elsewhere.

EDITIONS

1 London, 1704. *Opticks: or, a Treatise of the Reflexions, Refractions, Inflexions, and Colours of Light. Also Two Treatises of the Species and Magnitude of Curvilinear Figures.* The two treatises added were *De quadratura* and *Enumeratio.* It contains queries 1–16. The Advertisement of the work carries the date 1 April 1704 and the initials I.N.; Newton's name does not appear on the title page, or elsewhere. The work was presented to the Royal Society on 16 February 1704. An edition also appeared in 1704 consisting of the text of the *Opticks* alone. Re-issued in facsimile in Brussels, 1966.

2 London, 1706. The first Latin edition of the *Optice*, made by Samuel Clarke for a fee of £500 and seen through the press by A. de Moivre. The two mathematical treatises were retained and seven new queries were added, numbered from seventeen to twenty-three. The edition is known in two states. In query 20 Newton had written of space: 'Annon spatium universum, sensorium est entis incorporei, viventis, et intelligentis?' (Is not infinite space the sensorium of a Being incorporeal, living and intelligent?) (p. 315). It must have struck Newton that to call space the 'sensorium of God', without any qualification, was too bold a claim. Consequently, he chose to substitute for page 315 a cancel in which he spoke of infinite space ('spatio infinito') as 'tanquam sensorio suo' (which is as it were his sensorium). He failed, however, to modify the whole edition and copies with the missing *tanquam* have been found in the Babson collection, the Bodleian Library and the ULC. But worse, from Newton's point of view, an uncancelled copy found its way to Leibniz, who lost no time in accusing Newton of claiming that space is an organ of God.

3 London, 1717. Second English edition. The accompanying Advertisement carries the date 16 July 1717 and notes that the 'Mathematical Tracts publish'd at the End of the former Edition' are omitted as 'not belonging to the Subject'. Nor have they been included in any edition of the *Opticks* since published. Eight new Queries, mainly on the topic of the ether, were added. They were not, however, simply added on to the twenty-three Queries of 1706 but were inserted as wueries 17 to 24; the new Queries of 1706 thus became, in 1717, Queries 25 to 31. The work was re-issued in 1718.

4 London, 1719. Second Latin edition.

5 Amsterdam, 1720. The first French edition, *Traité D'Optique*, translated by Pierre Coste from the second English edition. In two volumes it contains a preface by Coste, had been checked by Desaguliers, and had been undertaken 'par l'ordre d'une grande Princesse' (Princess Caroline).

6 London, 1721. Third English edition, a simple reprint of 3.

7 Paris, 1722. The second French edition and, according to Guerlac (1981, p. 156), 'the handsomest edition of the *Opticks* printed in Newton's lifetime, or indeed later'. The edition was edited by Pierre Varignon and included changes proposed by de Moivre and authorised by Newton. Re-issued in facsimile in 1955.

8 London, 1730. Fourth English edition, 'corrected by the Author's own Hand' and with citations to demonstrations contained in the recently published *Lectiones opticae* but omitted from the *Opticks*.

9 Lausanne and Geneva, 1740. Latin.

10 Graz, 1747. Latin, published with the *Lectiones opticae* (1729); re-issued 1765.

11 Padua, 1749. Latin, published with the *Lectiones opticae* (1729); re-issued 1773.

12 London, 1782. Included in Horsley, vol. IV; reissued in 1964 (Stuttgart–Bad Cannstatt).

13 Paris, 1787. The third French edition in a translation 'Faite par M---' who was in fact the famous French revolutionary leader Jean-Paul Marat. Somewhat ironically the work was 'Dédiée Au Roi'. 'An excellent translation', according to C. C. Gillispie (1980, p. 320).

14 Leipzig, 1898. The first German edition, translated by W. Abendroth.

15 Moscow/Leningrad, 1927. The first Russian edition, translated by S. I. Vavilov and re-issued in 1954.

16 London/New York, 1931. A reprint of the fourth English edition with a foreword by A. Einstein and an introduction by E. T. Whittaker. The first English edition to appear for 200 years.

17 London/New York, 1952. 16, together with a preface by I. B. Cohen and an analytical table of contents by Duane Roller. As a Dover paperback the edition has been reprinted several times and is currently in print (Newton, 1952).

CONTENTS

Reference throughout will be made to the fourth edition of 1730, as published by Dover in 1952. The work is divided into three books.

OPTICKS

Book I

Newton set out, beginning with a number of definitions and axioms, to present the main properties of both light and colour. It is divided into two parts.

PART I

The 'Design' of the book, Newton began, was 'not to explain the Properties of Light by Hypotheses, but to propose and prove them by Reason and Experiments.' To this end he started with the following definitions and axioms.

Definitions I–VIII (pp. 1–4): rays of light; refrangibility; reflection; angle of incidence; refraction; sines of incidence, reflection and refraction; simple, homogeneal, similar rays of light, and compound, heterogeneal and dissimilar rays of light; primary colours.

Axioms I–VIII (pp. 5–20): angles of reflection, refraction and incidence lie in the same plane; angles of incidence and reflection are equal; refracted ray and point of incidence; angle of refraction less than angle of incidence; sine of incidence is in a given ratio to the sine of refraction; reflecting and refracting surfaces produce point images of point objects; converging rays produce real images; diverging rays produce images at the point of divergence.

Propositions I–VIII (pp. 20–111) deal mainly with the nature of light and include the following:

prop. I: lights which differ in colour differ also in degrees of refrangibility;

prop. II: sunlight consists of rays of different refrangibility;

prop. VI: Snell's law;

prop. VII: the perfection of telescopes is restricted by the different refrangibility of light rays.

Proof throughout is mainly 'by experiments'.

PART II

Eleven propositions (pp. 113–91) dealing mainly with the nature of colour are presented. They include the following:

prop. I: colours are not caused by the modification of light;

prop. II: homogeneal light has its proper colour corresponding to its degree of refrangibility;

prop. V: the whiteness of the sun's light is compounded of all the primary colours;

prop. VII: all the colours in the universe are either produced by homogeneal lights or compounded from them;

prop. VIII: to explain the colours produced by prisms;

prop. IX: to explain the colours of the rainbow;

[415]

prop. XI: a beam of sunlight can be compounded from coloured lights.

As in Part I, proof is mainly 'by experiments'.

Book II

It is divided into four parts and is concerned mainly with interference phenomena.

PART I

'Observations concerning the Reflexions, Refractions, and Colours of thin transparent Bodies' (pp. 193–225).

Observations 1–16 deal with such thin transparent bodies as 'two slightly convex prisms' pressed together, and a plane telescope object pressed against a convex glass. The resulting rings are measured, counted and described under a variety of conditions.

In the above observations 'a rarer thin Medium' was terminated by a denser medium as with 'Air or Water compress'd between two Glasses'.

Observations 17–24 are more concerned with 'the Appearances of a denser Medium thin'd within a rarer, such as are Plates of Muscovy Glass, Bubbles of Water, and some other thin Substances terminated on all sides with air'. Again the emphasis is on the coloured rings produced.

PART II

'Remarks upon the foregoing Observations' (pp. 225–44). It contains an analysis of the material described in the previous part. He claimed the new material supported the earlier conclusions derived from his prism experiments.

PART III

Twenty propositions are stated on 'the permanent Colours of Natural bodies, and the analogy between them and the Colours of thin transparent Plates' (pp. 245–88). They include the following:

prop. II: the least parts of almost all natural bodies are in some measure transparent;

prop. VIII: the cause of reflection is not the impinging of light on the solid or impervious parts of bodies;

prop. IX: bodies reflect and refract light by one and the same power;

prop. XI: the velocity of light;

prop. XIII: why does the surface of thick transparent bodies reflect part of the light incident upon them and refract the rest?

props XIV–XX: theory of fits.

PART IV

Newton presented thirteen observations on 'the Reflexions and Colours of thick transparent polish'd Plates' (pp. 289–315).

OPTICKS

Book III
PART I

The heading 'Part I' appeared first with the second English edition of 1717. There is no Part II. Although the heading was dropped from the two French editions of 1720 and 1722, it was retained in the second Latin edition of 1719 and all subsequent English editions. It presents eleven observations on 'the Inflexions of the Rays of Light and the Colours made thereby' (pp. 317–39). The observations conclude:

> When I made the foregoing Observations, I deigned to repeat most of them . . . and to make some new ones for determining how the Rays of Light are bent in their passage by Bodies . . . But I was then interrupted, and cannot now think of taking these things into further Consideration. And since I have not finish'd this part of my Design, I shall conclude with proposing only some *Queries*, in order to a further search to be made by others.

There followed, after 1717, thirty-one queries (pp. 339–406).
Query 1 Do not bodies act upon light at a distance?
Query 2 Do not rays differing in refrangibility also differ in flexibility?
Query 3 Do not rays of light move sometimes like an eel?
Query 4 Do not rays of light bend before they fall on bodies?
Query 5 Bodies and light interact.
Queries 6–11 The heat queries.
Queries 12–16 The physiological queries.
Queries 17–24 The ether queries.
Query 25 Double refraction.
Query 26 Have not rays of light several sides?
Query 27 The phenomena of light are not explicable in terms of modifications of light rays.
Query 28 Light is not a 'pression of motion through a fluid medium'.
Query 29 Are not light rays small bodies emitted by 'shining substances'.
Query 30 Are not gross bodies and light interconvertible?
Query 31 Action at a distance; attraction and repulsion; occult qualities; inertia, etc.

RECEPTION AND INFLUENCE

Cohen has noted how, in his investigations of eighteenth-century experimental science, he found few references to *Principia* but many to the *Opticks*. Stephen Hales, for example, in his *Vegetable Staticks* (1727), quoted from the *Opticks* fifteen times without ever once referring to *Principia*. Part of the reason for the relative popularity of the *Opticks* lay, undoubtedly, in its accessibility. Compared with only two vernacular editions of *Principia* to appear in the eighteenth century, the *Opticks* is known in six English and three French editions. Nor was it expressed in the formidable, mathematical language deliberately selected by Newton in *Principia* to discourage casual readers.

The *Opticks* was, however, much more than accessible. Contained within its pages were the details of an exciting new scientific programme. Whereas *Principia* primly declined 'to frame' hypotheses, the *Opticks* was rich with speculation; whereas *Principia* was a treatise reporting the definitive results of a project long completed, the *Opticks* appeared as a manifesto posing challenging problems on which work had scarcely begun. The science of the *Opticks* was experimental and, though quantitative, avoided the elaborate mathematical formalism displayed in *Principia*. In addition, and particularly in the Queries, it spoke of a world occupied by 'solid, massy, hard, impenetrable, movable Particles' which were, in turn, directed by a number of unknown 'attractive and repelling powers'. The task facing the eighteenth-century scientist was to show how a number of outstanding problems in chemistry, optics, physiology, astronomy and dynamics could be resolved in terms of Newtonian particles and powers.

Much of eighteenth-century science can, in fact, be seen in these terms. Hales in the field of physiology, Robert Smith on optics, Benjamin Franklin working on newly-reported electrical phenomena, iatrophysicists such as John Freind, and chemists like C. F. Wenzel and J. B. Richter, all sought to follow Newton's guide. Their work met with varying success. For some, the iatrophysicists for example, there seemed to be no clear way to link the unobservable particles of Newton with the grosser manifestations of disease. For others, such as the chemists, it proved to be more than usually difficult to develop a quantified discipline. There were successes none the less. Franklin, for example, threw much light on electrical phenomena in a self-consciously Newtonian approach to his problems, as did Hales.

There remains the issue of Newton's theory of light as presented in the *Opticks*. Much of this lay long ignored. Because of a number of plausible and well-known objections to the corpuscular theory, many Continental scholars chose to work instead on the wave theory of light. Many of Newton's experiments were accepted but reinterpreted in more congenial ways. English scholars remained loyal throughout the century but, with the discoveries of Thomas Young at the beginning of the nineteenth century and their development by the mathematical physicists of Paris, they too began to adopt varieties of the wave theory. By 1830 it was difficult to find anyone other than the ever-loyal Sir David Brewster willing to support traditional Newtonian optics unreservedly. If, however, the details of Newton's optics have long been discarded, and such is the inevitable way of science, it must still be conceded that the Newtonian vision of science displayed in the *Opticks* is still very much with us.

Nor was it only in the domain of science that the influence of the

Opticks can be detected. Nicolson (1966), in her important study of eighteenth-century verse, has described the eagerness with which the poets greeted Newton's optical researches, and the excitement with which they described his discoveries. Such eagerness, however, like Newton's theory itself, did not long outlast the century.

See also Poetic tradition; Wave theory of light

Optics, writings

Title	Found in
1 *The invension of figures for reflections at right angles* (Waste Book, 1664)	MP, I, pp. 551–4
2 Miscellaneous early calculations on Cartesian ovals (Waste Book, 1664)	MP, I, pp. 555–8
3 *Of Colours* (QQP, 1665)	QQP, pp. 430–3, 452–63
4 *Of Refractions* (Mathematics Notebook, 1665–6)	Hall (1955, pp. 36–43; MP, I, pp. 559–75)
5 *Of Colours* (Chemistry Notebook, 1666)	QQP, pp. 466–89
6 *On Rainbows* (1665–6)	MP, III, pp. 543–9
7 *The refraction of light at a spherical surface* (1666)	MP, I, pp. 577–85
8 Isaac Barrow's *Lectiones XVIII*, 1669	
9 *Lectiones opticae* (1670)	Shapiro (1984)
10 *Theoremata optica* (Waste Book, 1671)	MP, III, pp. 514–20
11 *Problem of twofold refraction resolved* (Waste Book, 1671)	MP, III, pp. 528–30
12 *Of ye coloured circles twixt two contiguous glasses* ('closer to 1672 than to 1666', Westfall)	Westfall (1965, pp. 181–96)
13 Papers on light and colour (*PT*, 1672–6)	
(a) 'New Theory about Light and Colours' (*PT* 80, 19 February 1672, pp. 3075–87)	Horsley, IV, pp. 295–308; PLNP, pp. 47–59; C, I, pp. 92–102
(b) 'An accompt of a new catadioptrical telescope invented by Mr Newton' (*PT* 81, 25 March 1672, pp. 4004–10)	PLNP, pp. 60–6
(c) 'Mr Newton's letter . . . containing some more suggestions about his new telescope and a table of apertures and charges for the several lengths of that instrument' (*PT* 82, 22 April 1672, pp. 4032–4)	Horsley, IV, pp. 276 7; PLNP, pp. 68–70; C, I, pp. 123–5
(d) 'Answer to some objections made by an ingenious French philosopher (Adrien Auzout) to the new reflecting telescope' (*PT* 82, 30 March 1672, pp. 4034–5)	Horsley, IV, pp. 278–81; PLNP, pp. 70–1; C, I, pp. 126–9

Title	Found in
(e) 'Considerations . . . concerning the catadioptrical telescope, pretended to be improv'd and refined by M.Cassegrain' (*PT*, 83, 20 May 1672, pp. 4056–9)	Horsley, IV, pp. 281–3; *PLNP*, pp. 72–5; C, I, pp. 153–5
(f) 'Some experiments propos'd (by Sir Robert Moray) in relation to Mr Newton's theory of light . . . together with the observations made thereupon by the author of that theory' (*PT*, 83, 20 May 1672, pp. 4059–62)	*PLNP*, pp. 75–8; C, I, pp. 136–9
(g) 'First reply to I. G. Pardies' (*PT*, 84, 17 June 1672, pp. 4901–3, Latin)	Horsley, IV, pp. 308–10 (Latin); *PLNP*, pp. 83–5, 90–2 (Lat./Eng.); C, I, pp. 140–4 (Lat./Eng.)
(h) 'A series of quere's propounded by Mr Isaac Newton, to be determin'd by experiments . . . concluding his new theory of light and colours' (*PT*, 85, 15 July 1672, pp. 5004–5)	*PLNP*, pp. 93–4; C, I, pp. 208–10
(i) 'Second reply to I.G.Pardies' (*PT* 85, 15 July 1672, pp. 5014–18, Latin)	Horsley, IV, pp. 314–19 (Latin); *PLNP*, pp. 99–103, 106–9 (Lat./Eng.); C, I, pp. 163–71 (Lat./Eng.)
(j) 'Reply to Hooke' (*PT*, 88, 18 November 1672, pp. 5084–103)	Horsley, IV, pp. 322–42; *PLNP*, pp. 116–35; C, I, pp. 171–88
(k) 'Reply to Huygens' (*PT*, 96, 21 July 1673, pp. 6087–92)	*PLNP*, pp. 137–42; C, I, pp. 290–5
(l) 'Further reply to Huygens' (*PT*, 97, 6 October 1673, pp. 6108–11)	Horsley, IV, pp. 349–52; *PLNP*, pp. 143–6; C, I, pp. 264–6
(m) 'First reply to F.Linus' (*PT*, 110, 25 January 1675, p. 219)	*PLNP*, p. 150
(n) 'Second reply to F. Linus' (*PT*, 121, 24 January 1676, pp. 501–2)	Horsley, IV, pp. 353–5; *PLNP*, pp. 153–4; C, I, pp. 356–8
(o) 'Reply to W.Gascoin' (*PT*, 121, 24 January 1676, pp. 503–4)	*PLNP*, pp. 155–6; C, I, pp. 407–11
(p) 'Third reply to F.Linus' (*PT*, 123, 25 March 1676, pp. 556–61)	Horsley, IV, pp. 360–6; *PLNP*, pp. 157–62; C, I, pp. 421–5
(q) 'Reply to A.Lucas' (*PT*, 128, 25 September 1676, pp. 698–705)	Horsley, IV, pp. 366–72; *PLNP*, pp. 169–76; C, II, pp. 76–81
14 *Discourse of Observations* (1672, read to the RS on 20 January, 3 and 10 February 1676)	*PLNP*, pp. 202–35

Title	Found in
15 *An hypothesis explaining the properties of light discoursed of in my several papers* (read to the RS on 9 December 1675)	*PLNP*, pp. 178–90; *C*, I, pp. 362–86
16 *Fundamentum opticae* (*c.*1694)	
17 *An instrument for observing the moon's distance from the fixt stars at sea* (1699, read to the RS 28 October 1742)	*PLNP*, pp. 236–8
18 *Opticks* (1704 + queries 1–16)	
19 *Optice* (1706 + queries 25–31)	
20 *Observations concerning the medium through which light passes, and the agent which omits it* (1715–17)	Guerlac (1967, pp. 40–57)
21 *Opticks* (1717 + queries 17–24)	

P

Paget, Edward (1656–1703)

A junior Fellow and contemporary of Newton at Trinity. In 1682 Newton was instrumental in obtaining for Paget the mathematical post at Christ's Hospital. He submitted a testimonial in which he declared Paget to be 'very sober and industrious . . . He understands ye several parts of Mathematiks', which he had learned 'by his own inclination, and by his own industry without a Teacher' (*C*, II, p. 373). Newton also turned to Flamsteed for help in Paget's cause.

Paget played a minor role in the production of *Principia*. It was he in 1684 who carried to London, and Halley, Newton's demonstration of the inverse square law. But, despite Newton's testimony to Paget's sobriety he was later reported to have turned to drink. He abandoned his post at Christ's Hospital in 1695 and left the country for India. He returned home to die in 1703.

Relations between Newton and Paget seem to have been good. He instructed Halley in 1687 to present to Paget a copy of *Principia* (*C*, II, p. 481) and a little later, in a letter to Flamsteed (*C*, III, p. 164), he spoke of a visit to Greenwich with Paget and 'another friend', a far from common term in Newton's correspondence.

See also Christ's Hospital

Paradoxical Questions concerning the Morals and Actions of Athanasius and his followers

---

The Sotheby 1935 PC *Catalogue* described various drafts of the *Paradoxical Questions*. Some were in 'several states' and, in all, there were about 30,000 words or 120 pages of imperfect, un-numbered and confused manuscript. Brewster (vol. II, pp. 273–5) was the first to publicise the treatise and to quote from a sixty-two page manuscript. It was published in full for the first and only time by McLachlan (1950) and probably dates from the late 1670s.

It is in many ways the strangest of all Newton's works. A passionate document, it is also instantly readable. Sixteen questions are posed and discussed. The tone of the piece is set by the first such question: is it true, Newton seriously asked, that Arius died at Constantinople 'in a bog house miserably by the effusion of his bowels the day before he was to have been absolved from excommunication?' Clearly false, he declared, on the two grounds he would use over and over again in the piece. If it was true, why did the story only begin to appear twenty-four years after the death of Arius? Secondly, as it first appeared in the writings of Athanasius, a bitter enemy of Arius, no trust can be placed in the source.

Thereafter, Newton settled down, in the manner of a modern invest-igative journalist, to evaluate the charges laid against Athanasius 1,200 years before. The bulk of the work is devoted to the unexpected question of whether or not Athanasius had murdered Arsenius, a Meletian bishop. Newton seemed unworried by the fact that Athanasius had faced such charges before an imperial court many centuries before and been acquitted. And, indeed, with his usual polemical skill, and his great command of the sources, he did succeed in building up a formidable case against Athanasius.

According to the traditional account, Arsenius was merely in hiding, part of a plot to discredit Athanasius. He was eventually found by Athanasius and produced in court. Not so, insisted Newton. It was a letter from Pinnes, the superior of a monastery, produced in court. Pinnes claimed to have seen Arsenius and to know where he was hiding. The letter, Newton insisted, was a forgery. In any account, if the defence was true, why had it only emerged, in the writings of Athanasius, many years later? Arsenius had been murdered, Newton concluded, and Athanasius was undoubtedly the murderer.

And so Newton proceeded from one charge to another. At all times totally innocent of his own outrageous bias and unaware of the unre-liability of much of the evidence he marshalled against Athanasius, Newton had no difficulty finding him guilty on all counts.

Details of the supposed crimes of Athanasius can be found in Chapter XXI of Gibbon's *Decline and Fall*.

See also Athanasius

Parker, George (1697–1764)

Parker's father was the first Earl of Macclesfield, the famous Thomas Parker, George I's Lord Chancellor, who was successfully impeached in

1725 for mishandling Chancery funds. One of Newton's pall-bearers, he had settled earlier in 1716 at Shirburn Castle in Oxfordshire.

It was there that his son George, trained in mathematics and science by de Moivre and William Jones, built a superb observatory stocked with some of the finest instruments in the land. One of his assistants was James Bradley (1693–1762), a future Astronomer Royal. Also resident at the Castle for many years was William Jones. As Jones had inherited the papers of Collins, with its rich correspondence, they in their turn passed to the Macclesfield family. They have remained ever since at Shirburn Castle. Rigaud published the bulk of Collins's letters in 1841 but the collection itself is not available for public inspection and remains out of reach of even the most eminent of scholars.

Parker himself left one permanent mark on British life; he successfully introduced in 1751 a Bill to introduce the Gregorian calendar into Britain.

Parliament

Newton stood three times for Parliament and was elected twice.

CONVENTION PARLIAMENT, JANUARY 1689–JANUARY 1690

It was called by William III to settle the succession problem. The Senate of Cambridge University met on 15 January 1689 to elect two members. The results were:

Sir Robert Sawyer	125 votes
Mr Newton	122 votes
Mr Finch	117 votes

No doubt Newton's role in the Alban Francis affair increased his standing in the University. There is no evidence that Newton spoke in debate, although there is an oft-repeated anecdote that he once asked an usher to close a window. Whether he spoke or not, Newton had a very clear understanding of what was going on in Parliament as he left a fairly full account of the proceedings, as they affected Cambridge, in a series of letters sent to John Covel, the Vice-chancellor.

1701 PARLIAMENT, DECEMBER 1701–JULY 1702

Newton did not stand for the 1690 Parliament. Presumably it was to support his patron Halifax and the Whigs that Newton sought election for the 1701 Parliament – he voted for them throughout the Parliament's short life. The result of the election was:

Mr Henry Boyle	180 votes
Mr Newton	161 votes
Mr Hammond	64 votes

After the election there was a complaint from the defeated candidate that the East India Company had been buying votes, including Newton's. Hammond issued a pamphlet on the subject, *Considerations upon Corrupt Elections of Members to Serve Parliament*. Newton did not stand for the 1702 Parliament.

1705 PARLIAMENT

Why Newton allowed himself to be persuaded to run once more for election is unknown. Presumably it was at the call of Newton's patron, Lord Halifax. To help his election campaign he was publicly knighted by Queen Anne on April 16 in Trinity College, just a few weeks before the election on May 17. Newton is also known to have paid several visits to Cambridge to solicit votes. The results were far from impressive:

Hon. Arthur Annesley	182 votes
Hon. Dixie Winsor	170 votes
Mr Godolphin	162 votes
Sir Isaac Newton	117 votes

Last in a field of four could not much have pleased the newly knighted Newton. He never stood again nor, at the age of sixty-three, did he express any regret at the end of his political career.

See also Thirteen Letters . . . to John Covel

Pearce, Zachary (1690–1774)

The son of a distiller, Pearce was educated at TCC, where he served as a Fellow until his appointment in 1718 to the Bishopric of Rochester. With an interest in chronology, he seems to have befriended Newton in the last few years of his life when he was serving, in his role as Rector of St Martin-in-the-Fields, as Newton's parish priest. He has left a valuable account of a visit to Newton a few days before his death. He found him writing his *Chronology*, 'without the help of spectacles'. Newton told Pearce he was preparing the *Chronology* for the press, read him parts of the work, and continued discussing chronological problems for about an hour.

Pellett, Thomas (1671–1744)

Educated at Cambridge, Pellett qualified as a physician. He practised in London and eventually served, from 1735 to 1739, as President of the College of Physicians. In 1727 he was asked by the heirs to the estate to examine Newton's papers, to determine whether they contained anything publishable. Why Pellett was chosen for this difficult task is no longer clear. After just three days' examination he concluded that the *Chronology* was certainly fit for publication and four other works were worthy of consideration. Otherwise Pellett was content to dismiss the remaining manuscripts with such comments as 'foul draughts of the Prophetic stile' and 'not fit to be printed'. Pellett's inventory was published in Charles Hutton's *Mathematical and Philosophical Dictionary* (1795, vol. II, pp. 155–7) and in William Davis's edition of *Principia* (1803, vol. III, pp. lv–lx).

See also Portsmouth Collection

Pemberton, Henry (1694–1771)

Pemberton was one of the many ambitious young scientists of the period who chose to pursue their career under Boerhaave in Leyden. He qualified in medicine in 1719 and went on to further studies in Paris and at St Thomas's Hospital in London. He also taught himself mathematics along the way. On his return to London Pemberton seems to have set about making himself known to Newton. In 1722 he published in the *PT* a paper attacking Leibniz's mechanics and expressing his own unqualified support for Newton. This was sufficient to gain an introduction to Newton shortly afterwards through the good offices of Richard Mead.

Within the space of a year Pemberton had been invited to edit the third edition of *Principia*. Why Pemberton was chosen, and precisely when Newton decided to go ahead with his vague plans for a new edition of *Principia*, are not known. Thirty-one letters from Pemberton to Newton have survived. They are published in *C*, VII, and show that at eighty-one Newton was in no mood to consider any radical changes to his work. Pemberton was to be no Cotes. He strove, none the less, to leave his mark on the text. He proposed to include work of his own on the lunar nodes, but Newton preferred to use similar material prepared by John Machin. Pemberton did manage to persuade Newton to squeeze his name into the *Scholium* following prop. XXXIII of Book III, where reference is made to a 'Mr Machin . . . and Dr Henry Pemberton, separately found out the motion of the nodes by a different method' (p. 463). Unfortunately for Pemberton's reputation, the

Scholium has become better known for containing in the Cajori edition a glaring error. A 'Professor Gresham', an inversion of Machin's title in fact, has come to claim equal credit with Pemberton and Machin for their work on the lunar nodes.

The only other reference to Pemberton in the text is to be found in the Preface, where Newton expressed his gratitude to 'Henry Pemberton M.D., a man of the greatest learning in these subjects'. Judging from the absence of the acknowledgment from the drafts of the Preface, it looks very much as if Newton needed some nudging at this point. If Newton was short in praise, he was as generous as ever in matters of money and bestowed two hundred guineas on Pemberton for his services.

Pemberton seemed reluctant to allow his special relationship with Newton to end with the appearance of *Principia* (1726). The obvious step would be to prepare an English translation of *Principia* and so Pemberton proceeded, announcing in March 1727 his plans to publish such a work. He even threw in the suggestion that the translation had been authorised by Newton. The appearance of Andrew Motte's translation of *Principia* in 1729 forced Pemberton to abandon his plans. He did, however, continue with one of the earliest commentaries on Newton's Work, *A View of Sir Isaac Newton's Philosophy* (1728), a study described by I. B. Cohen (1956, p. 209) as 'one of the three outstanding popular introductions to Newtonian science of the eighteenth century'. Again, Pemberton could not resist claiming that Newton had 'approved the . . . treatise, a great part of which we read together' (Preface). Conduitt told a different story. Newton had merely glanced at the text; 'Pemberton should not have said so much as he does on that subject', he commented.

After his years of service to Newton, Pemberton turned to chemistry and medicine. In 1728 he was appointed Professor of Physics at Gresham College, London, and from 1739–46 he worked for the College of Physicians on a pharmacopoeia. He also produced a *Course of Chemistry* published posthumously in 1771 together with a biographical preface by James Wilson.

Pemberton died without issue. His papers, including those connected with his work on *Principia*, despite appeals by Rigaud in 1836, de Morgan in 1854 and Cohen in 1963, have yet to be traced.

Pepys, Samuel (1633–1703)

The well-known diarist and Admiralty official, Pepys found himself involved with Newton on a number of occasions. Unfortunately his diary runs only for the period 1660 to 1669 and ends long before he was ever aware of Newton. As President of the Royal Society from 1684 to

1688 it was the name of Pepys that was placed on the title page of *Principia* underneath the Society's imprimatur, although Pepys's role in its production was only nominal. They probably came into greater contact through their common interest in Christ's Hospital.

Much more dramatic, however, was the contact established between them in 1693 at the height of Newton's breakdown. Without any warning Pepys received in September 1693 a letter from Newton informing him: 'I never designed to get anything by your interest . . . but am now sensible that I must withdraw from your acquaintance, and see neither you nor the rest of my friends any more' (C, III, p. 279). Pepys immediately seems to have got on to a Cambridge friend, John Millington, to check on Newton's health. Millington met Newton a few days later in Huntingdon, found him well and received from him an apology for transmission to Pepys (C, III, pp. 281–2).

Shortly afterwards in November Pepys approached Newton with a supposedly mathematical problem. Whether this was Pepys's pay-off for Newton's intemperate letter of September, or a mere coincidence, is not clear. Which was the more likely, Pepys asked, throwing a six with six dice (A), two sixes with twelve dice (B) or three sixes with eighteen dice (C)? In his reply Newton, after regretting he had not been given a problem of 'greater moment', and after eliminating a couple of ambiguities, offered a general solution requiring no computation. The answer was A, for 'A has all chances of sixes . . . but B and C have not all the chances on theirs. For when B throws a single six or C but one or two they miss of their expectations' (C, III, pp. 293–6).

Pepys confessed, a fortnight later, that he could not fully understand the force of Newton's argument. Would he be prepared to let him have the computations. By this time Newton had begun to realise that Pepys was more concerned with his chances at the gaming table than with probability theory. Consequently, amongst the computations of his answer, he began to introduce himself the language of the wager. Thus, given one throw for a stake of £1,000, what should the gambler be prepared to wager. Upon six dice he should wager no more than £618 13s 4d, and on twelve dice no more than £665 0s 2d (or £665 2s 5d, as corrected by Turnbull), and for eighteen dice, Newton concluded, his expectation would be still less (C, III, pp. 298–301).

The prudent Pepys had one further query before, presumably, launching himself on the gaming tables of London. Would it make any difference, he asked Newton, if twelve dice was thrown from a single box, or 'twice with 6 dyes at a time out of one Box, or at once out of 2 Boxes with that Number in each' (C, III, pp. 301–2). Once more Newton willingly and politely sorted out Pepys's queries before concluding the correspondence with the offer, 'If there be anything else, pray command' (C, III, pp. 302–3).

Peyton, Craven

Peyton succeeded Sir John Stanley as Warden of the Mint in 1708 and continued to hold the post until 1714. The son of Sir Robert Peyton and married to a daughter of the Earl of Bath, Peyton was returned to Parlaiment in 1705 as the Member for one of the Duke of Newcastle's seats. With such a background it is unlikely that anyone could have worked harmoniously with a Newton demanding total control of the institution he commanded.

Peyton quickly revealed his power and independence by successfully introducing in Parliament an amendment to the Coinage Act which gave him an account of £100 per annum to be operated separately from any of the Master's funds and to be used for the suppression of coiners. Further challenges to Newton's authority were persistently made by Peyton. A major issue in 1711 concerned the collection by the Mint of silver plate to be used for coining. Who should be allowed to receive plate and issue receipts for its collection? As Master, Newton claimed the sole right. Peyton, as Warden, demanded parity and, using his Parliamentary connections, gained it. After two defeats Newton won the third encounter in 1713 when Master and Warden backed different candidates for the vacant post of Assay Master.

In the last months of Queen Anne's reign the issues between the two came to a head over the Mint accounts for 1713. Mint accounts were always complex and led to endless disputes over whether individual items should be counted as coining expenses or deemed to be repairs to equipment. The challenge to Newton's account was directed by Peyton, a lapsed Whig, and Tory ministers who appeared keen to gain Newton's office for their own disposal. With the accession of the Hanoverians and the return of the Whigs, Peyton's own position became untenable and before the end of the year he had been replaced by Sir Robert Sanford, a loyal Whig.

The surface victory was insufficient for Newton. The Warden's independent account was abolished and much time was spent preparing draft after draft of the 1713 accounts in order to show that his administration had been perfectly proper and untainted by extravagance. Despite his final disappearance from the Mint, Peyton remained one of the few opponents of Newton to gain, however temporarily, convincing and substantial victories.

Philalthes, Eiraneus

Described by Dobbs as 'the last great philosophical alchemist' (1975, p. 179), he has been identified as George Starkey, several of whose

[429]

works Newton possessed. *Clavis* seems to have relied heavily upon views expressed by Philalthes in his *Secret's Reveal'd* (1669).

Philosophical Notebook

This important Notebook was described in the PC Cambridge *Catalogue* of 1888 as 'A common-place book written from both ends with "I.N. Trin.Coll. Cant.1661" at the beginning.' It had earlier been marked by Thomas Pellet 'Not fit to be printed 26 Sept 1727.' And nor has it been.

The Notebook consists of two quite distinct parts. The first thirty and the final forty pages consist of little more than notes taken from the texts prescribed for Cambridge students in the 1660s. Thus, in the first thirty pages notes were taken from:

Aristotle, *Organon*, in Greek with Latin headings;

Johannis Magirus, *Physiologiae peripeteticae* (1645, Peripatetic physics), in Latin;

astronomical notes in English.

The rear of the Notebook contains notes from:

Aristotle, *Ethics*, in Greek;

Daniel Stahl, *Axiomatica philosophica* (1645), a compendium of Aristotelian philosophy;

Eustachius of St Paul, *Ethica* (1654);

Gerardus Vossius, *Rhetorices* (1631);

some notes in English from Descartes.

The central forty-eight pages of the Notebook contain a separate work of a markedly different quality. Entitled *Quaestiones quaedam philosophicam* (Certain Philosophical Questions), it shows Newton attempting to comprehend such basic categories of nature as attraction, gravity, motion, fire and light.

The original thirty-seven headings eventually increased to seventy-three. Some of these, like 'Of fluidity, stability, humidity, & siccity', remained no more than headings; others, like the entries on 'Colors' and 'Motion', expanded so much that they had to be spread out over several pages. Some entries were merely reports of what others had said; others began to query such reports, raise objections, pose problems and state views of his own. In general terms, the *QQP* can be seen as Newton's evaluation, at several different levels, of the competing physical systems of Descartes and Gassendi.

The entries are variable in quality. Some are quite minimal. Thus 'Touching' merely notes: 'A man has been deprived of his feelings, Sir Kenelm Digby.' Others are trivial. Surely, even in Newton's day, it was unnecessary to point out under the entry 'Sympathy and Antipathy' that: 'To one palate that is sweet which is bitter to another.'

Elsewhere there is more substance. For example, the entry 'Of ye first matter' contains Newton's rejection of the view that matter can be constituted by 'mathematicall points'. What lacked dimensions, he argued, could not constitute body and, therefore, 'ye first matter must be attoms'. On the question of the nature of light, he rejected the Cartesian view that it operated by 'pression', on the grounds that 'for then we should see at night' and, further, 'a little body interspersed could not hinder us from seeing'.

More space was devoted to colour than to any other topic. Newton was still, at this stage, thinking in terms of a modification theory. Writing on coloured bodies, he supposed that:

> Ye slowly moved rays being seperated from ye swift ones by refraction, there ariset 2 kinds of colours viz: from ye slow ones blew, sky colour, & purples. from ye Swift ones red, yellow – from them which are neither moved very swift nor slow ariseth greene but from ye slow & swiftly moved rays mingled ariseth white grey & black. (QQP, pp. 432–4)

Newton had not, at this point, concluded that light consists of rays of unequal refrangability; he had, rather, taken the less radical step of arguing that the colours of bodies arise from the manner in which the speed of light rays is modified as they fall on and are refracted by the surfaces of bodies.

Since its examination by Pellet in 1727, the Notebook was ignored until 1948, when Hall published the first account of its structure and contents. He also made it clear that it was a key text for understanding the development of Newton's early thought. Since Hall's seminal paper, the Notebook has been much discussed. The most important part of the Notebook, the section QQP, was finally published in full, with an extensive commentary, by McGuire and Tamny (1983). They argue that 'it was most likely begun in early 1664, but not earlier than the long vacation (summer) of 1663'. The closing date they assign to 'middle or late 1665' (QQP, pp. 6–8).

The Notebook is to be found in the PC in the ULC (Add. MS 3996).

Philosophical Transactions

The PT, in which Newton in 1672 launched his scientific career, was not the first scientific periodical to appear. The Academia del Cimento of Florence began to print its proceedings in 1657, while the Journal des sçavans first appeared in Paris on 5 January 1665. In contrast the first issue of the PT is dated 27 March 1665. The Academia del Cimento, however, survived only until 1667, while the Journal des sçavans, while still in existence, initially opened its pages to historians and lawyers as well as scientists. With the above reservations in mind, the PT can be described more accurately as the first, still surviving, purely scientific periodical.

Its roots are unexpected. It began as a commercial venture of Henry Oldenburg, first secretary of the Royal Society, who sought to supplement his salary of £40. In this way the early issues are presented as edited extracts from Oldenburg's correspondence with the scientists of Europe. Before his death in 1677 he had published 136 issues. The *PT* continued to be edited by the secretary of the Society until 1752. Only then did the Royal Society accept responsibility for the periodical and place its editorial management in the hands of a specially-appointed committee.

Newton's first paper to appear in the *PT* was his famous account of his discoveries concerning light and colour published in issue 80 in February 1672. This was followed in the following month with a report of his newly-invented reflecting telescope. Over the next four years a further fifteen papers followed. Also following were expressions of increasing exasperation from Newton to Oldenburg about the 'vain disputes' he was being drawn into. Consequently when he sent his *Hypothesis of Light* to the Royal Society in 1675 he refused to allow it to be published in the *PT*.

Thereafter Newton's appearance in the pages of *PT* tended to be rare and to serve polemical rather than scientific purposes. They also tended to be published anonymously and include the following.

1 Newton's solution to Bernoulli's brachistochrone problem was published in the January 1697 issue under the title '*Epistola missa ad . . . Montague . . . in qua solvuntur duo problemata mathematica a Johanne Barnoullo* (sic)' ('Letter sent to . . . Montague . . . in which two mathematical problems from Johann Bernoulli are solved') (pp. 384–8).

2 '*Scala graduum caloris*' ('A graduated scale of heat') appeared in the *PT* for March 1701 (pp. 824–9). Just why Newton felt it necessary to publish such an innocuous piece anonymously is not known.

3 On the other hand, there are no doubts why he chose to publish the 'Account of the Book entituled *Commercium Epistolicum*' (1715, pp. 173–224) anonymously.

4 Further anonymous solutions to problems of Bernoulli appeared in the January–March issue of 1716 (pp. 399–400) under the title '*Problematis mathematici . . . solutio generalis*'.

5 Edmond Halley published in *PT* (1721) his 'Some remarks on the allowances to be made in astronomical observations for the refraction of the air'; it included Newton's *Tabula refractionum siderum ad altitudines apparentes* composed in 1695.

6 Newton's final, and characteristically anonymous, contribution, 'Remarks upon the observations made upon a chronological index

of Sir Isaac Newton', appeared in the July–August 1725 issue of the *PT* (pp. 315–21).

7 There was, however, a posthumous publication, 'An instrument for observing the moon's distance from the fixt stars at sea'. It appeared in *PT* October–November 1742 (pp. 155–6).

Pilkington, Mary (b.1647)

Newton's half-sister, the daughter of Barnabas Smith and Newton's mother Hannah. In 1666 she married Thomas Pilkington of Belton, Rutlandshire. They had four children, Hassilwood (b.1667), Thomas (b.1668), Mary (b.1670) and George (b.1672). After the death of her husband Thomas, Mary seems to have been supported by regular quarterly payments of £9 from Newton. In 1723 he stood surety for a £20 loan to his nephew Thomas. On his death three surviving Pilkingtons, Thomas, Mary and George, were amongst Newton's heirs and must consequently have inherited over £3,000 each.

Pitcairne, Archibald (1652–1713)

Born and educated in Edinburgh, Pitcairne studied mathematics under David Gregory and went on to study medicine in Paris and Rheims. Apart from a brief interval as Professor of Medicine at Leyden from 1692–3, Pitcairne taught and practised medicine in Edinburgh.

Pitcairne was the key figure who introduced into Britain the iatrophysical approach to medicine. 'All diseases', he declared, 'consist in a Change of the Quantity of Fluids, or a Change of their Velocity, or a Change in their Quantity and Texture.' He thus saw the hydraulic approach as the way to introduce mathematics into medicine and make it a Newtonian science. Although many younger physicians found his work stimulating, not everyone relished the idea of doctors curing their patients by solving equations, and the basic iatrophysical principles were attacked in the anonymous work *Apollo Mathematicus: or the Art of Curing Diseases by the Mathematicks, According to the Principles of Dr.Pitcairne.*

Pitcairne visited Newton in Cambridge in 1692. He was shown and allowed to take away with him a copy of *De natura acidorum*. Notes taken by Pitcairne of their conversation were later used to complete Newton's copy of the work.

Plume, Thomas (1630–1704) and the Plumian Chair

Archdeacon of Rochester from 1679, Plume left in his will the income of £1,900 a year from his estate in Balsham to endow a chair in astronomy and experimental philosophy at Cambridge. His generosity was reported to have been stimulated by reading Huygens's *Cosmothereos*, a work loaned him by Flamsteed. Although Flamsteed was keen to have a say in the statutes, and even hoped to appoint his assistant John Witty to the chair, he was pre-empted by Bentley and Newton who between themselves had already drafted the statutes and appointed Roger Cotes as first Plumian professor in 1706 without consulting anyone. Cotes was succeeded in 1716 by his cousin Robert Smith, yet another Newtonian, who held the chair until 1760.

Poetic tradition

The initial poetic response to Newton was undoubtedly eulogistic. His death in 1727 led to the almost immediate production of such pieces as James Thomson's *To the Memory of Newton* (1727), Richard Glover's *A Poem on Newton* (1728) and J. T. Desaguliers's *The Newtonian System of the World* (1729). There was thus much talk of the 'first of men', 'our philosophic sun' and the 'beloved of Heaven', amongst much other extravagant hyperbole. More, however, can be found than hyperbole.

There was, first, a quite unambiguous acceptance of Newton's work as science. 'How just, how beauteous the refractive law', Thomson had written, while at the same time referring to Newton's achievement in pursuing 'The comet through the long elliptic curve' and in expelling from the heavens 'whirling vortices and circular spheres' (Heath-Stubbs and Salman, 1970, pp. 138–9). That the observations were often mathematical, or were derived from complex measurements, in no way seemed to distress the eighteenth-century poet. Rather, it was felt, and repeated endlessly of the account of light presented in the *Opticks*, that the results were quite amazing. Or, in Thomson's words, 'Did ever poet image aught so fair' (Heath-Stubbs and Salman, 1970, pp. 138–9).

Thomson was the first to celebrate Newton's untwisting of the 'whitening undistinguished blaze' into 'the gorgeous train/Of parent colours':

First the flaming red
Sprung vivid forth; the tawny orange next;
And next delicious yellow

and so on through the spectrum until:

the last gleamings of refracted light
Died in the fainting violet away.

(HEATH-STUBBS and SALMAN, 1970, p. 139)

Similar rolls of colours were called by many of Thomson's contemporaries and can be seen in Nicolson (1966, pp. 20–54).

The spectrum permitted numerous variations. It was not, however, the only aspect of Newtonian science attractive to poets. Some, like Henry Brooke (1703–83), wrote of the air and 'Its springy tension and elastic spring' (Nicolson, 1966, p. 67). Another, Sir Richard Blackmore (1650–1729), was also attracted to the atmosphere:

> Let curious Minds, who would the Air inspect,
> On its Elastic Energy reflect. (NICOLSON, 1966, p. 66)

Others wrote of atoms, of attraction and of comets. Some, even, like J. T. Desaguliers, could imply that Newton had discovered all truth, and that Nature:

> 'Gainst Mathematics she has no Defence,
> And yields t'experimental Consequence. (NICOLSON, 1966, p. 136)

It was left to Pope, as ever, to puncture such inflated optimism. As well as writing the celebrated epithet:

> Nature and Nature's laws, lay hid in Night:
> God said, Let Newton be! and all was light.

Pope also warned that Newtonian science was limited:

> Could he, whose rules the rapid Comet bind,
> Describe or fix one movement of his Mind.
> (*Essay on Man*, II, lines 34–5)

And in the *Dunciad* (IV, lines 647–52) he identified deeper ills:

> See Mystery to Mathematics fly!
> In vain ! they gaze, turn giddy, rave, and die.
> Religion blushing veils her sacred fires,
> And unawares Morality expires.
> For public Flame, nor private, dares to shine,
> Nor human Spark is left, nor Glimpse divine!

Pope's quarrel lay not with Newton, nor even with science. It was rather the excesses of science he sought to identify and those over-enthusiastic Newtonians who:

> Superior beings, when of late they saw
> A mortal Man unfold all Nature's law,
> Admir'd such wisdom in an earthly shape,
> And shew'd a NEWTON as we show an Ape.
> (*Essay on Man*, I, lines 31–4)

A later generation would emerge lacking all such restrictions in their condemnation both of Newton and his science. Thus, Wordsworth in the *Prelude* (V, lines 88–90) spoke of a dream in which he was offered a stone and a shell.

The stone:

Was 'Euclid's Elements:' and 'This', said he,
'Is something of more worth'; and at the word
Stretched forth the shell.

Wordsworth was still at the stage of attributing to science (the stone) less worth than art and poetry (the shell). Such a viewpoint could tolerate science as a less significant activity and grant it an existence independent of poetry. Some of Wordsworth's contemporaries, however, would take a much harsher line and see art and science as so destructive of each other as to bar their coexistence. The two leading figures in this aspect of the Romantic movement in Britain were William Blake and John Keats.

While the poets of the eighteenth century had been deeply impressed by Newton's achievements in analysing nature, the later Romantics found almost any analysis of nature incompatible with its appreciation. Hence the bitter dismissal of the science of optics by Keats in *Lamia* (II, lines 229–37):

Do not all charms fly
At the mere touch of cold philosophy?
There was an awful rainbow once in heaven:
We know her woof, her texture; she is given
In the dull catalogue of common things.
Philosophy will clip an Angel's wings,
Conquer all mysteries by rule and line,
Empty the haunted air, and gnomed mine –
Unweave a rainbow.

The reference to Newton is unmistakable.

Less clear is the reaction of Blake. At one level Blake saw Newton, together with Locke and Bacon, as prophets of the materialism and industrialism so characteristic, he thought, of his age. Thus, in his *Jerusalem*, he railed against the 'cogs tyrannic',

Moving by compulsion each other, not as those in Eden, which,
Wheel within Wheel, in freedom revolve in harmony and peace.

(I, lines 19–20)

This unhappy condition, Blake argued, had been produced by the 'Schools and Universities of Europe' in which he found 'the Loom of Locke' washed by 'the Water-wheels of Newton'.

Blake's distress at the new age extended further than a mere concern with the emergence of industrial pollution. He was, in fact, more aroused by what he termed the 'Philosophy of the Five Senses'. Beginning with Bacon, it had been followed by Locke and Newton with their rejection of 'inspiration and Vision' and their obsession with experiment and mathematics. 'God forbid,' Blake lamented, 'that Truth should be Confined to Mathematical Demonstration', for the end of such 'Epicurean or Newtonian Philosophy . . . is Atheism' (Nicolson, 1966, pp. 170–1).

In any case, Blake added, the results of science were quite insignificant:

The Atoms of Democritus,
And Newton's particles of Light,
Are sands upon the Red Sea shore,
Where Israel's tents do shine so bright.

(HEATH-STUBBS and SALMAN, 1970, p. 165)

Another Romantic poet critical of Newton was Coleridge. He found him 'exceedingly superficial . . . a mere materialist . . . a lazy Looker-on on an external World'. Resorting to mathematics, Coleridge advanced the equation 'the Souls of 500 Sir Isaac Newtons' would go to the making up of a Shakespeare or a Milton' (Meadows, 1969, p. 163). Only Shelley amongst the Romantics seemed to take science seriously. His views were, however, too idiosyncratic to be ever part of a tradition. References to Newton, though favourable, tended to be somewhat inaccurate; thus, his declaration in the notes to *Queen Mab* that 'the consistent Newtonian is necessarily an atheist'.

Romantic hostility to science in general or Newton in particular failed to survive long amongst the optimism of the Victorians. Thus Macaulay, in his essay on Bacon (1837), spoke of the benefits of science:

It has lengthened life; it has mitigated pain; it has extinguished diseases; it has increased the fertility of the soil; it has given new securities to the mariner; it has furnished new arms to the warrior . . . it has lighted up the night with the splendour of the day . . . it has accelerated motion; it has annihilated distance . . . These are but parts of its fruits, and of its first-fruits; for it is a philosophy which never rests . . . which is never perfect. Its law is progress.

Similar views were expressed by Tennyson in his *Locksley Hall* (1842) where, when he 'dipt into the future', he saw:

the heavens fill with commerce, argosies of magic sails,
Pilots of the purple twilight, dropping down with costly bales;

and noted, also:

Science moves, but slowly slowly, creeping on from point to point.

Such views could foster a tradition in which little more than the occasional encomium would emerge; a recipe for doggerel rather than verse. In this tradition there is the verse of a 'modern poet' on the Westminster Abbey monument quoted by Brewster (1831, p. 326):

Hark where the organ, full and clear,
With loud hossanahs charms the ear;
Behold, a prism within his hands,
Absorbed in thought great Newton stands.

In modern verse, with the exception of *The Torch-bearers*, an ambitious poem by Alfred Noyes, Newton is little met with. When he does appear it is, more often than not, as in Aldous Huxley's *Fifth Philosopher's Song* (Heath–Stubbs and Salman, 1970, lines 266–7), that he has been selected as the impersonal example of the scientific genius to match the equally impersonal selection of Shakespeare as the supreme artistic genius.

Polarisation

Light and sound travel from one place to another. But how? One obvious suggestion is that they should move through a medium of some kind in a wave-like manner. Such a notion was picked up and developed with considerable sophistication by a number of leading seventeenth-century scientists. For no very obvious reason it was assumed that sound and light moved in the same way. As sound travelled in longitudinal waves in which the vibrations take place in the direction of propagation of the waves, it was assumed that light behaved in the same manner. Such a view was not without its difficulties. One, in particular, stressed by Newton and other opponents of the wave theory, arose out of the strange behaviour of light as it passed through crystals of Iceland spar. The resulting doubly-refracted beams of light seemed to require, Newton argued, light to have a 'permanent Virtue in two of their Sides which is not in their other Sides' (*Opticks*, Query 29). No one, however, could see how longitudinal waves could have such a property.

A further troublesome property was described by the French physicist, Etienne Malus, in 1808. Examining the setting sun one day through a crystal of Iceland spar as it was reflected from a nearby window, he noted that as he turned the crystal round one of the images grew dimmer and finally disappeared. At this point Malus, a good Newtonian, with Query 29 in mind, supposed that light particles, like magnets, had opposite poles. Under certain conditions, Malus argued, light particles of one pole would be selected and light would thereby become polarised. Just this, he thought, had happened with the light reflected from the window.

It was at once clear to all that there was no way in which longitudinal waves could ever be polarised in this manner. Leading wave theorists like Thomas Young were thus forced to concede that polarisation 'appears to be much more easily reconcilable with the Newtonian ideas than those of Huygens' (Steffens, 1977, p. 139). Newton's triumph was short lived and five years later Young's doubts were seen to be somewhat premature. The basic error all along had been to suppose that light moved longitudinally. At approximately the same time Thomas Young and Augustin Fresnel proposed an alternative model in which light consisted of transverse waves vibrating in all directions, at right angles to the direction of the propagated wave.

With such a model the polarisation of light waves became a relatively simple matter and the wave theory of light began to look increasingly attractive. Indeed, after the work of Young and Fresnel in 1818, while some committed Newtonians maintained their allegiance, they would find no new recruits to their cause.

See also Double refraction; Wave theory of light; Young, Thomas

---

Polignac, Cardinal Melchior de (1661–1742)

A French diplomat who paid for the experiments of Truchet in 1721 to check Newton's theory of light and colour. He was also present. Though, perhaps, a convert to Newton's views on light, he remained a Cartesian to the end, as witnessed by his incomplete and posthumously published poem, *Anti-Lucrèce* (1748).

See also Newton in France

Pope, Alexander (1688–1744)

The greatest of the Augustan poets, Pope was approached by John Conduitt in 1727 and asked to compose a suitable couplet for a planned monument to Newton to be erected in Westminster Abbey. Pope responded with:

All nature and its laws lay hid in night
God said: Let Newton be! and all was light.

For some reason an epitaph composed by Fatio was preferred: 'Qui genus humanum ingenio superavit' (Who surpassed all men in genius). Pope, however, must have been reluctant to waste a good couplet and, suitably modified, published it in 1735. In the form:

Nature and Nature's laws lay hid in night:
God said, Let Newton be! and all was light.

it has become the best known and most frequently quoted verse on Newton.

See also Poetic tradition

[439]

Portraits, medals, busts and statues

PORTRAITS

The first puzzle about the Newton portraits is their sheer number. Excluding doubtful portraits and copies, seventeen pictures still remain. What on earth was the supposedly secretive and cautious Newton hoping to gain by posing so frequently for the fashionable artists of his day? It was not a cheap pastime. Sir Peter Lely charged £60 for a full-length portrait in 1671, while John Riley was not much cheaper at £40 in the 1680s. Why then should the middle-aged Newton commission Kneller to paint him in 1689 at a price of half a year's salary? His mother was dead so it could not have been for her. Nor, as he kept the painting for the rest of his life, as he did with the 1702 Kneller, were they commissioned for anyone else.

Of the seventeen, only seven of the portraits seem to have been painted for a known purpose. The Loggan (1677) and the Vanderbank (1726) were meant to appear in books; two others, Jervas (1703) and Kneller (1720), were commissioned as gifts to the Royal Society and Varignon respectively. The remaining three, Thornhill (1710) and two late Knellers, were commissioned by and for others: Richard Bentley and John Conduitt. This still leaves another ten portraits unaccounted for. Surely Newton could not have had them all painted for his own satisfaction?

Some hints of the meaning of such portraits to the international scientific community of his day can be gleaned from the *Correspondence*. It was apparently not unknown for the leading figures of the day to distribute to each other not only their books but their portraits as well. Thus Pierre Varignon in Paris, first through the Abbé Conti and secondly through de Moivre, approached Newton in 1715 with the request for a portrait; not an original he emphasised, a copy would suffice. Newton ignored the request for several years until in 1720 when, keen to gain Varignon's support on a number of issues, he commissioned Kneller to produce a new portrait. An original was presumably a sign of the high esteem in which he held Varignon.

One who lacked such esteem was the mathematician Johann Bernoulli. He too had approached de Moivre asking for a portrait. Newton described his response in a letter to Varignon written in 1721:

Mr De Moivre has told me that Mr Bernoulli desires a picture of me: but he still has not publicly acknowledged that I had the method of fluxions and moments in the year 1672 . . . that I gave a true rule for differentiating differentials . . . in 1693 . . . that in 1669 . . . I had a method for accurately squaring curved lines . . . If he will submit on those points so as to entirely remove the cause of disputes, I will not readily refuse [him] my picture. (*C*, VII, p. 165)

Bernoulli failed to earn his portrait. Were then these other portraits commissioned as gifts to be handed as rewards to his faithful followers and offered as inducements to those whose support could not be completely relied upon?

One other possibility is that particular portraits were commissioned to mark certain exceptional occasions. The appointment in 1700 to the Mastership of the Mint, the election in 1703 to the Presidency of the Royal Society and the knighthood in 1705 are all events which, it might be supposed, Newton would have wished to commemorate in the permanency of oil. In this way Kneller (1702), Jervas (1703) and Gandy (1706) could all have been produced to record well-documented public events. There could perhaps have been, also, more private needs of Newton which were best satisfied on canvas.

Perhaps, however, on a comparative basis, the seventeen or so portraits of Newton are by no means exceptional for the times. Wimsatt (1965), for example, noted sixty-six primary types of Alexander Pope portraits; a sufficient number, incidentally, to catch the attention of Voltaire, who reported having seen Pope's portrait displayed in twenty of the houses he visited.

Several other portraits must be considered doubtful. One such, owned by the Cambridge bookseller W. Heffer & Sons (RSW, p. 847), has been variously attributed to William Hogarth and Michael Dahl. It has also been identified as a copy of the Seeman (1725) or the Vanderbank (1725). Another portrait, in the National Portrait Gallery, has a history going back to the early nineteenth century and was once thought to have been painted by Vanderbank (RSW, p. 830). It is now, however, thought to be neither by Vanderbank, nor even to be the missing Dahl, but rather a copy of the Vanderbank (1725). A third portrait, signed and dated 1669 by Henry Cook (1642–1700) and at present in St Catherine's College, Cambridge, is not thought to be authentic. Equally doubtful are the portraits by Sir Peter Lely (1665) and John Riley.

The portraits, doubtful and genuine alike, spawned a vast number of copies and prints. To list, identify and distinguish the items of this complex tradition would require a monograph of its own. The fullest listing is to be found in D. E. Smith (1927b) based on his impressive collection housed in the library of Columbia University, New York.

In addition to the actual portraits painted of Newton, and the print tradition they inspired, there are also a large number of imaginative paintings depicting important events in Newton's life or representing some aspects of Newton the man. Of these, the following are amongst the best known.

1 Sir Peter Lely (1618–80). Sir Isaac Newton when Bachelor of Arts in Trinity College, Cambridge.
2 1794, George Romney. Newton displaying the prismatic colours.
3 1795, William Blake. Newton.
4 George Cruikshank (1792–1878). Sir Isaac Newton's courtship.
5 1859, Frederick Newenham. Isaac Newton at the age of twelve.
6 1870, John-Adam Houston. Newton investigating light.
7 c.1869, Hosai. From an entirely different tradition, a Japanese print of Newton watching an apple fall to the ground. He is in western dress and described as 'Isaac Newton, very great head of school but not pompous'. The print belongs to Stillman Drake and was part of a series depicting great men of the West. It can be seen in *Scientific American*, August 1980, p. 122.

A checklist of the known portraits, with some of their basic data can be conveniently displayed as in the accompanying table.

PORTRAIT MEDALS

It is the convention of commemorative medals that the front or obverse face presents a portrait of the person honoured while the reverse displays an appropriate design. D. E. Smith (1912) has illustrated and described nineteen such medals of Newton. The following are amongst the best known.

1 1731, John Croker. Bronze and silver: obverse, bust of 'Isaacus Newtonus' looking left; reverse, a seated figure with winged head holding a plan of the solar system, and the motto 'Felix.Cognoscere Causas'. It carries Newton's date of death as the old style 1726 (RSW, p. 622; Babson *Catalogue*, p. 200; Smith, 1951, vol. I, p. 400).
2 1739, Jacques Roettiers. Bronze and silver: obverse, bust of 'Isaacus Newtonus'; reverse, a seated figure as in 1 above and the motto 'Erit qui demonstret in quibus coeli partibus errent' (There will one day be someone who can demonstrate the movements of comets). It is a quotation from Seneca, *Quaestiones naturae* (Book VIII, chapter 26). The medal was cast at the expense of Thomas Hammond for presentation to his friends. It continued to be struck throughout the century. Smith (1951, vol. I, p. 401), for example, displays one such medal with the date 1774 but with the different motto 'Quaeritur huic alius' (Another is sought for him), taken from *Aeneid*, Book V, line 378. The original Roettier can be seen illustrated in the Babson *Catalogue* (1950, p. 200), and in Greenstreet (1927).
3 1820, George Mills. Silver: obverse, bust of Newton looking right and the inscription 'The Astronomical Society of London Instituted MDCCCXX', and the motto 'Nubem pellente mathesi' (Mathematics banishes the cloud); reverse, the telescope of William

PORTRAITS, MEDALS, BUSTS AND STATUES

Known portraits of Sir Isaac Newton

Date & Artist	Location	Comment
1 1677, D. Loggan	Lost	Reported to have been prepared for a proposed book by Newton on his theory of light and colour
2 1689, G. Kneller (two versions)	Portsmouth Estate Kensington Palace	There is no known reason for the portrait
3 1702, G. Kneller	National Portrait Gallery	Originally part of the Portsmouth Estate but sold in the 1936 Sotheby sale for £800 and donated to the National Portrait Gallery
4 1703, C. Jervas	Royal Society	Although commissioned in 1703, it was not actually donated to the Society until 1717
5 1706, W. Gandy	Lost	Known only from an 1848 lithograph by G. B. Black. There is a copy in the D. Smith Collection at Columbia University, New York. The reason for the portrait is unknown
6 1710, J. Thornhill	TCC	Commissioned by Richard Bentley, the Master of Trinity
7 1710, J. Thornhill	Portsmouth Estate	Presumably commissioned by Newton
8 1714, C. Richter	Lost	A miniature, known only from a 1785 engraving in the D. Smith collection (RSW, p. 682)
9 1718, T. Murray	TCC	History and purpose unknown
10 1720, G. Kneller	Petworth House	Presented by Newton to P. Varignon
11 1723, G. Kneller	Portsmouth Estate	Commissioned by John Conduitt
12 1725, J. Vanderbank (two versions)	Royal Society TCC	Donated by C. B. Vignoles in 1841 Given by R. Smith in 1766 In an engraving by George Vertue it was used at the frontispiece of *Principia* (1726)
13 1725, E. Seeman	TCC	Presented by T. Hollis. Not thought to be an original portrait but a copy of another work
14 1725, J. Vanderbank	Royal Society	Obtained in 1950
15 1726, J. Vanderbank	Royal Society	Donated by Martin Folkes FRS in the mid-eighteenth century
16 Late, G. Kneller	Lost	A wigged portrait commissioned by John Conduitt
17 Late, M. Dahl	Lost	Referred to by George Vertue as late and 'in his own hair'

Herschel and the motto 'Quicquid nitet notandum' (Whatever shines through is of note). The medal was struck from time to time to honour distinguished astronomers. Greenstreet (1927, p. 180) has noted that when the Society was awarded its Royal Charter in 1831 it ordered a much-improved medal, similar to that of Mills, but designed by the chief engraver to the Mint, William Wyon (1795–1851). The Mills medal is illustrated in the Babson *Catalogue* (1950, p. 200).

4 1826. Sir Francis Chantrey (obverse) and Sir Thomas Lawrence (reverse).

5 The Royal Medal of the Royal Society, awarded since 1826, displays Roubillac's TCC statue on the reverse.

6 Trade tokens. Large numbers of trade tokens have been issued at various times in the past in response to persistent shortages of small change. One such period was 1787–97. Local tradesman would issue their own farthings, halfpennies and pennies, with indications on them precisely where they would be honoured. Their reverse usually showed such standard emblems as Britannia, a portcullis, a caduceus or a cornucopia. They could also depict the heroes of the nation. Millions were issued during this period and a fair number have survived with Newton on the obverse and a standard emblem on the reverse. The Babson Library has two such tokens payable in Hull and London, while Smith (1927c, p. 180) lists one token payable in Hull and London, and a second payable in London, Bristol and Lancaster. They are apparently not much appreciated by collectors and can consequently be picked up quite cheaply.

7 Two other items listed in Smith 1927c, are of some interest.

(a) A tin medal signed L.B., with Newton's bust on the obverse and, on the reverse, 'Sir Isaac was born at Woolsthorpe in the Soke of Grantham . . . and educated at the Free Grammar School of King Edward the Sixth.Grantham.' It is thought to have been issued by the School and is to be found in the Grantham Museum. A plaster replica is in the Babson Library.

(b) A so-called calendar medal, with a calendar for the year 1822 on the reverse and a bust of Newton on the obverse. It is to be found in the Babson Library.

BUSTS

The surviving busts of Newton include the following.

1 D.Le Marchand. An ivory bust; at least two identical busts were thought to have been sculpted at the same time (RSW, p. 687).

2 1718, D.Le Marchand. Ivory bust in the British Museum (RSW, p. 752). A second bust portraying a bewigged Newton is reported

to have been sculpted at the same time. Its whereabouts is unknown.

3 1718, D.Le Marchand. An ivory plaque in alto-relievo, was presented to KCC by Keynes.

4 1720, D.Le Marchand. Mounted on wood, in profile, in basso-relievo, it is to be found in the Babson Library. It was long thought to have been by Van der Hagen, a pupil of Rysbrack, but is now thought by some authorities to have been carved by Le Marchand (Babson *Catalogue*, p. 48).

5 In 1935 the Royal Society purchased an ivory medallion of Newton, by Le Marchand, similar to 4 above.

The occasions for these items by Le Marchand, and their subsequent history, is as yet unknown. Newton's Inventory describes 'a figure cut in ivory of Sir Isaac in a glass frame' which could well have been one of the pieces above.

6 1727, M. Rysbrack. In March 1727, at Conduitt's request, Rysbrack prepared Newton's plaster death mask. He, himself, used the mask to aid him in his work on the Westminster Abbey monument and on his 1734 bust. Five copies are known today:

(a) Royal Society, donated by a Professor Hunter in 1839;

(b) TCC;

(c) Laurence Hutton Collection, Princeton University Library;

(d) in 1951 a death mask was owned by Walter Krieg, Vienna;

(e) Babson Collection, presented in 1951 by the Trustees of the Boston Athenaeum. As the Athenaeum obtained the mask in 1834 from a granddaughter of Thomas Jefferson, it is thought that the mask may well have belonged at one time to Jefferson himself.

One of the masks, presumably (c) or (d), was sold at the 1936 auction of the PC. Also known is an iron death mask, based on Rysbrack's work, donated by Frank Baxter to the National Portrait Gallery in 1925.

7 1729, M. Rysbrack. A marble bust, known as the Conduitt bust, it can be seen displayed in Hogarth's *The Indian Emperor* (1730) and in Esdaille (1928). Mrs Esdaille attributed the bust to Roubillac but this is certainly an error and, following Webb (1952), the work is now assigned to Rysbrack. The bust is in the possession of the Portsmouth family.

8 1733, M. Rysbrack. A stone bust produced for Lord Cobham's Temple of British Worthies at Stowe, Bucks. It can be seen in Pevsner (1976, p. 13) and Webb (1952).

9 1734, M. Rysbrack. A marble bust produced for Queen Caroline's Temple at Richmond, Surrey. It is at present in Kensington Palace in the Royal Collection. It can be seen in Webb (1952) and the Babson *Catalogue*.

10 N. Guelfi. A stone bust, very similar in pose to 7 above. It seems that the original commission was given to Guelfi but, at some point he was dropped in favour of Rysbrack who adopted Guelfi's stone designs for his marble busts. Guelfi's work was somehow obtained by Alexander Pope, who left it in his will to Lord Mansfield. It is now to be found at Scone Palace, Perthshire, and can be seen illustrated in Webb (1952).

11 1737, L. Roubillac. A marble bust in the Royal Society.

12 1739, M. Rysbrack. A terra-cotta bust, in the style of 8 and 9 above. It was sold by Rysbrack in 1756 to Sir Edward Littleton, of Teddesly, Staffordshire, and remained with the Littleton family until it was auctioned in 1932 at Spinks. It can now be found at TCC and is illustrated in Webb (1952).

13 1751, L. Roubilliac. A marble bust commissioned by Robert Smith for the Wren Library in TCC, where it can still be seen.

14 1828, Edward Hodges Baily. A marble bust, after Roubilliac, transferred from the Tate to the National Portrait Gallery in 1957.

15 1874, William Calder Marshall. In Leicester Square, London, there stands the James Knowles statue of Shakespeare. Around him are busts of famous early residents of the area – John Hunter, Joshua Reynolds, William Hogarth and Newton, whose home was once on the east side of the neighbouring St Martin's St. Newton's face is barely distinguishable; the weather and exhaust fumes have so worn away his features as to leave little more than a flat and pitted surface.

STATUES

There are surprisingly few statues of Newton. Only the following are known.

1 1755, L. Roubillac. TCC.

2 1858, W. Theed. St Peter's Hill, Grantham, Lincolnshire (Greenstreet, p. 75).

3 1870, Joseph Durham. On the front of the Museum of Mankind, Burlington Gardens, London, and seated over the central portico, are statues of Newton, Jeremy Bentham, John Milton and William Harvey.

4 1897, Cyrus Edwin Dallin. Bronze, sited in the reading room of the Library of Congress, Washington. It is thought to be the only free-standing statue of Newton in the US. A second statue, one of fourteen great scientists, can be seen sited in the archway of the west portal of Riverside Church, New York City.

MISCELLANEA

Newton's image was also displayed during the eighteenth century upon a number of smaller, more personal items. A couple of such pieces are to be found in the Babson Library and are listed in the Babson *Catalogue* (1955, p. 80).

1 A sardonyx ring, dating from about 1790, and displaying a comet and a bust of Newton. It was once the property of Sir John Herschel.

2 An eighteenth-century gold and cornelian seal with an intaglio Newton bust. It is probably the work of W. Berry.

Also known are a number of pieces by Josiah Wedgwood. In 1776 Wedgwood succeeded in developing a fine white artificial jasper suitable for, amongst other things, cameos, portraits and bas reliefs. Also available for the production of busts from 1770 onwards was an improved blackware named *basaltes*. With these new materials at his disposal Wedgwood was able to offer an incredible number of statues, heads, busts, cameos, medallions and much more besides. All sixty-four Roman emperors from Caesar to Constantinus could be had, as could thirty-four Kings of England, sixty-seven French monarchs and, at three-pence a head, 257 Popes from St Peter to Pius VII. Famous poets, artists, philosophers and scientists were also portrayed and amongst them were a number of figures of Newton. The 1779 Wedgwood and Bentley Catalogue lists the following items (Mankowitz, 1966, pp. 213–64).

1 Cameos. Item 1,685 Sir Isaac Newton, head; 1,686 the same; 1,687 the same, smaller, from his own ring.

2 Intaglios. Item 20 Sir Isaac Newton, head; 96 head, small, from a ring that belonged to himself; 284 head.

The somewhat mysterious ring referred to in 1 and 2 above is not listed in Newton's Inventory or any other primary source.

3 Heads in either black *basaltes*, or blue and white jasper, in various sizes and selling from one shilling to a guinea. Newton appears as item 5 in the Philosophers, Physicians, etc., series and was available in three sizes.

4 Busts, in black *basaltes*. Busts of Newton of 18, 15, 10 and 7 inches high were on offer.

Other items were added later to the Wedgwood range. Some of the above items are listed in the Babson *Catalogue* and can be seen illustrated in Kelly (1970, p. 52) and Dawson (1984, p. 82).

A number of Staffordshire pottery figures of Newton have been identified. One of these is listed in the Babson *Catalogue* (1955, p. 84) and is dated *c*.1770. By Ralph Wood and 12½ inches high, it shows a standing Newton next to a celestial globe resting on three books. From the top book a sheet of paper protrudes showing a comet dated 1680. The left hand once held a telescope.

While Wedgwood and other Staffordshire potters may no longer issue medallions and busts of Newton, his image may still be occasionally found in such popular forms of modern art as advertising. One such example can be seen in the inside cover of *History Today* for January 1971, with the Rysbrack bust of 1734 standing over the claim that 'Newton would have appreciated the *Financial Times*'.

See also Public monuments

Portsmouth Collection

ORIGIN

Newton died intestate on 20 March 1727, a presumably deliberate act by an ailing octogenarian who had had ample warning of his mortality. Although the motivation for his decision has long been lost, its consequences are still with us. In the absence of any will his papers became the subject of greedy squabbles between Newton's rapacious kin, and have since been scattered around the world.

The initial aim of the eight Smiths, Pilkingtons and Bartons who rushed to London was to get their hands on the share of the £30,000 cash available to them. However, before the money could be dispersed, it was first necessary to satisfy the Mint that Newton owed them no money. To do this would require an audit of the accounts and a check on the coinage minted for several years before. Until these and other bureaucratic procedures had been fully discharged, Newton's fortune lay tantalisingly beyond them. Unless, that is, someone could be persuaded to stand surety for the vast sums involved. Only John Conduitt was in a position to put up such a bond.

But for such trouble and risk Conduitt would clearly have to be rewarded. He consequently chose to take for himself the largely unknown quantity of Newton's surviving papers. The remainder of the family were suspicious, tempted strongly to settle for an immediate award of about £3,000 each, yet fearful they might be yielding their rights in assets which might ultimately prove to be more valuable. A compromise was reached between the two parties, with Conduitt receiving all papers and manuscripts while ceding to the heirs all profits which might arise from any future publication of the papers. An agreement was drawn up accordingly stating:

That the papers and manuscripts be first perused by the parties and such as are treatises be afterwards examined by Dr Pellett and printed if thought proper by him . . . and sold to the best advantage. That Mr Conduitt . . . pass the account with the Crown . . . In consideration of which he shall have such papers which shall not be thought proper to be printed, giving bond that if ever he shall publish any or make any advantage thereof to be accountable for the same.

Conduitt thus put up a further bond of £2,000 to allay the rustic suspicions of his wife's cautious relatives.

What did Conduitt get in return? The answer was soon available but disappointing. Newton had died on 20 March. By 18 May Conduitt had freed the estate from the Crown and distributed the liquid assets. The executors – Catherine Conduitt, Benjamin Smith and Thomas Pilkington – invited Pellett to examine the papers and report on their suitability for publication. In late May he advised there was nothing fit to print except the *Chronology*, immediately sold to a willing bookseller for £350, and four other possible manuscripts: the original draft of what turned out to be Book III of *Principia*, published in 1728 as *De mundi systemate* at a profit of £31 10s 0d.; *Observations*, published in 1733; the manuscript of *Paradoxical Questions*, published eventually in 1950; and an 'imperfect mathematical tract'. On other documents Pellett passed such unambiguous judgments as 'Not fit to be printed', 'Foul papers relating to Church matters'. His brief inventory was in fact published in 1795 by Charles Hutton and reprinted in Davis (1803, vol I, pp. lv–lx). They were the first indications of the wealth of material contained in what came to be known as the PC.

Conduitt died in 1737 and the papers passed to his wife, Catherine. Unlike Pellett, she was keen to see some of her uncle's theological papers in print but, before her death in 1740, all she could do was to add a codicil to her will directing her heirs to seek the advice on this question of Dr A. Sykes. It was a bad choice; Sykes was too old and sick to do anything more than glance at the papers before his death in 1756. By this time the papers had passed to Catherine's only child, a daughter also called Catherine. She had married in 1740 the Hon. John Wallop, Viscount Lymington. In 1743 his father became the first Earl of Portsmouth and was eventually succeeded by his son as the second Earl. In this way the papers passed into the possession of the Portsmouth family and found their way to the family seat at Hurstbourne Park, Hampshire. And there the bulk of them were to remain, unread, unexamined, undisturbed and, even, unknown for another 200 years.

EARLY ACCESS

As mentioned already, Sykes examined the collection in the mid-eighteenth century. He arranged for some eleven manuscripts to be sent to him in London shortly before his death. For some reason they were never returned to the Portsmouth family but found their way to the

Rev. Jeffrey Ekins, the executor of Lady Lymington's estate. They remained in the Ekins family for another century before being presented in 1872 to New College, Oxford.

Others were less fortunate. Robert Smith, working on the papers of Roger Cotes in 1750, seemed genuinely unaware of the mass of relevant material available. Castillioneus sought in vain for Newton's *Dictionarium Biblicum*, while the historian Edward Gibbon in 1748 tried to find Newton's papers on the Athanasian fathers. His enquiries led nowhere.

The first serious Newtonian scholar to be allowed access was Samuel Horsley, while preparing his collected edition of Newton's works. He spoke of great difficulty in procuring access and when it came in 1779 it was really too late, as the first volume of his work had actually appeared. In any case, Horsley was not really the man to delve too deeply into Newton's papers, and he ended up including only published material in the five volumes of the supposedly *Opera omnia*. He did, however, prepare a preliminary catalogue of the collection.

Edmund Turnor was also allowed to inspect the collection and in 1806 included in his *Town and Soke of Grantham* material collected by Conduitt on the early life of Newton. It was the first previously unpublished material taken from the Portsmouth Collection to appear in print.

Francis Baily was the next scholar of note to use the collection while preparing his *Account* of Flamsteed published in 1835. But, he noted, his search of the papers had thrown no light 'on the special object of my inquiries'. The only material he actually published from the PC was a letter from John Wallis to Newton dated 9 January 1699.

It was thus left to Sir David Brewster to be the first to make substantial use of the collection. He applied in 1837 to 'the honourable Newton Fellowes, one of the trustees of the Earl of Portsmouth, for permission to inspect the manuscripts and correspondence of Sir Isaac Newton'. In June 1837 Brewster went to Hurstbourne Park where, assisted by Fellowes, he examined material 'calculated to throw light on Newton's early and academical life'. The material appeared in Brewster, vol. I.

Before he began his second volume he obtained a collection of papers selected and arranged by Fellowes. Brewster never actually seems to have had the free run of the collection. What he saw, however, contained 'much new information respecting the history of *Principia*'.

The great virtue of Brewster was that he published an enormous amount of new material on a wide variety of topics taken directly from the PC. Flamsteed's letters to Newton, Newton's religious views, draughts of the General *Scholium*, the full correspondence with Halley on the publication of *Principia*, and many other letters were published for the first time. Newton was beginning to take on his modern complex image. But Brewster's modest but impressive use of the PC led to no new onslaught on the unpublished papers. It was assumed that Brewster had been through the papers and published everything of value; what remained was either trivial or irrelevant. Until some idea of the extent of the papers was established, they would very likely continue to be ignored. A first step in this direction was taken in 1888.

THE CAMBRIDGE *Catalogue* OF 1888

In 1872 the fifth Earl of Portsmouth, Isaac Newton Wallop, decided to transfer that part of his collection which was exclusively scientific to Cambridge. It has been suggested that a fire at Hurstbourne Park reminded the Earl of the vulnerability of the papers in his possession; 'I would rather cut off my hand than sever my connection with Newton which is the proudest boast of my family', he wrote in 1872. It was first necessary to catalogue the papers. To this end they were moved in bulk to Cambridge where for sixteen years J. C. Adams, G. D. Liveing, H. R. Luard and G. G. Stokes worked on their classification.

Newton's copies of *Principia*, together with about 1,000 pages of notes and calculations showing the development of the work, were handed over to the University Library. Also transferred were the Waste Book and other mathematical manuscripts. Retained by the Portsmouth family were all Newton's writings on chronology, theology, history, alchemy and the personal details gathered by Conduitt.

In 1888 Adams *et al.* published their Cambridge *Catalogue*. It was divided into fifteen sections and covered: maths; chemistry; chronology; history; miscellaneous; letters; books; papers; correspondence about the publication of Flamsteed's work; correspondence between Conduitt and Fontenelle; drafts of Conduitt's life of Newton; letters relating to Newton after his death; papers of Newton's family and the Mint; books and papers not by Newton; complimentary letters to Newton by distinguished foreigners.

Surprisingly, its publication had little impact on Newtonian research. Only Rouse Ball's 1893 study of *Principia* revealed any systematic use of the Portsmouth papers. One reason for their neglect, Cohen (1971, p. 12) has proposed, is the *Catalogue*'s tendency 'to mask or to conceal rather than to reveal the nature of the treasures the Portsmouth Collection contains'. The Waste Book, for example, is described as 'A common-place book . . . with calculations by Newton . . . contains Newton's first idea of fluxions', with no mention at all that the notebook is an important source of Newton's early ideas on dynamics.

In a perverse and quite unexpected way it required the actual dispersal of the bulk of the PC for scholars to appreciate the riches it contained. This event took place in 1936.

SOTHEBY SALE 1936

On 13 and 14 July 1936 at 34–5 New Bond St, the Portsmouth family disposed of virtually all their remaining Newton papers. It has been rumoured that they were under pressure from death duties and the need to pay for a divorce. The 144-page *Catalogue*, with sixteen plates, was prepared by John Taylor and sold for 7s 6d; today it is unlikely to sell for under £100. Divided into twelve sections it covered the following ground: alchemy, 120 unprinted lots; letters to Newton, 31 lots; letters from Newton, 22 lots; personal, 35 lots; Conduitt's notes, 10 lots; chronology, 5 unprinted lots; theology, 44 mostly unprinted lots; calculus, 14 lots; autograph miscellanea, 30 lots; other, 10 lots; Mint papers, 329 unpublished lots.

The sale raised £9,030. It is difficult even to begin to conceive how much the collection would raise today. As nothing of any substance has come back on to the market in recent years, it is impossible to be certain of the current value of the collection. Despite this it seems clear that if the Portsmouth family had delayed the sale until the 1970s they would have been collecting for the sale of the 650 lots a sum approaching a million pounds.

DISPERSAL

Details of the fate of most of the major items are known and can be listed as follows.

J. M. Keynes – most of the alchemy manuscripts ended up with Keynes, 57 out of 120, and are now in KCC. They are listed in Dobbs (1975). Keynes also bought, with a single exception, all Conduitt's notes.

Lord Wakefield bought all 329 Mint lots and presented them to the Mint.

Sir Robert Hadfield bought and presented the Halley letters to the Royal Society.

Peter Rosenbach bought the Kneller portrait which he presented to the National Portrait Gallery.

Y. Yahuda bought the bulk of the theological manuscripts, which he donated to the Jewish National and University Library, Jerusalem.

Emmanuel Fabius of Paris purchased thirteen lots, which have remained unavailable for examination.

A modern catalogue has been under preparation for some time by Peter Spargo.

CONTENTS

Estimates have varied considerably, but an often-quoted analysis breaks the material down into:

Theology and chronology	1,400,000 words
Alchemy	550,000 words
Mint and coinage	150,000 words
Various scientific papers	1,000,000 words
Miscellaneous	500,000 words
TOTAL	3,600,000 words

LATER NEWTONIAN SCHOLARSHIP

The extraordinary advance which has taken place in Newtonian scholarship since 1945 is ultimately based on the PC. Such scholars as A. R. Hall, I. B. Cohen, A. Koyré, F. Manuel, M. J. Dobbs, D. T. Whiteside, J. Herivel and R. S. Westfall have spent many years analysing the several million words of the collection. It has enabled them to do a number of things, three of which particularly stand out. It has, first, allowed scholars to piece together the great collections of Newton's *Correspondence* (1959–77, 7 vols), *Mathematical Papers* (1967–1981, 8 vols) and the planned writings on optics. Secondly, it has proved possible, as in Cohen (1971) and Cohen and Koyré (Newton, 1972) to explore in unrivalled detail the development of major works of Newton. And, less fundamentally perhaps, it has made it possible to see, and in some detail at that, the extraordinary diversity and depth of Newton's interest.

As a result of this material, more is known about Newton than any other scientist of the period. Indeed, he comes over as one of the best-documented figures, scientific or otherwise, of the period 1640–1730.

Praxis

An unpublished alchemical manuscript in Newton's hand, it runs to about 5,000 words and is to be found in the Babson Institute. Westfall (RSW, p. 529) has judged it to be 'the most important alchemical essay Newton ever wrote'. It is a late manuscript composed some time in 1693.

Pricked and dotted letters

Newton's dotted fluxional notation first appeared in the manuscript of *De quadratura* (1692) and was first used in print in Wallis's *Algebra* (1693, vol. II).

See also Fluxions, fluents and moments; Mathematical notation

Prideaux, Humphrey (1648–1724)

Educated at Oxford, an orientalist, Prideaux served as Dean of Norwich from 1702. He was the author of *The Old and New Testament Connected in the History of the Jews and Neighboring Nations*, 2 vols (1716–18), a work owned by Newton. Prideaux held views quite distinct from Newton. He claimed Bishop Usher's chronology to be 'the exactest . . . that had ever been published' and insisted, in conflict with Newton, that the Assyrian civilisation was older than the Jewish. Ironically, it was as a supplement to a seven-volume French translation of this work that the pirated French edition of Newton's *Short Chronicle* first appeared in 1725.

Apparently it was correspondence between Prideaux and the Bishop of Worcester, William Lloyd, in 1713 on the nature of the ancient calendar, and shown to Newton, which stimulated him to prepare a draft of his own views on the subject. It was published in the *Gentleman's Magazine* (1755) and is known under the title 'Form of the Most Ancient Year'.

Primitive sphere

The key to Newton's astronomical dating of ancient chronology lay with the primitive sphere. By this Newton meant the system of asterisms adopted by the Greeks to describe the heavens; the familiar system of such constellations, in fact, as Orion, Taurus, Aries, Andromeda, etc. The question Newton wanted answered was how old was this traditional sphere and how had it been constructed.

The fullest account of the sphere is to be found in the *Phaenomena* of Aratus, a still-extant astronomical poem dating from the third century BC. It is based on an earlier but lost work of Eudoxus from the fourth century BC. None of the names in Aratus, Newton noted, related 'to ye war at Thebes or Troy'. Rather, the celestial constellations related to 'persons who flourished in ye age wch ended with the Argonautic expedition'. It seemed to Newton to follow that the sphere was put into the form known to Aratus at about the same time as the Argonauts' expedition. If he could date the sphere, he would immediately have a firm date for the Argonauts.

The point was of enormous significance to chronologists. According to Herodotus there had been just one generation between the voyage of the Argonauts and the fall of Troy. Once having dated the fall of Troy a firm chronology for the Mediterranean seemed to follow, for had not Aeneas founded Rome a few years after Troy's collapse? All, thus, seemed to hang on the crucial issue of the date of the Argonauts' voyage, a date Newton hoped to calculate astronomically.

See also Chronological principles

Principia

CHRONOLOGY

1684 January. Meeting at the RS between Christopher Wren, Robert Hooke and Edmond Halley in which the problem of deriving the laws of celestial motion from the inverse square law was raised.
August. First visit of Halley to Newton in Cambridge. Newton claimed to have demonstrated that planets moving in accordance with the inverse square law would move in elliptical orbits.
November. The tract *De motu* sent to Halley in London via E. Paget. Second visit of Halley to Cambridge.
December 10. Halley reported to the RS that he had seen 'a curious treatise *De motu*' and that Newton had promised to enter it in the Register.
1685 February 23. A letter from Newton to Francis Aston, secretary of the RS, thanking him 'for entring in your Register my notions about motion'.
Summer. Book II completed.
1686 April 28. Book I presented to and dedicated to the RS.
May 19. RS announced its intention to publish *Principia*.
May 22. Beginning of Halley–Newton *Principia* correspondence. Newton informed of Hooke's claim for some acknowledgment of his priority.
June 2. Halley instructed by the RS to publish *Principia* 'at his own charge'.
June 7. Proof of 'first sheet of your book' sent to Newton.
June 20. Newton announced to Halley that he had intended *Principia* to consist of three books but that he had decided to suppress the third.
July 5. Royal Society imprimatur granted.
July 14. Newton agrees to restore *Principia* Book III.
1687 March 1. Newton sends Book II by coach to Halley in London.
April 4. Halley received Book III.
July 5. Newton informed by Halley that he had 'at length brought your book to an end'.
Principia reviewed by Halley in *PT*, no. 186.
1688 Further reviews appeared in *Journal des Sçavans, Bibliothèque universelle* and the *Acta eruditorum*.

1690 April. A list of *errata* and *addenda* to the *Principia* was taken by Fatio to Holland and a copy presented to Huygens.

1691 December. Fatio announced his plans to edit a new edition of *Principia*.

1694 January. David Gregory completed his *Notae in Newtoni Principia*. May–July. Various memoranda of Gregory describe numerous improvements and corrections Newton was proposing to include in any new edition of *Principia*.

1701 Johann Groening included in his *Historia cycloeidis* the annotations given to Huygens in 1690.

1706 David Gregory was shown by Newton an annotated *Principia* 'corrected for the press'.

1708 March 25. Gregory reported that Newton 'has begun to reprint his *Principia*'.
June 10. Bentley sent to Newton a specimen of the first sheet of the new edition.

1709 Roger Cotes appointed editor.
October 11. Newton sent Cotes the 'greatest part' of the corrected *Principia*.

1712 November 23. Whole work printed, apart from a few lines.

1713 January 6. Corrected prop. X of Book II sent to Cotes.
March 2. Concluding *Scholium generale* sent to Cotes.
May 12. Cotes completed his Preface.
June 18. Printing completed.

1714 Amsterdam reprint of *Principia* (1713).
Review published in *Journal des sçavans*.

1715 Review published in *Acta eruditorum*.

1718 Review published in *Mémoires de Trevoux*.

1723 Second Amsterdam reprint of *Principia* (1713).
Decides to prepare a third edition of *Principia*.
Henry Pemberton appointed editor of a proposed third edition of *Principia*.

1726 March 25. Royal Privilege granted.
March 31. *Principia* published.
Review appeared in *Acta eruditorum*.

1729 London. English translation of 1726.

1739–42 Geneva. Three-volume Jesuit edition of 1726.

1756/9 Paris. French translation of 1726 by the Marquise du Chastellet.

1760 Geneva. Reissue of the Jesuit edition.

1777 London. Translation of Book I of 1726 by Robert Thorp.

1779–82 London. An edition of 1726 was included in Horsley (1779–85), vols II–III.

1780–5 Prague. A two-volume reissue of the Jesuit edition.

1789 Prague. A reissue of 1780–5.

1802 London. A reissue of 1777.

1803 London. A revision of 1729 by William Davis.

1819 London. A reissue of 1803.

1822 Glasgow. A four-volume reissue of the Jesuit edition.

1833 Glasgow. A two-volume reissue of the Jesuit edition.

1848 New York. A revision of 1729 edited by N. W. Chittenden.

1849 New York. A reissue of 1848.

1850 New York. A reissue of 1848.

1858 New York. A reissue of 1848.

1871 Glasgow. A reprint of 1726 edited by Sir William Thomson and Hugh Blackburn.

1872 Berlin. A German translation of 1726 by J. P. Wolfers.

1874 New York. A reissue of 1848.

1885 New York. A reissue of 1848.

1915–16 Petrograd. A Russian translation of 1726 by A. N. Kriloff.

1927–31 Lund. A two-volume Swedish translation of 1726 by C. V. Charlier.

1930 Tokyo. A Japanese translation of 1726 by Kunio Oka.

1934 Berkeley. A revision of 1729 by Florian Cajori.

1946 Berkeley. A reissue of 1934.

1947 Berkeley. A reissue of 1934.

1952 Chicago. A reissue of 1934 by *Encyclopedia Britannica*.

1953 London. A facsimile edition of 1687, second issue.
A reissue of 1952.

1955 Chicago. A reissue of 1952.

1956 Bucharest. A Roumanian translation of 1726 by Viktor Marlian.

1960 Berkeley. A reissue of 1934.

1962 Berkeley. A two-volume paperback edition of 1934.

1963 Chicago. A reissue of 1952.
Berlin. A facsimile edition of 1872.

1964 Stuttgart–Bad Cannstatt. A facsimile edition of 1779–82.
New York. A facsimile edition of 1848.
New York. A facsimile paperback edition of 1848.

1965 Brussels. A facsimile edition of 1687, first issue.

1966 Paris. A facsimile edition of 1756/9.
Berkeley. A reissue of 1962.

1968 London. A facsimile edition of 1729.

1969 London. A reissue of 1777.

1972 Cambridge. A two-volume *variorum* edition of 1726 prepared by I. B. Cohen and A. Koyré.

1973 Berkeley. A reissue of 1934.

ORIGIN AND PRODUCTION

Principia (1687), as a work rather than a set of ideas, began some time in August 1684 with a visit by Halley to Newton in Cambridge. According to de Moivre's 1727 account:

> After they had been some time together, the Dr asked him what he thought the Curve would be that would be described by the Planets supposing the force of attraction towards the Sun to be reciprocal to the square of their distance from it. Sr Isaac replied immediately that it would be an Ellipsis, the Doctor struck with joy & amazement asked him how he knew it, Why saith he I have calculated it, Whereupon Dr Halley asked him for his calculations without any further delay, Sr Isaac looked among his papers but could not find it, but he promised him to renew it, & then to send it him.

Halley's question was not an idle one but dates, he later told Newton, from a meeting with Hooke and Wren earlier in the year when the same problem had been posed.

> I declared the ill success of my attempts; and Sr Christopher to encourage the Inquiry, sd that he would give Mr Hook or me 2 months to bring a convincing demonstration therof, and besides the honour, he of us that did it, should have from him a present of a book of 40s. Mr Hook said that he had it, but that he would conceale it for some time that others triing and failing, might know how to value it, when he should make it publick. (*C*, II, p. 442)

Newton at least kept his promise and sent to Halley in London by the hand of Paget in November the manuscript since known as *De motu*.

The stimulus of Halley's visit and question seemed to be sufficient to start Newton on the writing and research which would eventually lead to *Principia*. Halley visited Newton once more in Cambridge in November and on his return to London he announced to the Royal Society on 10 December 1684: 'Mr Halley . . . had lately seen Mr Newton at Cambridge, who had shewed him a curious treatise, *De motu*; which, upon Mr Halley's desire, was . . . promised to be sent to the Society to be entered upon the Register.' Such a manuscript had been received by 23 February 1685 when it was duly entered into the Society's Register.

Nothing more is heard for well over a year. On 21 April 1686 Halley informed the Society that Newton's 'Treatise on Motion' was almost ready for the press and a week later on 28 April the Society received a manuscript entitled *Philosophiae naturalis principia mathematica*, Book I of *Principia*. Halley was asked to report on the work and on 19 May the Society announced its intention to print the work. The task of actually printing the work was 'intrusted' to Halley. Although in May the Society announced its intention to publish *Principia* at its own charge, it was ordered on 2 June that 'Mr Newton's book be printed, and that Mr Halley undertake the business of looking after it, and printing it as his own charge; which he engaged to do'. The reason for the Society's sudden withdrawal of financial backing for Newton was simply that the Society was virtually bankrupt. They had recently published Francis Willoughby's *De historia piscium* (1686) which had exhausted the Society's funds and was proving difficult to sell. Unable to pay their own staff, let alone finance another expensive work, the Society offered copies of Willoughby to its secretaries in place of salary. Halley, at this time a man of independent means, was accordingly instructed to finance the new project. He appears not to have resisted.

Of the period between February 1685 and April 1686, between *De motu* and Book I of the *Principia*, a period in which Newton, at his most creative, tackled and solved the deepest problems of dynamics, virtually nothing is known. There are a few work sheets but no letters nor any eye-witness accounts of Newton's mode of work. Presumably, in isolation, Newton worked continuously in Trinity on reshaping *De motu* into the authoritative treatise on dynamics it became in *Principia*.

Mention of a second book is first heard in a letter from Halley to Newton dated 7 June (*C*, II, p. 434). The reference was undoubtedly to *De motu corporum: liber secundus* (LL-2). It would, Halley noted, make the 'Mathematical part . . . acceptable to all Naturalists, as well as Mathematiciens'. He was clearly pleased that the inclusion of more discursive material would 'much advance the sale of ye book'.

Newton replied on 20 June (*C*, II, p. 437) with the further news that *Principia* would consist of three, not two, books. Book III would deal with the system of the world. Newton, however, had less welcome news for Halley. He had heard, partly from Halley himself, but probably from others as well, that Hooke was already publicly making claims to have anticipated the inverse square law. Consequently, he informed Halley:

> The third I now designe to suppress. Philosophy is such an
> impertinently litigious Lady that a man has as good be engaged in
> Law suits as have to do with her. I found it formerly so & now I
> no sooner come nearer her again but she gives me warning.

He would, however, as a concession to Halley, allow the title to remain unchanged.

It remained for Halley to make yet one further contribution to the publication of *Principia* by persuading its author of the folly of mutilating his text. Thus on 29 June Halley replied, arguing that Newton should not allow himself to be influenced by envious rivals. 'The Gentlemen of the Society' were 'much troubled' by the news, Halley continued, and, he reminded Newton, it was Book III that would have brought

Principia to the attention of 'those that will call themselves philosophers without Mathematicks, which are by much the greater number'.

Within a fortnight Newton had calmed down sufficiently to see the force of Halley's arguments. On 14 July he wrote to him, somewhat apologetically, agreeing he had over-reacted and proposing to 'compose ye present dispute' by adding a *Scholium* to proposition IV. The printing of Book I began. By November 1686 Flamsteed had heard from Halley that '13 sheets . . . are wrought of', 104 pages, and that 'We shall have the piece in good time, though the press proceed by Mr Newton's order very slowly.'

Nothing more was heard until the 1 March 1687, when Newton wrote to Halley that he was sending Book II by coach to London. Halley acknowledged receipt on the 7th. In the following month, on 4 April, Halley received Book III. Using two printers Halley was able to inform Newton on 5 July that he had 'at last brought your book to an end'.

MANUSCRIPT

Written in the hand of Humphrey Newton it is 460 pages long and can be found in the library of the Royal Society. Written on one side only, it contains corrections in the hands of both Isaac and Humphrey Newton as well as that of Halley. It is not a draft but a final copy. It must therefore be assumed, knowing Newton's method of work, that earlier drafts were made. This view is supported by the absence of the corrections and cancellations typical of a dictated manuscript, particularly a manuscript as technical as *M*. Humphrey Newton must therefore have had before him a draft of some kind from which he copied *M*.

It should also be noted that, in Newton's words, Humphrey did not understand 'what he copied' and is therefore even less likely to have been capable of taking dictation. The drafts have nevertheless not been traced and could well have been destroyed by Newton.

HALLEY'S ODE

Absent from *M*, it appeared first in *Principia* (1687) and continued to appear, modified by Bentley, in the editions of 1713 and 1726. Motte (1729) simply ignored the Ode. It was first printed in an English translation by an otherwise unknown Eugenio in Benjamin Martin's *General Magazine of Arts and Sciences*, 1755, vol. I, p. 4. The original, together with later changes, was first printed in Rigaud (1838, Appendix 15) and can also be found in Brewster, MacPike (1932), Newton (1972) and Albury (1978).

It was claimed quite early that Halley's Ode was based on a comparable work by James I on Tycho Brahé. More recent scholarship has sought as a source the famous poem of Lucretius, *De rerum natura*, from the first century BC. Albury (1978) has even claimed to identify specific lines taken straight out of Lucretius.

The sixty-six lines of the poem at first sight seem quite straight-forward. Halley began by listing some of the advances made by Newton. He explained how the stars move in 'motionless ellipses', that comets are no longer 'a source of dread', that the course of the seasons, the tides – all these things which once appeared so strange – were at last understood. Surely, Halley concluded, we could celebrate in verse the man who did all this. For:

> Nearer the gods no mortal may approach.

Could Bentley have had anything more than Halley's Latin style to object to?

It could well have been the Epicureanism implicit in the original that Bentley found unacceptable. For, example, Halley begins with lines 3–5:

> Here ponder too the Laws which God,
> Framing the universe, set not aside
> But made the fixed foundations of his work

suggesting that God was constrained by Law. Bentley's change empha-sised that God had made the Law. Or, again the suggestion that science dispels fear of the heavens:

> nor longer do we quail
> Beneath appearance of bearded stars (lines 16–17)

was simply dropped altogether.

On Halley's attitude, Conduitt reported: 'Bentley altered Halley's verses when he printed *Principia*. Halley told me that Sir Isaac Newton made him hope that in Pemberton's edition his verses would be printed from his own copy, but complained they were not.'

PREFACE

Carrying the date 6 May 1686, or in new style 1687, it contains a generous and much-deserved expression of thanks to 'the most acute and universally learned Mr.Edmund Halley'. It also contains a clear statement of what Newton took to be the subject of natural philosophy. He was concerned with natural powers, 'chiefly those things which relate to gravity, levity, elastic force, the resistance of fluids, and the like forces, whether attractive or impulsive'. From these forces 'other phenomena' would be demonstrated. That is, from the mathematical propositions of the first two books he would derive, in Book III, 'the motions of planets, the comets, the moon and the sea'. He regretted that he was unable:

to derive the rest of the phenomena of Nature by the same kind of reasoning from mechanical principles, for I . . . suspect that they may all depend upon certain forces by which the particles of bodies, by some causes hitherto unknown, are either mutually impelled towards one another, and cohere in regular figures, or are repelled and recede from one another. These forces being unknown, philosophers have hitherto attempted the search of Nature in vain; but I hope the principles here laid down will afford some light either to this or some truer method of philosophy.

The somewhat cryptic remarks of the above paragraph represent a persistent theme in Newton's thought. Several times, as with the abandoned *Conclusio*, the *Scholium Generale*, and Query 31 of the *Opticks*, he returned to the difficult problem of attempting to talk credibly of unknown forces. In a draft of the Preface further details were offered. It exists in two states. One, a holograph draft (MS 3965) in the PC in the ULC, is incomplete but much interlineated and corrected. Newton felt it important enough to have a copy made by an amanuensis. It has been published for the first and only time by the Halls (pp. 302–8) in both the original Latin and English translation.

To illustrate the unknown forces he had in mind Newton spoke of the ways in which 'solvents, salts, spirits and bodies either act upon one another or not'. This was in terms of 'certain forces by which the particles of bodies . . . wither are impelled towards one another and cohere, or repel each other and fly apart'. Of such forces he could do little but speculate. One force, he considered, could impel adjacent particles towards each other and, though strong, operate only at short range. There could also be a second force which 'drives particles away from each other' which, although weaker than the attractive force, operated over greater distances. Thus, when two particles were a certain distance apart the weaker repulsive forces would be more potent than the stronger attractive forces.

Brief additional Prefaces were also added to the two later editions of *Principia*. In the second edition (1713), dated 28 March 1713, he merely noted that there were 'many emendations and some additions' and, in a line or two, listed some of them. No word of thanks was offered to the editor, Roger Cotes, who contributed his own long and important Preface.

The Preface to the third edition of 1726 was dated 12 January 1726 and did note the care taken by the editor, Henry Pemberton. Again, he made a brief mention of the changes and additions made.

[462]

COTES'S PREFACE TO THE SECOND EDITION OF 1713

When the question of a Preface arose early in 1713, Cotes was initially in some doubt what to include. He first thought of an attack on Leibniz's dynamical treatise, *Tentamen* (1689), but much preferred an alternative proposal that either Newton or Bentley should prepare a Preface that Cotes would then loyally 'own . . . and defend'. Bentley, however, told Cotes that he should undertake the task himself, while Newton, after some initial hesitation, warned Cotes to 'spare ye name of M. Leibniz'. He also declined to read it before its publication. He informed Newton that he would 'add something . . . concerning the manner of Philosophising' and indicate in particular how the Newtonian approach differed from the Cartesian.

Cotes has been accused, with some justification, of misrepresenting Newton's notion of gravity. Unaware of Newton's *Letter to Boyle* (1679) and his *Letters to Bentley* (1694), he spoke witheringly of those who 'would have the heavens filled with a fluid matter', while of gravity he insisted that it was just as much a primary property of bodies as 'extension, mobility, and impenetrability'. Yet, to Bentley, Newton had insisted: 'You sometimes speak of gravity as essential and inherent to matter. Pray, do not ascribe that notion to me' (*C*, III, p. 240). Earlier, to Boyle, he had spoken of an 'etherial substance' diffused through all space. Oddly enough Newton accepted the misrepresentation of his views without complaint, public or private.

On two other topics Cotes was more accurate. The first was a strong attack launched against Cartesian physics in general and the vortex theory of planetary motion in particular. The second was a commitment to providentialism, with the claim that 'this world, so diversified with that variety of forms and motions we find in it, could arise from nothing but the perfectly free will of God directing and presiding over all'

SCHOLIUM GENERALE (GENERAL *SCHOLIUM*)

The General *Scholium* was introduced into the second edition of *Principia* (1713). It was sent to the editor, Roger Cotes, on 2 March 1713 with the comment: 'I intended to have said much more about the attraction of the small particles of bodies, but upon second thoughts I have chosen rather to add but one short Paragraph about that part of Philosophy' (Edleston, 1850, p. 147). From the five drafts surviving in the PC in the ULC (MS 3965, ff. 357–65) it was clearly an important expression of Newton's late views. Two drafts have been printed by the Halls (pp. 348–64) in both the original Latin and in English translation.

One reason for the new *Scholium* was to answer criticisms raised by Leibniz and Berkeley against the general cosmology of *Principia*. Newton had been accused, for example, of presenting God as no more than an incompetent watchmaker incapable of making a clock which did not need his regular attention each time it broke down. Newton chose to reply by presenting in some of his finest prose his own conception of God. It is not a creed many Christians today will find attractive.

Newton rejected the idea that the true nature of God consisted in his possession of the familiar attributes of perfection; it lay rather in his 'dominion'. For, he declared, 'a being, however perfect, without dominion, cannot said to be Lord God'. We may well admire him for his perfections but 'we reverence and adore him on account of his dominion'.

Further, this dominion was exercised 'in a manner not at all human, . . . in a manner utterly unknown to us'. We know God only through his works, 'by his most wise and excellent contrivances of things'. There seems little room in Newton's austere theology for anything like a personal God. Indeed, he went out of his way to dismiss such an option. God, he insisted, 'is utterly void of all body and bodily figure, and can therefore neither be seen, nor heard, nor touched'.

From God, Newton turned to gravity. In often-quoted words, he declared his failure to have discovered any cause for gravity. As, he insisted, 'I frame no hypotheses', any attempt to speculate about possible causes had no place in experimental philosophy; 'it is enough', he concluded the point, 'that gravity does really exist, and act according to the laws which we have explained'.

The *Scholium* concluded with an intriguing paragraph, presumably the item referred to in the letter to Cotes above. He spoke of 'a most subtle spirit which pervades and lies hid in all gross bodies'. It is through this spirit, Newton proposed, that bodies cohere, 'light is emitted, reflected, refracted, inflected, and heats bodies', sensations are excited, electric bodies repel and attract, and the will operates. A formidable list, and one demanding some explanation. Newton merely concludes, however: 'But these are things that cannot be explained in few words'. What precise explanation he had in mind can perhaps be seen in the drafts of the *Scholium* printed in the Halls. In version C, for example, twelve propositions are asserted in which many powers are attributed to the 'electric spirit'. It is, for example, 'a medium most active and emits light' (prop.6), and it also accomplishes nutrition (prop.12). Disappointingly, however, the published drafts are no more generous in the provision of details of these processes than is the *Scholium* itself.

The text of the *Scholium* is readily available in any of the various editions of Cajori's *Principia*.

CONCLUSIO

At one time Newton intended to complete the first edition of *Principia* (1687) with a *Conclusio*. Two versions have survived in the PC in the ULC (MS 4005), the former in Newton's hand, the latter by an amanuensis with Newton's amended corrections added. It has been published for the first and only time in both the original Latin and English translation in the Halls (pp. 320–47). It was, however, never completed nor was it ever sent to Halley.

Whereas in the 1670s Newton had been trying to develop a natural philosophy in which light, heat, gravity, and much more besides, were transmitted throughout space by means of an etherial medium, in the *Conclusio* Newton began to speak of a universe of forces. Nature he saw as uniform. Consequently, he declared, 'Whatever reasoning holds for greater motions, should hold for lesser ones as well.' As the motion of the heavens are controlled by the 'attractive forces of larger bodies', so too were lesser motions dependent on 'lesser forces as yet unobserved, of insensible forces'. Thus, in addition to the known forces of gravity, electricity and magnetism, Newton insisted that it would be rash to deny there were not 'still more kinds'. In particular, he went on to list 'the motions of the particles in hot bodies, in fermenting bodies, in putrescent bodies, in growing bodies, in the organs of sensation and so forth'. He added further material, mainly chemical, and similar to that used in Query 31 in the *Opticks*, to make his case.

Something of this approach was retained in the Preface to *Principia* (1687), with its speculation that Nature depends upon 'certain forces by which the particles of bodies, by some causes hitherto unknown, are either mutually impelled towards one another . . . or are repelled and recede from one another'.

RULES, HYPOTHESES AND PHAENOMENA

There are considerable differences between the opening of Book III as it appears in the three editions of *Principia*. In the final edition there are four 'Rules of reasoning' (*Regulae philosophandi*, RP), six phaenomena and one hypothesis. By contrast, the first edition had merely nine hypotheses. The development from 1687 to 1726 can sound most confusing when put into words but can be readily gathered from the simple table, with arrows tracing the history of the various propositions, dashes indicating the absence of the proposition from the text, and a solid line distinguishing between methodological principles and more substantive propositions.

Newton's well-known saying, 'I frame no hypotheses', looks distinctly odd against the evidence of the nine hypotheses of 1687. The truth is that Newton used the term hypothesis in more than one sense.

PRINCIPIA

Development of propositions between 1687 and 1726 editions of *Principia*

1687		1713		1726
Hyp.1	→	*RP* 1	→	*RP* 1
Hyp.2	→	*RP* 2	→	*RP* 2
Hyp.3		– – – – –		– – – – –
– – – – –		*RP* 3	→	*RP* 3
– – – – –		– – – – –		*RP* 4
Hyp.4	→	Hyp.1	→	Hyp.1
Hyp.5	→	Phen.1	→	Phen.1
– – – – –		Phen.2	→	Phen.2
Hyp.6	→	Phen.3	→	Phen.3
Hyp.7	→	Phen.4	→	Phen.4
Hyp.8	→	Phen.5	→	Phen.5
Hyp.9	→	Phen.6	→	Phen.6

Consequently he sometimes found it necessary to adjust his language. Certainly, his use of the term in 1687 conveyed little, with hypotheses 1–2 being methodological principles, hypothesis 3 affirming the unity of matter, and the remaining hypotheses 4–9 expressing truths about the solar system. It is not surprising that with such a mixture of propositions, Newton felt some need to reclassify them when he came to revise *Principia*. The result in 1713 was the fairly obvious distinction between methodological principles (RP), a hypothesis in the sense of something he could not demonstrate, and phaenomena, which could be justified.

The content of the various propositions can now be indicated.

Hypotheses 3 and 4

Hyp.3 (1687) stated: 'Any body can be transformed into another, of whatever kind, and all the intermediate degrees of qualities can be induced in it.' Koyré has suggested that it was probably dropped because it conflicted with the claim made in the Queries of 1706 that God had created atoms of different shapes and masses (Koyré, 1965, p. 263n).

Hyp.4 (Hyp.1) 'That the centre of the system of the world is immov-

[466]

able.' Newton states the proposition without proof, merely adding that it is 'acknowledged by all'.

RPs 1–4

RP 1 Only true and sufficient causes should be admitted to explain natural things, or, more gandly, 'Nature . . . affects not the pomp of superfluous causes.'

RP 2 To the same natural effects, the same causes must be assigned. Examples listed are respiration in both beasts and men, the descent of stones in America and Europe, and light in the sun and in a fire.

RP 3 Only those qualities of bodies which admit of neither intensification nor remission, and which belong to all bodies are universal qualities. Examples offered are impenetrability, motion, extension and mutual gravitation.

RP 4 If propositions have been 'inferred by general induction from phenomena as accurately or very nearly true', they could be accepted even if we can imagine 'contrary hypotheses'.

RP 5 Koyré (1965, pp. 271–2) has pointed out that Newton had in fact drafted a fifth rule. It is distinctly anti-Cartesian in that it denies that I sense 'that any idea whatever may be innate'. He went on to emphasis that things which cannot be 'demonstrated from the phenomenon nor follow from it by the argument of induction' were merely hypotheses. It is not known why Newton failed to include the proposed fifth rule in *Principia*.

Phenomena 1–6

Phen.1 The area and harmonic laws for Jupiter's satellites.

Phen.2 The area and harmonic laws for Saturn's satellites.

Phen.3 The five primary planets orbit the sun.

Phen.4 The harmonic law holds for the five primary planets.

Phen.5 The area law holds for the primary planets with respect to the sun, but not with respect to the earth.

Phen.6 The area law holds for the moon with respect to the earth.

HOOKE IN *Principia*

The *scholium* to Book I prop.IV originally read: 'in what follows I intend to treat more at large of those things which relate to centripetal force decreasing as the squares of the distances from the centres.' Having drafted the *scholium*, Newton heard from Halley on 22 May 1686 that Hooke 'seems to expect you should make some mention of him, in the preface'. Newton replied five days later that 'there is noe one proposition to which he can pretend'. Rather than leave it at that, Newton sent Halley on 14 July the revised *scholium* which later appeared in *Principia* (1687) and all later editions. It did indeed mention Hooke, and it did also attribute to Hooke the view that centripetal forces decrease as the squares of the distances from the centres. Newton went on to add, however, that such a view was known to Halley and Wren as well as Hooke. He further hinted that once Huygens had published his *De horologio oscillatorio* the result should have been obvious to all. It is clear that while Hooke did receive his acknowledgment, he is unlikely to have found it satisfactory. No other mention is made of Hooke in Book I.

Nor did he occur elsewhere in the first edition of 1687. Fifteen references are to be found in the second edition of 1713 and twelve in the final edition of 1726. All, however, occur in Book III and are no more than references of observations of comets made by Hooke.

A not dissimilar treatment was accorded Leibniz.

CLASSICAL *scholia*

It is abundantly clear from the classical *scholia* that Newton's own view of his major work, *Principia*, and the source of his most important ideas, is very different from that of later commentators. In the 1690s he had begun to contemplate a second edition of *Principia* and accordingly had started to assemble corrections, revisions and additions. One such set of additions, conveniently described as the classical *scholia*, was drafted as *scholia* to propositions IV to IX of Book III. These propositions are at the very heart of Newton's system of the world, for they establish gravity as the ruling force of the solar system and go on to demonstrate several of its essential features.

In May 1694 David Gregory visited Newton at Cambridge, making various 'annotations physical mathematical and theological' while he was there. He probably received at the same time the *scholia* intended for the second edition of *Principia* and which are now in the Royal Society (Gregory MS 247). Similar material was found in the PC. David Gregory actually used some of this material, although without acknowledgment, in the preface to his *Astronomia physicae et geometrica elementa* (1702).

The point of the planned *scholia* was to show that the essential elements of Newtonian science were explicitly argued for by the scientists of classical times. In particular he sought to identify four specific beliefs in the writings of the ancients. Of the first, atomism, there is no cause for surprise. The claim, however, that the Pythagorean and Ionian philosophers held 'bodies are compound of atoms' is unwarranted. Not content with tracing atomism back to the sixth-century BC Ionian philosopher Thales, Newton went on to identify its founder as 'Moschus the Phoenician whom Strabo declares older than the Trojan war'.

He claimed, secondly, that the ancients recognised that gravity was a universal force and that it was proportional to the quantity of matter involved. His main source for such a view was Lucretius and the first

book of *De rerum natura*. More unusual, however, was his third claim
that the ancients, the Pythagoreans in particular, had discovered the
inverse square law. The evidence for this he found in the Pythagorean
discovery 'that the same tension upon a string half as long acts four
times as powerfully'. The Pythagoreans hid their talk of the solar system
in discourse about musical tones. The lyre had seven strings and so
corresponded to the sun and the six planets; Apollo was known as
Hebdomagetes, ruler of the seven, and thus united his role as solar god
and musical deity. Pythagorean talk of the music of the spheres was
thus for Newton another way of discussing how the gravitational force
of the sun decreased inversely as the square of the distance.

Newton went on to make a final point about the cause of gravity. In
the draft *scholium* to proposition IX he commented:

> Thales regarded all bodies as animate, deducing that from magnetic
> and electrical attractions. And by the same argument he ought to
> have referred the attraction of gravity to the soul of matter . . . And
> in the same sense Pythagoras, on account of its immense force of
> attraction, said that the sun was the prison of Zeus, that is, a body
> possessed of the greatest circuits. (MCGUIRE and RATTANSI, 1966, p. 119)

In an alternative version Newton noted:

> Those ancients . . . taught that a certain infinite spirit pervades all
> space into infinity, and contains and vivifies the entire world. And
> this spirit was their supreme divinity . . . In him we live and move
> and have our being. (MCGUIRE and RATTANSI, 1966, p. 120)

God was thus, as well as the order of the universe, the cause of gravity.

Why did not Newton incorporate the *scholia* into later editions of
Principia? Perhaps, suggested McGuire and Rattansi (1966, p. 121), he
'considered these enquiries too speculative, or too incongruous with his
inductive natural philosophy, to be made public'. Even though he may
not have published them, Newton's views were nevertheless made available to Gregory, Maclaurin, Fatio and probably others.

See also Gravity; Moschus

LEIBNIZ *scholium*

In the first edition of *Principia* (1687), Book II, prop. VII, Newton wrote:

> In letters which went between me and that most excellent geometer,
> G.W.Leibniz, 10 years ago, when I signified I was in the knowledge
> of a method of determining maxima and minima, of drawing
> tangents, and the like . . . that most distinguished man wrote back
> that he had also fallen on a method of the same kind, and

communicated his method which hardly differed from mine, except in his form of words and symbols. (CAJORI, p. 655)

There could hardly be a clearer admission, made without qualification, that Leibniz had independently established a good many of Newton's own results. In the second edition of *Principia* (1713) Newton merely added to the above passage, following on from 'words and symbols', the phrase 'and the concept of the generation of quantities'.

Not surprisingly Leibniz took the passage to mean what it said and accordingly he informed the Abbé Conti in 1716 that Newton, thirty years before, 'had assigned to me the invention of the differential calculus independently of himself' (*C*, VI, p. 308). Newton's first reaction was to deny that the *scholium* meant any such thing. He took the opportunity of the publication of Raphson's *History of Fluxions* (1716) to add the comment: 'But in the paragraph referred unto I do not find one word to this purpose.'

But even this was not enough. Newton must have brooded on the supposed slight long and hard, for in the third edition of *Principia* (1726), ten years after Leibniz's death, he took the extreme course of substituting a new *scholium* in which no mention was made of Leibniz or his work. Instead, Newton used the *scholium* to establish his own priority claims on the basis of a treatise composed in 1671 and a letter to Collins in 1672 (Cajori, pp. 251–2). No indication was given that new material was being incorporated or that old material had been cut. The alteration was, however, noted by the anonymous reviewer in the *AE* (1726). Surprisingly, no comment was made.

BASIC DATA ON PUBLICATION AND CONTENTS OF *Principia* (1687, 1713, 1726)

	1st edition	*2nd edition*	*3rd edition*
Length	511 pp.	492 pp.	536 pp.
Date of publication	5 July 1687	11–14 July 1713	31 March 1726
Editor	E. Halley	R. Cotes	H. Pemberton
Price, and number printed	9s, *c*.400	15s, 750	1,250
Published in	London	Cambridge	London
Printer	Sam Smith (3-line) J. Streater (2-line)	Cornelius Crownfield	William & John Innys

PRINCIPIA

	1st edition	2nd edition	3rd edition
Imprimatur	S. Pepys	—	Royal privilege
Frontispiece	—	—	Three-quarter length portrait; *Pinxit* J. Vanderbank 1725; *Sculpsit* G. Vertue 1726
Dedication	*Illustrissimae societati regali – serenissime rege Carolo II*		
	Potentissimi monarche Jacobi II	*Augustissimae reginae Annae*	*Auspiciis serenissimi regis Georg II*
Ode	Halley's Ode	As corrected by R. Bentley	As corrected by R. Bentley
Preface	Unsigned and undated	Signed Is. Newton, dated *Dabam Cantabrigiae, e Collegio S. Trinitatis, Maii 8.1686*	
	—	Signed Is. Newton, dated London, March 28, 1713	
	—	Signed Roger Cotes, dated Cambridge, May 12, 1713	
	—	—	Signed Is. Newton, dated London, Jan. 12, 1726
Index	—	*Index capitum totius operis*, compiled by Cotes	
Corrigenda	—	—	*Corrigenda*
Text	Definitions I–VIII *Scholium* on absolute space, time and motion Axioms I–III, corollaries I–VI, *scholium* Book I: The motion of bodies, sections I–XIV Book II: The motion of bodies in resisting mediums, sections I–IX Book III: System of the world:		
	Hypotheses I–IX	*Regulae philosophandi* I–III Hypothesis I Phenomena I–VI	*Regulae philosophandi* I–IV Hypothesis I Phenomena I–VI
	Propositions I–XLII	Propositions I–XLII	Propositions I–XLII

	1st edition	2nd edition	3rd edition
	—	*Scholium generale*	*Scholium generale*
Index	—	*Index rerum alphabeticus*, compiled by Cotes	
Errata	*Errata*	*Errata*	—

REVIEWS

Principia (1687)

There were four published reviews of *Principia* (1687).

1 *Philosophical Transactions*, 1687, no. 186, pp. 291–7; reprinted in *PLNP* (pp. 405–11). Not only did Halley finance, edit, publish and distribute *Principia*, he also reviewed it, anonymously, in *PT*. It is little more than a summary interspersed with expressions of praise of 'this incomparable author' who had 'discovered' so many and 'so Valuable Philosophical Truths, as . . . were never yet owing to the Capacity and Industry of any one Man'. It was the first expression of the many extravagant and often quite absurd eulogies which would over the centuries be linked with Newton's name.

2 *Bibliothèque universelle*, March 1688, vol. 8, pp. 436–50. Anonymous but attributed by Axtell (1965, pp. 152–61) to Locke. It consists of nothing more than the headings of the sections of Books I and II translated into French. There is also a summary of Book III, and an introductory paragraph which has been reprinted in Cohen (1971, p. 146n).

3 *Acta eruditorum*, June 1668, pp. 303–15. Anonymous. The most detailed and serious of the four reviews. It was comprehensive enough to provide many in Europe without access to *Principia* itself with a fairly full account of its contents.

4 *Journal des sçavans*, August 1668, p. 128. Anonymous. Although it conceded that *Principia* was 'une Mécanique la plus parfaite qu'on puisse imaginer', fundamental objections were none the less raised. Newton's hypotheses were dismissed as arbitrary, unproven and belonging to geometry rather than mechanics. It was recommended that he write a second work in which he substituted 'vrais mouvemens en la place de ceux qu'il supposés'.

Principia (1713)

Principia (1713) collected three reviews.

1 *Journal des sçavans*, March 1715, pp. 157–60. It was actually a review of the Amsterdam (1714) reprint. Anonymous and quite matter of fact. The critical comments of the 1688 review are not repeated and in their place a number of favourable comments were substituted.

His account of absolute space and time, for example, 'ne laisse rien a desirer'.

2 *Mémoires de Trevoux*, February 1718, pp. 466–75. A critical account in which the familiar contrast between Newton as profound mathematician and implausible physicist is once more made. The reviewer goes further and challenges Newton's famous Moon test (Book III, *Scholium* to prop.IV) and his judgment that the earth is flattened at the poles.

3 *Acta eruditorum*, March 1714, pp. 131–42. The only review which bothered to collate the two editions and to appreciate the significant nature of the changes introduced. The reviewer summarised the General *Scholium* and went on to doubt the value of Newton's 'subtle spirit' discussed there. The references annoyed Newton. He replied in his anonymous *Recensio* (1715) that the editors 'are perswading the Germans that Mr. Newton wants Judgement'.

Principia (1726)

There was only one review of *Principia* (1726), in *Acta eruditorum*, February 1726, pp. 73–6. It contained a note of the new material incorporated in the new edition. The omission of the Leibniz *scholium* was noted, although without comment.

EDITIONS

1   London, 1687

The precise date of publication is taken to be 5 July, for on that day Halley sent Newton forty copies with the request that he put them 'into the hands of one or more of your oldest booksellers'. He further recommended that they be offered to the trade in quires for 6s (5s for cash) and that they be sold to the public for 7s unbound and 9s 'bound in calves' leather and lettred'. The size of the edition is generally agreed to be not less than 300 and 'may have been 100 more than this' (Munby, 1952a).

There were two issues, distinguished only by their title page. The first carries the imprint:

Jussu Societatis Regiae ac Typis Josephi Streater. Prostat apud
    plures Bibliopolas. Anno MDCLXXXVII.

It is known variously as the first, Streater, 'plures' or, because of the length of the printer's imprint, the two-line issue. Halley seems initially to have decided, in addition to his financial and editorial duties, to distribute the work himself. The task must soon have proved too irksome to pursue for Halley quite early on handed the duties of distribution to the London bookseller, Sam Smith, who inserted the following three-line cancel on the title page:

Jussu Societatis Regiae ac Typis Josephi Streater. Prostat Venales apud Sam.Smith ad insignia Principis Walliae in Coemeterio D.Pauli, aliosq; nonnullos Bibliopolas. Anno MDCLXXXVII.

It is known variously as the second, Smith, 'venales', three-line of Continental issue. This final description arises from the suggestion made in 1927 by Zeitlinger that Smith exported his copies to the Continent. Such a supposition would fit well with what is known of Smith's trade. It is also confirmed by the fact that few copies of Smith are known in contemporary English binding (Munby, 1952a). Of the possible 400 or so copies printed, it is thought that no more than fifty carry Smith's cancel.

One other feature of the title page is the imprimatur granted by Samuel Pepys in his role as President of the Royal Society. Since 1631 the government had sought to control publication, first by Star Chamber decree and later by Acts of Charles II (1662) and James II (1685). Licences for publication had to be sought and could only be granted by such figures as the Archbishop of Canterbury, the Vice-chancellors of Oxford and Cambridge and, after the grant of a royal charter, the President of the Royal Society.

A census conducted by H. P. Macomber in 1953 identified 189 surviving copies, forty-six of which carried the three-line imprint; 124 copies are in Europe, sixty-three in the US and one each in Australia and South Africa. The greatest concentration is, unsurprisingly, Cambridge with its thirty-one copies. Seven of these are in Trinity, five in King's and a further four in the ULC. The earliest known copy is to be found in Cambridge, a presentation copy to Emmanuel College with the date 13 July 1687 inscribed within. The earliest known Smith copy is in Nijmegen, Holland, with the inscription, 'Ex libris Adriani Verwer, 1687'.

A number of other special copies have been identified. Halley presented copies to James II, Robert Boyle and Edward Paget, none of which seems to have survived. Two copies presented by Newton to Trinity College and Emmanuel College, both specially bound in panelled calf with a distinctive fleuron in each corner did, however, survive. Other presentation copies with their location when known, were made to John Locke (Trinity College), John Flamsteed (Royal Society), Lord Halifax (Louisville, Kentucky), Humphrey Babington (?) and Fatio (Bodleian).

Newton's own copy, specially bound and much annotated, is in Trinity College. Newton had another copy specially bound with interleaved blanks on which he could enter corrections and proposed additions. It can be seen in the ULC. There are reasons to believe that Newton had other interleaved and annotated copies. Traces remain, though the works themselves appear to be lost. Annotations in Newton's hand have, however, been identified in the copies of Locke, Halifax, Fatio, and unidentified works in the Babson Collection and Australia. Annotations are also known, although not in Newton's hand, in Bentley's copy (TCC) and John Craig's (Fisher Library, New South Wales). There is also a very heavily annotated copy in the University of Texas which Cohen (1971, p. 203) allows could well have been Halley's missing copy. 'The handwriting', he noted, 'bears some strong resemblances . . . although there are some divergences.'

Principia soon became an expensive and rare work. Hooke's copy was auctioned for £2 3s 6d in 1703 while Sir William Browne complained in 1707 that he had been forced to pay two guineas for a copy. But it was not simply the difficulty of finding a copy that led Newton to contemplate producing a second edition. Almost as soon as the work had appeared Newton had begun assembling corrections, modifications and additions which he obviously intended to include in any new edition. By the 1690s the alterations were clear enough in his mind and on paper for him to show them to members of his group of young mathematicians. So organised were they that David Gregory in July 1694 could draw up a six-page manuscript listing the changes Newton proposed to make (C, III, pp. 384–9). Fatio, also, made extensive notes on Newton's proposed changes and had no hesitation in informing scholars like Huygens of them.

Both Gregory and Fatio saw themselves as editors of any new edition. Newton's interest in the project, however, was variable. Even without the added duties incurred from 1696 by his move to the Mint, it was clear that Newton was in no hurry to publish. When, in 1708, he was ready to move, Gregory was dead and Fatio had fallen out of favour. The task was initially undertaken by the unlikely figure of the Master of Trinity, Richard Bentley, the foremost classicist of the century. When asked later why he had entrusted the task to someone who understood little of the technical detail, Newton replied that Bentley 'was covetous and loved mony & therefore I lett him that he might get mony'. By June 1708 Bentley was in a position to send Newton an eight-page sample of the new edition. Shortly afterwards, while remaining as publisher, Bentley handed over the editorial duties to Roger Cotes, a young Trinity mathematician.

2 Cambridge, 1713

Printed in an edition of 750 copies, it was sold in quires for 15s and bound for a guinea. Bentley's accounts have survived and show that the total cost of the printing came to £117 4s 1½d. He sold 375 copies to various booksellers and individuals at an average cost of 13s each. The printer C. Crownfield took a further 200 copies at 11s each. This yielded Bentley a profit of £200 while still holding a substantial stock for future sale. Some of these were in fact presentation copies. Twelve were given to Cotes and a further six to Newton. There is also a distribution list in Newton's papers of another seventy or so recipients. It covers most of the great libraries, scientific institutions and Courts of Europe. Individuals listed include Cassini, de la Hire, Varignon, Bernoulli, Leibniz and Machin. But even this list is incomplete as it contains no reference to the copies known to have been presented by Newton to Queen Anne personally on 27 July 1713, nor a copy he sent to Yale University.

The most significant feature remains the number of changes introduced into the edition. Rouse Ball (1893) noted that, of the 494 pages of *Principia* (1687), '397 are more or less modified in the second edition'. Changes include 'the propositions on the resistance of fluids, Book II, section VII props 34–40; the lunar theory in Book III; the propositions on the precession of the equinoxes, Book III. prop. 39; and the propositions on the theory of comets, Book III, props 41, 42'. In addition there was a completely new *Scholium generale*. Also included for the first time were a table of contents (*Index capitum totius opera*), which did no more than list the section headings of the first two books, and a rather sketchy index (*Index rerum alphabeticus*). Cotes also provided an important preface in which he undertook to explain and defend Newton's account of gravity.

No census has been taken of the second edition.

3   Amsterdam, 1714

The 750 copies of *Principia* (1713) clearly did not meet the demand for *Principia*, particularly the Continental demand. Consequently 'une compagnie des libraires' of Amsterdam undertook to fill the gap.

4   Amsterdam, 1723

As the reprint of 1714 had failed to meet demand, a second reprint was issued by another company of booksellers. It also contained as a supplement the *Analysis per quantitatum series* published by William Jones in 1711.

5   London, 1726

The third and final edition of *Principia*, edited by Henry Pemberton and published in an edition of 1,250 copies. It was printed in three different sizes:

  1,000 copies on Demy (24.2 × 18.2 cm) bound in calf, the small paper edition;

  200 on General Royal (29 × 22.2 cm) bound in calf, the large paper edition;

  50 on Superfine Royal (34 × 23 cm) bound in red or green morocco, the largest paper edition.

The largest paper issue in its sumptuous Harleian binding was clearly intended to be a presentation copy. Of the original fifty Macomber has traced thirty-four, many of which were presentation copies. They include the copies of James Bradley (Bodleian), Christopher Turnor (Cambridge, Mass.), John Conduitt (*Bibliothèque Nationale*, Paris), Sir Hans Sloane (Royal Society), Fontenelle (King's College, Cambridge), J. F. Fauquiere (Queen's College, Cambridge) and Littleton Powys (Andrade's copy, sold in 1965 for £900).

A detailed list of the changes made in 1726 was first published by J. C. Adams in Brewster (1855); they are of far less significance than the comparable changes made in 1713. The Leibniz *scholium* (Book II, lemma II) was eliminated, Machin's account of the motions of the lunar nodes (Book III, following prop.XXXIII) was added, some experiments of Desaguliers dating from 1719 were included in Book II, section VII after the *scholium* to prop.XL, astronomical data was revised and the material at the beginning of Book III was re-organised. But, compared to 1713, there were, in Cohen's phrase, no 'bold and exciting innovations'.

6 Geneva, 1739–42

The so-called 'Jesuit' edition in three volumes. Its editors, F. Jacquier and T. Le Seur, were both clearly stated on the title page to be Minims, a Franciscan and not a Jesuit order. It proved to be an extremely useful edition containing a 'perpetuis commentariis illustrata', much of which had been provided by Jean-Louis Calandrini (1703–58), Professor of Mathematics at the University of Geneva.

Each volume contains a separate book of *Principia*. The third volume contains in addition:

Traité sur le flux et reflux de la mer, by Daniel Bernoulli;

De causa physica fluxis et refluxis maris, by Colin MacLaurin;

Inquisitio physica in causam fluxus ac refluxus maris, by Leonard Euler.

These were the three prizewinning essays submitted in 1724 to the *Académie des sciences* to resolve 'the Problem relating to the Motion of the Tides from the theory of gravity'. The final volume also contains a long *Introductio ad lunae theoria Newtonionam* (vol. III, pp. 375–677).

The edition is also noteworthy in containing a comprehensive *Index propositionum totius operis* (vol. III, pp. 678–703), the most comprehensive to be published before Cohen and Koyré's definitive edition of 1972 (Newton, 1972).

With its rich editorial content, extensive summaries and detailed index, the Jesuit edition remains the most ambitious ever published. It is still a desirable and useful work. Not surprisingly it was reissued in a number of countries and in a variety of forms during the following century. Indeed, between 1727 and 1871 and excluding translations, the only editions of *Principia* published were Jesuit editions. There were four such reissues:

    1 Geneva, 1760: an 'Editio altera longe accuratior & emendatior', 3 vols;

2 Prague, 1780–85: in two volumes with a commentary by Johannes Tessanek;

3+4 Glasgow, 1822, in 4 vols, and Glasgow, 1833, in 2 vols: both editions were edited by J. M. F. Wright.

7 *London, 1780–1*

Horsley included the edition of 1726 in his *Opera* (1779–85, vols II and III). Cohen (1971, p. 199) has noted that Horsley was one of the few editors to have incorporated material from the *Notae* of David Gregory into his edition. It was reissued in Stuttgart–Bad Cannstatt in 1964.

8 *Glasgow, 1871*

Sir William Thomson and Hugh Blackburn, professors of physics at Glasgow University, decided, 'as all editions of the *Principia* are now out of print', to reprint the final edition of 1726 without note or comment. The reason for their work, Thomson's biographer has revealed (Thompson, 1910, p. 480), was 'to have available copies to award as prizes to University students'.

9 *London, 1953*

A thousand copies of a facsimile of the three-line edition of 1687 were published by Dawson's of Pall Mall at a price of two guineas. They were the first copies of *Principia*, excluding translations, to appear in England since Newton's death. It was also only the second time that the first edition of 1687 had been printed.

10 *Brussels, 1965*

A reprint of *Principia* (1687) in the *Culture et Civilisations* series.

11 *Cambridge, 1972*

The definitive *variorum* edition, in two volumes, edited by I. B. Cohen and A. Koyré. It presents the text of 1726 together with any earlier versions recorded in the editions of 1686 and 1713. Also noted are significant versions of the text found in *M*, or any of Newton's annotated or interleaved copies. In addition, Cohen and Koyré have collected in ten appendices an enormous amount of editorial matter.

TRANSLATIONS

1 *London, 1729*

The first and still the only complete English translation ever made was completed by Andrew Motte and published in two volumes by his brother, Benjamin Motte. All later English translations are little more than variants, and often inferior variants, of Motte's work.

Motte's achievement is somewhat surprising as it was widely assumed that Pemberton, ideally placed in 1727 as the editor of *Principia* (1726) and self-proclaimed confidant of the aging Newton, would produce such a work. It was an assumption shared by Henry Pemberton himself. As early as March 1727, almost before Newton was cold, he announced his plans. They were repeated in the preface to his *A View of Sir Isaac Newton's Philosophy* (1728). Motte first publicly announced his plans in the *Journal des sçavans* for June 1727 and repeated them in England in the following year.

The race was clearly on and both contestants lost no time in claiming for their unfinished works the special authority which only Newton's name could provide. Motte made the most unlikely claim that his translation had been made 'sous les yeux et suivant les avis de M.Newton'. Pemberton, probably with more justification, responded by insisting that his work contained 'sans doute vrai sens de l'auteur'.

That the outsider Motte completed his translation first suggests strongly that he had begun the enterprise long before Newton's death. The fact that he used earlier *Principia* editions in his translation reinforces this view and suggests that he began his work, at least in a preliminary way, before the appearance of the third edition in 1726.

Having won the race, Motte was unwilling even to recognise Pemberton's existence. His name was omitted from the acknowledgments Newton made in the preface to *Principia* (1726). Also, with an elaborate dedication to Sir Hans Sloane, President of the Royal Society, Motte was clearly seeking to bestow on the work an authority it neither needed nor had earned.

In addition to Motte's translation the work also includes a translation of Newton's *System of the World*. Whether this is by Motte is unclear. It also contains, separately paginated, John Machin's *The Laws of the Moon's Motions*.

Machin was probably closely involved in the preparation of the translation. One of the mysteries of the work is an appendix claiming to contain 'explications (given by a friend) of Some Propositions in the Book, not demonstrated by the Author'. The eight-page appendix then proceeds to explicate Book I, prop.91, cor.2 and the *Scholium* to Book II, prop.34 by showing how, for example, fluxions can be used to find the force of attraction of a sphere. The author was undoubtedly knowledgeable about Newton's work, for the material included in the appendix is similar to papers in the PC only recently published. Motte is unlikely to have had any such access to Newton's thought and papers. Machin, on the other hand, was highly thought of by Newton and could well have had access to his unpublished papers.

The work has been so successful that later scholars have been deterred from attempting a rival translation. They have settled instead for 'revisions' and 'corrections'. Thorp in 1777, Davis in 1803, Chittenden in 1848 and Cajori in 1934 have all firmly based their work on Motte. When Cohen and Koyré were considering attempting for the first time in 250 years to add to their critical edition of *Principia* a new English translation, they concluded eventually that, although Motte sometimes translated too freely, interpolated his own expressions, mixed editions and used unfamiliar expressions, he remained 'sound, literate and generally accurate'. He was, in any case, preferable to the 'modernisation' of Florian Cajori. Consequently, there seemed no immediate need for a new translation. Cohen, however, did issue in 1968 a two-volume facsimile reprint of Motte (1729) to which he contributed a valuable introduction. It was, surprisingly, Motte's first reprint in 240 years.

2 Paris, 1756/1759

The first and still the only French translation ever made. It was carried out by the Marquise du Chastellet, friend of Voltaire, with the help of A. C. Clairaut. Although the first issue does have a date of 1756 on its title page, it is very rare and may well have been, according to Cohen (1971), 'a preliminary edition, not made available for general sale to the public'. He had managed to trace only twelve. The 1759 is certainly the major edition.

In two volumes, the first volume contains, in addition to Book I and II, a 'preface historique' and a poem by Voltaire. The second volume contains Book III and, separately paginated, 'Exposition abregée du système du monde, et explication des principaux phenomenes astronomiques tirée des Principes de M.Newton' (pp. 1–116). This was supplied by Clairaut. There was also 'Solution analytique des principaux problemes qui concernent le système du monde' (pp. 117–286).

As the Marquise died in 1749, it is evident that considerable responsibility for the final form of the translation must rest with Clairaut. One extraordinary feature of the work is that the title page carries on it the title '*Principes mathématiques de la philosophie naturelle* par feue Madame la Marquise du Chastellet'. Nowhere is the name of Newton mentioned. Indeed, as a result, it has even been listed in catalogues as an original work by the Marquise. When Newton was referred to in the preface the further extravagant claim was made that 'on trouvera souvent Newton plus intelligible dans cette traduction que dans l'original; et même dans la traduction Angloise'.

It was also pointed out that the translation had been 'revûe par M.Clairault' and that, although the Marquise had made all the calculations herself, they had been checked and sometimes revised by Clairaut.

A facsimile was issued in Paris in 1966.

3 London, 1777

The first revision of Motte, together with an extensive commentary, was made by Robert Thorp, a Northumberland clergyman. Only the first volume dealing with Book I ever appeared. It is described by Cohen as 'with lavish notes . . . one of the best texts to use for anyone who wishes to make a careful study of Newton's *Principia*'. It was reprinted in 1802 and is available also in a modern edition, with an introduction by Cohen, published in London in 1969.

4   London, 1803

A second revision of Motte by William Davis. It was re-issued in 1819. Published in three volumes, it was originally issued as a part work: six issues at 4s each, published on the first of each month. It also contained a life of Newton by the editor and, in Volume III:

1   *The System of the World* (1728), pp. 1–82;
2   *A Short Comment on the Principia*, by William Emerson, pp. 89–175;
3   *A Defence of the Principia*, by William Emerson, pp. 177–92;
4   *The Laws of the Moon's Motion*, by John Machin, pp. 195–230.

Volume I contained Thomas Pellett's *A Catalogue of Sir Isaac Newton's Manuscripts*, pp. lv–lx.

5   New York, 1848–85

Six editions were published, four by Daniel Adee in 1848, 1849, 1874 and 1885, one by Putnam in 1850, and one by Ivison and Phinney in 1858. All sold for $4.50 and differed only in their title page. The edition was based on Motte (1729) and carried a fifty-two-page life of Newton by N. W. Chittenden, as well as his *The System of the World* (1728). All editions carry the dedication 'To the Teachers of the Normal School of the State of New York'. The New York editions were the only English translations of *Principia* to appear between 1819 and 1934. Why *Principia* should be in so much demand in New York remains unclear. The editor noted that the work was 'generally unknown' in the US, partly, he added, because the work had hitherto been inaccessible, in Latin and expensive. The work itself was put forward not so much as a treatise in mathematical physics but as 'the noblest illustration of what Man may be, and may do'. Until the work of P. J. Wallis (1977 and 1978), it had been incorrectly assumed that the New York editions of *Principia* had all been published in the puzzlingly short two-year interval, 1848–50.

6   Berlin, 1872, Mathematische Principien der Naturlehre

A complete German translation, with a commentary by J. P. Wolfers. It was reissued in facsimile in Darmstadt in 1963.

7   Petrograd, 1915–16, Matematicheskia nachala naturalnoi filosofi

A Russian translation by A. N. Kriloff. It was first published as fascicules IV and V of the *Nokolaevski morskoi akademi* (Bulletin of the Nicholas Naval Academy). More than a third of the volume is taken up with some 200 notes and supplements covering historical, philological and mathematical topics. As most copies were destroyed in the 1917 Revolution it is now a work of some rarity. Consequently the last copy to be auctioned, in the Honeyman sale in 1980, fetched £1,800.

8 Lund, 1927–31, Naturvetenskapens matematiska principer

A three-volume Swedish translation by C. V. Charlier. Based upon *Principia* (1726), it also contains a number of variant readings from the earlier editions of 1687 and 1713, an historical introduction and a large number of analytical notes.

9 Tokyo, 1930, Purunshipia by Nyu Ton

A Japanese translation by Kunio Oka.

10 Berkeley, 1934

The fourth revision of Motte was made by Florian Cajori. He died in 1930 before the work could be completed. The final editing was therefore done by R. T. Crawford who noted that it had been Cajori's aim to render 'certain parts into modern phraseology and to append historical and critical notes'. It also contains *The System of the World*. The notes are indeed useful and would undoubtedly have been fuller if Cajori had lived long enough to complete his work.

The policy of modernisation worked less well. The substitution of 'inversely as the square root of' for 'reciprocally in the subduplicate ratio of' is both harmless and acceptable as a modernisation. It has, however, been objected that Cajori failed to carry his programme through and modernise all obsolete expressions and failed to define adequately those which remain. At some points he has altered the text while giving no indication of his innovation. It is, in Cohen's judgment, 'neither Newton's original version nor a truly modern text; hence it serves neither a modern reader nor the historian' (Cohen 1968, p. xii). Never the less it has become the standard modern English version and it is likely to be from Cajori that most readers of today will gain their first-hand knowledge of Newton's text. It has been reissued several times (1946, 1947, 1960 and 1962); since 1952 it has been available also in a two-volume paperback. Cajori has also been issued several times, bound with *Opticks* and Huygens's *Treatise on Light*, under the imprint of the *Encyclopedia Britannica*'s 'Great Books of the Western World' series.

11 Bucharest, 1956 Principiile matematice ale filozofiei naturale

A Roumanian translation by Viktor Marlian.

EXCERPTS AND COMMENTARIES

From the beginning of the eighteenth century onwards the bulk of readers have derived their knowledge of *Principia* not directly from the pages of Newton, or indirectly from Motte's translation. Too much mathematical competence was demanded for such an approach. Instead, the interested reader turned to the commentaries, summaries, excerpts and paraphrases which emerged in large numbers to help the mathematically less-sophisticated. The history of this secondary literature remains to be written; its outlines, however, have been traced. It divides naturally into three phases.

Eighteenth century

Here the main aim was to get the basic Newtonian ideas and texts to an audience who were unfamiliar with Latin and maths and were unlikely even to see a copy of *Principia*. Inevitably philosophy and cosmology took precedence over mechanics and mathematics, and material from the *Opticks* and other texts would be included as well. The first texts were in Latin.

1 John Keill (1701), *Introductio ad veram physicam*. The first Newtonian physics textbook. It was based on lectures given at Oxford since 1694. An English edition appeared in 1720 under the title *An Introduction to Natural Philosophy*.

2 David Gregory (1702), *Astronomiae physicae et geometricae elementa*, 2 vols. 'A well documented but unimaginative attempt to graft the gravitational synthesis . . . of Newton's Principia onto the findings of traditional astronomy' (*DSB*). It was reissued in 1726 and in English translation, *The Elements of Astronomy, Physical and Geometrical* (1715 and 1726). It contained Newton's *Theory of the Moon's Motion* and, without acknowledgment, the so-called classical *scholia*.

3 William Whiston (1710), *Praelectiones physico-mathematicae*. Based on Whiston's Cambridge lectures, it contained substantial extracts from *Principia*.

4 John Maxwell (1715), *A Discourse Concerning God*. The first English work to contain translations of parts of *Principia*; it contained the first complete English translation of the General *Scholium*.

5 William Whiston (1716), *Sir Isaac Newton's Mathematick Philosophy More Easily Demonstrated*. Forty lectures read at Cambridge for 'the use of the young students there'. It was a translation of his *Praelectiones* (1710) above. The first English work to contain sizeable and comprehensive extracts from *Principia*, it was reissued in 1728.

6 W. J. 'sGravesande (1720), *Introductio ad philosophiam Newtonionam*, 2 vols. It was quickly translated into English, with two rival editions appearing in the same year as the original Latin version: J. Desaguliers, *Mathematical Elements of Natural Philosophy*, the official version; and John Keill's *Mathematical Elements of Physics*. Yet a third translation by Edmund Stone appeared in 1735. 'sGravesande

issued an abridgment, *Philosophiae Newtonianae institutionis* (1723). Translated into Dutch and French as well as English, some twenty-four editions in one form or another had appeared before 1760. It was clearly one of the main channels through which Newton's ideas were spread throughout Europe.

7 Henry Pemberton (1728), *A View of Sir Issac Newton's Philosophy*. Described by Cohen (1956, p. 209) as 'one of the three outstanding popular introductions to Newtonian science in the 18th century'.

8 P.L.M. de Maupertuis (1732), *Discours sur les différentes figures des astres*. 'The first Newtonian treatise by a Frenchman' (Hall, 1983, p. 348).

9 Francesco Algarotti (1737), *Il Newtonianismo per le dame*. First published in Naples, it was rapidly translated into French, *Le Newtonianism pour les dames* (1738), by de Castera, and into English, *Sir Isaac Newton's Philosophy Explained for the use of Ladies*, by Mrs Elizabeth Carter. It was also translated into German (1745), Dutch (1767), Swedish (1782) and Portuguese. Thirty editions in seven languages were published in thirteen towns before 1791, making Algarotti's work the most popular of all eighteenth-century introductions to Newton's work.

10 J. T. Desaguliers (1733–4), *A Course of Experimental Philosophy*, two vols. A work which sought to avoid mathematical complexity by concentrating on experimental demonstrations of Newtonian mechanics, a solution adopted by many later writers. It was reissued in 1744 and 1763.

11 Voltaire (1738), *Élémens de la philosophie de Newton*. Together with his *Lettres sur les anglais* (1733), this did much to introduce basic Newtonian concepts into France.

12 Cadwallader Colden (1746), *An Explication of the First Causes of Action in Matter and of the Causes of Gravity*, New York. One of the first American discussions of Newton's work.

13 Colin Maclaurin (1748), *An Account of Sir Isaac Newton's Philosophical Discoveries*.

14 Tom Telescope (1761), *The Newtonian System of Philosophy Adapted to the Capacities of Young Gentleman and Ladies . . . Six Lectures Read to the Lilliputian Society*. Its author has been variously identified as Oliver Goldsmith and John Newbery (1713–67), the publisher of the work. It was enormously successful, with editions appearing in Dutch, Swedish and Italian. It was also published in America. Twenty-two editions are known, with the last appearing in London as late as 1838. Some of the later editions also carry an additional piece by 'William Magnet'.

15 Robert Thorp *et al.* (1765), *Excerpta quaedam e Newtoni principiis . . . cum notis variorum*. A straightforward selection from the Latin text of *Principia*.

Nineteenth century

By the early 1800s there was no longer a pressing need for general introductions to Newtonian philosophy. By this time Newton's principles had either been absorbed or discarded. The general public sought enlightenment on new discoveries in geology, the chemistry of Lavoisier, and an understanding of the 'fluids' of magnetism and electricity. Those who were interested in Newton were the growing and never-before-known generation of young scientists and engineers who required some introduction into the formal principles of Newtonian mechanics. The need was met by a large number of seemingly identical works, some typical examples of which are listed below.

16 John Carr (1821), *The First Three Sections of Newton's Principia with Copious Notes and Illustrations . . . Deductions and problems.* Designed for the use of students, it was reissued in 1825 and 1826.

17 J. M. F. Wright (1830), *The Principia of Newton (First Three Sections) With Notes, Examples and Deductions.* This is the same Wright who edited the Glasgow editions of *Principia* of 1822 and 1833.

18 J. H. Evans (1834), *The First Three Sections of Newton's Principia.* In 1835 Evans published a comparable work on the ninth and tenth sections of *Principia*'s Book I. Thereafter the five sections were combined in one work and published together in 1837, 1843, 1855 and 1871.

19 William Whewell (1846), *Newton's Principia, Book I, Sections I, II, III.* Printed in the original Latin with notes and commentary.

20 Percival Frost (1854), *Newton's Principia, Sections I,II,III with Notes . . . Problems.* There were later editions in 1854, 1863, 1878, 1880, 1883 and 1900. The most widely used of all such works. It was from Frost, for example, that a distant young New Zealand student who entered Trinity College, Cambridge, in 1895 first gained his detailed knowledge of Newtonian mechanics. The student was Ernest Rutherford (1871–1937) and his annotated copy of Frost was exhibited during the Royal Society's 1971 celebrations of the centenary of his birth.

21 Lord Brougham and E. J. Routh (1855), *Analytical View of Sir Isaac Newton's Principia.* The most comprehensive and impressive work of this genre, it still contains the fullest analysis of *Principia* available in English. It is available in a facsimile reprint edited by Cohen (1972).

22 Ferdinand Rosenberger (1895), *Isaac Newton und seine physikalischen Principien.* The fullest account of Newton's scientific thought ever published.

Representing a different tradition, two nineteenth-century works began the historical study of *Principia*.

23 S. P. Rigaud (1838), *Historical Essay on the First Publication of Sir Isaac Newton's Principia*.

24 W. W. Rouse Ball (1893), *An Essay on Newton's 'Principia'*.

Twentieth century

With the final appearance of Frost in 1900, the demand for detailed analyses of technical aspects of Newtonian mechanics seemed to disappear. Modern scholars have continued to study the history of *Principia* and have been concerned to publish the basic documents. Extracts have continued to appear, but the commentary has largely disappeared. In its place there has emerged the collections of essays, ostensibly linked with particular occasions, but of variable quality and interest. They include the following.

25 E. von Schweidler and K. Zindler (1899), *Vorreden und Einleitungen zu klassischen Werken der Mechanik*. It includes *Principia* extracts, pp. 7–44.

26 P. Jourdain (1914), *Abhandlung über jene Grundsätze der Mechanik*. It contains *Principia* extracts translated into German by A. von Oettingen, pp. 3–28.

27 F. Enriques and U. Forti (1925), *Principi di filosofia naturale*. No complete Italian translation of *Principia* has ever appeared. This work contains in translation the axioms, definitions, *regulae philosophandi* and large parts of Book I and III.

28 H. J. Beth (1932), *Newton's Principia*. No Dutch translation of *Principia* has yet been made. Beth's work, however, fills the gap by providing a summary containing a number of excerpts in Dutch.

29 H. S. Thayer (1953), *Newton's Philosophy of Nature*. Amongst other items it contains from *Principia* the definitions, axioms, *scholium* on absolute space, time and motion, General *Scholium*, *regulae philosophandi*, Cotes' preface and various items on gravity.

30 A. R. and M. B. Hall (1962), *Unpublished Scientific Papers of Isaac Newton*. Selected from the PC, it contains much background material and early drafts of work which eventually appeared in *Principia* including: *De motu corporum, definitiones*; *De motu sphaericorum in fluidis*; a suppressed *Conclusio*; several alternative versions of the *Scholium generale*. All texts were printed in both English and Latin.

31 Alberto Pala (1963), *Antologia*. Italian extracts from *Principia*.

32 John Herivel (1965), *Background to the Principia*. An invaluable work which prints in full, in both Latin and English, many early drafts of material incorporated in *Principia*.

33 Alberto Pala, *Principi mathematici della filosofia naturale di Isaaco Newton*. Extracts from *Principia* published in Italian in the *Classici della sienza* series.

34 I. B. Cohen (1971), *Introduction to Newton's Principia*. The definitive account of the publication of *Principia*.

With reference to the numerous memorial volumes of collected essays, three in particular stand out.

35 W. J. Greenstreet (1927), *Isaac Newton 1642–1727*. A volume published for the Mathematical Association to commemorate the bicentenary of Newton's death. Amongst other items it contains the following papers of especial interest:

> D. Smith: 'Two unpublished documents of Newton';
>   'Portraits of Sir Isaac Newton';
>   'The portrait medals of Sir Isaac Newton';
> H. Zeitlinger: 'Newton bibliography';
> D. C. Fraser: 'Newton and interpolation';
> J. Proudman: 'Newton's work on the theory of the tides';
> J. T. Milne: 'Newton's contribution to the geometry of conics';
> H. Hilton: 'Newton on plane cubic curves'.

36 F. E. Brasch (1928), *Sir Isaac Newton 1727–1927*. A bicentenary evaluation of Newton's work produced by the History of Science Society. Of especial interest are the following four papers:

> F. Cajori: 'Newton's twenty year delay in announcing the law of gravitation';
>   'Newton's fluxions';
> L. C. Newell: 'Newton's work on alchemy and chemistry';
> F. E. Brasch: 'Newton's first critical disciple in the American colonies'.

37 Robert Palter (1970), *Annus mirabilis of Sir Isaac Newton 1666–1966*. The proceedings of a conference held at the University of Texas to commemorate the tercentenary of Newton's *annus mirabilis*. It contains the following important studies:

> A. R. and M. B. Hall: 'Newton and the theory of matter';
> D. T. Whiteside: 'Success and strength of Newton's early mathematical thought';
> R. S. Westfall: 'Uneasy fitful reflections on fits of easy transmission';
> I. B. Cohen: 'Newton's second law and the concept of force in the *Principia*';
> F. Haskell: 'The apotheosis of Newton in art'.

PRICE

Principia could not long be bought for its initial price of 9s. A shortage of copies pushed the price up to about £2 a copy at the close of the century. The publication of the second and third editions satisfied the demand of most readers and the price of first editions dropped considerably. A copy belonging to Martin Folkes was auctioned in 1756 for only

4s. First editions carried no premium in the eighteenth century. In so far as there were any collectors interested in *Principia*, it was the third edition they sought and, if possible, a largest-paper Harleian copy.

The pattern persisted. Most first editions before 1900 sold for no more than two or three guineas, while before 1914 no copy ever reached £10. Prices rose in the inter-war years, with the average price settling at about £50. Special copies like Halifax's fetched £250 at auction in 1937, while Keynes paid £85 in 1936 for an uncut three-line issue.

Prices continued to rise in the 1950s, with good copies beginning to command £200. In the 1960s prices of £1,000 began to be heard of. In 1965 Andrade disposed of his magnificent collection of Newtoniana, including sixteen *Principia*. They fetched £6,648, with £2,400 on a two-line imprint and £2,200 on a three-line imprint.

A decade later another great collection, that belonging to J. B. Honeyman, was also auctioned. Honeyman also had sixteen *Principia* but, sold in 1980, they commanded £34,370. Three first editions went for £12,500, £8,000 and £7,000 respectively. Although nothing in public has yet exceeded the £12,500 needed to buy a unique copy of the two-line imprint at the Honeyman sale, prices on offer in catalogues have been noted at £14,000 (1979) and even, in 1982, of £17,850. It is doubtful, however, whether such high prices would be realised for anything other than an exceptional copy.

Other editions of interest are Motte's translation and the very rare Russian translation of 1915, both of which command prices of up to £2,000, much higher prices in fact than copies of either the second or third editions, still found for well under £1,000.

JAMES II

In 1687 a special presentation of a copy of *Principia* was made by Halley to James II. It was accompanied by a brief summary of the work, together with an account of Newton's theory of the tides prepared by Halley.

'If ever a book was worthy the favourable acceptance of a Prince', Halley told James, then *Principia* with its 'great discoveries' was the most suitable. Aware that James might find the work difficult, or, in Halley's more diplomatic language, 'being sencible of the little leisure which care of the Publick leaves to Princes . . . a short Extract of the matters contained' had been prepared. Halley also offered to return and discuss any problems James might have with the text.

There is no evidence that James had any interest in Newton's work. In any case, with his kingdom collapsing about him, James hardly had time for any such discussions. The copy itself is lost.

Halley's 'Discourse presented . . . to the late King James' was later published in *PT*, No. 226, March 1697, pp. 445–57. It has been published more recently in Cohen (*PLNP*, pp. 412–24). The work can also be found bound in Pepys's copy of *Principia* in Magdalene College, Cambridge, a unique copy.

DIFFICULTY

It has long been a widespread belief that certain scientific theories and works are so difficult as to be intelligible to only a few very brilliant minds. In our own day comments made by Bertrand Russell and Sir Arthur Eddington have suggested that *Principia mathematica* (1910–13, 3 vols) and the general theory of relativity have been mastered by no more than half a dozen people, most of whom are dead or have been driven mad by the effort.

Similar beliefs seemed to have been regularly expressed about *Principia* in Newton's day. One story, for example, told by Martin Folkes, described a Cambridge undergraduate pointing Newton out in the streets as 'a man who has writt a book that neither he nor anyone else understands'. Newton himself added to the legend by declaring that not even Halley 'understood that part relating to fluids' and that he had deliberately made the work abstruse 'to avoid being baited by little Smatterers'.

Those who did wish to master the book were prepared to pay for the insight. Sir William Petty's claim, that he would have given £500 to be the author and £200 simply to understand it, may well have been rhetorical. Others were more literal, with Halifax, for example, paying John Machin fifty guineas for tuition on *Principia*. Others like Humphrey Babington saw time rather than money as the key; he declared that he 'might study seven years' before understanding 'anything of it'.

Some who knew Newton asked him directly how to tackle the work. Thus to R. Bentley's query he offered a formidable reading list together with some more general advice: 'At ye first perusal of My book it's enough if you understand ye propositions with some of the Demonstrations wch are easier than the rest . . . they will afterwards give you light into ye harder.' After working on the first sixty pages in this way Bentley was then advised to 'pass on to ye 3rd Book and when you see the design of that you may turn back to such Propositions as you shall have a desire to know' (*C*, III, pp. 155–6).

Locke was another who sought help. He first approached C. Huygens with the query as to whether or not he could safely assume the soundness of Newton's mathematical demonstrations. So assured, he became, according to Desaguliers, 'Master of all the Physicks' and 'the first who became a Newtonian philosopher without the help of geometry'. Locke approached Newton in 1690 and received from him 'A Demonstration That the Planets, by their gravity towards the Sun, may move in Ellipses' (*C*, III, pp. 71–7).

While it would be fatuous to pretend that *Principia* is not a difficult work, it is also too easy to exaggerate its obscurity. The mathematicians of Newton's day found no especial difficulty in the work. Much now of its language is strange to the modern physicist, as are a good many of the mathematical techniques deployed in the work. If such difficulties are discounted, then *Principia* can hardly be classed as any more difficult than any other original and comprehensive treatise of mathematical physics.

CONTENTS AND ARGUMENT

Definitions and axioms

After the various dedications, prefaces and Halley's Ode, *Principia* proper begins with eight definitions, an important *scholium* and three laws of motion.

DEFINITIONS I–VIII (CAJORI, PP. 1–12)

I   The quantity of matter, or mass, Newton defined as the product of its density and volume. Consequently, air of double density in twice the space would have four times as much mass. Newton pointed out that he had excluded from the definition 'a medium, if any such there is, that freely pervades the interstices between the parts of bodies'. Finally, he distinguished mass as the quantity of matter (inertial mass) from weight (gravitational mass), while insisting that mass was proportional to weight, 'as I have found out by experiments on pendulums'. It has been objected that the definition is circular, on the grounds that it is impossible to define density independently of mass.

II   The quantity of motion, momentum in the terminology of today, was defined as the product of a body's mass and velocity.

III *Vis insita*, innate force of matter or, in today's terminology, inertia, was defined as 'a power of resisting, by which every body . . . continues in its present state, whether it be of rest, or of moving uniformly forward in a right line.' (*See also* Inertia)

IV   By impressed force Newton meant 'an action exerted upon a body, in order to change its state'. He was careful to point out that the force was 'the action only' and did not persist in the body once the action had been completed.

V   'A centripetal force is that by which bodies are drawn or impelled, or any way may tend, towards a point as to a centre'. (*See also* Centripetal force)

VI–VIII The absolute quantity, the accelerative quantity and the motive quantity of centripetal force were defined respectively.

SCHOLIUM (CAJORI, PP. 6–12)

Although Newton offered no definitions of such basic concepts as space, time, motion and place, he objected to the common view that they arise 'from the relation they bear to sensible objects'. Instead, he argued, 'true time' was 'absolute . . . and mathematical', and space was absolute, 'always similar and immovable' without reference to anything else. Motion was also presented in absolute terms. (*See also* Absolute space, time and motion)

AXIOMS OR LAWS OF MOTION (CAJORI, PP. 13–28)

1 Every body continues in its state of rest, or of uniform motion in a right line, unless it is compelled to change that state by forces impressed upon it.

2 The change of motion is proportional to the motive force impressed; and is made in the direction of the right line in which the force is impressed.

3 To every action there is always opposed an equal reaction. (*See also* Laws of motion)

In the accompanying six corollaries Newton presented the parallelogram of forces (Cor.1), argued that momentum was conserved (Cor.3), and claimed that the motions of bodies in the same space are the same 'amongst themselves, whether that space is at rest, or moves uniformly in a right line' (Cor.5).

The section was concluded by a *Scholium* in which, amongst other points, Newton set out to demonstrate the equality of action and reaction as presented in the third law above. Using two suspended balls, the ancestor of the executive toy known today as Newton's cradle, he measured the results of their collisions and found that 'when the bodies concurred together directly, equal changes to the contrary parts were produced in their motions, and, of consequence, that the action and reaction were always equal'.

Book I The Motion of Bodies

SECTION I (LEMMAS I–XI; CAJORI, PP. 29–40)

It contains Newton's doctrine of limits. Areas were taken to be the limits of sums of inscribed or circumscribed parallelograms whose 'breadth . . . be supposed to be diminished, and their number to be augmented in infinitum' (lemma II). In the concluding *scholium* Newton explained his choice of method. Demonstrations by the method of indivisibles, he conceded, were shorter; they were, however, 'somewhat harsh, and . . . less geometrical'.

SECTION II (PROPS I–X; CAJORI, PP. 40–55) THE DETERMINATION OF CENTRIPETAL FORCES

Newton began by showing that 'The areas which revolving bodies describe by radii drawn to an immovable centre of force . . . are proportional to the times in which they are described' (prop.I).

Consider the diagram. Let a body move by its innate force from A to B in one unit of time; in the same time, if allowed to continue, it would move from B to c (law I). As the triangles SAB and SBc have equal bases and the common altitude S it follows that a body moving from A to c will have swept out equal areas in equal times. But now suppose that when the body reaches B 'a centripetal force acts at once . . . and, turning aside the body from the right line Bc, compels it . . . along the right line BC'. But, again, the triangles SAB and SAC are equal, and once more the radius vector has swept out equal areas in equal times. A similar effect will be produced as the body moves from C to D. Finally, Newton concluded, allow the number of triangles to be increased, and their breadth diminished *ad infinitum*, then 'their ultimate perimeter ADF will be a curved line'.

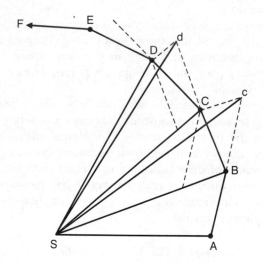

Newton had thus shown that bodies moving under the influence of a centripetal force will obey Kepler's area law and sweep out equal areas in equal times. In prop.II he derived the converse that bodies which move in any curved line and which observe Kepler's area law are under the influence of a centripetal force. It was further argued (prop.IV, corollary VI) that, given also Kepler's harmonic law, 'centripetal forces will be inversely as the square of the radii'.

SECTION III (PROPS XI–XVII; CAJORI, PP. 56–67) THE MOTION OF BODIES IN ECCENTRIC CONIC SECTIONS

In props XI–XIII Newton posed the problem, if a body moves in an eccentric conic section (ellipse, parabola or hyperbola), what is the law of centripetal force tending to the foci of the figures? He demonstrated that in all cases the centripetal force varied inversely as the square of the distance. He thus claimed, in corollary I to prop.XIII, to have proved that bodies governed by centripetal forces which vary inversely as the square of the distance move in conic sections. The converse was also claimed.

SECTIONS IV–V (PROPS XVIII–XXIX; CAJORI, PP. 68–108)

In a purely technical manner Newton dealt with methods for determining elliptical, parabolic and hyperbolic orbits given a focus (section IV) and without a focus (section V).

SECTION VI (PROPS XXX–XXXI; CAJORI, PP. 109–16)

In prop. XXXI Newton tackled Kepler's problem: 'To find the place of a body moving in a given ellipse at any assigned time.' Noting the difficulty of the problem, Newton added, in an accompanying *scholium*, a further and simpler solution by approximation.

SECTION VII (PROPS XXXII–XXXIX; CAJORI, PP. 117–27)

Bodies did not always, Newton noted, move in 'curved lines'. He therefore, assuming a centripetal force varying inversely as the square of the distance, set out to show how far a body will fall rectilinearly in a given time (prop.XXXII), and how to determine the time of descent of a body falling from a given place (prop.XXXVI). Finally, in prop.XXXIX, and assuming 'a centripetal force of any kind', it was shown how to determine a body's velocity at any point, and the time it will arrive at any point.

SECTION VIII (PROPS XL–XLII; CAJORI, PP. 128–34)

The situation was made completely general and Newton considered the orbits of bodies acted upon by 'any sort of centripetal force'.

SECTION IX (PROPS XLIII–XLV; CAJORI, PP. 135–47)

Newton noted that previously he had dealt with 'the motions of bodies in immovable orbits' and that in section IX he would consider the motions of bodies whose orbits revolved around their centres of force. In prop.XLV he set out to determine the motion of the apsides in nearly circular orbits. It was established that, under certain conditions, the apsides will advance 1° 31′ 28″ in each revolution. He noted, however, that the moon's apse was about twice as fast.

SECTION X (PROPS XLVI–LVI; CAJORI, PP. 148–63)

So far, Newton noted, he had dealt exclusively with 'the motion of bodies in orbits whose planes pass through the centre of force'. In section X he proposed to consider 'motions in eccentric planes'. Also considered were the oscillations of pendulums.

SECTION XI (PROPS LVII–LXIX; CAJORI, PP. 164–92)

Newton considerably deepened the range of *Principia* at this point. He began by emphasising that his previous assumption that bodies were attracted to an immovable centre may be a fiction. By law III, attraction between bodies was always 'reciprocal and equal' and consequently neither of the bodies 'is truly at rest'. He first proved that 'Two bodies attracting each other mutually describe similar figures about their common centre of gravity' (prop.LVII). A further generalisation was attained with prop.LXVI when the behaviour was raised of 'three bodies, whose force decreases as the square of the distance' attracting each other. In twenty-two corollaries Newton not only raised the three-body problem but made the first coherent attempts at its solution. In the process several of the inequalities of the moon were identified and analysed.

SECTION XII (PROPS LXX–LXXXIV; CAJORI, PP. 193–213) THE ATTRACTIVE FORCES OF SPHERICAL BODIES

Previously Newton had written as if he were dealing with point masses. How, at last, he asked would 'spherical bodies consisting of Particles' act upon each other? The answer came, in prop.LXXV, that they would act as if their masses were located at their centres. Consequently, it was necessary to point out that the inverse square law ranged between the centres of bodies.

SECTION XIII (PROPS LXXXV–XCIII; CAJORI, PP. 214–25) THE ATTRACTIVE FORCES OF BODIES WHICH ARE NOT SPHERICAL
SECTION XIV (PROPS XCIV–XCVIII; CAJORI, PP. 226–33)

Book I concluded with an account of the motions of 'very small bodies when agitated by centripetal forces'. It is of note for its application, consciously evoked, to the phenomena of light. His aim, however, he insisted, was not to consider the nature of light, or even whether light rays were bodies, but to determine 'the curves of bodies which are extremely like the curves of the rays' (Cajori, pp. 230–1). Snell's law was derived (prop.XCIV), and diffraction, along with a number of other optical properties, was considered.

Book II   The Motion of Bodies in Resisting Mediums

SECTIONS I–IV (PROPS I–XVIII; CAJORI, PP. 235–89)

Newton began by considering three ways in which a medium may resist moving bodies: in the ratio of their velocities (sect.I); as the square of their velocities (sect.II); and partly in the ratio and partly as the square of their velocities (sect.III). Sect.IV opened up the question of the circular motion of bodies in resisting mediums under the conditions that the medium's density varied inversely as the distance from an immovable centre and the centripetal force was as the square of the density (prop.XV). Throughout these sections, and indeed throughout the whole Book II, it is seldom clear where mathematics ends and physics begins. In the concluding *scholium* to sect.I he noted 'that the resistance of bodies is in the ratio of the velocity, is more a mathematical hypothesis than a physical one'; elsewhere he was less explicit.

LEMMA II (SECT.II; CAJORI, PP. 249–51)

This contains Newton's approach to the calculus represented by his method of moments.

SECTION V (PROPS XIX–XXIII; CAJORI, PP. 290–303)

The general principles of hydrostatics are presented. On the assumption that 'a fluid be composed of particles fleeing from each other', and with forces inversely proportional to distances of their centres, then the density will be as the compression, a form of Boyle's law (prop.XXIII).

SECTION VI (PROPS XXIV–XXXI; CAJORI, PP. 303–26)

Newton moves on to consider 'The motion and resistance of pendulous bodies'. Three cases are discussed: pendulous bodies 'resisted in the ratio of the moments of time' (props XXV, XXVIII); in the ratio of their velocity (prop.XXVI); and as the square of their velocities (props XXVII, XXIX). In corollary VII to prop.XXIV Newton made the important claim of the equivalence between the inertial and gravitational mass of bodies. The claim was based upon 'experiments made with the greatest accuracy' in which Newton compared the mass of bodies with 'the weights of the same bodies in different places'. Everywhere, he declared, he found 'the quantity of matter in bodies to be proportional to their weight'.

In the concluding *scholium* Newton demonstrated how 'the resistance of mediums' could be found 'by pendulums oscillating therein'. In impressive detail he recorded the results obtained with a 10½ ft pendulum. He also reported the results of a further pendulum experiment which seemed to count against the existence of the ether (Cajori, pp. 325–6).

SECTION VII (PROPS XXXII–XL; CAJORI, PP. 327–66)

The longest section of *Principia*, it deals with 'The motion of fluids, and the resistance made to projected bodies'. The final *scholium* reported the results of fourteen experiments in which various wax and lead globes were allowed to descend in water-filled wooden vessels 9½ ft and 15½ ft. In other experiments globes filled with mercury and with air were dropped from the top of St Paul's. He found that the times of descent of the bodies, in both water and air, agreed with his theoretical predictions.

Projected bodies, Newton proposed, were resisted 'in a ratio compounded of the squared ratio of their velocities, and the squared ratio of their diameters, and the simple ratio of the density of the parts of the system' (prop.XXXIII). The insight has been retained in modern textbooks as Newton's law of fluid friction (Pitt, 1977, p. 258).

Prop.XXXIV and the following *scholium* dealt with the problem of the form of the solid of least resistance.

SECTIONS VIII–IX (PROPS XLI–LIII; CAJORI, PP. 367–96)

The final two sections deal largely with wave motion. It is first demonstrated (prop.XLI) that pressure was not normally 'propagated through a fluid in rectilinear directions'. It would become his strongest argument against the wave theory of light. On wave motion itself he demonstrated that a wave's velocity varies as the square root of its breadth (prop.XLV), how to find a wave's velocity (prop.XLVI) and how to find the wavelength (prop.L). The following *scholium* dealt with how to calculate the speed of sound.

In the concluding sections, 'The circular motion of fluids', Newton chose to deliver a powerful attack against the Cartesian theory of vortices (prop.LII and *scholium*, prop.LIII and *scholium*). The attack is based, in part, on the hypothesis with which the section opens (Cajori, p. 385): 'The resistance arising from the want of lubricity in the parts of a fluid, is . . . proportional to the velocity with which the parts of the fluid are separated from one another.'

Book III   System of the World

RULES OF REASONING IN PHILOSOPHY I–IV (CAJORI, PP. 398–400)

I   A version of Ockham's razor, claiming the need to admit only those causes of natural things which are both 'true and sufficient to explain their appearances'.

II Principle of uniformity that to the same 'natural effects we must . . . assign the same causes'.

III The principle of primary qualities that qualities of bodies admitting neither of 'intensification nor remission' are to be taken as 'the universal qualities of all bodies whatsoever'.

IV The principle of induction that 'propositions inferred by general induction from phenomena' are accurate 'or very nearly true'.

PHENOMENA I–VI (CAJORI, PP. 401–5)

I Circumjovial planets observe Kepler's area and harmonic laws.

II So do the circumsaturnal planets.

III The planets orbit the sun.

IV The planets observe Kepler's harmonic law.

V The planets observe, in their solar orbit, Kepler's area law.

VI The moon, in its terrestrial orbit, observes Kepler's area law.

PROPOSITIONS (CAJORI, PP. 406–547)

Props I–III The circumjovial planets, the planets and the moon all obey the inverse square law with respect to the sun.

Props IV–XII Newton here deals with the nature and operation of gravity and includes: the moon test (prop.IV); that gravity and centripetal force are one and the same (*scholium* to prop.V); that 'all bodies gravitate towards every planet' (prop.VI); gravity between bodies proportional to the matter they contain (prop.VII).

Props XIII–XIX Features of planetary orbits.

Prop.XX 'To find and compare together the weights of bodies in the different regions of the earth', as determined by observations of pendulums at various sites around the world.

Prop.XXI The equinoctial points go backwards and the earth's axis nutates.

Props XXII–XXXV The main features of the moon's complex motions are presented and include: perturbations caused by the sun (prop.XXV); diameter of lunar orbit (prop.XXVIII); variation of the moon (prop.XXIX), nodes (props XXX–XXXIII); inclination of lunar orbit to ecliptic (props XXXIV–XXXV). Also included (Cajori, pp. 464–7) is John Machin's *The Motion of the Moon's Nodes*.

Props XXXVI–XXXVII Tides, as caused by the sun (prop.XXXVI) and the moon (prop.XXXVII).

Prop.XXXVIII 'To find the figure of the moon's body.'

Prop.XXXIX 'To find the precession of the equinoxes.'

Lemma IV–lemma XI and props XL–XLII Comets: they are more remote than the moon (lemma IV); move in 'some of the conic sections' and obey Kepler's area law (prop.XL); to determine a comet's parabolic orbit from three observations; the comet of 1680; the nature of comets; their tails, atmosphere and coma (prop.XLI).

General *Scholium* Vortices, God, ether, gravity, hypotheses.
Also included are the following hypotheses.

Hypothesis I That the centre of the system of the world is immovable
(following prop.X; Cajori, p. 419).

Hypothesis II On the motion of the equinoctial points (before
prop.XXXIX; Cajori, p. 489).

OBSERVATIONAL TESTS AND PROBLEMS

While it was clearly impossible to perform simple experiments in the
laboratory to test Newton's claims for universal gravitation and its
operation through the inverse square law, it was none the less quite
possible to probe their plausibility and accuracy in the heavens themselves. The eighteenth century consequently became a time of great
drama for mathematical physicists as they sought to measure *Principia*
against the heavens. Four problems in particular were to emerge as
serious challenges.

The inequality of Jupiter and Saturn

In 1625 Kepler observed that the positions of Jupiter and Saturn were
not in agreement with accepted values for their mean motion. The
disagreement appeared to be progressive, with Jupiter accelerating and
Saturn slowing down. Halley took up the problem in 1695 and, using
ancient texts, judged that in the last 1,000 years Jupiter had advanced
its position 2° 19' while Saturn had been retarded some 0° 57'. If the
processes were allowed to continue, more than the validity of Newtonian
mechanics was at stake; the solar system itself would collapse, with
Jupiter leaving the system and Saturn falling into the sun. The inequalities, Halley thought, might arise from the mutual attraction between
the two planets.

A further attempt was made on the problem in 1748 and 1752 when
the *Académie des sciences* challenged the mathematicians of Europe to
derive the inequalities rigorously from the assumption of universal gravitation varying inversely as the square of the distance. The prize was
awarded to Euler on both occasions but, despite making important
contributions to the theory of planetary perturbations, the solution to
the main problem eluded him.

The first new insight into the problem was glimpsed by J. H. Lambert
(1728–77) in 1773. A more careful examination of the records revealed
that the observed changes were not progressive and that after a certain
time Jupiter began to decelerate and Saturn to accelerate. This, in theory,
by suggesting a periodic system, should be enough to maintain the
stability of the solar system; there remained the problem of deriving the
process from *Principia*.

It was left to Laplace in 1784, almost a century after the publication of *Principia*, to provide the solution. The process, he argued, was generated by the near identity of five revolutions of Jupiter with two of Saturn's orbits, 59 years, and led to a cyclic variation in the conjunctions of the two planets with a period of 900 years. Laplace was well aware of the implications of his work. 'The irregularities of the two planets appeared formerly to be inexplicable by the law of universal gravitation – they now form one of its most striking proofs' (Pannekoek, 1961, p. 302).

The shape of the earth

In Book III, prop.XIX, Newton tackled the problem of how to find 'the proportion of the axis of a planet to the diameters perpendicular thereto'. He concluded that 'the diameter of the earth at the equator is to its diameter from pole to pole as 230 to 229'. The implications of the calculation were clear: the earth was an oblate spheroid, flattened at the poles and elongated at the equator; further, geodetic measurements should verify the claim by revealing that the length of one degree of meridian was shorter at the equator than at the poles.

In one of the earliest examples of 'big science', the *Académie des sciences* began to organise in the 1730s two expeditions charged with making precisely these measurements. Pierre Bouguer and La Condamine travelled to Peru in 1735 to make the equatorial measurement, while in the following year de Maupertuis and Clairaut left for Lapland where they would collect the relevant polar figures. The final results were not available until 1743. They clearly revealed, however, the soundness of Newton's initial calculations. While at 66° north in Lapland a degree was found to contain 57,395 toises (1 toise equals 1.949 metres), at Quito on the equator a comparable degree measured only 56,768 toises.

Halley's comet

A second successful confirmation of Newtonian theory was obtained with regard to the return of Halley's comet. Halley had claimed that the comet of 1682 was the same as the comet of 1531 and of 1607. It would return, he predicted, at Christmas 1758. It was necessary, however, for the credibility of Newtonian mechanics, for astronomers to show that they could predict accurately such a precise feature of the comet's orbit as the time it would reach perihelion. The calculations were undertaken by Clairaut, with the assistance of Mme Lepaute, and turned out to be so elaborate that Clairaut began to fear that they would only be completed long after the comet had been and gone. He was finally able to claim in late 1758 that, because of the gravitational attraction exercised by Jupiter and Saturn, the comet would require an extra 618 days to complete its orbit. Perihelion was predicted for 13 April 1759.

The comet was, in fact, first sighted on Christmas day 1758 in Dresden by the amateur astronomer G. Palitsch; perihelion was observed in

March 1759, close enough to Clairaut's predicted date to be seen as a major triumph for Newtonian theory.

Motion of the lunar apsides

The extremities of the major axis of the orbit of a planet are known as apsides and the imaginary line joining them is accordingly known as the line of apsides. In the case of the moon the line connects the lunar apogee and perigee. In Book I, prop.XLV, Newton had calculated that, in the case of the moon, the line of apsides would advance 1° 31′ 14″ each month. In the third edition of *Principia* (1726) the figures were changed to 1° 31′ 28″ and the further comment was added: 'The apse of the moon is about twice as swift.' It is sometimes claimed that Newton refused to admit errors in his work. In this case he actually drew the reader's attention to a mistake he was unable to correct himself.

The issue was tackled by Clairaut, Euler and Jean d'Alembert in the late 1740s and early 1750s in response to the inevitable problems set by the societies of the day. Clairaut's first attempts led precisely to the same figures Newton had derived long before. So recalcitrant did the problem appear to Clairaut that at one point he even considered modifying the inverse square law. Under certain conditions, he proposed, another term should be added which varied inversely as the fourth power of the distance.

Such moves soon proved to be premature. Shortly afterwards Clairaut discovered a number of neglected terms which, when added, harmonised the predicted calculations with the observed movements of the lunar apogee.

Cajori (p. 649) has claimed that Newton had in fact 'overcome the difficulty' he displayed so prominently in 1726.

BOOK II, PROPOSITION X

Proposition X deals with how an object under uniform gravity will move in a medium which resists 'as the product of the density of the medium and the square of the velocity'. In example I he considered the problem of finding the density of a medium which would permit a body to move in a semicircle. In August 1710 Johann Bernoulli informed Leibniz that he had discovered something wrong with this particular example. Bernoulli was convinced that Newton's error demonstrated his failure to have fully mastered the calculus. He did not inform Newton of the error immediately, hoping perhaps that the same error would be repeated in the awaited second edition of *Principia*.

And so it would if Nicolas Bernoulli, Johann's nephew, had not visited Newton in London in September 1712 and informed Newton of his uncle's discovery. Newton claimed to de Moivre that the mistake was a simple one. The error was spotted and eliminated by October and the corrected text sent to Cotes on 6 January 1713. Cotes replied the same day that he was well satisfied. No acknowledgment was made to either Bernoulli in the forthcoming *Principia* (1713), an omission Bernoulli and Leibniz found quite intolerable.

BOOK I, PROPS XI–XIII AND THE INVERSE PROBLEM OF CENTRAL FORCES

In origin, *Principia* began in August 1684 with a visit to Cambridge by Halley. He asked Newton what path a planet would adopt if it was attracted to the sun by an inverse square law. Newton answered that it would be an ellipse and, he added significantly, he had 'calculated it'. Simplifying somewhat, and allowing 'ISL', 'EO', 'CS', and '→', to stand for inverse square law, elliptical orbit, conic section, and implies respectively, Newton had claimed in 1684 to be able to prove:

$$\text{ISL} \rightarrow \text{EO} \tag{A}$$

It would be natural to assume that when *Principia* finally did appear in 1687 it would contain a proof of (A).

Robert Weinstock (1982), an American mathematical physicist, has recently argued that no such proof is to be found anywhere in *Principia*. What *is* to be found, at prop. XI, is a proof of the proposition that if a body moves in an elliptical orbit under the influence of a force directed to one focus of the ellipse, then that force will indeed vary inversely as the square of the distance (Cajori, pp. 56–7):

$$\text{EO} \rightarrow \text{ISL} \tag{B}$$

Similar results were claimed in props XII–XIII for hyperbolic and parabolic orbits respectively. This allows (B) to be generalised as:

$$\text{CS} \rightarrow \text{ISL} \tag{C}$$

But (B), which is proved, is not the same as (A). Where then, asked Weinstock, is the proof of (A)? To his amazement he could find no such proof; nor could he find any acknowledgment of its absence in contemporary studies of *Principia*.

At one point, Weinstock has noted, in cor. I to prop. XIII, Newton did seem to offer a proof. There, it is claimed, that from the last three propositions (props XI–XIII) it follows that bodies 'urged by the action of a centripetal force that is inversely proportional to the square of the distance . . . will move in one of the conic sections' (Cajori, p. 61), or:

$$\text{ISL} \rightarrow \text{CS} \tag{D}$$

But, despite Newton's use of the phrase 'it follows that', the proposition (D) is merely asserted and offered without proof. Nor is it the case that, as Newton claimed:

$$CS \rightarrow ISL \; . \rightarrow . \; ISL \rightarrow CS \qquad\qquad\qquad\qquad (E)$$

The step is no more permissible than the claim that from the proposition 'All lions are carnivores' it follows that 'All carnivores are lions.'

The absence of a proof had been noted much earlier in 1710 by Johann Bernoulli. Newton had failed to demonstrate, he argued, how to derive curves from forces, the so-called inverse problem, and went on to offer his own proof. Newton himself, at about the same time, must have become aware that the position was unsatisfactory, for a brief supplement was sent to Roger Cotes in October 1709 for inclusion in the planned second edition of *Principia* (*C*, V, pp. 5–6). Although the addition has been taken by Hall (*C*, V, p. 6) as 'Newton's first direct proof of the inverse problem of motion', Weinstock has dissented, arguing that the addition to cor.I of prop.XIII merely demonstrated that '*if* the inverse-square orbit is a conic section, then that conic section is uniquely determined by initial conditions' (Weinstock, 1982, p. 611).

If Newton did not, in *Principia* or elsewhere, offer a solution of the inverse problem, who did? In his survey of the problem, Aiton (1964) has noted that two solutions by Bernoulli and Jakob Hermann were presented in 1710 to the Paris *Académie*. Ironically, Bernoulli's solution was taken from *Principia* Book I, prop.XLI, and involved little more than a translation of Newton's geometric approach into the language of analysis. It remains unclear why Newton failed to take the step himself.

Priority dispute

1666 October 1666 Tract composed.

1669 *De analysi* written and shown to I. Barrow and J. Collins.

1671 *Methodus fluxionum* composed.

1672 December 10. Newton revealed to Collins that he possessed a general method of 'drawing tangents to all curve lines' (*C*, I, p. 247).

1673 January–March. Leibniz visited London and met Oldenburg.
April 6. Oldenburg sent Leibniz a report on the state of British mathematics prepared by Collins. It referred to Newton's method of infinite series without revealing any of its details.

1675 Autumn. Leibniz developed the basic ideas of his differential calculus (Hofmann, 1974, pp. 187–201).

1676 June 13. *Epistola prior* sent to Leibniz; it was received by him on August 16.
July. Oldenburg sent Leibniz an *Abridgement* of the *Historiola*.
October. Leibniz spent ten days in London. He met Collins, who showed to him his copy of *De analysi* and the *Historiola*.

October 24. *Epistola posterior* sent to Leibniz; it was received by him in June 1677.

1682 Leibniz published his *De vera proportione circuli* (*AE*), his study of the quadrature of the circle by means of infinite series.

1684 Leibniz published his *Nova methodus pro maximis et minimis* (*AE*), his first publication on the calculus. It was restricted to differentiation and, because of its sparse presentation, was described by the Bernoulli brothers as 'an enigma rather than an explication' (Boyer, 1959, pp. 207).

1685 Material from 1676 *Epistola prior* was summarised in John Wallis's *Algebra*. No reference was made to fluxions or to differentiation.

1686 Leibniz published his *De geometria recondita* (*AE*), a work as compressed as the *Nova* (1684), and containing his first account of integration.

1687 Section I of Book I of *Principia* contained details of Newton's method of 'first and last ratios'.

1691 E. Halley and J. Raphson shown *Methodus fluxionum* (1671) by Newton.
De quadratura composed.

1693 A brief account of fluxions was published in Wallis's Latin *Algebra*, vol.II; it also contained the first public description of Newton's dot notation.

1696 Bernoulli published his brachistochrone challenge problem.
L'Hopital published his *Analyse des infiniment petits*, the first textbook on the differential calculus.

1697 January 30. Newton communicated his solution of Bernoulli's problem to Montague and published it anonymously in the February *PT* (*C*, IV, pp. 220–7).

1699 Wallis included in vol.III of his *Algebra* the full texts of the two *Epistola* of 1676.
Fatio published his *Lineae brevissimi* in which he commented:

> Whether Leibniz, the second inventor, borrowed anything from him, I prefer that judgment be not mine, but those who have seen Newton's letters and his other manuscripts. Nor will . . . the active exertions of Leibniz in everywhere ascribing the invention of the calculus to himself, impose upon any person who has examined those papers as I have done.

1700 Leibniz reviewed Fatio's *Lineae* (1699) in the *AE* and insisted upon the priority of his *Nova* (1684); he conceded that 'Newton had gone much further' in *Principia*.

1704 Newton published his *De quadratura* and *Enumeratio* as appendices to the *Opticks*. He noted in the Advertisement: 'In a letter written to Mr. Leibniz in . . . 1679 . . . I mention'd a Method by which

I had found some general Theorems about squaring Curvilinear Figures'.

1705 Leibniz reviewed anonymously in the *AE* the mathematical papers of the *Opticks*. A rather obscure comparison was made between Newton and Honoré Fabri. Both had used alternative mathematical techniques: Newton had used fluxions rather than differentials; Fabri had substituted 'the advance of movements for the method of Cavalieri'.

1710 John Keill published *The Laws of Centripetal Force* (*PT*) in which he asserted Newton's priority and went on to charge Leibniz with having published Newton's 'arithmetic of fluxions . . . having changed the name and symbolism'.

1711 Newton's *De analysi* and *De quadratura* were published in *Analysis per quantitatum series*.

February 21. Leibniz complained to Hans Sloane, Secretary of the RS, against the accusations made against him by Fatio (1699, *Lineae brevissimi*) and Keill (1710, *The Laws of Centripetal Force*) (*C*, V, pp. 96–7).

April 3. Keill drew Newton's attention to Leibniz's 1705 review in the *AE* (*C*, V, p. 115).

May. Keill replied to Leibniz in an apparently conciliatory manner. He still insisted, however, that Newton was 'the first discoverer' of the differential calculus and that details of his discovery had been sent to Leibniz by Oldenburg in 1676 (*C*, V, pp. 133–49).

December. A second complaint to Sloane from Leibniz about the 'unjust braying' of Keill (*C*, V, pp. 207–8).

1712 March 6. A Committee of the RS was set up to evaluate the competing claims of Keill and Leibniz.

April 24. The Committee reported to the RS in favour of Newton (*C*, V, pp. xxvi–xxvii).

1713 January 29. The Report of the RS and the accompanying documentation were published under the title *Commercium epistolicum*. Leibniz's attention was drawn to the piece by Bernoulli on May 27 (*C*, VI, pp. 1–5).

February–March (*AE*). Bernoulli, convinced of Newton's incomplete understanding of the process of differentiation, published details of an error in prop.X of Book II of *Principia*.

May–June (*JL*). Keill published an anonymous *Lettre de Londres* in which the Newtonian case was stated in relatively moderate terms. The same issue of the *JL* also contained a French translation of the RS report of 24 April 1712.

July 29. Leibniz published his anonymous reply, *Charta volans* (*C*, VI, pp. 15–19), to the RS report of 24 April 1712. It appeared as a separate pamphlet and, together with a German translation of the report, in *AE* and, in a French translation, the *JL*. Reference was made to the 'judgment of a leading mathematician' that 'the true way of differentiating differentials was not known to Newton until long after it was familiar to others'.

November–December (*JL*). Leibniz published some brief anonymous *Remarques* in reply to Keill's *Lettre de Londres* in the May–June *JL* of 1713 (*C*, VI, pp. 30–2). He had begun to adopt a harder position. Newton was unaware of the differential calculus in 1687, Leibniz argued, as can be seen by the mistake identified by Bernoulli in the February–March *AE* of 1713. The material published in Wallis's *Algebra*, vols II (1693) and III (1699), was merely Leibniz's own work recycled.

1714 February–August. Unsuccessful attempts were made by John Chamberlayne to reconcile Leibniz and Newton (*C*, VI, pp. 71, 103–4, 126–7, 140, 152–3, 159, 173).

Newton drafted, but did not publish, a lengthy reply to Leibniz's *Charta volans* of July 1713 (*C*, VI, pp. 80–90). He claimed to have mastered higher-order fluxions by 1672; Leibniz's own results derived ultimately from James Gregory and Newton himself.

July–August (*JL*). Keill published his *Réponse* to the *Remarques* (November–December 1713) of Leibniz. The text was cleared with Newton (*C*, VI, pp. 113–14, 128–30, 135, 135–9, 142), and incorporated several of his suggestions.

1715 April 1715–April 1716. Further attempts at a reconciliation were made by the Abbé Conti (*C*, VI, pp. 215, 250–3, 285–8, 295–6, 304–12, 322–4); they were as unsuccessful as the earlier attempts of Chamberlayne in 1714.

February (*PT*). Newton published the anonymous *Account*, his fullest account of the development of his own mathematical ideas and their relationship to Leibniz's work (Hall, 1980, pp. 263–314).

Joseph Raphson published his *History of Fluxions* in which he claimed incorrectly that Newton had revealed his fluxional method to Leibniz in 1676.

1716 A number of foreign ambassadors, including the Hanoverian minister and the husband of George I's mistress, Baron Kilmansegge, were called to the RS to examine the papers assembled for the *CE*. Unimpressed by such documents, they recommended Leibniz and Newton should communicate directly.

February. Conti communicated to Newton the challenge problem posed by Leibniz; Newton's solution was published in the *PT* (*C*, VI, pp. 290–2).

July (*AE*). *Epistola pro eminente mathematico*, an anonymous piece by Bernoulli, edited by C. Wolf, and supposedly written on behalf of Bernoulli. The confused Bernoulli made the fatal mistake of referring to a particular formula as 'mine' (*meam*); he later argued it was a misprint for 'that' (*eam*).

November 14. Death of Leibniz.

1717 Newton added to an enlarged *History of Fluxions* (Raphson, 1715) some *Observations* (*C*, VI, pp. 341–9) and Leibniz's letter to Conti of March 1716 (*C*, VI, pp. 304–12). By this time Newton was claiming to have invented the 'Methods of Series and Fluxions in the Year 1665', and was unwilling to allow an independent discovery for any published results of Leibniz.

May 17. Keill drew Newton's attention to the *Epistola pro eminente mathematico* of Bernoulli (1716) and the 'impudence of Bernoulli' of speaking of himself in such a dishonest way (*C*, VI, pp. 385–6). Keill went on to produce a lengthy reply, read and checked by Newton, which would remain unpublished until 1720.

1718 De Monmort served as intermediary between Bernoulli and Newton (*C*, VI, pp. 435–8, 443).

May 2. Keill reported to Newton that Bernoulli had denied that he was the author of the *Epistola pro eminente mathematico* (1716) (*C*, VI, pp. 443–4).

Newton was shown by des Maizeaux the proofs of vol. II of his *Recueil* (*C*, VI, pp. 454–63). He proposed a number of amendations and additions, some of which des Maizeaux adopted.

1719 June 24. Bernoulli informed Newton 'in the name of everything sacred to humanity' that he had never commented anonymously on Newton or his works (*C*, VII, pp. 42–6).

September 29. Newton accepted Bernoulli's assurances and joined with him in wishing to see an end to the dispute (*C*, VII, pp. 69–70).

November. Newton offers des Maizeaux's bookseller twelve guineas to defer publication of the *Recueil* for six months.

December 10. Bernoulli replied to Newton's letter of September in an equally friendly manner. Why, he asked, was his name no longer entered on the list of foreign members of the *RS*? Newton arranged for its immediate restoration (*C*, VII, pp. 75–9).

1720 The *Recueil* of des Maizeaux finally appeared. It contained, amongst much else, several of Newton's earlier dismissive references to Bernoulli. Des Maizeaux also claimed, despite Bernoulli's denials, that he was the 'leading mathematician' referred to in Leibniz's *Charta volans* (1713).

1721 February 5. Bernoulli complained to Varignon of the descriptions of him in the 1720 *Recueil* of des Maizeaux as 'a pretended mathematician', 'a novice' and 'a knight-errant' (*C*, VII, pp. 130–2).

In letters to Varignon in August and September (*C*, VII, pp. 141–2, 160–5), Newton insisted that his quarrel was with Leibniz, not Bernoulli.

August. John Keill died.

1722 A second edition of the *CE* appeared with the *Account* of February

1715 included in a Latin translation as the *Recensio*, plus some additional material. It was to be Newton's last public word on the dispute.

July 28. Bernoulli informed Varignon that he expected an apology from Newton over the accusations made against him in the 1720 *Recueil*; further, Newton should instruct his 'bande' to cease their harassment.

December 22. Death of Varignon.

Nicholas Hartsoeker in his *Recueil de plusieurs pièces de physique* (Amsterdam, A Collection of Several Pieces on Physics) once more spoke of Bernoulli pompously describing himself as 'an excellent mathematician'.

1723 January 26. Bernoulli, in his final approach to Newton, asked him to disown the report of Hartsoeker in his *Recueil* of 1722 (C, VII, pp. 218–21). Newton made no reply, and with Bernoulli's letter the dispute, begun in 1699 with the *Lineae*, finally ended.

1761 James Wilson in Benjamin Robin's *Mathematical Tracts*, vol. II first revealed that Newton was the author of the *Account* of February 1715.

Prisms

In his papers and published works Newton referred to several prisms he had bought and worked with. Attempts have been made to distinguish and identify the various prisms used. Six extant prisms have been claimed for Newton.

1 One was presented to the British Museum in 1927 by the Rev H. T. Inman of Grantham, a descendant of Newton. According to Mills (1981, p. 30) it is probably post-1700 and 'of much better quality and higher refractive index and dispersion than any he worked with in the early years'.

2 Three prisms in the Treviso Museum near Venice were supposedly acquired by Algarotti. Examination by Cohen (1957), however, suggested they were made in Italy for Algarotti.

3 There are two further supposedly Newtonian prisms in the Whipple Science Museum, Cambridge. One was donated by TCC, the other by the Cavendish. Neither, according to Mills (1981), matches any of Newton's descriptions of his prisms.

He reported the purchase of the following prisms.

1 'In the beginning of the year 1666 . . . I procured me a triangular glass prism, to try therewith the celebrated phenomena of colours.' So began Newton in his first paper on light and colour in 1672.

2 His first prism, according to a note made by Conduitt from a lost

manuscript, was purchased in 1664 at the Stourbridge fair to try out Descartes's theory of colour.

3 The Fitzwilliam Notebook records the purchase of three prisms in 1667.

4 Certain experiments in the *Opticks* require two 90° prisms. The prism used in the 1672 paper had an angle of 63°12'. Other experiments require four 60° prisms.

5 In a conversation with Conduitt on 31 August 1726 Newton recalled the purchase of a prism at 'Sturbridge fair' in August 1665.

5 is undoubtedly incorrect as Newton was in Woolsthorpe in August 1665. Doubts have also been raised about the accuracy of 1 by Hall (1948), who has argued that Newton mistakenly wrote '1666' for '1665'. As he had claimed elsewhere to have arrived at his theory of colours in January 1666, he is unlikely to have done so immediately after first examining 'the celebrated phenomena'.

See also Experimentum crucis

Problems for Construing Equations

The manuscript was sent by Newton to John Collins on 20 August 1672. A copy made by Collins passed, via William Jones, to the Macclesfield Collection. The original was returned to Newton and eventually to the ULC as Add. MS 3963.9, pp. 70–106. 'I think 'em not fit to be seen by any but your selfe', Newton had told Collins (*C*, I, p. 231), a view presumably shared by Horsley who examined them in 1777 and declined to publish them. They were published for the first and only time in *MP*, II, pp. 450–516.

The work is mainly concerned with the geometrical resolution of algebraic equations, presenting material for the resolution of quadratic, cubic, biquadratic and higher-order equations. The material was refashioned and re-used in the unpublished *De constructione problematum geometricorum* of some time around 1705 (*MP*, VIII, pp. 200–18).

Prolegomena ad lexici prophetici partem secundam, in quibus agitur De forma sanctuarii Judaici . . . commentarium

---

An unpublished manuscript of about 20,000 autograph words, it is to be found in the Babson Institute Library, Wellesley, Massachusetts. Contained in the work are six sketches drawn by Newton and showing details of the Temple. One such drawing can be seen in Manuel (1963, p. 148), Babson (1935, p. 214) and RSW (p. 347). A partial text, also unpublished, is said to be included in Yahuda MS 14. A shortened account was published as Chapter 5 of *Chronology (1728)*.

See also Solomon's temple and the cubit

Prophetic figures

A manuscript from the Yahuda Collection in Jerusalem consisting of seventy prophetic figures taken from the Bible and other near-Eastern literature. In a second section, entitled 'The Proof', Newton set out to show how the figures of prophecy should be interpreted. Westfall (RSW, p. 327) quotes as an example the figure of the balance as it occurs in the 'ye third Seale' (Revelation 6). He objected to the claim that it stood as 'an emblem of famin'. No such authority, Newton declared, could be found 'in scripture or other authentic writings'. Further, famine is shown in the Bible by 'ye tearing of doggs', as in Jeremiah 15:3, while the balance, when it does appear, is used to denote justice or judgment (Job 31:4; Daniel 5:27). Newton concluded by claiming to have found 'ye same purpose in ye doctrine of ye Indian interpreters'.

Propositiones, de motu

This was the title assigned by S. P. Rigaud to Newton's *De motu* which he published for the first time in his *Historical Essay* (1838), Appendix I. It was later published once more, still in its original Latin, by W. W. Rouse Ball in his *An Essay on Newton's Principia* (1893, pp. 35–51).

Rigaud had taken the text from the Register of the Royal Society, vol. 6, where it had been entered some time between December 1684 and February 1685. Untitled in the Register, Rigaud gave the work the above title. It is not significantly different from the four other known manuscripts of *De motu* and is, according to Herivel (1965, p. 257), 'essentially a copy' of *De motu corporum in gyrum*.

See also De motu; Principia, Origin and production

Providentialism

In 1692 Richard Bentley delivered the inaugural series of Boyle Lectures under the title *A Confutation of Atheism from the Origin and Frame of the World* in which he sought to show that the Universe could neither be created nor continue to exist without 'the Power and Providence of a Divine Being'. In this view he was wholly supported by Newton.

Providentialism did not begin with Newton and Bentley. The works of Robert Boyle, for example, are rich in such ideas. Another who sought to reveal the divine providence was Walter Charleton in his *The Darkness of Atheism* (1652). Note, he pointed out, the orbit of the earth. If it had been placed closer to the sun, it would have been burnt up; placed further away, it would have been too cold to support life. Charleton went on to distinguish the heathen, who 'absurdly dreamed that all effects are inevitably produced . . . by natural causes', from the Christian, with his awareness 'that the precise and opportune contingency of every individual event proceeds from . . . providence' (Westfall, 1973, p. 70).

Newton made it clear in his 1693 *Four Letters . . . to Dr Bentley* that he was not on the side of the heathens with their 'absurd' dreams in the supremacy of natural causes. Four points in particular were stressed by Newton.

1 How could the original matter of the universe have developed into two quite distinct kinds of body: a shining sun, and several opaque planets? Only by, he answered, the 'Contrivance of a voluntary Agent' (*PLNP*, p. 282).

2 Gravity could account for the descent of planets towards the sun. What, though, could impress on them their 'transverse Motions'? And why, given their angular momentum, did all the planets lie in the same plane, and revolve in the same direction? It can only have been 'the Effect of Counsel' (*PLNP*, pp. 284–5). The argument was repeated in the General *Scholium* (Cajori, p. 544) and in Query 31 (*Opticks*, p. 402).

3 While Newton was unimpressed by Bentley's claim that the 'Inclination of the Earth's Axis' showed the hand of Providence, he conceded that 'the diurnal Rotations of the Sun and Planets . . . could hardly arise from any Cause purely mechanical' (*PLNP*, p. 289).

4 Newton had supposed that originally matter was 'evenly spread through the Heavens' and had formed the solar system under the influence of gravity. But how could such a situation ever have arisen? Only with the aid of a Deity (*PLNP*, p. 311).

Newton also deployed more familiar providential arguments. In Query 31 he recognised the 'Uniformity in the Bodies of Animals' as having arisen from the 'Wisdom and Skill of a powerful ever-living Agent' (*Opticks*, pp. 402–3).

In the 1706 Latin *Opticks* Newton seemed to be assigning a further role to God in the universe. In Query 31 he had written of the manner in which 'Motion . . . is always upon the Decay'. Consequently there is a necessity for 'conserving or recruiting it', a process which took place through such active principles as gravity, or through 'the dictates of a will'. He further spoke of some 'inconsiderable Irregularities' in the solar system, arising through 'the mutual Actions of Comets and Planets upon one another', which would occasionally demand a 'Reformation' of the system (*Opticks*, p. 402).

The point was seized upon by Leibniz in his correspondence with Clarke. Newton and his followers, Leibniz scoffed, seemed to have a 'very odd' idea of God. Could not God have had the foresight to endow the universe with a 'perpetual motion'? Resorting to the fashionable image of the clockmaker, an image which would be deployed *ad nauseam* in the following century, Leibniz went on to ask whether God really needed to wind up his watch from time to time? Or, whether he was really obliged to clean it now and then by an 'extraordinary concourse' (Alexander, 1956, p. 11)? The official Newtonian answer to the point, presented by Clarke, was that ''tis not a diminution, but the true glory of his workmanship, that nothing is done without his continual government and inspection' (Alexander, 1956, p. 14).

Newton's providentialism brought him into conflict with the orthodox mechanical philosophy of his day. Given the restrictions mentioned above, it was no longer plausible to maintain that all observable events could be explained solely in terms of the mechanist's paradigm of matter and motion. In this form providentialism has continued to be an attractive option to a number of scientists. Thus, in an echo of Charleton's argument, Freeman Dyson (1979, pp. 250–1) has noted how fortunate we are in the strength of the nuclear force. Any stronger and protons would have bound together making hydrogen a rare element and so preventing the formation of stars like the sun; any weaker and hydrogen 'could not have burnt at all and there would be no heavy elements'. While unwilling, as a modern rather than an eighteenth-century scientist, to claim that 'the architecture of the universe proves the existence of God', Dyson was prepared to conclude that it is 'consistent with the hypothesis that mind plays an essential role in its functioning'.

Publication

Newton's attitude to the publication of his work, and his actual publishing record, stand out in marked contrast to the behaviour normally practised by scientists. It is, to begin with, remarkable that the greatest mathematician of the day published nothing at all in mathematics until 1704, when he was sixty-two. Also of interest is Newton's decision to delay publication of the *Opticks*, one of the most famous works in the entire scientific canon, for thirty years.

On a more general level, four points stand out as being peculiarly Newtonian and untypically scientific.

1 In proportion to the amount of material Newton assembled, he

published very little. Several whole treatises remained unpublished until long after his death. The *Methodus fluxionum*, completed by the early 1670s, and Newton's fullest account of fluxions, appeared for the first time in 1736. Again, the *Lectiones opticae*, completed in the 1670s, received a posthumous publication. There were also, of course, a number of theological and historical works which Newton completed but failed to publish. While there may have been sound reasons for such unwillingness in the field of theology, the only pressures capable of inhibiting scientific publication can have been personal ones.

2 When he did decide to publish, the task was invariably handed over to a friend or colleague. Three editors worked on *Principia*, Clarke translated the *Opticks*, Whiston dealt with the *Arithmetica universalis* and Jones handled in 1711 the other mathematical treatises. There were several others called in to undertake Newton's editorial duties and most received from the author an abundance of advice. Newton was clearly in no way indifferent to the accuracy, appearance and quality of his work; he was also prepared to work on texts and even, sometimes, to follow advice. Having said this, the point remains that he was more comfortable working through a front man. Often this was carried to the extreme, as with the *Arithmetica universalis*, of not even having his name on the title page.

3 Indeed, as a third point, much of Newton's work was issued anonymously and often in a manner intending to deceive.

4 Perhaps the most characteristic feature of Newton's behaviour was his inability to contemplate publication of his work without, at the same time, complaining to anyone who would listen about the folly of his ways. Newton's syndrome was first seen in 1673 and was precipitated by the mildly critical reception accorded his *New Theory about Light and Colour*. Such 'incongruities', Oldenburg advised, could be ignored. Newton's reaction was extreme. 'I intend to be no further sollicitous about matters of Philosophy', he wrote to Oldenburg, adding that he refused to do 'anything more in yt kind' (*C*, I, pp. 294–5). When he did, in 1675, publish new material he reminded Oldenburg of his earlier decision: 'I had formerly purposed never to write any Hypothesis of light & colours, fearing it might be a means to ingage me in vain disputes: but I hope a declar'd resolution to answer nothing that looks like a controversy . . . may defend me from yt fear' (*C*, I, p. 361). To Hooke, four years later, a similar point was made: 'But yet my affection to philosophy being worn out . . . I must acknowledge myself averse from spending that time in writing about it which I think I can spend otherwise more to my own content and the good of others' (*C*, II, p. 302). Halley too, in the course of publishing *Principia*, received similar complaints: 'Philosophy is such an impertinently

litigious Lady that a man had as good be engaged in Law suits as have to do with her. I found it so formerly and now I no sooner come near her again but she gives me warning' (*C*, II, p. 437). The same excuses were being offered to Wallis in 1695; he declined to publish his *Treatise of Light and Colours*, the future *Opticks*, least it create him 'some trouble' (*C*, IV, p. 116). In later life, when pressed about a point, he would respond in a different manner, insisting that it was so long since he had considered such matters that his views could be of no interest. Thus, Conti was told in 1716, 'I have left off Mathematicks 20 years ago' (*C*, VI, p. 285). Two years later the similar, if somewhat inflated, excuse was presented to Varignon: 'It is now above 40 years since I left of all Correspondence by Letters about Mathematicks and Philosophy, and therefore I say nothing further to you about these matters' (*C*, VII, p. 3).

One further aspect of Newton's behaviour, seen on several occasions, involved an initial commitment to the publication of a particular work, followed some time afterwards by the abandoning of all such plans. It was first seen in 1670 with his *Observations on Kinckhuysen*. When completed, he agreed to its publication, specifying only that his contribution should remain anonymous. Shortly afterwards he seemed to lose interest in the project and, buying out the publisher/bookseller, Moses Pitts, deposited the manuscript amongst his private papers, where it remained unseen and unread for 200 years. Later in the 1670s Newton seemed to be considering a major treatise on light and colour. Hooke was informed of the plan in December 1677 (*C*, II, p. 239). Whether obstructed by a fire, or whether due to other reasons, nothing materialised. In 1692 events repeated themselves. He had sent Locke in 1690 his *An Historical Account of Two Notable Corruptions of Scripture* and agreed to its anonymous publication in Holland. Even at such a distance, and in such a form, the planned publication was too disturbing for Newton to contemplate for long and in February 1692 he wrote to Locke: 'Let me entreat you to stop their translation and impression so soon as you can for I designe to suppress them' (*C*, III, p. 195).

Also of note are the number of abandoned works found in Newton's papers. It might be thought that many scholars begin works they fail to complete, and, indeed, for every work published there are dozens of discarded or unfinished manuscripts. Few, however, of these texts are works of genius. It is, thus, difficult to see what could have prevented Newton from both completing and publishing his *De methodis*, a work which, when laid aside in 1672, would have revolutionised European mathematics. Several other mathematical works were laid aside by Newton. In most cases it seems that nothing more subtle was involved than a change in interest of Newton's part. Thus *De computo serierum* and *Mathesos universalis specimina* were abandoned in 1684 when he began work on *Principia*; *De methodis*, on the other hand, could well have been discarded to allow Newton a free hand in the 1670s on problems of alchemy. Once started on such projects Newton tended to work on them single-mindedly until the next one came along to attract him. When it would be, and how long it would last, were unpredictable. It could be a query, a letter, a visit or a book. The effect, whatever the source, was always the same and would involve the dropping of current work in favour of the enthusiastic pursuit of a new project.

See also Anonymity

Public monuments

The growing appreciation of Newton's genius harmonised well with a major change in artistic tolerance and expression. Pevsner has pointed out that, while 'It has always been customary in monarchies to erect monuments to kings or princes after their death', nothing comparable was contemplated for commoners, whatever their achievement, before the eighteenth century. The 'first monuments to national genius', as it happened, were British. Poet's corner at Westminster Abbey, for example, dates from the 1730s (Pevsner, 1976, p. 13).

Few figures were better suited for this emerging awareness of national genius than Newton. Consequently he inspired quite early on a number of elaborate monuments. The best-known of these monuments are described below.

WESTMINSTER ABBEY

The earliest public monument to Newton was unveiled in the Abbey in 1731. Newton's kin had been persuaded, with some reluctance, to spend £500 on a suitable tomb. M. Rysbrack was therefore commissioned to work on a design prepared, under the supervision of John Conduitt, by William Kent. It can still be seen in the nave to the left of the pulpit.

Newton is seen reclining on a sarcophagus. On its front in *basso-rilievo* are putti bearing a prism, a reflecting telescope, a balance, a furnace and some newly-minted coins. Two more putti are holding a scroll on which can be seen a diagram of the solar system and a converging series. The reclining Newton has his elbow supported by four books labelled *Divinity*, *Chronology*, *Optica* and *Phil.Princ.Math*. Behind him there stands a large black pyramid on which is engraved a number of constellations through which the path of the 1681 comet can be traced. Also visible is the solstitial colure shown at the point Newton presumed the Argonauts to have adopted. The accuracy of the iconography is undoubtedly due to Conduitt's supervision.

Missing, though, are two of the most familiar of all Newtonian icons

– the apple tree and the Pope couplet. This latter omission is surprising, for Conduitt had approached Pope and received from him the verse:

All nature and its laws lay hid in night
God said, 'Let Newton be!' and all was light.

There is even a sketch by Conduitt of the tomb with Pope's couplet inscribed on its side. For reasons unknown, the couplet was dropped and replaced by a lengthy list of Newton's achievements followed by the epitaph contributed by Fatio de Duillier: *Sibi gratulentur mortales, tale tantumque extitisse humani generis decus* (Let mortals rejoice that there has existed so great an ornament of the human race).

The monument is not to everyone's taste. Westfall (RSW, p. 874) has dismissed it as a 'baroque monstrosity'. Pevsner's more considered judgment noted that: 'The composition is entirely baroque, yet there is nothing sensational or indeed operatic about this monument. What it has of oratory is nowhere excessive' (Pevsner 1957, p. 396).

STOWE

Kent and Rysbrack in the early 1730s had been commissioned by Lord Cobham, one of Marlborough's generals, to work on a Temple of British Worthies for the gardens of his house at Stowe in Buckinghamshire. His plan was for three temples dedicated in turn to Ancient Virtues, Modern Virtues and British Worthies. The last of the three consists of a semi-circular row of busts. Along with such 'worthies' as Locke, Bacon, Milton, Gresham and Shakespeare, Newton's statue was included. It carries the inscription informing us, amongst other things, that Newton had been made by God for the specific purpose of understanding his works.

It is this work that Pevsner describes as 'the first monument to national genius built specially as such'. It is illustrated in Pevsner (1976, p. 13).

RICHMOND

Something comparable to Stowe was planned in the early 1730s by Queen Caroline for her Richmond home. In 1734 she ordered from Rysbrack busts of Newton, Locke, Boyle, Clarke and Wollaston for a specially-designed grotto. The busts were apparently lost for many years until in 1922 Mrs Arundel Esdaille noted busts of Locke, Newton and Clarke at Kensington Palace. Those of Boyle and Wollaston, she was told, were in one of the greenhouses. The Newton bust can be seen in the Babson *Catalogue* (1950) where it appears as the frontispiece.

TRINITY COLLEGE, CAMBRIDGE

Standing in the ante-chamber to the chapel there stands a full-length white marble statue of Newton. Gowned, he stands holding a prism and, in Brewster's phrase, 'looking upwards with an expression of deepest thought'. Inscribed on the pedestal is the line *Qui genus humanum ingenio superavit* (Who surpassed all Mankind by his genius). The statue is known by many who have never seen it through the well-known lines of Wordsworth:

> Where the statue stood
> Of Newton, with his prism and silent face,
> The marble index of a mind for ever
> Voyaging through strange seas of thought alone.

> (*Prelude*, III, lines 61–4)

The statue was sculpted by L. F. Roubillac and commissioned by Robert Smith, Master of Trinity, at a cost of £500. It was unveiled on 4 February 1755.

For a further £500 Smith commissioned a stained glass window for the south windows of the Wren Library. Designed by Cipriani and executed by Peckitt of York, it was sited in 1774. Paying no attention whatever to chronology, it shows Newton in the company of Sir Francis Bacon about to have a laurel chaplet placed on his head by George III!

The library also contains a plaster bust of Newton by Rysbrack presented by Sir Thomas Barlow in 1932, and a marble bust by Roubilliac which was part of the Smith commission of 1755. Since 1943 the Library has also housed the remaining 860 volumes of Newton's library.

Trinity contains, in addition to a number of important portraits, a collection of memorabilia. These include a lock of Newton's hair, various astronomical instruments and a plaster copy of Rysbrack's death mask.

Also to be seen in Cambridge, in the Hall of Peterhouse, is a stained glass window, depicting Newton, designed by Ford Madox Brown and dating from 1870.

GRANTHAM

At 1 p.m. on 21 September 1858 a procession and band met at the Grantham Grammar School and proceeded to St Peter's Hill. Along with the civic dignitaries were Sir David Brewster, the Master of Trinity College, Lord Brougham, the Bishop and local MPs; leading them were the boys from the Grammar School, with the head boy carrying a copy of *Principia* and flanked by two other boys holding a reflecting telescope and a prism.

At St Peter's Hill waiting to be unveiled was Theed's statue. Cast in a light bronze it stands 12-feet high on a 14-foot pedestal. It shows Newton pointing with his right hand to a scroll held in his left and displaying a diagram taken from *Principia*. The statue took two tons of bronze to cast, one half of which was presented in the form of old cannon by Queen Victoria. Its cost, £1,630, was raised by public subscription, with Grantham contributing £600 and Queen Victoria £100.

At the unveiling ceremony Brougham sat upon a chair said to have belonged to Newton and to have been used by him when he wrote *Principia*. The head boy and his consorts, as if at some pagan ceremony, carefully placed their three sacred relics upon three covered tables placed before the statue. After the unveiling and a speech by Brougham a formal dinner was held in the Exchange Hall.

Illustrations of the scene and a full report can be found in *Illustrated London News*, Supplement, 2 October 1858, vol. XXXIII, no. 99.

LIBRARY OF CONGRESS, WASHINGTON

Overlooking the main reading room there stands a full-length bronze statue sculpted by C. E. Dallin. It can be seen in F. Brasch (1928).

WOOLSTHORPE

The most enduring and significant monument to Newton remains his home at Woolsthorpe. The property of the National Trust since 1943, and open to the public between April and October, it still shows a few signs of Newton's presence. The sundials he built as a boy are no longer there, but a descendant of the original apple tree still flourishes. Also of interest are some geometrical carvings in the stonework of a window in the north bedroom discovered in 1947. They presumably were inscribed by Newton.

See also Residences

BOULLÉE

Newton inspired a number of grandiose but never-realised monuments. Particularly prone to such flights of fancies were the *savants* of the Enlightenment and the French Revolution. Supreme amongst the dreamers is the figure of the French architect E. L. Boullée. In 1784 he proposed an enormous spherical cenotaph. Its top surface would be pierced with holes through which the light could pass in daytime and stars be seen by night. It would carry the legend *Esprit sublime: Genie vaste et profond. Être divin*. Newton. The rationale for his design he explained: 'O Newton as by the extent of your wisdom . . . you determined the shape of the earth; I have conceived the idea of enveloping you in your own discovery.'

EPONYMIC MONUMENTS

Statues and busts are just one way to mark a man's intellectual achievements. It has long been the convention in science to name the intellectual tools of the discipline after their discoverer. In this way, over the centuries, science has taken on a vocabulary of its own, with such items as Bunsen burners, Sims specula, Boyle's law, Euclidean geometry, the islets of Langerhans, Skewes' number and the Grignard reaction. Sometimes the eponymy is so unobtrusive, with terms for example like kilowatts and Mach numbers, as to be scarcely discernible.

Hence an inspection of any science dictionary will soon turn up such items as Newton's rings, Newton's laws of motion, Newton's law of cooling, Newtonian telescope, Newton's laws of fluid friction and, perhaps, a few more obscure items. If the scientist is eminent enough he is likely to qualify for a further degree of eponymy and have a standard unit in a field related to his work named after him. In this way in the SI system the standard unit of force is named the newton.

For the truly eminent there remains an even higher degree of eponymy. Here the name is linked with one or other of the great natural divisions of science. With Euclidean geometry, Linnean systematics, Darwinian biology, Hippocratic medicine, Aristotelian logic there is inevitably to be found Newtonian mechanics.

Pulleyn, Benjamin

Although it is widely assumed that Newton's tutor at Cambridge was Isaac Barrow, the mathematician, it was in fact Pulleyn. Little is known about him other than that he was Regius Professor of Greek from 1674–86 and that he was known in Cambridge as a 'pupil monger', that is, someone keen to make extra money by taking extra pupils. To this end he was reported to have taken fifty-seven pupils, including Newton, between 1661–4.

No account has survived of how the two got on and whether their relationship was more nominal than active.

Q

Quaestiones quaedam philosophicam

See Philosophical Notebook

Queries

The first edition of the *Opticks* (1704) contained sixteen queries. A further seven were added to the first Latin edition of 1706, and another eight to the second English edition of 1717. As the numbering of the queries changed in the 1717 edition their identification can be somewhat confusing. The arrangement of the queries can be summarised as in the diagram, with the arrows indicating continuity and the first appearance of a set of queries indicated by underlining.

1704		*1706*		*1718*
Queries 1–16	→	Queries 1–16	→	Queries 1–16
		Queries 17–23	↘	Queries 17–24
			→	Queries 25–31

The Queries contain some of Newton's most influential and speculative writing. Although presented in the *Opticks* without explanation or comment, Newton referred to them in his *Account* (1715):

> Mr Newton in his Optiques distinguished those things which were made certain by Experiments from those things which remained uncertain, and which he therefore proposed in the End of his Optiques in the form of Queries. (HALL, 1980, p. 312)

While *Principia* itself may have been read in full by few eighteenth-century scholars, there is ample evidence that the queries were well known to a wide circle of readers. Chemists, theologians, physiologists and physicians proved to be as interested in the text as the student of optics.

The actual queries themselves can be summarised as follows.

Q.1   Do not bodies act on light at a distance, bend its rays, and 'act strongest at the least distance?'

Q.2–Q.4   The properties of rays of light.

Q.5   Bodies and light act mutually on each other.

Q.6–Q.11   Light and heat.

Q.12–Q.16   Light and the physiology of vision.

Q.17–Q.24   The ether queries.

Q.17 Light as waves, fits of easy reflexion and transmission.

Q.18 Two-thermometer experiment as proof of the ether's existence.

Q.19 Refraction.

Q.20 Inflexion.

Q.21 Gravity, attraction and the elastick force of the ether.

Q.22 Density of the ether.

Q.23 The ether's role in vision and hearing.

Q.24 The role of the ether in 'Animal Motion'.

Q.25–Q.26   Double refraction.

Q.27   The 'Phaenomena of Light' are not to be explained by 'new Modifications of the Rays'.

Q.28   Objections to wave theory of light and to a dense fluid medium; rejection of hypotheses in natural philosophy; limits of mechanism and a list of fundamental questions; space is the Sensory of God.

Q.29   Rays of light are 'very small Bodies emitted from shining Substances', a view which allows many of the properties of light to be explained.

Q.30   Bodies and light are interconvertible.

Q.31   Small particles of bodies capable of acting at a distance, as can be seen in a number of chemical and physical processes; evidence for the view that 'All Bodies seem to be composed of hard Particles'; Hauksbee's experiments; motion and its need of certain active principles; matter also, made in the beginning by God from 'solid, massy, hard, impenetrable, moveable Particles', in need of 'certain active Principles'; examples of the divine providence in the universe.

Queries Regarding the Word Homoousios

This short text was first published by Brewster (vol. II, p. 532), who listed twenty-two *quaere*; McLachlan (1950, pp. 44–7) published a slightly longer list of twenty-three *quaere*. The questions are posed but not answered. There can, however, be no doubt of the answer Newton expected. Typical questions posed are as follows.

Q.2 Whether the word homoousios 'ever was in any creed before the Nicene'.

Q.4 Was not the creed passed against the council's will?

Q.6 Did not the term mean only that Christ was the 'express image' of the Father?

Q.13 Whether the worship of the Holy Ghost was known before the Council of Sardica?

Q.22 Were not St Athanasius, St Hilary, St Ambrose . . . all Papists? The manuscript is in KCC, Keynes MS II, and is similar to a number of other texts in the Yahuda collection (Yahuda MSs 15.3–15.5, 15.7). Westfall dates them all to the post-1715 period. All are uncompromisingly Arian and concerned with Newton's great obsession, the church history of the fourth century.

R

Raphson, Joseph (?–died before 1715

In the absence of a *DNB* entry and with no other apparent source, little is known about the life of Raphson. He was elected to the Royal Society in 1689 and met Newton in Cambridge in 1691, shortly before attending the University in the following year as a Fellow-Commoner. No correspondence between the two, if indeed it ever existed, has survived.

In 1715, some time after his death, there appeared the work by which he is still remembered, the ninety-six page *The History of Fluxions*. It is, in Hall's words, 'both an apologia for Newton and an exposition of the methods of the calculus' (1980, p. 224). It was based on the two mathematical tracts published in the *Opticks* (1704), and earlier works of Craig (1693) and Cheyne (1703). Raphson's failure to refer to Jones (1711) would suggest that the work was complete by 1711. This interpretation is supported by the claim made by Newton to Bernoulli (*C*, VII, p. 80): 'Mr Ralphson wrote and printed before the Commercium Epistolicum came abroad and his book was in the press before I knew of it, and I stopt it coming abroad for three or four years.'

The work itself is both partisan and inaccurate. Newton is reported to have informed 'some of the best Mathematicians of Europe' of his method of fluxions. Leibniz's calculus had a 'less apt and more laborious Method of Notation' while Newton, in *Principia*, had deployed 'innumerable Applications' of his calculus.

A second edition of Raphson's work, bearing the same title page and date, appeared in 1718. Newton took the opportunity to add to it an Appendix (pp. 97–123). It contained the following.

1 Letter from Leibniz to Conti, 25 November 1715, *C*, VI, pp. 250–5.
2 Letter from Newton to Conti, 26 February 1716, *C*, VI, pp. 285–90.
3 Letter from Leibniz to Conti, 29 March 1716, *C*, VI, pp. 304–14.
4 Newton's *Observations* on 3, May (?) 1716, *C*, VI, pp. 341–52.
5 Letter from Leibniz to Newton, 7 March 1693, *C*, III, pp. 257–60.

[522]

6 Letter from Wallis to Newton, 10 April 1695, *C*, IV, pp. 100–2, extracts.

7 Two short extracts from Wallis (1693) and Fatio (1699).

The letters were reprinted in des Maizeaux (1720). No indication was given that the Appendix was the work of Newton.

Raphson was also responsible for the English translation of Newton's *Arithmetica universalis* (1707), published posthumously in 1720 under the title *Universal Arithmetick*.

See also Priority dispute

Rationes

L. T. More (1962, pp. 642–3) quotes from a manuscript, presumably from the PC, 'giving seven *Rationes* or *reasons* against' the traditional doctrine of the Trinity. He quotes three reasons.

1 *Homoousion* is unintelligible. 'Twas not understood in the Council of Nice . . . nor ever since.

6 The Father is God, creating and a person; the Son is God, created and a person; and the Holy Ghost is God, proceeding and a person.

7 The Person is intellectual substance therefore the three Persons are three substances.

See also Argumenta; Queries Regarding the Word Homoousios

Reflection

In *Opticks*, Book II, part III, prop. VIII, Newton went to some lengths to show that, contrary to common sense, reflection is not caused by 'the impinging of Light on the solid or impervious parts of Bodies'. Three main arguments were advanced.

1 Reflection takes place when light passes from glass into air, even when the adjacent air is drawn away by a vacuum pump.

2 Why should light passing through glass with an angle of incidence greater than '40 or 41 Degrees' be totally reflected? It would be absurd to suppose, Newton argued, 'that Light at one degree of obliquity should meet with Pores enough in the Air to transmit the greater part of it, and at another degree of obliquity should meet with nothing but parts to reflect it wholly'.

3 A prism could be so inclined that blue light emerging from another prism would be totally reflected while red light was 'pretty copiously transmitted'. Once more Newton asked, if reflection was caused by parts of the glass, why did blue light 'wholly impinge

on those parts, so as to be all reflected, and yet the red find Pores enough to be in great measure transmitted'.

The conclusion Newton drew was that reflection was effected 'not by a single point of the reflecting Body, but by some power of the Body which is evenly diffused all over its Surface, and by which it acts upon the Ray without immediate Contact'. Thus, once more, Newton had been led away from a straightforward mechanical explanation in terms of the impact of particles, into the language of power.

See also Mechanical philosophy

Regulae differentiarum

In 1676 Newton began to consider the problem of interpolation. The result of his labours was the brief treatise *Regula differentiarum*, described by Whiteside as 'hastily composed, extensively cancelled and much over-written' (*MP*, IV, pp. 36). Soon abandoned, Newton never returned to the manuscript. It was first published 251 years later by D. C. Fraser (1927, pp. 78–84) and has since appeared in *MP*, IV, pp. 36–50.

The manuscript contains three precepts. The first two claim:
1 how to construct 'intermediate positions' from the 'foreknowledge of a few terms set equally distant from one another in some table to be constructed';
2 a similar method was used to cover the cases 'when the intervals between the numbers to be intercalated are unequal in length'.

The work concluded with an attempt 'to embrace everything in one single general rule'.

See also Methodis differentialis

Regulae pro determinatione Paschae

Unpublished, although Brewster (1860, vol. II, p. 312) gives some idea of its contents. He noted two copies in the PC.

It presumably used arguments similar to those found in *Observations* (1733), chapter XI. He argued for a date of 34 for the Passion. His reasoning was ingenious and depended upon a close knowledge of the Gospels, a commitment to astronomical dating and, perhaps, his experience down on the farm.

Newton noted the Gospel description of Christ and the disciples walking through fields of ripe corn during the Passover, two years before the Passion. If the corn was ripe then, Newton argued, Passover must have been late that year and therefore it could not have been the year 31, when it fell very early on March 28. In the following year Passover fell on April 14, a possible date for ripe corn. Consequently, Newton argued that the Passion of two years later was most likely in the year 34.

See also Calendrical writings

Residences

WOOLSTHORPE

Seven miles south of Grantham in Lincolnshire and half a mile north-west of Colsterworth there can still be found the two-storey grey stone building Newton was born and grew up in. The house and the attendant manor came into the hands of Newton's grandfather Robert in 1623. It passed to his father, another Issac, who held the manor for just the year prior to his death in 1642. Newton lived there until he was sent to school in Grantham in 1654. In 1661 Newton went up to Cambridge. Thereafter he never, despite numerous visits to Woolsthorpe, really lived there; his longest stay at home would have been during his flight from Cambridge and the plague in August 1665, when he spent much of the following eighteen months at the manor.

The income of the estate was valued at £30 p.a. in 1623. Figures quoted later range from £50 to £150 p.a. but never make clear over what property they range. Do they, for example, include property left him by his mother? After his death the estate went to his nephew John, who quickly sold it to a Thomas Alcock, who in turn disposed of it equally quickly for £1,600 in 1733 to Edmund Turnor. The house remained in the Turnor family until 1943 when 'On the initiative of the Royal Society the owner of Woolsthorpe Manor, Major Turnor, agreed to part with the property for a sum well below its market value provided its preservation as a national monument was assured' (*Pilgrim Trust Annual Review* 1943). A further sum was made available from the Pilgrim Trust to put the property in order and in 1943 it was handed over to the National Trust.

The house itself is situated in the valley of the Witham. Two early sketches have survived. One, made by Stukeley, is now in the Royal Society and can be seen reproduced in Manuel (1980, p. 79); the other, also dating from the eighteenth century, can be seen in Westfall (RSW, p. 54). Both sketches obscure the basic fact that the house is T-shaped, with the kitchen in the stem and the bulk of the house in the cross-bar. Stukeley visited the house in the 1720s and described it as:

> Built of stone . . . and a resonable good one. They led me upstairs, and shewed me Sir Isaac's study, where I suppose he studied when

in the country in his younger days . . . I observed the shelves were of his own making, being pieces of deal boxes . . . There were some years ago two or three hundred books in it, of his father-in-law Mr Smith. (TURNOR, 1844, p. 176)

The house was repaired in 1798 and over the front door Edmund Turnor had erected a stone tablet proclaiming, over the family arms, 'In this Manor House Sir Isaac Newton was born 25 December 1642'. Turnor also installed, in the upstairs room, on the left of the staircase, a sign recording the fact that 'Sir Isaac Newton, son of Isaac Newton, Lord of the Manor of Woolsthorpe was born in this room on 25 December 1642'. Also to be seen, over the fireplace, is a sketch of an apple tree, and the well-known Pope couplet.

Outside the house two features have been traditionally associated with Newton. Of these the most famous is the apple tree. The tree, as reported by Brewster in 1831, was standing until the 1820s, when it was destroyed by a strong wind. The tree presently to be seen in the garden is thought to be a descendant of the tree Newton sat under during his *annus mirabilis*. The other feature of the house was the presence of sundials designed and built by Newton. Two dials, missing their styles, were reported by Brewster in 1831 to be still *in situ*. They were removed, however, in 1844 by the Rev. Charles Turnor and donated to the Royal Society and Colsterworth Church.

In 1947 the National Trust decided to open a window blocked up some 250 years before to avoid paying the window tax. Found in the east window of the room of Newton's birth were some geometrical drawings. They were first described by Robinson (1948), and as the earliest mathematical doodles of the young Newton they have been pronounced quite trivial by Whiteside (1964a).

Despite such rich associations the house has been dismissed by Pevsner as 'architecturally undistinguished' (1964, p. 499).

GRANTHAM

Newton was at school in Grantham from late 1654 until the spring of 1658. During this period, excluding obvious breaks for holiday, he lived with apothecary Clark in the house next to the George Inn on the High St. He probably lodged there because Clark's wife and Newton's mother were close friends. Also present in the house were the Storer children, Arthur, Edward and their sister, children of his wife's first marriage. While Newton seemed not to have got on terribly well with the two boys, there is some evidence that he contemplated marriage with their sister, later known as Mrs Vincent.

When Newton returned to school in the autumn of 1660 after an unhappy time spent on the farm, he changed his lodgings. For some unknown reason he moved into the house of his headmaster, Mr Stokes. He stayed with him until he moved to Cambridge in the spring of 1661.

CAMBRIDGE

Newton was admitted to Trinity College on 5 June 1661 as a sub-sizar; he remained in residence as scholar, Fellow and professor until 20 April 1696. During this time he occupied various sets of rooms. Despite, however, a careful search of the records by Edleston (1850), and some ingenious speculation by Adrian (1963), only the location of the final set of rooms is known with any certainty.

He is first known to have shared rooms with someone he found disagreeable. In 1663 he met John Wickins, a student with a similar problem, and it was agreed that they should room together. Of these rooms, Edleston (1850, p. xliii) has noted, there is no mention.

On his election in 1667 to a minor Fellowship, Newton was assigned the room described in the college records as the 'Spirituall chamber'. Although none too clear about its location, Edleston has suggested that 'it may have been the ground-room next the Chapel, in the north-east corner of the great court' (1850, p. xliii). But, even if this were the correct location, it would be no guarantee that Newton actually lived there. Fellows were allowed to rent out their rooms and live elsewhere and there is, in fact, a record from the summer of 1668 of the sum of £1 11s 0d being paid to Newton as rent. He could well have chosen to remain with Wickins, also a Fellow of Trinity, in other rooms, and to rent out his own rooms as and when they were in demand.

There are two further pieces of evidence strongly suggesting that Newton did not long occupy the 'Spirituall chamber'. The first comes from Stukeley, who noted that in 1669 Newton occupied rooms on the north side of the Great Court between the Master's Lodge and the Chapel. Arguments were proposed by a later Master, Lord Adrian (1963), in support of Stukeley. He took as his basic data Newton's published account of experiments with prisms carried out in the mid-1660s. The experiments, carried out in late March or early April, required rooms 22 feet wide into which the sun, 44° 56' high in the sky, could penetrate. Only the south-facing rooms on the north side of the Great Court were both wide enough and oriented in the right direction to satisfy these conditions. Accurate though Adrian's data may be, it remains inadequate. Newton's study at Woolsthorpe also measures 22 feet, and also points in the right direction. The experiments described could therefore have been carried out at Woolsthorpe during Newton's absence from Cambridge in the plague years of 1665 and 1666.

It is only with Newton's final set of rooms, located on the first floor on the east side of the Great Court, between the Great Gate and the Chapel, and looking out over Trinity St, that there exists any reliable documentary evidence. They are described in the Junior Bursar's Book for 1683 as occupied by Newton. Edleston has suggested that 'the most probable supposition is that he went into them in the summer of 1679'. Adrian (1963, p. 23) thinks he may well have been in the rooms as early as 1676.

They can be seen in the Loggan engraving of 1690. Steps running down from Newton's rooms to the garden below and to Trinity St are clearly visible. Also visible is the laboratory reported by Humphrey Newton to be 'on the left end of the garden . . . near the east end of the chapel'. This has been identified by Dobbs (1975, pp. 98–9) with the two-storey wooden structure visible in the Loggan print at the chapel end of the garden. There were also reports of an observatory. It apparently consisted of no more than a reflecting telescope mounted at the head of the stairs.

It is these rooms, E3 in the numbering of today, to which visitors are referred when they enquire about the location of Newton's rooms. Since Newton's time they have been occupied at one time or another by Lord Macaulay, William Thackeray, J. G. Frazer, Lord Adrian and C. D. Broad.

See also Loggan, David

LONDON

Newton moved from Cambridge to London in 1696 on his appointment as Warden of the Mint. In his thirty-one years in London he occupied five houses.

1 He first moved into the Warden's house in the Tower of London. It proved too noisy and smoky.

2 Consequently in August 1696 Newton moved to a house in Jermyn St, near St James's Church, Piccadilly. The site was reported by More (1962, p. 456) to be occupied by Jules's Hotel and to bear a commemorative plaque.

3 In late 1709, for unknown reasons, Newton moved to Chelsea. It cannot have been satisfactory, for within a few months he moved once more.

4 In September 1710 Newton occupied a three-storey house in St Martin's St. It lay south of what was then termed Leicester Fields and is now known as Leicester Square. A nineteenth-century drawing of the house can be seen in Westfall (RSW, p. 670). It was demolished in the early 1920s and the site is now occupied by the Public Library of the City of Westminster. Newton's residence in St Martin's St is commemorated by a bust in the public gardens in Leicester Square. Sculpted by William Calder Marshall, it was

placed there in 1874, together with busts of several other famous residents.

Newton's rent of £100 per annum was a substantial one for the times. For this he received a substantial house, excluding servant's quarters, of eight rooms. He shared the house, until her marriage in 1717, with his niece, Catherine Barton. There were also six staff: a housekeeper, a cook, a footman, two maids and a Mr Woston, whose duties were unspecified. They presumably occupied the top floor. The bedrooms of Newton and Catherine, together with his study, were sited on the first floor; the ground floor contained two parlours and a dining room.

The house seemed well stocked, with forty plates, fifty chairs, eleven pictures and the surprising figure of over 250 prints. Another curious feature was the prevalence of crimson. Newton's bedroom contained a crimson mohair bed, crimson curtains and crimson hangings, while, downstairs in the back parlour, crimson chairs with crimson cushions could also be found.

Some of the house has survived. When it was pulled down in the 1920s parts of the wainscoating and trim were rescued by the antiquarian firm of Phillips. It can now be seen in the library of the Babson Institute, Wellesley, Massachusetts, where an attempt has been made to reconstruct Newton's room in St Martin's St.

5 Given reasonable health, Newton would presumably have spent the rest of his life in St Martin's St. In 1725, however, he was advised by his physicians to seek the more salubrious air of Kensington. Although the eighty-two-year-old Newton was reluctant to leave his home of the past fifteen years, he finally, under pressure from his physicians and the Conduitts, conceded. Yet, despite his move, Conduitt later admitted, 'no methods that were used could keep him from coming sometimes to town'.

The house stood to the west of Church Lane, now named Kensington Church St, and was known as Orbell's Buildings. They were demolished in the 1890s and the site is now occupied by Bullingham Mansions. It was, however, in Orbell's Buildings that Newton died two years later in 1727. An illustration of the house can be seen in Rattansi (1974, p. 87). The only present sign of Newton's stay in the area appears to be a window in memory of Newton in St Mary Abbots Church, Kensington.

Rigaud, Stephen Peter (1774–1839)

Rigaud's father had been an observer of George III at Kew. He himself spent his entire career at Oxford, first as a student at Exeter College, and subsequently as Savilian Professor, initially of Geometry but from 1827 of Astronomy.

In the 1830s modern Newtonian scholarship began, with publications from Sir David Brewster, Francis Baily and Rigaud. Original documents were examined, manuscripts sought and new positions established. Thus Rigaud's *Historical Essay on the First Publication of Sir Isaac Newton's 'Principia'* (1838) not only demonstrated for the first time that *Principia* was the kind of thing which could have a history but went on to publish some of the relevant documents. Contained in twenty-three valuable appendices (pp. 1–80) were many of the primary documents on the history of *Principia*. They include: the first publication of the pre-*Principia* tract, *Propositiones de motu*; the fluxions tract dated 13 November 1665; six letters from Newton to Halley over the period 20 June 1686 to 1 March 1687 and two from Halley to Newton (22 May 1686 and 29 June 1686); extracts from various other letters of Newton; Halley's review of *Principia*; and, amongst much else, the original uncorrected Latin verse of Halley contributed to the first edition of *Principia*. It would be many years before another scholar followed Rigaud's lead.

Rigaud also had access to the Macclesfield Collection at Shirburn Castle, probably the last serious scholar to be so privileged. The result was his invaluable *Correspondence of Scientific Men of the Seventeenth Century* (1841, 2 vols), a work which contained a rich selection of letters from Newton, Barrow, Flamsteed, Collins, Wallis, and many others.

Roberval, Gilles Personne de (1602–75)

In addition to his work on the cycloid and other curves, Roberval, Professor of Mathematics from 1634 at the *Collège de France*, also published on gravity. He expressed his views in his curiously titled, *Aristarchi Samii de mundi systemate* (1644, The System of the World of Aristarchus of Samos), a supposedly Latin version of an Arabic translation of a lost Greek work – in such a manner did mid-seventeenth-century Catholic scientists express their Copernicanism – in which he sought to explain gravity in terms of a universal ether or fluid. He also spoke of attractive forces. Although Newton possessed a copy of the work and had presumably read it, there is no indication that Roberval exercised any real influence over the development of Newton's dynamics.

Newton was never the less somewhat sensitive on the point. In 1712, in the *Memoirs of Literature*, Leibniz had attacked those who followed Roberval and claimed that bodies attract each other. Had such thinkers, he asked, substituted miracles for natural causes? Newton took the reference, quite accurately, to be an attack on his own dynamics and consequently began to draft a reply (*C*, V, pp. 298–302). It was never sent.

See also Attractive and repulsive forces

Rohault, Jacques (1620–75)

The son of a wealthy wine merchant, Rohault moved in Cartesian circles in the Paris of the 1640s. From the mid-1650s he gave weekly lectures and demonstrations. He is mainly remembered, however, for his influential textbook, *Traité de physique* (1671). It proved to be one of the main channels through which the details of Cartesian physics were disseminated and maintained throughout Europe from the 1670s to well into the eighteenth century. Rohault became available in England in T. Bonet's Latin translation of 1674 in 1682. The publication of *Principia* in 1687 seems if anything to have stimulated demand. Samuel Clarke, a Newtonian, issued a new Latin translation in 1697, which was re-issued in 1702, 1708, 1710 and 1739. His brother, John Clarke, felt there to be sufficient demand to publish in 1723 an English translation and to require two further editions in 1729 and 1735.

Why, in England, with Newton's influence so dominant, were seven editions of a Cartesian textbook called for? One simple answer is that textbooks continue, whatever their theoretical stance, until replaced by something as good. *Principia* itself was too difficult ever to serve as a textbook, while the numerous expositions it inspired were too general and philosophical to compete with Rohault.

One other factor helps to explain the continuing demand for Rohault's work. Beginning in Clarke's Latin translation as endnotes and developing into extensive footnotes, Rohault's text carried an ever-increasing amount of Newtonian commentary. How, it was asked in the footnotes, could comets drift effortlessly through planetary vortices? Some idea of the situation can be seen from the full title of the 1723 English edition: *Rohault's System of Natural Philosophy Illustrated with Dr. Samuel Clarke's Notes taken mostly out of Sir Isaac Newton's Philosophy.* Illustrations from Rohault showing how Clarke argued against the Cartesian dismissal of attraction, and the Cartesian position on motion, space and time are included in Koyré (1965, pp. 170–2, 198–200).

Romney, George (1734–1802)

With Gainsborough and Reynolds, Romney was one of the leading portrait painters of eighteenth-century Britain. He is remembered in the popular mind for his affair with Lady Hamilton and the mildly risqué portraits he produced of her in various historical guises.

In 1793 he painted 'Milton and his Two Daughters' for which he sold the reproduction rights for fifty guineas. The success of the Milton led Romney to plan a series of historical paintings. They would include Bacon gathering snow for his experiments, the aged Wren being carried into St Paul's and 'Newton Displaying the Prismatic Colours'. The Newton was painted in 1794 and sold, or bought in perhaps, at the first sale of his work in 1807 for £42. In 1902 it was described as the property of a Mr Tankerville-Chamberlayne M.P.

Roubillac, Louis Francois (*c.*1705–62)

Born in Lyon, Roubillac studied sculpture in Paris and settled in England some time in the 1730s. His work, together with that of M. Rysbrack and P. Scheemakers, came to dominate eighteenth-century British sculpture. He produced many busts and executed a number of elaborate tombs, none more so than the remarkable monument to Handel in Westminster Abbey in which he is shown conducting a celestial orchestra.

He was commissioned by Robert Smith to produce a full-size statue of Newton for Trinity College. It was completed in 1755 and can still be seen today standing in the ante-chamber to the chapel. He also sculpted a number of marble busts, including one of Newton, which stand today in the Wren Library of Trinity College. The Royal Society possesses another copy.

See also Public monuments

Routh, Edward John (1831–1907)

Educated at London University and Peterhouse, Cambridge, Routh seems to have spent the rest of his life after 1855 in Cambridge coaching as many as 100 pupils a year in the rigours of the mathematical tripos. He was also the author of two formidable and widely-used textbooks: *The Dynamics of a System of Rigid Bodies*, 1860; and *A Treatise on Analytical Statics*, 1891–2.

In 1855, having shown no previous interest in historical questions, he collaborated with Lord Brougham on the production of their *Analytical View of Sir Isaac Newton's Principia*.

See also Brougham, Henry

Royal Society

One of the distinctive features of modern science, and indeed of modern learning in general, has been the emergence of various societies. Initially they tended to be provincial groupings like the *Accademia Secretorum Naturae* founded in 1560 and based in Naples, the *Accademia dei Lincei* founded in 1600 in Rome, the Florentine *Accademia del Cimento* established in 1657, and the Oxford Philosophical Society formed in 1651. In the 1660s however two great national societies were founded: the Royal Society of London established in 1662; and, four years later in Paris, the *Académie des Sciences*. Both were under Royal patronage. While the French *Académie* was well-funded by Louis XIV and Colbert, the Royal Society received little from Charles II beyond his goodwill and patronage. Funds were derived initially from the one shilling a week subscription Fellows were supposed to contribute. Few however did and in its early years the Society was chronically short of money. So poor was the Society that it was unable in 1687 to pay for the publication of Newton's *Principia*.

Newton's own contact with the Society began in 1671. Newton had told a number of friends about his newly-invented reflecting telescope, and somehow, perhaps through John Collins, news of the discovery reached the officers of the Society. They were curious enough to ask to see the new model and late in 1671 Isaac Barrow took one to London for them to examine. Newton was told by Oldenburg in the following January that his invention had been examined by some of the 'most eminent in Opticall Science and practise, and applauded by them'. Further, he had been proposed as a candidate for the Society by Seth Ward and on 11 January 1672 he was elected accordingly. Newton replied shortly afterwards expressing his gratitude to Ward and promising that he would repay the honour by 'communicating what my poore & solitary endeavours can effect towards ye promoting your Philosophical designes' (*C*, I, p. 80).

The result was that in February Newton submitted the first of the seventeen papers he would publish over the next four years in the *Philosophical Transactions* of the Society. Newton clearly had not planned to publish as extensively on his theory of light but, pressed by Oldenburg and others, and with growing irritation, he replied to the many queries and objections his work had provoked. However, by March 1673, after nine contributions to the *PT* in a year, Newton took the radical step of resigning from the Society. Thus, he wrote to Oldenburg: 'I desire that you will procure that I may be put out from being any longer Fellow of the Royal Society: for though I honour that body, yet since I shall neither profit them, nor (by reason of distance) can partake of the advantage of their assemblies, I desire to withdraw' (*C*, I, p. 262).

Oldenburg replied that the distance between Cambridge and London had not increased since Newton joined the Society and went on to offer to relieve him from the 'burden' of his quarterly payments. Newton did not press the issue of his resignation. He did, however, inform Oldenburg in June 1673 that he intended 'to be no further solicitous about matters of Philosophy'.

Later, in early 1675, fearing his Cambridge Fellowship was about to end, Newton raised with Oldenburg once more the question of dues, pleading a contracting income. The crisis failed to develop and it proved unnecessary for Newton to press his claim. He continued to reply to objections made to his work throughout 1675 and 1676 and in early 1675, while on a visit to London, he paid three visits to the Society. Thereafter contacts with the Society were minimal until 1684, when Newton began to work on *Principia*.

Although the Society lacked sufficient funds to publish *Principia*, they authorised the President, Samuel Pepys, in June 1686, to license the printing of the book. Consequently *Principia* carried the imprimatur of 'S.Pepys, Reg.Soc. Praeses' on its publication in July 1687. Newton, also, chose to dedicate the work to the Society.

After Pepys had resigned in 1688 he was followed by a series of mainly aristocratic Presidents under whom the Society languished. It was clearly time the Society's affairs were directed by a scientist of both standing and vision. The obvious candidate was Newton. He had moved from Cambridge to London in 1696 as Warden of the Mint. In 1697 he was elected to the Council of the Society, as he was again in 1699. Whether he was too busy with the re-coinage or whether there were other reasons to keep him away, Newton seems not to have attended a single council meeting. The suggestion has been made that with Hooke frequently in attendance, ever ready to challenge any claim or thought of Newton, meetings of the Society could not have looked at all attractive to the new Warden of the Mint. When Newton did attend the Society early in 1699 to describe a sextant he had invented, he was met with the familiar claim from Hooke that the instrument had been invented by him some years before. But Hooke was sick and aging, and died finally in March 1703. When Lord Somers retired from the Presidency later in the year, the way was at last open for Newton, if he so wished, to offer himself for the post. There is some evidence that influential Fellows preferred Sir Christopher Wren for the post but, ten years older than Newton, he had no interest in the position.

Newton's election to the Presidency in November 1703 was not without opposition. Of the thirty or more members who voted, only twenty-four cast their vote for Newton. The first change made by the new President was immediate, and arose from his duties at the Mint. Occupied with official duties on a Wednesday, the day the Council and

Society normally met, Newton switched the day to a Thursday. The Council of the Society have continued so to meet ever since.

As at the Mint, so with the Royal Society, Newton took his duties seriously. The most obvious change was that, unlike his noble predecessors, he attended meetings regularly. Whereas his immediate predecessor, Lord Somers, had attended not a single Council meeting during his five years of office, Newton attended 161 out of the 175 meetings held between his election in 1703 and the end of 1726. He also took the trouble to attend most Ordinary meetings. There was inevitably more to Newton's ministry than attendance.

To begin with he had a vision of the Society which he, with only limited success, sought to implement. The details were set out in his *Scheme for establishing the Royal Society*, seven drafts of which can be found in the PC in the ULC (Add. MS 4005.2) and which was published for the first time by Brewster (vol. I, pp. 102–4). The main point of the scheme was the appointment of several paid professional demonstrators who would work in five main fields: mathematics and mechanics, astronomy and optics, biology, botany, and chemistry. With their aid, a determined effort could be made to discover 'the frame and operations of Nature'. As early in Newton's period of office as December 1703 Francis Hauksbee, the first appointed demonstrator, performed experiments on air pumps. Until his death in 1713 Hauksbee continued to work as a paid demonstrator. In 1707 a second demonstrator, James Douglas, began to perform dissections for the Society. Later, in 1714, two replacements are first heard of, J. T. Desaguliers and William Cheselden, for the physical and biological sciences respectively.

Although Desaguliers and Hauksbee were undoubtedly grateful for whatever patronage they received, and while Hauksbee in particular performed experimental work of some significance, the scheme itself failed to develop as Newton had imagined. Money was not sufficiently available to the Council to pay full-time demonstrators. Payments were invariably small, infrequent and made on an *ad hoc* basis. The Council itself lacked the will to employ fully a serious worker and preferred to pay someone for actual work carried out. Nor was Newton beyond taking the demonstrators to be no more than his own private servants, responsive to his every bidding. In any case there is always something slightly suspect in the idea that the 'operations of nature' are more likely to reveal themselves to an organised public campaign rather than to a private individual effort. Of the demonstrators appointed by the Society, only Hauksbee produced work of genuine insight and distinction.

Against this, of course, it must be appreciated that anything that distracted the Society from its concern with such issues as the therapeutic value of 'cows piss drank to about a pint' could only be an improvement. Under Newton's direction the Society was guided to some of the more central problems of science; it did not, however, succeed in finding any especially significant solutions. Newton thus rescued the Society from the distractions of the virtuosi rather than succeeding in establishing it as a major centre of scientific research.

On Newton's assumption of office a further and more pressing problem presented itself, namely the actual location of the Society. On 12 December 1660, a fortnight after the Society's foundation, the Society met in Gresham College and decided to meet there weekly 'till further order'. By the beginning of the eighteenth century the building was in need of demolition and consequently in 1705, after several previous warnings, the Society was requested to find new quarters. Approaches were made to Queen Anne, the Mercer's Company and the Trustees of the Cotton Library for grants of land or for free quarters, but none seemed willing to offer the Royal Society charitable bequests. In some haste Newton and Sloane, the Society's Secretary, arranged in 1710 for the purchase, from Dr. E. Browne, the son of Sir Thomas Browne, of two houses in Crane Court for the sum of £1,450. Suggestions were made by some Fellows that Newton and Sloane had acted high handedly. An anonymous pamphlet appeared calling for the dismissal of the Council, but Newton and his colleagues had little difficulty in gaining re-election at the 1710 annual meeting.

Thereafter there was little opposition to Newton. Sloane resigned in 1713 and was succeeded as secretary by Halley. He was later joined in the post by such faithful Newtonians as Brook Taylor, Machin and James Jurin. Surrounded by disciples, the Society could not but help becoming Newton's personal fief. On two occasions in particular Newton so manipulated the Society that his own personal views on matters of public importance came to be expressed as the supposedly impartial judgments of a public body. The first and most important arose out of the dispute between Newton and Leibniz over their claims to have invented the calculus. Let us settle the issue once and for all, Newton proposed. Let us set up an independent committee of the Royal Society to examine all the correspondence, documents and other relevant material. A committee was set up including such undisputed Newtonians as Halley, Machin, Aston, Taylor and de Moivre; unsurprisingly it reported in 1712 in the *Commercium epistolicum* that 'we Reckon Mr.Newton the first inventor'. It turned out that much of the report was not only derived from biased judges but was actually written by Newton himself. Far from being an independent report issued by an organisation concerned with the truth, it was little more than a personal plea trading under the name of a supposedly public body.

Again, in his dealings with Flamsteed, Newton found it prudent and profitable to present his case as if it were the considered judgment of an independent committee. Referees appointed by the Society to supervise the publication of Flamsteed's work inevitably tended to be Newton's nominees and consequently, and typically, allowed Newton to act with the authority of the Society in virtually any way he chose.

Newton, never the less, remains the greatest and most honoured of all the Society's presidents and his image and presence are still carefully preserved. Not only does it possess three portraits by Vanderbank, and one by Jervas, a reflecting telescope made by Newton, a bust by Roubilliac, an ivory medallion carved by Le Marchand, a solar dial taken from Woolsthorpe, and a death mask, but also a host of such minor memorabilia as a supposed lock of hair, an armchair and a watch which may have once belonged to Newton. The Society is even richer in manuscripts, letters and documents once belonging to or connected with Newton. Of these the most significant are concerned with the publication of *Principia* and include that most valuable of all scientific texts, the manuscript of *Principia*.

Rules for Interpreting the Words and Language in Scripture

The text has been published as part of Appendix A of Manuel (1974, pp. 116–22). It is derived from 'a 550-page manuscript . . . Yahuda MS.I' and is to be found in Jerusalem. It is followed by two related pieces: *Rules for methodising/construing the Apocalyps* (pp. 119–21), and *Rules for interpreting the Apocalyps* (pp. 122–5). As presented by Manuel, and beginning with an untitled introduction (pp. 107–16), the various items seem to be part of a single work.

Some fifteen rules are proposed, the observance of which would, even today, eliminate much fanciful nonsense. It is difficult to see, for example, how such a surprisingly popular work as the prophecies of Nostradamus could ever survive such a test. Thus, a single meaning should be assigned to words in any one vision; prophecies should apply to the more significant events of an age and should not be held to predict the trivial and the obscure; the more literal use of words should be preferred, as should the simpler of any competing interpretations. Only the fifteenth rule, "To chose those interpretations which . . . most respect the church and argue the greatest wisdom and providence of God', would be likely to provoke any opposition from a modern secular critic. The rest are, for the most part, rules accepted by any scholar when he faces an obscure and difficult text.

See also Interpretation and purpose of prophecy

Rysbrack, John Michael (1694–1770)

The son of an Antwerp landscape painter, Rysbrack settled in London in 1720. His work, with that of L. F. Roubillac and Peter Scheemakers, dominated eighteenth-century British sculpture. He produced busts of Walpole, Pope and Sloane, while his equestrian statue of William III in Bristol has been described as the finest of its kind of the period.

Most of the public monuments erected to Newton after his death came from the hands of Rysbrack. The first, designed by William Kent and supervised by John Conduitt, was the baroque sarcophagus erected in Westminster Abbey in 1731. He also produced busts for the Temple of British Worthies at Stowe and for Queen Caroline's Temple at Richmond. Both date from the 1730s. The former can be seen in Pevsner (1976, p. 13) while the latter was chosen as the frontispiece to the Babson *Catalogue* (1950).

Rysbrack was also entrusted with the preparation of Newton's death mask. Five plaster copies are known; one is in the Royal Society, another is in TCC, while a third was disposed of in the 1936 Sotheby sale. The British Museum possesses an iron mask based on Rysbrack's work, which it acquired in 1925.

See also Public monuments

S

Saint-Simon, Henri (1760–1825)

Born into an old and noble family, his great uncle was the famous chronicler of the court of Louis XIV. Saint-Simon led a varied and dramatic life. He fought in the American revolution, was imprisoned by Robespierre in his own country's revolution, failed in various businesses, attempted suicide and wrote extensively and prophetically on the emergence of the industrial estate.

Saint-Simon first unfolded his vision of the new world in his *Lettre d'un habitant de Genève a l'humanité* (1802). In this and other works he pursued one of the prevalent fantasies of the time, that a religion of Newton should be set up, better to direct the affairs of man and society. Only a society in which science occupied a fundamental position could achieve order and stability. He proposed, therefore, to locate supreme rule in the hands of 'the twenty-one elect of humanity' which would be called the Council of Newton. It would be made up of three mathematicians, three physicists, three chemists, three physiologists, and three each from the painters, musicians and authors of the world. They would be more than just leaders. Saint-Simon insisted that they also be endowed with spiritual authority. To this end temples would be built containing a mausoleum in honour of Newton to which all would have to make a pilgrimage once a year and to which children would be brought shortly after birth. It would be surrounded by laboratories, workshops and colleges.

Saint-Simon presented the scheme as if it were a divine vision. The voice of God spoke to him renouncing Rome as 'headquarters of my church' andcontinued with the announcement, 'I have placed Newton at my side, to control enlightenment and command the inhabitants of the planets'.

See also Attitudes to Newton

Sampson, Ralph Allan (1866–1939)

Educated at the Liverpool Institute and St John's College, Cambridge, Sampson served as Professor of Mathematics at Durham University from 1893 until 1910, when he was appointed Astronomer Royal of Scotland. As an astronomer he is best known for his *Tables of the Four Great Satellites of Jupiter* (1910). His connection with Newton arose in 1904 when, for some not very clear reason, he was selected by the Syndics of the Cambridge University Press to be Editor-in-Chief of a proposed complete edition of Newton's scientific work and correspondence. It was not an inspired choice. Planned in six volumes of 600 pages each, it was expected to take six years. Although a detailed prospectus was drawn up, little else seems to have been done. In 1923 Sampson explained his lack of progress (Sampson, 1924, p. 318).

> Perhaps I ought not to have undertaken it . . . In 1904 . . . I had on my hands a very heavy piece of work, the Theory and Tables of Jupiter's Satellites, which I might never have finished had I allowed any other task to take priority of it. As often happens, it took more time than was anticipated. The conclusion was assured in 1910; and, had nothing intervened, I should then have taken up actively the edition of Newton . . . But in the same year I was transferred to Edinburgh where different demands upon my time have never allowed me to think of it again.

See also Correspondence

Sanderson, Robert (1587–1663)

Sanderson was educated at Oxford, where he served briefly from 1646–8 as Regius Professor of Divinity. Out of favour during the Commonwealth, he returned to office as Bishop of Lincoln with the Restoration.

His most famous work was the logic textbook, *Logicae artis compendium* (1618), a work last printed in 1841 when it was still being used by university students. Newton was advised by his uncle William Ayscough to work on Sanderson's textbook before going up to Cambridge. According to Conduitt, when Newton attended his tutor Benjamin Pulleyn's classes he was found to know the text better than his teacher.

Scala graduum caloris (A scale of degrees of heat)

The *Scala* was the first published anonymously in the March–April issue of the *PT* (1701, pp. 824–9). It is also to be found in Castillioneus, *Tome*

II (1744) and, more conveniently, in both the original Latin and English translation in *PLNP* (pp. 259–68).

The scale runs from 0, when 'water begins to freeze', to 192, the 'degree of heat of live coals in a small kitchen fire . . . that burn without using bellows'. On this scale the 'heat of the human body is 12' and that of boiling water 34. The table was constructed by means of a linseed oil thermometer. When placed in snow the oil took up 10,000 parts, but when heated by a human body, boiling water and melted tin, the oil was found to occupy the space of 10,256, 10,705 and 11,516 parts respectively. Assuming the 'degrees of heat of the oil proportional to its rarefaction', and assigning the temperature of the human body an arbitrary value of 12, Newton was able to calculate the temperature of boiling water to be 33 and the melting point of tin as 72.

Newton developed a second technique to check his initial results. It involved comparing the time taken by a piece of red-hot iron to cool to body heat with the time taken by attached particles of various metals to harden. The results of this second approach, Newton noted, 'had the same ratio among themselves with those found by the thermometer'.

The paper seems to have had little impact. When, in 1714, Daniel Fahrenheit (1686–1736) sought to construct a mercury thermometer, he adopted a quite different scale. Newton's scale was too concerned with the very hot temperatures to be more than of passing interest. The paper was, however, issued three times in English translation in the eighteenth century (1738, 1747 and 1775), as well as being translated into Dutch (1740) and French (1742).

Schooten, Frans van (1615–60)

Both his father, Frans the elder (1581–1646), and his half-brother, Petrus, were well-known mathematicians of the period. Frans the younger served as Professor of Mathematics at Leyden where he taught Huygens, Hudde, de Witt and de Sluse.

His significance as a mathematician lies basically with his dissemination of the works of Descartes, particularly his *Géométrie* (1637). It was a difficult work and, written in French, was largely inaccessible to provincial scholars like Newton. A Latin translation by van Schooten in 1649 helped to make the work more available; much more important, however, was the second edition, in two volumes, published in 1659–61 together with related texts and commentaries, a work described by Westfall as 'the century's most influential mathematical publication' (RSW, p. 23). It was through this work of van Schooten that Newton, some time in 1664, first tackled the complexities of modern analysis. When, many years later in 1691, Newton was asked by Bentley which books should be read before tackling *Principia*, the reply came: 'peruse such Problems as you will find scattered up and down in ye Comment-aries on Cartes's Geometry . . . of Francis Schooten' (*C*, III, p. 155).

Scottish kin

In 1725 Newton, in conversation with James Gregory, the brother of David Gregory, declared: 'Gregory, I believe you don't know that I am connected with Scotland', and went on to report that his grandfather was a gentleman from East Lothian who had come to London with James I, lost all his money there and left Newton's father in 'mean circumstances'. A doubtful Gregory replied that he had 'never heard of a gentleman of East Lothian of that name'. Thomas Reid took the question up later in the century and wrote in 1784 that he had located a baronet's family in the area with the name Newton and that they recalled Newton contacting them earlier in the century. They had not replied. Brewster took up the issue once more in the 1820s and reported that, despite a careful search amongst the papers of the Newtons of Newton, East Lothian, 'no document whatever has been found that can throw the least light upon the matter' (1831, Appendix I). There was, however, a surviving oral tradition affirming the connection.

See also Ancestry

Seeman, Enoch (1694–1744)

Born in Danzig, the son of a portrait painter, Seeman followed his father's trade in England.

There hangs in TCC a head-and-shoulders portrait of Newton dated 1726. Although undoubtedly by Seeman, some doubt has been expressed about whether it is an original portrait or merely a copy of the portrait in the National Portrait Gallery, which it strongly resembles. Either way it presents a more vital and carefully drawn face than its supposed original (RSW, pp. 860, 831).

It was presented to Trinity by Thomas Hollis.

See also Portraits, medals, busts and statues

Sendovigius, Michael (1566–1646)

A Moravian or a Pole, Sendovigius met in 1603 Alexander Seton, a Scot who was thought to have learned the secret of transmutation. Sendovigius later married Seton's widow and so gained his manuscripts.

Newton owned a copy of his *Nouvelle lumière chimique* (1691, New light on Chemistry) and took extensive notes from it. There is also a 12,000-word manuscript in Newton's hand entitled *Sendovigius explained* (Keynes MS 55).

Dobbs (1975, pp. 157–60) has detected in Sendovigius an important influence on the development of Newton's alchemy. Sendovigius had spoken of a 'Chalybs' or 'Magnet', 'created of itself from nature, which knows how to draw the rays of the sun'. In some unknown way Newton took the passage to refer to antimony and its various reguli. In consequence much effort and time was spent in mastering the literature on antimony and pursuing its chemistry in the laboratory.

See also Antimony

Shaw, George Bernard (1856–1950)

Shaw's final play, *In Good King Charles's Golden Days*, was written for the 1939 Malvern festival. He described its origin to Hesketh Pearson.

> He told me that he had really wanted to write a play on George Fox . . . Then he had thought: why not introduce Isaac Newton? –'an astonishing creature with a terrific memory, the most prodigious feat of which, a chronology of the world, was reduced to absurdity by his assumption that the world was created in 4004 B.C. Then Shaw's mind had played him a trick about Charles II, the cleverest monarch who had ever sat on the English throne. Finally, he had decided to introduce all three, with a few of Charles's mistresses thrown in to relieve 'the intellectual tension.' The result is entertaining. (PEARSON, 1948, pp. 414–15)

The play is in two acts, with the first set in the library 'in the house of Isaac Newton in Cambridge'. Present are Mrs Basham, his housekeeper, a Mr Rowley, who turns out to be Charles II, three of his mistresses – the Duchesses of Cleveland and Portsmouth, and Nell Gwynn – Charles Fox the Quaker, Godfrey Kneller the artist, and the future James II as Duke of York. The second and much shorter act takes place between Charles and Queen Catherine. The time is 1680.

Pearson's claim that the play is 'entertaining' and 'the most satisfying thing he had done since *Saint Joan*' can be questioned. Indeed, with no dramatic interest, it requires an unquenchable passion for all things Newtonian to tempt the reader to the play's end. The play is highly anachronistic, a fact appreciated by Shaw as much as anyone and justified by him with his reference to the 'prophetic quality of his anachronisms'.

While the anachronisms are not unduly disturbing, other references to Newton can be more irritating. Thus, Charles speaks to his mistress:

[543]

'We must not waste anymore of Mr Newton's time, Mistress Gwynn, He is at work on fluxions.' Newton is shown for the most part as the stereotypical scientist. Absent-minded and impractical, he finds it difficult even to multiply three by seven. In the end he adds their logs and concludes the result 'must be less than 22 and more than 20'.

Shaw, however, knew a fair amount about Newton. He was aware of the dog Diamond, that Newton had based his chronology on the precession of the equinoxes, and had written on the prophecies of Daniel and on alchemy. He was also aware of the correspondence between John Locke and Newton, giving Newton the line 'I will not have Mr Locke and his friends accuse me of having relations with women'.

Probably the best line of Act I arises when the Duchess of Portsmouth seeks to persuade Newton to make an aphrodisiac for her. 'I do not deal in love potions', Newton responds. Farce also enters the play, with a fight between Newton and the Duke of York. The first act ends with the entrance of Kneller, who begins to argue with Newton that 'motion in a curve is a law of nature' and that space, time and the universe are all curved.

The play was first staged at Malvern on 12 August 1939. It entered the West End on 9 May 1940 and ran until the Blitz closed all London theatres. Newton was played by Cecil Trouncer. It was revived at the People's Palace in the East End of London in 1948 and played once more at Malvern in 1949. Thereafter it seems to have been ignored. Nor has it apparently ever been performed professionally in the US.

Shelton, Thomas (1601–50)

The author of *Short Writing* (1626) and *Tachy-graphy* (1635), works which went through twenty-two editions before 1710. Shelton's system of shorthand was used by Hartlib, Hooke, Locke and, above all, by Pepys in his diary. Newton had a copy of the 1660 edition of *Tachy-graphy* and used shorthand in a number of his notebooks. There are brief shorthand entries in the Morgan and Trinity Notebooks. More significant is the list of sins presented in the Fitzwilliam Notebook.

In the system, consonants are represented by simple straight lines and curves, vowels by dots placed in any of five positions. In addition there were 256 arbitrary characters for common words and a large number of contractions. Although it was originally designed for the transcription of sermons, it seems to have been used more commonly, as with Newton and Pepys, to provide some minimal security for private and sensitive material.

Simon, Richard (1638–1712)

The son of a Dieppe blacksmith, Simon, first at the Oratory, then as a *curé* at Belleville, and finally after 1682 as an independent scholar, introduced a radically new approach to the Bible. His chief works, in translation, were *Critical History of the Old Testament* (1682), *Critical History of the New Testament* (1689) and *Critical Enquiries into the Various Editions of the Bible* (1684). All were in Newton's library.

For Simon the available biblical texts were historical texts which had been, like any other texts, modified, corrupted and altered over the centuries. It was the task of the 'critical' scholar, using his knowledge of tradition, chronology and philology, to restore the true text. It was an approach which Newton, suspicious of the Trinitarian tone of parts of the Bible, found attractive. Simon himself, though far from orthodox, was no Unitarian. His critical approach, never the less, provoked much opposition.

Sizar

The term sizar, according to the *Oxford English Dictionary*, probably derives from the word 'size' meaning 'bread and ale'. It refers to the Cambridge custom of awarding certain students free 'sizes' – board – and tuition in return for a certain amount of domestic service. The comparable Oxford term was *servitor*. Trinity in the seventeenth century normally admitted thirteen sizars, three of whom served the Master and the remainder the ten most senior Fellows.

Newton was actually described as a sub-sizar, students who bought their own food and who were then rewarded for their services by paying a reduced fee. Why Newton's mother, believed to have a substantial income of about £700 p.a., should have chosen to send her son to Cambridge in this manner is not known. While it is generally assumed that Newton found his lowly position embarrassing, there is in fact no hard evidence for such a view.

Smith, Barnabas (1582–1653)

'Mr Smith a neigbouring Clergyman, who had a very good Estate, had lived a Bachelor till he was pretty old, & one of his parishioners adviseing him to marry He said he did know where to meet with a good wife: the man answered, the widow Newton is an extraordinary good woman.' In this way, according to Conduitt, did Barnabas Smith approach Newton's mother Hannah. After consulting her brother William, she agreed to Smith's proposal, even though it meant that she would have to leave her three-year-old son to be brought up by his grandmother.

Conduitt's account was not quite accurate, for Smith had been married before and, indeed, widowed for only a year. He was a man of substance and education. An Oxford M.A. and an income of £500 a year, as well as the living of North Witham bought for him by his father in 1610, placed Smith much further up the social scale than the illiterate Newtons. There were three children from the marriage; the son Benjamin inherited all his father's lands while the two girls, Mary and Hannah, received £500 each. Newton seems to have acquired the two to three hundred theological works reported to have been seen by Stukeley at Woolsthorpe. He also acquired a large 1,000 page commonplace book which eventually became his Waste Book. Newton's mother had seen to it that her prospective husband settled some land on her son.

It is tempting to suppose that the young Newton, deprived of his mother, developed some hostility to his stepfather. Such a supposition, attractive as it might be, is wholly speculative. No accounts have survived of how they felt to each other. The only evidence quoted comes from a 1662 entry in Newton's Fitzwilliam Notebook: 'Threatening my father and mother Smith to burne them and the house over them.'

Smith, Benjamin (b.1651)

Newton's half-brother, the son of his mother Hannah and stepfather Barnabas Smith. He had three children, Hannah, Benjamin (1700–76) and Newton (d.1728), each of whom, as one of Newton's heirs, inherited over £3,000 on his death in 1727. Although it is natural to suppose Newton would have felt some hostility to his half-brother, there is no actual evidence for such a supposition.

Smith, Benjamin (1700–76)

Newton's nephew, the son of his half-brother Benjamin. As a young man, Benjamin was considered to have been somewhat wild. For a time he lived with Newton, who was said to have denounced his nephew's morals and character, although he gave him £500 shortly before his death; as one of Newton's heirs, he stood to inherit over £3,000. He was admitted into orders after 1727 and, in 1733, published his uncle's Observations.

Smith, Hannah (d.1679)

Newton's mother, born Hannah Ayscough, she married her first husband, Isaac Newton, shortly before his death in 1642. She brought with her lands in Sewstern, Leicestershire, valued at £50 p.a. Widowed soon after her marriage and with a posthumous child, she remarried in 1645 the sixty-three-year-old Barnabas Smith, rector of North Witham. Hannah left her three-year-old son with his grandmother in Woolsthorpe and moved the three miles to her new husband's home. She returned to her son after her second husband's death in 1653, bringing with her two half-sisters and a half-brother for the ten-year-old Isaac.

Despite much speculation, little is known of the relationship between Newton and his mother. She is known to have wished to turn Newton into a farmer, removing him from his Grantham school in 1659 to help her manage the family estate. It took the persuasive power of her brother William and Newton's headmaster, Stokes, to persuade her to allow her son to return to school to prepare for Cambridge.

One mystery about Newton's Cambridge days is why his mother sent him up to Trinity as a sub-sizar. With the inheritance from two husbands and her own dowry she is assumed to have had an income of several hundred pounds a year. Why, then, should Newton spend his undergraduate days paying his way by waiting on others? Whether this was her innate meanness, hostility to her son, financial embarrassment or the belief that it would be good for Newton, remains a mystery.

To what extent was she responsible for her son's character? In his 1980 *Portrait of Isaac Newton*, Manuel has argued that Hannah was 'the central figure in his life' (p. 25); his fixation on her was 'absolute'. The loss of his mother, he went on, 'was a traumatic event . . . from which he never recovered'. Consequently he responded to those who threatened his intellectual property with 'a violence commensurate with the terror and anger generated by his first searing deprivation'. Leibniz, Bernoulli and Hooke were simply re-runs of the theft by Barnabas Smith of his mother. Her death in 1679 released him from this pressure and permitted 'the period of prodigious creativity' of the 1680s which led to *Principia*.

There is no hard evidence of the relationship between mother and son apart from the list recorded by Newton in his Fitzwilliam Notebook and the nomenclator of the Morgan Notebook. Manuel makes the most of this somewhat sketchy evidence; it has failed to convince other biographers.

Westfall, for example, has asked why Newton chose to leave Woolsthorpe and his mother in 1661. She clearly wanted him to stay and manage the estate; Newton opted instead for a distant Cambridge career. Again, if he was so attached to his mother why did he not follow the expected career of most undergraduates and return, if not as a farmer, to a living around Grantham?

The fact is that Newton seems to have deliberately kept a fair distance between Hannah and himself. Excluding the extended stay in Woolsthorpe during the plague years of 1665–7, Newton is known to have made only three visits to his home before Hannah's death in 1679: autumn 1668; summer 1672; and spring 1678. There were four other times – the spring of 1671, 1673, 1675 and 1677 – when Newton was absent from Cambridge long enough to have gone home, and he may well have visited Hannah on one or more of these occasions. 'More vogorous displays of filial affection have been recorded', Westfall (RSW, p. 340) commented.

No letters from Newton to his mother have survived, nor have any eye-witness accounts of their relationship. One letter from Hannah has survived, but it is no more than an acknowledgment of a letter and some cloth from Newton. He was, however, present at her death. According to Conduitt's account she caught a fatal fever and Newton 'sate up all night with her, gave her all her Physick himself, dressed up all her blisters with her own hands'. She was buried on 4 June 1679.

Smith, Robert (1689–1768)

The son of a clergyman, Smith first entered Trinity in 1708 where his cousin, Roger Cotes, was Plumian Professor of Astronomy. Smith succeeded his cousin in the Plumian chair in 1716 and held the post until 1742 when, following the death of Richard Bentley, he was elected Master of Trinity. As Master he commissioned the Roubillac statue and bust of Newton, still to be seen in Trinity, for a fee of £500, and went on to commission the rather odd stained-glass windows for the Trinity Library. His name is perhaps best known today through the Smith's prize, founded by him to be awarded to the two junior B.A.s who had made 'the greatest progress in mathematics and natural philosophy' in the previous year.

Appointed the executor of Cotes, Smith prepared for publication his cousin's posthumous *Harmonia mensarum* (1722) and his *Hydrostatical and Pneumatical Lectures* (1738). He also commissioned from P. Scheemakers the Cotes bust still to be seen in Trinity. The Cotes papers left by Smith to the Rev. E. Hawkins eventually found their way to Trinity in 1779 and later formed the basis for the important publication of Edleston (1850).

Smith was a Newtonian and in his *A Compleat System of Opticks* (1738) sought to present a bold theory based on Newtonian ideas of attraction and repulsion expressed without any of the reservations and doubts their founder customarily inserted. The work proved successful and, translated into German (1755), French (1767) and in an abridged English version (1778), came to be seen as the standard account of Newtonian optics.

Smith, Samuel

A London bookseller at St Paul's Churchyard from 1681–1703. He began his career as an apprentice to Moses Pitt but later, in partnership with Benjamin Walford, set up as an independent bookseller. He served as bookseller to the Royal Society and is also thought to have dealt in the distribution of Continental books in Britain and the sale of British books to Europe. It was this same 'Sam Smith' who issued the three-line imprint of *Principia* (1687) and who was probably responsible for its European distribution.

See also Principia, Editions

Snell, Willebrod van Roijen (1591–1626) and Snell's law

A Dutch mathematician, Snell followed his father in 1615 as Professor of Mathematics at the University of Leyden. Some time afterwards he formulated the law, ever since identified with his name, that, as light passes from one medium to another, the ratio between the sine of the angle of incidence and the sine of the angle of refraction is constant:

$$\frac{\sin i}{\sin r} = k$$

for any pair of media.

Snell's work remained unpublished, confined to a long-lost notebook, until Descartes first revealed the law in his *La dioptrique* (1637). The charge of plagiarism was raised against Descartes in 1662 by Isaac Vossius; it was later confirmed by Huygens in 1691. Further research has been more generous to Descartes. While it is true that Descartes was made aware of Snell's result's some time after 1632, it is equally clear 'from Descartes' correspondence that he already had the sine law in 1626 or 1627' (Sabra, 1981, p. 102).

Newton stated the law in the *Opticks* (1704) as axiom V, in the form 'The Sine of Incidence is either accurately or very nearly in a given Ratio to the Sine of Refraction', and went on to discuss it at some length at prop. VI, Book I. The law had also been discussed in the *Optical Lectures* (1669–71), where Newton attributed the discovery to Descartes. When, however, he came to discuss the law in *Principia* (1687, Book I, sect.XIV), the attribution had been changed to Snell.

Snyder, John de Monte

When, some time after 1837, Sir David Brewster began to examine Newton's papers in the PC, he came across Snyder's *The Metamorphosis of Planets*. First published in German in 1663, a language unfamiliar to Newton, it had been transcribed from an unknown English source, in Newton's hand, into a sixty-two-page manuscript of about 22,000 words (Yale University Medical Library). To Brewster's dismay the manuscript turned out to be a long allegorical piece so typical of much alchemical literature; as such it called for the same hermeneutical skills Newton had deployed against the prophecies of Daniel and St John. Thus, for example, where Snyder had described Jupiter mounting upon a 'nimble eagle', Newton, in notes on the manuscript (Keynes MS 58), wrote instead of the more familiar language of the chemistry of tin (Dobbs, 1983, pp. 169–72).

Solomon's Temple and the cubit

In three separate works Newton turned his attention to the size and structure of the Temple of Solomon. One of them, *Prolegomena lexici*, in the Babson Institute, has never been published; the other two, *Chronology* (1728), chapter five, and *Dissertation upon the Sacred Cubit* (1737), were published posthumously. These are by no means casual essays but closely-argued tracts showing mastery of a complex and extensive literature. It may even have been to pursue such studies, Westfall has speculated, that Newton began to learn Hebrew (RSW, p. 346).

As to the purpose of this considerable intellectual activity, no hint is given in the published *Chronology* or *Dissertation*. The arguments are presented as pure studies in metrology and archaeology. Newton was not, however, the kind of man to need such hobbies, however intellectual and demanding they may be. What then was the point of this activity?

In *Chronology* he uninformatively introduced his discussion of the Temple with the phrase 'it may not be amiss to give a description of that edifice' (Horsley, V, p. 236). Westfall (RSW, p. 346) has explained how Newton came to see that a knowledge of Jewish practices, just as much as revelation, were needed to understand fully the divine prophecies. He is unclear, however, whether Newton's concern with the details of the Temple was directed to some end or merely something he became obsessed with. Manuel, in contrast, has claimed to have recognised 'the secret purpose of this research' (Manuel, 1963, p. 162). Just as prophecies were:

> Hieroglyphs for the facts of future history, every part of the earthly abode of the Law had its correspondence in the heavenly Jerusalem of the next world. The Temple of Solomon was the most important embodiment of a future extra-mundane reality, a blueprint of heaven; to ascertain every last fact about it was one of the highest forms of knowledge, for here was the ultimate truth of God's kingdom expressed in physical terms.

Manuel offers no documentation in support of his claim, and in a later work spoke somewhat differently. In Manuel (1974, pp. 92–3) chapter five of *Chronology* is described as having been undertaken 'in order to explain the vision of the Temple in the Apocalypse'.

Whatever the motivation, Newton's researches were impressive. All measurements in both Hebrew and Greek Bibles were examined and analysed. He soon found that he could make no sense of published accounts of the Temple until he had first gained some understanding of the ancient units of measurement. This involved Newton in the further major research undertaking of determining the precise length of the cubit as it is used in the Book of Ezekiel to describe the Temple. The issue was complex enough to lead Newton to change his mind on more than one occasion. Thus the length of the cubit was variously recorded by Newton as:

Chronology: '21½ or about 22 inches of the English foot';
Dissertation: vulgar cubit, 20.79 English inches;
    sacred cubit, 2.05 English feet;
Prolegomena: between 2.6 and 2.8 English feet.

See also *A Dissertation upon the Sacred Cubit of the Jews*

Souciet, Etienne (1671–1744)

A Jesuit theologian and antiquary, Souciet was a leading member of the *Académie des inscriptions et belles-lettres*. When the Abbé Conti arrived in Paris in the early 1720s with a copy of Newton's *Short Chronicle* he showed it to a number of scholars, including Souciet. A number of queries were drawn up by Souciet and passed on to Newton via John Keill. A brief reply was passed back to Souciet via Brook Taylor. From this Souciet must have inferred the fact, not openly displayed in the *Short Chronicle*, that Newton's chronology was astronomically based.

Once Newton's manuscript had appeared in the pirated edition of Nicolas Freret in 1725, Souciet felt himself free to comment as he wished. The result was his *Recueil de dissertations critiques* (1726), a lengthy critical survey of Newton's twenty-page manuscript. He dismissed Newton's astronomical and historical arguments and went on to reject the law of regnal length. Newton, he concluded, was some 530 years in error.

See also A Short Chronicle; Chronological principles

South Sea Bubble

In 1711 Robert Harley, the Earl of Oxford, founded the South Sea Co. to trade with Spanish America. By 1720 the National Debt had risen to £50 million. Taking inspiration from the financial dealings of the Scottish financier John Law in Paris, Sir John Blunt proposed that the South Sea Co. should take over the National Debt. It would offer for each £100 of National Debt, stock in the company worth £100. As long as there was confidence in the company and the value of the stock continued to rise there would be profits for everyone. The plan was approved by Parliament in February 1720 and by June £100 stock was selling for £1,050. Amongst the contributors were Pope, Swift and Kneller. When the crash came in September they lost virtually their entire investment. Others, wiser in the ways of the world, like the Duke of Marlborough and the Duchess of Kendal, made substantial profits.

Did Newton fall, like many of his friends, for what Pope termed 'lucre's sordid charms'? The answer is that he clearly did. On his death he held £10,000 of South Sea stock: £5,000 capital stock valued at £5,200; and £5,000 of annuities valued at £5,000. Earlier he had held much more. On 8 August 1722 he instructed the company to pay the interest on his stock of £21,696 6s 4d to his agent (*C*, VII, p. 210). What happened to the £11,000 difference? Hall (*C*, VII, pp. 95–7) has warned that it was common practice for Mint officials to invest, at their own risk and for their own gain, any available surplus Mint funds. Consequently, not all the £21,696 6s 4d held in 1722 need have belonged to Newton; he could simply have been farming the interest.

Is it possible to work out whether Newton lost or gained from the Bubble? Catherine Barton was reported to have put her uncle's losses as high as £20,000. De Villamil (1931, pp. 19–35), however, has argued that the loss could have been no more than a paper loss. Westfall, in contrast, has argued that such a loss was 'not impossible' (RSW, p. 862). He noted that in 1724 Newton held stock worth £11,000 in the East India Company. Three years later, at his death, the stock had been disposed of. Had it gone to repay the Mint the £11,000 borrowed and consumed in the Bubble?

The documented transactions between Newton and the Company are few and can be listed as follows.

1 1 September 1713. Newton held £2,500 of stock at 3 per cent (*C*, VI, p. 27).

2 19 April 1720. Fauquiere, Newton's agent, was empowered to sell £3,000 of his stock (*C*, VII, p. 96).

3 June 1720. £1,000 of stock bought (*C*, VII, p. 358).

4 27 July 1720. Instructions were issued to transfer annuities worth £650 into capital stock (*C*, VII, p. 96).

5 8 August 1722. Instructions were given to pay the 3 per cent dividend on his holdings of £21,696 6s 4d to Fauquiere (*C*, VII, p. 210).

6 5 May 1727. Newton's Inventory listed as part of his estate £5,000 capital stock at 104, and £5,000 annuities at 97½ with a dividend of 2½% due on Lady Day (de Villamil, 1931, p. 55).

See also Finances; Inventory

Sozzini (Socinus) Fausto Paulo (1539–1604) and the Socinians

A native of Sienna, Sozzini had already established a reputation in theology when he settled in Poland in 1580. He found there an already-existing tradition of Unitarian belief which had been introduced in the 1550s by G. Blandrata, a Piedmontese physician. Sozzini met considerable opposition but, shortly after his death, several of his disciples formulated in 1605 the so-called Rakovian Catechism. It denied the doctrine of the Trinity, original sin, predestination and justification by faith alone. Given the general weakness of the Polish crown, Socinianism managed to survive for more than a generation, but by the mid-century their churches were closed, their congregation expelled. It was not the end, for Unitarian beliefs emerged in England, Holland and Germany. In England they were first associated with John Biddle (1615–62), a Gloucester school teacher, who in between imprisonment and exile wrote against the validity of the Trinity.

Spence, Joseph (1699–1768)

Professor of Poetry at Oxford (1728) and from 1742 the Regius Professor of Modern History. A close friend of Pope, he collected many stories of the poet which were first published, together with tales of other contemporary celebrities, in his *Anecdotes* (1820). It contains a number of since-famous anecdotes of Newton, not all of them reliable. It is Spence, for example, who absurdly noted that Newton could not fathom the accounts of the Mint.

Stewart, John

Professor of Mathematics at the University of Aberdeen, Stewart translated into English the two texts *De quadratura* and *Enumeratio* which had first appeared in *Opticks* (1704). Published in 1745 under the title *Two treatises* in an edition of 350 copies, it was being remaindered two years later at 3s a copy.

Stirling, James (1692–1770)

Of Jacobite stock, Stirling was educated at Balliol, but as he refused to take the oath he could not graduate. As one of the young mathematicians brought to Newton's attention he received considerable support and patronage.

Newton was impressed by Stirling's *Lineae tertii ordinis Neutonianae* (1717) in which four new cubic curves were added to the seventy-two described by Newton in his *Enumeratio* (1704). After its publication Stirling spent some time in Venice and was thereafter known as the Venetian. Newton encouraged him to return to London and actually paid for his return journey in about 1724. Although it seems some effort was made by Newton to obtain a suitable academic post for Stirling, he was unsuccessful. Nor did Stirling have any better fortune on his own in 1746 when he applied for the mathematics chair at Aberdeen. Consequently Stirling worked mainly in mining, in which field he helped to re-organise and manage the Lanarkshire lead mines.

See also Enumeratio

Stokes, John

The headmaster of the Free Grammar School of King Edward VI, Grantham, during Newton's attendance there. According to Stukeley he played a crucial role, together with Newton's mother's brother, William Ayscough, in persuading Newton's mother that 'it was a great loss to the world . . . to bury so promising a genius in rustic employment . . . that the only way whereby he could either preserve or raise his fortune must be by fitting him for the University'. So convinced was Stokes of his case that he even offered to waive the forty-shilling school fees. He also, when Newton did return to school at Grantham in 1660, took him as boarder into his own house.

Storer, Edward and Arthur

The Storer boys, with their unnamed sister, lived with their step-father apothecary Clark at the same time Newton lodged there during his Grantham schooldays. There are a couple of references to the brothers amongst the sins listed in the Fitzwilliam Notebook. He confessed to 'Stealing cherry cobs from Eduard Storer' and to 'Beating Arthur Storer.'

In later life Edward became a tenant of Newton at Woolsthorpe, while Arthur, from Maryland in the US, communicated observations on the comet of 1680 which were eventually quoted in *Principia*, Book III, prop.XLI.

There was also a Storer sister, unnamed, who as Mrs Vincent later reported on her youthful affair with Newton.

Streete, Thomas (1622–89)

Of Irish origin, Streete worked in London in the Excise Office under Elias Ashmole until 1666, when he joined the survey of London made necessary by the Great Fire. Streete worked as an astrologer, as well as producing the popular textbook *Astronomia carolina* (1661), of which both Newton and Flamsteed owned copies. The work is of significance for Newton's thought in that it inspired Newton in the ULC Notebook to record his earliest astronomical observations. Streete stated Kepler's first and third laws but recorded the second area law only in the modified form proposed by Ismael Boulliau. Streete's account was taken from Ward (1656).

See also Kepler, Johann and Kepler's laws

Stukeley, William (1687–1765)

Born in Holbeach, Lincolnshire, the son of an attorney, Stukeley was educated at Cambridge. He went on to complete his medical education in London and after several years in practice in Boston, Lincolnshire, he moved in 1717 to London. In addition to his work as a physician, Stukeley joined the Royal Society, and from 1718 to 1727 spent nine years as the first secretary of the Society of Antiquaries, a society he had helped to found. It is of course as an antiquarian that Stukeley is mainly remembered. His *Itinerarium curiosum* (1725) is still much consulted, while his studies of Stonehenge and Avebury in 1740 and 1743, with his attempts to identify them as Druid temples, are no sillier than many recent publications.

Stukeley first met Newton in 1718. Despite the difference in their ages, and perhaps due to their common Lincolnshire background, the two became friends, with Stukeley paying regular visits to Newton's house in St Martin's St. The relationship was not without its problems. There was a coolness between them for 'two to three years' following Halley's resignation from the secretaryship of the Royal Society, when, against Newton's wishes, Stukeley unsuccessfully stood against Dr James Jurin for the vacant post. Apart from this hiatus, relations seem to have been good between the two men. Stukeley made good use of his friendship and it is largely due to him that much of the detail of Newton's later life has been preserved.

In 1726 Stukeley abandoned London and medicine, moving to Grantham to spend the rest of his life as a country clergyman. The town of Grantham, a few miles from Newton's home at Woolsthorpe, was ideally situated to enable Stukeley to gather from the few survivors who had known Newton as a boy their fading memories. It was thus Stukeley who was the sole witness to Mrs Vincent's account of her youthful affair with Newton. It was also Stukeley who, in 1726, recorded from Newton one of the fullest accounts of the famous story of the apple tree.

Stukeley provided Conduitt with some of the material he had collected and it eventually found its way into the PC. Stukeley himself gathered his own material into a ninety-page manuscript dated 1752; it contained details of Newton's family history, and sketches of Newton, Colsterworth church and the Woolsthorpe Manor. The manuscript, as the property of Stukeley's great-great-great-grandson, Oliver S. F. St. John, was eventually sold by Sotheby's in 1931. It was shortly afterwards presented to the Royal Society and, edited by A. Hastings White, was published in 1936 under the title *Memoirs of Sir Isaac Newton's Life*.

Sullivan, J. W. N. (1886–1937)

Sullivan began his career as a businessman, while educating himself in his spare time and at University College, London. After the First World War he worked as a freelance writer, producing a number of scientific biographies and popular science works.

One of these biographies, before his early death from disseminated sclerosis in 1937, was his posthumous *Isaac Newton 1642–1727* (1938). It has been singled out for praise by Westfall and linked with de Morgan as 'correctives to Brewster' (1965b, pp. xliv–xlv). The link seems too weak to hold, as Sullivan's biography is entirely derivative. His only original claim is his strange view that 'science never seemed to [Newton] particularly important' (Sullivan, 1938, pp. 43–4), a claim which fails to stand up to the most gentle of analyses.

Sundials and dialling

Stukeley reported of Newton how:

> Diligent he was in observing the motion of the sun, especially in the
> yard of the house where he lived, against the walls and roofs,
> wherein he would drive pegs, to mark the hours and half hours
> made by the shade, which by degrees from some years observations
> he had made very exact, and anybody knew what o'clock it was by
> Isaac's dial, as they ordinarily called it. (STUKELEY, 1936, p. 43)

It was a skill and interest he retained throughout his life for, as Conduitt
noted:

> To the time of his death he retained this custom of making constant
> observations in the rooms he chiefly used where the shade of the
> sun fell; and I have often known him both at Kensington and in St
> Martin's St, when anyone asked what o'clock it was, tell
> immediately by looking where the shadow of the sun touched as
> exactly as he could have by his watch.

Two other signs of his interest are various entries on dialling in his
notebooks and the construction of a number of dials.

Brewster reported in 1831 (p. 344) that two dials made by Newton
could still be seen at his old home at Woolsthorpe, although 'the styles
of both are wanting'. Two dials, perhaps the two seen by Brewster,
were moved later in the century. The first was taken from the south
wall in 1844 and presented by the Rev. Christopher Turnor to the Royal
Society. The second dial, supposedly cut when Newton was nine, was
removed in 1877 to the Colsterworth Church. There were, apparently,
many more less permanent dials constructed by Newton.

Sykes, Arthur Ashley (1684–1756)

A 'latitudinarian divine', according to the *DNB*, he was educated at
Corpus Christi, Cambridge. He served as rector in various parishes
around Essex and Cambridgeshire but is mainly known as a regular
contributor to the many theological controversies of the century. The
British Museum catalogues some eighty of Sykes's pamphlets on these
themes.

Some time in the late 1750s Lady Lymington (Kitty Conduitt) decided
to implement her mother's will and have the Newton papers in her
charge examined and possibly published. For no very clear reason the
task was assigned to the aged Sykes. He was, however, too frail and ill

[557]

by this time and, although he seems to have examined some of the papers, nothing came from the venture.

See also Portsmouth Collection

T

Tables for Renewing and Purchasing of the Leases of Cathedral Churches and Colleges, &c. (1686)

This thirty-nine-page anonymous set of tables was long thought to have been the work of Newton. It was presumably this belief which accounts for the nine further editions called for by 1758. A final eleventh edition was published in 1808. It was thus left to Edleston (1850, p. lvi) to point out that the *Tables* had not been prepared by Newton; it did, however, contain a certificate signed by Newton, dated 10 September 1685, guaranteeing the accuracy of the tables. The author was, in fact, George Mabbot, Manciple of KCC. This did not stop publishers of the 1729 and later editions adding the half-title 'Newton's Tables'.

Somewhat confusingly Newton did, during the period 1674–8, draw up a set of tables 'of the fines to be paid for renewing any number of years lapsed in a lease for twenty years', for use by the Trinity College Bursar. The tables were used by the College until 1700. They are entitled *Tabula redemptionalis ad reditus Collegii SS. Trinitatis accomodata* and are included in a notebook, *Notitia E*, once belonging to Humphrey Newton, Bursar of Trinity from 1674–79, and still to be found in TCC.

Tabula refractionum siderum ad altitudines apparentes

On 15 March 1695 Newton sent to Flamsteed his completed *Tabula*. It was first published by Halley in his 'Some remarks on the allowances to be made in astronomical observations for the refraction of the air' in *PT* (1721, p. 169) and is reproduced in *C*, IV, p. 95. An earlier *Tabula* had been sent to Flamsteed in November 1694 and is reproduced in *C*, IV, p. 49.

The effect of atmospheric refraction on light passing through the earth's atmosphere is to elevate slightly the observed position of heavenly bodies. The effect is a complex one and depends upon variations in the density of the atmosphere and the relation between varying density and refractive power. Newton began by assuming that the density of the atmosphere 'decreases uniformly from ye earth upwards to the top' (C, IV, p. 61). Tables compiled on this assumption in 1694 proved to be inaccurate. Consequently, Newton substituted the assumption expressed in *Principia*, Book II, prop.XXII that 'the density of any fluid is proportional to the compression' and that if the parts of the fluid obey the inverse square law, then, 'if the distances from the centre be in harmonic progression, the densities at these distances will be in geometrical progression'. The results, however, were no more accurate than before. The fault he soon realised, as he told Flamsteed in February 1695, lay in the fact that 'the rarefaction and condensation of ye Air by heat and cold seems to have a much greater hand in ye phenomena of refractions, than we are yet aware of' (C, IV, p. 86). Having taken this particular factor into account, Newton prepared his final set of tables and submitted them accordingly to Flamsteed.

The *Tabula* itself lists the refraction, in minutes and seconds, met with at altitudes from 0° 0' to 90° in steps of 15' from 0° to 2°, of 30' from 2° to 10°, and of 1° thereafter.

Taylor, Brook (1685–1731)

Brook Taylor, as he seems invariably to have been called, came from a well-to-do family. Educated at Cambridge, he was elected to the RS in 1712 and served as its Secretary from 1714–18. He is first heard of in Newtonian circles in 1712 when, a sure sign of favour, he was appointed to the RS committee set up to examine the priority dispute between Leibniz and Newton. Thereafter he seems to have made himself available as and when Newton needed him. He thus found himself a minor player in the priority dispute, answering Bernoulli's 1716 charge of plagiary with a similar complaint of his own (*PT*, 1719). The issue was the discovery of the so-called Taylor's theorem, formulated by Brook Taylor in his *Methodus incrementorum* (1715, Method of Increments) and claimed by Bernoulli to be an earlier result of his own. In actual fact the theorem had been known to James Gregory some 40 years before.

Telescopes

The telescope was introduced into modern science in the early years of the seventeenth century. Developed by Dutch instrument and spectacle makers, its potential was dramatically revealed by Galileo in 1610 with his discovery of the moons of Jupiter, the mountains of the moon, and several other unsuspected features of the heavens. Galileo had used, as did all other early observers, a refracting telescope. Astronomers soon began to realise that such telescopes suffered from a number of inherent defects. As the refractive index of glass is different for light of different colours, images formed by simple lens will suffer from chromatic aberration; that is, the image will be surrounded by coloured fringes. Spherical aberration was also present, making it impossible to focus the rays of light at an exact point. One solution was to use lenses with the smallest possible degree of curvature. This would, however, increase their focal length and require the construction of very long telescopes. Astronomers responded to the challenge and began to construct telescopes well over a hundred feet long. Adrien Auzout of the Paris Observatory had even begun to consider the construction of a thousand-foot long refractor.

The first to diagnose the theoretical limitations of the refractor was Newton in his first paper on *Light and Colors* published in 1672 (*C*, I, pp. 92–102). As, he noted, 'light itself is a heterogeneous mixture of differently refrangible rays', any glass which collected 'any one sort of rays into one point' could not at the same time collect rays of different refrangibility. But as, Newton pointed out, 'the angle of reflection of all sorts of rays was equal to the angle of incidence', it should be possible to construct a telescope 'to any degree of perfection imaginable, provided a reflecting substance could be found' as good as glass.

By 1668 he had produced a telescope 6 inches long which, with a magnification of forty, was as powerful as a six-foot refractor. With it he was able to see the satellites of Jupiter and the phases of Venus. A second instrument, described as 'passably better', was made in 1671 and sent to London, where it was demonstrated at a meeting of the Royal Society on 11 January 1672. It brought back Oldenburg's first letter to Newton (*C*, I, p. 173), a nomination from Seth Ward for a Fellowship of the Society, and recognition not only from London but from Huygens and Europe. The reception offered to his telescope no doubt encouraged Newton to communicate more of his work.

Newton was something more than just the designer of his telescopes. He actually built them himself. Talking to Conduitt in 1726, he recalled how 'he had made it himself and when I asked where he had got his tools said he made them himself and laughing added if I had staid for other people to make my tools and other things for me, I had never made anything of it'. In recognition of such facts the Royal Society has possessed for many years a Newtonian reflector with the description: 'The original reflecting telescope made by Sir Isaac Newton with his own hands in 1671.' It had been presented to the Society in 1766 by Messrs Heath and Wing, Mathematics Instrument Makers of the Strand, London.

There is clearly something wrong with the inscription. The original telescope was made in 1668 not 1671. Also, why did a telescope sent to the Society in 1671 need to be presented to them in 1766? The documentary and optical evidence has been examined recently by A. A. Mills and P. J. Turvey (1979) in some detail. They point out that there is no evidence that Newton presented either instrument to the Society. A catalogue drawn up in 1678 did, however, refer to 'A reflecting telescope. Contrived by Mr Isaac Newton'. Yet, some time after 1700, the telescope could no longer be found at the Society. It is next heard of in 1737 when Algarotti saw it in the window of Heath and Wing in the Strand; it was seen once more in 1758. The telescope was moved finally in 1766 when on the 6 February Heath and Wing presented it to the Society.

Examination of the telescope by Mills and Turvey has shown it to have a focal length of 8.25 inches. Yet the instrument sent by Newton to the Society in 1671 had a focal length of only 6.25 inches, a discrepancy too large to be ignored. Mills and Turvey have consequently argued that the Royal Society's telescope is the first such instrument to be built by Newton.

There remains the question of priority and originality. For the first time Newton had to face the reaction of Hooke, who immediately let it be known that he had made a 'little tube about an inch long' as early as 1664. It fitted in the fob and performed better than any 50-foot instrument. He had failed to develop it himself, he explained, because most of his time had been spent on urgent duties imposed on him by the destruction caused by the Great Fire.

Also linked with the new design was James Gregory. His *Optica promota* (1663) described such an instrument. Newton possessed a copy of the work, although he told Collins later that he had only received it in May 1672 (*C*, I, p. 153). Further, it has to be conceded that only Newton built a working telescope. Gregory, and others, merely spoke of the possibility. As one of the key questions was whether it was possible to find 'a reflecting substance' capable of being polished and reflecting as much light as glass transmits, design alone was no more than a beginning. Finally, Gregory's design differed from Newton's model in an important manner. There is thus no need to feel that Gregory's contribution to telescope design, as in mathematics, has been unfairly obscured by Newton. The actual designs of Newton and Gregory, together with the earlier refracting telescope, can be seen below as Figs 1, 2 and 3.

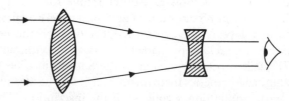

Fig. 1 Galilean refracting telescope

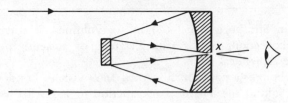

Fig 2 Gregorian reflecting telescope

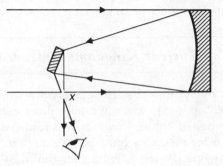

Fig. 3 Newtonian reflecting telescope

The telescope was described in the *Opticks* (pp. 102–7). A concave copper alloy, of Newton's own design, was used instead of the traditional object glass. Its diameter was 'about 25 *English* inches' and the length of the instrument a mere 6¼ inches. The magnification was between 30 and 40.

See also Aberration

Tentamen de motuum coelestium causis (An Essay on the Causes of Heavenly Motion)

Leibniz published his essay in the *AE* (1689, pp. 82–96). It contains an attempt to explain planetary motion by assuming the existence of various vortices. Leibniz later claimed to have written it before reading *Principia* (1687). An amended version, in which several misprints were corrected, was published in the *AE* (1706, pp. 446–51).

Newton drew up a set of *Notes on Leibniz's Tentamen* in which he critically examined hypotheses I, II, VII, IX–XII, XIV–XVI and XIX of the *Tentamen* (*C*, VI, pp. 116–18). Keill was also turned loose on the paper. Leibniz's celestial dynamics and the response of the Newtonians is fully discussed in Aiton (1960, 1962).

Theatrum chemicum

Published in Strasburg (1659–61) in six volumes, it consisted of an enormous collection, by Lazarus Zetzner, of ancient, medieval and Renaissance alchemical tracts.

Newton bought a copy on his April 1669 visit to London for £1 8s 0d. It was sold at the Thame Park auction in 1920. Six years later it turned up in a Sotheran's catalogue where it was described by Zeitlinger as 'very copiously annotated'. Sold for £50 in 1926, it has disappeared completely from view and must therefore remain one of the most sought-after items from Newton's library.

The Chronology of Ancient Kingdoms Amended (1728)

Newton's last work is today little thought of; 'Hardly worth reading' according to More (1962, p. 615), while Westfall, more extravagantly, has described it as 'a work of colossal tedium . . . read today only by the tiniest remnant who for their sins must pass through its purgatory' (RSW, p. 815). It was never the less a work Newton must have taken seriously judging by the time he spent on it and the number of drafts he is said to have prepared; Whiston reported there were eighteen drafts of the first chapter, although Pearce's claim of sixteen drafts of the entire work is scarcely credible. Two manuscripts have survived, both in the ULC (Add. MS 3987 and Add. MS 3988); a further 180,000 words on 448 pages of draft-sections of the *Chronology* (lots 225–6) were disposed of in the 1936 Sotheby sale to G. Wells.

The origin of the work is well known. Newton had worked on chronological problems for many years. There are, for example, New College manuscripts dating from 1680 in which the basic dating of the *Chronology* had already been established. Why, then, did the octogenarian Newton decide to collect his manuscripts together and put them into a publishable form? The answer lies with the earlier and unauthorised appearance of the *Short Chronicle* in 1725 and the critical comments it had received from the Paris savants.

His initial reaction, as always, was to avoid public dispute; 'At his time of life', he told Pearce, 'it was too late to enter into a controversy.' He must soon have changed his mind, stimulated by Pearce perhaps, the last in a long line of willing helpers, to organise his manuscripts. The Advert to the first edition commented that Newton 'was actually preparing it for the press at the time of his death'. To say this, however, may not be to say very much. Often in the past Newton had prepared works for the press, only to decide at the last moment to defer publication. Much of the *Opticks*, to quote just one example, was ready for the press twenty years or more before it finally did leave his hands in 1704. It is more than likely that without Newton's death in 1727 the *Chronology* would have remained unpublished.

The work is divided into six chapters, although Conduitt noted that 'The sixth chapter was not copied out with the other five which made it doubtful whether he intended to print it.'

1 Chronology of the Greeks.
2 Of the Empire of Egypt.
3 Of the Assyrian Empire.
4 Of the two contemporary Empires of the Babylonians and the Medes.
5 A description of the Temple of Solomon.
6 Of the Empire of the Persians.

The *Chronology* contains the fullest published account of Newton's chronological theories. Much of the basic argument is to be found in the first half of chapter 1. In general terms it was 'to make Chronology suit with the course of Nature, with Astronomy, with Sacred History, with Herodotus . . . and with itself'. Following these principles, Newton modestly admitted, could lead to errors of a year or two or even, at the very worst, as many as five or ten. Rest assured, he added, errors would certainly be no greater than twenty years!

Traditional chronologists such as Diodorus Siculus (first century BC) had accepted that before the Trojan war there were:

> No certain foundations to rely upon: but from the Trojan war . . . there were eighty years to the return of the Heraclidae [the Dorian Greeks] into Peloponnesus, and that from that period to the first olympiad there were three hundred and twenty-eight years, computing the times from the kings of the Lacedaemonians.
> (HORSLEY, V, p. 36)

The first Olympiad was a dateable event. The battle of Thermopylae of 480 BC had taken place in the first year of the seventy-fifth Olympiad. Therefore the first Olympiad must have been celebrated 296 years before in 776 BC. But this would mean, following Diodorus, that the Trojan war had been waged some 408 years earlier in the early twelfth century (1184 BC). Newton found this date quite unacceptable. The Temple of Solomon had been founded in 1019 BC, considerably later, and thus seemed to be in conflict with his deep conviction that the kingdom of Israel was the oldest of all civilisations. Unable to enlarge the chronology of the Jews, Newton chose instead to reduce the dimensions of Greek history. This was carried out in two stages.

To begin with, he noted, 'All nations, before they began to keep exact accounts of time, have been prone to raise their antiquities' (Horsley, V, p. 28). This was done in the simplest of ways and involved no more than systematically exaggerating average regnal lengths. Thus, Newton claimed, amongst the Egyptians, Greeks and Romans, average regnal lengths were taken to be 'equipollent to generations of men, and three generations to a hundred years' (Horsley, V, p. 37). But, Newton argued, whenever well-documented king lists were examined – the kings of England or France for example – they were found to have no more than an average regnal length of nineteen to twenty years. If a figure of this magnitude was accepted, Newton realised, a chronology of a quite different kind could be constructed.

Between Thermopylae (480 BC) and the return of the Heraclidae, seventeen Spartan kings had reigned. If their average regnal length had been the twenty years proposed by Newton, then the Heraclidae would have returned to the Peloponnesus in about 820 BC. Add also the eighty years demanded by Diodorus and Newton at last had an acceptable date for the Trojan war of about 900 BC.

It would, however, be as well to have some supporting evidence. This Newton sought, in a quite original way, from astronomy. Troy had fallen one generation later than the voyage of the Argonauts. If a voyage date of about 930 BC could be in some way rigorously derived, the new chronology would begin to look extremely attractive. To find such a derivation Newton began with Chiron who, he claimed, had prepared a sphere for the Argonauts on which he had located the equinoctial and solstitial points in the fifteenth degree of the constellations of Cancer, Chelae (Scorpio), Capricorn and Aries. Yet, in about the year 145 BC, the astronomer Hipparchus had noted that the equinoctial point was in the fourth degree of Aries. Comparing his observation with previous results recorded by Meton and Euctemon in 431 BC, Hipparchus was able to conclude that the equinoctial and solstitial points were not constant features of the heavens but retrogressed around the ecliptic. Hipparchus went on to calculate the rate of this precession somewhat inaccurately at 1° a century. A more accurate figure known to Newton was 1° each seventy-two years.

With this figure it was a simple matter to calculate the exact date of the Argonaut's expedition. Between Meton and the voyage there had been a precession of some 7°. At seventy-two years a degree, 504 years must have elapsed and therefore the Argonauts must have sailed in the year 935 BC, precisely one generation before the fall of Troy. The result was, apparently, an impressive confirmation of Newton's restructuring of ancient chronology. The rest of the book was mainly concerned to show how the chronology of the rest of the ancient world could be fitted into the new structure.

Impressive though Newton's results may have appeared, they were, as many contemporaries suspected, quite bogus. All depended upon the soundness of being able to identify the sphere of the Argonauts and, if so, being able to take the further step of locating on that sphere precisely where, assuming them to be so capable, they had marked the solstitial and equinoctial points. However accurate the remaining assumptions may have been, without the solid support of Chiron's sphere they could lead nowhere. And, indeed, the sphere was not only grossly anachronistic but based on little more than fanciful readings of dubious texts.

The *Chronology* is known in the following editions.

1 London, 1728. Edited by John Conduitt and 'superintended by' Thomas Pellet and Martin Folkes. It also included the *Short Chronicle* and was published in Dublin at the same time. 346 pp.
2 Paris, 1728. A French translation by François Granet; it also contains the *Short Chronicle*.
3 Delft, 1737. A Dutch translation prepared by A. de Vryer; reissued in Leyden in 1763.
4 Meiningen, 1741. A German translation prepared by P. G. Huebner; reissued in 1745.
5 Lausanne and Geneva, 1744. A Latin translation appeared in *Tome* III of Castillioneus.
6 Venice, 1757. An Italian translation prepared by P. Rolli.
7 London, 1770. Remainder sheets from the 1728 edition were reissued with a new title page, and to which was added 'a Letter from the Rev. Zachary Pearce, the present Lord Bishop of Rochester, written in 1754 to the Rev. Dr Hunt, the Hebrew Professor at Oxford'.
8 London, 1785. Included in vol. V of Horsley, with notes, and in the 1964 Stuttgart–Bad Cannstatt facsimile reprint.

See also A Short Chronicle; Chiron; Chronological principles

Theed, William (1804–91)

The son of a painter, also named William Theed (1764–1817), who specialised in classical themes and who also served as a designer for Wedgwood. The younger Theed trained as a sculptor under E. H. Baily and was responsible for such visible items as the colossal statue of Sir William Peel in Calcutta, Gladstone in Manchester, and the Africa group on the Albert Memorial. Theed was also selected by the citizens of Grantham to provide them with a statue of Newton. Theed's 12-foot bronze figure of a standing Newton, at a cost of £1,630, was unveiled by Lord Brougham in Grantham on 21 September 1858.

See also Portraits, medals, busts and statues

The Language of the Prophets

Only brief extracts have so far appeared from this 50,000-word manuscript presently to be found in KCC as part of the Keynes Collection (McLachlan, 1950, pp. 119–26). It is claimed by Westfall (RSW, p. 349n) to be, in fact, two distinct manuscripts, one dating from about 1680 and the second coming from the 1705–10 period. The latter is seen by Westfall as a 'major revision' of his treatise on Revelation of the 1670s. The former is a more general account of prophetic language similar to that contained in Chapter 2 of *Observations upon the Prophecies*. As presented by MacLachlan the work is divided into the following chapters.

1 Synopsis of prophetick figures.
2 The dayly worship described.
3 The prophecy of opening the Sealed Book and sounding the Trumpets described.
4 The prophecy of the Eaten Book described.
5 Of the Kingdoms and Churches which are the subject of sacred prophecy.
6 The prophecy of the Epistles to the seven Churches described.
7 The prophecy of the opening of the first six Seales explained.
8 The prophecy of the opening of the seventh Seale explained.
9 The prophecy of the woes of the voices of the three last Trumpets explained.

The Lawes of Motion

The manuscript, partly in the hand of Newton and partly in the hand of John Wickins, derives from loose sheets in the PC and is to be found in the ULC (MS 3958.5). It consists of two sheets folded to make eight pages. The work itself is divided into three sections entitled: 'How solitary bodyes are moved'; 'How bodys are reflected'; and 'Some observations about motion'. The text was first published in *C*, III, pp. 60–6, and thereafter in Halls (pp. 157–64) and Herivel (1965, pp. 208–18).

The subject of the work is not the laws of motion as Newton came to describe them in *Principia* (1687) but, following on from the Waste Book, the rules governing the impact of bodies. At last he could tackle cases in which two rotating bodies collide. In paras 10 and 11 he presented the general solution to how 'any two reflecting bodies', with any 'quantity of their progressive and angular motions' and with their 'point and plane of contact' given, 'shall be reflected'. It was, according to Herivel (1965, p. 84), an 'impressive proof of his dynamical genius'.

There remains some doubt about the date of composition. The Halls have favoured 1666 as the most plausible, while Herivel has done no more than to accept that it must have been written by 1669. Turnbull, in *C*, III, however, proposed an admittedly conjectural date of 1672.

See also Of Reflections

Theologiae gentilis origines philosophicae

The manuscript of this unpublished work has been described by Westfall as 'chaotic . . . a confused, missorted mass, half Latin and half English, half in Humphrey's hand and half in Newton's' (RSW, p. 351n). It dates from the 1680s and is to be found in the Yahuda Collection in Jerusalem (MS 16.2).

For Newton the religions and pantheons of the ancient peoples were all built on the same basic pattern. All began with twelve gods, derived from the seven planets, the four elements and the quintessence. These gods, in turn, became 'divinised ancestors'. Certain patterns of deification were universal. Thus, all peoples established a female deity variously named as Venus, Aphrodite, Ishtar or Astarte. All, also, took one god as supreme and the ancestor of the rest. He was invariably taken to be an old man associated with, amongst other things, time and the sea.

Behind this facile 'astronomical theology', Newton claimed to have identified 'another religion more ancient than all of these'. It was a religion 'in which a fire for offering sacrifices burned perpetually in the middle of a sacred place. For the Vestal cult was the most ancient of all' (RSW, p. 354). Because, however, 'men are ever inclined to superstition', this original religion was corrupted by later generations by such innovations as ancestor worship and idolatry. Prophets, like Christ, were sent, not to impart any new revelation, but to recall mankind back to the original, true religion.

The treatise is, according to Westfall, 'the most important theological treatise Newton ever composed'; he describes it as 'the first of the deist tracts' (Westfall, 1983, p. viii) and has recently discussed it at some length in Wagar (1982).

Theological Notebook

The catalogue of the PC compiled in 1888 noted 'A theological Commonplace Book written from both ends, in Newton's hand.' It was one of the items acquired by J. M. Keynes at the 1936 Sotheby sale and is now to be found in the library of KCC (K. Ms 2). The cover carries the note 'Sep 25, 1727, Not fit to be printed. Tho Pellett'. And nor has it been, apart from the few extracts included in McLachlan (1950, pp. 127–41).

As in several other notebooks, Newton chose to record different sets of entries at the front and rear of the book. There are no dated entries, although it is likely to belong to the early 1670s. With entries in English and Latin, much of the Notebook is empty. Only 104 pages carry entries, with the remaining 220 blank apart from the occasional subject heading.

The front of the book, paginated in arabic numerals, contained mostly notes from the patristic literature. The longest entry, *De Trinitate*, nine pages long, shows Newton already making a careful study of the original sources – Athanasius, Gregory, Jerome, Augustine, etc. – of accepted Christian belief. Other entries included *De Athanasio*, *De Arrianis et Eunomianis et Macedonianis*, *De nominibus Dei* and *De Deo uno*, headings which suggest the precise topics which were coming to obsess Newton's theological imagination.

At the rear of the book, paginated in Roman numerals, Newton placed mostly Biblical notes. Again the drift of his thought is quite apparent in the space devoted to each of the headings; *Deus Filius*, for example, required more than the original two pages allowed for it. Entries also show that Newton was laying the foundations for his formidable Biblical knowledge. Whatever views he would later adopt, it would be clear that they would be based on solid scriptural evidence. Thus, on the question of the subordination of Christ, Newton noted, 'see Acts 2.33.36. Phil 2.9.10. I Pet 1.21. John 12.44. Rom 1.8 & 16.27. Acts 10.38 & 2.22. I Cor 3.23. & 15.24,28. & 11.3. 2 Cor. 22, 23' (f. XIII^v).

The Original of Monarchies

The work has been published for the first and only time in Manuel (1963, pp. 198–221). Similar material can be found in the Bodleian Library and in the pages of *The Chronology* (1728). The autograph manuscript is to be found in KCC in the Keynes Collection (MS 146). On the basis of handwriting evidence the work has been assigned to the early 1690s.

Newton began *The Original* with an account of how families joined together into cities, and how cities in turn became kingdoms headed by a monarch. The style is that of the conjectural historical sociology found in the more familiar writings of John Locke and Sir Robert Filmer. Such history, however, was merely the framework within which he could seek to establish a more fundamental thesis, namely the priority of the Kingdom of Israel over all other ancient kingdoms. The main tool deployed was his law of regnal length. It enabled him to reduce drastically the many thousands of years claimed for their history by the scholars of Egypt, Chaldea and most other ancient kingdoms. Thus, to take one example, the 244 years claimed by Roman historians for the seven kings who preceded the Consuls was reduced by Newton to 'ninety or a hundred years' (Manuel, 1963, p. 212).

Newton was thus able to reduce, quite convincingly, the great antiquity claimed for the Kingdom of Egypt. He found it less easy to make a plausible case for his claim that Israel was more ancient than the Egypt which held it in bondage. Quoting Exodus (1:9; 5:12, 14) and the Psalms (CV:24), Newton argued that Egypt at that time consisted of 'several small kingdoms' and that, though in bondage, Israel was in fact a larger and mightier kingdom. It remained for Newton to show that these small kingdoms grew into a single monarchy, but at this point the manuscript abruptly ends.

See also Chronological principles; The Chronology of Ancient Kingdoms Amended

---

Theory of the Moon's Motion

If the only bodies in the solar system were a perfectly spherical earth and moon it would be a simple matter to predict at any time the position of the moon. The observer would need to know the initial position of the moon, its mean motion and the basic dimensions of the orbit. In such a universe the moon would return predictably to any specific point on its orbit – its apogee, for example – at regular intervals. In reality the moon weaves a much more complex path about the earth and instead of returning to the same point in its orbit at equal intervals, it displays a more variable and formidable pattern. Such orbital variations are known to astronomers as inequalities, and to account for such inequalities and other perturbations the modern astronomer has found it necessary to analyse the moon's orbit 'into about 150 principal periodic motions along the ecliptic, and about the same number perpendicular to it: there are also about five hundred smaller terms' (Payne-Gaposchkin, 1954, p. 131). At this point it becomes apparent to the observer why Newton once confessed to Machin that 'his head never ached but with his studies on the moon'.

In the present work Newton sought to list the rules needed to compute some seven such inequalities and perturbations found in the lunar orbit. They cover:

1 the annual equation;
2 the position of the lunar apogee relative to the sun;
3 the relation of the lunar nodes to the sun;
4 equation of centre;

5 the variation;

6 'The summ of the distances of the Moon from the Sun, and of the Moon's Apoge from the Sun's Apoge' (*C*, IV, p. 325);

7 'Say also As the Radius to the sine of the distance of the Moon from the Sun so is 1' 30" ± 31 to the seventh equation' (*C*, IV, p. 325).

While items 1, 4 and 5 were well known to astronomers, the remaining entries originated with Newton. They were judged by Baily, in 1837 (p. 743), to be only 'a rough numerical approximation to the formulae *now* in use for denoting the true place of the moon in her orbit'.

The work is known in the following editions.

1 Oxford, 1702. It was first published by David Gregory in Latin in his *Astronomia physicae et geometricae elementa* (Elements of astronomy, physical and geometrical, pp. 322–6). It was also contained in the second edition of 1726 and in the modern reissue of 1972. As no Latin text is known, it is argued by Cohen that the work had been translated – by Gregory himself perhaps – from Newton's surviving English text.

2 London, 1702. At the same time as Gregory published a Latin translation, the original text appeared in a brief and extremely rare pamphlet. It begins with a five-page section, 'To the Reader', by an unidentified author. The translator is unknown and amongst those proposed, the names of Halley, Gregory and Desaguliers are the most prominent. Two manuscripts are known: one in the PC in the ULC (MS 3966) in Newton's hand and dated 27 February 1700; the second, a copy made by Gregory, is in the library of the RS.

3 London, 1704. Edited by John Harris and included, under the heading *Moon*, in his *Lexicon technicum*. It is missing the initial 'To the Reader' and has been slightly 'altered or edited'. Harris also included the text in the later editions of 1708, 1716, 1725 and 1736.

4 London, 1705. It was printed, in English translation, in *Miscellanea curiosa*, and was retained in the later editions of 1708 and 1726.

5 Cambridge, 1707. Whiston reprinted for the first time in his Cambridge lectures, *Praelectiones astronomicae*, the Latin text of 1702.

6 London, 1715. A two-volume translation of 1 above, reissued in 1726 and in a modern reprint in 1972.

7 London, 1715. A translation by Whiston was included in the English edition of 5 above; it is also to be found in the 1728 reissue and in the modern reprint of 1972.

8 London, 1784. It was included in Horsley, vol.III, and is also available in the 1964 reprint.

9 London, 1837. Baily included the Latin pamphlet in the *Supplement* to his 1835 *Account of . . . Flamsteed*.

10 Cambridge, 1967. The text of the PC manuscript was published by J. F. Scott in *C*, IV, pp. 322–7.
11 London, 1975. A modern critical facsimile edition, edited by I. B. Cohen and including both English and Latin texts.

The System of the World

The title is misleading and can apply to Book III of *Principia* or the posthumous work of that title first published in 1728. It is the latter text which is to be considered here.

The work was intended originally to appear as the second of the two books which would together constitute *Principia*. It would carry the title *De motu corporum liber secundus*. But by the summer of 1685 Newton had expanded *Principia* to three books, with the original second book appearing as Book III. At the same time Newton decided to change the character of Book III. Originally, he noted in the introduction to Book III, he had planned a popular piece which 'might be read by many'. But, fearing the disputes such a work might provoke, he chose to produce a more mathematical work which would be readable only to those who had mastered the first two books.

Having therefore no immediate use for the completed *System* he had Humphrey Newton copy out part of the text and deposited it in the ULC on 29 September 1687 in the supposed fulfilment of his obligations as Lucasian Professor. The manuscript (Dd 4.18) is titled *De motu corporum liber*. A number of copies are known to have been made. One, made by Cotes is in TCC; another complete copy is in Clare College, Cambridge. There may also be a copy in the Macclesfield Collection.

Nothing more seems to have been heard of the work until after Newton's death in 1727. In the following year there appeared, by an unknown hand, an English translation of the work. This was followed in the same year by the publication by Conduitt of the Latin text based on Newton's original manuscript. With the title, *De motu corporum (Liber secundus)*, no longer making any sense, Conduitt changed it accordingly to *De mundi systemate*. Some sections of the work were incorporated into Book III of *Principia* and are listed in Cohen (1971, p. 329).

The work begins with a general account of centripetal force (paras 2–6). The discussion is non-mathematical. Beginning with para.7 Newton turns to consider the dynamics of the solar system. The latter part of the work is devoted to two long discussions of the theory of tides (paras 38–54) and the nature and dynamics of comets (paras 58–78). A concluding section discusses the problem 'The relation between the velocity of a comet and its distance from the sun's centre being given, the comet's orbit is required.'

The work is known in the following editions.

1 London, 1728. Anonymous English translation. References to *Principia* in the text were eliminated as 'the great work . . . appears to have been put into a very different form after this Tract was written . . . This alteration caused so much confusion in the citations, that it was thought best to leave them all out.' Some, however, escaped the cull. The suggestion by Cajori (p. 679) and others that the translation was made by Andrew Motte is confidently dismissed by Cohen (Newton, 1969, pp. xii–xiii). What had he to hide? Why should he give the work to F. Fayram to publish and not prefer his brother and regular publisher, Benjamin Motte?

2 London, 1728. The first Latin edition, edited by Conduitt from Newton's original manuscript (Add. MS 3990), entitled *De mundi systemate liber Isaaci Newtoni*. Citations to *Principia* were included and collated.

3 London, 1731. A reprint of the Latin text of 1728.

4 London, 1731. A second edition of the English translation of 1728. Citations to *Principia* were restored and, as with the Latin editions, collated with the third edition of Principia (1726). Asterisks were used to mark passages 'identical to portions of the later *Principia*' and marginal cross references were made to Motte's English translation of *Principia* (1729). The second edition is therefore 'of far more value . . . than the first' (Newton, 1969, p. xiii).

5 London, 1737. A third English translation. It was published by Benjamin Motte and reissued in 1740.

6 Lausanne and Geneva, 1744. A reprint of the Latin text of 1728 included in Castillioneus, *Tome* II.

7 London, 1779–85. A reprint of the Latin text in Horsley, vol. III; reprinted once more in Stuttgart–Bad Cannstatt (1964). Horsley introduced the custom, later followed by Cajori, of numbering each paragraph in sequence from 1 to 78. The concluding cometary problem and its solution were unnumbered. No further Latin edition has since appeared.

8 London, 1803 and 1819. English translation included in the two editions of *Principia* edited by William Davis.

9 New York, 1848–85. English translation included in the various editions of *Principia* edited by N. W. Chittenden.

10 Berkeley, 1934. Modernised English translation by F. Cajori published with his edition of *Principia* and included in all later editions.

11 London, 1969. A photo-reprint of the second English edition of 1731 with a valuable introduction by Cohen. It also contains the front matter of the first English edition of 1728.

Thirteen Letters from Isaac Newton to John Covel (1848)

On 22 January 1689 Newton and Sir Robert Sawyer took their seats in the Convention Parliament at Westminster as elected members for Cambridge. Between 12 February and 15 May Newton sent fourteen letters to Covel, Vice-chancellor of the University, informing him of any significant parliamentary proceedings and advising him on the University's response. None of Covel's replies have been traced.

Some of the material sent back to Cambridge, such as the news that the King 'was willing the Hearth Money Tax be taken away', could have been of no more than passing interest. On two more persistent themes, however, Newton did more than simply report parliamentary proceedings.

The first concerned the oath of allegiance due from all loyal subjects to the new monarch, William III. Some, Newton knew, would feel that an earlier oath made to James II remained binding as long as he lived. Arguments were therefore offered to Covel (21 February 1689) to deploy amongst the reluctant. Allegiance was due to James, Newton argued, only as long as such allegiance was the law of the land. Quoting statutes of Edward III and Henry VII, as well as judgments of Lord Chief Justice Hales, he concluded that it is 'treason to be in arms against a king de facto . . . tho it be in behalf of a king de jure'.

Later, on 16 March, Newton revealed that it was unlikely that the oath would be imposed on anyone already 'in preferments'. Only those about to take up future preferments would have to swear the oath. The compromise was defeated in the Lords, but Newton on 29 March was still able to offer to Covel the expectation that the Bill would be 'mollified in committee'. His optimism was misplaced; the oath was imposed on all.

The second main issue to concern Newton was the struggle to confirm the University's statutes. Did Covel want any changes made, he asked. Oxford had already submitted their proposals; would not Covel respond? As no reply appears to have been received by Newton, he made several proposals of his own, including 'entituling Professors to livings annexed to their Professorships, granting one book of every printed copy and restoring the rights of University Preachers' (7 May 1689).

The edition of the thirteen letters (a fourteenth written jointly with Sawyer (15 May 1689) was excluded) was published by Dawson Turner in a slim thirty-page volume without any editorial comment at all in 1848. It was edited from originals in his possession and is now in TCC. The full correspondence is available in C, III, pp. 10–24.

Thomson, James (1700–48)

Thomson was a Scot, educated at Edinburgh University, who came to London in 1725. His most durable verse, *Rule Britannia*, is taken from his masque *Alfred* (1740).

He was one of the first British poets to oppose the artificiality of Augustan verse and to express a new feeling for nature. It is instructive to compare his attitude to Newton with that proclaimed by the Romantic poets a century later. He was, in fact, one of the earliest to attempt to identify and express in verse particular aspects of the Newtonian canon which most illuminated nature.

Thus in his *To the Memory of Newton* (1727) he identified light in general, and the colours of the spectrum in particular, as having a special interest. In this he would be followed by most eighteenth-century poets. Before Newton, he declared, light had 'shone undiscovered' and it was Newton who:

> To the charmed eye educed the gorgeous train
> Of parent colours. (lines 101–2)

This led him to the oft-repeated 'roll of colours':

> First the flaming red
> Sprung vivid forth; the tawny orange next;
> And next delicious yellow; by whose side
> Fell the kind beams of all-refreshing green.
> Then the pure blue, that swells autumnal skies,
> Ethereal played; and then, of sadder hue,
> Emerged the deepened indigo . . .
> While the last gleamings of refracted light
> Died in the fainting violet sway. (lines 102–11)

Not for Thomson a Keatsian dismissal of the basic facts of optics; rather the more enthusiastic response:

> Did ever poet imagine aught so fair (line 119)

and the simple reaction:

> Seen, Greenwich, from thy lovely heights, declare
> How just, how beauteous the refractive law. (lines 123–4)
> (Heath-Stubbs and Salman, 1970, p. 139)

See also Poetic tradition

Thornhill, Sir James (1675–1734)

A highly successful painter of his day, he was knighted in 1722, the first British-born artist to be so honoured. From 1718 Thornhill served as History Painter to George I. A decorative painter in the baroque manner, his work can be seen in the Dome of St Paul's, Greenwich Hospital, Queen Anne's bedroom at Hampton Court and Blenheim. He was also the father-in-law of Hogarth.

Thornhill twice painted Newton's portrait. The first was commissioned by Richard Bentley in 1710 and remains where it was first hung. Newton is shown three-quarter length in his own short hair, *contraposto*, with open neck and simple robe (RSW, p. 701; Manuel, 1980, p. 334).

The second portrait, also dated 1710, was presumably commissioned by Newton, for it passed through Catherine Barton to the Portsmouth family at Hurstbourne Park. He is shown seated, three-quarter length, with sparser hair than the Bentley portrait. His gown is more elaborately embroidered and Newton looks much frailer. The result is less pleasing than the Bentley portrait. With less hair to conceal the shape of his skull there is revealed a massive brow and an extended, and perhaps, even pointed occiput; it seems far too large for his frail body (RSW, p. 704).

See also Portraits, medals, busts and statues

Thorp, Robert (1737–1812)

Thorp was educated at Cambridge and, after graduating in the 1760s, succeeded his father as rector of Chillingham in Northumberland. He went on to hold a number of livings in the area while also being appointed, in 1792, Archdeacon of Northumberland.

Thorp was one of the three editors of the Latin 'excerpta' from *Principia* published in 1775. In the following year he issued a prospectus announcing a two-volume translation of *Principia* for those, 'who, with a moderate skill in mathematical learning, are desirous of being acquainted with the Philosophical Principles of . . . Newton as they are delivered in his own writings'. It would also contain a commentary, and the two volumes would cost two guineas. In actual fact only the first volume, dealing with Book I, ever appeared. First published in 1777, it was reissued in 1802; both editions are extremely rare. It is also available in a 1969 facsimile reprint.

The translation, though based on Motte's edition of 1729, is considered by Cohen (Newton, 1969, p. iv) to be 'notably improved and amended'. Further, he declared, for anyone wishing to follow Newton's reasoning and 'to comprehend this great treatise on its own terms, there is no better work . . . available in English'. Its only rival is the more comprehensive Jesuit edition of 1739–42.

See also Principia, Translations

Tides

The connection between the tides and the moon seems to have been made first in the West in the first century BC by the Stoic, Posidonius, and in the East in about 770 AD by Tou Shu-Meng. There were, however, alternative visions which sought, for example, to equate the tidal cycle with some form of terrestrial respiration, and which would prove to be even more tempting than the prosaic observations of the Stoics. When Kepler, in the *Astronomia Nova* (1609), sought to develop a lunar tidal theory, he found his work dismissed by Galileo as mere astrology. Galileo went on to argue that tides were caused by the earth's motion, both daily and annual, and constituted the strongest evidence of the Copernican system. Against such views, the influential figure of Descartes presented tidal motion in a purely mechanical manner within his general theory of vortices. No one before Newton seems to have considered that the sun, as well as the moon, could exert its influence over the tides.

Newton's analysis of tidal motion can be found in *Principia*, Book III, props XXIV and XXXVI–XXXVII, and *The System of the World*, sections 38–54. It was an analysis, a modern authority has declared, which afforded 'the firm basis on which all subsequent work has been laid' (Darwin, 1911, p. 89). A detailed analysis of Newton's work has been provided by Aiton (1955, pp. 207–14).

Tractatus de quadratura curvarum

One of the most frequently published of Newton's mathematical papers, work on it began in 1691 in a letter to David Gregory. On 7 November 1691 Gregory had written to Newton sending him 'my method of squaring figures, published three years ago but now clarified by examples. If only I might be allowed to know your method too, which, as I have subsequently gathered, differs little from mine' (*C*, III, p. 176). Newton replied later in the month and, characteristically, began his reply with references to work of twenty years before. Newton seldom missed an opportunity to impress on his colleagues just how long ago he had anticipated them all. Gregory's letter did more than elicit Newton's standard response and seems to have stimulated him to make one more attempt to present his work in a definitive and acceptable form. The result was the first draft of *De quadratura* (*MP*, VII, pp. 24–128), worked on into 1692. As with so many of his other mathematical works, Newton found it impossible to sustain enough interest in the manuscript to complete it.

It was, however, shown to several colleagues. Fatio saw it, as did Gregory, who noted in 1694 that the tract 'develops that matter astonishingly and beyond what can readily be believed' (*C*, III, p. 338). Extracts also appear to have been sent to John Wallis (*C*, III, pp. 222–9), who published them in the second volume of his *Opera* (1693, pp. 391–6). A further copy was made by Halley (*C*, IV, p. 165).

De quadratura was next heard of when it appeared in print as an appendix to the *Opticks* (1704). In an Advertisement to the work Newton noted that he had described to Leibniz in 1679 'a Method by which I had found some general Theorems about squaring curvilinear figures'. What, however led him to publish his method, he went on, was that others had started to publish results derived from a manuscript he had lent out some years before. Consequently, he had decided to publish the work himself. The reference is to George Cheyne and the publication of his *Fluxionum methodus inversa* (1703). The result, when it did appear, proved to be a revised and abbreviated version of the incomplete manuscript of 1691–2 (*MP*, VIII, pp. 92–159). Incredible as it may seem, at the age of 62, Newton had published his first mathematical work.

The work is significant in a number of ways. At the level of notation the manuscript of 1691–2 saw for the first time the use of Newton's dotted fluxional notation. The notation was preserved in the published version of *De quadratura* (1704). Also used was a capital Q to stand for the process of quadrature, rather than the summation sign $\int$ adopted by Leibniz in his published work. On a more substantive issue, *De quadratura* contained the first published statement of the binomial theorem, discovered by Newton some forty years before.

The text of *De quadratura*, in its published form, is in two parts. In the first part Newton, in the manner of *De analysi*, demonstrated how infinite series could be deployed to determine the quadrature and rectification of curves. In the second part he returned to the topic of fluxions, discussed at greater length in his then unpublished *De methodis*.

The 'Method of Fluxions', he noted, had been discovered in 'the years 1665 and 1666'. He chose in *De quadratura*, to develop the method in terms of the 'prime and ultimate ratios' first met with in *Principia*, Book I, sect.I. Thus, in his new approach:

> Fluxions are very nearly as the Augments of the Fluents generated in equal but very small Particles of Time, and, to speak accurately, they are in the first Ratio of the nascent Augments; but they may be expounded in any Lines which are proportional to them.
> (MIDONICK, 1968, vol. 2, pp. 189–90)

Newton illustrated his terminology in the accompanying diagram. Let
the areas ABC and ABDG be produced by the uniform motion of the
ordinates BC and BD, and let the line VTH touch the curve at C and
meet bc and BA at T and V. Thus the ordinate BC, the abscissa AB
and the curve ACc will have as augments Ec, Bb and Cc. Therefore the
sides of the triangle CET 'are in the Prime Ratio of these Nascent
Augments', and the fluxions of AB, BC and AC are 'as the Sides CE,
ET, and CT of the Triangle CET'.

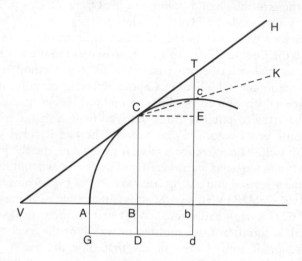

Alternatively, the fluxions could be taken as 'the ultimate Ratio of the
Evanescent Parts'. In this case it is assumed that the ordinate bc returns
to its original site BC; as it does so CK will more closely approach the
tangent CH and the 'Evenescent Triangle CEc in its ultimate form
becomes similar to the Triangle CET'. Accordingly 'the Evenescent
Sides CE, Ec, and Cc, will be ultimately to one another as are CE, ET,
and CT the Sides of the other Triangle CET' and, in conclusion, 'the
Fluxions of the Lines AB, BC and AC are in the same Ratio'.

The terminology is far from memorable and difficult to control. Its
application can, however, be seen in a simple example taken from *De
quadratura* in which Newton demonstrated how to find the fluxion x^n of
a uniformly flowing quantity x.

In the same time that the Quantity x, by flowing, becomes $x + o$,
the Quantity x^n will become $(x + o)^n$, that is, by the Method of
Infinite Series,

$$x^n + nox^{n-1} + \frac{n^2 - n}{2} oox^{n-2} + \text{etc.}$$

And the Augments o and

$$nox^{n-1} + \frac{n^2 - n}{2} oox^{n-2} + \text{etc.}$$

are to one another as 1 and

$$nx^{n-1} + \frac{n^2 - n}{2} ox^{n-2} + \text{etc.}$$

Now let these Augments vanish, and their ultimate Ratio will be 1 to nx^{n-1}, and therefore the Fluxion of the Quantity x is to the Fluxion of the Quantity x^n as 1 to nx^{n-1}. (MIDONICK, 1968, vol. 2, p. 193)

The work has proved to be one of the more popular of Newton's mathematical texts and is known in some thirteen editions, details of which can be listed as follows.

1 London, 1704. Included in the first edition of the *Opticks*, separately paginated. It was retained in the first Latin edition of 1706 and thereafter dropped from all further editions.

2 Paris, 1707. De Monmort wrote to Newton in 1709 informing him that two years before he had had one hundred copies of the work especially printed and distributed to French scholars unable to find a copy of *Opticks* (*C*, IV, p. 534).

3 London, 1710. John Harris published the work in vol. II of his *Lexicon technicum*, the first English translation to appear, under the heading 'Quadrature of Curves'.

4 London, 1711. A lightly corrected text was published by William Jones in his *Analysis per quantitatum series* and was included in the 1723 Amsterdam reprint.

5 Lausanne and Geneva, 1744. It was included in Castillioneus, *Tome* I.

6 London, 1745. A second English translation published in John Stewart's *Two Treatises*.

7 Uppsala, 1762. A reprint taken by Daniel Melander from Jones (1711).

8 London, 1779. Included in vol. I of Horsley and its 1964 Stuttgart–Bad Cannstatt reprint.

8 Leipzig, 1908. German translation by G. Kowalewski.

10 Moscow/Leningrad 1937. Russian translation by D. D. Mordukay-Boltovsky in his Russian edition of Castillioneus (1744, *Tome* I).

11 Bologna, 1938. A partial Italian translation by Ettore Carruccio; reprinted in 1962.

12 New York, 1964. Facsimile reprints of 3 and 6 above, edited by Whiteside.

13 Cambridge, 1976 and 1981. Included in MP, VII and MP, VIII are the Latin/English texts of the earlier versions of 1691–2, together with the additions and revisions incorporated into the final version of 1704.

Extracts have been published in Midonick (1968) and Struik (1969).

Trinity College, Cambridge

Newton was admitted as a sub-sizar at Trinity on 5 June 1661. He matriculated on 8 July. Trinity could well have been chosen by his uncle, William Ayscough, himself a Trinity man; alternatively, Humphrey Babington, a fellow of Trinity and rector of Boothby Pagnell, a few miles from Woolsthorpe, could have been responsible.

As a sub-sizar Newton would have been expected to serve on the Fellows and perhaps even some of the wealthier students. No record of his attitude to his status has survived. As for his social life, the Fitzwilliam Notebook reveals that Newton did in fact frequent taverns and play cards. 'Lost at cards twice 15s 0d', 'At the tavern twice 3s 6d', 'At the tavern several other times £1 0s 0d' are all items of expense carefully listed in his 1665 accounts. Another surprising side of the undergraduate Newton is his role of Trinity money-lender. The same Fitzwilliam Notebook also reveals a list of carefully itemised loans to his fellow students at Trinity.

Newton's studies at Trinity can be followed in his ULC Notebook. It began with such orthodox courses as Aristotelian physics, ethics, metaphysics and the rhetoric of Vossius. At some point, which cannot be dated exactly, the Aristotelian entries of the Notebook were replaced by notes from Descartes, Charleton, Boyle and other modern writers. It is also while a Trinity undergraduate that Newton's mathematical interests first reveal themselves. He bought in 1664 a number of mathematical texts, while the Waste Book's first mathematical entries date from this same period.

On 28 April 1664 Newton ceased to be a sizar on his election to a Trinity scholarship. The election was not trivial for it was only scholars who could proceed to become Fellows. Nor were they awarded annually, and if Newton had failed to be elected in 1664 it is unlikely that he would have remained at Cambridge. He later described the struggle to Conduitt.

> When he stood to be a scholar of the house his tutor sent him to Dr Barrow to be examined, the Dr examined him in Euclid wch Sir I. had neglected & knew little or nothing of and never asked him about Descartes's Geometry wch he was master of. Sr I. was too modest to mention it himself and Dr Barrow could not imagine that anyone could have read that book without first being master of Euclid, so that Dr Barrow conceived then but an indifferent opinion of him but however he was made a scholar of the house.

Why Newton should have won a scholarship after such a miserable showing is unclear. Westfall (RSW, pp. 102–3) has supposed the presence of a patron in the background, although whether it was Benjamin

Pulleyn, Newton's tutor, Humphrey Babington, Barrow himself, or some other figure, is unknown.

However, with the scholarship Newton's career at Trinity advanced with some rapidity. The relevant landmarks are:

January 1665 awarded BA

2 October 1667 elected minor Fellow of Trinity

7 July 1668 awarded MA; elected to major Fellowship

29 October 1669 elected to the Lucasian chair of mathematics

One further problem remained, namely the need for Newton to take orders if he wished to remain indefinitely at Cambridge.

The crisis would have come for Newton in 1675. If by this time he had not been ordained a clergyman of the Anglican church he would be forced to resign his Fellowship and chair. The rule was a strict one and invariably enforced. But, although Newton had previously affirmed his belief in the Thirty-nine Articles when he was elected to the Lucasian chair, the increasing conviction of his Unitarian beliefs precluded him from making any deeper commitment. Two, and only two, Trinity Fellowships were exempt and both of these had been filled. It seemed to Newton that his Cambridge days were about to end. In January 1675 he wrote to Oldenburg informing him that as 'I am to part wth my Fellowship, & as my incomes contract' he wished to be excused payment of his RS membership fees (C, VII, p. 387).

Fortunately for Newton, and Trinity, help came from an unknown quarter. On 27 April 1675 a dispensation was granted by the Crown to the Lucasian Professor against taking orders unless, of course, he so wished. Who had moved the Crown to act so? For Westfall (RSW, pp. 333–4) only Barrow had sufficient interest in Newton's career and influence at Court to arrange the dispensation.

Newton remained in Cambridge for a further twenty-one years before moving to London in 1696 to take up the appointment as Warden of the Mint. He did not immediately resign his chair but continued to draw the salaries of his Fellowship and chair for a further five years. At the beginning of 1701 he appointed William Whiston his fully-paid deputy in the Lucasian chair. Finally on 10 December 1701 he resigned both Fellowship and chair, to be succeeded shortly afterwards by Whiston.

Though Newton had made his home in Trinity for thirty-five years, he seems to have left Cambridge with no regrets. Certainly he did not rush back at regular intervals to see old friends, nor does his surviving correspondence burst with letters to his Cambridge colleagues of half a lifetime. In actual fact Newton seemed to make few friends during his long Trinity residence. He was undoubtedly on more than professional terms with his senior colleagues, Humphrey Babington and Isaac Barrow. Of his own generation only the names of John Wickins and Francis Aston suggest themselves as possible friends. Humphrey Newton, who observed him at first hand in the 1680s, reported that he had 'few Visters, excepting 2 or 3 Persons, Mr Ellis of Keys, Mr Lougham (also called Laughton) of Trinity, & Mr Vigani, a Chymist, in whose Company he took much Delight and Pleasure at an Evening, when he came to wait upon Him'.

If Newton had few friends to show for thirty-five years' residence, he had even fewer students to show for a Fellowship of twenty-nine years. His first student, St Leger Scroope, was assigned to Newton on 2 April 1669. Presumably, it was not a task he much enjoyed for it was not until June 1680 that he was assigned George Markham, his second pupil. Neither student, fellow-commoners both, matriculated or graduated. He took on a third and final student later in the 1680s.

Humphrey Newton has left a note on the demands made on Newton to lecture. 'When he read in the schools he usually staid about half an hour; when he had no auditors, he commonly returned in a 4th part of that time or less.' Or, alternatively: 'When he read in the schools as Lucasianus Professor, where so few went to hear him, and fewer that understood him, that ofttimes he did in a manner, for want of hearers, read to the walls.' Despite Newton's later fame, only three students later reported having attended Newton's lectures. One was Whiston. A second, Henry Wharton, reported receiving instruction from Newton 'amongst a select Company in his own private Chamber'. The final figure, Sir Thomas Parkyns, recalled being invited by Newton in the 1680s to attend 'his publick lectures'.

Newton's life at Trinity was thus not dominated by social pursuits, nor was his time given to fulfilling heavy teaching duties. It was devoted to work. Humphrey Newton, who lived with him in the 1680s for several years, noted that Newton was distracted by no recreations. Even a casual walk could not be entertained as he considered 'all hours lost that was not spent in his studies'. Only the occasional lecture could entice him from his chamber. Otherwise he worked day after day 'till two or three of the clock' in the morning, and 'sometimes . . . until five or six'.

Newton's connection with Trinity is also apparent in the actual fabric of the College. As a Fellow Newton contributed to the building of the Wren Library. The old library had burned down and Barrow, as Master, wished to create in Trinity a building as splendid as the recently-completed Sheldonian Theatre in Oxford. Newton contributed £40 to the library fund in 1676 and in 1680 loaned a further £100 to the fund. He also donated in 1706 a pendulum clock worth £50 to the Trinity Observatory built over the Gate-House.

It is however with the more visible public monuments erected after his death that the Newton–Trinity connection is most apparent. Bentley's successor as Master, Robert Smith, a distinguished Newtonian himself, commissioned a statue from L. F. Roubillac to stand in the ante-chamber to the chapel. It was unveiled in 1755. Roubillac also sculpted a bust of

Newton which now stands in the Wren Library. A further commission of Smith, to Peckitt of York, produced the commemorative stained-glass windows still to be seen in the south window of the Wren Library. The library also contains a large number of Newton memorabilia. Its greatest treasure, however, is the remaining 860 volumes of Newton's library housed in the Wren Library since 1943. Trinity is also the home of a number of Newton portraits. They include the Thornhill (1710), Murray (1718), Vanderbank (1725) and the Seeman (1725).

Details of Newton's life at Trinity, the dividends he drew as a Fellow, and the times he was actually in residence, drawn from Edleston (1850), are shown in the accompanying table.

Newton's life at Trinity

Year	Exit	Redit	Dividend	Weeks resident
1668		Sept. 29	£15	
1669	Nov. 26	Dec. 8	£25	52
1670			£20	49½
1671	April 17	May 11	£16 13s 4d	48
1672	June 18	July 19	£16 13s 4d	48½
1673	March 10	April 1	Nil	49½
1674	August 28	Sept. 5	£25	51
1675	Feb. 9	March 19	£25	46
	Oct. 14	Oct. 23		
1676	May 27	June 1	£25	50½
1677	Feb. 20	March 3	£12 10s 0d	43½
	March 26			
	April 26	May 22		
	June 8			
1678	May 6	May 27	£25	49
1679	May 15	May 24	£25	38
		July 19		
	July 28	Nov. 27		
1680	March 11		£25	36½
	April 28	May 29		
1681	March 15	March 26	£25	49
	May 23			
1682	Feb. 21	Feb. 28	£12 10s 0d	46½
	April 8	April 29		
	May 10			

Year	Exit	Redit	Dividend	Weeks resident
1683	March 17 May 21	May 3	£12 10s 0d	46
1684	—	—	£25	52
1685	March 27 June 11	April 11 June 20	£25	51
1686	—	—	£12 10s 0d	52
1687	March 25		£12 10s 0d	45
1688	March 30 June 22	April 25 July 17	Nil	45
1689	—	—	Nil	19
1690	March 10 June 22	Feb. 4 April 12 July 2	Nil	29½
1691	Sept. 12 Dec. 31	Sept. 19	£12 10s 0d	44½
1692		Jan. 21	£12 10s 0d	49
1693	May 30	June 8	£25	49½
1694	—	—	Nil	49
1695	Sept. 14	Sept. 10 Sept. 28	£34	50
1696	March 23 April 20		£34	27½
1697	—	—	Nil	0
1698	—	—	£34	½
1699	—	—	£34	0
1700	—	—	£37	0
1701	—	—	£40	0
1702	—	—	—	2

Trinity College Notebook

One of the least significant of the notebooks. It was first noted by Brewster in the PC, who published extracts from it in the *Memoirs* (1855). Sold in the Sotheby sale of 1936, it was later purchased from Maggs Bros in 1949 by the Pilgrim Trust and donated to TCC.

Inscribed on the fly-leaf is the entry, 'Isaac Newton, Martij, 1659'. This is followed by a page in Shelton's shortwriting on the ancestry of his grandmother Ayscough. The rest of the notebook is divided into two main parts. The first, with the heading *Utilissimum prosodiae supplementum* is a simple Latin word list, while the second part consists of a set of accounts covering the period at Trinity from 1661 onwards.

They present a similar picture to the Fitzwilliam Notebook. Newton's role as money-lender is documented, with amounts ranging from one shilling to a pound loaned to fifteen people. There is also a record of books bought and the price paid for them. 'Sleidan's 4 Monarchies' cost him a shilling (a reference to *De quatuor monarchis* of Johan Sleidan) while 'Schrevelius his lexicon' cost him in about 1665 as much as 5s 4d (*Lexicon manuale Graeco–Latinum et Latino–Graecum*, 1657, by Cornelius Schrevelius).

The accounts contain, in addition, a number of more conventional domestic items such as 'cherries, Tarte, Custourde, Herbs and washes, Beere, cake, Milke'. There are also references to a chamber pot bought for 2s 2d, Stilton for 2s, and a set of chessmen. These expenses Newton described as 'impensa propria' while the earlier list on cherries and milk was dismissed as 'otiose – frustra expensa'.

See also Fitzwilliam Notebook; Notebooks

Trinity Observatory

In February 1706 it was decided to build an observatory over the Gate-House of Trinity College. Cotes noted in 1708 that 'Sir Isaac Newton gave orders for ye makeing of a Pendulum Clock which he designed as a present to our new observatory . . . I believe Sir Isaac's clock can cost him no less than £50'.

By 1715 the clock had still not been delivered. It took a further appeal from Cotes to Newton before the clock, signed R.Street, London, and dated 1708, finally arrived at Trinity. In 1952 it was reported still to be in the Master's Lodge.

The Observatory fared less well. It was pulled down in 1797, although it had been little used for many years before that date. The print of the Observatory, engraved by R. West in 1739, can be seen in Price (1952).

Truchet, Jean, also known as Père Sebastien (1657–1729)

Born in Lyon, he was both a Carmelite brother and a well-known engineer who had worked on the hydraulics of Versailles and the Orléans canal. In 1719, before Cardinal de Polignac, Fontenelle, Varignon and others, he repeated successfully some of Newton's experiments on light. Truchet informed Newton of his work (*C*, VII, pp. 111–18) in 1721; 'A deep and ardent eagerness . . . to try those experiments which you bring together so brilliantly in your treatise', he reported to Newton, had struck him on reading an English edition of the *Opticks* (1704). Newton's reply has not survived.

Turnbull, Herbert Westren (1885–1961)

Turnbull was educated at TCC, where he was second wrangler in 1907 and Smith's prizeman in 1909. After a period teaching mathematics in Hong Kong and at Repton School, he was appointed Regius Professor of Mathematics at the University of St Andrews and continued to hold the post until his retirement in 1950. By this time he had established his reputation as a historian of mathematics with the invaluable *James Gregory: Tercentenary Memorial Volume* (1939) and the still-useful *The Mathematical Discoveries of Newton* (1945). Shortly afterwards in 1947 he was invited by the RS to undertake the task of editing Newton's correspondence. Some initial editorial work had been begun by H. C. Plummer before his death in 1946. Accepting Plummer's basic plan, Turnbull began the lengthy editorial tasks which led to the publication in 1959 of the first volume of the correspondence. Two further volumes appeared, in 1960 and 1961 respectively, before ill health forced him to resign from the project. He died shortly afterwards.

Turner, Dawson (1775–1858)

As Turner's father was the head of a Yarmouth bank, he was sufficiently provided throughout his life to indulge his interests in botany, antiquities and as a bibliophile. In botany he is best known for his work on the cryptograms, *The Natural History of Fuci* (1809–19, 4 vols). He also published a number of works on local history, edited ancient manuscripts and collected letters. After his death some 40,000 letters and manuscripts were auctioned in 1859 for over £6,500.

Amongst this collection were the letters sent by Newton to John Covel in 1689 from the Convention Parliament. Turner published them, without editorial comment, in the slim volume *Thirteen Letters from Isaac Newton to John Covel* (1848).

Turnor, Edmund (1755–1829)

The son of a gentleman, Turnor was able to pursue his interest in local history and antiquities as he wished. After Trinity College, Cambridge, and the Grand Tour he became a Fellow of the Royal Society in 1786 and served as M.P. for Midhurst in Sussex from 1802 to 1806.

The Turnor family had purchased the Woolsthorpe Manor from Thomas Alcock in 1733 for £1,600. In 1806 Edmund Turnor published his *Collections for the History of the Town and Soke of Grantham*. It contained (pp. 154–86) much hitherto unpublished primary material concerning Newton's life and work. In particular Turnor made available the following items.

1 A brief account of the history of Woolsthorpe (pp. 157–8).
2 Memoirs of Sir Isaac Newton, sent by Mr Conduitt to Monsieur Fontenelle, in 1727 (pp. 158–66).
3 Sir Isaac's Funeral, from the *Gazette* of Tuesday 4 April 1727 (p. 167).
4 Newton's pedigree submitted to the College of Arms (pp. 168–9).
5 Affidavit made by Newton before a Master in Chancery, in proof of, and accompanying his Pedigree (pp. 170–1).
6 A conversation between Sir Isaac Newton and Mr Conduitt on 7 March 1725 (pp. 172–3).
7 Letter from Dr Stukeley to Dr Mead dated Grantham 26 June 1727, containing memoirs of Newton's life collected at Grantham and Colsterworth (pp. 174–80).
8 Extracts from the Journal Books of the Royal Society, relating to Sir Isaac Newton, dating from 23 December 1671 to 8 January 1713 (pp. 181–6).

U

ULC Add. MS 4000

The Notebook carries the date '166³₄ January'. It contains the following.

1 Mathematical annotations from the works of Viete, Oughtred, Wallis, van Schooten and Huygens. Many of these have been published in *MP*, I.

2 Some of Newton's earliest writings on the calculus and the evaluation of derivatives (*MP*, I).

3 *Of Refractions*; optical notes on the grinding of hyperbolic and elliptical lenses. Parts of the manuscript were published in Hall (1955, pp. 36–43); the balance can be seen in *MP*, I, pp. 559–76.

Unitarianism

Modern Unitarianism emerged in the sixteenth century as one of the many new religious traditions of the Reformation. Its roots were, of course, ancient and go back to Arius and the Arian heresy condemned by the Council of Nicaea in 325 AD; indeed, the name Arian was still in wide use in Newton's day. Another common name was Socinian. This derived from Fausto Sozzini, around whom, in late sixteenth-century Poland, there grew up a body of doctrine, echoed in the Rakovian catechism of 1609, which rejected the Trinity, original sin, baptismal regeneration, predestination and justification by faith. Unitarianism was a broad movement and to say of two believers that they were both Unitarians was not necessarily to say they had much in common.

Newton was not alone in his circle to embrace Unitarian beliefs. William Whiston and Samuel Clarke were both Unitarians, as was Hopton Haynes, a colleague at the Mint. The reasons Newton offered for his beliefs were mainly scriptural. God's name, he declared, was never used to refer to more than one of the Trinity and if used without restriction referred always to the Father. As for Christ, Newton insisted, by expressing his dependence on God, and by acknowledging the superiority of God, and that foreknowledge belonged to God alone, he was clearly a subordinate being. Newton could quote Biblical texts endlessly to show there was no warrant for Trinitarian beliefs. He could also produce a mass of historical evidence to show that such beliefs only entered into the church in the fourth century, after the Council of Nicaea.

Such beliefs were not to be subscribed to casually in Newton's day. The Act of Toleration of 1688 specifically excluded from its protection those who spoke against 'the Blessed Trinity'. A later Act of 1689 barred all such from holding public office. Whiston was in fact one who fell under this ban when he was dismissed in 1711 from his Cambridge chair. It even seemed that Newton too, at one point, would be forced to abandon his academic career. In 1675 however a dispensation, allowing holders of the Lucasian chair to continue in their college Fellowship without taking orders, freed Newton from any such threat.

Some theologians have sought to impose a neat classification on a clearly complex body of belief held by men reluctant to commit themselves to dogma. They thus distinguish between:

1 Arians, who claim of Christ that he was begot by God, existed before time began, is to be worshipped, and that through him God created all things;

2 Socinians, who still see Christ as an object of prayer, but who deny that he existed before his appearance on earth;

3 humanitarians, who, most radically of all, see Christ merely as an exceptional man, undeserving of worship.

Given such a classification, Newton would most accurately be described as an Arian.

V

Vacuum

Newton presented arguments for the existence of the vacuum, or, in the terminology of seventeenth-century physicists, the void, in both *Principia* and *Opticks*. In the second edition of *Principia* (1713) Newton introduced two new corollaries to proposition VI of Book III. Corollary III argued that 'All spaces are not equally full', on the grounds that, if they were, 'neither gold, nor any other body could descend in air'. Corollary IV went on to draw the conclusion that 'If all the solid particles of all bodies are of the same density, and cannot be rarefied without pores, then a void, space, or vacuum must be granted.' At one time Newton seems to have considered introducing into Book III, at the beginning, a set of *Definitiones*. Amongst them was a *Definitio* II which defined vacuum as 'every place in which a body moved without resistance' (ULC Add. MS 3965, f.437). Along with other related revisions they were not in fact incorporated.

Further arguments were presented in *Opticks*, Book II, part III. Here the issue was the opaqueness and transparency of bodies. He began by noting (prop.II) that 'the least part of almost all natural bodies are in some measure transparent'. Opaqueness, he went on in prop.III, is due to the 'discontinuity of parts', as witnessed by the fact that 'opake Substances become transparent by filling their Pores with any Substance of equal . . . density with their parts'. Paper dipped in water is cited as an example. Conversely, transparent substances can be made opaque 'by evacuating their pores, or separating their parts', as with, for example, 'Horn by being scraped, Glass by being reduced to powder'.

Further use was made of the density argument in prop.VIII. It was noted that while gold was nineteen times heavier than water, it was still rare enough 'to admit Quicksilver in to its Pores, and to let Water pass through it'. Newton concluded that gold must have 'more Pores than solid parts, and by consequence that Water has above forty times more Pores than Parts'.

Against Newton's commitment to the void there lay the arguments of the Cartesians and Leibniz. For Descartes, with his identification of body with extension, there could be no void. It had been ruled out by definition. In a similar way, Leibniz's rejection was based on metaphysical assumptions. In his second letter to Clarke he maintained that 'the more matter there is, the more God has occasion to exercise his vision and power. Which is one reason . . . why I maintain there is no vacuum at all' (Alexander, 1956, p. 16). Another reason, involving an appeal to the principle of sufficient reason, insisted that, if there were a void, God would have had no reason to prefer any one particular proportion of matter to empty space.

Such arguments meant little to Newton. The Cartesian identification of matter and extension was rejected in *De gravitatione* on the grounds that it led to atheism (Halls, pp. 142–3). The objections of Leibniz were dealt with in the *Leibniz–Clarke Correspondence* (Alexander, 1956, p. 21) where they were dismissed as equally theologically unsound.

Vanderbank, John (*c.*1694–1739)

The son of the Dutch portrait painter, Peter Vanderbank, he was born in England and seems to have inherited the practice of Kneller.

There is a certain amount of uncertainty about how many of the surviving portraits of Newton come from Vanderbank. Portraits 1–3 below are all signed and generally accepted as authentic.

1 1725. This was the portrait used as a frontispiece to the third edition of *Principia* (1726). It was presented to the Royal Society by C. B. Vignoles (1793–1875), a leading civil engineer of his day, in 1841. It now hangs in the Lift Hall of the Society's rooms (RSW, p. 803); another version, hanging in Trinity College, Cambridge (RSW, p. 810), was presented to the College by Robert Smith in 1766. It shows a seated Newton in a velvet coat with his own shoulder-length hair. He presents a dull, listless appearance, with his hands hanging loosely by his sides and a vacant expression on his face.

2 1725. In 1950 the Royal Society obtained a study in oils on paper of Newton's head. Somewhat extravagantly, Manuel has commented that Newton's 'lips have become loose and almost sensual, the eyes bulge, the face is puffy, and creased, the hair is unkempt. If there was cruelty in this man, Vanderbank caught it' (1980, p. 382). It is reproduced in colour in *Endeavour*, 1956, p. 131.

3 1726. Probably Newton's final portrait (RSW, p. 818; Manuel, 1980, p. 367). It was donated to the Royal Society by Martin Folkes, President of the Royal Society from 1741 to 1752. An unattractive picture, it shows Newton dressed formally in elaborate wig and gown sitting down holding a book in his left hand. His face looks

bloated and withdrawn. Behind him can be seen the emblem of the snake, encoiled in a circle, swallowing its own tail, and known as ouroboros to alchemists. What significance it had for Vanderbank is not clear.

4 1726. Bequeathed by a John Hatsell (d.1820) to the British Museum, it was transferred to the National Portrait Gallery in 1871, where it was thought to be a Vanderbank. It shows a three-quarter-length seated Newton with his right hand resting on the chair and his left hand turning the pages of a mathematical treatise. It is undoubtedly the third edition of *Principia* (1726) as the open pages in the portrait show diagrams on opposite pages found only in this edition. On the table there also can be seen an unopened *Opticks*. To one side there stands a globe, while carved on the side of the table the crossed bones of the Newton family arms can be clearly seen. Similar versions can be seen at Trinity and in the Babson Collection. It is reproduced in Westfall (RSW, p. 831). It is no longer thought to be by Vanderbank but rather a copy of the earlier portrait of 1725.

5 Also attributed at some time to Vanderbank is the portrait (RSW, p. 847) owned by the Cambridge booksellers W. Heffer and Sons.

The Babson *Catalogue* (p. 203) lists unsigned portraits, located in the collections of the Marquis of Bute, the Babson Institute Library, Amherst College, and a further portrait of TCC purchased in 1850, as 'formerly attributed to Vanderbank, but possibly by Enoch Seeman'.

See also Portraits, medals, busts and statues

Varenius, Bernhard (1622–50)

A German physical geographer, Varenius was educated at the universities of Königsberg and Leyden. He is remembered for his two works: *Descriptio regni japonicae* (1649), one of the earliest Western works on Japanese geography; and *Geographia universalis* (1650), a work still of interest because its second edition was edited and revised by Newton in 1672. It is in fact the first book to appear with Newton's name on the title page.

See also Geographia universalis

Variantes lectiones apocalypticae

A collation of about twenty different versions of Revelation. Judging by a letter to the Biblical scholar John Mill, the work was complete by 1694 (*C*, 3, pp. 305–7).

Manuel (1974, pp. 93–4) describes the work as 'a closely written notebook . . . that contains variant readings of the Apocalypse, verse by verse, gathered together from every conceivable manuscript and printed edition he could lay his hands on'.

The notebook is to be found in the Yahuda collection, Jerusalem (Yahuda MS 4).

See also Mill, John

Varignon, Pierre (1654–1722)

As a Professor of Mathematics at the Collège Mazarin and Professor of Greek and Latin at the Collège de France, Varignon was a figure of some authority in French science when, beginning in 1714, Newton began to seek support from his colleagues in France in his priority dispute with Leibniz. Consequently, in 1713, Newton began a correspondence with Varignon, sent him a copy of the second edition of *Principia* (1713) and, shortly after, proposed him for membership of the Royal Society. Later, several copies of various editions of the *Opticks* were sent to Varignon and, finally, in 1720 he received the ultimate sign of Newton's favour, a portrait.

Twenty-two letters have survived, with the bulk of them originating from the period 1718 to 1722 and concerned with the priority dispute. Beginning in 1718, Varignon strove to resolve the differences between Newton and Bernoulli. He sent, with Newton's later approval, a copy of the *Opticks* (1717) to Bernoulli. And thereafter, for four years, he attempted to explain to each participant that insults and slights they detected in letters and books were non-existent or not intended. Despite some initial success, he died in December 1722 with Bernoulli and Newton still hurling studied insults in each other's direction.

One other aspect of the correspondence concerns a second French edition of the *Traité d'optique* (1722), a task supervised by Varignon. Completed in July 1722, not long before Varignon's death, it has been described as the 'handsomest' edition of the *Opticks* ever produced.

Vegetation of Metals

This alchemical manuscript of Newton is dated by Westfall to the year 1669. It is described in Dobbs (1975, p. 247) as a 'draft of a Short Treatise, incomplete . . . about 4500 words, 12 pp. Autograph'. It is one of the few manuscripts to have escaped Keynes and is to be found in the Burndy Library, Norwalk, Connecticut.

It contains an important restriction Newton was often tempted to place on the cruder forms of the mechanical philosophy of his day. He accepted the 'sensible changes wrought in the textures of the grosser matter' but went on to insist that there were 'more subtle secret and noble' processes in nature. What he had in mind was a subtle ether, formed from metallic vapours as they are released into the air. The ether they form became, for Newton, 'Natures universall agent, her secret fire, the only ferment and principle of all vegetation. The material soule of all matter' (RSW, p. 306). Westfall has claimed to see in Newton's *Hypothesis of Light* (1675) traces of the *Vegetation of Metals*.

Vellum Manuscript

The manuscript was first described by H. W. Turnbull in the *Manchester Guardian* of the 3 October 1953. It was partially published by Hall (1957, pp. 62–71) and published in full by Herivel (1961, pp. 410–16). Thereafter, it has been reprinted by Herivel (1965, pp. 183–91) and *C*, III, pp. 46–54. The original manuscript, on which Newton had jotted down a number of calculations, is to be found in ULC (MS 3958, f. 45). It comes from the 1665–6 period.

It contains a number of calculations of the ratios between the force of gravity and the centrifugal forces produced by the daily rotation of the earth and by the earth's annual orbit around the sun. The conclusions reached are that 'the force of a body from the sun is to the force of its gravity as one to 3749 or thereabouts', and 'the force of the Earth from its centre to the force of gravity as one to 144 or thereabouts' (Herivel, 1965, p. 185). But as Newton soon became aware that he had taken, probably from Galileo, an incorrect figure for the rate at which a body falls under gravity, he set about recalculating it himself. Using a conical pendulum he established that a body falls 196 inches in one second, roughly twice the value initially assumed. Consequently he revised the above ratios of 1:3,749 and 1:144 to 1:7,500 and 1:300.

Velocity of light

It was widely assumed in antiquity that light travelled instantaneously. Thus, Aristotle in *De anima* (On the Mind) spoke of light as if it were a state the medium acquired instantaneously from the presence of a luminous object. It was all very similar, Aristotle explained, to the manner in which water froze instantaneously. A similar position was adopted by Descartes in his *Traité de la lumière*; the parts of matter were so closely in contact, Descartes argued, that a push at any part was instantaneously felt by all other parts.

There were others, however, like Galileo, who suspected that light had a finite speed. Attempts to measure this speed by terrestrial experiments proved fruitless and it was not until 1677 that Ole Romer, using observations of the satellites of Jupiter, detected a measureable velocity of about 225,000 km a second. Newton noted Romer's result in the *scholium* to prop.XCVI of Book I of *Principia*. It was also noted in the *Opticks*, Book II, part III, prop.XI, that 'Light is propagated from luminous Bodies in time, and spends about seven or eight Minutes of an Hour in passing from the Sun to the Earth.'

Newton was largely unconcerned about the precise value assigned to the velocity of light. He did work out, however, in section XIV of Book I of *Principia*, that the velocity of light is greater in a denser medium than in a rarer medium. Consequently, light should travel faster in water than in air. The hypothesis proved easier to derive than to test. It required the ability to measure accurately the speed of light on the earth, a power first demonstrated in 1849 by Armand Fizeau. In the following year J. B. Foucault used similar techniques to demonstrate that light in water travels with a speed of 223,000 kilometres a second, while in the air its speed was the faster 298,000 kps. Newton, and with him the corpuscular theory of light, were clearly wrong. The experiment was widely seen as an *experimentum crucis*, with the power to decide authoritatively and immediately between the corpuscular and wave theories of light. Subsequently, for the rest of the century the wave theory was seen as the only viable theory of light, and with the death of Sir David Brewster in 1868 the corpuscular theory lost its last notable supporter.

See also Corpuscular theory of light; Wave theory of light

Velocity of sound

In *Principia*, Book II, section VIII, Newton discussed 'motion propagated through fluids'. He proved in proposition XLVIII that 'the velocities of pulses propagated in an elastic fluid are in a ratio compounded of the square root of the ratio of the elastic force directly, and the square root of the ratio of the density inversely'. In modern symbolism this would be expressed by the formula:

$$c = \frac{k}{\rho}$$

where c is the velocity of sound, k is the elasticity of the medium and ρ its density. He went on to show in the following proposition XLIX how, given 'the density and elastic force of the medium', we could find the velocity of the waves. Making certain reasonable assumptions, he concluded the argument in proposition L by calculating the velocity of sound to be 968 English feet per second (fps). In support of his theoretical calculations, Newton triumphantly recorded the results of experiments carried out in the cloisters of Neville's Court in Trinity. He measured the distance an echo travelled in the cloisters and found it to be 416 ft and also carefully adjusted a pendulum to swing precisely in time with the echo. Newton found that the echo was slower than a pendulum 5½ inches long but faster than one 8 inches long. This meant the velocity of sound must lie between 920 and 1,085 English feet per second. Newton's calculated figure of 968 fps fitted beautifully into these limits and seemed to be one more sign of the awesome power of the Newtonian system. Earlier measurements of Giles Roberval and Marin Mersenne of 600 fps and 1,474 fps respectively could be dismissed as hopelessly wrong.

Newton's triumph remained short-lived. In 1704 William Derham performed some simple observations on the difference in times between the arrival of the sight and sound of an object some miles distant. Careful measurements by Derham, which Newton readily accepted, yielded a velocity for sound of 1,142 fps, well outside Newton's calculations and his measurements. By this time Newton was preparing a revised second edition of *Principia* for publication. It is intriguing to note Newton's response to the conflict between theory and the intractable facts of nature. He was clearly unwilling to accept any fault in his theoretical deductions, nor could he find anything to query in Derham's simple observations. Consequently, it has been claimed, he began to fudge and to shape his material with the freedom of a sculptor shaping his clay. Some have found this behaviour shocking, with Westfall, for example, declaring Newton's response at this point 'one of the most embarrassing passages in the whole *Principia*' (RSW, p. 735). It has also been included in Broad and Wade's recent study of 'fraud and deceit in the halls of science' (Broad and Wade, 1983).

It had not taken Derham to make Newton realise something was wrong with his figures. New experiments performed in the cloisters of Trinity led him in 1694 to raise the limiting velocities to 984 fps and 1,109 fps. Derham's work could thus only confirm Newton in his doubts and give him a mark to measure his theory by. When scientists find theory and experience in conflict they suspect first that their theory is incomplete. Newton was no exception and consequently began to consider which factors had been ignored in his initial calculations. He settled finally on two. He also began with a newly-calculated velocity of sound of 979 fps.

His earlier calculations, he insisted, had made no allowance for what he termed 'the crassitude of the solid particles of the air, by which the sound is propagated instantaneously'. Such particles, Newton estimated, were separated from each other by about the diameters of nine particles. It was therefore necessary to add '$\frac{979}{9}$, or about 109 feet, to compensate for the crassitude of the particles of the air'. The result was a velocity of 1,088 fps. This was still short of Newton's target. He turned next to consider the effect of water vapour in the atmosphere. Water clearly had a 'spring' to that of air. Assuming the atmosphere to consist of ten parts air to one part vapour then, Newton concluded, the velocity of sound will be increased by 'the entire ratio of 21 to 20'. Carrying through the necessary calculations, Newton concluded that 'sound will pass through 1,142 feet in one second of time'. As if he had suddenly been informed of the fact, Newton went to note in triumph that 'it actually appears that sounds do really advance in one second of time about 1,142 feet'.

Newton's behaviour was certainly disingenuous at this point. He had known of Derham's figure of 1,142 ft for several years and quite deliberately manipulated his calculations to produce just this figure. He was right, however, to suppose that unknown factors were present and that, in the light of his knowledge, the notions of the crassitude of the atmosphere and the presence of water vapour were not implausible in themselves. And, indeed, when Laplace, a century later, analysed the situation once more, he did succeed in identifying an unknown factor. Rather, where Newton was at fault was in his presentation of a number of measurements as reliable when they were nothing more than casual estimates. Air to water was 1 to 870, atmosphere to water was 10 to 1, and air particles to the intervals between them were 1 to 9; all were presented as if they arose from careful experiments and measurements. In actual fact Newton was free to vary these figures considerably. In this way the ratio of the density of water to the density of air had started at 1:850 in *Principia* (1687), later took the values 1:900 or 1:950, but in the second edition of *Principia* became for no apparent reason 1:870. The reason, however, soon became apparent for it was just this value which yielded the value of 1,142 fps.

It was an odd exercise to undertake, for there was nothing especially authoritative about the figure of 1,142 advanced by Derham. It was in fact an average figure derived from a number of observations. There would thus have been no cause for worry if Newton's revised calculations had been a little wayward. Such margins of error, however, seemed unacceptable to Newton, who selected the values of his variables accordingly.

The issue was cleared up finally by Laplace in 1817. He realised that heat would be produced by the compression produced by the passage of sound waves. When taken into account it yielded, with no spurious accuracy, the value predicted by theory for the velocity of sound waves.

See also Derham, William

Vigani, John Francis (1650–1712)

Born in Verona, Vigani studied metallurgy and pharmacy. He arrived in Britain in 1682 and shortly afterwards took up residence in Cambridge and began to give private chemistry lessons. In 1703 his position was officially recognised by the University when he became Cambridge's first professor of chemistry.

Vigani was described by Humphrey Newton as one of Newton's few personal Cambridge friends. He was one of the two or three who regularly saw Newton and 'in whose company he took much delight and Pleasure at an Evening'. The 'Pleasure' did not last, for, according to Catherine Barton, despite Newton's pleasure 'in discoursing with him on chemistry', all contact was broken when Vigani tried to tell Newton a loose story about a nun. Vigani was elsewhere described by de la Pryme as a 'drunken fellow'.

Newton possessed a copy of Vigani's *Medulla chymiae* (1682), the 1683 second edition. His copy is dog-eared and annotated on two pages. It is now in the University of Wisconsin Library. Further details about Vigani can be found in Coleby (1952).

See also Friends

Vincent, Mrs (b.1645)

Née Storer, she was the step-daughter of apothecary Clark, Newton's Grantham landlord, and the niece of Humphrey Babington. William Stukeley spoke to her in the late 1720s when she was over eighty. She described Newton as a 'sober, silent, thinking lad' and went on to reveal for the first time that Newton had 'entertained a love for her . . . but her portion being not considerable, and he being a fellow of a college, it was incompatible with his fortunes to marry'. Stukeley and Mrs Vincent are the sole sources for the story. The relationship inspired a nineteenth-century engraving by George Cruikshank entitled 'Sir Isaac Newton's courtship'. It can be seen in Rattansi (1974, p.16).

See also Chastity

Voltaire (1694–1778)

Already when he arrived in England in 1726 for a prolonged stay, Voltaire was a figure of European stature. Like many other of his journeys, this one was a flight from some threat to his life or liberty.

The threat came from the Chevalier de Rohan, who had been challenged by Voltaire to a duel. The Chevalier, distressed by the thought of duelling with a commoner, resorted instead, by that curious logic known only to aristocrats, to ordering his servants to find and beat the insufferable Voltaire. Arriving in May 1726, he remained for three years, and some years later he published a description of what he had seen in his *Letters concerning the English Nation* (London, 1733; Voltaire, 1980). The French original, *Lettres philosophiques*, appeared in the following year in Amsterdam. The work is, above all, an attack on French society through the device of extolling the virtues of English politics, religion and science, real or imagined, which were clearly not to be seen in France.

One of the main contrasts Voltaire sought to establish and explore was that he claimed to identify between French and English science; between, in effect, the science of Newton and the science of Descartes. Although sympathetic to the achievements of Descartes, Voltaire went on to expound and proclaim what he took to be the superior system of Newton. Vortices were fanciful, as was the plenum, and attraction was 'the mainspring which keeps the whole of nature in motion', Voltaire declared in support of Newton (Voltaire, 1980, Letter 15). Of Newton's optics he spoke with enthusiasm of the man who had dissected 'a single ray of light with more dexterity than the most skilful surgeon dissects the human body' (1980, p. 83). He also discussed Newton's work in mathematics and chronology.

It must be said that 250 years later, Voltaire's account, though brief, is accurate and reads well. Although he did not actually meet Newton, he spoke to such leading Newtonians as Henry Pemberton and clearly was familiar with the ideas and details of both Cartesian and Newtonian science. He was also familiar with many details of the private life and character of Newton, which he had no hesitation in publishing for the first time. The story of the falling apple was first revealed by Voltaire in the earlier work *An Essay on Epick Poetry* (1727), and repeated in the *Letters* (1980, p. 75). Also mentioned are Newton's Arianism (p. 42), the *annus mirabilis* (p. 75) and his chastity (p. 70). In a later work, *Dictionnaire philosophique* (1757), Voltaire first publicised the view that would echo down the centuries, that Newton had gained public advancement, not 'by his great merit', but through the appeal of his 'charming niece' to Charles Montague, the Chancellor of the Exchequer.

Voltaire returned to France in 1728. Soon after, in 1733, he began his famous love affair with the remarkable Marquise du Chastellet. It lasted until her death. Much of their time was spent at her chateau at Cirey in Champagne. Together they experimented and studied the natural philosophy of their day. The result of this labour on Voltaire's part was his *Les elémens de la philosophie de Newton* (1738). It was a work written to make available the principles of Newtonian science 'to minds with little practice in these matters' and covered his theology, optics and mechanics. At the same time the Marquise was working on her French translation of *Principia*, to which Voltaire contributed a nine-page *preface historique* and a poem on 'la physique de Newton'. The Marquise died in 1749, several years before the translation appeared. By this time Voltaire's scientific mission was complete and the rest of his life was dominated by issues of another kind.

See also Chastellet, Marquise du; Newton in France

Vortex theory

The theory of vortices is linked most closely with the name of Descartes. It is described most fully in Part III of his *Principia philosophiae* (1644). Descartes was a member of the first generation of physicists who had come to see that there was nothing at all natural about circular motion. Left to themselves, bodies moved uniformly in straight lines. Consequently, the motion of the heavenly bodies in circular orbits clearly revealed the presence of an external force.

Descartes began with two basic assumptions: the universe was a plenum; and matter had been endowed with motion by God. But if there were no empty spaces for bodies to move into, how was motion possible? Only, Descartes answered, by each body moving in a closed circuit, and by moving instantaneously into the space vacated by a contiguous body. The result would be a number of vortices. One such vortex is the solar system. Contained in it are some fourteen smaller vortices of the planets and their satellites.

Vortex theory proved remarkably attractive and long lived. Both Huygens and Leibniz, for example, continued to subscribe to some form of vortex theory throughout their lives. Thus Huygens, writing in 1688, after he had read *Principia*, noted: 'Vortices necessary; [without them] the earth would run away from the sun; but very distant the one from the other, and not, like those of M.Des Cartes, touching each other' (Koyré, 1965, p. 117). And Leibniz, equally post-*Principia*, in his *Tentamen* (1689) spoke of planets being carried through the heavens by the motion of a fluid ether.

It was thus left to Newton to mount the first plausible attack on Cartesian vortices. In Book II, section IX, of *Principia* he turned to the subject of 'The circular motion of fluids'. In the *scholium* to prop.LIII, Newton concluded that 'planets are not carried round in corporeal vortices', for such vortices do not observe Kepler's area law. Further, in cor.VI to prop.LI, Newton demonstrated that as 'the vortices will not be confined by any certain limits; but by degrees run into each other', the system will be unstable.

Vossius, Gerardus Johannes (1577–1649)

One of the foremost classical scholars and theologians of his age. Educated at the University of Leyden, he was appointed in 1622 Professor of Rhetoric, Chronology and Greek. He resisted two attempts to attract him to England, despite his supposedly Arminian tendencies, moving instead in 1632 to the newly-founded Amsterdam Atheneum.

Vossius wrote a number of books on rhetoric, one of which, his *Rhetorices* (1631, Rhetoric), was used by Newton as a textbook during his Cambridge student days. Notes taken from the book were entered into his Philosophical Notebook, although Newton seems to have advanced no further than the second of the five books.

Wallis, John (1616–1703)

The son of a clergyman, Wallis was educated at Emmanuel College, Cambridge. He later served as Savilian Professor of Geometry at Oxford from 1649 until his death in 1703. He flourished under the Commonwealth, deciphering for Cromwell the coded messages of Charles I. He carried on as cryptographer for Charles II, while later he could be found deciphering messages between Louis XIV and his ambassador in Poland for William III. Having worked successfully for the Stuarts, the Commonwealth and the House of Orange, Wallis arranged for his grandson, William Blencowe, to succeed him on his death.

As a pure mathematician Wallis's most important work was his *Arithmetica infinitorum* (1655), the first significant British work on the calculus. Newton talking to William Derham, acknowledged the influence of Wallis, commenting that, on his return to Cambridge in 1666 'Mercator's Logarithmotechia and what Dr Wallis published about yt time, revived his thoughts of these matters' (RSW, p. 203).

Through the labours of Collins, Wallis was quickly initiated into the insights obtained by Newton on the very problems he had tackled more than a decade before. Collins, for example, copied and sent to Wallis the important work of Newton, *De analysi* (1669). Wallis, in his turn, saw to it that Newton's ideas were published, however inadequately, in some form or other. Thus, his *Algebra* (1685) described Newton's work on infinite series, while the Latin version of the work published in 1693 (*Opera*, vol. II) described Newton's method of fluxions and displayed for the first time Newton's dot notation. In the third volume, published in 1699, Wallis published for the first time Newton's *Epistola posterior* (1676) and other previously unpublished items of correspondence.

Also surviving is a remarkable letter from Wallis to Newton dated 10 April 1695 (*C*, IV, p. 101) in which Newton found himself sternly rebuked for failing to publish his work. He had heard, he began, that Newton had completed a 'Treatise about Light, Refraction and Colours';

he had also heard, from Holland, that Newton's fluxions were there described as 'Leibnitz's Calculus Differentialis'. Consequently, he warned Newton: 'You are not so kind to your Reputation (& that of the Nation) as you might be, when you let things of worth ly by you so long, till others carry away the Reputation that is due to you.' Newton's reply is lost but, from the sense of Wallis's response Newton must have deployed his stock answer, namely, that it 'may occasion some Letters (of Exceptions)'. Wallis dismissed the objection abruptly. It was up to Newton, he insisted, whether he chose to reply. In any case, did he not get as many letters from friends importuning him to publish. Further, he warned, 'some other may get some scraps of ye notion, & publish it as his own; & then 'twill be His, not yours'. What of the objection that the work was incomplete, imperfect? 'I own that Modesty is a Vertue; but too much Diffidence . . . is a Fault. And if men will never publish ought till it be so perfect as that nothing more can be added to it: themselves and the publicke will both be loosers' (*C*, IV, pp. 116–17). Unfortunately Newton's reply to Wallis's blunt speaking has not survived. It clearly had no impact upon him, for it took Newton another nine years to decide finally to print his 'Treatise about Light, Refraction and Colours' as the *Opticks* (1704).

Walton, Brian (1600–61)

A clergyman who in 1660 was made Bishop of Chester. His major work was the enormous *Biblia sacra polyglotta* (1655–7, 6 vols), with versions of the Bible in Hebrew, Greek, Syriac, Ethiopian (translated into Latin), Chaldean, Samaritan, Arabic, Persian and Latin. Newton possessed a full set and clearly used it frequently.

Ward, Seth (1617–89)

The son of an attorney, Ward was educated at Cambridge University. After serving as Savilian Professor of Astronomy at Oxford from 1649 to 1661, Ward sought ecclesiastical preferment as, from 1662, Bishop of Exeter and, from 1667, Bishop of Salisbury. Ward was a founder member of the Royal Society and had earlier, in Oxford, belonged to the Invisible College and the Philosophical Society. It was Ward, in 1672, after receipt of Newton's telescope, who proposed Newton for membership of the Royal Society.

As an astronomer Ward is best known for his *Astronomia geometrica* (1656), in which he followed Ismael Boulliau in his treatment of Kepler's second area law. It was probably from Ward that later astronomers like Thomas Streete and Vincent Wing gained their knowledge of Boulliau.

Waste Book

Thomas Pellet reported that he had found amongst Newton's papers in 1727 'A folio commonplace book, part in Sir Isaac's hand'. It was next heard of in the Cambridge PC *Catalogue* of 1888: 'A commonplace-book, written originally by B. Smith D.D.; with calculations by Newton written in the blank spaces. This contains Newton's first idea of fluxions.' Little more was heard of the common-place book until the 1960s.

The book itself is enormous. Newton's step-father, B. Smith, had numbered the pages up to 1,194 without exhausting the capacity of the book. He had entered the date 12 May 1612 and had obviously intended to use it as a theological notebook. Of his original intention, only the headings and a few completed entries bear witness. Consequently, when Newton inherited the book, presumably in the mid-1650s, all verso pages were blank and most of the recto pages carried no more than a single theological term. The title, Waste Book, is Newton's own; its significance, however, has long been lost. The earliest dated Newton entry is 20 January 1664 (1665?).

Although H. W. Turnbull referred to the work in *C*, I, no systematic extracts from the notebook appeared before Herivel's (1965, pp. 128–82) detailed analysis of the work's dynamical writings. Extensive extracts from the mathematical entries appeared shortly afterwards in *MP*, I. Judged by Cohen to be 'one of the primary manuscript repositories of Newton's early scientific and mathematical ideas' (1971, p. 12), the actual Waste Book itself is to be found in the ULC as part of the PC (MS 4004).

Wave theory of light

As soon as it was realised that light travelled, the question of the nature of that travel inevitably arose. One early model developed by the Stoics in the third century BC took light to be propagated through a pervasive *pneuma* as a pressure wave.

> According to Chrysippus . . . sight is due to the light between the observer and the object observed being stretched conically . . . In this way the signal is transmitted to the observer by means of the stressed air, just as (by feeling) with a stick. (SAMBURSKY, 1956, p. 138)

The same image of a man feeling with a stick was later used by Descartes.

> Light is in the bodies which we call luminous, nothing but a certain

movement or action that is very quick and very violent which passes to our eyes through the mediation of the air . . . in the same way as the movement or resistance of bodies, which this blind man encounters, passes to his hand through the mediation of his stick. (SABRA, 1967, p. 55n)

Newton had considered Cartesian theories of light in his early *QQP* and objected that 'light cannot be by pression . . . for yn wee should see in the night well or better yn in ye day'. Further objections were raised in Query 28 of the *Opticks*. There Newton pointed out that if light was 'Pression propagated without actual Motion, it would not be able to agitate and heat the Bodies which refract and reflect it'. Further, with 'Pression', unlike light, we are able to see around corners.

A more sophisticated wave theory was formulated by Robert Hooke in his *Micrographia* (1665) and further developed by Christian Huygens in his *Traité de la lumière* (1690). The theory required the existence of a homogeneous medium through which light could be propagated. Within this medium, Hooke argued:

Every pulse or vibration of the luminous body will generate a Sphere which will continually increase and grow bigger, just after the same manner . . . as the waves or rings on the surface of water do swell into bigger and bigger circles about a point of it, where, by the sinking of a Stone the motion was begun. (HOOKE, 1961, pp. 56–7)

Newton's most important objection, repeated in several places, was that any wave theory must be incompatible with the rectilinear propagation of light. Thus, in Query 28 in the *Opticks*, Newton noted that waves, whether they be sound waves or water waves, 'bend manifestly'. Bells and cannons can be heard from the other side of a hill, sounds can be propagated as readily in crooked pipes as in straight ones, but 'Light is never known to follow crooked Passages nor to bend into the Shadow. For the fix'd Stars by the Interposition of any of the Planets cease to be seen.'

Further doubt was raised in Newton's mind about the viability of the wave theory by the strange phenomenon of double refraction, first observed in Iceland spar by E. Bartholin in 1663. Huygens in 1690 confessed his inability to account for all the features of Iceland spar in terms of his wave theory. Newton took up the challenge and in Query 29 proposed a solution requiring the assumption that we could talk of and distinguish between the different sides of light rays. Yet, he pointed out, 'its difficult to conceive how the Rays of Light, unless they be Bodies, can have a permanent Virtue in two of their sides which is not in their other Sides'.

Largely due to the authority of Newton, most eighteenth-century British physicists remained hostile to wave theories of light. Consequently, when, in 1800 Thomas Young began to challenge Newtonian assumptions, he found his work so violently attacked that the publisher of his lectures asked to be released from the contract. Young, in turn, abandoned science for medicine. Before he did, however, he made one of the two fundamental discoveries which would shortly do much to revive interest in the wave theory. In May 1801 he discovered 'the general law of the interference of light' and went on to show that with its aid he could readily account for 'the colours of striated surfaces and the colours of thin plates'. 'Radiant light', he roundly declared, 'consists in Undulations of the luminiferous Ether.'

The second major discovery was made in 1810 by Etienne Louis Malus with his paper on *La théorie de la double refraction de la lumière dans les substances cristalisée*, in which he introduced into science the notion of the polarisation of light. The immediate effect of Malus's work was to reinforce Newtonian assumptions. Young in an anonymous review of Malus's work admitted his inability to account for the phenomenon of polarisation in terms of the wave theory. The difficulty facing Young and other physicists was that they had all unquestioningly assumed that light waves were propagated longitudinally; in other words, like sound, light waves were propagated by means of alternate compressions and rarefactions along its direction of motion. As Young quickly saw, there is no obvious way to polarise longitudinal waves.

It took Young a further seven years to see how the wave theory and polarisation could fit together. In a letter to Arago in 1817 he proposed that if light be allowed to be propagated transversely, that is, to be displaced at right angles to the direction of the wave's propagation, then polarisation no longer conflicted with the wave theory of light. Young's insight was most fruitful, and in the hands of several leading French mathematical physicists was widely deployed to explain many previously puzzling properties of light. Some British physicists, the loyal Sir David Brewster for example, remained faithful to Newton. In his *A Treatise on Optics* (1831) he used throughout the language of particles and forces and even at the end of his life in 1868 he was still raising objections to the wave theory. He could not, he told John Tyndall, 'think the Creator guilty of so clumsy a contrivance as the filling of space with ether in order to produce light' (Steffens, 1977, p. 147).

By this time J. B. Foucault had carried out his supposedly crucial experiment on the nature of light. Wave theorists had predicted that light would travel slower in water than in air; Newton had made the converse prediction. In 1850 Foucault found that while light travelled four miles in air it had only travelled three miles in water. Thus, while the report of one *experimentum crucis* in 1672 had established Newton's account of light and colour, another *experimentum crucis* carried out nearly two centuries later finally overturned one major part of that account.

See also Double refraction; Interference; Polarisation; Velocity of light

Westfall, Richard Samuel (1924–   )

Educated at Yale, Westfall has served since 1960 as Professor of the History of Science at the University of Indiana, Bloomington. In the 1960s he published, amongst other items, an important series of papers on Newton's early studies on light and colour. These were followed by a detailed study of Newton's dynamics in his *Force in Newton's Physics* (1971). Such items were, never the less, only parts of a much lengthier and more ambitious project. When in 1959 the first volume of Newton's *Correspondence* appeared, Westfall began 'serious work' on a new and fully-documented biography of Newton. The result, *Never at Rest*, appeared twenty years later in 1980.

See also Biography

Whiston, William (1667–1752)

The son of a parish priest, Whiston was educated at Cambridge. He served for some years as Fellow of Clare, chaplain to the Bishop of Norwich and rector of Lowestoft. In 1703 he was selected by Newton to succeed him in the Lucasian chair. However, unlike Newton, he was incapable of concealing the unorthodox and even heretical views which attracted him throughout his life. In about 1705 Whiston began to doubt the Athanasian doctrine of the Trinity. Further reading confirmed his suspicions, as they had done Newton's many years before, and with no thought of the consequence he began to inform various Bishops and Archbishops of his new discovery. Letters from him and tracts produced would end with the familiar 'In the name of the Father, and of the Son, and of the Holy Spirit', accompanied with the *erratum* 'delete "of the Son"'. Whiston clearly could not long survive. The Vice-chancellor refused his imprimatur to one of Whiston's tracts and on 31 October 1710 he was sacked from his Chair and banished from the University. To Newton, who found it difficult to publish even his mathematical works, such public posturing on matters theological must have been deeply distasteful. Thereafter Whiston spent his life arguing for a number of unorthodox theological positions becoming, in time, accepted as an eccentric rather than persecuted as a heretic. He survived through his writings and lectures. In later life he received a pension of £40 a year from Queen Caroline and a further £20 from Sir Joseph Jekyll, the Master of the Rolls.

If others were prepared to tolerate Whiston, Newton wanted nothing to do with him. Thus the proposal to elect him to the Royal Society in

1720 was dismissed by Newton. Whiston, for his part, left a far from flattering picture of Newton.

> So did I then enjoy a large portion of his favour for twenty years together. But, he then perceiving that I could not do as his other darling friends did, that is, learn of him without contradicting him, when I differed in opinion from him, he could not in his old age bear such contradiction, and so he was afraid of me the last thirteen years of his Life. (*Memoirs*, 1749, p. 249)

Whiston wrote extensively on both scientific and theological matters. His *Praelectiones astronomia* (1710) and its English translation, *Sir Isaac Newton's Mathematick Philosophy More Easily Demonstrated* (1716; reissued 1728) – Whiston's Cambridge lectures – was one of the first works designed to present, in English, Newtonian physics in a popular form. His earlier *Theory of the Earth* (1696) was dedicated to 'summo viro Isaaco Newtoni' and was clearly Newtonian in inspiration. In 1707 Whiston was given the task of editing Newton's *Arithmetica universalis*. A reluctant author, Newton refused to allow his name to appear on the title page, and unfairly complained to Conduitt that Whiston had introduced so many errors that the work had later to be republished.

Whiston also seems to have been the first explicitly and publicly to reveal Newton's Arianism. In his *A Collection of Authentick Records belonging to the Old and New Testament* (1727–8) he noted that Newton had long held that:

> Arianism is no other than the Old uncorrupt Christianity . . . This was occasionally known to those few who were intimate with him all along; from whom, notwithstanding his prodigiously fearful, cautious, and suspicious Temper, he could not always conceal so important a Discovery. (RSW, pp. 649–50)

One curious incident, and one suggesting that Newton did not immediately break with Whiston after his dismissal from Cambridge in 1710, concerned Whiston's nephew, whom Newton employed in his house. On one occasion £3,000 in bank bills was stolen from the house; on another occasion one hundred guineas were taken from his desk. Whiston's nephew was suspected but, according to Conduitt, Newton refused to prosecute him (RSW, p. 652).

Though Whiston recognised Newton's mathematical genius (he could see 'almost by Intuition, even without Demonstration'), he was not prepared to be so fulsome about Newton's chronological work. 'A sagacious Romance' he declared and went on to write his *Confutation of . . . Newton's Chronology*, which he added as an appendix to his *Authentick Records*. After examining all the evidence assembled by Newton, Whiston proposed to raise the date of the Argonauts' expedition by a century rather than reducing it as Newton wished.

In many ways Whiston and Newton were remarkably similar. Both were mathematicians, both had deep interests and displayed great learning in theology, church history and chronology, and both had occupied the same Cambridge chair. Both also held unorthodox religious beliefs in an age which might tolerate, but in no way favour, any who chose to support publicly such beliefs. There were also substantial differences, however. Whereas Newton was prudent and secretive, Whiston was rash and open, characteristics which permitted the success of the one as they inevitably led to the downfall of the other. If any would care to speculate on how Newton would have developed if he had not been so cautious and introverted, they need look no further than the career of Whiston. A cautious Whiston may never have developed the genius of a Newton; a rash Newton could, however, have easily become as wasteful with his talents as a Whiston.

Whiteside, Derek Thomas (1932–   )

After graduating from the University of Bristol Whiteside has spent virtually all his academic career at the University of Cambridge where, since 1976, he has occupied the position of Reader in the History of Mathematics. Whiteside established his reputation with his 'Patterns of mathematical thought in the later seventeenth century' (1961b). Thereafter, he has devoted himself to the narrower field of Newton's mathematical works. The first results appeared in 1964 with the publication of *The Mathematical Works of Isaac Newton* (1964–7, 2 vols), in which Whiteside included English editions of six previously published works of Newton. More importantly, however, he had already begun to prepare for publication the confused mass of Newton's mathematical papers. Much of this had never been properly examined since the death of Newton in 1727. The result of Whiteside's labours lie in the eight volumes of the *Mathematical Papers* (1967–81), one of the century's more durable scholarly achievements.

Wickins, John (d.1719)

With no *DNB* entry, little is known about Wickins except at the points when his life connected with the public career of Newton. Yet Wickins must have been Newton's closest friend for some twenty years and, as 'chamber fellows', he must have come to know Newton and his way of life better than anyone else.

Wickins' son, Nicolas, described how they came to share rooms.

My father's first chamber-fellow being very disagreeable to him, he retired one day into the walks, where he found Mr Newton solitary and dejected. Upon entering into discourse, they found their cause of retirement the same, and thereupon agreed to shake off their present disorderly companions and chum together, which they did as soon as conveniently they could, and so continued as long as my father staid at college. (MORE, 1962, p. 206)

As Wickins stayed in Trinity as a Fellow until 1684, when he was given a living at Stoke Edith, near Monmouth, it must at least be assumed they found each other's company congenial.

Of the stories Wickins told his son about Newton, all Nicolas could remember was that his hair was 'turning grey, I think, at thirty', was forgetful of his food, and drank Leucatello's Balsam when he felt ill. But Wickins must have known a good deal about Newton's method of work, for he served as his amanuensis on the 1672 paper on light and colours, on the *Lectiones opticae* deposited in the ULC in 1674, and on several other manuscripts. On these great events, however, both Wickins and his son have remained silent.

Wilkins, John (1614–72)

An early influence on Newton, Wilkins was the son of an Oxford goldsmith. Ordained after graduating from Oxford in 1631, he was later appointed Warden of Wadham College, Oxford, in 1648. A well-known Parliamentarian, he married Cromwell's sister in 1656, and in 1659 was appointed by his nephew, Richard Cromwell, to the Mastership of TCC. His tenure was short for, with the Restoration in 1660, he was dismissed immediately. Clearly a survivor, Wilkins was back in office in 1668 as Bishop of Chester.

Wilkins was the author of *Mathematical Magic* (1648), a work similar in tone and style to such books of today as Lyall Watson's *Supernature* (1973). In the same naive manner as Watson, Wilkins reported on the wonders of his day and would breathlessly describe such items as the latest perpetual motion machine or a lamp that had been burning continuously for 1,500 years. It also contained accounts of simple mechanical experiments and simple machines such as water mills. The Morgan Notebook of Newton contains extracts from Wilkins and clearly reveals his early interest in the practical aspects of mechanics.

Wing, Vincent (1619–68)

The son of a small landowner, Wing worked variously as a surveyor, astrologer, compiler of almanacs, and the author of popular textbooks of astronomy. He began as a traditional geocentrist but by 1651 he had been converted to the heliocentric views of Copernicus. Newton possessed a copy of Wing's *Astronomia Britannica* (1669), a work which followed Seth Ward's formulation of Kepler's second law. Newton's copy carries on two rear end-papers extensive notes compiled about 1670. One interesting comment attributed 'the disturbance of the moon's orbit from its theoretical elliptical shape' to the action of the solar vortex which compressed the 'terrestial one bearing the moon by about 1/43 of its width'. Newton had by 1670 yet to question seriously the vortex theory of Descartes.

Winthrop, John (1606–76)

Educated at Trinity College, Dublin, and the Inner Temple, Winthrop emigrated to America, where he served eventually as Governor of Connecticut from 1660–76. In 1662 he was elected to the Royal Society and thus became the first American Fellow of the Society. He was also the first to construct a large telescope in the Colonies. It was in fact with his 3½-ft reflector, donated to Harvard in 1672, that Thomas Brattle made the cometary observations reported by Newton in *Principia* (1687).

Described in the *DSB* as the 'first scientific investigator of note in British America', his tastes ran more to alchemy than planetary observation.

Winthrop, John IV (1714–79)

The descendant of the John Winthrop above, he graduated from Harvard in 1732, where he later served from 1738–79 as Hollis Professor of Mathematics and Natural Philosophy in succession to Isaac Greenwood.

Winthrop obtained a copy of the third edition of *Principia* in 1739 and lectured on its mechanics as well as attempting to check its basic assumptions against his own planetary observations. In particular, he did his best to observe the various transits of Venus (1761, 1769) and Mercury (1740, 1743, 1769) visible in North America in the latter part of the century. From such observations he derived a figure of 8″.68 for the solar parallax, the best of his day.

See also Newton in America

Works

In the accompanying table are listed 119 of Newton's more important works. Included are published and unpublished works, fragmentary texts and complete books. The list is far from complete. It is doubtful, however, if anything of any great significance has been omitted. Also noted are the dates and places of first publication and, if appropriate, similar data is recorded for the first English translation. If the work is available in one of the standard Modern compilations (*MP*, *PLNP*, *C*, etc.), an appropriate reference has been entered. Fuller details about the works listed can be found in the separate entry for each text entered under the work's title as listed here. In a very few cases no further entry has been provided; in that case, as with item 19, reference has been made to another entry where further information can be found.

Newton's more important works

Title	Publication details
1 *A Demonstration that the Planets, by their Gravity towards the Sun, may move in Ellipses*	A document of the early 1680s, it first appeared in *Life of Locke*, 1830, vol. I, by Lord King; *C*, III, pp. 71–7
2 *A Description of an Instrument for Observing the Moon's Distance from the Fixt Stars at Sea*	Sent to Halley in 1700, the paper disappeared until 1742 when it appeared in *PT* (No. 465, pp. 155–6); *PLNP*, pp. 236–8
3 *A Dissertation upon the Sacred Cubit of the Jews*	Known only in an edition edited by T. Birch (1737) and, in Latin translation, in Castillioneus, *Tome* III (1744)
4 Alchemical Notebook	Unpublished and to be found in the Yahuda Collection, Jerusalem
5 *An Account of the Book Entituled Commercium epistolicum*	First published anonymously in *PT* (No. 342, pp. 173–224) and in 1722 in a Latin translation as the *Rencensio*; Hall (1980, pp. 263–314)
6 *An Historical Account of Two Notable Corruptions of Scripture*	Although originating in 1690 in two letters to Locke, it was first published by an unknown editor in 1754; *C*, III, pp. 83–144 contains a third previously unpublished letter
7 *An Hypothesis Explaining the Properties of Light* (second paper on light and colours)	Read to the RS in December 1675, it was first published in Birch (1757); *PLNP*, pp. 177–99

Title	Publication details
8 *A Problem in College Administration*	A manuscript of 1708 in TCC published for the first and only time in *Isis* (1958)
9 *Argumenta and Twelve Points on Arian Christology*	Unpublished manuscripts from the PC; extracts have appeared in More (1962, p. 642) and RSW (pp. 315–16)
10 *Arithmetica universalis* (Universal Arithmetic)	First published anonymously in 1707 in an edition edited by W. Whiston; first English edition, edited by J. Raphson, was published in 1720; *MP*, V, pp. 54–491
11 *A Scheme for Reformed Spelling*	The first and only edition was published by R. W. Elliott in *Modern Language Review* (1954)
12 *A Short Chronicle from the First Memory of Things in Europe to the Conquest of Persia by Alexander the Great*	Issued first in Paris in 1725 in a French translation by N. Freret, the original text was edited and published by J. Conduitt in 1728
13 *A Short Scheme of the True Religion*	An unpublished manuscript from the PC; extracts have appeared in McLachlan (1950)
14 *Chemical Dictionary*	An unpublished notebook located in the Bodleian Library, Oxford
15 Chemistry Notebook	An unpublished notebook located in the ULC as part of the PC
16 *Classical Scholia*	Drafts of proposed but never used additions to *Principia*; located in the RS Library, extracts were first published in Gregory (1702) and, more recently, in McGuire and Rattansi (1966)
17 *Clavis* (The Key)	An alchemical manuscript located in KCC; it has been published in full in both Latin and English translation in Dobbs (1975)
18 *Commercium epistolicum D. Johannis Collins et aliorum* (The Correspondence of John Collins and others)	Published by the RS in 1713; an augmented second edition appeared in 1722
19 *Concerning the Amendmt of English coins* (*see* Mint, Recoinage)	Unpublished manuscript located in Goldsmith's Library, University of London.

Title	Publication details
20 *Conclusio*	Several manuscript drafts exist of an unused Conclusion to *Principia*; they have been published in both Latin and English translation in Halls
21 *Considerations about Rectifying the Julian Kalendar*	An unpublished manuscript from the PC; extracts were published in Brewster
22 *De aere et aethere* (On Air and Ether)	A manuscript from the PC first published in Halls
23 *De analysi per aequatione numero terminorum infinitas* (On Analysis by Means of Equations with an Infinite Number of Terms)	Although widely distributed amongst mathematicians from 1669 onwards, it was first published in Latin in Jones (1711), and in English translation in Stewart (1745); *MP*, II, pp. 206–47
24 *De computo serierum* (On the Computation of Series)	A manuscript from the PC dating from 1684; it was published for the first and only time in both Latin and English translation in *MP*, IV, pp. 590–616
25 *De constructione problematum geometricum* (On the Construction of Geometrical Problems)	An item from the PC dating from about 1706; it was published for the first and only time in both Latin and English translation in *MP*, VIII, pp. 200–19
26 *De gravitatione et equipondio fluidorum* (On the Gravity and Equilibrium of fluids)	A manuscript from the PC dating from the late 1660s; it was first published in both Latin and English translation in Halls
27 *De methodis fluxionum et serierum infinitorum* (On the Methods of Fluxions and Infinite Series)	Composed in the period 1670–1, it was first published in an English translation in Colson (1736); the original Latin text first appeared in Horsley; *MP*, III, pp. 32–353
28 *De motu corporum, definitiones* (On the Motion of Bodies, Definitions)	An item from the PC first published in Latin and English translation in Halls
29 *De motu corporum in gyrum* (On the Motion of Revolving Bodies)	First published, in Latin, by Rigaud (1838) from a manuscript in the RS and in English translation from a PC manuscript by Herivel (1965)
30 *De motu corporum in mediis regulariter cedentibus* (On the Motion of Bodies in Uniformly Yielding Media)	An item from the PC first published in Latin and English translation by Herivel (1965)

Title	Publication details
31 *De motu corporum, liber primus* (On the Motion of Bodies, Book I)	Extracts from Newton's Lucasian lectures of 1684 have been published by Herivel (1965) and in *MP*, VI
32 *De motu corporum, liber secundus* (On the Motion of Bodies, Book II)	Published as 34 below.
33 *De motu sphaericorum corporum in fluidis* (On the Motion of Spherical Bodies in Fluids)	An item from the PC first published in both Latin and English translation in Halls
34 *De mundi systemate* (On the System of the World)	Published first in an anonymous English translation in 1728 under the title *The System of the World*; the original Latin text, in an edition prepared by John Conduitt, also appeared in 1728 (*see The System of the World*)
35 *De natura acidorum* (On the Nature of Acids)	Published first in both Latin and English translation in the 1710 edition of John Harris's *Lexicon technicum*; *C*, III, pp. 205–14
36 *De ratione temporis quo grave labitur per rectam data duo puncta conjungentem, ad tempus brevissimum quo, vi gravitatis, transit ab horum uno ad alterum per arcum cycloidis* (On the Ratio of the Time in which a Weight will fall in a Straight Line joining Two Points, and the shortest Time in which, by the Force of Gravity, it will pass from one to Another by a Cycloidal Arch)	Newton's answer to Bernoulli's challenge problem of 1696 was published anonymously in 1697 in *PT* (*see* Bernoulli's problems)
37 *Determination of Longitude* (*see* Longitude)	Evidence submitted to a House of Commons Committee; was first published in the *House of Commons Journal* (1714); *C*, VI, pp. 161–3
38 Determination of the form of solid of least resistance	Proof of prop. XXXIV of Book II of *Principia* was sent to David Gregory in 1694 (*C*, III, pp. 380–3); it was first published in the 1888 Cambridge *Catalogue* of the PC
39 *De vi electrica* (On the Electric Force)	An item from the PC published for the first and only time in both Latin and English translation in *C*, V, pp. 362–9

Title	Publication details
40 *Discourse of Observations*	Read to the RS in January 1676, the *Discourse* was first published in Birch (1757); *PLNP*, pp. 202–35
41 *Enumeratio linearum tertii ordinis* (An Enumeration of Cubic Curves)	First published in Latin in *Opticks* (1704), and in an English translation in the *Lexicon technicum* of John Harris in 1710; *MP*, VII, pp. 588–645
42 *Epistola prior* and *Epistola posterior* (First Letter and Second Letter)	Two letters to Leibniz dated 13 June 1676 and 24 October 1676 respectively; they were first published in their original Latin in Wallis (1699) and in English translation in *C*, II
43 *Essay on the Preparation of Star Reguluses* (*see* Antimony)	Alchemical manuscript located in KCC; published in full in Dobbs (1965, pp. 249–50)
44 Fitzwilliam Notebook	An unpblished notebook from the Fitzwilliam Museum, Cambridge
45 'Form of the most ancient year'	It was published for the first and only time in the *Gentleman's Magazine* (1755)
46 *Four Letters from Sir Isaac Newton to Dr Bentley*	The correspondence of 1692–3 was first published by Bentley's grandson, R. Cumberland, in 1756; *PLNP*, pp. 279–312
47 *Fundamenta opticae* (Fundamentals of Optics)	Unpublished draft of Book I of the *Opticks* dating from the 1690s and located in the PC
48 *Geographia universalis* (Universal Geography)	A work by Bernard Varenius edited and published in 1672 in Cambridge by Newton; an English translation appeared in 1733
49 *Geometria curvilinea* (The Geometry of curves)	An item from the PC dating from about 1680 and published for the first and only time in both Latin and English translation in *MP*, IV, pp. 420–484
50 *Geometria libri tres* (Geometry in Three Books)	A manuscript from the PC dating from the 1690s and published for the first and only time in Latin and English translation in *MP*, VII, pp. 248–400

Title	Publication details
51 *Gravia in trochoide descendentia* (The Descent of Heavy Bodies in Cycloids)	A manuscript from the PC and dating from the 1670s, it was published in both Latin and English translation in Halls (pp. 170–80)
52 *Index chemicus* (Index of Chemistry)	An unpublished notebook located in KCC
53 *Irenicum*	An unpublished manuscript in KCC; extensive extracts were published by McLachlan (1950)
54 Latin Exercise Book	An unpublished notebook in private hands
55 *Lectiones opticae* (Optical Lectures)	Newton's Lucasian lectures deposited in ULC and published in 1729; *see also* 56 and 76
56 *Lectures on Optics*	A second manuscript of 55 above published in 1973 in a facsimile edition edited by Whiteside (Newton, 1973)
57 *Letter to Robert Boyle*	Written in 1679 and published first in Boyle (1744); *PLNP*, pp. 249–54
58 Letter to Montague (*see* Bernoulli's Problems)	The solution to Bernoulli's problem of 1696 sent to Montague in January 1697; *C*, IV, pp. 220–9 (*see also* 36 above)
59 *Mathesos universalis specimina* (Specimens of a Universal System)	Dating from 1684 and located in the PC, the manuscript was published for the first and only time in both Latin and English translation in *MP*, IV, pp. 526–90
60 20 May 1665 Tract 14 May 1666 Tract 16 May 1666 Tract	All three tracts were published for the first time in *MP*, I, pp. 272–80, 390–4
61 *Methodis differentialis*	First published in the original Latin in Jones (1711); the first English translation appeared in Fraser (1918); *MP*, VIII, pp. 244–55
62 Morgan Notebook	Unpublished notebook located in the Pierpont Morgan Library, New York; extracts have appeared in D. Smith (1927a)
63 'New Theory about Light and Colours' (First paper on light and colour)	First published in *PT* (1672). *PLNP*, pp. 47–59
64 13 November 1665 Tract	*MP*, I, pp. 382–90
65 *Observations*	First published as an appendix to Raphson (1718); *C*, VI, pp. 341–9

Title	Publication details
66 *Observations Concerning the Medium through which Light passes, and the Agent which Emits it*	An unpublished manuscript from the PC; extracts were published by Guerlac (1981)
67 *Observations on Kinckhuysen*	Although composed in 1670, the manuscript remained unpublished until 1968 when it appeared in *MP*, II
68 *Observations upon the Prophecies of Daniel and the Apocalypse of St John*	First published in 1733 in an edition edited by Benjamin Smith; there is a modern edition edited by Whitla (1922)
69 *October 1666 Tract: To resolve Problems by Motion*	First published in Halls; *MP*, I, pp. 400–48
70 *Of an Universal Language*	Dating from 1661, it was published for the first and only time by R. W. Elliott in *Modern Language Review* (1957)
71 *Of Colours*	The first twenty-two pages of the Chemistry Notebook, they have been published in *QQP*
72 *Of Reflections*	Extracts from the Waste Book published in Herivel (1965, pp. 133–5)
73 *Of Refractions*	Optical notes taken from the notebook ULC Add. MS 4000 and published in Hall (1955) and *MP*, I
74 *Of Violent Motion*	Extracts from *QQP* published in Herivel (1965, pp. 121–7)
75 *Of ye Coloured Circles twixt Two Contiguous Glasses*	First published by Westfall (1965)
76 *On Circular Motion*	First published by Hall (1957)
77 *Optical Lectures*	A partial and anonymous translation of 55 above appeared in 1728
78 *Opticks*	First published in English in 1704; Samuel Clarke's Latin translation appeared in 1706
79 *Papers on Light and Colour*	Some seventeen papers were published by Newton in the period 1672 to 1676 in the *PT* following the initial appearance in the *PT* of 63 above; *PLNP*, pp. 47–176

Title	Publication details
80 *Paradoxical Questions Concerning the Morals and Actions of Athanasius and his Followers*	A manuscript from the PC, dating from the 1670s; extracts were first published in Brewster; a much fuller version appeared in McLachlan (1950)
81 Philosophical Notebook	An unpublished notebook from the PC; part of the notebook, the *QQP* section, has been published in full by McGuire and Tamny (1983)
82 Praxis	An unpublished alchemical manuscript located in the Babson Institute
83 *Principia*	Three editions appeared during Newton's lifetime – 1687, 1713 and 1726; Andrew Motte's English translation was published in 1729
84 *Problematis mathematicis anglis nuper propositi solutio generalis* (General Solution to a Recently Proposed Mathematical Problem about Angles; see Bernoulli's Problems)	Newton's proposed solution to Bernoulli's second challenge problem was published anonymously in *PT* (1715)
85 *Problems for Construing Equations*	A manuscript of the 1670s first published in *MP*, II, pp. 450–516
86 *Prolegomena ad lexici prophetici partem secunda, in quibus agitur de forma sanctuarii Judaicii . . . commentarium* (Preface to the Prophetic Language to which is added a Commentary on the Form of the Sanctuary of the Jews)	Unpublished manuscript in the Babson Collection
87 *Prophetic Figures*	An unpublished manuscript from the Yahuda Collection, Jerusalem
88 *Propositiones: de motu* (Propositions on Motion)	The title assigned by Rigaud (1838) to 29 above
89 *Quaestiones quaedam philosophicae* (Certain Philosophical Questions)	The most significant part of Newton's Philosophical Notebook; it has been published in full in McGuire and Tamny (1983)
90 Queries 1–31	Queries 1–16 appeared initially in *Opticks* (1704); further queries were added to the editions of 1706 and 1717
91 *Queries regarding the Word homoousios*	A short text located in KCC; it was published in slightly different versions in Brewster, and McLachlan (1950)

Title	Publication details
92 *Rationes* (Reasons)	An anti-Trinitarian tract from which extracts were taken and published by More (1962)
93 *Recensio libri qui inscriptis est Commercium epistolicum* (An account of a Book called the Commercium epistolicum)	A Latin translation of 5, published in the second edition of 18 (*see An Account of a Book entituled Commercium epistolicum*)
94 *Regulae differentiarum* (Rules of Interpolation)	Dating from 1676, the manuscript was first published in Latin and in English translation in D. C. Fraser (1927); MP, IV, pp. 36–50
95 *Regulae pro determinatione paschae* (Rules for Determining Easter)	An unpublished manuscript from the PC first described by Brewster
96 *Remarks upon the Observations made upon a Chronological Index of Sir Isaac Newton*	An anonymous reply to French critics of 12; it was published in the PT (1725)
97 *Rules for Interpreting the Words and Language in Scripture*	A lengthy manuscript located in the Yahuda Collection, Jerusalem; extracts have been published in Manuel (1974)
98 *Scala graduum caloris* (A Scale of the Degrees of Heat)	First published anonymously in PT (1701) PLNP, pp. 259–68
99 *Sendovigius Explained* (*see* Sendouigius)	Unpublished 12,000-word alchemical manuscript located in KCC
100 *State of the Gold and Silver Coyns of this Kingdom* (*see* Mint, Guineas)	21 September 1717 and published first in *The Daily Courant* for 30 December 1717; C, VI, pp. 415–18
101 *Tables for Renewing and Purchasing Leases*	First published in 1686 but, despite frequent attributions, the work is not by Newton
102 *Tabula refractionum siderum ad altitudines apparentes* (Table of Stellar Refractions at Different Apparent Altitudes)	Composed in 1695, it first appeared as part of a paper published by Halley in PT (1721); C, IV, p. 95
103 *The Chronology of Ancient Kingdoms Amended*	Newton's major contribution to chronology first appeared, edited by John Conduitt in 1728; there is no modern edition
104 *The Language of the Prophets*	An unpublished 50,000-word manuscript located in KCC
105 *The Lawes of Motion*	A manuscript from the PC dating from the late 1660s; it was published first in C, III, pp. 60–6
106 *Theologiae gentilis origines philosophicae* (Philosophical Origins of Gentile Philosophy)	An unpublished manuscript of the 1680s; it is to be found in the Yahuda Collection, Jerusalem

Title	Publication details
107 Theological Notebook	An unpublished notebook located in KCC
108 *The Proof*	An unpublished manuscript from the Yahuda Collection, Jerusalem, dealing with prophecy
109 *Theoria lunae* (Theory of the Moon)	First published in Gregory (1702); see 110
110 *Theory of the Moon's Motion*	Published as a pamphlet in 1702, an unsigned translation of 109
111 *The System of the World*	An anonymous English translation of 34 first published in 1728
112 *Thirteen Letters from Isaac Newton*	Newton's reports from the Convention Parliament of 1689 were first published by Dawson Turner in 1848; *C*, III, pp. 10–25
113 *Tractatus de quadratura curvarum* (A Treatise of the Quadrature of Curves)	Composed in the early 1690s, the treatise was published first in Latin in *Opticks* (1704); it first appeared in English in 1710 in John Harris's *Lexicon technicum*; *MP*, VII, pp. 24–129; *MP*, VIII, pp. 92–159
114 Trinity College Notebook	Unpublished notebook located in TCC
115 ULC Add. MS 4000	An unpublished notebook in the PC; extensive extracts have appeared in *MP*, I
116 *Variantes lectiones apocalypticae* (Variant Readings in the Apocalypse)	An unpublished manuscript from the Yahuda Collection, Jerusalem
117 *Vegetation of Metals*	An unpublished alchemical manuscript located in the Burndy Library, Norwalk, Connecticut
118 Vellum Manuscript	First described by H. W. Turnbull in the *Manchester Guardian* of 3 October1953; it was published, partially by Hall (1957) and in full in Herivel (1965, pp. 183–91)
119 Waste Book	An unpublished notebook from the PC, rich in material on Newton's early advances in mathematics and mechanics; extensive extracts have been published in the *MP*, *passim*, and in Herivel (1965, pp. 128–82)

Y

Young, Thomas (1773–1829)

The son of a wealthy Quaker, Young possessed one of the most original and remarkable intellects ever to work in British science. He was educated at Cambridge (where his precocity gained him the name 'Phenomenon' Young), St Bartholomew's, in London, Edinburgh and Göttingen. By this time he had acquired the command of several modern languages, the languages of classical antiquity, and had begun the study of oriental languages. When in 1814 he came across a copy of the Rosetta Stone, he began at once the work which would lead eventually, at the hands of Champollion, to the first modern decipherment of a hieroglyphic text.

He began his scientific career in medicine and succeeded almost immediately, in 1793, in describing the phenomenon of visual accommodation. He also worked in the field of acoustics. Further work led to the discovery of the later-termed Young's modulus, one of the most enduring and basic tools of engineering and materials science.

In 1801 he joined the staff of the newly formed Royal Institution as Professor of Natural Philosophy. In the same year he announced that, by reflecting on 'the beautiful experiments of Newton', he had formulated 'the general law of the interference of light'. This, in turn, had led him to establish 'almost incontrovertibly the undulatory system of light' (Steffens, 1977, pp. 115–16). Young's basic claim was that if light did consist of a periodic wave motion then, when two beams intersect, some waves are likely to reinforce each other and others to cancel one another. He sought for, and claimed to have found, the effect. His most famous discovery in this context, although Young himself paid little attention to it, was the well-known two-slit experiment.

Young had thus become the first serious British scientist to set himself apart from the traditional Newtonian corpuscular view of light. Young attempted to soften somewhat the sharpness of the break by claiming, and not without justification, that Newton himself had been tempted by various aspects of the wave theory. The ploy failed, however, to provide him with adequate protection from the hostility of the still-powerful Newtonians. Was the world of science, Henry Brougham asked in the *Edinburgh Review* (1802–3, pp. 450–1), 'to be as changeable in its modes, as the world of taste, which is directed by the nod of a silly woman, or pampered fop?' Young's work was dismissed as containing 'nothing which deserves the name, either of experiment or discovery, and . . . destitute of every species of merit'. Unhappy at the Royal Institution and disillusioned by the hostility directed against his work, Young abandoned in 1803 a full-time career in science and returned to the practice of medicine.

Scientists did in fact have stronger grounds for dismissing Young's work than mere conservatism. There still remained the problem of double refraction and Iceland spar, as troublesome to the wave theory in 1800 as it had been to Huygens in 1690. The problem was compounded by the discovery in 1809 by Etienne Malus of the equally puzzling phenomenon of polarisation. Young, once more, held the key to the problem, with his proposal that light was composed of transverse rather than longitudinal waves. It was a suggestion which, taken up by the French mathematical physicist Augustin Fresnel in 1818, would finally dispose of the last objection to the wave theory of light.

See also Interference; Polarisation; Wave theory of light

Bibliography

ADRIAN, LORD (1963) 'Newton's rooms in Trinity', *Notes and Records of the Royal Society*, vol. 18, pp. 17–24.

AITON, ERIC J. (1954) 'Galileo's theory of the tides', *Annals of Science*, vol. 10, pp. 44–57.

AITON, ERIC J. (1955) 'The contributions of Newton, Bernoulli and Euler to the theory of the tides', *Annals of Science*, vol. 11, pp. 206–23.

AITON, ERIC J. (1960) 'The celestial mechanics of Leibniz', *Annals of Science*, vol. 16, pp. 65–82.

AITON, ERIC J. (1962) 'The celestial mechanics of Leibniz in the light of Newtonian criticism', *Annals of Science*, vol. 18, pp. 31–41.

AITON, ERIC J. (1964) 'The inverse problem of central forces', *Annals of Science*, vol. 20, pp. 81–99.

AITON, ERIC J. (1972) *The Vortex Theory of Planetary Motions*, London, Macdonald.

ALBURY, W. R. (1978) 'Halley's Ode on the *Principia* of Newton and the Epicurean revival in England', *Journal of the History of Ideas*, vol. 39, pp. 24–43.

ALEXANDER, H. G. (ed.) (1956) *The Leibniz–Clarke Correspondence*, Manchester, Manchester University Press.

ANDRADE, E. N. da C. (1935) 'Newton's early notebook', *Nature*, vol. 135, p. 360.

ANDRADE, E. N. da C. (1950) *Isaac Newton*, London, Max Parrish.

ANDRADE, E. N. da C. (1953) 'A Newton collection', *Endeavour*, vol. 12, pp. 68–75.

ANDRADE, E. N. da C. (1954) *Sir Isaac Newton*, London, Collins.

ANDRADE, E. N. da C. (1959) 'Introduction', in Newton, Sir Isaac, *The Correspondence of Isaac Newton*, vol. I, edited by Turnbull, H. W., Scott, J. F. and Hall, A. R., Cambridge, Cambridge University Press, pp. xv–xxiv.

ATKINSON, W. D. (1952) 'William Derham', *Annals of Science*, vol. 8, pp. 368–92.

AUBREY, JOHN (1972) *Brief Lives*, Harmondsworth, Penguin.

BIBLIOGRAPHY

AXTELL, J. L. (1965) 'Locke's review of the *Principia*', *Notes and Records of the Royal Society*, vol. 20, pp. 152–61.

AXTELL, J. L. (1969) 'Locke, Newton and the two cultures', in Yolton, J. (ed.) *John Locke: Problems and Perspectives*, Cambridge, Cambridge University Press, pp. 165–82.

BABSON INSTITUTE (1950) *A Descriptive Catalogue of the Grace K. Babson Collection of the Works of Sir Isaac Newton and the Material Relating to him in the Babson Library, Babson Park, Mass.*, New York, Herbert Reichner. (*See also* Macomber, 1955.)

BABSON, R. W. (1935) *Actions and Reactions*, New York, Harper.

BAILY, FRANCIS (1835) *An Account of the Revd John Flamsteed, the first Astronomer-Royal, compiled from his own Manuscripts, and other authentic documents, never before published. To which is added, his British Catalogue of Stars, Corrected and Enlarged*, London.

BAILY, FRANCIS (1837) *Supplement to the Account of the Revd John Flamsteed, the first Astronomer-Royal*, London.

BAILY, FRANCIS (1966) *An Account of the Revd John Flamsteed* and *Supplement to the Account of the Revd John Flamsteed*, a photo-reprint of Baily (1835) and (1837), excluding the stellar catalogue, London, Dawsons.

BALL, W. W. ROUSE (1893) *An Essay on Newton's 'Principia'*, London, Macmillan; (1972) New York, Johnson Reprint Corp.

BANVILLE, JOHN (1982) *The Newton Letter*, London, Secker & Warburg.

BASALLA, GEORGE (1968) *The Rise of Modern Science*, Lexington, Mass., D. C. Heath.

BINDMAN, DAVID (1977) *Blake as Artist*, Oxford, Phaidon.

BIRCH, THOMAS (1756–7) *The History of the Royal Society of London*, 4 vols, London.

BLUNT, ANTHONY (1938–9) 'Blake's "Ancient of days". The symbolism of the compasses', *Journal of the Warburg and Courtauld Institutes*, vol. 2, pp. 53–63.

BOAS, MARIE and HALL, A. RUPERT (1958) 'Newton's chemical experiments', *Archives internationales d'histoire des sciences*, vol. 11, pp. 113–52.

BORENIUS, TANCRED (1936) 'A Venetian apotheosis of William III', *Burlington Magazine*, vol. 69, pp. 244–5.

BOSS, V. I. (1972) *Newton and Russia, the Early Influence 1698–1796*, Cambridge, Mass., Harvard University Press.

BOYER, CARL B. (1959) *The History of the Calculus and its Conceptual Development*, New York, Dover.

BOYER, CARL B. (1968) *A History of Mathematics*, Chichester, John Wiley.

BOYLE, ROBERT (1744) *The Works of the Honourable Robert Boyle*, 5 vols, edited by Birch, Thomas, London.

BRASCH, F. E. (ed.) (1928) *Sir Isaac Newton, 1727–1927*, Baltimore, Williams & Wilkins.

BIBLIOGRAPHY

BRASCH, F. E. (1952) 'A survey of the number of copies of Newton's *Principia* in the United States, Canada, and Mexico', *Scripta mathematica*, vol. 18, pp. 53–67.

BREWSTER, SIR DAVID (1831) *The Life of Sir Isaac Newton*, London, John Murray.

BREWSTER, SIR DAVID (1855) *Memoirs of the Life, Writings and Discoveries of Sir Isaac Newton*, 2 vols, Edinburgh, Thomas Constable & Co.; (1965) New York, Johnson Reprint Corp.

BROAD, W. and WADE, N. (1983) *Betrayers of the Truth*, London, Century Publishing.

BROUGHAM, LORD HENRY and ROUTH, E. J. (1855) *Analytical View of Sir Isaac Newton's Principia*, London, Longman, Brown, Green, and Longmans; (1972) New York, Johnson Reprint Corp.

CAJORI, FLORIAN (1928) 'Newton's twenty years' delay in announcing the law of gravitation', in Brasch, F. E. (ed.), *Sir Isaac Newton, 1727–1927*, Williams & Wilkins, pp. 127–88.

CHILD, J. M. (1920) *The Early Mathematical Manuscripts of Leibniz*, Chicago, Open Court.

CHURCHILL, M. S. (1967) 'The Seven Chapters, with explanatory notes', *Chymia*, vol. 12, pp. 29–57.

COCHRAN, WILLIAM (1981) 'Who remembers David Brewster?' *New Scientist*, vol. 93, pp. 815–17.

COHEN, I. BERNARD (1956) *Franklin and Newton*, Philadelphia, American Philosophical Society.

COHEN, I. BERNARD (1957) 'I prismi del Newton e i prismi dell 'Algarotti', *Publ. dell'Istituto Nazionale di Ottica*, series IV, no. 276.

COHEN, I. BERNARD (1962) 'The first English version of Newton's "Hypotheses non fingo"', *Isis*, vol. 53, pp. 379–88.

COHEN, I. BERNARD (1963) 'Pemberton's translation of Newton's *Principia*, with notes on Motte's translation', *Isis*, vol. 54, pp. 319–51.

COHEN, I. BERNARD (1964), '"Quantum in se est": Newton's concept of inertia in relation to Descartes and Lucretius', *Notes and Records of the Royal Society*, vol. 19, pp. 131–55.

COHEN, I. BERNARD (1968) 'Introduction', *The Mathematical Principles of Natural Philosophy of Sir Isaac Newton Translated into English by Andrew Motte*, 2 vols., vol. 1, pp. i–xvii, London, Dawsons.

COHEN, I. BERNARD (1969), 'The French translation of Isaac Newton's *Philosophiae naturalis principia mathematica* (1756, 1759, 1766)', *Archives internationales d'histoire des sciences*, vol. 72, pp. 37–67.

COHEN, I. BERNARD (1970) 'The American editions of Newton's *Principia*', *Harvard Library Bulletin*, vol. 18, pp. 345–58.

COHEN, I. BERNARD (1971) *Introduction to Newton's Principia*, Cambridge, Cambridge University Press.

COHEN, I. BERNARD (1972) 'Introduction', *Analytical View of Sir Isaac*

BIBLIOGRAPHY

Newton's Principia, Broughman, Henry, and Routh, E. J., pp. v–xvi, New York, Johnson Reprint Corporation.

COHEN, I. BERNARD (1974) 'Newton, Isaac', in *Dictionary of Scientific Biography*, New York, Charles's Scribners Sons, pp. 41–103.

COHEN, I. BERNARD (1980) *The Newtonian Revolution*, Cambridge, Cambridge University Press.

COLEBY, L. J. M. (1952) 'J. F. Vigani', *Annals of Science*, vol. 8, pp. 46–60.

CRAIG, SIR JOHN (1946) *Newton at the Mint*, Cambridge, Cambridge University Press.

CRAIG, SIR JOHN (1953) *The Mint*, Cambridge, Cambridge University Press.

CRAIG, SIR JOHN (1963) 'Isaac Newton and the counterfeiters', *Notes and Records of the Royal Society*, vol. 18, pp. 136–45.

CROSLAND, M. P. (ed.) (1971) *The Science of Matter*, Harmondsworth, Penguin.

CROSLAND, M. P. (1978) *Historical Studies in the Language of Chemistry*, New York, Dover.

CUNNINGHAM, W. (1912) *The Growth of English Industry and commerce in Modern Times. Part I: Mercantile System*, Cambridge, Cambridge University Press.

DARWIN, G. H. (1911) *The Tides*, London, John Murray.

DAVID, F. N. (1957) 'Mr Newton, Mr Pepys and dyce', *Annals of Science*, vol. 13, pp. 137–47.

DAWSON, AILEEN (1984) *Masterpieces of Wedgwood in the British Museum*, London, British Museum Publications.

DE MORGAN, AUGUSTUS (1885) *Newton: his Friend: his Niece*, London; (1968) London, Dawsons.

DE MORGAN, AUGUSTUS (1914) *Essays on the Life and Work of Newton*, Chicago, Open Court.

DESCARTES, RENÉ (1954) *The Geometry*, New York, Dover.

DE VILLAMIL, RICHARD (1931) *Newton: the Man*, London, Gordon D. Knox; (1972) New York, Johnson Reprint Corp.

DITCHBURN, R. W. (1980) 'Newton's illness of 1692–3', *Notes and Records of the Royal Society*, vol. 35, pp. 1–16.

DOBBS, B. J. T. (1975) *The Foundations of Newton's Alchemy*, Cambridge, Cambridge University Press.

DREYER, J. L. E. (1924) 'Address delivered by the President, Dr. J. L. E. Dreyer, on the desirability of publishing a new edition of Isaac Newton's collected works'. *Monthly Notices of the Royal Astronomical Society*, vol. 84, pp. 298–304.

DUBBEY, J. M. (1962) 'The introduction of the differential notation to Great Britain', *Annals of Science*, vol. 18, pp. 37–48.

DUHEM, PIERRE (1954) *The Aim and Structure of Physical Theory*, translated by Wiener, P., Princeton, Princeton University Press.

DYSON, FREEMAN (1979) *Disturbing the Universe*, New York, Harper & Row.

EDLESTON, J. (1850) *Correspondence of Sir Isaac Newton and Professor Cotes, including letters of other eminent men, now first published from the originals in the Library of Trinity College, Cambridge*, Cambridge, J. W. Parker; (1969) London, Frank Cass.

ELLIOTT, R. W. (1954) 'Isaac Newton as a phonetician', *Modern Language Review*, vol. 49, pp. 5–12.

ELLIOTT, R. W. (1957) 'Isaac Newton's "Of an Universal Language"', *Modern Language Review*, vol. 52, pp. 1–18.

ESDAILLE, K. A. (1928) *The Life and Works of Louis Francois Roubiliac*, Oxford, Oxford University Press.

FERGUSON, J. (1976) *Dr Samuel Clarke*, Kineton, The Roundwood Press.

FIGALA, KAREN (1977) 'Newton as alchemist', *History of Science*, vol. 15, pp. 102–37.

FOSTER, C. W. (1928) 'Sir Isaac Newton's family', *Reports and Papers of the Architectural Societies of the County of Lincoln, County of York, Archdeaconries of Northampton and Oakham, and County of Leicester*, 39, Part 1.

FRASER, D. C. (1927) *Newton's Interpolation Formulas*, London, C. and E. Layton.

FULTON, JOHN (1961) *Bibliography of Robert Boyle*, Oxford, Clarendon Press.

GAGE, JOHN (1971) 'Blake's Newton', *Journal of the Warburg and Courtauld Institutes*, vol. 34, pp. 372–7.

GAGNEBIN, BERNARD (1949) 'De la cause de la pesanteur. Mémoire de Nicholas Fatio de Duillier présenté à la Royal Society le 26 février 1690', *Notes and Records of the Royal Society*, vol. 6, pp. 106–60.

GALTON, FRANCIS (1962) *Hereditary Genius*, London, Collins.

GARDNER, MARTIN (1952) *In the Name of Science*, New York, Putnam.

GASKELL, P. and ROBSON, R. (1971) *The Library of Trinity College, Cambridge: a Short History*, Cambridge, Cambridge University Press.

GEOGHEGAN, D. (1957) 'Some indications of Newton's attitude towards alchemy', *Ambix*, vol. 6, pp. 102–6.

GILLISPIE, C. C. (1960) *The Edge of Objectivity*, Princeton, Princeton University Press.

GILLISPIE, C. C. (1980) *Science and Polity in France at the End of the Old Regime*, Princeton, Princeton University Press.

GJERTSEN, D. (1984) *The Classics of Science*, New York, Lilian Barber.

GRANT, ROBERT (1852) *History of Physical Astronomy, from the Earliest Ages to the Middle of the Nineteenth Century*, London, Baldwin.

GRAY, G. J. (1907) *A Bibliography of the Works of Isaac Newton*, Cambridge, Bowes & Bowes.

GREAVES, JOHN (1737) *Miscellaneous Works of Mr John Greaves*, 2 vols, edited by Birch, Thomas, London.

BIBLIOGRAPHY

GREENSTREET, W. J. (ed.) (1927) *Isaac Newton (1642–1727)*, London, G. Bell & Sons.

GUERLAC, HENRY (1967) 'Newton's optical aether. His draft of a proposed addition to his Optics', *Notes and Records of the Royal Society*, vol. 22, pp. 45–57.

GUERLAC, HENRY (1981) *Newton on the Continent*, Ithaca, Cornell University Press.

HALL, A. RUPERT (1948) 'Sir Isaac Newton's notebook, 1661–1665', *Cambridge Historical Journal*, vol. 9, pp. 239–50.

HALL, A. RUPERT (1955) 'Further optical experiments', *Annals of Science*, vol. 11, pp. 27–43.

HALL, A. RUPERT (1957) 'Newton on the calculation of central forces', *Annals of Science*, vol. 13, pp. 62–71.

HALL, A. RUPERT (1960) 'Newton's first book', *Archives internationales d'histoire des sciences*, vol. 13, pp. 39–61.

HALL, A. RUPERT (1980) *Philosophers at War*, Cambridge, Cambridge University Press.

HALL, A. RUPERT (1981) 'Review of Westfall' (1980), *New Scientist*, vol. 90, p. 172.

HALL, A. RUPERT (1982) 'Further Newton Correspondence', *Notes and Records of the Royal Society*, vol. 37, pp. 7–34.

HALL, A. RUPERT (1983) *The Revolution in Science 1500–1750*, London, Longman.

HALL, M. B. (1970) *Nature and Nature's Laws*, London, Macmillan.

HALL, MARIE BOAS (1975) 'Newton's voyage on the strange seas of alchemy', in Righini, Bonelli and Shea, W. R., *Reason, Experiment and Mysticism in the Scientific Revolution*, New York, Science History Publications, pp. 239–46.

HANKINS, T. L. (1970) *Jean d'Alembert: Science and the Enlightenment*, Oxford, Clarendon Press.

HARRIS, JOHN (1710) *Lexicon technicum*, vol. 2; (1966) New York, Johnson Reprint Corp.

HARRISON, JOHN (1978) *The Library of Isaac Newton*, Cambridge, Cambridge University Press.

HARRISON, JOHN and LASLETT, PETER (1965) *The Library of Locke*, Cambridge, Cambridge University Press.

HASKELL, FRANCIS (1963) *Patrons and Painters*, London, Chatto & Windus.

HASKELL, FRANCIS (1970) 'The apotheosis of Newton in art', in Palter, R. (ed.), *The Annus mirabilis of Sir Isaac Newton 1666–1966*, Cambridge, Mass., MIT Press, pp. 302–21.

HEATH–STUBBS, JOHN and SALMAN, PHILLIPS (eds) (1984) *Poems of Science*, Harmondsworth, Penguin.

HERIVEL, JOHN (1960) 'Halley's first visit to Newton', *Archives internationales d'histoire des sciences*, vol. 13, pp. 63–5.

HERIVEL, JOHN (1961) 'Interpretation of an early Newton manuscript', *Isis*, vol. 52, pp. 410–16.

HERIVEL, JOHN (1965) *The Background to Newton's Principia. A Study of Newton's Dynamical Researches in the Years 1664–84*, Oxford, Clarendon Press.

HESSE, MARY (1965) *Forces and Fields. The Concept of Action at a Distance in the History of Physics*, Totowa, New Jersey, Littlefield, Adams & Co.

HESSEN, BORIS (1931) 'The social and economic roots of Newton's *Principia*', *Science at the Crossroads*, London, Kniga.

HISCOCK, W. G. (ed.) (1937) *David Gregory, Isaac Newton, and their Circle. Extracts from David Gregory's Memoranda 1677–1708*, Oxford, printed for the editor.

HOFMANN, J. E. (1974) *Leibniz in Paris 1672–1676*, Cambridge, Cambridge University Press.

HOOKE, ROBERT (1935) *The Diary of Robert Hooke, M.A., M.D., F.R.S., 1672–1680*, edited by Robinson, H. W. and Adams, W., London, Taylor & Francis.

HOOKE, ROBERT (1961) *Micrographia*, New York, Dover.

HOWSE, DEREK (1980) *Greenwich Time*, Oxford, Oxford University Press.

HOYLE, F. and WICKRAMASINGHE, N. C. (1978) *Lifecloud*, London, J. M. Dent.

HOYLE, F. and WICKRAMASINGHE, N. C. (1979) *Diseases from Space*, London, J. M. Dent.

HUYGENS, C. (1962) *Treatise on Light*, New York, Dover.

JACOB, M. C. (1976) *The Newtonians and the English Revolution 1687–1720*, Ithaca, Cornell University Press.

JACOB, M. C. (1978) 'Newton and the French prophets', *History of Science*, vol. 16, pp. 134–42.

JACOB, M. C. and GUERLAC, HENRY (1969) 'Bentley, Newton and providence (the Boyle lectures once more)', *Journal of the History of Ideas*, vol. 30, pp. 307–18.

JOHNSON, L. W. and WOLBARSHT, M. L. (1979) 'Mercury poisoning: A probable cause of Isaac Newton's physical and mental ills', *Notes and Records of the Royal Society*, vol. 34, pp. 1–9.

JONES, WILLIAM (ed.) (1711) *Analysis per Quantitatum Series Fluxiones ac Differentias: cum enumeratione Linearum Tertii Ordinis*, London.

KAHN, DAVID (1966) *The Codebreakers*, London, Weidenfeld & Nicolson.

KARGON, R. H. (1966) *Atomism in England from Newton to Hariot*, Oxford, Clarendon Press.

KELLY, ALISON (1970) *Wedgwood Ware*, London, Ward Lock.

KEYNES, J. M. (1946) 'G.B.S. and Isaac Newton', in Winsten, S. (ed.), *G.B.S.90*, London, Hutchinson, pp. 106–9.

BIBLIOGRAPHY

KEYNES, J. M. (1947) 'Newton, the man', in Royal Society, *Newton Tercentenary Celebrations*, Cambridge, Cambridge University Press, pp. 27–34.

KOESTLER, ARTHUR (1959) *The Sleepwalkers*, London, Hutchinson.

KOYRÉ, ALEXANDRE (1957) *From the Closed World to the Infinite Universe*, Baltimore, Johns Hopkins University Press.

KOYRÉ, ALEXANDRE (1965) *Newtonian Studies*, London, Chapman & Hall.

KOYRÉ, ALEXANDRE (1968) *From the Closed World to the Infinite Universe*, Baltimore, The Johns Hopkins Press.

KOYRÉ, ALEXANDRE (1973) *The Astronomical Revolution*, Ithaca, Cornell University Press.

KOYRÉ, ALEXANDRE (1978) *Galileo Studies*, Hassocks, Sussex, Harvester Press.

KOYRÉ, A. and COHEN, I. B. (1961) 'The case of the missing *tanquam*: Leibniz, Newton and Clarke', *Isis*, vol. 52, pp. 555–66.

KOYRÉ, A. and COHEN, I. B. (1962) 'Newton and the Leibniz–Clarke correspondence, with notes on Newton, Conti and des Maizeaux', *Archives internationales d'histoire des sciences*, vol. 15, pp. 63–126.

LANDES, D. S. (1983) *Revolution in Time*, Cambridge, Mass., Harvard University Press.

LARMOR, JOSEPH (1924) 'On editing Newton', *Nature*, vol. 113, p. 744.

LEVEY, MICHAEL (1980) *Painting in 18th century Venice*, London, Phaidon.

LODGE, SIR OLIVER (1960) *Pioneers of Science*, New York, Dover.

LOHNE, J. A. (1960) 'Hooke versus Newton. An analysis of the documents in the case of free fall and planetary motion', *Centaurus*, vol. 7, pp. 6–52.

LOHNE, J. A. (1965) 'Isaac Newton: The rise of a scientist 1661–1671', *Notes and Records of the Royal Society*, vol. 20, pp. 125–139.

LOHNE, J. A. (1967) 'The increasing corruption of Newton's diagrams', *History of Science*, vol. 6, pp. 69–89.

LOHNE, J. A. (1968) '*Experimentum crucis*', *Notes and Records of the Royal Society*, vol. 23, pp. 169–99.

LYONS, SIR HENRY (1944) *The Royal Society 1660–1940*, Cambridge, Cambridge University Press.

MCGUIRE, J. E. (1966) 'Body and void and Newton's *De mundi systemate*: Some new sources', *Archives for History of the Exact Sciences*, vol. 3, pp. 206–48.

MCGUIRE, J. E. and RATTANSI, P. M. (1966) 'Newton and the "pipes of Pan"', *Notes and Records of the Royal Society*, vol. 21, pp. 108–43.

MCGUIRE, J. E. (1968) 'Force, active principles, and Newton's invisible realm', *Ambix*, vol. 15, pp. 154–208.

MCGUIRE, J. E. (1970) 'Atoms and the "Analogy of Nature": Newton's Third Rule of Philosophizing', *Studies in the History and Philosophy of Science*, vol. I, pp. 3–58.

MCGUIRE, J. E. (1977) 'Neoplatonism, Active Principles and the Corpus

Hermeticum', in *Hermeticism and the Scientific Revolution*, edited R. S. Westman and J. E. McGuire, Los Angeles, University of California Press.

McKie, D. and de Beer, G. (1952) 'Newton's apple', *Notes and Records of the Royal Society*, vol. 9, pp. 46–54, 333–5.

McLachlan, Herbert (1950) *Sir Isaac Newton: Theological Manuscripts*, Liverpool, Liverpool University Press.

Macomber, H. P. (1952) 'Principia census', *Isis*, vol. 43, p. 126.

Macomber, H. P. (1953) 'A census of the owner's of copies of the 1687 first edition of Newton's *Principia*', *The Papers of the Bibliographical Society of America*, vol. 47, pp. 269–300.

Macomber, H. P. (1955) *A Supplement to the Descriptive Catalogue of the Grace K. Babson Collection of the Works of Sir Isaac Newton*, Wellesley, Mass., Babson Institute (*see also* Babson Institute, 1950).

MacPike, E. F. (ed.) (1932) *Correspondence and Papers of Edmond Halley*, Oxford, Clarendon Press.

MacPike, E. F. (1937) *Hevelius, Flamsteed and Halley; Three Contemporary Astronomers and their Mutual Relations*, London, Taylor & Francis.

Mankowitz, Wolf (1966) *Wedgwood*, London, Spring Books.

Manuel, Frank (1963) *Isaac Newton, Historian*, Cambridge, Cambridge University Press.

Manuel, Frank (1974) *The Religion of Isaac Newton*, Oxford, Clarendon Press.

Manuel, Frank (1980) *A Portrait of Isaac Newton*, London, Frederick Muller.

Meadows, A. J. (1969) *The High Firmament*, Leicester, Leicester University Press.

Merton, Robert (1965) *On the Shoulders of Giants*, New York, Free Press.

Midonick, Henrietta (1968) *The Treasury of Mathematics*, 2 vols, Harmondsworth, Penguin.

Mills, A. A. (1981) 'Newton's prisms and his experiments on the spectrum', *Notes and Records of the Royal Society*, vol. 36, pp. 13–36.

Mills, A. A. and Turvey, P. J. (1979) 'Newton's telescope: an examination of the reflecting telescope attributed to Sir Isaac Newton in the possession of the Royal Society', *Notes and Records of the Royal Society*, vol. 33, pp. 133–55.

Mills, A. A. (1982) 'Newton's Water Clocks and the Fluid Mechanics of Clepsydra', *Notes and Records of the Royal Society*, vol. 37, pp. 35–61.

Mitford, Nancy (1959) *Voltaire in Love*, London, Hamish Hamilton.

More, L. T. (1962) *Isaac Newton: a Biography*, New York, Dover.

Morison, S. E. (1936) *Harvard College in the 17th Century*, 2 vols, Cambridge, Mass., Harvard University Press.

Munby, A. N. L. (1952a) 'The distribution of the first edition of

Newton's Principia', *Notes and Records of the Royal Society*, vol. 10, pp. 28–39.

MUNBY, A. N. L. (1952b) 'The Keynes collection of the works of Sir Isaac Newton at King's College, Cambridge', *Notes and Records of the Royal Society*, vol. 10, pp. 40–50.

NEWTON, SIR ISAAC (1779–85) *Isaaci Newtoni opera quae existant omnia*, 5 vols, edited by Horsley, Samuel; (1964) Stuttgart–Bad Cannstatt.

NEWTON, SIR ISAAC (1952) *Opticks or a Treatise of Reflections, Refractions, Inflections and Colours of Light*, with a preface by Cohen, I. B. and an introduction by Whittaker, E. T., New York, Dover.

NEWTON, SIR ISAAC (1959–77) *The Correspondence of Isaac Newton*, 7 vols, edited by Turnbull, H. W., Scott, J. F. and Hall, A. R., Cambridge, Cambridge University Press.

NEWTON, SIR ISAAC (1962a) *Sir Isaac Newton's Principles of Natural Philosophy and His System of the World*, 2 vols, edited by Cajori, Florian, Berkeley, University of California Press.

NEWTON, SIR ISAAC (1962b) *The Unpublished Scientific Papers of Isaac Newton. A Selection from the Portsmouth Collection in the University Library, Cambridge*, edited by Hall, A. R. and Hall, M. B., Cambridge, Cambridge University Press.

NEWTON, SIR ISAAC (1964–7) *The Mathematical Works of Isaac Newton*, 2 vols, edited by Whiteside, D. T., New York, Johnson Reprint Corp.

NEWTON, SIR ISAAC (1967–81) *The Mathematical Papers of Isaac Newton*, 8 vols, edited by Whiteside, D. T., Cambridge, Cambridge University Press.

NEWTON, SIR ISAAC (1969) *A Treatise of the System of the World*, 1731 edition, with an introduction by Cohen, I. B., London, Dawsons.

NEWTON, SIR ISAAC (1972) *Isaac Newton's Philosophiae naturalis principiae mathematica, the 3rd Edition with Variant Readings*, edited by Koyré, A. and Cohen, I. B., Cambridge, Cambridge University Press.

NEWTON, SIR ISAAC (1973) *The Unpublished First Version of Isaac Newton's Cambridge Lectures on Optics 1670–2*, with an introduction by Whiteside, D. T., Cambridge, Cambridge University Library.

NEWTON, SIR ISAAC (1975) *Isaac Newton's 'Theory of the Moon's Motion' 1702)*, with an introduction by Cohen, I. B., London, Dawsons.

NEWTON, SIR ISAAC (1978) *Isaac Newton's Papers and Letters on Natural Philosophy*, 2nd revised edition, edited by Cohen, I. B., Cambridge, Mass., Harvard University Press.

NEWTON, SIR ISAAC (1983) *Quaestiones quaedam philosophicae – Certain Philosophical Questions: Newton's Trinity Notebook, Cambridge*, edited by McGuire, J. E. and Tamny, M., Cambridge, Cambridge University Press.

NEWTON, SIR ISAAC (1984) *The Optical Papers of Isaac Newton. Vol. I: The Optical Lectures 1670–2*, edited by Shapiro, A. E., Cambridge, Cambridge University Press.

NICOLSON, M. H. (1966) *Newton Demands the Muse*, Princeton, Princeton University Press.

NOYES, ALFRED (1937) *The Torch-bearers*, London, Sheed & Ward.

NURMI, M. K. (1957) 'Blake's "Ancient of Days" and Motte's frontispiece to Newton's *Principia*', in Pinto, V. de Sola (ed.), *The Divine Vision*, London, Gollancz.

PALTER, R. (ed.) (1970) *The Annus mirabilis of Sir Isaac Newton 1666–1966*, Cambridge, Mass., MIT Press.

PANNEKOEK, A. (1961) *History of Astronomy*, London, Allen & Unwin.

PAYNE-GAPOSCHKIN, C. (1954) *Introduction to Astronomy*, Englewood Cliffs, New Jersey, Prentice-Hall.

PEARSON, HESKETH (1948) *Shaw*, London, Reprint Society.

PEMBERTON, HENRY (1728) *A View of Sir Isaac Newton's Philosophy*, London.

PEVSNER, N. (1957) *The Buildings of England: London I: The Cities of London and Westminster*, Harmondsworth, Penguin.

PEVSNER, N. (1964) *The Buildings of England: Lincolnshire*, Harmondsworth, Penguin.

PEVSNER, N. (1976) *A History of Building Types*, London, Thames & Hudson.

PIGHETTI, CLELIA (1960) 'Cinquant' anni di studi newtoniani (1908–59)', *Rivista Critica di Storia della Filosofia*, fascicoli II–III, pp. 181–203; 295–318, Florence.

PIPER, JOHN (1982) *Images of the Poet*, Oxford, Clarendon Press.

PITT, V. H. (1977) *The Penguin Dictionary of Physics*, Harmondsworth, Penguin.

PRICE, DEREK DE SOLLA (1952) 'The early observatory instruments of Trinity College, Cambridge', *Annals of Science*, vol. 8, pp. 1–12.

PRICE, DEREK DE SOLLA (1960) 'Newton in a church tower: the discovery of an unknown book by Isaac Newton', *The Yale University Library Gazette*, vol. 34, pp. 124–6.

RAPHSON, JOSEPH (1718) *History of Fluxions*, London.

RATTANSI, P. M. (1972) 'Newton's alchemical studies', in Debus, A. G. (ed.), *Science, Medicine and Society*, 2 vols, New York, Science History Publications, pp. 167–82.

RATTANSI, P. M. (1974) *Isaac Newton and Gravity*, London, Wildwood House.

RICHARDSON, A. E. (1947) 'Woolsthorpe Manor House', *Notes and Records of the Royal Society*, vol. 1, pp. 34–5.

RIGAUD, S. P. (1838) *Historical Essay on the first Publication of Sir Isaac Newton's Principia*, Oxford; (1972) New York, Johnson Reprint Corp.

RIGAUD, S. P. (1841) *Correspondence of Scientific Men of the Seventeenth Century . . . in the Collection of . . . the Earl of Macclesfield*, 2 vols, Oxford.

ROBINSON, H. W. (1948) 'Notes on some recently discovered

geometrical drawings in the stonework of Woolsthorpe Manor House', *Notes and Records of the Royal Society*, vol. 5, pp. 35–6.

ROSENBERGER, FERDINAND (1895) *Isaac Newton und seine physikalischen Principien*, Leipzig, J. A. Barth.

ROUTLEDGE, ROBERT (1894) *A Popular History of Science*, London, George Routledge & Sons.

ROYAL SOCIETY (1947) *Newton Tercentenary Celebrations*, Cambridge, Cambridge University Press.

RUSSELL, J. L. (1964) 'Kepler's laws of planetary motion: 1609–1666', *The British Journal for the History of Science*, vol. 2, pp. 1–24.

SABRA, A. I. (1967) *Theories of Light from Descartes to Newton*, London, Oldbourne.

SABRA, A. I. (1981) *Theories of Light*, Cambridge, Cambridge University Press.

SAILOR, D. B. (1964) 'Moses and atomism', *Journal of the History of Ideas*, vol. 25, pp. 3–16.

SAMBURSKY, S. (1956) *The Physical World of the Greeks*, London, Routledge & Kegan Paul.

SAMPSON, R. A. (1924) 'On editing Newton', *Monthly Notices of the Royal Astronomical Society*, vol. 84, pp. 378–83.

SCOTT, J. F. (1952) *The Scientific Work of René Descartes*, London, Taylor & Francis.

SCRIBA, C. J. (1964) 'Mercator's Kinckhuysen-translation in Bodleian Library at Oxford', *British Journal for the History of Science*, vol. 2, pp. 145–58.

SHAW, W. A. (1896) *Select Tracts and Documents illustrative of English Monetary History*, 1626–1730, London.

SHAW, W. A. (1935) 'Sir Isaac Newton's Mint Reports'. *Select Tracts and Documents Illistrative of English Monetary History 1626–1730*, London, George Harding.

SMITH, D. E. (1912) *The Portrait Medals of Sir Isaac Newton*, Boston, Mass., Athenaeum Press.

SMITH, D. E. (1927a) 'Two unpublished documents of Sir Isaac Newton', in Greenstreet, W. J. (ed.), *Isaac Newton (1642–1727)*, London, G. Bell & Sons, pp. 16–34.

SMITH, D. E. (1927b) 'Portraits of Sir Isaac Newton', in Greenstreet, W. J. (ed.), *ibid.*, pp. 171–8.

SMITH, D. E. (1927c) 'The portrait medals of Newton', in Greenstreet, W. J. (ed.), *ibid.*, pp. 179–80.

SMITH, D. E. 1951–3 *History of Mathematics*, 2 vols, New York, Dover.

SPARGO, P. E. (1972) 'Newton's library', *Endeavour*, vol. 31, pp. 29–33.

SPARGO, P. E. and POUNDS, C. A. (1979), 'Newton's "Derangement of the Intellect". New light on an old problem', *Notes and Records of the Royal Society*, vol. 34, pp. 11–32.

STEFFENS, H. J. (1977) *The Development of Newtonian Optics in England*, New York, Science History Publications.

STRUIK, D. J. (ed.) (1969) *A Source Book in Mathematics, 1200–1800*, Cambridge, Mass., Harvard University Press.

STUKELEY, WILLIAM (1936) *Memoirs of Sir Isaac Newton's Life*, London, Taylor & Francis.

SULLIVAN, J. W. N. (1938) *Isaac Newton 1642–1727*, London, Macmillan.

TAYLOR, F. S. (1956) 'An alchemical work of Sir Isaac Newton', *Ambix*, vol. 5, pp. 59–84.

TAYLOR, JOHN (1936) *Catalogue of the Newton Papers sold by Order of Viscount Lymington*, London, Sotheby & Co.

THACKRAY, ARNOLD (1970) *Atoms and Powers*, Cambridge, Mass., Harvard University Press.

THAYER, H. S. (ed.) (1953) *Newton's Philosophy of Nature*, New York, Hafner.

THOMPSON, S. P. (1910) *The Life of William Thomson, Baron Kelvin of Largs*, 2 vols, London, Macmillan.

TURNBULL, H. W. (ed.) (1938) James Gregory Tercentenary Memorial Volume, Edinburgh, Royal Society of Edinburgh Publications.

TURNBULL, H. W. (ed.) (1939) *James Gregory: Tercentenary Memorial Volume*, London, G. Bell & Sons.

TURNBULL, H. W. (1945) *The Mathematical Discoveries of Newton*, London, Blackie & Son.

TURNOR, EDMUND (1806) *Collections for the History of the Town and Soke of Grantham, containing authentic Memoirs of Sir Isaac Newton, now first published from the original MSS in the possession of the Earl of Portsmouth*, London, William Miller.

TURNOR, CHARLES (1844) 'An account of the Newtonian dial presented to the Royal Society', *Proceedings of the Royal Society*, 13 June 1844.

VOLTAIRE (1980) *Letters on England*, Harmondsworth, Penguin.

WAGAR, W. W. (ed.) (1982) *The Secular Mind*, New York.

WALLIS, P. J. (1978) 'The popular American edition of Newton's *Principia*', *Harvard Library Bulletin*, vol. 26, pp. 355–60.

WALLIS, P. and WALLIS, R. (1977) *Newton and Newtoniana 1672–1975*, London, Dawsons.

WATSON, F. J. B. (1953) 'An allegorical painting of Canaletto, Piazetta and Cimaroli', *Burlington Magazine*, vol. 95, pp. 362–5.

WATSON, LYALL (1973) *Supernature*, London, Hodder & Stoughton.

WEBB, M. I. (1952) 'Busts of Sir Isaac Newton', *Country Life*, 24 January 1952, pp. 216–18.

WEINSTOCK, ROBERT (1982) 'Dismantling a centuries old myth: Newton's *Principia* and inverse-square orbits', *American Journal of Physics*, vol. 50, pp. 610–17.

WESTFALL, R. S. (1958) *Science and Religion in Seventeenth Century England*, New Haven, Yale University Press.

BIBLIOGRAPHY

WESTFALL, R. S. (1962) 'The foundations of Newton's philosophy of nature', *British Journal for the History of Science*, vol. 1, pp. 171–82.

WESTFALL, R. S. (1963) 'Short-writing and the state of Newton's conscience', *Notes and Records of the Royal Society*, vol. 18, pp. 10–16.

WESTFALL, R. S. (1965a) 'Isaac Newton's coloured circles twixt two contiguous glasses', *Archive for History of Exact Sciences*, vol. 2, pp. 181–96.

WESTFALL, R. S. (1965b) 'Introduction', Facsimile Reprint of Brewster (1855), New York, Johnson Reprint Corporation.

WESTFALL, R. S. (1970) 'Uneasily fitful reflections on fits of easy transmission', in Palter, R. (ed.), *The Annus mirabilis of Sir Isaac Newton, 1666–1966*, Cambridge, Mass., MIT Press, pp. 88–104.

WESTFALL, R. S. (1971a) *Force in Newton's Physics*, London, Macdonald.

WESTFALL, R. S. (1971b) *The Construction of Modern Science*, New York, John Wiley.

WESTFALL, R. S. (1972) 'Newton and the hermetic tradition', in Debus, A. G. (ed.), *Science, Medicine and Society*, vol. 2, New York, Science History Publications, pp. 183–98.

WESTFALL, R. S. (1973) 'Newton and the fudge factor', *Science*, vol. 179, pp. 751–8.

WESTFALL, R. S. (1975) 'The role of alchemy in Newton's career', in Righini, B. and Shea, W. R. (eds), *Reason, Experiment and Mysticism in the Scientific Revolution*, New York, Science History Publications, pp. 189–232.

WESTFALL, R. S. (1980) *Never at Rest*, Cambridge, Cambridge University Press (1983) paperback edition.

WHITESIDE, D. T. (1961a) 'Newton's discovery of the general binomial theorem', *Mathematical Gazette*, vol. 45, pp. 175–80.

WHITESIDE, D. T. (1961b) 'Patterns of mathematical thought in the later seventeenth century', *Archive for History of Exact Sciences*, vol. 1, pp. 179–388.

WHITESIDE, D. T. (1964a) 'Isaac Newton: Birth of a mathematician', *Notes and Records of the Royal Society*, vol. 19, pp. 53–62.

WHITESIDE, D. T. (1964b) 'Newton's early thought on planetery motion', *British Journal for the History of Science*, vol. 2, pp. 117–37.

WHITESIDE, D. T. (1966) 'Newton's marvellous year: 1666 and all that', *Notes and Records of the Royal Society*, vol. 21, pp. 32–41.

WHITESIDE, D. T. (1970) 'The mathematical principles underlying Newton's *Principia*', *The Journal for the History of Astronomy*, vol. 1, pp. 116–38.

WHITESIDE, D. T. (1976) 'Newton's lunar theory: from high hope to disenchantment', *Vistas in Astronomy*, vol. 19, pp. 317–28.

WHITLA, WILLIAM (1922) *Sir Isaac Newton's Daniel and the Apocalypse with an Introductory Study . . . of Unbelief, of Miracles and Prophecy*, London, John Murray.

BIBLIOGRAPHY

WILLEY, BASIL (1972) *The Seventeenth Century Background*, Harmondsworth, Penguin.

WIMSATT, W. K. (1965) *The Portraits of Alexander Pope*, New Haven and London, Yale University Press.

ZEITLINGER, H. (1927) 'A Newtonian bibliography', in Greenstreet, W. J. (ed.), *Isaac Newton (1642–1727)*, London, G. Bell & Sons, pp. 148–90.

Alphabetical list of entries

[641]

Index

In the index below page numbers in italics indicates that a specific entry devoted to the subject can be found at that place.

INDEX

INDEX

INDEX

INDEX

[655]

INDEX

Motte, Andrew, 94, 148, 266, *331*, 373, 427, 478–9, 482, 488, 574, 577
Motte, Benjamin, 478, 574
Mouton's method, 128
Murray, Thomas, *373*
Musgrave, James, 309

National Portrait Gallery, 290, 443, 445–6, 452, 542, 594
National Trust, 517, 525–6
Neale, Thomas, 208, 248, 359, *374*
Neile, W., 186
Newberry, J., 484
Newcastle, Duke of, 429
New College, Oxford, 183
Newell, L. C., 487
Newenham, F., 442
New Theory about Light and Colours, 123–4, 178, 226, 320, 326, *374–7*, 419, 512, 619
newton, 377
Newton, Anne, 314
Newton as experimentalist and observer, *377–80*
Newton, Humphrey (Bursar of TCC), 559
Newton, Humphrey, *380*; as amanuensis, 165, 460, 573; as biographical source, 177–8, 185, 204, 223–4, 227, 233, 263–4, 297, 328, 379, 583, 600
Newton in America, 217, 242, 323, 340, 372, *380–2*, 613
Newton in France, 336, 347, 376, *382–4*, 414, 480, 498–500, 587, 595
Newton in Italy, *384–5*
Newton in Japan, *385*
Newton in Russia, 94, 125, *385–6*
Newton, Isaac (1606–42), 19, 197, 346, *386*, 525
Newton, John, of Colsterworth (1707–37), 19, 196–7, 255, *386*
Newton, John of Westby (d. circa 1544), 19, *386*
Newton, John of Westby (d. 1562), 19
Newton, John of Woolsthorpe (1665–1725), 19
Newton, Richard of Woolsthorpe (d. 1588), 19
Newton, Robert of Woolsthorpe (1570–1641), 19, *387*
Newton, Sir Isaac (1642–1727), appearance, *28*; artistic interests, *37*; attitude to publication, 511–14, 604–5; biographies, *74–83*; breakdown, *88–90*; chastity, *104–6*; death, 110, *152–3*; diet, *178*; drinking and gambling; finances, *201–3*; fire, *204–5*; friends, *222*; funeral, *225–6*; generosity, *227–8*; hair, 89–90, 516, 537; health, *254*, 355–6; *heirs*, 255; humour, *263–4*; inventory, *275–7*; knighthood, *292–3*;

life and career, *314–19*; as MP, *424–5*; at Mint, *358–68*; residences, *525–9*; Royal Society, *533–7*; TCC, *582–6*; works, *614–23*
Newton, Sir John (1629–99), 19, *387*
Newton, Sir John (1651–1734), 19, 58, 313, 387
Newton, Sir Michael, 19, 225, 314, 387
Newton, Samuel, 340
Newton's rings, 205–7; *387–9*
Nicaea, 21, 36, 42, *389*, 590
Nicole, F., 187–8
Nichols, J., 217
Nicolson, M., 419
Nicomedes, 186
Norris, I., 399
Norris, Lady, 105, *389–90*
Norton, T., 10, 38
Nostradamus, 275
Notebooks, *390–1*
Noyes, A., 178, 231, *391–2*, 438
Nutshell theory of matter, *392–3*

Observations, *394*, 619
Observations Concerning the Medium, *394–5*, 421, 620
Observations on Kinckhuysen, 25, 121, 288, 290, 342, 344, *395–6*, 420
Observation upon the Prophecies of Daniel . . . and St John, 98, 262, 274, 276, *396–99*, 449, 524, 568, 620
Occult causes and qualities, 353, *400–01*
Oettingen, A. von, 486
October 1666 Tract, 213, 337, 342, *401–02*, 620
Of an Universal Language, *402–03*, 620
Of Colours, 194, 387, 391, *403–04*, 419, 620
Official appointments, *404–05*
Of Reflections, 349, *405–06*, 620
Of Refractions, 1, 344, *406*, 419, 620
Of Violent Motion, 349, *406–07*, 620
Oka, Kunio, 385, 482
Oldenburg, Henry, 136, *407–08*; CF, 128; correspondence with: Gascoigne, 226; Hooke, 257–9; Leibniz, 15, 16, 122, 189, 502; Newton, 22, 24, 130, 138, 178–9, 262, 326, 329, 345, 512; and PT, 432, 561; and Royal Society, 376, 533–4
On Circular Motion, 130, 279, 350, *408*
One pound note, *409*
Optatus, 311
Optical Lectures (Lectiones opticae), 98, 124, 194, 261, 328, 387, *409–11*, 414, 419, 512, 619–20
Opticks, 25, 85, 90, 94, 98, 140, 159, 168, 188, 212, 223, 227, 251, 262, 283, 309, 335, 337, 353, 377, 378, 382, *411–19*, 421, 482, 510, 511, *519–20*, 592, 620; *An Hypothesis*, 24; Book I, Part I,

[659]

INDEX

[661]